The Whiskey BIBLE

A Complete Guide to the World's Greatest Spirit

NOAH ROTHBAUM

Workman Publishing
New York

Copyright © 2025 by Noah Rothbaum
Illustrations copyright © 2025 by Tom Woolley

Hachette Book Group supports the right to free expression and the value of copyright. The purpose of copyright is to encourage writers and artists to produce the creative works that enrich our culture.

The scanning, uploading, and distribution of this book without permission is a theft of the author's intellectual property. If you would like permission to use material from the book (other than for review purposes), please contact permissions@hbgusa.com. Thank you for your support of the author's rights.

Workman
Workman Publishing
Hachette Book Group, Inc.
1290 Avenue of the Americas
New York, NY 10104
workman.com

Workman is an imprint of Workman Publishing, a division of Hachette Book Group, Inc. The Workman name and logo are registered trademarks of Hachette Book Group, Inc.

Design by Becky Terhune
Additional photo credits can be found on page 628

The publisher is not responsible for websites (or their content) that are not owned by the publisher.

Workman books may be purchased in bulk for business, educational, or promotional use. For information, please contact your local bookseller or the Hachette Book Group Special Markets Department at special.markets@hbgusa.com.

Library of Congress Cataloging-in-Publication Data
Names: Rothbaum, Noah author
Title: The whiskey bible / Noah Rothbaum.
Description: First edition. | New York : Workman Publishing, 2025. | Includes index.
Identifiers: LCCN 2024059318 (print) | LCCN 2024059319 (ebook) |
  ISBN 9781523512706 hardcover | ISBN 9781523532582 epub
Subjects: LCSH: Whiskey--Handbooks, manuals, etc. | LCGFT: Handbooks and manuals
Classification: LCC TP605 .R682 2025 (print) | LCC TP605 (ebook) | DDC
  663/.52—dc23/eng/20250227
LC record available at https://lccn.loc.gov/2024059318
LC ebook record available at https://lccn.loc.gov/2024059319

First Edition September 2025

Printed in Shenzhen, China (APO) on responsibly sourced paper.

10 9 8 7 6 5 4 3 2 1

CONTENTS

Introduction — v
1 Whiskey 101 — 1
2 American Whiskey — 53
3 Scotch Whisky — 195
4 Irish Whiskey — 305
5 Canadian Whisky — 367
6 Japanese Whisky — 415
7 World Whiskey — 455
8 Enjoying Whiskey — 481
9 A Whiskey Timeline — 520
10 Classic and Modern Whiskey Cocktail Recipes — 551
Sources & Further Reading — 587
Acknowledgments — 590
Index — 592

INTRODUCTION

I can only hope that I'll never be marooned on a desert island with just a single bottle of liquor. Because even though I evaluate, study, and, yes, drink whiskey for a living, I do not have a favorite brand.

There are just too many wonderful whiskies to choose from.

I do gravitate towards certain flavor profiles or brands that suit my personal preferences. But while *I* enjoy those whiskies, *you* might not. That's the funny thing about whiskey: It's like art. You get to decide what excites you—and what turns you off.

Identifying the best whiskey *for you* goes beyond the simple Google search to land on some liquor expert's top ten list. That's why I wrote this book: to help you find your own way within the world of whiskey so you can fully enjoy it. There are no shortcuts when it comes to selecting a whiskey. Price, age, and reputation mean only so much. But if it was that easy, learning about and tasting whiskey wouldn't be nearly as fun.

Consider me your knowledgeable (and nonjudgmental) friend who wants to empower you with the tools, knowledge, and resources that will help you understand and appreciate whiskey.

I've organized the world of whiskey by geography, since, traditionally, where a whiskey is from dictates how it is produced and ultimately how it tastes. In each chapter, you'll find essential information, history, and advice, plus a section on the key whiskey brands that hail from each country. This taxonomy is meant to make

the world of whiskey more approachable and allow you to explore these different whiskey-rich regions. I, of course, suggest perusing these pages while enjoying a favorite dram.

What you are holding in your hands is the result of my life's work. But that work doesn't involve drinking alcohol from morning till night. I don't have an appetite for liquor like legendary drinkers Winston Churchill, Ernest Hemingway, or Charles Bukowski. Yes, I sometimes like to taste whiskey in the morning when my palate is fresh, but again, my apologies, most days my cup is filled with coffee. (No, not Irish Coffee, just regular coffee.)

Like any job, being a whiskey expert means finding a sensible work-life balance that allows you to be productive while not killing your passion and interest for the subject. While I may not be tasting whiskey 24/7/365, I do spend many of my waking hours thinking about, reading about, talking about, and writing about drinks.

Through the lens of liquor, I have had to immerse myself in the study of biology, chemistry, tax laws, and even dense federal regulations—subjects I never thought I'd find interesting or even approachable. But in order to separate marketing hype and lies from fact, I spent much of the last several years searching archives for arcane or obscure information to prove or disprove general whiskey assumptions.

In the roughly twenty-five years I've been reporting on and writing about drinks, I've learned that the vast majority of our collective drinks knowledge comes from ad copy generated by marketing machines that drives liquor sales—and much of it is far from the truth.

The only way to understand whiskey's full story and why we drink what we do is to combine deep archival research with visits to modern distilleries. My wonderfully bizarre career has necessitated that I travel the world—from Scotland's barley fields to Tokyo's Highball bars to Kentucky's rickhouses—to learn about and taste an incredible array of spirits and cocktails. And what I've found in doing that work is, to build off Mark Twain's famous bon mot, that the true story is not only stranger than fiction, it is also more interesting.

Like many folks, I discovered the joys of drinking whiskey in college. In the late 1990s, I was fortunate enough to do an internship at *Food + Wine* magazine and I worked under the then-new associate editor Pete Wells, who went on to become the editor of the food section of the *New York Times* and was later the paper's restaurant critic.

It was during my time at the magazine that I learned that the Irish whiskey category was much bigger than just Jameson and Bushmills. I learned about the new whiskies from the upstart Cooley distillery in the middle of the island and even tasted the incredibly rare Knappogue Castle Irish Whiskey 1951 vintage, which cost an astounding $600 a bottle. (Now, of course, that's a relative bargain for such an old and delicious whiskey—a

recent search found that it was now going for as much as $4,999. You can read more about Knappogue Castle on page 353.)

The experience of working at *Food + Wine* opened my eyes to the nascent world of cocktails and whiskey that was just rebuilding after decades of decline. I feel incredibly fortunate to have been at the right place at certainly the right time.

After that experience, I went back to college knowing that I wanted to be a writer, and that I wanted to write about drinks. The one problem was that almost no publication wanted to regularly publish stories about spirits and cocktails. At the time, hard alcohol had been desperately trying to catch up to the popularity of beer and wine, which had become increasingly dominant. And of all the spirits, the situation for whiskey was by far the worst, and its prospects for the future were the dimmest. If you went into a bar, your choice of whiskey was fairly limited and was often poured from an oversize plastic bottle that was kept out of sight. All of the attention was being lavished on imported vodka, which seemed sexy and cool. Whiskey, by contrast, seemed old, stodgy, and tired.

But you can't have a revival without first having a downfall, and around the millennium folks started coming into the industry with some creative and innovate ideas. I remember going to WhiskyFest in 2001 and hearing John Glaser talk about what he was envisioning for his startup brand Compass Box. (See page 302 for more on Compass Box.) He had worked at Diageo on Johnnie Walker and wanted not only to shake up the blended Scotch category, but reinvent it. To put it bluntly, his ideas were revolutionary and questioned the status quo—to me, this was exactly the kind of spark whiskey needed to compete with vodka and craft beer.

Another regular fixture of WhiskyFest was Jim Beam's grandson Booker Noe (see page 122), who was working to change the fate of the American whiskey industry with his innovative and delicious small-batch bourbons, including Booker's, Knob Creek, and Basil Hayden. While it wasn't easy, he finally was able to get the industry to embrace and celebrate the inherent differences that can occur when you age whiskey.

While I was certainly right about whiskey coming back, I would have never believed what has transpired over the last twenty-five years, and how incredibly popular the spirit has become around the globe. It's nothing short of a miracle.

WHISKEY 101

While Scotland, Ireland, and Kentucky have long been famous for making whiskey, the spirit is now widely produced in many countries around the world, including Australia, France, India, Israel, Italy, and Mexico.

Whiskey's ubiquity begs the question of where it originally comes from. Well, that's not any easy question to answer and one that is, no surprise, quite contentious. The two most *likely* spots where it was first made are Ireland and Scotland. What we can say definitively is that no matter the region where whiskey was born, the liquor essentially evolved from a simple spirit produced by industrious farmers looking to turn excess grain into alcohol. What came off their early stills certainly wouldn't qualify as whiskey today and in many ways was more like gin. Over the centuries, however, these protospirits slowly evolved into the familiar and complex amber elixir that we know and love today.

Thanks to whiskey's nebulous history, distillers, marketers, regulators, politicians, bartenders, and drinkers argued about what is and what is not whiskey for more than a century. Fortunately, most people can now—finally—agree on a basic definition for the spirit, along with generally how to make it.

Here are the main traits that make whiskey whiskey—and how it differs from other major spirits.

IT'S WHISKEY IF:

IT IS MADE FROM GRAIN. What kind of grain? That depends on local regulations and/or customs. Whiskey is commonly produced from corn, rye, barley, and wheat. Some distillers use oats, millet, or even spelt to make whiskey. The base, depending on the type of whiskey, can be just one type of grain or a blend of different types of grains.

THE GRAIN IS MADE INTO A MASH. This is done by grinding it up and cooking it with hot water. With the help of enzymes, this process converts the grain's stores of starch into sugar, which is much easier to ferment and turn into alcohol.

THE RESULTING LIQUID IS FERMENTED WITH YEAST. This creates a low-alcohol "distiller's beer," which is sometimes also called "wash."

Whiskey vs Whisky

One of the most maddening whiskey-related debates is the spelling of the word itself—is it whiskey or whisky?

The current convention is for any nonspecific reference, as well as whiskey produced in the United States and Ireland, to be spelled with an *e*. However, whisky produced in Scotland, Canada, Japan, India, Israel, and Australia is whisky without an *e*. Then, of course, there are many famous exceptions to the rule. (For example, Maker's Mark bourbon, which hails from Loretto, Kentucky, and George Dickel from Tullahoma, Tennessee, call themselves whisky.) And there are some countries, such as Mexico, where producers decide for themselves which spelling of the word they prefer.

In Ireland, whiskey is usually spelled with an e.

Like many topics in the whisk(e)y world, its fans have taken a fairly inconsequential thing and built it into an issue loaded with meaning and bubbling with drama. So naturally, I'm going to do the same here, with a twist.

It doesn't matter how you spell the word. Not even a little.

The whole conflagration around the spelling is particularly ridiculous given that the origin of the word *whiskey* is the Latin *aqua vitae* (water of life). To go from Latin to the Gaelic *uisge beatha* (pronounced ISH-keh BA-ha) to the modern term *whisk(e)y* required several major linguistic leaps and significant transliterations. After this less-than-streamlined process, any case for what's authentic or correct is pretty baseless. Around the globe and throughout modern history, both spellings have been used without regard to geography or these supposed spelling rules.

This silliness notwithstanding, I tried to keep to the modern usage and conventions of *whiskey* and *whisky* throughout this book. If I'm not speaking about a specific area, I use the generic *whiskey*. Given my mini rant here, I fully admit it may seem pointless to continue this charade. And yet it may seem even more confusing to use just one version of the term given that the spelling conventions in various countries are nonetheless dogmatically followed today and some "experts" are enraged if you refer to Scotch as "whiskey" and bourbon as "whisky." So, here we are. Still.

In Scotland, whisky is usually spelled without an e.

Aged whiskey is "dumped" from a barrel and will then be filtered and bottled.

THE "DISTILLER'S BEER" IS THEN PUMPED INTO A STILL. The distilling process is the main difference between making beer and whiskey.

THE DISTILLING HAPPENS IN A STILL. Depending on the whiskey brand and where it's made, a distiller will use a pot still, a column still, a hybrid pot/column still, or a chamber still.

IT IS AGED IN A WOODEN BARREL. The kind of barrel and how long the whiskey ages is based, again, on local regulations and traditions, as well as the climate, which will help determine when the whiskey is fully mature.

IT'S DEFINITELY NOT WHISKEY IF:

IT IS MADE FROM SUGAR OR MOLASSES (LIKE RUM) OR FROM GRAPES (LIKE BRANDY).

IT IS VODKA. Vodka can be made from grains but can't be called whiskey because it is not barrel-aged and it rarely meets all the specific whiskey regulations in a given country. More importantly it's designed to be odorless and flavorless, so it mixes with a range of ingredients. Whiskey, though, is produced to have abundant inherent aromas and flavors that are refined and enhanced by barrel aging.

A (Very) Brief History of Whiskey

We're currently in the midst of a whiskey boom, but the fortunes of whiskey have been cyclical, to say the least, with just as many busts as bonanzas and no shortage of high-wire drama along the way.

But first, whiskey had to be created. And that was a long process that began centuries ago, an evolution built through contributions from around the globe. So, full disclosure: What follows isn't comprehensive. It can't be. Not without even more pages than you have before you. But within each chapter is a much deeper dive into each country's and region's particular whiskey origins and backstories. This opening chapter is an attempt to set the larger stage for those smaller stages to come.

Let's start at the start. Long before there were small batch bourbons or sought-after Japanese blends or even single malts from Scotland, there were farm-made spirits that probably tasted very little like modern whiskey—but they were a harbinger of things to come. With this in mind, the first questions to ask are really: Can we even know where whiskey came from? Can anywhere claim to be the one true home of whiskey?

In 1808, Eli Barnum & Benjamin Brooks patented their wooden chamber still design.

It would be a marketer's dream to say, "Yes! We [insert country, region, or town] definitively created whiskey and everyone else followed in our footsteps." But the answer you usually get about whiskey's origin—like so many things about whiskey—depends on who you ask and what country you're in at the time. The true origin stories are both surprising and yet make sense, and require a raucous voyage around the globe to truly understand.

People have been making distilled spirits for thousands of years. David Wondrich, the world's foremost cocktail historian (and a friend and colleague), likes to point out that the basics of distilling are really not all that hard to learn. You can make an improvised still out of objects and materials easily found in a well-stocked basement, hardware store, or junkyard. This means the bar to distilling alcohol is not terribly high, even with pre-industrial materials. And that many of these early stills were not meant to last for eons and were destroyed a long time ago.

And to be clear, ancient spirits shouldn't be confused with the modern version of whiskey we know and love. Early liquor wasn't made in modern state-of-the-art distilleries but on basic small stills, which produced a completely different flavor profile. Also, the resulting alcohol wasn't typically aged in barrels. Perhaps most importantly, this proto-alcohol was originally considered a medicinal concoction thought to hold magical healing powers and maybe even the secret to living forever!

♦ BELLY UP TO THE ANCIENT BAR

People in Europe, Asia, and the Middle East have been making alcohol for many thousands of years—Dr. Patrick McGovern thinks that the Natufian culture in Western Asia might have been making a beer of some sort since as early as 13,000 BCE. (He has found evidence of alcohol being made in 7,000 BCE in China's Yellow River Valley, which is south of Beijing.) But these early beverages were usually made from a base of fruit, barley, or honey and then fermented into a style of beer and wine.

The next giant step in the development of whiskey was the advent of distilling, which wouldn't emerge for several thousand years. When, exactly? No one is really sure. Evidence has been found that stills were being possibly used as far back as the fifth century BCE in Mesopotamia. At a site called Tepe Gawra, some earthenware pots have been found that could have actually been used as simple stills. Some archaeologists and spirits experts have speculated that there may have been distilling even earlier in China, India, and across Southeast Asia. However, much more scholarship is needed to explore the early roots of distilling and possibly even reevaluating previous finds with distillation in mind. Ultimately, over the following centuries the art of distillation becomes well known in many parts of the world and Europeans began distilling in earnest.

No matter where these early distillers were located, they produced spirits for a number of perhaps surprising

Historically, pot stills were used by distillers around the world to make a range of spirits.

reasons—from creating perfumes to making medicinal essences. There were also monks and alchemists trying to discover a "water of life" that would provide longevity and good health. Some of their early stills were made of wood, clay, or even dried hollow gourds. Grains or fruit would be fermented and then distilled in these contraptions, which would be heated directly over a fire.

Around the thirteenth century, distillers in Ireland had started making a protowhiskey from local barley and other grains, such as oats and rye. This seminal *uisge beatha* certainly didn't taste like Bushmills or Jameson—they were flavored with a range of local botanicals, even honey. In many ways, the first whiskey is more closely related to gin than you might expect. Ultimately, around the 1400s these early European distillers went from making medicinal tinctures to recreational drinks. A true liquor boom followed over the next few hundred years, which led to the rise of dedicated distillers. Depending on what was locally available, these distillers used grapes and other fruits, sugarcane, or grain. Many of the well-known differences that make vodka or bourbon what they are came centuries later. Most of the spirits made during this period were likely similar in style to one another—products of a time when there were no rules, expectations, or standards.

One of the earliest known records of apparent whiskey making appears in the *Red Book of Ossory*, which we think was created in the fourteenth century by Bishop Richard de Ledrede, who lived in Kilkenny, Ireland. The manuscript includes a recipe for making aqua vitae and currently resides in the collection of St. Canice's Cathedral in Kilkenny. That mention alone gives Ireland some claim to its self-proclaimed status as the ancestral home of whiskey.

On the other hand, the earliest written reference to whisky distilling in Scotland dates to 1494 and was found in the official Exchequer Rolls, the daily budget and financial account statement for Scottish King James IV. In them is a simple note marking a transaction with a local distiller: "To Friar John Cor, by order of the King, to make aqua vitae VIII bolls of malt." Some experts and historians think that the good friar lived in Lindores Abbey, about 50 miles (80 kilometers) north of Edinburgh (where a Scotch distillery exists today).

To be fair, neither Ireland's nor Scotland's whiskey references are particularly detailed and could refer to some other type of distilled spirit—"aqua vitae" more or less included the whole liquor category as well as other things like water-of-life serums. There's also a confounding mention in Chaucer's *Canterbury Tales* of the late fourteenth century, about distilling beer in Britain, which is the first step in making whiskey. This timeline for whiskey could be turned on its head tomorrow if someone discovers a rare manuscript from a different time, one that puts Scotland or—brace yourself—even England first.

What's indisputable is that Ireland and Scotland are closely linked in many ways, including geography and early migration, and so share a ton of common DNA and history. It's more than plausible that distilling knowledge, along with these early spirits, traveled the 12 miles (19 kilometers) that separate Northern Ireland from the Scottish island of Islay. Repeatedly.

It's important to remember, also, that folks distill what's at hand. In fact, the practice of distilling tends to catch on when farmers realize they can turn what they grow into liquor. The advantages are glaring: Distilling transforms produce or grain into a product much easier to store, and one that tends to increase in value. You can sell liquor or barter it for other goods and services, even in winter when the fields are bare. Successful farms are really just successful businesses—and one way to ensure profitability is to hold down costs and keep spoilage and waste to a minimum.

Thanks to these advantages, over the next several centuries whiskey became very popular with farmers across Scotland and Ireland and then in the US and Canada, but it was far from the most popular spirit. Arrack (a palm sap-, rice-, or molasses-based alcohol from Goa and southeast Asia), rum, gin, and Cognac were far more sought-after and their consumption much more widespread.

Phylloxera insects derailed European wine, brandy, sherry, and port production in the late 1800s.

♦ PHYLLOXERA: AN UNLIKELY ALLY

What allowed whiskey to really catch on was the assistance of an unlikely ally: a tiny little insect called phylloxera. The grapevine-loving pests showed up in Europe in the late 1800s, and like a hoard of unruly tourists they wreaked havoc and upset the locals. But this was no spring break gone awry—phylloxera systematically and effectively destroyed Europe's vineyards. The insects greedily consume a vine's nutrients at root level before it can produce grapes, leaving fields full of depleted and half-dead plants in their wake.

And although it feels obvious, it must be said nonetheless: If there are no grapes, there can be no wine.

The phylloxera scourge was a horrific scenario for winemakers and wine drinkers, but it wouldn't have been so entirely awful if the destructive insects didn't also take out several other heavyweight drinks, including sherry, port, and Cognac. The damage to the grapes was perhaps only surpassed by the damage to the reputations of these noble beverages. In order to stay alive, some brands resorted to all manner of shortcuts, including blending in lesser-quality potato-based alcohol from Germany. These practices (or rumors of them) justifiably scared off

Thanks to the work of the so-called Men of Tain at the Glenmorangie distillery and their colleagues across Scotland, by the turn of the twentieth century, Scotch had established itself on the world liquor map.

The temperance movement swept across the Unites States in the 1800s and culminated in the passage of the Volstead Act.

not just drinkers but also doctors who prescribed fortified wine and spirits to cure maladies.

Life without these essential beverages was almost too much to bear for many residents of the United Kingdom and Europe. While grape growers searched for a solution, thirsty people searched for other things to drink. As you'd expect, many discovered the joys of whiskey for the first time during the phylloxera outbreak—and it was a massive boon to the Scotch, Irish, and American whiskey industries. In fact, it transformed whiskey from a farm product to an international bestseller. According to the *Scotch Whisky Industry Record*, Scottish distillers made nearly 14 million liters (3.7 million gallons) of alcohol in 1870. By 1900, they were making nearly 22 million liters (5.8 million gallons) annually.

Ultimately, a hearty rootstock found in Texas saved the day (reinforcing the age-old adage not to mess with Texas), but it took several years to replant vines and thus end the phylloxera outbreak. In that time, whiskey proved that it wasn't just a bench warmer but an all-star that could hit clean up and carry the whole damn team on its back. Cognac, sherry, and port suddenly found themselves trying to regain their starting spot behind an unheralded upstart named whiskey.

♦ **TEMPERANCE, PROHIBITION, AND WAR**

The twentieth century proved tumultuous for whiskey distillers. There was a danger yet more deadly than phylloxera on the horizon: temperance. Around the globe and especially in the United States, the temperance movement was becoming ever more powerful as a broad array of Americans began to see the value in banning the production of alcohol. Like reproductive rights are today, it was a polarizing issue that led to a number of states passing laws that banned the sale of alcohol. The movement culminated with the passage in 1919 of the Eighteenth Amendment to the US Constitution (the federal prohibition of alcoholic beverages), along with the Volstead Act to support the amendment, which made the manufacture, transportation, and sale of alcohol illegal. Ultimately, it would take a global economic depression of epic proportions to end Prohibition thirteen long years later.

Prohibition effectively destroyed the American whiskey industry, but its effects were more mixed for whiskey distillers in Canada, Scotland, and Ireland. It was also undeniably responsible for the styles of whiskey we drink today. And, outsized as Prohibition's impacts were on the development of the global whiskey trade, it wasn't the only impediment: The century was also marked by two horrific world wars and an influenza pandemic. Because of these world-altering events, distillers were barely able to function for decades, and some had to rebuild completely several times. By the late 1940s, as the world was piecing itself back together, the international whiskey industry was at a crossroads. In

While the United States was supposed to be bone-dry during Prohibition, a network of bootleggers and speakeasies ensured no Americans went thirsty.

Heirloom Grains

To make its Jaywalk Heirloom rye whiskey, a few years ago the New York Distilling Company had to resurrect a ghost.

With the help of Cornell University's seed savers program, the Brooklyn-based distillery discovered the historic Horton rye, which had last been grown in New York State a century ago. While each Horton rye plant is smaller than most modern commercially available varieties, it was prized for its crème brûlée and cinnamon notes.

Convinced that this variety would make more flavorful whiskey than commercially available ryes, the New York Distilling Company commissioned a farmer in the Finger Lakes area of upstate New York to propagate the ten seeds of Horton it received from Cornell. Fortunately, they were able to harvest a small amount of the rye and learn that it fully lived up to its reputation for flavor. Over the past few years, the distillery has been able to increase the amount of Horton it grows and now harvests more than 250 acres (101 hectares) of the grain each year.

The New York Distilling Company isn't the only distiller to use an heirloom rye variety. In fact, one of the greatest developments to come out of the craft distilling movement has been the discovery and use of once-lost grains that were popular with distillers in previous centuries. Not only do these varieties tend to have more flavor than modern commodity grains that are bred for high yield and consistency, but heirloom grains are sometimes easier to distill and also reflect the terroir of an area (see page 42).

To encourage more distillers to work with local farms, there are a number of associations around the country that have set up special designations with standards that require the use of local grains. For instance, to qualify for the Empire Rye program you have to use a base of at least 75 percent grains grown in New York State.

This trend, over time, will likely lead even more distillers, large and small, to use heirloom grains as they become easier to find and buy in larger quantities.

Distillers are increasingly making whiskey from flavorful heirloom grains.

the wake of one major upheaval after another, whiskey producers were left in a quandary. What kind of whiskey did people want? Or did they want whiskey at all? The process of answering those questions resulted in seismic changes in the distilling and drinks business in the second half of the century, forcing producers to completely rethink not just their business plans but how they produced their whiskey.

The whisky that ended up winning the day in the aftermath of World War II was smooth and quaffable blended Scotch, which became almost ubiquitous, while staples like Irish whiskey and American rye nearly disappeared completely. But while blended Scotch had a moment in the 1950s and '60s, the 1970s would bring gloom again to the industry. Tastes changed with the cultural upheaval caused by disagreements between generations, and Scotch began to be considered fusty compared to vodka, which could be mixed with just about anything and had a Scandinavian cool factor.

♦ HIPSTERS DISCOVER THE JOY OF WHISKEY

As the twentieth century came to a close, whiskey had managed to beat the odds and had stuck around, if only at the margins at times. But the vodka boom of the 1980s was almost too much for whiskey distillers to compete against.

With a far different history from whiskey and a massive base audience in Russia, Eastern Europe, and Scandinavia, vodka became a global bestseller in the

By the late 1990s, the hipsters coming of age discovered the joys of drinking whiskey.

second half of the twentieth century. The clear spirit had gone from near obscurity to become the drink of choice in the United States. Fast forward to the late 1990s and it seemed there was a distinct chance that all whiskey would be relegated to the sidelines. Currently, three out of every ten bottles of liquor sold in the States are vodka. That's how it's been for decades, and it will likely continue that way for the foreseeable future.

The benefit of falling so far out of favor was that whiskey was primed for a comeback. The ubiquity of vodka led to a next generation of drinkers who had no interest in their parents' Screwdrivers, Cape Codders, or Greyhounds. But whiskey, that seemed new and cool. Like the joy that comes with discovering a Stan Getz album in your grandparents' record cabinet, tasting a dusty bottle of Scotch or rye from the back of the liquor cabinet was a similar revelation.

Making Whiskey

No matter where in the world it's produced, all whiskey is always made from grains, which are fermented, distilled, and then aged in a wooden barrel. But that doesn't mean all whiskey is made exactly the same way. There are, in fact, huge differences in how whiskey is produced among different countries and brands. The devil, as they say, is in the details.

To truly understand a particular whiskey, you need to know about more than just how it tastes. Including, for example, how it was made and from what, and for how long it aged in a barrel before it ended up in the bottle you bought. That means understanding the key ingredients, the steps of distillation, and all the wild-card factors that go into creating your favorite dram.

♦ IT'S ALL ABOUT THE GRAINS

Historically, distillers were farmers who made whiskey from whatever local grain was available. The differences among those grains (basically, more or less starch) dictated how they made their whiskey and its eventual flavor.

As alcohol became a viable industry, distillers moved off the farm and typically stopped growing grains themselves. Most large whiskey companies today work with a network of suppliers to buy loads and loads of grains. For a sense of scope, take Corby, the giant distillery in Windsor, Ontario, which uses 120,000 metric tons of corn and 10,000 metric tons of rye (132,000 and 11,000 US tons, respectively) each year.

Nowadays you can find whiskey made from all kinds of grains (including Corsair Quinoa Whiskey), but distillers generally stick to barley, corn, rye, or wheat. Depending on the type of whiskey they're making, these grains are either distilled separately or combined and then distilled.

Regardless of whiskey type, none of today's distillers, large or small, currently use genetically modified grains. Most brands use grains that have been bred the old-fashioned way to have a set of desirable attributes, such as a high yield and resistance to disease.

♦ HOW GRAIN AFFECTS FLAVOR

It's hard to overestimate the role that grain plays in creating a whiskey's flavor. Single malt Scotch tastes like single malt Scotch because it's made from barley—if it was made from corn or any other grain it would have a completely different flavor. In many ways, the same flavor impact can be seen in bread—if you make a recipe with corn flour and

One of the few universal whiskey rules is that it has to be made from grain.

Is Whiskey Green?

From cars to clothing to furniture, we have become more and more concerned with the sustainability of how things are made in our increasingly overheated world. Whiskey is certainly not exempt from this all-important discussion—and frankly has some work to do.

The industry is a long way from calling itself green, given the variety and quantity of natural resources distilleries draw on. The bigger distilling conglomerates, in particular, consume enormous quantities of water and energy in the spirit-making process. And most American whiskey makers churn through huge numbers of oak barrels that cannot—by federal regulations—be reused to make bourbon or rye in the United States. Add in the environmental costs of shipping glass bottles around the world and it's clear a lot of change is necessary for the industry to become more sustainable.

However, there are some long-practiced green initiatives in the industry that can be built on. Traditionally, distilleries have sold or given away their spent grain after the distilling process is finished. All you need to make alcohol is the starch inside the grain. All the other parts of the corn, rye, or barley are essentially byproducts. Instead of ending up in landfills, these leftovers are perfect for feeding livestock. The spent grain does need to be trucked away, which is a factor. For this reason, some companies have invested in anaerobic digesters instead. These high-tech systems use bacteria to turn the spent grain into biofuel. The biofuel is then burned to heat up the stills for the next batch of whiskey. It's an innovation, and a good one, but it does have a lot of up-front costs to amortize over the lifetime of the system, making it less practical for many smaller brands. Maker's Mark bourbon was the first American whiskey to install one of these systems back in 2008.

You could definitely argue that reselling once-used wooden barrels from the United States to be used for aging other whiskies and spirits is a green practice. But the salutary effects of this idea are mitigated somewhat by the need to ship many of these casks around the world, which involves the burning of fossil fuels. So, not ideal.

A more encouraging development is that giant liquor company Diageo has started building carbon neutral distilleries around the world, including its new Bulleit Bourbon facility in Shelbyville, Kentucky, which will limit carbon emissions by using electrode boilers to create all the steam for its stills and will buy renewable electricity from the local power authority. Diageo has also pledged to use 30 percent less water by 2030 to make its different alcoholic beverages. In 2019, rival industry titan Pernod Ricard pledged to reduce its carbon footprint by half by 2030 and be net zero by 2050.

If there's hope, it's in the whiskey industry once again returning to its roots to overcome a massive challenge. After all, whiskey originated as part of a perfect,

At Westward Whiskey in Portland, Oregon, the leftovers from its distilling process are used to feed cattle at a nearby dairy farm.

multifaceted, and ingenious zero-waste production process on small farms. Liquor provided farmers a way to turn their grain, something notoriously hard to store, into a shelf-stable commodity. The spent grain from the distilling process was used as cattle feed in many whiskey-producing areas, leading to animal excrement that was an important renewable source of fertilizer, which enriched the land to support the very grains that would begin the distilling process anew. When you ran a farm, zero waste wasn't just a noble idea or a theory to test but the difference between surviving the winter or not. And that seems an apt metaphor for the climate moment we're racing toward. If the whiskey industry is to adapt and survive, it will need to revisit its sustainable roots for inspiration to solve its bigger environmental challenges.

Whiskey is at its core an agricultural product and the industry depends upon a global network of farmers.

then make it again with rye flour, you'll be able to tell the two loaves apart immediately. Distillers have the added advantage of being able to work with a single grain or blend them together, which creates a vast palette of flavors.

Each grain has its own flavor notes and attributes. Here's a quick breakdown of the four most popular for distilling.

CORN has an inherent sweetness and creaminess. It's also relatively easy to ferment and distill. It contains lots of starch, which means it produces a lot of alcohol.

RYE is harder to ferment and distill than corn, but it tends to have big spice notes, including cinnamon and black pepper, and a rich mouthfeel.

BARLEY has a kind of breakfast cereal note (think Grape-Nuts), which is especially present when peated. Most importantly, the grain contains a high level of the enzymes that turn starch into sugar. This is why distillers often add some malted barley to their mash bills—to help with the fermentation process.

WHEAT is generally used in conjunction with other grains to make whiskey because it has less flavor (think of wheat bread, which is fairly innocuous). But wheat has the advantage of giving a spirit a silkier mouthfeel.

The large whiskey brands usually buy commodity grains, which ensures a consistent, steady supply. But a growing number of distilleries have been able to create even more flavors by identifying and propagating heirloom seeds that fell out of favor decades or even centuries ago. These historic grain varieties also allow a whiskey to reflect its terroir (the characteristics of the place where the grain is grown; see page 42) and have become a powerful marketing point of pride.

♦ TO MALT OR NOT TO MALT?

Scottish single malt is one of the most famous and popular types of whiskey in the world. But what does single malt mean? The term *single* means the whisky is from just one distillery, while the *malt* part is a bit less straightforward. It refers to the base grain, malted barley.

Distillers traditionally malted barley so that it would be easier to ferment. It's full of starch, but you need to transform the starch into more easily fermentable sugar to make alcohol. Barley is a kind of magical grain because it has a very high diastatic value, which means each kernel already has the enzymes within it to convert starch to sugar. But to activate this conversion process, you need to trick the grain into thinking it's about to sprout by wetting it down. Then, in order to stop the seeds from actually growing, you need to essentially bake the grain. The process of wetting and heating is called malting. This is where some Scotch can get its smoky flavor. Many distilleries heat the barley over a pungent peat fire. The smoke generated imbues the grain with rich notes reminiscent of a fireplace, tires, or for some drinkers, adhesive first aid bandages.

Today, most whiskey brands use a large commercial company called a maltster, which treats the grain and delivers the finished malted barley right to the distillery. Before the late 1960s, creating malted barley was a lot more labor intensive and many distilleries used the so-called floor malting process.

Floor malting involves spreading the barley out on the floor and spraying it with water, then turning it periodically to aerate the grain and keep it from getting moldy. To do this you use a big wooden paddle that looks like it could double as a giant pizza peel used to slide pies in and out of industrial ovens. Workers who used to malt barley all day every day would supposedly develop one shoulder that was larger than the other. This was colloquially called monkey shoulder, which

Traditionally, distillers in Scotland and Ireland floor malted their barley in order to convert the grain's starches to sugar. Some modern distilleries, including Benriach, pictured above, continue to use the historic process today.

is where the brand Monkey Shoulder gets its name. A few Scotch distilleries, including Bowmore on Islay and Balvenie in the Scottish Highlands, continue to floor malt their barley today.

At one point in nineteenth-century Ireland, distillers were taxed by how much malted barley they used. But distillers are a resourceful lot, so they started using a mix of malted and unmalted barley, which over time evolved into the signature flavor of Irish whiskey.

In Scotland, logs of peat are cut from bogs and are then burned to dry the malted barley.

All this begs the question of why other types of grain aren't malted. Well, the other key grains don't have the same high diastatic value as barley, so they're not typically malted. In fact, malted barley's enzymes are so good at converting starch into sugar that the grain is added to the mash bill of most bourbons and many ryes, to help fermentation along.

Peat's Role in Malting

While Scotch distilleries on the island of Islay today are famous for smoking their barley over peat fires instead of drying it in ovens, the practice was once far more widespread across Scotland and Ireland. (Brands like Bushmills and Glenmorangie even used to make peated whiskies.) This tracks, because peat bogs, which are a mix of water and decaying organic matter (plants, leaves, bark, and moss), are found in both countries and across Europe. The peat-smoking process is fairly straightforward: Blocks of the peat are cut from a bog and then left to dry out. The dried blocks are burned like wood logs, with the soaked barley spread out above the fire atop a giant fine screen, allowing the smoke of the peat fire to channel up through the grain. The barley is not only dried by the fire's heat but now also has a smoky aroma that will come through in the whisky. (I've tried some of the barley that the Islay distillery Laphroaig uses and it's like eating smoked Grape-Nuts—the grain makes a delicious snack!)

Some distillers are now experimenting with smoking their grains over other types of fires. For its Brimstone Whiskey, Texas-based Balcones roasts blue corn over fires of local scrub oak. This process not only gives the whiskey a sense of place but also a unique

Sour Mash

You often hear the term *sour mash* thrown around by distillers and whiskey aficionados. (It will definitely come up if you're talking about Tennessee whiskey!) While it sounds at first like something bad, it just means that the distiller reserves a bit of the liquid distilling leftovers from the still, called backset or stillage, and adds it the next time they cook grains. In some ways, it's kind of like making sourdough with a "mother." But despite the name of this process (and despite the results in sourdough bread) sour mash doesn't add a sour tang to the whiskey. It got its name because this liquid is very acidic and helps lower the pH of the next batch of mash, which keeps bacteria from forming and the yeast happy and able to do its job. This process helps to ensure that the yeast is consistent from batch to batch and doesn't mutate, which would change the flavor of the finished whiskey. Most American whiskey distillers use a sour mash process, but a handful of new brands, such as Kentucky's Wilderness Trail and Peerless, are made using a process called sweet mash, in which each batch is started completely from scratch. Despite its name, this process does not actually make a sweeter whiskey. It's labor intensive, but the proponents of the sweet mash process say that it allows more of the flavor from the grain to come through in the finished whiskey and also creates a softer mouthfeel.

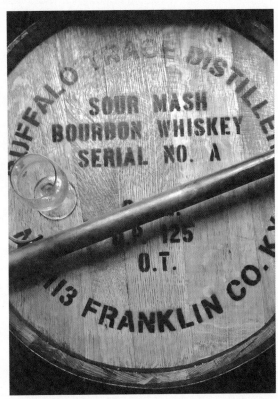

Nearly all the bourbon produced across the United States is made using the so-called sour mash process.

profile. The smoke flavor absolutely carries through to the finished whiskey.

In the same way that the heat of a hot pepper can be measured in Scoville units, the smokiness of a whiskey (made up of phenol compounds) has its own measure: phenolic parts per million (PPM). Bruichladdich's super smoky Octomore 8.3 set the bar for whiskey in 2017 when it registered an incredible 309 PPM rating. (Sipping one of the Octomore releases is like inhaling a campfire with your nose just inches from the logs.) Fortunately, most Islay whiskies clock in far below that, around 50 PPM.

♦ HOW WATER AFFECTS FLAVOR

For decades, a major part of whiskey brand marketing has involved touting a unique water source for a given distillery. Usually, there's a sacred spring or a well spoken about in hushed but reverential tones typically reserved only for a long-deceased distiller. I've had the privilege of accompanying various whiskey distillers and brand ambassadors as they've eagerly shown me their mythical water sources, to which I have paid my respects. This sometimes means hiking a good way up a steep hill through a beautiful but unremarkable Scottish field to see a very small stream quietly and serenely gurgling. And I appreciate the crucial attention to detail (but the hike less so).

So, does water really matter when making whiskey?

In short, absolutely. From the cooking of the grains (called mashing) to the cooling of the alcohol vapors in the still, to the proofing down of the finished spirit, you literally can't make whiskey without water. And because making whiskey is highly nuanced, the composition of the water used is important.

The most desirable water contains significant amounts of a few key minerals, including calcium, magnesium, and zinc, which all help with the fermentation process. According to Todd Leopold, master distiller of Leopold Bros. in Denver, Colorado, if you don't have enough of these elements for the yeast, the "metabolism shuts down" and the fermentation essentially stops. But he is also quick to add that this almost never happens in a modern distillery

Distillers need a consistent and reliable source of water, which is why historically distilleries, like Royal Brackla, have been located near springs and rivers.

The chemical compounds in water are essential for successfully fermenting grains to make whiskey.

because the water is tested, and then treated, if necessary, to ensure that it has the right chemical makeup. In fact, some distillers like to start with very soft water, which is essentially pure, and add the desired minerals to it. But the rule above all is that the water used by a distiller must be consistent, and the biggest brands have invested in technology that ensures there is no variance in their water supply.

Kentucky distillers in particular like to make a big deal about their water being filtered through limestone, often crediting this geological feature in part for the success of their whiskey industry. While the limestone certainly helps give water a significant amount of calcium and magnesium, Kentucky is far from the only place in the world with limestone deposits. The limestone shelf under Kentucky continues for hundreds of miles beyond its borders.

Before public water systems were built, distillers had to establish their own reliable water sources. That said, when major brands began selling millions upon millions of cases of whiskey, a single spring just couldn't provide enough water. This is why many of the bigger companies around the world use municipal water sources—tap water. These brands take the extra step of testing the municipal water and treating it in various ways to ensure it has the right chemical makeup to ensure consistency of flavor in the whiskey.

♦ MASHING

Water's dance partner in the early distilling stage is grain. Once distillers have decided on their mash bill (the percentage of different grains they will use or just a single grain), the grains are then sent through a mill. The goal is to break down the protective barriers around each kernel's stash of starch and create a rough grind of the grain, which is a mix of husk, bran, and flour. (Most large distilleries now have their own mills, but at the dawn of the industry distillers would bring their grain to a local miller.) The crushed grain is then cooked in hot water in giant metal tanks called mash tuns, which produces a porridgelike concoction. If you're using more than one type of grain, generally the corn goes into the tun first, since it needs to cook longest and at the highest temperature. Then later the rest of the grains are added in stages at increasingly lower temperatures—with the malted barley generally added last. And though it's the last guest to arrive at the party, it is actually the most important. Malted barley is a bona fide superhero because each kernel contains essential enzymes to convert starches to sugar—a process that is technically called saccharification. (If you're making whiskey from a mash bill that doesn't includes malted barley you need to add commercially produced enzymes in order to convert the starch into sugar.) Why does this all matter? You need sugar, not starch, to make alcohol. Depending upon the type of whiskey you're making, the whole mashing process takes somewhere between thirty minutes and an hour.

This is where the road forks in whiskey making. In Scotland and Ireland, the mash is strained and the sugary liquid, or wort (pronounced "wert"), is fermented. If pot still whiskey makers don't filter out the spent grain (using a tank called a lautering tun), it will end up in the still and may burn, which gives the whiskey a bad taste. But in the United States, many whiskey distillers ferment the sugary liquid and the spent grain together. They are able to do this since most American whiskey distillers use a column still, which allows you to skip the filtering step. This method is known in the industry as distilling on the grains, which is a key difference from how many other countries make their whiskey. This is the way that German distillers make alcohol and is something that immigrants from that country brought to the US in the 1800s.

♦ FERMENTATION

The next crucial step in the distilling process is to ferment the wort, or sugary liquid, by adding commercial yeast to it. The yeast consumes the sugars in the wort and produces heat, carbon dioxide gas, and—more importantly—alcohol.

Most distilleries have giant steel or wooden fermentation tanks that are several stories tall. (In Scotland, these containers are called "washbacks.") Corby, the enormous Canadian distillery in Windsor, Ontario, has a massive building that holds thirty-nine fermenters, each four stories tall, with a collective capacity of 40,000 gallons (1,500 hectoliters). No matter the size, fermenters give off heat and a huge amount of carbon dioxide, which is why they are usually open on top or have a system to suck out the CO_2. This is no joke, since the gas, if not handled correctly, can cause a fermenter to explode. Short of that, it can literally knock you out if you stick your head too far into one of these tanks. (This is not hyperbole—I peered a bit too deeply into the fermenters at Bushmills in Northern Ireland and felt lightheaded and woozy for the next ten minutes or so.)

After bubbling and foaming for between two and five days, the yeast is done with its job and the fermentation

In whiskey distilleries, the fermentation process takes place in large wooden or stainless-steel tanks.

The fermentation process is incredibly important, since it doesn't just create alcohol but also chemical flavor compounds. Four Roses in Lawrenceburg, Kentucky, seen above, even uses five different yeast strains to make its bourbon.

is complete. The resulting alcoholic concoction, traditionally called distiller's beer in America or the wash in the UK, has an alcohol level somewhere between 6 and 9 percent ABV. It's essentially beer at this stage, but without the hops that give a standard pilsner or IPA its signature flavor and bitterness. This is a key point to understand about whiskey: You can't make it without first making beer. Because of this, the best whiskey distillers usually have a background in brewing beer and strongly believe that this isn't a step to merely complete but is essential in developing flavor compounds.

How Yeast Affects Flavor

Legendary Kentucky distiller Jim Beam was known to take some of the company's yeast home with him for safekeeping, despite his family's complaints about its strong smell.

He "drove a Cadillac car back and forth from the distillery to Bardstown, a jug of family yeast sitting in the front seat next to him," wrote his great-grandson Fred Noe in his memoir *Beam, Straight Up*. "That yeast was a Beam heirloom, passed down through the generations, and it turned the mash into alcohol. You see, you have to use the same yeast to keep your whiskey consistent and tasting right and he wasn't about to let it out of his sight. No room for error on that subject."

It used to be said that there was at least one member of the Beam family working at every distillery in Kentucky. While that was probably a bit of an exaggeration (though not by much), the family's yeast strain was used by a number of different companies where various Beam family members worked. But here's the funny thing about yeast: It is a living organism that mutates readily. So, while Heaven Hill's yeast came with Earl Beam, the company's original distiller back in 1935, it has certainly changed over time. On a molecular level, the original yeast and what's used by the company today are no doubt still similar, but today's yeast has transformed enough that it produces whiskey that likely tastes very different from what was made decades ago.

If you don't have a family yeast strain and want to distill whiskey, you can buy commercially available yeast, which is exactly what many brands have done and is a standard practice for new distilleries. You can also specify how quickly you want your fermentation to last (generally the longer the mash ferments the more flavor compounds are generated) and even what flavors you want in the resulting spirit, including fruity, floral, or even grassy. On the other hand, some craft and larger distillers are currently experimenting with reviving lost yeast strains that were used in the past. (Some large companies used to keep yeast libraries and a number of these collections have been rediscovered recently.) When these come of age, we'll have a true sense of what whiskey tasted like decades ago.

At most large distilleries nowadays, there's a high-tech lab devoted to maintaining the purity of the yeast and propagating new batches of it. Several "mother" batches are always maintained in a freezer along with several more samples kept off-site, just in case all of a distillery's yeast supplies somehow get contaminated.

♦ DISTILLATION

No matter whether you're in Kentucky, the Scottish Highlands, or Goa, India, all whiskey is made in some kind of still.

The lightly alcoholic liquid resulting from fermentation, called the wash or distiller's beer (strained or still containing grains), is pumped into the still. The liquid is heated and its alcohol component vaporizes and separates from its water content. The alcohol vapor is then cooled, and it condenses back into a liquid. That is the very, very short version of distillation, but is how it's basically done around the world.

Pulling the lens back, it's fair to question why anyone would bother doing all of this. It's a lot of fairly exacting work, the primary goal of which is to exponentially increase the proof of an alcoholic beverage, allowing distillers to convert grains into a shelf-stable product while at the same time increasing its value. And then, yes, translate that value into money.

Distillers prize copper pot stills for the flavorful and complex spirit that they produce. The stills pictured above were installed in the new Tullamore D.E.W. distillery that opened in 2014.

The Pot Still

The oldest and most traditional still used today is the classic onion-shaped copper pot still. While its design and the shiny copper that makes it iconic are aesthetically pleasing and definitely eye-catching, pot stills have endured for centuries, largely unchanged, because they have real practical advantages.

The copper actually pulls stinky sulfur and mercaptan compounds as well as some phenolic compounds from the alcohol and makes the spirit smell and taste better. And the shape of the still plays a huge role in the spirit it produces. As the pot still boils, the alcohol component of the liquid wash is turned into a vapor, which rises to the top of the chamber. This happens because the boiling point of the alcohol (78.3° Celsius, 173.14° Fahrenheit) is much lower than the higher boiling point of water (100° Celsius, 212° Fahrenheit). If the angle of the exit pipe is very steep, it's hard for the vapor to leave the still. As a result, it condenses back to liquid and falls back into the pot. The process essentially begins again and the alcohol is vaporized again and heads to the top of the

Four Types of Stills

While there are countless whiskies on the market today, most of them are made in either a pot still or a column still. Some brands use both kinds of stills and blend the whiskies together. The latest development is a hybrid column/pot still that many craft distillers now use, which offers the best attributes of each still design. Naturally, there are additional features and modifications that distillers have made to these three main designs. Recently, the Leopold Bros. distillery in Denver, Colorado, resurrected the three-chamber still, which was an important innovation that bridged the pot and column still eras in the United States and was very popular for both bourbon as well as rye distillers in the nineteenth century. The illustrations below show how these four stills work.

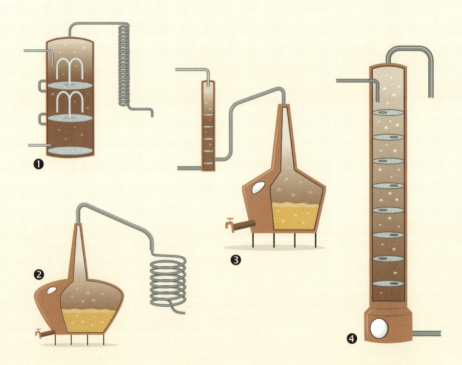

1. Three-Chamber Still: Steam is pumped into the bottom chamber while the distiller's beer enters the top chamber. The combination of high pressure and a long slow distillation, results in a rich and elegant spirit. **2. Pot Still:** The distiller's beer is heated up in a copper pot. Since alcohol boils at a lower temperature than water, it turns into a vapor and escapes from the top of the still. **3. Hybrid Still:** The distiller's beer is heated in a pot still and the alcohol vapor is routed into a column still to further refine the spirit. **4. Column Still:** Steam is pumped continuously into the bottom of the column and makes its way to the top. The distiller's beer is pumped into the top of the column and makes its way down through a series of perforated plates.

still to escape. The more times this reflux process takes place, and thus the more contact the spirit has with the copper, the more chemical compounds are stripped from it and the smoother and lighter it becomes. Conversely, if it's easier for the alcohol vapor to leave the still, the bigger, bolder, and more unctuous the finished whiskey will be.

Traditionally, this precious vapor ultimately escaped the pot still and condensed in a spiral-shaped copper tube (called the "worm," for obvious reasons) that sits in cold water or is covered with a cooling jacket. The clear alcohol that comes off of the condenser is collected and distilled a second time or third time.

In Scotland, the first still used is called a wash still and its partner, for the second distillation, is called a spirit still. The first distillation produces what are known as "low wines," which are roughly between 20 and 35 percent alcohol by volume. The second distillation increases the proof of the alcohol even higher, to at most 70 percent alcohol by volume and further smooths out any rough edges.

Most Scottish distillers stop at just two distillations, but they can go further if they choose to, which generally creates a lighter whisky. The Scotch brand Auchentoshan famously distills its single malts a third time. (This fact is useful when a know-it-all at a bar is spouting off about how Scotch *must* be distilled only twice.)

On the other hand, most Irish distillers do three distillations for their whiskey, which gives it a true

Whiskey brands around the world generally buy their stills from just a few companies, including Kentucky's Vendome.

smoothness. The three Irish stills are in order of use, the wash still, the feints still, and, finally, the spirit still.

At the heart of most single malt distilleries is a fairly standard copper pot still model. In fact there is a good chance that it was probably made by the Forsyths firm, located right in the heart of the Scottish distilling industry, in Speyside. The typical pot still has a broad round base, which was traditionally used because it allowed the wash or distiller's beer to be boiled quicker (kind of like the difference between using a wide frying pan versus a narrow stock pot), along with a conical top.

But if you look closely at stills around the industry, you'll see that each brand has a slightly different design. Midleton in Ireland has giant pot stills that each hold 75,000 liters (19,800 gallons). Scottish Macallan has very short pot stills, while Glenmorangie has the tallest ones in Scotland, which is why the company sometimes uses giraffes in its marketing. Why do these differences exist? Sometimes it has to do with mundane details such as how distillers were taxed, but in many cases, no one is exactly sure what led to a historic brand's original still design. I'd tend to assume it had to do with practical concerns and limitations, such as an entrepreneur's budget when building a distillery or the height of the room that housed a still. (New brands that use pot stills face similar challenges, which can cost at a minimum $300,000 for even a small copper pot still. But the price really depends upon the still's size, how it's made, and where the coppersmith is located.)

To complicate matters, many brands originally bought their pot stills secondhand from another distillery or even from a company making perfume or essences. And while the differences between the stills are small, they can have a big effect on the finished whiskey.

While pot stills are used widely today, they are not particularly efficient. A full distillation can take roughly four to eight hours to finish and then you have to clean the still to remove the compounds the copper has removed from the alcohol. Usually distillers give the copper several hours to cool down and dry off before it can be used again. But distillers actually prize the pot still for its inefficiency, which results in the unique spirits it can make. Meaning: Pot stills don't produce a completely neutral spirit,

leaving in ample compounds such as congeners and esters, which help produce flavor.

Pot stills require a steady fire or other heat source under the pot the whole time they're boiling a distiller's beer or wash, to keep it at a consistent temperature. Historically, this was not an easy or safe task, given that the spirit and vapor are highly flammable. (There have been some catastrophic accidents and horrific fires over the years.) Fortunately, today pot stills are usually not heated by "direct fire," but are instead powered by steam jackets or coils that are far more consistent, less labor intensive, and much safer. (This is roughly like the difference between boiling water in a teakettle on a gas burner versus using an electric stove to heat it up.)

After the final distillation, what you have is a perfectly clear, flavorful spirit—but not yet whiskey. To call it whiskey, it must first be poured into wooden barrels (also called casks) and allowed to age. How long it ages depends on the rules and traditions of the country, region, or state where it's produced. The cask is an incredibly important step—it gives the spirit its beautiful color and much of its flavor.

The Column Still

In the late 1700s and early 1800s, there was a push to come up with an alternative to the classic pot still that would be far more efficient and less labor intensive. After all, the amount of whiskey a pot still can produce depends on the size of the pot. If you want to

Barrel Entry Proof

A crucial consideration that is often skipped over in explanations of how whiskey is made is barrel entry proof. While the term sounds technical and something only whiskey superfans might obsess over, it's hugely important. Barrel entry proof is the alcohol level of the spirit when it goes into the barrel—which has a big effect on not just the flavor the whiskey pulls from the barrel but ultimately how the finished whiskey tastes.

According to US federal regulations, unaged whiskey can be at most 125 proof (62.5 percent alcohol by volume) when it goes into a barrel. The closer the alcohol is to that level, the stronger the finished whiskey will be and the more water you can potentially add when you're bringing it down to bottling strength. (In this scenario, you need fewer barrels and not as many warehouses.) While this practice is great for maximizing profits, it isn't always ideal for producing flavorful whiskey. A lower barrel entry proof generally creates a whiskey with a richer texture, which may be due to the fact that some of the flavor compounds in the barrel staves are alcohol soluble and others are water soluble. In order to get the full benefits of aging in wood,

The alcohol level of the spirit going into the barrel plays a large role in how the finished whiskey will taste.

you need the right balance of water and alcohol to get both kinds of flavor compounds. These benefits are perhaps why until 1962 the federal government set the barrel entry proof at 110 (55 percent alcohol by volume).

A number of brands now choose to set a much lower barrel entry proof. Michter's proudly uses a barrel entry proof of 103 (51.5 percent alcohol by volume) to make its bourbon and rye, because they think it begets a richer and smoother whiskey at that alcohol level. If you haven't tasted them yet, they have an uncommon richness, which I think is due in part to the lower barrel entry proof.

Barrel entry proof is less of an issue for distillers in Scotland, Ireland, and really any other place that uses a pot still. Unlike a column still, a pot still can't make very high proof alcohol. So most unaged whiskey made on a pot still goes into the barrel at around 125 proof.

Column stills are very effective at producing a river of alcohol in a very short amount of time.

sometimes also referred to as a beer still, a patent still, or a Coffey still. The column shape—specifically its height—is key to how it works. Inside the still, at regular intervals, are horizontal round copper plates, which completely block off the column but are perforated with a pattern of holes. The plates essentially cut the column into a vertical stack of individual chambers. The column itself doesn't have to be made of copper, which makes it less costly to build.

The distiller's beer is continually pumped into the top of the still while steam continually rises up from the bottom. When the steam meets the distiller's beer, it boils the liquid. Thanks to the lower boiling point of the alcohol (78.3° Celsius, 173.14° Fahrenheit) compared to the higher boiling point of water (100° Celsius, 212° Fahrenheit), the alcohol leaves the solution as a vapor and makes its way up the column. (The water makes its way down to the bottom of the column where it is collected and turned into steam.)

As the alcohol vapor enters the next chamber it's cooled down by the significantly increase the amount of whiskey you make, you need to either build a bigger still, buy a second one, or run the still you have night and day. The thinking at the time was that there had to be a better way.

In 1830, Aeneas Coffey, then Inspector General of Excise in Ireland, patented a design for his version of a continuous column still, which—you guessed it—is a giant column. It's distiller's beer making its way down the column—the higher up the column you go, the cooler the temperature.

The alcohol turns back into a liquid and the process begins once again. The solution is boiled by the steam that is making its way up the column and the alcohol vapor escapes into the next chamber above—each chamber is essentially a unique and full distillation. The process is very similar to reflux in a pot still. When the alcohol vapor finally reaches the top of the column, it's usually routed to what's called a "doubler" or "thumper" that both increases the proof of the alcohol and also continues to remove water molecules and unwanted compounds. Finally, the alcohol vapor is routed into a condenser, where for the last time it is turned into a liquid and the spirit is ready to be aged in a wooden barrel.

Unlike a pot still, a column still is an incredibly versatile tool and can be used to make pure alcohol or to make flavorful whiskey, like bourbon or rye—the number of plates or chambers determine how neutral the finished spirit will be. Generally, as the alcohol goes further up the column, the smoother and lighter it becomes, because the copper plates have stripped away the impurities, including the sulfides, mercaptans, congeners, aldehydes, and esters. Column stills are incredibly efficient and can produce truly high proof alcohol—like 160 proof (80 percent alcohol by volume) or higher.

Depending on the size of the brand, their column stills can be tremendous and produce a virtual river of alcohol. The tallest of Jack Daniel's six stills in its Lynchburg, Tennessee, distillery is 76 feet (23 meters) tall and runs twenty-four hours a day, seven days a week. At the heart of Heaven Hill's distillery is a trio of 70-foot (21-meter) behemoths, which run almost continuously year-round.

The Hybrid Column/Pot Still

Today, many craft distillers have eschewed the classic pot still *and* the column still. Instead they use a hybrid model that combines the two in a Frankenstein contraption consisting of a pot still with a small column on top of it. With a hybrid still, you can use just the pot or the pot as well as the column. This setup gives a distiller a lot of flexibility, which many craft brands need since they produce a huge range of spirits. You can use it as a column still to make high proof neutral grain spirit for vodka and gin or configure it as a pot still to make single malt whiskey.

How Stills Affect Flavor

A still not only increases the proof of an alcoholic liquid but also strongly influences how it will taste. The configuration of a still and the way a distiller uses it determines the character of a finished whiskey. In short, the still is an important component in making good whiskey.

At the heart of a distiller's skill is knowing their still inside and out and using its design advantageously to produce a unique spirit. A good analogy is how the crafty Boston Celtics basketball players used to know every inch of the

Whiskey is now produced in many countries, but there are just a handful of still designs. St. George Spirits in the Bay Area uses hybrid stills to make its single malt.

A Barrel By Any Name

BOURBON BARREL
200 liters
(53 gallons)

HOGSHEAD
approx. 250 liters
(66 gallons)

PUNCHEON
approx. 500 liters
(132 gallons)

wooden floor in the old Boston Garden. Supposedly, they knew all the spots that caused a ball to take an unusual bounce. That intimacy and understanding led to the type of game-changing steals that delivered them championship after championship.

COLUMN STILLS The more times a spirit is run through a column still, the more flavor-producing compounds, including esters and congeners, are stripped out of it and the closer it gets to vodka. You could age a neutral grain spirit like vodka in a wooden barrel for years, but it won't ever evolve into a rich or flavorful whiskey. So there is a balance between removing the harsher, less advantageous compounds and retaining enough to produce a spirit that will ultimately turn into a complex and delicious whiskey.

With a column still you can produce very high proof alcohol. If you're trying to maximize profits you could make your whiskey from the highest proof grain spirit regulations allow (in the United States, that's 160 proof, or 80 percent alcohol by volume). You'd then add water to the distillate before it went into the barrel (see Barrel Entry Proof, page 31). While your accountant may love this plan, because you'd wind up with more barrels to sell, distilling to a

SHERRY CASK/BUTT
approx. 500 liters
(132 gallons)

PORT CASK OR PIPE
approx. 500 liters
(132 gallons)

MADEIRA DRUM
approx. 600 liters
(172 gallons)

Whiskey by the Barrel

The American oak bourbon barrel is the workhorse of the whiskey industry and is used by distillers around the globe. Here are the cooper's names for its different parts and pieces.

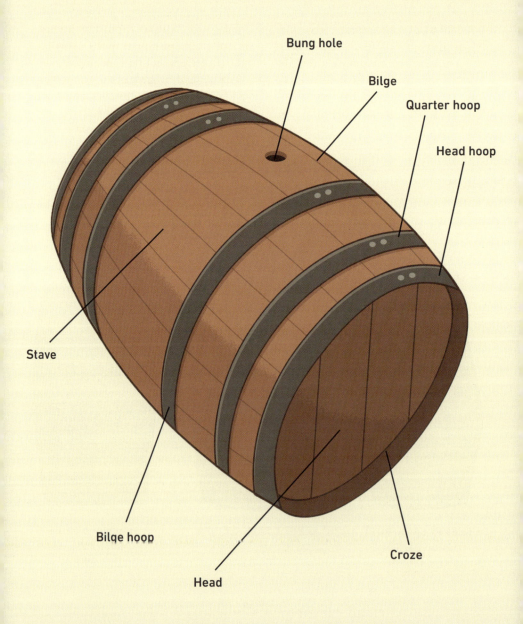

lower proof will generally create more flavor compounds and a richer mouthfeel in the finished whiskey.

POT STILLS: Pot stills come in all kinds of shapes and sizes, and for whiskey making are almost always constructed out of copper. There are small 50-liter (13-gallon) pot stills that look like shiny onions and humungous 75,000-liter (19,800-gallon) models the likes of which can be found at the Midleton Distillery in Cork, Ireland, which uses that size still to make Redbreast Single Pot Still Whiskey, as well as elements of Jameson's blends. In general, the easier it is for the spirit vapor to escape the still and condense back into a liquid, the heavier and oilier the whiskey will become. The more difficult it is for vapor to escape the still (leading to more reflux), the lighter the whiskey will ultimately become.

The way you use a pot still will also have a big effect on the spirit it produces. I'm not just talking about how many times you distill a spirit. How much you fill the still with wash, known as the fill line, will affect the distillation and the heaviness of the resulting spirit. Pot stills are made of copper because copper naturally removes impurities from a spirit. The more copper contact the spirit has, the more chance the metal has to work, and the lighter the spirit.

Temperature also needs to be taken into consideration here. After a distillation, most distillers allow the pot still to rest for twenty-four hours. That way it can cool down and the copper can be scrubbed of the copper sulfate that forms during each distilling run. If you don't allow the pot still to cool down and thoroughly clean it but instead run it almost constantly, like the historic Mortlach distillery in Dufftown, Scotland, you'll get a very heavy spirit. Mortlach would taste completely different if the stills were not run around the clock. However, now its unique flavor profile is sought-after by whisky blenders who think it gives a base note to a Scotch blend—so the distillery's copper won't be resting anytime soon.

Pot still distillers also need to decide how much of each run they'll keep. The spirit that comes off the still at the beginning and the end of each batch are called the heads and the tails, respectively. They often contain types of alcohol or compounds you don't want to drink, or are in fact dangerous to drink, like the alcohol methanol.

The heart of the run, or middle part, is the best tasting and most prized. Think of it as almost like making a cup of tea. As the tea bag first steeps you get fairly light flavors, which give way to the deepest, richest part of the brew. But if you steep the tea leaves too long, you'll start to get bitter and astringent notes. Similarly, a distiller doesn't want the beginning or the end of the run, only the heart. But there are no hard lines between these parts—the distiller must decide when the moment to start and stop is just right, a process known as "making cuts." The smaller the heart, the less whiskey you get from each run, and the more expensive it is to make. However, if you greedily try to keep as much as possible and remove just the worst bits at the beginning and the end, the resulting whiskey won't be as good. (If you don't make *any* cuts or don't make deep enough cuts, you could potentially kill someone, which is why making liquor at home or drinking homemade moonshine is a very risky proposition.) Most distillers find a balance between these two competing considerations. And don't worry about waste—the heads and the tails are not thrown away but are added to the next batch to be redistilled.

♦ MATURATION

A spirit doesn't become a whiskey until it has been aged. While the clear, unaged alcohol that results from distillation has a lot of inherent flavor, it picks up even more flavor—along with its color—from the wooden barrel it is aged in. Depending on the country where it's being produced, there are specific rules and regulations about the type of cask (read: barrel/wood container) that can be used and how long the whiskey must mature before it can be called whiskey.

In additional to their crucial flavor compounds, barrels are also a boon to distillers because they're sturdy and durable. And their curved sides mean they can be rolled, which is a great help when moving them around warehouses and on and off ships. For decades, American whiskey distillers have used a standard 201-liter (53-gallon) American

The type of wood a barrel is made from will directly affect the flavor of a whiskey aged in it. Yamazaki in Japan, for example, uses a range of barrels, including ones made from American, Spanish, and Japanese oak.

The Great Sherry Cask Myth

A number of famous Scotch brands don't age their whisky in used bourbon barrels, but in Spanish sherry casks instead.

Sherry itself is aged in a system called a solera, where the fortified wine is moved incrementally through a succession of casks. The idea with a solera is that the barrels are never completely drained, and that each batch is a complex mix of old and younger sherry. Which is a great system for producing sherry, but not for producing sturdy barrels. Because sherry makers will use a barrel until it practically falls apart, these barrels are not ideal for a Scotch distiller to use secondhand. This begs the question of how single malt Scotch is aged in sherry butts.

A number of Scotch whiskies are aged in casks that have first been seasoned with Spanish sherry.

Historically, the United Kingdom was a huge buyer of sherry and port, which were wildly popular until the late 1800s. Back then, sherry would be shipped in wooden barrels to British merchants, who would do the bottling themselves. The empty barrels would be taken to a local distiller who would refill them with whisky. This was done because the whisky aged in sherry barrels had a particularly delicious flavor, with notes of raisins and a pleasant dryness. But the sherry trade now isn't what it used to be, and since 1986 what sherry is sent to the UK is now required to be shipped in bottles, not barrels. Scotch producers found themselves in a seemingly impossible bind—where could they get these special casks?

Whisky makers must now pay for new barrels to be filled with sherry, which is aged in them for a few years. The sherry, which tends to be pretty low quality, is ultimately dumped out and turned into vinegar or distilled into neutral grain spirit. The barrels are then shipped to Scotland, where they're refilled with soon-to-be Scotch. It's not exactly a straightforward process, and a number of brands either imply or outright claim that their whisky is aged in barrels from a traditional solera system, which is highly unlikely and generally untrue. The more honest brands, such as The Macallan, perhaps the most famous sherried single malt, are up front about their barrels being "seasoned" with sherry. (The Macallan even bought a Spanish cooperage and a 50 percent stake in Bodegas Grupo Estévez to guarantee the consistency of its barrels.)

oak barrel that stands 35 inches (89 centimeters) high.

At the start of the craft distilling boom some distillers experimented with smaller barrels, such as 38- or 57-liter (10- or 15-gallon) sizes, in an attempt to increase wood contact and thus speed up the aging process. But the aging process doesn't really work that way, and I wasn't particularly impressed with the resulting whiskies, since they were sometimes too astringent, didn't have the depth of flavor, and were kind of thin. Fortunately, most distillers now use the standard 201-liter (53-gallon) barrel.

Outside the Unites States, you see a wider range of barrel sizes. Most Scottish whisky makers buy used bourbon barrels and fill them with unaged spirit. Sometimes two bourbon barrels will be taken apart and then the staves are joined together to form a jumbo "hogshead" that can hold 549 liters (145 gallons) and is 48 inches (122 centimeters) tall. If Scotch distillers aren't using a bourbon barrel, they'll generally age their whisky in a cask, or "butt," that has been seasoned with Spanish sherry, which holds 500 liters (132 gallons) and is 50 inches (127 centimeters) tall. A range of other sizes and shapes of barrels are used, which add their own flavor and twist on the maturation process.

♦ THE BOURBON BARREL'S SECOND ACT—IN SCOTLAND

Whisky lovers in the United States buy more Scotch than in any other country on Earth. The US also plays an important role in Scotch production.

The Scotch Whisky Association stipulates that Scotch whisky must be produced and aged in Scotland, so what does the United States have to do with it? Well, American distillers can only use a new oak barrel to make bourbon, rye, and Tennessee whiskey. But after they're used once, there's still quite a bit of life in these casks, so they're sold to distillers around the globe who fill them with a range of spirits.

The Scotch industry is the largest buyer of American whiskey barrels. Not only is it much more affordable to buy a used barrel in lieu of a new one—a new barrel currently costs between $300 and $400 while a used one is about $200—but the tannins of the virgin oak can overwhelm an

American whiskey producers supply used barrels to brands around the world that reuse them to age a range of spirits.

elegant single malt. A used barrel contributes just enough oak influence and allows the inherent flavor of the whisky to shine through. (Over the years, a handful of Scotch brands have experimented with using new oak barrels, but they haven't really caught on.)

Scottish distillers like used American bourbon barrels for another reason that has nothing to do with their cost. Each barrel contains about 5 liters (about 1 gallon) of American whiskey soaked into its staves. The precise amount of whiskey in the wood depends on a few variables, including how expertly the barrel was emptied and the age of the barrel. Over time, the American whiskey trapped in the wood mixes with the Scottish spirit. So, for those folks who think Scotch is somehow superior to American whiskey, I would remind them that in many of their favorite single malts is a bit of good old American bourbon, rye, or Tennessee whiskey.

The use of American whiskey barrels by Scotch distillers took off in the 1960s. These secondhand barrels were so in demand that there were not enough of them to go around—Scottish whisky makers needed about 1.5 million barrels a year at the time. "Twenty years ago, you couldn't give a used whiskey barrel away, and distillers took to burning them just to reclaim the metal hoops," wrote Ernest L. Clark in a piece titled "Bourbon-Barrel Boom Brings Bleat," which ran in Louisville, Kentucky's *The Courier Journal* newspaper in 1965.

With the crash of whiskey sales around the world not many years later, American whiskey makers once again had trouble getting rid of their used barrels, which were often turned into planters or chipped up. Eddie Russell, master distiller at Wild Turkey, once told me that by the year 2000 the brand had 30,000 used barrels it couldn't sell. They were finally shipped off to a company that paid a nominal amount for them before turning the casks into flooring. Now that the whiskey business is booming again, used American oak barrels are in short supply.

Barrels: More than Just Fancy Shipping Containers

The last major pieces to the whiskey-making puzzle come down to how long the whiskey is aged, where it is aged, and in what it is aged. These three factors might actually be more important than even what grains were used to make the spirit. And we've known this definitively for more than a century, thanks to the conclusions of a remarkable and groundbreaking eight-year study of whiskey maturation undertaken by, of all entities, the US Bureau of Internal Revenue in 1898. The government researchers looked at thirty-one barrels of unaged bourbon, rye, and corn whiskey produced around the country in all kinds of stills and from different recipes. Every year samples were taken from each cask as it aged, and scientifically evaluated in a lab. The findings are fascinating—for example, whiskey aged in a heated warehouse developed more flavor compounds and is richer than whiskey aged in an unheated warehouse, which tends to have a lighter body.

Is There Terroir in Whiskey?

Over the past few years, a lot of brands have been tossing around the term *terroir*. It's a concept that winemakers like to talk about, which makes them sound sophisticated and fancy. But it more or less just means earth. *Dirt*.

The idea is that every vineyard—based on the soil, the hours of sunshine and amount of rainfall or wind, and other factors for that exact tract of vineyard land—is unique and can result in slight but important differences in the finished product.

For whiskey the idea is very similar—where the grain comes from, the chemical makeup of the water, and the specific conditions under which the whiskey ages will all have significant impacts on how it tastes.

But does the concept of terroir actually exist or is it just a term professional and amateur whiskey experts like to throw around? Well, sunshine, high humidity, and heat (or conversely shade, low humidity, and cold) certainly have a huge effect on how a whiskey ages—both the speed of maturation and the chemical processes that happen during that period. (A stiff briny wind will also play a role in how a whiskey tastes.) I also believe that grain, water, and yeast can have local characteristics that can create a taste of place. However, for me, this is where the argument for terroir existing in whiskey begins to fall apart (at least for now). The industry is generally focused on consistency and mass production, which is usually at odds with using ingredients that retain any sense of place. But given that this is a complex discussion, let's go through the major factors and how they affect the terroir of whiskey from developing.

GRAIN: Many large and small brands buy their grain from the same large agricultural conglomerates. The type of corn, rye, barley, or wheat is often what everyone else is using that season and can come from anywhere—from down the road or another continent entirely. While a distiller can now request a certain moisture content or starch level in a particular load of grain, they can't typically ask for a selection of local characteristics. Commodity grain, by its very definition, is supposed to be consistent from batch to batch without any deviations.

H2O: Water can absolutely be an important source of flavor. Local characteristics vary from place to place—just think about the amount of lather you get when you wash your hair in New York (soft water with low mineral content) compared to when you shower in Los Angeles (harder water with higher mineral content). Historically, local water likely made a huge difference in how a whiskey tasted. Not only does the water itself have its own flavor, but its chemical makeup directly affects the rate and the success of the fermentation process. But today many distillers either treat their water with a reverse osmosis process to make it as neutral as possible or get it from a municipal water authority that treats the water for them. So, if most bourbon distillers in a certain area are pulling their water from the same public source

There are many factors that play into whether a whiskey truly reflects where it comes from, including the grain, the fermentation process, and how it's aged.

rather than using their own private springs, wells, or rivers, the water is not going to have a big impact on flavor.

FERMENTATION: Yeast is another factor to consider. Wild yeasts would definitely be localized and give your whiskey a unique flavor. However, they're very unpredictable and difficult to use. Because of this, most brands prefer a commercially available (lab-grown) yeast strain that they work hard to keep pure.

THE AGING PROCESS: This leaves the barrels. Sure, local oak would make a big difference in flavor, but most of the wood used for barrels currently comes from the same places and is turned into barrels by the same few large coopers.

OK then, maybe the question is: Could you possibly do things differently to get a true sense of terroir in your finished whiskey? Absolutely.

Some brands, including Westland in Seattle, Washington, WhistlePig in Vermont, Leopold Bros. in Denver, Colorado, Buffalo Trace in Kentucky, Waterford in Ireland, and Glenmorangie in Scotland, have experimented with growing their own grains from proprietary or heirloom seed strains, or even building barrels from local species of oak. These changes have had major and profound effects on the flavor of their whiskey—you can really taste the difference.

While a major brand would currently have a hard time sourcing an heirloom strain of corn, rye, or barley in large enough quantities, it will be a viable option in the near future. High Wire Distilling in Charleston, South Carolina, is the perfect case in point. The distillery resuscitated the heirloom Jimmy Red corn strain and now harvests about 2 million pounds (907,000 kilograms) of the grain each year for its acclaimed (and very delicious) Jimmy Red Straight Bourbon Whiskey.

While the ideas around whiskey terroir are being explored seriously by a growing number of distillers each year, it will take significant changes in the way we make whiskey and what we make it from for more of these truly local drams to be widely available.

A barrel isn't just a container but contributes a range of flavor compounds to the whiskey.

Alcohol is a solvent, so as it ages it slowly breaks down the wood cells of the barrel and draws out a lot of the sugars and some of the other flavorful compounds in the wood. When you taste notes of vanilla, hints of baking spice, and a whisper of crème brûlée in a whiskey, what you're really tasting are flavor compounds from the barrel.

So, the longer a spirit ages in a barrel, the more flavor compounds it draws from the wood. The optimal amount of aging time is, of course, widely debated and depends on personal preference and a number of other variables. For American whiskey, I often find six to eight years is ideal because it allows a lot of the spirit's own flavor to come through and a lot of the sugars in the wood have broken down and been integrated into the spirit. (I'm not alone in this belief—a number of veteran distillers also cite six to eight years as their favorite whiskey age.) For Scotch and Irish whiskey, it's a bit harder to give a range because most distillers age their whiskey in used barrels. As a result, there are very good 10-year-old whiskies and also incredible 50-year-old whiskies. But there is a limit—if whiskey ages too long in a barrel, the only thing you'll taste is astringent and mouth-puckering wood.

Location, Location, Location

Where a barrel ages is also of great importance. The climate and weather are a huge factor in a spirit's rate of maturation—fluctuations in temperature and humidity play a critical role in driving the spirit in and out of the wood of a barrel. As the temperature heats up, the pressure inside the barrel begins to build and pushes the spirit into the wood staves. Then, when the temperature falls, the pressure inside the barrel decreases and the spirit is drawn back out of the staves and takes with it sugar and flavor compounds from the wood. According to Andrew Wiehebrink, director of spirit research and innovation at famed cooperage Independent Stave Company, for optimal aging you don't want sudden temperature spikes. Rather, for a rich and complex whiskey long sustained weather changes that allows the spirit to pull as much as possible from the barrel are ideal.

The location of the warehouse may also play a role in the ultimate flavor of a whiskey—for example, you usually only find a briny tang in a spirit aged by the ocean. Even different microclimates inside a barrel warehouse will have a big effect on how the whiskey ages and ultimately tastes. (The Father of Small Batch Bourbon, page 122.)

No matter where you age whiskey, every year it matures in the barrel you're losing a certain percentage of it to evaporation. This is traditionally called the angel's share. In cooler climates, it's alcohol that evaporates, while in warmer places it's water. So, in Ireland or Scotland whiskey goes down in proof (strength) as it ages due to loss of alcohol, and in the United States and Canada it goes up in proof due to loss of water. The evaporation also means that the liquid remaining in the cask gets ever more concentrated, which affects the final flavor and texture of the whiskey. One final factor is the increasing airspace in the barrel during evaporation, which allows oxidation to change the flavor of the whiskey as well. The air also plays a role in creating pressure in the barrel, which causes the spirit to be drawn in and out of the staves.

Zen and the Art of Barrel Aging

The particular kind of barrel used to age whiskey naturally greatly affects its flavor. In the United States, bourbon, rye, and Tennessee whiskey producers have to use a new barrel made from oak. They often use American white oak (*Quercus alba*), which has plenty of sweetness and vanilla notes.

No matter the origin of the staves, the inside of a whiskey barrel is either toasted or charred. The type of wood used, the flavors you're after, and the type of whiskey you're making will determine how you'll want the cooperage to treat the interior of the barrel. The flames during toasting or charring caramelize some of the sugars in the wood and help break down the barrels different flavor compounds. (To put it in flavor terms, imagine the difference between eating a raw English muffin versus one that has been toasted.) The charring process helps the wood release sweetness as well as the vanilla and baking spice notes found in many whiskies. The layer of charcoal created on the inside of the barrel is also a natural filter that pulls out impurities and mellows the spirit.

Generally, a new oak barrel is charred on the inside before it is filled with new-make spirit for aging.

Some distillers instead like to use a barrel made from tighter-grained French oak (*Quercus robur*), which can contribute dark chocolate or rich plum notes. Another popular option are casks that have previously held a different kind of alcoholic beverage, such as wine, port, sherry, or even mezcal, each of which add a significant and noticeable flavor of their own to the whiskey. Occasionally, a brand will put their new spirit in one of these flavorful types of barrels, but more often they're part of the finishing of a whiskey after it's already been aged once. Starward in Australia likes to use freshly emptied red wine casks for some of its different whiskies, which give the liquor an elegant mouthfeel and a big note of jammy fruit.

Casks made from Japanese mizunara oak (*Quercus mongolica*), which imparts a note of sandalwood, are particularly sought-after and hard to come by. However, the wood can be harvested from trimmed limbs or a tree that falls from natural causes. The American bourbon brand Angel's Envy spent years looking for someone to sell them one of these barrels to finish their bourbon. Finally, a broker got them an extra-large mizunara oak barrel, and they produced 1,200 bottles of a special whiskey, which originally had a suggested retail price of $350. (It was worth the effort—that whiskey now sells for about ten times that price.)

A newer trend is trying to find local varieties of oak for barrels that add a unique flavor to the spirit, giving it a bit of terroir. This term is now increasingly used for whiskey. (See Is There Terroir in

Whiskey?, page 42.) One of the brands trying this is Westland American Single Malt in Seattle, Washington, which has been sourcing Garry oak (*Quercus garryana*) literally from people's backyards, since the wood is no longer commercially grown. This is, of course, much harder than simply ordering a standard barrel from a cooper, but it gives the whiskey a very different, unique flavor. I expect we'll see more brands trying to find local and heirloom oak varieties for barrels.

Aging whiskey in two or even three different types of barrels is also becoming more common, and is done by many brands in Scotland and Ireland. This is a finishing technique popularized by single malt brands Balvenie and Glenmorangie that has become an important tool for distillers around the world to create new flavors (see The Perfect Finish, page 241).

Still other brands and coopers are experimenting with the basic design and construction of the barrel. Some of the more innovative ideas include creating grooves in the barrel staves to increase the amount of wood contact with the spirit, which could perhaps speed up the maturation process. Glenmorangie Single Malt Scotch, which has arguably done more than any other brand to push the envelope of barrel aging, once even used trees for some of its casks that were sourced from the Ozark mountains and had only grown on shady slopes. The thinking was that, as a result of being deprived of direct sunshine, the grain of the wood would be tighter and the spirit would have a harder time entering and exiting the staves. These barrels were hideously expensive to produce and needed to be specially tracked as they were first used to age bourbon, then emptied, and finally sent to Scotland. Ultimately, they were used to make the brand's Astar Whisky.

Maker's Mark bourbon, which had produced basically just one product since its founding in 1953, came out with Maker's Mark 46 in 2010. This pioneering product was made by adding a rack of additional ten seared French oak staves inside a barrel filled with its regular mature bourbon.

♦ FILTRATION

Vodka makers like to brag about the number of times their liquor has been filtered, along with the type of filtration system used, which can run the gamut from charcoal to diamonds. But filtration isn't only a part of producing vodka, it's also an essential step to making whiskey, one that at a minimum rids the final product of the barrel char particles. All whiskey is filtered in some manner. This can include anything from gentle straining to more invasive procedures that remove chemical compounds and/or alter the color of the whiskey.

Many brands start by running their whiskey through mesh, paper, or cloth filters, while others use charcoal. The Lincoln County Process famously used by Jack Daniel's involves allowing the whiskey to make its way through a vat of freshly made charcoal, which naturally filters out impurities. (See page 64.) This is also one reason whiskey is

Unless whiskey is bottled at cask strength, it is mixed with some water to bring it down to a specific alcohol level.

aged in barrels that have been charred on the inside—that interior layer of charcoal helps to remove unwanted compounds from the whiskey.

Other brands use different filtration processes to remove or lighten a whiskey's color and even temper its flavor—a practice commonly used for a number of other spirits, including rum and cristalino tequila.

Additionally, most of the big brands of whiskey around the world use some form of chill filtration right before the whiskey is bottled. The liquor is chilled down to below freezing, at which point lipids, proteins, and impurities drop to the bottom and can be removed. Why bother? Without chill filtration, thanks to the lipids, a whiskey can get cloudy if it gets too cold while shipping, or if

Proof vs ABV

What is the big deal about proof anyway? Does it matter? Should we care?

In the United States, the proof of a spirit is twice its alcohol by volume (ABV). That means if a whiskey is 100 proof, 50 percent of its volume is alcohol and 50 percent is water. In the US, all whiskey must be at least 80 proof (40 percent alcohol by volume) by federal regulation, although there is no maximum limit and some cask strength bottlings clock in well above 120 proof (60 percent alcohol by volume).

Here's why it matters: As a rule, the higher the proof, the more flavor a whiskey contains. You could drink it neat, but to bring the ABV down to a more enjoyable level and reveal a whiskey's full flavor potential, I would suggest adding a small amount of water. This might sound counterintuitive, I know, but the addition of water triggers a chemical reaction that releases more aromas and flavors. Don't believe me? Pour yourself two glasses of the same high proof whiskey (well over 90 proof). Add a little water (like a teaspoon or two) to one and then compare them. I promise you'll see a big difference.

A higher proof whiskey can sometimes work better in cocktails because it can handle the ice dilution from shaking or stirring, and its flavor won't disappear behind the other ingredients. But like many things about drinking whiskey, the amount of water you add (if any) is a personal choice and really depends on the specific dram. There are 80-proof (40 percent alcohol by volume) whiskies that taste best to me with a splash of water and some potent 120-proof (60 percent alcohol by volume) cask strength whiskies that need nothing. That's why if I haven't tasted a whiskey before I'll try a sip neat and then decide if I need to add a splash of water, ice, or soda.

you add frigid water or ice. Proponents of this process argue that this is a necessary step because consumers would complain if their whiskey got hazy. But there are many critics of chill filtration, who claim it robs a whiskey of some flavor and changes the mouthfeel, which is why they prefer whiskies made without it. Distillers can avoid this step altogether by bottling the whiskey at a minimum of 92 proof (46 percent alcohol by volume), since at that level of alcohol the lipids will remain soluble. The problem is that lipids aren't soluble in water, so at lower proof they turn into particles and fall out of the solution, which creates this so-called flocking.

♦ **BLENDING**

Consistency is one of the biggest challenges facing large-scale distillers. Blending is an essential practice for ensuring a whiskey tastes the same because it mitigates the differences from barrel to barrel. While the flavor of a given whiskey might change ever so slightly from year to year, consumers of big-brand whiskey expect the bottle they buy today to be indistinguishable from the one that they bought last year. So if a whiskey maker is successful, a drinker shouldn't notice any discernible differences in their favorite dram.

But when we talk about blending, the term means vastly different things depending on where the whiskey is produced. In some places the technique has a negative connotation, though that's hardly a universal interpretation.

Here's what it means to blend in a few key whiskey-producing countries.

SCOTLAND: Scotland is famous for its blended Scotches like Johnnie Walker, Chivas Regal, and Dewar's, which are made from a combination of mature single malts from different distilleries and grain whisky, which is generally produced on a large column still from a mash that mostly contains corn or wheat. Some blenders age the mixture in wooden barrels so the components can "marry" together.

Unless you buy a *single barrel* bottle, Scottish single malts are also blends—in this case a combination of a number of barrels of whisky from a single distillery. Keep in mind that the age on the label of a Scotch reflects only the youngest whisky in the bottle. So even a single malt might contain various ages of the same whisky.

CANADA: In terms of blending, Canada generally follows the practices of Scotland. Many of the country's most famous brands are a combination of a wide range of different kinds of fully mature whiskies, like straight rye, straight corn, and even single malt, with a base whisky that is usually made from corn or wheat.

UNITED STATES: In the US, blending has a terrible reputation. This is because low-quality and low-cost blended whiskey have traditionally been sold when straight bourbon or rye is in short supply. Why is this so bad? Imagine mixing two or three bottles of vodka with a bottle of your favorite straight bourbon and adding some food coloring. Yeah, I don't want to drink that either! But some companies are now making high-end blends of straight whiskies, which can be delicious.

And just like with single malt Scotch, unless you buy a single barrel bottle, every bourbon or rye you buy is a blend of a number of barrels of the same distiller's whiskey.

♦ **COLORING**
Consistency in big-brand whiskey isn't just about flavor—the whiskey also needs to look the same from year to year. One bottle can't be darker or lighter than another bottle of the same whiskey. The tricky part of this equation is that the color of a whiskey traditionally comes from aging it in a charred oak barrel. (Like all spirits, whiskey comes off the still perfectly clear.) How can a distiller reliably

In a number of countries, whiskey makers are allowed to add so-called spirit caramel to adjust the color of their products. However, this practice is not allowed in the US.

control the color of whiskey across tens of thousands or more bottles? In some countries you can add what is called spirit caramel.

This substance isn't actually caramel but a coloring agent that can be used to create a uniform shade of whiskey. It's not supposed to add any flavor to the whiskey, although some purists aren't convinced that it lacks all flavor.

While distillers in Scotland, Canada, and Ireland are allowed to add spirit caramel to their whiskey, distillers in the United States aren't allowed to add any coloring but have the advantage of using new barrels, which contribute more color. Some countries, including Germany, require brands from every country to disclose on their label if spirit caramel has been added to a whiskey.

♦ PROOFING DOWN AND BOTTLING

The last step in producing whiskey is putting it in a bottle. But before a whiskey meets glass, it's usually first mixed with filtered water to "proof it down" to an enjoyable alcohol level. (Distillers want the water being added at this stage to be as neutral as possible, but it may just be from a municipal source.) As you add water to a spirit, the alcoholic strength naturally decreases and the flavor of the whiskey changes. I once sat in on a tasting as Old Forester set the proof for one of its limited editions—and the addition of even the tiniest bit of water significantly changed the bourbon. It was fascinating to see how the whiskey tasted so very different at each proof point.

Ideally, a brand's distiller or blender decides what proof is best for each barrel or batch of whiskey. But that doesn't really work if you have a multimillion-case brand that uses thousands of barrels a year. In that scenario, the brand decides what the house style will be and sets a proof level that they think works best overall for their whiskey. Obviously, the more water you add, the bigger the profit margins and the more bottles you will have to sell, which is why some whiskies have no doubt lowered their proof over the years.

On the other hand there are cask strength whiskies, which aren't proofed down at all and are generally more expensive because no water is added to the whiskey. These bottlings are generally at a much higher alcohol level and offer drinkers a different flavor perspective than the standard bottling of the same whiskey.

In many countries, the proof minimum for whiskey is 80 proof (40 percent alcohol by volume). But it's not a blanket international standard. In Australia, for example, the tax rates for liquor are very high and are determined by the proof of a whiskey. It's why some brands have offered bourbon that is below 80 proof (40 percent alcohol by volume) for sale in Australia—to keep the suggested retail price down. However, because of this lower proof, these special Aussie bourbons can't be sold in the United States as bourbon, or even labeled as whiskey.

AMERICAN WHISKEY

AMERICAN
Whiskey Landmarks

- **DISTILLERY**
- **DISTILLERY (NOT OPERATIONAL)**

1. Jack Daniel's distillery, Lynchburg, Tennessee
2. Old Overholt Broad Ford distillery, Connellsville, Pennsylvania
3. George Washington's distillery, Mount Vernon, Virginia
4. Stitzel-Weller Distillery, Louisville, Kentucky
5. Leopold Bros. distillery, Denver, Colorado
6. MGP distillery, Lawrenceburg, Indiana
7. Maker's Mark distillery, Loretto, Kentucky
8. Heaven Hill Bourbon Experience, Bardstown, Kentucky

9. Wild Turkey distillery, Lawrenceburg, Kentucky
10. Tuthilltown Spirits distillery, Gardiner, New York
11. Castle & Key, Frankfort, Kentucky
12. Churchill Downs Racetrack, Louisville, Kentucky
13. Buffalo Trace distillery, Frankfort, Kentucky
14. St. George distillery, Alameda, California
15. Dickel distillery, Tullahoma, Tennessee

blame *The Dukes of Hazzard.*

For far too long, whiskey in the United States was associated with moonshiners who worked during the dead of night to produce hooch that was so potent you could run your car on it. But moonshine only really became a thing in America in the late 1700s as a proper whiskey distilling industry—complete with rules, regulations, and taxes—was created. As a result, this unaged "white lightning" developed its own separate and distinct outlaw culture as well as a down-and-dirty production style. I too wouldn't worry about things like sanitation, high-quality ingredients, or barrel aging if federal agents were breathing down my neck!

Thanks to Hollywood and a killer theme song from Waylon Jennings, the reputation of these overall-wearing good ol' boys and the romantic notion of their Robin Hood–like resistance to unjust distilling laws and taxation has persisted long after the end of the *Dukes*'s seven-season run on TV. And the show had an unintended consequence that Uncle Jesse and his forebears distilling deep in the safety of the dense Appalachian woods were suddenly and mistakenly credited with originally creating bourbon, rye, and the rest of America's whiskey industry. Ultimately this thinking contributed to a thirty-year identity crisis for American whiskey with a number of brands leaning into this hillbilly fantasy for their marketing campaigns. As a result, up until recently, only the contributions of Kentucky and Tennessee to US distilling history were remembered and celebrated, while former whiskey stalwarts, including New York, Pennsylvania, Illinois, and Ohio, were largely forgotten and written out of the narrative. Thanks to this revisionist history, for decades America's whiskies were treated by drinkers like a joke or a novelty, which were far inferior to noble and dignified Scotch. The shame is that American whiskey is no less impressive or less authentic than any other type of whiskey.

In fact, because of fits and starts in popularity, various crises, and near-death episodes, the history of American whiskey is wildly interesting and nuanced. And surprisingly long: Whiskey has been produced in the United States for hundreds of years and its highs and lows often tracked those of the overall country. In very American fashion, the country's whiskey was created by people hailing from all over the world—some fleeing persecution and oppression, others brought to the US against their will and enslaved, and still others brimming with rebellion and wild ideas. The story of American whiskey doesn't just reflect the history of the United States, but tells a

There are more barrels of whiskey aging in Kentucky than there are residents of the state.

much more complicated tale about the growth of the country's modern society and its drinking culture.

American whiskey now typically takes up significant real estate in most liquor stores and is far and away the most popular kind of whiskey sold in the United States. (That is why it's here in Chapter 2, before Scotch.) But it wasn't that long ago, the late '90s, when I remember regularly standing in front of the small American whiskey section in my local liquor store for an uncomfortably long time, trying to decide between Jack Daniel's Tennessee Whiskey and the very similarly packaged Evan Williams Bourbon. At the time, it was frankly hard to decipher any difference between the two similarly packaged whiskies. Usually, the amount of cash in my wallet ultimately determined which bottle I bought.

I now see a lot of customers wrestling with the same predicament I did decades ago. Ironically, instead of scarcity there's now a plethora as American whiskey's fortunes have risen over the last two decades, but people have to answer the same essential question: How do you figure out which bottle to buy?

Read on for the tools that will help you decide as well as the story of how this one-time regional farm product became an international bestseller, and the backgrounds of your favorite brands.

While the story of American whiskey history may not exactly include flying Dodge Chargers jumping through burning hoops, it is actually quite a wild ride. So pour yourself a dram and sit back and enjoy.

Types of American Whiskey

While the United States is famous for making bourbon and rye, there are a host of other types of whiskies made across its fifty states. Here are the most important categories to know about.

♦ BOURBON

Thanks to a US congressional resolution in 1964, you can call a whiskey bourbon only if it is produced in the United States—just as Scotch can only be made in Scotland. This standard of identity is now recognized by forty-five countries around the world and codified by international trade agreements. However, there's a common misconception that bourbon must come from Kentucky. This is not true—it can be made anywhere in the United States. You can now get bourbons from New York, Texas, and California, but Kentucky is still far and away the biggest producer of bourbon. (At last check, there were more than 10

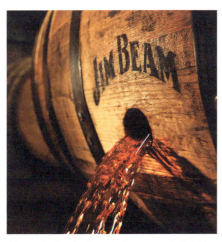

A key part of bourbon's production process is that it is aged in a new charred oak barrel.

Key Differences

It's no secret that Americans proudly like doing things their own way, even if most of the world takes a different approach (i.e., see the debate over the metric system). So, it should come as no surprise that distillers in the US have a few unique methods and traditions. Chief among these differences is the fact that most whiskey in America is aged in new charred oak barrels as opposed to reusing barrels, which is a common practice in most other major whiskey-producing countries. These new casks give the whiskey all of its color and make it relatively sweet, with plenty of vanilla and baking spice flavor notes. Another major difference is that most American whiskies are made from a mix of different grains, which are fermented and distilled together. And finally, most American whiskey is produced on a large and efficient column still. No matter the style, whiskey made in the US is practically designed to be used in cocktails and mixed drinks.

Total Consumption: Sales of American whiskey in the United States in 2023 totaled nearly 31 million 9-liter cases.

DEFINING BOURBON

- It must be produced in the United States.
- The mash (base grains) must be at least 51 percent corn.
- It has to be aged in a charred new oak barrel.
- The finished whiskey has to be at least 80 proof (40 percent alcohol by volume).
- No additives or coloring can be added.
- "Straight" bourbon must be aged for at least two years.

million barrels of bourbon aging in the Bluegrass State.)

No matter where in the United States it hails from, bourbon must be made from at least 51 percent corn. The rest of the mash (the base grains) is usually malted barley and either spicy rye or sweeter wheat. You can even use all four grains to make bourbon. The grains are cooked and fermented together, and the resulting "distiller's beer" is then pumped into a still.

Bourbon is now usually made in a column still (see page 28), but since it was first produced roughly two hundred years ago, distillers have used a range of stills to make it and still do! No matter what kind of still is employed, the spirit must adhere to specific regulations created by the federal government. In addition to those listed in Defining Bourbon, it cannot be more than 160 proof (80 percent alcohol by volume) when it comes off the still and no more than 125 proof (62.5 percent alcohol by volume) when the so-called "white dog" (unaged spirit) goes into the barrel for aging. Those federal regulations specify that bourbon must be "stored" (aged) in "charred new oak containers." In practice, this means unused wooden barrels constructed of American white oak that have been burned on the inside. After one day of aging, the result can technically be called bourbon, but it must age for at least two years before you can call it "straight" bourbon. (But, of course, you would have a very pale and thin-looking bourbon indeed, if you aged it for only a day.)

While there's a large range of flavors from one bourbon to another, most generally have an inherent sweetness from the corn and a very big vanilla note from the charred oak barrels. Bourbon is generally not smoky or peaty, like some brands of Scotch.

♦ RYE

Bourbon may now be synonymous with America itself, but the country's residents actually first drank rye whiskey. Unlike bourbon, you can make rye whiskey anywhere in the world—the term is not owned or protected by a single country. In fact, you can now buy rye whiskey made in a number of disparate locales, including Canada, England, Denmark, and Ireland.

And yet the US's rules for making rye whiskey are arguably the tightest. The federal government mandates that

AMERICAN WHISKEY

Before the United States was synonymous with bourbon, rye was its original signature whiskey.

rye whiskey must be made from at least 51 percent rye. Some distillers use an all-rye mash, while others like a mash of 95 percent rye and 5 percent malted barley or one that includes rye, malted barley, and corn, which is particularly popular with Kentucky distillers. Most rye whiskey brands now use a column still or a hybrid pot/column still (see page 28), but up to World War II it was common to use a three-chamber still (see sidebar). Like bourbon, in the US rye whiskey cannot be more than 160 proof (80 percent alcohol by volume) when it comes off the still and cannot be more than 125 proof (62.5 percent alcohol by volume) at the beginning of the aging process. It must also be aged in what the government calls "charred new oak containers," or unused wooden barrels that have been burned inside, which are generally made from American white oak. Similar to bourbon, it can technically be called rye whiskey after one day of aging, but it must age for at least two years before it can be called "straight" rye whiskey. Also like bourbon, rye whiskey must be at least 80 proof (40 percent alcohol by volume) when bottled, and adding coloring of any kind is strictly forbidden.

While bourbon is famous for its sweetness, rye tends toward a spicier profile and a more unctuous mouthfeel. Usually, the more rye the whiskey is made from, the spicier and bigger the flavor.

By the early 2000s, rye was almost yeti-like in its availability: There were lots of unconfirmed sightings but with scant evidence that it actually existed in the wild. Thanks to a perfect storm of factors, over the second half of the

DEFINING RYE

- The mash (base grains) must be at least 51 percent rye.
- It has to be aged in a charred new oak barrel.
- The finished whiskey has to be at least 80 proof (40 percent alcohol by volume).
- No additives or coloring can be added.
- "Straight" rye must be aged for at least two years.

George Dickel and Leopold Bros. teamed up to make a whiskey that combines rye whiskey made on a historic and rare three-chamber still with whiskey made on a column still.

The Rebirth of the Three-Chamber Still

Until recently, the only place you could see a three-chamber still was in old newspaper articles and vintage distilling manuals. Before World War II, however, this historic still design was particularly popular with rye distillers in the Mid-Atlantic states. (It had even been used for a time by some bourbon distillers in Kentucky.) While the three-chamber still is not very efficient, pumping out just a few barrels a day, it intentionally produces lower-proof alcohol with a higher amount of naturally occurring flavor compounds, resulting in a finished whiskey that was quite rich and complex.

Today, there are only a few three-chamber stills in existence. One was found in the boneyard of spare parts and old machinery at the Long Pond distillery in Jamaica, and is currently being refurbished.

Several years ago, pioneering Denver-based distiller Todd Leopold noticed that the three-chamber still was touted in a study undertaken by the Bureau of Internal Revenue and published in 1907. The more Leopold learned about the still's design, the more convinced he was of the need to re-create this important lost piece of distilling history.

He got his brother and business partner, Scott Leopold, on the bandwagon and they commissioned renowned Kentucky-based still maker Vendome Copper & Brass Works to build a three-chamber still for them. At great cost and with no guarantee that the still would work or that they would like the whiskey it produced, the Leopold brothers embarked on distilling three-chamber rye whiskey. It was the first time in decades the style had been made.

The first batch of their 100-proof (50 percent alcohol by volume) bottled-in-bond whiskey, produced in 2016 and released in 2021, was astonishingly good and sold out immediately. The brothers then partnered with Tennessee distillery George Dickel to produce a Collaboration Blend, which combines rye whiskey made on the Leopolds' three-chamber still with rye whiskey made on Dickel's column still. The idea for this blended whiskey came out of the Leopolds' research, which revealed that the two types of rye were sometimes combined by distillers back in the day.

Thanks to Leopold Bros.' success, a number of large and historic rye whiskey brands are currently considering building their own three-chamber stills. I'm now cautiously optimistic that we'll once again have a selection of these flavorful whiskies to drink.

twentieth century the demand for rye had almost completely dried up and production had almost completely ceased. Just a token amount was produced one day a year by a few bourbon distillers who kept a handful of rye whiskey brands alive. Thanks to the recent meteoric rise in popularity for it, rye is now typically produced one day a month by the big whiskey companies. (By comparison, bourbon is made 24/7 and just stops for scheduled maintenance and major holidays.)

♦ TENNESSEE WHISKEY

When it comes to Tennessee whiskey, no federal definitions or rules exist. Brands like Jack Daniel's and George Dickel technically qualify as bourbon, and could be labeled as such if their distillers wanted this designation. (In fact, several years ago Dickel began selling some of its whiskey as bourbon.) Instead, the Tennessee whiskey brands have carved out a niche category and have set up state standards that dictate how to make this kind of whiskey. These rules include that it must be produced and aged in Tennessee and filtered through maple charcoal before the whiskey is aged.

Whether these whiskies are in fact bourbon, regardless of how they're labeled, has engendered fierce and lengthy debates on social media among whiskey experts and aficionados. (Trust me when I say you don't want to raise this issue with American whiskey superfans.) Generally, the folks who insist that Tennessee whiskey is not bourbon but its own style, base their case

DEFINING TENNESSEE WHISKEY

- The whiskey must be produced in Tennessee.
- The mash (base grains) must be at least 51 percent corn.
- It must be filtered through maple charcoal before it's aged.
- It has to be aged in a charred new oak barrel.
- It must be aged in Tennessee.
- The finished whiskey has to be at least 80 proof (40 percent alcohol by volume).
- No additives or coloring can be added.
- "Straight" Tennessee whiskey must be aged for at least two years.

on how it tastes different because of the charcoal filtration process the spirit goes through. This is the point that Jack Daniel's argued with the federal government when its distillery reopened after Prohibition ended.

Why Is Jack Daniel's Charcoal Mellowed?

Jack Daniel's, far and away the most famous spirit brand in Tennessee, and perhaps in the United States, uses something called the Lincoln County Process to make its whiskey. It's the term you see repeatedly on its label or may hear on a commercial, but likely have no idea what it actually means—and there's no reason on earth why you should.

While the name could inspire a host of mysterious or creative theories, it actually refers to something mundane: a type of charcoal filtration. Thanks to Jack Daniel's enduring popularity and the fact that for many years it was the only whiskey distillery in the state, now all so-called Tennessee whiskies have to be charcoal filtered before aging.

Sure, most whiskey, no matter where it is produced in the world, is filtered in some manner, but the Lincoln County Process is unique in that it happens before aging and is certainly more invasive than other types of filters employed by many brands. Thanks to the charcoal, impurities, as well as some flavor compounds, are removed. If Jack Daniel's skipped this step, its finished whiskey would certainly taste very different.

Here's how it works: After Jack Daniel's makes its spirit, the distillate is dripped through giant vats that contain 10 feet (3 meters) of charcoal and two wool blankets that remove the dust from the alcohol. It takes ten days for the spirit to finally reach the bottom, where it's captured and poured into a new charred American oak barrel.

The distillery even makes its own charcoal by burning great piles of sugar maple wood, which is a prized material for making briquettes, since it's strong and has a subtle sweetness. (According to a piece in the trade publication *Bonfort's Wine and Spirit Circular* that ran in December 1905, this process is done outside "so as to avoid the creosote which develops in kiln-burned charcoal.") While the fire is controlled, it's still a risky maneuver so close to a facility producing millions of gallons of high proof alcohol each year. This is why the brand has its own fire department on-site, including a fire engine.

Tennessee whiskey brands Jack Daniel's and George Dickel make their own charcoal, which is an essential element of their production processes.

So why did Jack Daniel originally begin to charcoal filter his whiskey back in 1866? It was a costly and labor-intensive step that wasn't necessary. Well, no one is exactly sure why Daniel started doing it in the first place. The only reasonable explanation I can imagine for why the Lincoln County Process began was that the brand's original distillers were trying to remove something from the spirit. Was it an off smell? An odd flavor? We don't know. But I can tell you that an unwanted note usually intensifies as a whiskey ages, so it's better to remove it as soon as possible, and before aging begins.

According to newspaper advertisements at the beginning of the twentieth century, Jack Daniel's originally used a horizontal two-chamber wooden still before switching to giant column stills. Perhaps those early stills produced a funky "white dog" or maybe they scorched the grain residue in the liquor—both of which were common problems for American distillers in the 1800s. Charcoal filtering could be used to alleviate either problem and improve the whiskey's flavor.

In fact, according to an 1896 piece in the *Nashville American* about Lynchburg and Moore counties and the history of Jack Daniel's, charcoal "leeching" was reportedly done locally before the Civil War to remove "much of the impurities of the still—the verdi gris and the fusil oils." That reference would seem to prove my theory but, as with many mysterious elements of unique production protocol, we might never have definitive

Each drop of Jack Daniel's Tennessee Whiskey is filtered through 10 feet of homemade charcoal before it's aged in a barrel.

proof of why Jack Daniel's started mellowing their whiskey with charcoal. Furthermore, charcoal filtration wasn't an uncommon process in the early American whiskey industry.

In a memoir-like essay in *Bonfort's Wine and Spirit Circular* by George C. Buchanan, who was a whiskey broker and president of the Newcomb-Buchanan Company, he wrote that in early whiskey distilling most farm distillers made rough "high wines" that were blended together and redistilled. He added that: "Until about 1850 there was no other means of purifying this product than by the use of pulverized charcoal." An undated broadsheet from the New York Public Library's Liebmann collection, which looks to be from the 1800s, offers detailed instructions for this filtration process. It opens by saying: "Charcoal is the greatest absorbent in nature, and if it be put into the most impure, still burned, or stinking liquor of any kind, it will absorb all its flavor and other impurities, and render it perfectly flavorless and pure—we have then only to separate the liquor from the Coals, by straining it through sand, and it will be complete."

While Jack Daniel's doesn't use sand to remove the coal, it does employ a wool blanket layer to make sure none of the dust makes it into the barrel. Until I read this broadsheet, I could never understand the purpose of the cloth, which of course now makes a lot of sense.

Since Jack Daniel's is the most famous Tennessee whiskey, what the brand does tends to define how the entire state differentiates its whiskey from bourbon. In 2013, the company's entire production process was used by the Tennessee General Assembly to create a definition for the state's signature whiskey, which includes the requirement that it be "charcoal mellowed."

As we have seen, the practice of charcoal mellowing was not started by Jack Daniel's, even if the distillery's is now synonymous with the Lincoln County Process. So did Jack Daniel and his master distiller Nathan "Nearest" Green (see page 76) improve upon the process? Quite possibly, but we currently have no evidence of that happening.

♦ AMERICAN SINGLE MALT

The newest American whiskey category is single malt, which is just a few decades old. The first malt I heard about being produced in the United States was called The Notch. The whiskey debuted in 2000 and is made by the Triple Eight distillery on Nantucket Island, off the coast of Massachusetts. But the truth is that Steve McCarthy at Clear Creek distillery in Oregon and Lance Winters at St. George Spirits in the Bay Area had already been making pioneering single malts at the time. The category has now exploded—at last count the American Single Malt Whiskey Commission had nearly a hundred distillery members, who make a wide spectrum of whiskies. Whiskey Del Bac in Tuscon, Arizona, even smokes the malted barley for its Dorado single malt by toasting it over a fire made from local mesquite wood.

After years of lobbying by distillers, in December 2024, the federal government established an official and distinct category for American single malt. While this bureaucratic pronouncement might not sound like a big deal, it legitimizes this type of whiskey and ensures that there is consistency across the many distilleries making it.

The federal regulations require that

DEFINING AMERICAN SINGLE MALTS

- The mash (base grains) must be 100 percent malted barley.
- A single malt must be made at a single distillery.
- The whiskey has to be aged in a used, or a charred or uncharred new oak barrel.
- You're not allowed to add to the whiskey any neutral spirits, coloring, or flavoring, except spirit caramel.
- The finished whiskey must be at least 80 proof (40 percent alcohol by volume).

DEFINING CORN WHISKEY

- The mash (base grains) must be at least 80 percent corn.
- It does not need to be aged, but may be aged in a used or new oak barrel.
- It cannot be aged in a charred barrel.
- The finished whiskey has to be at least 80 proof (40 percent alcohol by volume).
- "Straight" corn whiskey must be aged for at least two years.

single malt be made exclusively from malted barley and produced at just one distillery. It must be both distilled and aged in the United States. Distillers can age the whiskey in a new charred or uncharred barrel. They also have the option, like Scotch makers, to age their whiskey in a used barrel, which is important since the flavor of new oak can overpower the delicate malt flavor. (A used barrel is also more economical and more sustainable.) If a whiskey is at least two years old, it can be sold as straight American single malt whiskey.

♦ CORN WHISKEY

While bourbon contains plenty of corn, there is a separate category for whiskey made from at least 80 percent corn—corn whiskey, sometimes also called white whiskey. The rules for producing corn whiskey are very similar to those for producing bourbon, except when it comes to aging. Corn whiskey doesn't have to be aged at all, or it can be matured in a new or used oak barrel. The barrel just can't be charred inside.

These are big differences—the other major American whiskey categories require aging in a barrel that is both charred and new. Generally, in America barrels can't be reused. I imagine that the federal government has written different aging regulations for corn whiskey because the spirit would be overwhelmed by the wood flavor from the barrels. It also may be a nod to corn whiskey's humble origins, when it was made on farms in small quantities. Interestingly, the federal government does not specify the type of corn you must use to make the spirit, even though different varieties would make a huge difference in the finished product. (In fact, Waco, Texas–based Balcones has won acclaim for its Baby Blue Whisky, which is made from locally grown roasted blue corn.)

Corn whiskey doesn't typically get much attention in the spirits world and is too often treated like the punch line to a stale joke. And there are just a handful of corn whiskies still available. But many sought-after bourbons, if they were bottled without being aged or if they were aged in an uncharred barrel, would be classified

as corn whiskies. The category certainly has its fans, who appreciate these smooth and creamy corn-laced spirits that aren't overly complicated. One of the most widely available corn whiskies is Heaven Hill's aptly named Mellow Corn. It may have a truly old-timey label, but make no mistake, the bottled-in-bond 100-proof (50 percent alcohol by volume) whiskey is quaffable and a guilty pleasure for a number of top bartenders.

♦ AMERICAN BLENDED WHISKEY

No one generally talks about blended whiskey made in the United States—and probably for good reason. It is not a small category, but it's held in very low regard thanks to the fact that most blends are a mix of straight bourbon and neutral grain spirit—essentially whiskey-flavored vodka. The federal regulations state that a blended whiskey must be at least 20 percent straight whiskey, which means it theoretically could be a staggering 80 percent neutral grain spirit. As a result, bottom-shelf brands like Fleischmann's Preferred or Seagram's 7 cost less than $15 a bottle—several dollars less than entry-level blended Scotches, like Clan MacGregor.

Blended whiskey has played an important role in American whiskey history. It was a stop-gap measure when bourbon and rye were in short supply after the repeal of Prohibition as well as during and after World War II. By adding neutral grain spirit to bourbon or rye distillers could stretch their supply of whiskey.

As you can imagine, the problem with American blended whiskey is that it doesn't have much flavor and is generally inferior to Irish, Scotch, or Japanese blends. Which begs the question: Why do those other blends taste so much better? The short answer is that, in those non-American blends, the base isn't neutral grain spirit but aged whiskey of some kind. It's an approach that could certainly be taken in the United States—the use of neutral grain spirit is not required. A few brands have already taken this route, including Blackened, High West, Keeper's Heart, and Milam & Greene. In the next few years, I suspect we'll see the rise of a new generation of blended American whiskies that don't use any neutral grain spirit but are instead a blend of straight whiskies.

DEFINING AMERICAN BLENDED WHISKEY

- The blend must contain at least 20 percent straight whiskey.
- The finished whiskey must be at least 80 proof (40 percent alcohol by volume).

American Whiskey History, Part I: Rise of an Empire

Although the United States didn't invent whiskey, the country has become synonymous with a couple of the spirit's bestsellers: bourbon and rye. The story of how these whiskies developed and evolved is as fascinating as they are delicious. Born from a simple means to preserve excess grain, along with the desire to get the most out of one's land and livestock, whiskey distilling developed into a massive US industry that sells millions of bottles a year that are prized by drinkers around the world. Its rise and development was also very American in that it was built by a wide range of immigrants, including Dutch, German, and Jewish people, as well as enslaved Black workers.

The story of whiskey development in the United States includes one dramatic twist after another, including a recent crash so severe the industry almost didn't recover. It's a history every bourbon and rye drinker should know.

♦ **AMERICA'S LIQUID HISTORY**

No one would blame you for thinking that once the English pilgrims stepped off the *Mayflower* onto North American

shores they immediately set up stills and began making bourbon and fixing Mint Juleps. And while that would make one hell of a yarn, bourbon—despite its recent claims—was not the first spirit made in the colonies. In fact, it wasn't produced anywhere in what would become the United States until the late 1700s.

We do know that Willem Kieft, director general of the Dutch Colony of New Netherland, set up the colonies' first still on Staten Island in New York harbor in 1640 and made some kind of booze from rye and corn. But you couldn't call his spirit whiskey—it was likely unaged and probably more of a cross between moonshine and vodka.

So, what did people drink in colonial times and early after independence? The answer may surprise you: rum.

The New England colonists were involved in a system of trade and production with Britain's Caribbean colonies, dubbed the triangular trade. At the time, sugar was an extremely sought-after commodity and very expensive. In Europe, sugar was traditionally made from beets, a labor-intensive process that didn't result in a large yield. To feed their continent's sugar rush, early European explorers quickly realized that the Caribbean islands would be the perfect place for growing sugarcane on a massive scale. However, they needed an army of laborers to work the fields and process the cane juice into sugar crystals. But these Caribbean islands had few residents at the time, so the colonists brought enslaved workers from Africa to these sugar plantations.

The triangle of the so-called triangular trade worked like this: Manufactured goods from England, Portugal, France, and other European countries were brought to Africa and exchanged for enslaved workers. The enslaved workers were transported from Africa to the Caribbean to make sugar. The finished sugar was sent to Great Britain and Europe, and the triangle was complete. An important role of the North American colonies was to receive the molasses from the sugar processing and turn it into rum. The rum was drunk in the colonies, but also sent to Great Britain and Europe.

The East Coast of what would become the United States was once dotted with rum distilleries. It might seem odd now given rum's association with tropical climates and cocktails, but it was originally the signature beverage of Bostonians. "By 1750, when the rum trade was at its height, there were sixty-three distilleries in Massachusetts, and the city of Newport, Rhode Island, alone had thirty distilleries. Nine hundred vessels traded in rum out of Boston," said H. F. Willkie, who ran production for Joseph E. Seagram & Sons in Kentucky, in a lecture to the Newcomen Society in 1947.

This unholy system of trade fell apart when the colonists on the East Coast decided that they were done with Britain's inherently unfair system of "taxation without representation," and revolted. While dumping tea into Boston Harbor was the opening act of the American Revolution, it was another beverage—rum—that was transformed by the break from Britain.

George Washington: America's First Celebrity Liquor Brand Owner

War hero George Washington, who parlayed his success leading the revolutionary army into the presidency of the new United States, was also the owner of a distillery that produced rye whiskey and fruit brandies—making him arguably the owner of the country's first celebrity liquor brand.

Washington was certainly not the typical liquor maker, but the rise and fall of his distillery helps explain the origins of the modern whiskey business in the United States. On the banks of the bucolic Potomac River sits his home and plantation, Mount Vernon. During his time owning it, the estate comprised 7,600 acres (3,076 hectares) and housed hundreds of enslaved people who worked the property.

The manager of the plantation was a Scottish immigrant named James Anderson, who suggested that Washington turn some of his rye grain into whiskey. A 2,250-square-foot (209-square-meter) distillery was ultimately constructed on the estate, with five copper pot stills that were heated directly over small fires. The actual work of making whiskey was done by Washington's enslaved workers. This was no side project, but a serious undertaking—the distillery produced 11,000 gallons (41,640 liters) of whiskey in 1799, which made the former president a handsome $7,500 profit (some $120,000 today). Later that year, Washington passed away at the age of sixty-seven, after a short illness.

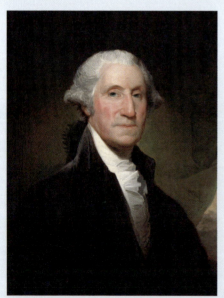

George Washington is famous for being a war hero and the United States' first president, but he was also a successful entrepreneur.

After his death the distillery was shut down. Ultimately it was destroyed in a fire, and was largely forgotten. In 2006, with the help of the Distilled Spirits Council of the United States, it was reconstructed and is now used to make spirits once again.

That is where the story usually ends, but if you dig deeper into the distillery's history it is emblematic of the whiskey industry's early struggles—and the country's ugly reliance on slavery.

After leaving the White House, George Washington owned a distillery on his plantation, Mount Vernon, which made rye whiskey.

Washington's will stipulated that his enslaved workers would be freed once his widow, Martha Washington, died. Fearing that she might be killed by the workers to invoke this clause, in December of 1800 Martha freed all the enslaved workers at the plantation that she could. (Some of the enslaved workers were owned by Martha's family and could not be freed by her but were required to be passed on to other members of her family.) But without Washington's enslaved workers it wasn't economically viable for Mount Vernon's distillery to continue and it closed in 1808, which shows just how much these early distilleries (and the United States economy in general) depended upon enslaved Black labor.

This aspect of Mount Vernon's history and the story of American whiskey is not usually discussed but is incredibly important—it helps explain how the country's spirits industry was, in many cases, built directly on the back of enslaved labor. These workers not only did the distilling and all the other related jobs but are *still* largely left out of the accepted history and given none of the credit for helping to create the country's whiskey industry.

Washington's rebuilt distillery now serves as a monument to him and to his industrious plantation manager, but it should rather be treated as a monument to honor the enslaved workers who actually made the whiskey—so they and all other enslaved distillers won't be forgotten again. May Washington's distillery stand forever.

After the colonies' improbable victory over their far larger and better-equipped overlord, the British crown naturally tried to prevent any supplies, including molasses, from reaching its former subjects. (One can easily imagine King George thinking: *Let's see how long they last without rum!*) But it turned out American pioneers were industrious in numerous ways—and were in no danger of going thirsty.

♦ THE BIRTH OF WHISKEY

Following independence in the late 1700s, everything that could be fermented and distilled in the young country was turned into alcohol, including apples, peaches, berries, and of course, grains. Farmers around the nascent country set up small stills to turn their excess crops into liquor, which could safely and efficiently be stored in a barn, sold, or bartered. One of the byproducts of grain distilling, the spent grain (essentially all the solids, including the husks and bran), made perfect animal feed. Animal waste was used as fertilizer for the grains, and the grain itself was distilled, closing the loop. The whole endeavor was sustainable and profitable.

Whiskey also had clear advantages over rum. After the revolution it wasn't just hard to get the raw ingredients for rum; without ties to Britain it was difficult to sell the finished spirit abroad, and even in the States. "Erratic supplies and higher prices for rum had encouraged a shift to beer, cider, and whiskey, but rum also suffered from rising nationalism," wrote W. J. Rorabaugh in his pioneering 1979 book *The Alcoholic Republic: An American Tradition*. "Imported molasses and rum were symbols of colonialism and reminders that America was not economically self-sufficient." The young federal government tried to help prop up the rum industry by instituting a tax on whiskey, which led to a rise in its retail price, but ultimately that scheme didn't work.

"Even this levy could not stop the drift of Americans from expensive rum distilled from imported molasses to cheap whiskey made from domestic grain," explained Rorabaugh, who noted that by the end of the century the situation only got worse for rum, with whiskey and domestic fruit brandies making up a third of all liquor consumed.

Thanks to rum's fading popularity and the onset of the Industrial Revolution, the American whiskey business was completely transformed in the first half of the 1800s. The widespread use of the sour-mash process (see page 21) helped streamline fermentation and ensured a more consistent finished product. As a result, the constellation of thousands of small farm distillers evolved into an increasingly sophisticated and organized industry. The result was fewer players, but each produced increasingly more whiskey on new and improved equipment.

♦ INVENTING BOURBON

Whiskey made in the United States is now classified and marketed in very specific terms and categories, but these are almost entirely a modern convention. The earliest distillers were

The Negligible Effect of the Whiskey Rebellion

Many barroom historians credit the Whiskey Rebellion at the end of the eighteenth century with forcing whiskey distillers out of western Pennsylvania and into the American South. This migration supposedly led to the beginning of the bourbon industry. But there are a few holes in this theory. It's helpful to consider why the distillers rebelled in the first place, and the timeline that followed.

George Washington's treasury secretary, Alexander Hamilton, imposed a tax for people who owned a still and produced liquor in the states of the Union. As you can imagine, this didn't go over well, particularly in a country that had just fought a war over unfair taxes. And while some farmers did leave Pennsylvania, their effect on distilling history is debatable.

Hamilton instituted the tax in 1791. Kentucky, with a population of seventy thousand, became a state the following year. Yet the Whiskey Rebellion took place over several years culminating in a 1794 insurrection. By the time the Pennsylvania farmers who took up arms realized they wouldn't win against Hamilton and his force of thirteen thousand men, Kentucky was already part of the Union and subject to the same taxes. Also, people were no doubt already making booze in Kentucky at the time.

In the late 1700s, distillers in western Pennsylvania revolted against the newly formed US government and its distilling taxes imposed by treasury secretary Alexander Hamilton.

Nathan "Nearest" Green, Jack Daniel's Teacher

There are no confirmed photos of Nearest Green. In this image, the man to the left of Jack Daniel (center) may be Green, or possibly his son George.

During the 1800s, it was common to find want ads in newspapers for plantation owners who would sell enslaved workers who could make liquor. Unfortunately, the names and histories of most enslaved distillers were not recorded.

One enslaved distiller whose name and life we do know about is Nathan "Nearest" Green, who taught Jack Daniel to distill. (Yes, *that* Jack Daniel.) When Daniel was a teenager, he began working on Rev. Dan Call's plantation in Tennessee, which is where Green was making whiskey. In 1866, after the end of the Civil War, Daniel officially started his eponymous distillery, and the Jack Daniel's brand now credits Green as its first master distiller.

It's hard to overemphasize what this means: In short, the bestselling American whiskey brand in the world was created by a formerly enslaved distiller.

Some of Green's relatives still work at the Jack Daniel's distillery in Lynchburg, Tennessee, and there is also a new brand called Uncle Nearest that was created to honor Green and is owned by Black Americans. Green's great-great-granddaughter, Victoria Eady Butler, is the brand's master blender.

Nathan "Nearest" Green is an incredibly important figure because he provides a tangible link to when much of the whiskey in the United States was produced by enslaved people.

Writer and entrepreneur Fawn Weaver started the Tennessee whiskey brand Uncle Nearest to celebrate Green's story.

certainly not confined by our current ideas and opinions. They made anything and everything they could reliably drink or sell. What they considered whiskey back then was probably quite different from how we define it now—and wouldn't likely qualify as straight bourbon or rye today.

So, where did our modern ideas and terms for whiskey come from? Many whiskey experts claim they can pinpoint the first person or area to produce bourbon, but there has been no definitive evidence to prove any one theory. (And no, the claim that Bourbon County, Kentucky, is where the spirit originated doesn't hold up.)

Personally, I don't think we'll ever truly know who first made what now qualifies as bourbon or rye. Nor does it matter, frankly. Many early farmer-distillers experimented with different grain combinations and distilling techniques—who is to say that one of them didn't technically make bourbon? My research found that the term *bourbon* in relation to whiskey started showing up in newspapers with some frequency in the 1820s and became much more common across the country in the 1830s. What we do know for certain is that corn grows well in Kentucky and rye thrives in the northeast and Mid-Atlantic states—and that's what shaped the types of liquor people living in those areas made.

♦ THE CIVIL WAR & AMERICAN WHISKEY'S UGLY HISTORY

The incredible growth of the American whiskey industry seemed unstoppable—before everything changed at 4:30 a.m. on April 12, 1861. For the next four years, the American Civil War tore apart the country, leaving the liquor industry in the same tatters the fighting made of everyday life and countless other burgeoning businesses.

Just as most agriculture work in the US South was done by enslaved people at the time, so too was the distilling (see George Washington: The Country's First Celebrity Liquor Brand Owner, page 70). Because the roots of the liquor industry and the slave trade were inextricably linked, the Civil War laid waste to that morally reprehensible arrangement.

Not only was the southern distillers' source of labor about to become much less certain, but the politics of the time changed the Confederacy's view of alcohol in general.

Distillers were soon cast as profiteers in the eyes of many of their neighbors, using precious resources to make booze instead of supporting the war effort. As a result, a movement to prohibit the production and drinking of alcohol became increasingly popular across the South. However, Megan L. Bever, writing in the *Journal of Southern History*, points out that the support for temperance was also connected to a much larger issue—the possibility that enslaved workers would be freed. Those who were enslaved, along with all people of color, were not allowed to drink alcohol in the antebellum South. Bever contends that many white Southerners were fine with drinking liquor if it was just white people doing it, but the idea of Black people having unfettered access to spirits was so terrifying that they were willing to outlaw alcohol for everyone.

♦ STILLS & DISTILLING BEFORE AND AFTER THE CIVIL WAR

Just like their brethren in Ireland or Scotland, the earliest distillers in the United States used a classic onion-shaped pot still heated directly over a fire to make their whiskey. And one might assume that American distillers never used anything else, but that couldn't be farther from the truth. In fact, over the past two centuries there have been quite a few different types of stills and pieces of distilling equipment used in the US. These advances in whiskey making can generally be split into two distinct eras, the periods right before and right after the Civil War.

The first half of the nineteenth century marked an era when the US began to come into its pre-industrial own. "From 1802 through 1815 the federal government issued more than 100 patents for distilling devices," wrote W. J. Rorabaugh in *The Alcoholic Republic: An American Tradition* (1979). "These patents were more than 5 percent of all patents granted."

One of the new designs that caught on in this period was something called a chamber still, which was made from two hollowed-out logs.

H. F. Willkie, head of production for Joseph E. Seagram & Sons in Kentucky, explained how the wooden chamber worked in a 1947 speech, noting that it was constructed from "an 8- to 10-foot poplar log, which was split, hollowed with an adze, and a copper pipe run from one end to the other." After distillation in the chamber still, the spirit would be redistilled in a copper kettle or pot still to make it smoother and remove any last impurities, as well as raise the proof of the alcohol.

While this log chamber still may sound crude (distilling in a tree?), it was a major step in US distillers creating their own type of whiskey, one distinct from Scottish and Irish traditions and methods. And the log chamber still was

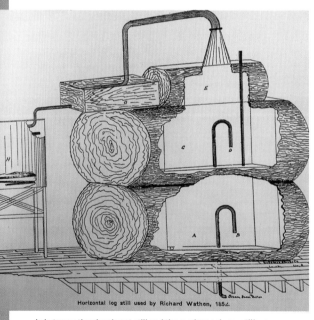

In between the classic pot still and the modern column still were a number of different still designs.

actually a giant technological leap forward that demonstrated a huge advantage over the pot still.

The log chamber still came about because American whiskey had a bad reputation for its burnt flavor at the time. American distillers traditionally like to distill their whiskey without filtering off the leftover grain fibers and husks. This, according to drinks historian David Wondrich, produces better-quality animal feed, which was incredibly important for the country's earliest farm distillers. The problem is that some of the spent grains would burn on the bottom of the pot still. According to a 1910 piece in *Bonfort's Wine and Spirit Circular*, using a chamber still "did away with the scorched flavor because the steam, while boiling the mash, did not scorch the meal, and the log and copper whisky rapidly grew in favor with consumers, and carried the fame of Kentucky to all parts of the United States."

Even Jack Daniel's used wooden stills until 1888, according to an advertisement the company published in the early 1900s: "The logs were mortised together," explained the ad copy. "There are probably none of these old-time stills left. They have long ago been replaced with copper [column] stills, which have proven more satisfactory and easier managed."

At the time, grains used for distilling were mashed and fermented in wooden barrels to create what was called distiller's beer. The distiller's beer was then pumped into the wooden still, which could hold about 100 gallons (379 liters). Interestingly, early on Kentucky distillers used homemade malted corn to convert the grain's starch to sugar. It wasn't until the 1870s that it was replaced by malted barley, which is still used today.

The change from malted corn to malted barley wasn't the only one to arrive after the Civil War. The Emancipation Proclamation and the freeing of enslaved workers led to a number of distilling innovations and mechanizations around the more labor-intensive distilling processes. For one, rather than fermenting in barrels—hot, back-breaking work—distillers began to use larger temperature-controlled fermenters, which allowed them to make bigger batches. Whiskey makers also began to grind their own grain instead of relying on local mills, which allowed them to vertically integrate this process and control more of their supply chain. Most brands today still have their own milling machines on site, opting to buy grain that comes whole from farmers.

The horizontal log stills ultimately evolved into a vertical version with one and then multiple chambers. The chamber still, no matter what it was made from, was usually used in conjunction with a doubler, which is essentially a small secondary still that looks like an old copper kettle. It smooths out the whiskey and increases its proof. Even as the wooden three-chamber stills were phased out—perhaps because they could blow up if subjected to too much steam—the doubler continued to be used by distillers with a range of different types of stills.

Cheat Sheet: American Whiskey Terms

Over the past several hundred years, American whiskey has developed its own specialized lexicon of expressions, designations, and turns of phrase. This language may be confusing at first, but most of these terms are pretty straightforward and make sense when explained. Here's my cheat sheet to sound like an expert.

BOTTLED-IN-BOND WHISKEY: If you see a whiskey that is labeled bottled-in-bond, odds are it's going to be delicious. The term dates back to the Bottled-in-Bond Act of 1897 (see Bottled-in-Bond American Whiskey, page 86), which created a rigorous federal standard for liquor. At the time, the quality of a lot of alcohol was dubious at best and deleterious at worst. Looking for bottled-in-bond on a label was an easy and effective way to guarantee purity and quality. For a whiskey to qualify as bottled-in-bond it must meet a number of stringent conditions, including that it's 100 proof (50 percent alcohol by volume), at least four years old, the product of a single distillery, produced in a single season, and aged in a federally bonded and secured warehouse.

CASK STRENGTH: Most whiskey is cut with water before it's bottled. The amount of water added determines the proof of the finished whiskey. When a whiskey is sold at cask strength, it has been bottled without the addition of any water—which usually indicates a very high alcoholic strength, like above 120 proof (60 percent alcohol by volume). The strength will vary widely from barrel to barrel. Cask-strength whiskies are sought after because, like fat, alcohol carries flavor, so these whiskies generally are very, very rich and complex. Most drinkers add some water to them in the glass, so that they open up and reveal their flavors. Given that these whiskies are more expensive to make, since the distillery is getting fewer bottles to sell, they are also usually quite a bit more expensive than standard 80-proof (40 percent alcohol by volume) release.

HIGH-RYE BOURBON: By federal regulation, bourbon must be made from a mash bill of at least 51 percent corn. Generally, the rest of the grain base is malted barley and rye. Each distiller figures out the exact percentages of each grain. Brands that produce a high-rye bourbon use more rye grain—generally between 20 percent and 35 percent rye. A high-rye bourbon will taste a bit more like rye, with a spice note on the palate and a more unctuous mouthfeel.

MASH BILL: All whiskey is made from grain, and the list of grains used by a distiller is called the mash bill. These grains will be mashed (mixed with hot water and enzymes) to convert their starches to sugar before being fermented and then distilled.

The American whiskey industry has its own nomenclature and terminology to describe its production processes and spirits.

RICKHOUSE: Rickhouse (or sometimes "rackhouse") is just a folksy nickname for a warehouse. You'll usually encounter this term in Kentucky.

SINGLE BARREL: A single barrel whiskey is made when the contents of one barrel are bottled. The number of bottles you get from a barrel depends on the size of the barrel, how many years the barrel has been aging, and the climate where the barrel has been stored. Single barrel whiskies have become very popular with aficionados and collectors because their availability is, by nature, limited and they often showcase an unusual flavor profile.

SMALL BATCH: A small batch whiskey is generally . . . made in a small batch. This means that only a few barrels of whiskey are emptied and their contents are then mixed together and bottled. But this begs the question of how many barrels qualify as a so-called small batch? The answer is that this is a relative term, which varies widely from brand to brand. Some small batch whiskies are made from a dozen barrels or less, while others are made from hundreds of barrels. As a result, the term sometimes has an actual meaning and sometimes is just marketing speak.

STRAIGHT: A straight bourbon or rye has been aged for at least two years in a charred new oak barrel. This is a term codified in federal regulations.

WHEATED BOURBON: The most common recipe for making bourbon calls for at least 51 percent corn plus malted barley and rye. A wheated bourbon, on the other hand, swaps the rye for wheat, which is less spicy and a bit smoother. There are only a handful of wheated bourbons on the market, including Maker's Mark, Old Fitzgerald, and Larceny.

WHITE DOG: In the United States, the unaged, clear spirit that comes off the still is sometimes referred to as "white dog." It's used interchangeably with the term "white whiskey."

(You can even find a number of distillers around Kentucky still using a doubler today.) In a 1945 book published by the Glenmore Distilleries Company, *The Spirit of Old Kentucky*, there's a sepia photo of its doubler with the description: "Looks a little like part of an old-fashioned locomotive, doesn't it? Actually, it's a 'doubler'—a highly efficient type of still which further distills and refines the first distillation."

High-volume continuous column stills made from metal were installed in many Kentucky distilleries in the 1880s. These far more efficient stills were based on Aeneas Coffey's innovative design, which he patented in 1830. The so-called Coffey still had transformed the Scotch industry and allowed Scotch to become the whiskey of choice for decades (See The Tax Collector Who Transformed Whiskey, page 212).

But right up until World War II, many American rye distillers put their own spin on the wooden chamber still, using a vertical three-chamber version made of steel and copper. It was much less popular with bourbon distillers, but prized by makers of rye because it allowed the spirit to retain a lot of flavor compounds, which translate into a complex and rich whiskey. (See page 63 for how the Leopold Bros. in Denver, Colorado, brought this piece of distilling history back to life.) The three-chamber still truly helped America create an international reputation for its rye whiskey, which really put the country on the world's distilling map.

The three-chamber still essentially worked like a stack of pot stills. But thanks to an incredible amount of heat and pressure that would build inside the chambers, it extracted more flavor compounds. To celebrate the first bottles of bonded Maryland rye available after Prohibition, a 1938 *Baltimore Sun* article offered a detailed step-by-step on how the region's signature spirit was produced. Readers no doubt needed a refresher since the whiskey hadn't been made in more than twenty years. "Each new batch of fermented wort enters the top chamber of the trio, placed one above the other," explained the author, William F. Conhurst. "Steam introduced into the bottom compartment heats the wort, causing hot vapors to rise into the second chamber and so boil that batch. This process is repeated for the third and or top chamber, from which vapors are condensed and collected into the 'high-wine' tank, which then holds whisky of about 100 proof." What this means is that the alcohol was slowly distilled several times before it left the still.

The three-chamber still was so well known it was often touted in newspaper advertisements for rye whiskey. Even the department store R. H. Macy's had a house rye whiskey brand called Old Whaler that it boasted in 1937 was made in the "old fashioned 'three chamber' still method." The store's 2-year-old, 93-proof (46.5 percent alcohol by volume) rye at the time sold for $1.58 for a quart bottle (about 1 liter). (But if you wanted to buy in bulk, you could get three bottles for $4.39 or a case of twelve for $17.56.)

The reign of the three-chamber still came to end with the onset of World War

II. American distillers phased them out in favor of column stills, which could efficiently and quickly produce the millions of gallons of high proof alcohol needed by the military-industrial complex for the war effort. I imagine many of the old three-chamber stills were scrapped and used to build warships, fighter planes, and tanks. After the war was over, American rye was made on column stills, which changed its flavor. The whiskey slowly began a fade-out that culminated in its near disappearance by the end of the twentieth century.

♦ WHISKEY COMES INTO ITS OWN

The late 1860s ushered in a new era of innovation in the United States that literally brought the country together—from national train lines to the standardization of time zones to the rise of advertising and marketing. Not to mention newly formed water companies that brought the country's vast rivers and streams right to people's homes—and to the nation's distilleries.

But despite this unification, most whiskey makers were still fairly small

In the late 1880s, Kentucky's E. H. Taylor and Sons distillery was producing some of the best whiskey in the United States.

The Recipe for Making Imposter Whiskey

During the late 1800s and early 1900s, if you ordered a glass of whiskey there was a great chance that what you would be served was actually just young whiskey or neutral grain spirit—basically vodka—that had been doctored up. Sadly, this was a fairly common practice and the ingredients added to make this so-called whiskey ran the gamut from stomach-turning to downright dangerous.

In 1874, a so-called "reformed liquor dealer" from Brooklyn named Oliver Cotter published his aptly titled book, *Adulteration of Liquors*, which examined what exactly was being added to whiskey. What he found was that creosote, sulfuric acid, red pepper, pellitory, caustic potassa, benzine, and nux vomica was being used in making these imposters.

The recipe that famous San Francisco bartender William "Cocktail" Boothby shares in the 1908 edition of his book *The World's Drinks and How to Mix Them*, is just as appetizing: "To one hundred gallons of proof spirit, add four ounces of pear oil, two ounces of pelargonic, thirteen drachms of oil of wintergreen (dissolved in the ether), one gallon of wine vinegar, Color with burnt sugar." It's amazing that anyone was willing to drink whiskey or hard spirits at the time.

and produced no more than a couple of barrels a day, which was enough to supply demand at the time. Whiskey at the time was largely sold by grocery stores that doubled as bar and liquor establishments. When Abraham Lincoln ran for president of the US, in the run up to the 1860 election the temperance movement drummed up a great controversy, objecting to the fact that Lincoln had run a bar. The future president naturally insisted that he only owned a grocery store and sold alcohol you could consume at home. In truth, it's quite possible that both sides were right.

While this system might sound odd today, it was absolutely necessary back in the 1800s. At the time, brands sold their whiskey by the barrel, and drinkers would have to go to the store to have a dram or buy a jug of whiskey. It was a bit like the big grocery stores of today (think: Whole Foods) that have a craft brew pub and/or a station where you can buy a six-pack or fill up a growler. And just like Whole Foods, which has its own line of coffee, grocers back then would often blend barrels of whiskey that they bought to create proprietary house blends. At the time, most drinkers didn't look for specific brands like we do today. For one, there wasn't usually a huge selection of spirits to buy. Most of the whiskey would have likely come from a company that would buy up barrels from several smaller distillers and combine them as well as possibly redistill the alcohol. These types of companies were called rectifiers and were quite common at the time since most distillers didn't have the supply or resources to run a brand on their own.

Contributing to the industry were a number of larger distillers who did actually have their own brands. One of these distillers, who would help pioneer brand marketing, was Colonel E. H. Taylor, who famously burned his name into the ends of his barrels and used shiny copper bands to set his casks apart.

The cask was really all Taylor and other distillers had in which to package their whiskey. It wasn't until 1870 that Old Forester introduced the first American whiskey to come in a sealed bottle from the distillery. We might take this advancement for granted now, but it was truly groundbreaking at the time. In many ways, the packaging of whiskey in sealed bottles helped settle the tremendous debate as to what was and what wasn't whiskey. When it was sold in barrels, there could be significant—and secretive—additions. Often, what was sold as whiskey had little or no actual whiskey in it (see Bottled-in-Bond American Whiskey, page 86). Producers could and did add all types of things to flavor and color neutral grain spirits (basically vodka). Some additives were harmless to drink, such as prune juice, while other stuff, including creosote, was quite dangerous to consume.

"It is a generally well understood fact that the thirsty individual who takes his glass of whiskey at any of even the first-class public bars, saloons, or parlors, does not know what he drinks," wrote Joseph Fleischman in his 1885 book, *The Art of Blending and Compounding Liquors and Wines*. "The moment a barrel of liquor leaves the bonded warehouse, the first thing thought of, and *done*, is to reduce its cost." Fleischman's slim volume proceeds to offer business owners advice for doing exactly that, with recipes for stretching a barrel of whiskey to squeeze the most profit from it.

These practices were certainly meant to improve the bottom line, but also because supposedly "all newly distilled liquors and spirits have a rough and pungent taste, which must be remedied before they can be used as beverages," explained Fleischman. "This is done by fruit-juices or flavors, which are mainly alcoholic extracts of fruits or other substances." Similar advice and recipes are found in a range of cocktail and distilling books from that time, including William "Cocktail" Boothby's classic *The World's Drinks and How to Mix Them* (1908).

Whiskey purity wasn't just an issue for the drinks industry, but for the medical community too. While this might sound like a joke now, during the 1800s alcohol was a common remedy prescribed by doctors for everything from a

Bottled-in-Bond American Whiskey

When I first started drinking whiskey more than twenty years ago, I would occasionally notice the term *bottled-in-bond* on labels. I figured that, like so many things printed on spirits or wine packaging, it was probably just marketing nonsense. It also struck me as suspect that the term seemed only to appear on many remarkably affordable whiskies.

I could not have been more wrong!

In fact, bottled-in-bond has a very specific meaning, and requires a distiller to jump through a series of very challenging federal hoops in order to use the designation on a label. The whiskey must be at least four years old and exactly 100 proof (50 percent alcohol by volume). It must be made during only one distilling season and the label must identify the distillery that produced it. (Usually the identifying number the distillery has received from the federal government is used for this, which is called a distilled spirits plant number, or simply a DSP number.)

While that all sounds fairly manageable, the next requirement is that the whiskey must be stored in a bonded warehouse. Traditionally, this means that the warehouse would have two locks on the door, one that the proprietors of the whiskey brand could open and one the government could open. Meaning both parties would have to be present to open the warehouse. (Now the government uses extensive auditing and inspections to ensure that the barrels aren't being removed early and, most importantly, that the right amount of taxes are being collected.)

This might all sound a little over the top and performative. We're talking about whiskey after all, not diamonds or ballistic missiles. But all these checks and balances actually make sense for the whiskey industry of the 1800s, when these bottled-in-bond procedures were created. Remember, at the time, it was difficult to know what exactly a bottle of whiskey contained, since it was often cut with or made from all kinds of dangerous ingredients. Ordering a whiskey in the 1800s could kill you.

You can understand, then, why some drinkers and distillers wanted a way to certify and ensure whiskey's purity. (Two locks on the door now sounds pretty reasonable.) Unsurprisingly, not everyone agreed on this idea since it was more profitable for a brand to sell imitation whiskey than to make and age the real stuff. However, a number of bourbon pioneers, like E. H. Taylor, were undeterred and pushed for the creation of the so-called Bottled-in-Bond Act, which was approved on March 3, 1897. In fact, Taylor was such a proponent of the new designation that he created a bottled-in-bond display for the 1904 St. Louis World's Fair, which was part of the National Pure Food Commission's exhibition.

The Bottled-in-Bond Act of 1897 was a watershed moment in American whiskey history and codified a set of distilling standards that are still used today.

For many years, the designation was the gold standard for distilling and ensured that a spirit was unadulterated. But by the 1980s and 1990s, the whiskey category was barely holding on, seemingly unable to convince new generations that it was still relevant. Even through these tough times, a number of brands continued to take the time and expend the effort to produce bottled-in-bond whiskies, including Rittenhouse, Old Overholt, and Jim Beam. But given whiskey's low profile at the time, these bottles were often stocked on the bottom shelves at liquor stores and sold for half the price of high-flying vodka brands. Savvy drinkers just shook their heads in disbelief and filled their shopping carts with as many of these bottled-in-bond whiskies as they could afford.

Over the past few years, the secrecy surrounding bottled-in-bond whiskey has faded, prompting brands to start raising their suggested retail prices. Perhaps more interesting is that, for the first time in decades, a whole new generation of bottled-in-bond whiskies have been introduced by brands including New York Distilling Company in Brooklyn and WhistlePig in Vermont. Bottled-in-bond whiskies are now sought after and have thankfully moved up from the bottom shelf to a place of more prominence behind a liquor store's register, where they will hopefully remain.

cold to back pain to anxiety to insomnia. However, the whiskey available could be very dangerous to drink and could actually be worse for a patient than their original problem.

In fact, Old Forester, which was developed by George Garvin Brown and his half-brother J.T.S. Brown Jr., was originally intended to be used as medicine. (When the brand launched it had an extra *r* in its name—Old Forrester—which was later removed for unclear reasons, but most likely to do with a copyright issue.) But since Old Forester was bottled by the distillers, doctors and patients could be sure that it was uncut and unadulterated. A small ad announcing the whiskey's availability at Gleason's Hotel in Little Rock, Arkansas, which ran in the *Daily Arkansas Gazette* in 1884, stated that the bourbon was "for family and medicinal uses." Old Forester was so successful, it led to the founding of the giant liquor conglomerate Brown-Forman, which to this day owns Old Forester, as well as a number of other brands, including Jack Daniel's and Woodford Reserve.

Why did it take so long for the whiskey industry to adopt bottles? The short answer is cost. Bottles were expensive to make back in the 1800s. Each one had to be handblown or blown into a mold. Fortunately, with the turn of the century came many manufacturing advancements, including a machine that could rapidly produce bottles. Thanks to these advances in mechanization, the spirits industry switched to selling bottles instead of barrels. The change happened to coincide with a movement to make sure food and beverages in general were safe to consume and accurately labeled, which culminated with the passage of the Pure Food and Drug Act in 1906.

By the end of the nineteenth century, whiskey had become a huge industry in the US. Modern distilling technology and scientific methods allowed brands to produce record amounts of spirits, so much so that during several years too much whiskey was made and warehouses overflowed with barrels. As a result, the industry lobbied the federal government to allow them to delay paying taxes for a number of years after distillation, so they had a chance of selling the excess before paying the taxes. This became the basis of our modern tax code for alcohol producers.

As the century came to a close, distilling was no longer a side hustle for farmers with excess grain. It was an independent and important part of the American economy.

♦ **THE BATTLE FOR PURITY RAGES ON**
One of whiskey's unsung champions was Dr. Harvey W. Wiley, chief chemist of the US Department of Agriculture from 1883 to 1912. While his name is largely forgotten now, he is in many ways the father of modern American whiskey, because his beliefs about how it should be produced and labeled are reflected in the regulations that we still follow today.

"He fought impurity, but he also fought dishonesty in labels," wrote the

Dr. Harvey W. Wiley, chief chemist of the US Department of Agriculture, fought against unscrupulous whiskey brands that took shortcuts and used all kinds of deleterious ingredients.

New York Times when Wiley died in 1930 at the age of eighty-five. "In pre-prohibition days he said that he believed 85 percent of the whiskey sold over bars in this country was adulterated."

Wiley insisted that the color of the whiskey should come from aging in a barrel and that the whiskey shouldn't be so distilled or redistilled that it lost all of its innate flavor. He believed above all that whiskey should not be blended with all kinds of additives. One of his chief concerns was keeping as many as possible of the naturally occurring flavor compounds in the whiskey, which at the time was a very contentious opinion. Essentially, Wiley's ideal for whiskey was very similar to our current definition of straight whiskey.

But in the late 1800s and early 1900s, Wiley's opinions were not universally supported. He was forced to wage an aggressive campaign against a number of companies that realized if Wiley was successful, they would have to change their production techniques or label their spirits differently, which would destroy their brands' reputations. One of Wiley's main adversaries was the National Wholesale Liquor Dealers' Association, which represented many of the rectifiers that wanted the rules around whiskey to be fairly loose.

Defining whiskey and ensuring its purity was ever more important because whiskey had suddenly become big business. Just as the demise of the colonial rum market at the close of the eighteenth century created an opportunity for whiskey distillers, the industry would now get a boost from the misfortune of Cognac. Beginning in the 1860s, a small insect called phylloxera had destroyed a great swath of vineyards in Europe. And without grapes it's hard to make Cognac—or wine, for that matter. In the late 1800s this was a huge problem. Cognac was wildly popular and was called for in numerous cocktail recipes.

Whiskey, of course, was more than happy to supply Cognac's customers. Distillers were thrilled to finally be able to step out of brandy's shadow and assume a starring role. Some of these brands were already trying to change the perception of American whiskey as a low-quality product by touting its heritage and the excellence of

The Immigrants Who Created American Whiskey

Historically, Scottish, Irish, and English immigrants were credited with building America's spirits industry. Which made a lot of sense, since distillers in Great Britain had produced spirits for centuries. But the truth is more complex and nuanced—in addition to the crucial toil of enslaved workers (see pages 72 and 73), America's distilling industry owes a great debt to a number of major immigrant groups who helped refine and create the main whiskey varieties we know and drink today.

The Dutch

From Amsterdam Avenue in Manhattan to the Spuyten Duyvil section of the Bronx, all over New York you can still find traces of America's early Dutch roots. The area was claimed by the Dutch Republic in the early 1600s and was controlled by the Dutch until 1664. You may be asking yourself *What the hell do the Dutch have to do with American whiskey?* Well, the answer is *more than you realize.*

The Dutch built one of the earliest distilleries in New Amsterdam, which was located on Staten Island in the middle of New York harbor. What did it make? Probably all kinds of liquor, including grain-based spirits. No matter what they produced, it was made to drink immediately, so none of it was barrel aged.

The production of grain-based spirits in New Amsterdam makes sense because the Netherlands is, of course, famous for its signature spirit, genever. But in the United States today genever is usually talked about in the same breath as gin. Yes, British gin is based on Dutch genever, but there are key differences between the two spirits. Gin is now made from a neutral base of grain alcohol, usually a wheat or corn spirit that is basically vodka, which is then infused with a range of potent botanicals, including juniper. Genever, on the other hand, was historically made from malted barley and other grains, including rye. And the botanicals aren't the star of the show here, but instead it's the grain spirit flavor. If you didn't know what you were drinking, you'd think it was some kind of unaged or young whiskey.

The Dutch built liquor distilleries when they arrived in New Amsterdam in the seventeenth century.

The experience and knowledge of making genever no doubt informed American distillers for decades. In many ways the Dutch spirit led not only to the British-made gin, but also to whiskey industry in the US.

The Germans

Given that Germany and the Netherlands are neighbors, it should come as no surprise that they shared distilling knowledge. Germany is also one of the world's biggest producers of rye grain, and the country has a tradition of turning it into a spirit called korn (from *kornbranntwein*). This spirit, almost unknown in the United States, is one of the forbears of American rye whiskey.

In a 1648 letter found in the collection of the Massachusetts Historical Society, Emmanuel Downing asks John Winthrop for his help making German whisky from rye and corn. "I have even now sold my horse to James Oliver for 10l to purchase the still, I pray remember me about the German receipt for making strong water with rye meall without maulting of the Corne, I pray keepe a copie, in Case the noate you send me should miscarye." This note, according to drinks historian David Wondrich, is incredibly important because it's the first reference in the North American colonies to making rye whiskey. (It was also written well before people began producing bourbon.)

Many of the United States' most important whiskey brands were started by immigrants from Germany, including Old Overholt, Jim Beam and George Dickel.

German immigrants became so known for whiskey distilling expertise that a want ad for "a person who understands the process and management of distilling whisky," that ran in the *Philadelphia Inquirer* on December 3, 1794, even specified "A German will be preferred."

Adding to the legacy of German immigrants is that many of the most famous American whiskies were created by Germans in America, including the talented and prodigious Beams. The family's influence was so vast that it used to be said that you couldn't have a distillery without at least one Beam on the payroll. For example, John Henry "Jack" Beam started Early Times, Charles L. Beam was master distiller for Four Roses, and when Heaven Hill opened in 1935 in Bardstown, Kentucky, a Beam—Joseph L. Beam in this case—was making the whiskey. (A Beam family member made the whiskey at Heaven Hill until fairly recently.) At last count there were eleven Beam family members in the Kentucky Distillers' Association's Bourbon Hall of Fame.

The Beam name was originally "Boehm," and all the modern distillers who consider themselves descendants can be traced back to one man: Johannes Jakob Boehm, later known as Jacob Beam. As far as we can tell, he likely came from Germany in the 1750s as a baby, although some believe he was born in southeastern Pennsylvania to immigrant parents. Either way, he no doubt spoke German and was familiar with Germanic drinking and food customs and culture.

Tennessee whiskey George Dickel was created by George A. Dickel, who hailed from Grünberg, Germany, and Old Overholt was created by Henrich Oberholtzer, the son of German immigrants. (His last name later became Henry Overholt.) Isaac Wolfe Bernheim (see the sidebar, pages 110–111) and his brother Bernard Bernheim came from Schmieheim (Baden), Germany, and went on to build a vast whiskey empire. And there were dozens and dozens of other distillers and liquor entrepreneurs who were German immigrants, or their children, often in Ohio, Pennsylvania, or Kentucky.

With the onset of World War I and then the horrors of World War II, many Americans tried to distance themselves from their Germanic roots, changing their names and family histories to leave out that heritage. In whiskey, it was no different. The narrative for the spirit was carefully edited, so the credit for distilling went to Scottish and Irish immigrants instead of Germans.

European Jews

The influx of Jewish immigrants to the United States in the 1800s completely changed the country and also revolutionized the liquor industry. Jews brought with them hundreds of years of distilling knowledge and alcohol business acumen. Thanks to their dietary laws, kashruth, Jews have traditionally produced their own alcohol. In addition, in the 1800s in a number of Eastern European countries, Jews ran the local taverns and distilleries.

During the 1800s and 1900s, Jews fled to the United States to escape anti-Semitism and to find a better life. Through Jewish immigrants already in the US, these new arrivals found jobs in the whiskey industry. Some, like Isaac Wolfe Bernheim, who left Germany, became fabulously successful and wealthy. In fact, there were so many Jews working in the liquor industry that many noted anti-Semites, including Henry Ford, supported a national prohibition of making and selling alcohol, in the form of a constitutional amendment, as a way of depriving these immigrants of a means of making a living and driving them from the country.

Jewish immigrants helped build the American whiskey industry and continue to run a number of important brands today, including Sazerac.

While Prohibition shut down the liquor industry outright, it thankfully didn't have the effect of forcing Jewish Americans to leave the country. And once Prohibition was repealed, Jews played an even more important role in the history of whiskey. Many of the biggest liquor companies were owned by Jews, including Schenley, Seagram's, and Jim Beam. While Schenley and Seagram's are no longer around, and Suntory bought Jim Beam, Jewish families still own Heaven Hill and Sazerac. There's also a new generation of Jewish distillers running craft distilleries across America.

While president of the United States, Teddy Roosevelt was a staunch supporter of Dr. Harvey W. Wiley, chief chemist of the Department of Agriculture, in his fight against unscrupulous distillers.

their spirits. These distillers, including Colonel E. H. Taylor, naturally supported Wiley and disapproved of the shenanigans that had long plagued the whiskey industry.

On the other side of the debate were the blenders (also known as rectifiers), who took a decidedly different approach to making whiskey. "The blender doesn't care whether the whisky is made in Kentucky or Indiana or Illinois—nor whether it is made in a log still or a continuous copper still—nor whether it is made from spring water or well water or pond water—nor whether it is run 100 proof or 180 proof," lamented a piece in *Bonfort's Wine and Spirit Circular* in September of 1906.

This was an especially important and topical issue because, at the turn of the century, consumers were incredibly interested in how their food and drinks were being made. The timing was perfect too, for Upton Sinclair's bestselling novel *The Jungle*, which exposed filthy and unsafe practices in the meat industry and was a sensation when it was published in 1906.

After years of debate and discussion in the media and in Congress, Wiley was ultimately successful. For his trailblazing work as a chemist to create and uphold standards of pure food and drink, he is often credited as the inspiration and driving force behind the wildly important Pure Food and Drug Act of 1906. Then, with the support of President Theodore Roosevelt and Attorney General Charles Joseph Bonaparte, Wiley was able to limit the use of the term *whiskey* to only straight whiskies. The result was that all the other kinds of whiskey on the market had to be labeled "blended whiskey," "imitation whiskey," or "compound whiskey," which wasn't exactly great for their sales and served to undermine their credibility and prestige. It's hard to claim your whiskey is wonderful

While president of the United States, Teddy Roosevelt was a staunch supporter of Dr. Harvey W. Wiley, chief chemist of the Department of Agriculture, in his fight against unscrupulous distillers.

when it's called imitation whiskey by the US government.

Given that politicians were involved, however, Wiley's pioneering work would get completely undone. The unraveling came by way of none other than President William Howard Taft, who declared in late December of 1909 that, basically, the term *whiskey* could be used for a wide range of spirits. Taft did carve out a special class for straight whiskey, but any other kind of whiskey would just have to state what it was made from on its label.

Taft's ruling stated: "The public will be made to know exactly the kind of whisky they buy and drink. If they desire straight whisky, they can get it by purchasing what is branded 'straight whisky.' If they are willing to drink whisky of neutral spirits, then they can buy it under a brand showing it; and if they are content with a blend of flavor made by the mixture of straight whisky and whisky made of neutral spirits, the brand of the blend upon the package will enable them to buy and drink that which they desire."

Something similar happened in the UK that same year. After a Royal Commission was convened and lengthy testimony heard from a wide variety of distillers, the definition that was settled on for the term *whisky* was disappointingly vague. (For more on the Royal Commission see page 214.)

Needless to say, Taft completely missed Wiley's point in establishing standards for whiskey, and perhaps also the larger aim of the Pure Food and Drug Act. (The president did concede that whiskey could not be made from molasses—that was a step too far, he decreed, and was rum.) Taft's ruling naturally upset all the distillers who were making whiskey the old-fashioned way and supported Wiley. The Rohr McHenry Distilling Co. in Wilkes-Barre, Pennsylvania, even decided to publish copies of the impassioned letter it had sent to President Taft about the dangers of allowing imitation whiskey to be sold, including one that found its way into Harvard's library. My favorite line from this screed is: "IT IS SO PURELY IMITATION, WHY NOT ALLOW THE CONSUMER TO PAY FOR IT WITH IMITATION MONEY?"

But there wasn't much time for Wiley or his opponents to recover from their battle. Whiskey drinkers would soon face an even tougher fight

The Real Reason You Pay Income Tax

Americans have Prohibition to thank for federal income tax. Seriously. To make up for the anticipated loss of tax revenue from the sale of spirits, beer, and wine, and all of their related industries, the 16th Amendment was added to the Constitution in 1913, which gave the government the power to establish a mandatory federal personal income tax. This measure helped to convince any reluctant members of Congress who had reservations about the economic viability of a temperance amendment to the Constitution. And while Prohibition was repealed long ago, most Americans will sullenly note that they're still required to pay federal income tax every year.

that would nearly destroy the entire industry—Prohibition.

♦ AMERICA'S WHISKEY DISTILLERS JOIN THE WAR EFFORT

Although the United States was a spectator for most of World War I, the horrifically bloody global conflict still had major ramifications for the American whiskey industry. During the war years, the newly formed Food Administration, led by future US President Herbert Hoover, was co-opted by Prohibitionist congressmen who tried to use the war as justification for turning America "bone dry."

And they succeeded. Just a few months after America officially entered the war, the government banned the importation of foreign liquor. This ban severely hurt Scotch distillers, who weren't sure how long the fighting would last but were desperate to sell what was in their warehouses and raise funds. In the name of preserving supplies for the war, the US Food Administration also instituted incredibly high taxes on liquor and, further, banned all distillation of liquor in America.

The result: On September 1, 1917, the nation's distilleries went silent, save the distillation of any grains that were already fermenting. A few distilleries were able to stay open to make high proof alcohol for the war effort, but the laws behind the ban meant death for many of the country's distilleries, which lacked the resources to ride out the war.

While these austerity measures were supposedly for the duration of the war only, ten days after the official armistice that ended it, Prohibitionists were able to pass the Wartime Prohibition Act, which forbade the sale of distilled spirits. The legality of this prohibition was subsequently upheld by a majority decision from the Supreme Court. All these measures culminated in the passage of a national alcohol ban, otherwise known as Prohibition.

♦ NATIONAL PROHIBITION

It's hard to overestimate the effect that Prohibition had on the American liquor industry and the country's larger drinking culture. Once the government-sanctioned dry period went into effect on January 17, 1920, it immediately became illegal to manufacture, transport, or sell alcohol. If you had a personal stash, you could still drink it. Very wealthy people were known to buy out whole liquor stores to stock their cellars right before Prohibition took effect. For example, US Treasury Secretary Andrew Mellon filled his house with cases and cases of Old Overholt whiskey, which his family conveniently owned.

It's now fashionable to look back at the Roaring Twenties with nostalgia for the Great Gatsby–style parties of lore, but living through the era was quite different. There was no guarantee that the government would ever allow the manufacture and sale of liquor again. For the whiskey industry, the thirteen years of Prohibition were an eternity. And keep in mind that some states had enacted their own prohibition laws long before federal Prohibition went into effect.

Add the distillery shutdown during World War I, and the whiskey industry was effectively shuttered for an even longer stretch than most folks realize.

In response to Prohibition, almost all the country's distilleries completely fell apart. Anything of value was sold and the rest was left to crumble. Just six lucky distilleries received government permits to bottle so-called medicinal whiskey. Somehow, amid the triumph of the temperance movement, the consumption of spirits was still commonly prescribed by doctors and dentists.

The way the system worked was that you could go to a pharmacy with a prescription, like you would for any other medication, and get a small bottle of booze. While Prohibition was able to stop the sale of recreational whiskey, it couldn't abolish the sale of medicinal whiskey. This loophole was exploited, and is one reason pharmacy chains grew big during this period.

As you might imagine, the number of "sick" people requiring extensive whiskey treatment was quite high. So high, in fact, that the six distillers still allowed to bottle spirits were running out of booze, and began buying up the mothballed brands to access their warehouses of barrels. These purchases drove a consolidation of the industry that led to a few companies owning the intellectual property of a huge number of their former competitors.

A case in point was Brown-Forman, which shrewdly bought the historic Early Times brand and its stock of whiskey in 1923. After repeal, Brown-Forman decided to focus on rebuilding just a few of the whiskies in its portfolio, which at that point contained more than a hundred brands—many of which they nabbed during Prohibition. Ultimately, these mergers and acquisitions weren't enough to keep up with the demand for medicinal whiskey at the time. To replenish rapidly diminishing stocks, the federal government instituted a "distiller's holiday" in 1929 that allowed authorized distillers to make more whiskey.

If you weren't able to get your hands on medical whiskey, your booze choices ranged from highly sought-after and expensive bootlegged bottles from Canada or Scotland to highly adulterated and possibly deadly concoctions from unscrupulous back-alley and backwoods moonshiners. Most of what the illicit stills turned out was high proof, very rough unaged spirits made from grain, fruit, sugar, or frankly anything the makers could get their hands on. The same broad spectrum of quality also existed for cocktails. Some of the best speakeasies were well stocked with liquor made before Prohibition or smuggled into the country after—the worst were serving shots of wood alcohol that could make you blind.

It's no wonder that, by the end of Prohibition, America's drinks culture was in shambles. Drinkers could barely remember what a proper whiskey was supposed to smell or taste like. So it's no surprise that many of the newspaper advertisements for spirits that ran in the late 1930s are essentially lessons on what to look for in a high-quality whiskey. In an attempt to gain instant credibility, and to disassociate themselves from Prohibition, many distillers also added the word *old* to their brand names and created sophisticated packaging.

One of the few beneficial effects of Prohibition was that it became popular to make cocktails at home. As you might imagine, the sales of shakers and barware were high during the famously dry period. Even President Franklin D.

During Prohibition the only way you could legally bottle whiskey in the United States was if it was to be used for so-called medicinal use.

Pappy Van Winkle: Myth versus Reality

There are few brands as mythologized as Pappy Van Winkle. Of all the questions I'm asked—by friends, family, acquaintances, even random strangers—I'm asked about Pappy the most. What shocks me about the brand is not its popularity but how little people tend to know about its actual history and production process. This knowledge is, in fact, incredibly important and might give you pause before spending thousands of dollars for a bottle of it.

Let's start with the facts. Pappy Van Winkle was an actual person. Julian "Pappy" Van Winkle was born on March 22, 1874, in Danville, Kentucky. He briefly attended Centre College in his hometown, but dropped out and began working in the (no surprise here) whiskey industry. At just nineteen, he started out by selling whiskey from a horse-drawn buggy to establishments around Kentucky, Ohio, Indiana, and West Virginia.

In the 1920s, he joined with Alex Farnsley to buy wholesaler W. L. Weller. They began to work closely with the A. Ph. Stitzel distillery, which had a sought-after medicinal whiskey license that allowed them to stay open and bottle alcohol during Prohibition. After Repeal, the two companies merged to form the formidable Stitzel-Weller. Thanks to their medicinal whiskey sales they had the money to build a huge state-of-the-art distillery in Louisville, Kentucky, in 1935, which reportedly cost $250,000. By 1937, the new facility was making 75,000 gallons (2,840 hectoliters) of spirit a day. The distillery was located on about 25 acres (just more than 10 hectares) and ultimately boasted fifteen vast unheated warehouses—Pappy insisted that every warehouse window be opened during the day for ventilation, and then closed at night. The company exclusively made bourbon, including Old Fitzgerald, Rebel Yell, W.L. Weller, Old Mammoth Cave, and Cabin Still.

The one brand that he didn't make or sell? Pappy Van Winkle. That would come later.

Pappy became quite famous, and even ran a series of advertisements in publications such as the *New Yorker* with his thoughts on the proper way to make whiskey—of which he had many and was quite happy to share. One of his opinions was that he didn't need any newfangled innovations and that whiskey should be made the old-fashioned way. There was even a sign hanging in his distillery that proclaimed in

During his lifetime, Julian "Pappy" Van Winkle was considered Kentucky's dean of distillers while he ran the Stitzel-Weller Distillery in Louisville.

a large Gothic font, "No Chemists Allowed." When Pappy was eighty-seven and the oldest active distillery executive, he was interviewed by the Associated Press: "'No chemist ever did anything for our business,' he says, emphasizing the remark with a flourish of his shillelagh. 'And you can tell them I said that.'"

Later in life each of Pappy's milestone birthdays was written up in local Louisville papers, who usually called him "Kentucky's dean of distillers." The Stitzel-Weller distillery, which is now owned by Diageo and is home to Blade and Bow Kentucky Straight Bourbon Whiskey, still features a plaque that states Pappy's famous axiom: "We make fine bourbon . . . at a profit if we can . . . at a loss if we must . . . *but always fine bourbon*."

On February 16, 1965, Pappy passed away at the age of ninety. Despite vowing never to retire, he did in fact retire just a few months before he died. Pappy's son, Julian Van Winkle Jr., succeeded him and became president of the distillery. Pappy left his family a $2 million estate, a veritable fortune at the time that would be worth almost $20 million today.

Now for the myths. If you're lucky enough to get a bottle of Pappy Van Winkle Bourbon (don't even dream about getting the rye, it's even scarcer), it was not made

Julian Van Winkle III has made his grandfather famous around the world with his line of Pappy Van Winkle bourbon and rye.

at the Stitzel-Weller distillery. In fact, there is no Pappy Van Winkle distillery and there never was one. (I'll give you a minute to let that sink in.)

Seven years after Pappy passed away, his family sold the Stitzel-Weller distillery and the whole business to the conglomerate Norton Simon for $20 million in stock—an enormous sum. Norton Simon renamed the facility the Old Fitzgerald distillery, after the most popular whiskey brand made there. It turned out to be an incredibly shrewd move for the family to sell—at the time the future of the American whiskey industry seemed bright. But just a few short years later, the industry suffered a catastrophic collapse. In fact, it was the perfect moment for the Van Winkles to exit the business. They were truly lucky to get out when they did.

According to family lore, what wasn't included in the sale was the intellectual property of the Old Rip Van Winkle brand, the one that pays homage to the famous Washington Irving story about a man who falls asleep for decades. While Pappy was alive, he never made any Old Rip Van Winkle whiskey and likely acquired the brand name around repeal.

Julian Van Winkle Jr., Pappy's son, had opposed the sale of the Stitzel-Weller distillery but ultimately voted for the deal. A few years later, he told the *Charlotte*

News, "I was left with no money problems. We continued to eat very well. The deal we got was very favorable for all stockholders." But he wasn't ready to retire, since he was only in his late fifties. So in October 1973, he created a new company called, you guessed it, the Old Rip Van Winkle distillery, which would make collectible ceramic decanters of bourbon. According to a small story in the *Courier-Journal*, it was announced "the bottles will be made by Hall China in Liverpool, Ohio, and the whisky will be bottled by Old Boone Distillery Co., Louisville." He hired Robert Walter, who was known in Louisville for his newspaper cartoon strip "You Be the Judge," to design the decanters. Where did the 7-year-old bourbon come from? He simply bought back some barrels from Norton Simon.

Julian Van Winkle Jr. also had a plan, one that showed he understood both quality and the whiskey lover's mindset: "The key to succeeding in this market is producing in limited quantities. If you think you can sell 3,500, put out 3,000. If you think you can sell 10,000, put out 8,000," he explained to the *Charlotte News* in 1975. "My motto has been: 'Something rare is something dear.' It's true about everything—not just whiskey bottles. No matter how high priced something is— within reason—it's more attractive if there are not too many to be had." While he was talking about selling decanters, his family used (and continues to use) this strategy to build momentum for their brands and create an almost obsessive collectability for their whiskey.

Julian Van Winkle Jr. ran the brand for several years, but it was an incredibly bad period in American whiskey history and would remain so for decades to come. The Van Winkle family continued to plug away, buying whiskey on the open market from a number of distilleries. But the family never actually made Pappy whiskey themselves or got back into the distilling business.

In 1981, Julian Van Winkle Jr. passed away and his son, Julian Van Winkle III, took over the company. There was just enough interest in American whiskey to keep the brand alive. While the family continued to sell ceramic decanters, they also began selling bourbon in regular glass bottles. In 1980, a special 11-year-old Old Rip Van Winkle Kentucky Bourbon was advertised in Louisville for just $10.49 a fifth—and that included a special Father's Day label.

Just as the twentieth century was coming to a close, Van Winkle had some whiskey with a bit more age than what he usually sold. With a stock brandy bottle and a gorgeous black-and-white professional photo of his grandfather, perhaps taken by a local newspaper photographer, Van Winkle launched the now-famous Family Reserve line of Pappy Van Winkle whiskies. It was a grandiose name for a new whiskey that had been bootstrapped together.

Throughout this entire period Julian Van Winkle III continued to buy whiskey from other distillers. In 2002, he signed a landmark agreement with acclaimed Frankfort, Kentucky, distillery Buffalo Trace to produce all of the Pappy Van Winkle whiskies going forward. It was a prescient move. Because of the huge rise in popularity of American whiskey that began at about that time, it has become ever more difficult and expensive to buy barrels from distillers.

And Buffalo Trace knows a thing or two about creating sensations. In the 2000s, it turned Sazerac 18 Year rye whiskey into arguably the original, modern trophy bottling that people hunted down in liquor shops. The company also turned Blanton's, Weller, Stagg, E. H. Taylor, and a number of other brands into highly sought-after whiskies that are now so popular they are on allocation, meaning only certain states and only certain bars and stores get them. (Julian Van Winkle Jr. would be quite proud that Buffalo Trace still uses his philosophy to build bestsellers.)

The Buffalo Trace production deal finally gave Pappy Van Winkle consistency and a house style. Before that, the flavor of Pappy varied widely from year to year. The partnership has spawned myriad conspiracy theories about how Buffalo Trace is producing Pappy. Questions abound: Is Pappy actually different from other Buffalo Trace whiskies? Did they create a completely different whiskey from scratch? While Buffalo Trace and Julian Van Winkle III obviously know the answer to this question, it is naturally a closely held secret. While there has been endless speculation in the industry about the exact provenance of Pappy's whiskey within the Buffalo Trace whiskey-verse, I imagine the truth is that Pappy Van Winkle is one of the company's preexisting whiskies—but it comes only from a specific part of one of their many warehouses. The place where the barrels age can greatly affect the flavor of the finished whiskey. Regardless, hopefully we'll see the Pappy supply increase and its price decrease.

Not to start another Pappy craze, but keep an eye out for pre-Buffalo Trace bottlings of Pappy Van Winkle. I imagine collectors will really want to add those whiskies to their collections.

Starting in 2002, the Buffalo Trace Distillery in Frankfort, Kentucky, began producing the Pappy Van Winkle line of whiskey.

Roosevelt had a regular happy hour in the White House, at which he insisted on making some of his signature cocktails for everyone, with varying results. While FDR may not have been a gifted mixologist, he did have his own sterling silver cocktail shaker with six matching cups. Before Prohibition, men and some women would do their drinking in proper bars. After repeal, bars were once again very popular, but people continued to make drinks at home, even buying bar carts for their living rooms and offices.

♦ REPEAL AND THE RISE OF THE FOUR GIANTS

After the repeal of Prohibition, the United States was, unsurprisingly, fully stocked with whiskey from the United Kingdom and Canada. Foreign distillers were naturally very excited (and ready!) for Prohibition to be over, because the United States was such a big and important market for spirits. The 21st Amendment repealing Prohibition was passed by the US Congress in February 1933, but it still had to be approved by a three-quarters majority of the country's then forty-eight states. About nine months later, the amendment was ratified at 5:31 p.m. eastern standard time on December 5, 1933.

This time between when the amendment passed and was ratified was a kind of blessing for entrepreneurs. It gave them almost a year to raise funds and draw up business plans for a host of new whiskey brands.

While money was still tight, the reopening of the US liquor industry was one of the few significant economic opportunities created during the country's Great Depression. It's no wonder that it attracted investors willing to roll the dice on new and unproven ventures—an American tradition dating back to well before Prohibition.

Soon after repeal, at least 150 new distilleries were built around the country, with another 200 reportedly given permits. The race to get product to market and establish a brand name was officially on.

One of these start-ups, Heaven Hill, was backed by the Shapira family, who were already fairly well known in Kentucky for their chain of small dry-goods stores. The head of the family, Max Shapira, came from Lithuania and started out as a peddler selling wares in rural Kentucky. Ultimately, he opened

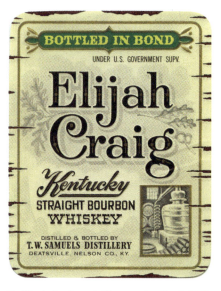

The Shapira family pooled its money together in 1935 and joined a few other investors to start Heaven Hill, which is now known for its Elijah Craig Bourbon.

Margie Samuels came up with the name Maker's Mark for the bourbon she and her husband, Bill Samuels, created in the 1950s.

several stores across the state, which were run by his sons. The family then built a distillery in Bardstown, Kentucky, with other investors, whom they soon bought out for $17,000. Heaven Hill continues today to make a large range of American whiskies, including stalwarts Evan Williams, Elijah Craig, Rittenhouse Rye, and Old Fitzgerald.

At the same time, a number of legendary American whiskey families suddenly found themselves without a distillery or a company. That included James Beauregard Beam, aka Jim Beam, who had spent Prohibition exploring different ventures, including running a rock quarry and a citrus grove. Fortunately for whiskey drinkers, none of those opportunities worked out for him. At the ripe old age of sixty-nine, and with the backing of a group of Deerfield, Illinois, investors, he started a new company, Jim Beam. However, while the Beams were able to get back into the whiskey business, they were no longer the owners of the company that bore their name.

The situation in which the Beams found themselves was hardly unique. Another famous distilling family, the Samuels family, found themselves in a similar predicament after the repeal of Prohibition. Now famous for creating the bestselling brand Maker's Mark, the Samuelses originally produced an altogether different bourbon, T. W. Samuels. After Prohibition, they were able to find investors to help

America's Forgotten Whiskey Capital

Today, Kentucky is the undisputed king of American whiskey. There isn't another area or state that can rival its number of distilleries, its deep and rich history, or the absolute river of whiskey it produces each year.

But until 1979, there was a different American whiskey capital: Peoria, Illinois.

On September 8, 1917, Peoria was called the "whiskey making center of the world" by papers across the United States, which were running front-page stories about how distilleries were forced to close because of the country's entry into World War I. That same day the Associated Press ran a piece that started, "Peoria, for more than half a century the whiskey making center of the United States, will lose its title of 'The Still City' early in September, at least for the duration of the war."

Peoria's five pre–World War I distilleries were: Atlas, Clarke Bros. & Co., Corning & Company, Great Western, and Woolner. All have been largely forgotten despite producing a huge amount of whiskey. From 1912 to 1917, these facilities collectively distilled nearly 30 million gallons (1.14 million hectoliters) of spirit a year on average. They collectively used 54,500 bushels (1,921 cubic meters) of corn each day and employed nearly 1,300 people. The city even boasted a minor league baseball team, of course called the Peoria Distillers. According to a story in the *Chicago Daily Tribune* from 1944, the distilleries in Peoria were making one out of every six bottles of American whiskey before World War II.

Ultimately, what dethroned Peoria wasn't Kentucky, but a common pair of enemies—vodka and changing tastes. By the late 1970s, being the home of American whiskey was nothing to boast about it. And it made little sense to keep pumping out barrels of whiskey when you couldn't sell what was already aging in your warehouses.

By the end of Peoria's reign, only Hiram Walker's hulking distillery, which was built in 1934, was left. What no doubt aided in the decision to close it down in 1979 was the existence of another huge Hiram Walker facility in Windsor, Ontario, right across the river from Detroit, Michigan. That distillery is currently one of the three largest in North America and makes roughly 75 percent of all Canadian whisky.

While it's, well, sobering that American whiskey fell so far out of favor that its largest distillery could close, what's more shocking is that few remember it existed in the first place. Peoria, Illinois, the whiskey capital of the world? Bourbon distillers in Kentucky are likely happy that Peoria and other Midwestern distillery locations, such as Cincinnati, Ohio, have been largely written out of history. The current Bluegrass narrative around whiskey's past tends to focus mostly on Kentucky. And if you don't dig any deeper, you might think that no other states ever made whiskey or did much of consequence for the industry.

Perhaps the saddest part of Peoria's history is that while whiskey distilling is now booming in many parts of the country, from Brooklyn, New York, to Berkeley, California, the city has yet to successfully tap into its own past and reestablish its credibility as one of the most important whiskey centers in the country. But there is hope: Peoria now has the Black Band distillery, which just may yet put the city back on the national spirits map.

Forget Kentucky—for decades Peoria, Illinois, was considered the whiskey-making center of the United States.

them restart their business, but about a decade later their investors forced the sale of their distillery and the Samuelses lost their eponymous brand. Bill Samuels Sr. and his wife, Margie Samuels, then bought a distillery in Loretto, Kentucky, and started their now-famous wheated bourbon Maker's Mark, which hit the market in fall 1958.

In many ways, the deck was stacked against the post-Prohibition whiskey upstarts—they were facing not one King Kong conglomerate, but four giant liquor companies. And together these four ruled the liquor industry with an iron fist, while building some of the world's largest distilleries.

Thanks to their Prohibition profits, the Canadian-based Seagram Company and Hiram Walker were able to construct huge facilities across the United States while also buying up a vast range of American brands. And although these distilleries were located in the United States, in many ways they were run as if they were still across the border making Canadian whisky. Both companies pushed blended whiskey brands containing a significant percentage of neutral grain spirit—because it was cheaper, easier, and faster than making straight bourbon or straight rye. And right after repeal, the goal was unambiguous: to increase supply; quality could come later. The plan worked, and over the next few years blends became very popular as straight whiskey brands struggled to restart.

But even when these Canadian companies made straight bourbon in the United States, the whiskey was much lighter and smoother in flavor and character—more like Canadian Club. "Walker's DeLuxe Straight Bourbon Whiskey is of lighter build than its Kentucky relations. Its body is better suited to today's American taste," proclaimed Hiram Walker's 1946 sales force textbook, "which has less and less liking for the harsh and the heavy."

Given the incredible dominance of the Seagram's and Hiram Walker brands, these subtle changes would have long-lasting consequences. Seagram's giant distillery in Lawrenceburg, Indiana, now known as MGP, produces whiskey for countless brands and arguably helped change the flavor profile of straight rye to make it more like it's done in Canada and less like the traditional American version. Canadian rye was usually made on a column still and was traditionally designed to be less unctuous and rambunctious than its spicier and bigger American cousin. (See The Giant Distillery That Powered the Craft Whiskey Movement, page 130.)

The counterweight to the Canadian behemoths were two American giants: National Distillers and Schenley, both with vast liquor holdings of millions of gallons of whiskey across many different distilleries and owning intellectual property rights to hundreds of brands. (Reportedly, National alone had 70 percent of the country's bottled-in-bond whiskey reserves and two hundred brands, including such stalwarts as Old Grand-Dad, Mount Vernon, and Old Overholt.) Once repeal took effect, both companies were positioned to dominate the American whiskey industry and remain incredibly powerful for decades to come. In 1933, Schenley was able to raise a fortune when its stock went public. According to *Time* magazine, National's stock price skyrocketed after repeal was ratified—from $17 a share to $117 in just a few months.

These four companies not only controlled the North American liquor game, but in many cases wrote the rules for how it would be played, including those codified in federal laws and regulations.

♦ NEW BARRELS AND THE BATTLE OF BOURBON VS RYE

The end of Prohibition meant that you could once again produce and sell whiskey in the United States. But exactly how were distillers supposed to make American whiskey? Repeal meant that the federal government had to standardize production methods for whiskey and create regulations that all US distillers would have to follow. Given the myriad special interests involved in the writing of the rules, the process was hardly straightforward. It was also emblematic of the long-running battle between bourbon and rye distillers, and between large and small operations.

While most of the largest Kentucky bourbon brands proudly produce rye whiskey today, that wasn't always the case. For most of whiskey history, the competition between bourbon and rye distillers was cutthroat. In a 1946 *New York Times* story about how Washington, DC, ran on bourbon—thanks to President Harry Truman's love of it—there's an anecdote about how some Kentuckians still called rye "bastard whiskey." The fault lines ran so deep that it's *still* hard to get old-time bourbon distillers to enjoy a glass of rye whiskey, or even say a kind word about it—even the rye made by their own distilleries.

In 1936, the newly formed Federal Alcohol Administration (FAA) issued regulations for spirits made in America. This wasn't just crucial for distillers, who needed the guidance to produce whiskey, but was also necessary for the Internal Revenue Service (IRS) to collect the right amount of taxes. Given the desperate economic conditions of the Great Depression, the government was keen for the liquor industry to start up as soon as possible and begin filling the US Treasury's coffers with tax dollars.

While distillers are now required to age bourbon and rye in new barrels, up until Prohibition many distillers simply refilled used barrels.

The 1936 rules were particularly important in the historical sense, as they're basically the same ones on the books today. And while some of these regulatory decisions were hotly debated at the time, there was one small rule that created a bona fide firestorm of controversy—the banning of used barrels.

The new regulations required the use of a "charred new oak container" (that is, an oak barrel) for making bourbon or rye, although distillers had historically aged their whiskey in used barrels at times. Not only was it more economical, but it was also a sustainable environmental practice. The FAA rules made the use of new barrels a standard practice. If you insisted on aging whiskey in used barrels, you were at a great disadvantage in what you could label the resulting whiskey. If you chose to go that route, the new-barrel rule ensured that your whiskey would be worth much less. (Corn whiskey, which is generally treated as an afterthought in the United States, was and still is exempt from this rule and can be aged in used and uncharred barrels.)

The new-barrel requirement for bourbon and rye was supposedly because "the Administration relied upon evidence adducted at public hearings to the effect that American type whiskey stored in new oak containers matures more satisfactory and more uniform than whiskey stored in second-hand barrels, and that consumers can be assured of uniform quality only when new containers are used." Which all sounds plausible, along with the statistics the FAA offered that indicated most distillers in the United States were already using new barrels to age their whiskey.

But when you dig deeper, a completely different story emerges. For one, the FAA statistic pointing to how most distillers were already using new barrels is fairly meaningless, given that Prohibition had just ended. If you made whiskey at the time, you *had* to use a new barrel because there were no used ones available. Also, any historical precedent about aging bourbon is kind of suspect—for a long time American distillers never purposely aged their whiskey. The new regs also conveniently ignored the fact that, until the early 1900s, distillers delivered their whiskey to bars and stores in the same barrel it was aged in, which meant that each new batch of whiskey had to use a new cask.

"Before the Civil War, little attention had been paid to aging, though

The char on the inside of a barrel filters out impurities from the whiskey as it ages.

Bourbon and rye whiskey are aged in brand-new oak barrels that have been charred on the inside.

distillers had discovered that whiskey left in charred oak barrels lost some of its sharpness and took on mellowness along with a golden color. Ordinarily, it was either sold in its natural white state or artificially colored with caramel," explained Seagram's H. F. Willkie.

According to a 1938 article by syndicated newspaper columnists Joseph Alsop and Robert Kintner, the Kentucky distillers liked using new barrels but also saw an advantage in the requirement because: "The northern rye whiskies are lighter, and, if they are not aged in old barrels, they taste like so much turpentine."

A new charred barrel is full of flavorful compounds, including vanillin and tannin, that can overwhelm certain types of spirits. By making the use of new barrels mandatory, the bourbon brands could undermine many large rye whiskey producers who liked to age their whisky in used barrels. The battle lines fell more or less between distillers in Kentucky and Maryland (for new barrels) versus distillers in Illinois, Indiana, Pennsylvania, and Ohio (against, although there were some notable exceptions).

Another important and perhaps more predictable issue that separated these two groups: money. Specifically, the retail price of their product. Whiskey aged in a used barrel was cheaper to produce by ten cents a gallon (4 liters), but it would command sixty cents to a dollar less per gallon on store shelves, according to *An Outline for Industry*, a 1944 book published by H. F. Willkie and Harrison C. Blankmeyer. Essentially keeping the retail price higher made better fiscal sense than lower production costs.

The Kentucky and Maryland distillers were backed by the coopers, who

Isaac Wolfe Bernheim

Isaac Wolfe Bernheim's rags-to-riches life story sounds more like the plot of a Hollywood movie than real life.

On March 23, 1867, an eighteen-year-old Bernheim left his home country of Germany on a steamboat called the *Hansa*, bound for New York. The voyage across the Atlantic in steerage was far from comfortable, and he mostly subsisted on boiled Irish potatoes. Since Bernheim didn't have a plate or a bowl, the kitchen would fill up his hat with steaming hot spuds, which he would eat on the ship's deck.

Things didn't exactly look up for Bernheim when he arrived in Manhattan. The job promised to him by his uncle didn't pan out, and worse, the American economy was still recovering after the Civil War. He wound up working as a peddler in rural Wilkes-Barre, Pennsylvania, working on foot, holding his dry goods in a sack balanced on a stick he rested across his shoulder.

Bernheim had grown up in a Jewish merchant family in Germany, but this job was a huge change for him. Despite having to adjust to his new country's customs and traditions, he was successful enough that he was soon able to buy a wagon and horse. This allowed him to increase his selection of products—but ultimately proved to be his downfall. The winters in Pennsylvania were frigid and, like a scene from a horror movie, his old horse suddenly died. By this point, his uncle had moved to Paducah, Kentucky, and fortunately offered him a job as a clerk in his new store.

A few months later Bernheim met Moses Bloom, who, with his business partner, Reuben Loeb, ran a wholesale liquor company called Loeb, Bloom & Co. It was a pivotal moment in Bernheim's life—his introduction to the whiskey business. Soon after joining the company as a bookkeeper, he was able to transition to a salesman job and brought his younger brother Bernard over from Germany to fill his original position. This not only kept Bernard out of the Franco-German War of 1870 but likely gave Isaac the idea for them to start their own liquor business. On January 1, 1872, after securing the financial backing of a local grocer, he did just that, creating Bernheim Bros.

Bernheim gives scant details about the whiskey business (or even his own drinking preferences) in his memoirs, but he does talk about how the sales of his new company were soon booming, allowing them to move the business to Louisville, Kentucky, in April 1888. Bernheim Bros. soon outgrew that space and bought a huge building on Main Street that had been constructed for the dry-goods business Bamberger, Bloom & Co. (The Bernheims sold their old building to another legendary bourbon company, W.L. Weller & Sons.)

The brothers ultimately built a giant distillery on more than 9 acres (3.6 hectares) that was conveniently located right next to the Illinois Central Railroad tracks. It included its own mill (with a daily capacity of 2,000 bushels [about 70 cubic meters]) and a power plant as well as seven warehouses that could hold up to one hundred thousand barrels of whiskey.

The Bernheim brothers created a number of brands, including their signature I.W. Harper. The first two initials came from Bernheim's own name, but no one is sure of the origin of Harper. It was likely chosen because it sounded generically Christian. Because of rising anti-Semitism in America at the time, a Jewish name on a whiskey bottle would have been a tough sell.

While Bernheim's contributions to the whiskey industry have been largely forgotten, he was hailed as one of the greats during his time. In a 1903 roundup of Kentucky distillers that appeared in *Bonfort's Wine and Spirit Circular*, it read: "Bernheim Bros. have been wonderfully successful, but this success has not been easily attained, and this notwithstanding the fact that I.W. Bernheim is beyond doubt one of the most remarkable merchants ever connected with the wine and spirit trade of the country."

One of the largely forgotten bourbon barons of the 19th century is Isaac Wolfe Bernheim who emigrated from Germany to the US in 1867.

In 1911, Bernheim retired from his company after selling his distillery to the United American Company, a move that appears to have been unexpected. The Owensboro, Kentucky, newspaper the *Messenger* admitted as much in a small item that ran on its second page about his retirement and the resulting shake-up in Bernheim Bros. management. The wording was blunt: "The changes in the company came as a complete surprise." What the *Messenger* didn't mention was that Bernheim got involved in a disastrous distillery deal in South Carolina, which required him to pay that state a fine of more than $34,000 in 1911. It is pure speculation, but perhaps this embarrassment is what made him retire.

In April 1945 at age ninety-six, Bernheim died and left his estimated $3 million fortune to an eponymous trust to turn his 13,000-acre (5,260-hectare) piece of land just outside Louisville into an arboretum, which was ultimately named the Bernheim Forest. He was buried on the property, which is still one of the area's most beautiful attractions.

So, what happened to Bernheim's brands? In 1918, Bernheim Distilling Company's giant distillery was sold at auction for what the *Courier-Journal* called "the ridiculously low price of $39,000." For an additional $5 the winning bidder, A. B. Flarsheim, vice president of Bernheim Distilling Company, also reportedly bought the company's brands trademarks, which included the brands Crestmore, Big Shanty Corn, and Old Roan.

While those whiskies are now forgotten, Bernheim's I.W. Harper is still available today, part of the portfolio of the giant liquor company, Diageo.

were keenly in favor of getting rid of used barrels. After repeal, beer brewers had begun to use steel kegs instead of the traditional oak barrels, which was a huge blow to America's cooperage industry. A switch by distillers had the potential to be a death blow, so it's little wonder the coopers were happy to pair up with the bourbon distillers in favor of new barrels.

It also helped, perhaps decisively, that the US senate majority leader at the time was Alben W. Barkley, from Kentucky, who pushed for the use of new barrels. "It's a comic but effective illustration of the power politics which sometimes makes Washington resemble a steaming compost heap, nourishing national policies at haphazard, like mushrooms," wrote Alsop and Kintner.

The large rye distillers fought back, of course, and were able to get the FAA to allow them to continue to age whiskey in used barrels. But there was a very large caveat: If they wanted the label to include the age of the whiskey—a key selling point—it would have to say it was aged in "reused cooperage."

While seemingly a footnote in whiskey history, this switch to new barrels helped precipitate the downfall of rye whiskey and almost entirely discredit the use of previously used barrels in American whiskey. The way things were done in Kentucky would essentially become the norm—any other style or method was basically written out of history.

Ultimately, the rules were changed to completely outlaw the use of used barrels, unless for the vague and hard-to-market category of "American whiskey." But the fight would have more rounds before it ended in total defeat for the proponents of used barrels. Some distillers had to break the rules and age whiskey in used barrels during World War II because of wood shortages.

In the late 1940s, the distillers who had been forced to reuse barrels wanted the treasury department to allow them to consider the whiskey they aged in used barrels as if it had been aged in new barrels. "The switch would mean a profit (because of the increased value that would result) of some $90 million for a few big distillers, mostly outside of Kentucky, who have 30 million gallons of whiskey in secondhand barrels," reported *Time* magazine in July 1949. The request and initial approval naturally enraged most of the large Kentucky producers, who fought hard against this plan.

"Their friends in Senate and House began to descend on the Treasury. At one time Secretary of the Treasury John Snyder had 24 members of the Senate and House in his office, each one trying to pound on the desk and outshout the others in denunciation of the inquiry of the ruling," reported Marquis Childs in a 1949 column that ran in the *Wilmington Morning News*. Ultimately, the whiskey aged in used barrels wasn't allowed to be labeled as straight whiskey. Several decades later, in the 1970s, after the demand for whiskey started to collapse, some distillers wanted to be able to reuse barrels, which would allow them to significantly lower their production costs. Again, their request was denied.

While distillers around the world are happy to buy used American whiskey barrels to age their whiskey in, if you want to make bourbon, rye, or single malt in the United States, you must age it in a new barrel. The rule still primarily benefits bourbon producers, since some rye and American single malt might actually benefit from aging in a used barrel. And if a distiller, brand ambassador, bartender, or know-it-all friend tries to tell you that Americans have *always* aged their whiskey in new barrels, know that old chestnut is nonsense.

♦ DISTILLERS GO BACK TO WAR

World War II is skipped over in the majority of books about spirits, since most distilleries were running twenty-four hours a day, seven days a week producing high proof alcohol for the war effort. In 1942, the US government estimated it needed 480 million gallons (18.2 million hectoliters) of 190-proof (95 percent alcohol by volume) ethanol. This almost pure alcohol would be turned into explosives and also used in the manufacture of synthetic rubber.

In 1942, the US War Production Board did a study and calculated that American brands had an inventory of about 550 million gallons (20.8 million hectoliters) of whiskey, a reserve they figured could last American drinkers until 1946 or 1947. That supply was quite an achievement, from an industry that had only had six years to rebuild and distill following the end of Prohibition. (In the late 1930s, some distillers were

After the United States entered World War II, distilleries across the country shut down to produce supplies for the military.

worried that too much whiskey had been produced, which turned out not to be a problem!) This calculation also no doubt helped the War Production Board decide that the distillers could

Distilleries across the United States modified their stills to make high-proof war alcohol, which was used for making explosives and synthetic rubber.

shut down their whiskey-making operations and instead produce high-octane alcohol to support the troops.

By September 1942, the distiller Schenley alone had thirteen whiskey distilleries involved in the making of 190-proof (95 percent alcohol by volume) war alcohol, and had just bought two more facilities. It had even come up with an ingenious process to convert a standard column still into a so-called packed column capable of producing the required high proof alcohol.

Not to be outdone, Schenley's chief rival, Seagram's, had its own design for converting its distilleries to support the war effort, and in 1943 reportedly managed to produce twice as much alcohol as they had the year before.

Schenley also used its laboratories, originally set up to propagate yeast and for quality control, to help produce the new wonder drug penicillin. In fact, the company became a leading producer of the antibiotic and ultimately created a new pharmaceutical division.

In 1943, the Distilled Spirits Institute (the industry's lobbying arm, now called the Distilled Spirits Council of the United States) ran a series of newspaper advertisements touting that "not a drop of whiskey has been made in months."

Although it might have been tough to buy your favorite bourbon or rye, you were meant to feel better because the ads showed how the "war-alcohol" was helping the troops, including in the form of the smokeless powder used to fire shells from Sherman tanks.

While the US government calculated that there were hundreds of millions of gallons of whiskey in warehouses, the liquor industry began to worry about a looming shortage. Shipping problems, increased consumption, and the growth of a black market for alcohol only served to justify their fears. (And then, of course, there was the annual natural evaporation from the barrels that shrank the stocks of whiskey.) Ultimately, some states and their distilleries instituted a form of rationing in the absence of a national restriction, which was never issued.

The ramifications of the changes wrought by World War II on the American whiskey industry are still felt today. The big war contracts for producing high proof alcohol overwhelmingly benefitted the larger companies, which could quickly retrofit their distilleries. This led to another wave of consolidation, as the four whiskey conglomerates—National Distillers, Seagram's, Schenley, and Hiram Walker—continued to gobble up many of their competitors, which had sprung up since the repeal of Prohibition. The acquisition trend had been going on for several years, with many smaller brands bought up in 1941 for their warehouses of whiskey. The looming war no doubt encouraged bigger brands to shore up their stocks and increase them where they could. (Rum producers were also a popular acquisition target because, while American whiskey distilleries were dedicated to helping the war effort, you could still make liquor for drinking in the Caribbean.)

According to a 1943 Scripps-Howard column by Thomas L. Stokes, even the US justice department was questioning whether the big four controlled too much of the industry and had essentially created a monopoly. "The curiosity of the Justice Department was aroused by the increasing size of the big units, their handsome profits, and their control of distribution outlets," wrote Stokes.

The technological innovations spawned by the war effort would also change the way whiskey was made after the war. The need for columns that could produce high proof spirits meant the traditional three-chamber still had reached the end of the line. By that point, it was used primarily for making rye in Maryland and in the other Mid-Atlantic states. To ramp up the production of war goods, the government paid for three-chamber stills to be replaced with column stills. As a result, rye was made on column stills after the war and its flavor profile was irrevocably changed, arguably leading to its near demise.

The emergency switch to producing war goods required brands to invent ways to ferment their grains quicker. Instead of the traditional four- or five-day process, fermentation soon could be completed in four or five hours. Speeding up a fermentation process means that flavors aren't allowed to develop—which is okay when you're making pure ethanol, since no one would ever drink it. However, these advances were no doubt used by some brands after the fighting stopped and they went back to producing whiskey.

As World War II ended, the American whiskey industry once again found itself scrambling to get product on store shelves. Many brands switched from making straight whiskies to producing bland blends—essentially stretching the stocks of straight whiskey by adding unaged neutral grain spirit (basically vodka). Thanks to their experience during the war, distillers were able to rapidly produce very high proof alcohol. It wasn't unusual for these blends to be 65 percent neutral grain spirits, including one called PM Blended Whiskey that was owned by National, whose newspaper ads touted it as something for "pleasant moments" that was also "priced modestly." I suppose these blends were better than having no whiskey at all, but they were just a stopgap measure. Given time to age, straight whiskies were widely available again and blended whiskies faded quickly into the background, where they remain today.

♦ SCHENLEY DISTILLERS AND A WHISKEY TAX FIGHT

Just as the whiskey industry was getting back on its feet, the threat of another war, in Korea this time, was clouding the horizon. It lasted just three years, but the Korean War had a huge (inadvertent) effect on the whiskey industry. The story begins with Lewis Rosenstiel, the head of Schenley, the giant liquor conglomerate he founded. Rosenstiel was known as an incredibly shrewd businessman, and, more precisely, a hustler who knew how to play all the angles and come out ahead.

In 1925, acting on a tip from none other than Winston Churchill that Prohibition was coming to an end, Rosenstiel bought the Schenley distillery in Pennsylvania, which had one of the few medicinal whiskey permits in the country. He bought up other brands as well, and proceeded to build up a tremendous stock of whiskey. Since no one knew if Prohibition would ever end, he was able to assemble a veritable empire at a wildly discounted rate. Rosenstiel's long shot, of course, came in and Lehman Brothers handled the IPO after repeal for his new company, Schenley Distillers, which raised $3 million. By 1935, just two years after repeal, the company had sales of $63 million, a huge sum at the time, especially in the wake of the Depression, which had laid waste to the country's economy, leaving millions of people unemployed for years.

As things began to heat up between the United States and the Communist bloc after World War II, Rosenstiel sensed another giant whiskey opportunity. He was convinced the country would soon go back to war and distilleries would once again be called upon to make high proof alcohol instead of whiskey, leading the demand and price for whiskey to skyrocket. So, he again would be ready with a huge stock of whiskey to make him another gigantic fortune. Based on his hunch, Rosenstiel directed his whiskey distilleries around the country to increase production and pack his warehouses full of barrels.

When the United States entered the Korean War in 1950 and distillers were once again asked to produce high proof alcohol, Rosenstiel no doubt felt vindicated and began to count his profits. Everything went according to plan except for one important detail: The Korean War didn't last very long, and American distillers were never asked to shut down their operations to make war goods exclusively. Even worse for Rosenstiel, there was no spike in demand for whiskey. Which meant there was no new fortune to be made by Schenley.

Rosenstiel suddenly found himself

sitting on an enormous supply of whiskey. This might not sound like a problem at first, but at the time the IRS considered whiskey to be fully mature at eight years old. When it reached that milestone, distillers were required to pay a tax of $10.50 on each gallon (4 liters). Rosenstiel knew it would take far longer than eight years to sell off his enormous whiskey reserves and didn't want to pay a giant tax bill without any hope of recouping the money quickly.

Backed into a corner, Rosenstiel did the only thing he could—he began an intensive lobbying effort to change the tax rules. His plan was to get the government to consider whiskey fully mature at twenty years old, which would give him a bit more breathing room to sell off his huge stock. While it took serious arm-twisting and likely the help of his slimy personal lawyer, Roy Cohn, Rosenstiel was able to get the tax code changed.

Naturally, the temperance movement was aghast. Elizabeth Smart, the legislative director of the Woman's Christian Temperance Union, estimated in an Associate Press story that the government wouldn't collect as much as $1.4 billion in taxes from distillers in the years to come. Most of that money would of course be owed by Schenley. Seagram's was also an opponent of this tax rule change, since according to an article in Time, "Schenley held 60% to 70% of all the old whisky in the U.S., hence would reap the major benefit."

Rosenstiel, for his part, was hailed as a miracle worker, whose successful efforts led to his company's stock price shooting up.

Although this was a tiny footnote in the annals of US congressional legislation, Rosenstiel's efforts had huge implications on American whiskey. Suddenly, it was economically feasible to age whiskey for a longer period of time. We arguably wouldn't have 10-year-old, 15-year-old, and 20-year-old American whiskies today without Rosenstiel. His insistence that older American whiskies should be treated like Cognac changed the trajectory of the American spirits industry. Rosenstiel's idea that premiumization would help drive American whiskey sales ultimately came to pass.

In 1951, the George Washington Carver Memorial Institute honored Lewis Rosenstiel with its Gold Award. He was introduced by legendary baseball player Jackie Robinson, who had received the award the previous year.

The Invention of Light Whiskey

To level the playing field for whiskey brands to compete with vodka, the federal government loosened regulations a bit in 1968 to allow distillers to make so-called light whiskey. This newfangled type of whiskey was distilled to a higher proof and aged in used barrels, which produced a spirit with a lot less flavor, character, and color. The first of these bland whiskies to be sold was Brown-Forman's Frost 8/80 Dry White Whiskey which took millions of dollars to create and debuted in late 1971. (The color and some of the flavor of the eight-year-old bourbon were also filtered out.)

A 1972 newspaper ad for Old Crow's brand-new Crow Light proclaimed: "Not a Bourbon. Lighter than Scotch. Smoother than Canadian." The brand even promised a money-back guarantee if you didn't like the whiskey. I imagine many folks took the brand up on that offer, given that this new category was hugely unpopular with drinkers and failed to save the whiskey industry. It didn't take long for Brown-Forman and the rest of the companies to discontinue the dozen or so light whiskey brands available and shut down this failed experiment.

One major reason for American whiskey's slump was that there was basically just one market at the time: Bourbon was barely sold outside of the United States. While the whiskey was technically available in more than a hundred countries, the truth was that exports in 1970 totaled just more than an embarrassing 2 million gallons (7.6 million liters), most of which went to the UK, West Germany, and France.

American Whiskey History, Part II: An Empire Falls

The decline of whiskey in the United States was dramatic, ugly, and sudden. After riding a roller coaster of extreme highs and grinding lows, the 1960s finally seemed to deliver a sustained period of growth for American whiskey. In fact, the future seemed incredibly bright for distillers.

"The next five years to 1965 will be a phase of mounting stability and quite possibly, unprecedented boom," wrote Sylvia Porter in her 1958 syndicated column titled "Liquor Industry Goes From Chaos to Boom."

Distillers were further helped by Congress, which, on January 7, 1964,

Thanks to sky-high foreign tariffs, American whiskey was just too expensive in most foreign markets. "Bourbon is virtually unknown outside the U.S., and the foreign governments would just as soon keep it that way," wrote syndicated newspaper columnist Milton Moskowitz in late 1971. Throughout the decade the industry worked hard to lower tariffs and open markets, but sales didn't grow enough to offset the downturn in domestic demand.

It got so bad that a number of whiskey companies started to buy brands that were outside the liquor category in order to diversify their holdings and revenue streams. Brown-Forman bought luggage maker American Tourister and dishware company Lenox. Other whiskey brands were forced to shut down temporarily, or just never reopened. In March 1983, the Owensboro *Messenger-Inquirer* reported that the state of Kentucky had just sixteen distilleries, down from forty-five in 1959. "I don't expect bourbon to come back," Joel High, the president of Medley Distilling Co., told the newspaper. "It will never hold the percentage of the market that it did. That's because there are so many more drinks on the market today."

Throughout the 1980s and '90s, High seemed prophetic, as sales of American whiskey continued to decline and the number of distilleries in Kentucky shrunk to below ten. Meanwhile, new premium vodka brands continued to be launched in the United States with great success, including Stolichnaya, Absolut, Ketel One, and Grey Goose.

It led many in the whiskey industry to ask if Americans would ever regain their taste for bourbon or rye.

passed a resolution that called bourbon whiskey "a distinctive product of the United States . . . unlike other types of alcoholic beverages, whether foreign or domestic." In theory, this placed bourbon on equal footing with other nationally protected spirits, including Cognac and Champagne in France, and Scotch in Scotland. It also prevented other countries from making bourbon, a serious concern because there were a number of "bourbons" already coming out of Canada and also Mexico. (A newspaper ad for a bourbon made by the D. M. distillery in Juárez proudly stated "Straight American whiskey made slowly and with care . . . in Mexico.")

This plan to make bourbon synonymous with the United States was, naturally, cooked up by Lewis Rosenstiel of Schenley Distillers who, if you recall, was sitting on a huge stockpile of mature whiskey. Back in 1958, right after he got the tax rules changed to protect his aging supply, he was interviewed by Sylvia Porter, who reported that Rosenstiel was sponsoring a Bourbon Institute "to promote sale of American straight bourbon around the globe and to work for international laws and treaties which will confine the name 'bourbon' only to bourbon whisky produced in our country." Rosenstiel wanted bourbon to be thought of as American in the same way that Scotch could only come from Scotland.

All of Rosenstiel's efforts appeared to be working, as American whiskey grew and grew in popularity. In April 1970, *The Wooden Barrel*, the newsletter of the Associated Cooperages Industries of America, included an item about record bourbon sales in the previous year. "Bourbon closed ten years of ardent competition in the distilled spirits market with the best year in its history," crowed Admiral William J. Marshall, president of the Bourbon Institute, in the piece. He credited advertising and marketing in making the achievement: "In a period of growing affluence, appreciation of the know-how of the American distiller and the quality of his product has grown accordingly."

But just under the surface of American society, serious problems were emerging that would tear apart the generational fabric of the country. While many Americans were seemingly happy in the 1950s to coast down the ideological middle of the road with President Dwight D. Eisenhower at the wheel and Ozzie and Harriet riding shotgun, in the 1960s and 1970s that was a much harder ideal to sell. The Vietnam War, the civil rights movement, and the women's liberation movement shattered the Technicolor fantasy that everything was just dandy. It turned out there were real problems in America and they would finally be dealt with—and Ozzie and Harriet didn't get a say.

The evolution of the Beatles is particularly telling of the seismic cultural changes taking place in the United States. In 1964, the Beatles' first live performance in the US was on *The Ed Sullivan Show* and they appeared in matching short haircuts and wearing suits while singing bubblegum rock. By the end of the decade, Americans were obsessed with the hippies that the Fab Four had turned into, complete with their long flowing hair and beards, who sang about peace, love, and a psychedelic future.

A similar change took place in what Americans drank. It was easy enough to imagine Ed Sullivan knocking back Old-Fashioneds and Whiskey Highballs, but "Sgt. Pepper's Lonely Hearts Club Band"? Not so much. As a result, domestic sales for bourbon and rye peaked in 1970 and then steeply declined for the next thirty years. What happened to whiskey was not out of line with the country's larger culture shift, but the surprise was how long these changes in taste lasted. (Hint: long enough to almost kill the American whiskey industry.)

You couldn't have drawn up a worse

Across the country you can now find hundreds of whiskey distilleries, like Frey Ranch in Nevada. But twenty-five years ago there were just a handful of companies left making whiskey.

set of problems for distillers. For starters, Americans begin to drink less overall beginning in the mid-1970s, with annual per capita consumption of alcohol continuing to shrink for the rest of the century. And when Americans did drink, they didn't drink whiskey. Everything from beer and wine to tequila, rum, and gin really took off. Basically, anything and everything aside from whiskey was popular. But it was the boom in vodka, the polar opposite of whiskey, that arguably did the most damage.

Vodka, with its chameleon-like ability to mix with virtually anything, took whiskey's top spot and became America's favorite spirit. In fact, it is still the bestselling spirit in the United States today, accounting for more than three out of every ten bottles sold.

♦ THE RISE OF SMALL BATCH BOURBON

If bourbon's fall from grace was dramatic, ugly, and somewhat sudden, its rebirth was unlikely, disorganized, and plodding.

For the same reasons that bourbon fell out of favor—including its inextricable link to the past, its insistence on using old-timey fonts and logos, and its supposedly antiquated production processes—the spirit appealed to the hipsters coming of age in the late 1990s and early 2000s.

This new generation associated vodka and its range of bestselling cocktails, including the Cape Codder, the Madras, and the Screwdriver, with 1980s yuppies—and even more damningly,

The Father of Small Batch Bourbon

Frederick Booker Noe was destined to work in the bourbon industry.

It might have had something to do with his grandfather, who was Jim Beam.

Noe went to the University of Kentucky to play football under legendary coach Bear Bryant, but left after only a year to return home and join the family business. By the early 1960s, he was running Jim Beam's smaller distillery in Boston, Kentucky. His cousin, Carl Beam, ran the company's larger and more famous distillery. Booker and Carl had always been rivals, often competing over how much whiskey they could produce from a bushel of corn.

I imagine that, in many ways, life for Booker was kind of boring. Beam didn't often change up its products, and Booker was curious by nature. When he was in his forties, he started to rethink all the common practices to make bourbon. And while that might not sound particularly shocking now, it was tantamount to heresy at the time.

The problem was that there was absolutely no incentive to change anything in the 1970s, '80s, or early '90s. The remaining bourbon drinkers were definitely not looking for innovations, or even slight deviations. Nor were liquor store owners, bartenders, or distributors, who were laser-focused on vodka and other types of spirits that were actually growing.

The goal of the whiskey industry had always been to figure out how to mass-produce the same whiskey over and over and over again—ensuring that all of the barrels in a given warehouse would taste very similar. But over the years, Booker noticed a few spots in various warehouses where the whiskey tasted . . . different. The barrels in these locations boasted rich flavors along with a depth and complexity that the standard Jim Beam White Label or Jim Beam Black Label just didn't have.

Noe began experimenting, investigating why some barrels tasted different from the rest. Traditionally, these special barrels weren't a mystery—they were trouble. While they tasted good, sometimes incredibly so,

Master distillery Booker Noe spent his life producing whiskey and his small batch collection made him a legend in his own time.

there wasn't anything you could do with them. Employees would enjoy clandestine glasses of them or they would be mixed together with dozens of other barrels to blend out their uniqueness. There was no real market for single barrel bottlings or small batch bourbons, so they were hardly prized.

It's worth noting that Noe had precious little say over what Jim Beam produced. His grandfather was indeed Jim Beam, but his family didn't own the company and the executives headquartered in Deerfield, Illinois, called the shots. And those suits made it pretty clear to Noe that they weren't interested in his ideas for new whiskies to sell. Fortunately, a few years later, someone who did care about what Noe had discovered walked right into his office.

Mike Donohoe was an unlikely savior. His gridiron hero days were behind him—he'd played sixty-four games as an NFL tight end for the Green Bay Packers and the Atlanta Falcons. After he retired, he started working in the liquor business on the sales side. When he met Booker, Donohoe had been with Jim Beam for just a few years. Around 1985, he was in Kentucky to see how the company's flagship whiskey brand was produced. After taking a tour of the distillery and one of its many warehouses, he met Noe in the late afternoon for a drink in his nondescript office.

"He poured some whiskey out of a jug. Poured water into it. And we start talking about football," recalls Donohoe. After discussing their careers, Donohoe said to Noe, "This doesn't taste like Jim Beam." Booker replied that it was indeed Beam whiskey. Then he revealed that every year he'd take a barrel from his favorite part of the "A" warehouse, right in the center of the building, and that's what he liked to drink himself.

"That was it," said Donohoe, who went home to Chicago not thinking much about Noe's special whiskey.

The following year, Donohoe and some of the other Beam executives were trying to come up with unique holiday gifts they could give their top distributors and liquor store owners instead of the traditional flowers or candy. "We couldn't give them Beam, since they sell Beam," said Donohoe. "That's a stupid gift."

What could they give them that was a bit more special and memorable? Suddenly, the special whiskey Noe had poured for Donohoe in Kentucky popped into his mind. "And I called him and I just said 'you know that stuff you gave me last year, could you get one hundred, 150 bottles of that?' He said, 'Yep.'"

And that's how Booker's Bourbon was born.

Donohoe and Noe had no budget for producing and packaging this special whiskey, but they were creative. Booker heard about a winery going out of business in Louisville, Kentucky, so they were able to buy cases and cases of brand-new wine bottles for almost nothing. Noe then created the label, which featured his now-legendary handwritten note. He signed and numbered every bottle himself. He also dipped the top of each bottle into wax.

The original Booker's Bourbon was bottled at cask strength, as it is today, and is generally around 120 proof (60 percent alcohol by volume). But the potency of the

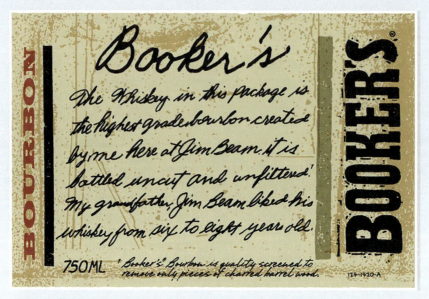

The original Booker's Bourbon release was sent out to 100 distributors and liquor store owners as a holiday present in December 1986.

spirit varies from bottle to bottle, since it depends on the strength of the whiskey in the individual cask selected.

In December 1986, about a hundred bottles of Booker's Bourbon were sent as gifts. The response was incredibly positive. The next year, Beam decided to try to sell the whiskey, producing about 1,800 bottles for the sales effort. Some nearly forty years later, a bottle of Booker's Bourbon fetches about $200.

Liquor store shelves are now packed with cask strength bottlings from whiskey distilleries around the world—but at the time Noe's idea was truly pioneering. This may sound like an obvious move, but the 1980s was a truly dire period for the whiskey industry, a time when many brands were trying to find ways to be more neutral, like vodka. It was actually visionary to believe that doubling down on bourbon's unique flavor and increasing its potency was the way to boost sales. Noe and Donohoe were simply looking for a memorable holiday present, but they unwittingly seeded the rebirth of American whiskey.

Distilling legend Elmer T. Lee dreamed up the single barrel bourbon Blanton's, which led to a whole new kind of whiskey.

their parents. Looking to define themselves in a new way, they eschewed the familiar mass-produced trappings and looked to their grandparents' generation for style and cultural inspiration. Is there any wonder that swing dancing, the Rat Pack, and fedoras came back into fashion? At the same time, there was a related movement to celebrate and buy supposedly authentic and traditional products.

Just as the hipsters rediscovered straight razors, cardigan sweaters, and bossa nova, they naturally started looking beyond the vodka section in the liquor store. What they found was a treasure trove of whiskey. The bottles on store shelves were reasonably priced and often contained whiskey that was from six to ten years old. These were flavorful whiskies that, for years, the brands literally couldn't give away.

But for bourbon to truly appeal to a large audience, it would need a new signature product to sell. Just as Scotch distillers had turned single malts into their star performers, what could American distillers use to attract drinkers? The answer, of course, was already hiding in their warehouses: small batch bourbons.

Just as Jim Beam's legendary distiller Frederick Booker Noe released his pioneering small batch bourbon, Booker's, another fortuitous thing happened around that time. In April of 1987, Beam acquired all of National Distillers and Chemical Corporation's liquor brands for $545 million, including stalwarts Old Crow, Old Overholt, and Old Grand-Dad. Along with the brands and distilleries came a huge stockpile of whiskey that was aging nicely as fewer and fewer people drank bourbon and rye. Given the success of Booker's Bourbon (see The Father of Small Batch Bourbon, page 122), in a stroke of sales and marketing genius Beam decided to use some of these mature National whiskies to help create its landmark Small Batch Collection. On store shelves, Booker's was soon joined by stalwarts Knob Creek, Basil Hayden, and Baker's. These bourbons took the world by storm and helped to reshape the perception of American whiskey.

At roughly the same time, Noe's fellow Kentucky distiller Elmer T. Lee, who worked at George T. Stagg (now called Buffalo Trace), also saw that the future of American whiskey lay in selling more expensive small batch and single barrel bottlings. He talked to his friends in the industry and tried to convince them of the idea, but according to his recollections no one was terribly interested in joining him.

Undeterred, Lee created Blanton's Bourbon, whose wild success was in part due to its simultaneous release in Japan, where it was an immediate hit. The overseas market helped sustain the brand while domestic demand grew at a slower pace. That it wasn't a universal hit may now sound surprising, since Blanton's has become prized by whiskey drinkers over the past few years and is nearly impossible to purchase. (If you can find it, it sells for three or four times its suggested retail price of $60.)

While neither Booker Noe nor Lee are alive today, I like to imagine them drinking small batch bourbon together somewhere, toasting the success of the American whiskey category, which they helped to bring back to life.

♦ THE REBIRTH OF RYE

To say that the resurgence of straight rye whiskey was an incredible long shot is something of an ode to long shots. Even fans of the historic spirit could never have predicted that it would once again be widely available, and celebrated.

A far more likely scenario, given its historic trajectory, was that rye would completely disappear from stores' shelves, cocktail

Itinerant master distiller David Pickerell was involved with a number of new rye whiskey brands, including Vermont's WhistlePig.

After creating St-Germain Elderflower Liqueur, Rob Cooper focused on bringing back rye whiskey and introduced the brand Lock Stock & Barrel.

books, and the collective memory of drinkers far and wide. But in a deep irony, it was bourbon distillers who actually kept rye alive. This was unexpected to say the least, as distillers of the two whiskies had been bitter rivals for decades. Business was so bad for bourbon distillers that they were grateful for the small amount they could make from rye sales. While they may have hated themselves for producing this reviled whiskey, the truth was that it helped keep the lights on.

Miraculously, in the early 2000s, hipster bartenders searching for any shred of surviving cocktail history, along with pioneering entrepreneurs looking for a new bestseller, saw value in straight rye. The problem was, there wasn't much of it around—most bars and liquor stores across the country didn't carry any of the whiskey. The rye available at the time mainly consisted of Rittenhouse Rye as well as Pikesville Rye, Old Overholt, Jim Beam Rye, and Wild Turkey Rye. Many of these were sold only in certain states or even in just a handful of cities, mostly around Maryland and Pennsylvania, since the Mid-Atlantic region was originally the home of rye whiskey and whatever dribble of demand remained for it came from those few places. While meager, those sales were just enough to keep these rye whiskies in production.

As rye whiskey slowly attracted more interest in the late 2000s, folks started launching new rye brands. There was just one big problem: Rye is much more annoying to produce than bourbon. Fermenters can overflow with foam and the mash is incredibly sticky and hard to clean off equipment—and few distillers had any real experience making it. Even if a brand wanted to buy it instead of making it, there wasn't a lot around to purchase. So, if an American distillery made rye whiskey—no joke—they did it just one day a year.

Around this time, one of the first rye whiskey evangelists I encountered was Robert Cooper. His family had been in the liquor business for more than a century and his father had created Chambord Liqueur and then the family sold it to Brown-Forman. Rob Cooper branched out on his own and started St-Germain Elderflower Liqueur, which was a sensation with bartenders. (Ultimately, Cooper sold that brand to Bacardi.) But his real passion was for rye whiskey, which at the time was so far under the radar that most people barely understood what it was or how it was different from Canadian whisky. So, Cooper set out to buy barrels from the few Kentucky distillers that made that style of whiskey. While they would have gladly sold him barrels, there was one small problem—there was no stock

Upstate New York's Hillrock was another of distiller David Pickerell's rye whiskey projects.

to be had. Ultimately, Cooper did find the warehouse of his dreams that was packed with plenty of barrels of mature rye, but it was thousands of miles away in Alberta, Canada, of all places.

Ralph Erenzo wanted to open a rock-climbing center but unwittingly helped start the craft distilling movement.

Canadians traditionally don't blend their ground grains together before fermenting, as do their American counterparts. Instead, the Canadian preference is to make several types of whisky and then blend them together before bottling. For this reason, distilleries in Canada had stocks of straight rye whisky that were waiting to be blended and bottled. Cooper, along with famed American distiller David Pickerell, realized around the same time that the only place on the planet with ample stocks of aged straight rye was across the border. Cooper used the Canadian rye whisky he purchased to start his Lock Stock & Barrel brand, while Pickerell used the whisky to help start Hillrock and WhistlePig whiskies.

Other entrepreneurs found a source of rye whiskey at the MGP distillery in Lawrenceburg, Indiana (see The Giant Distillery That Powered the Craft Whiskey Movement, page 130), which dates back to right after the repeal of Prohibition and was originally built by Seagram's. Still other early producers, including Allen Katz, the founder of the New York Distilling Company, built their own distilleries and patiently waited for their rye to mature. (Katz, in the meantime, sold a number of gins, including the acclaimed Dorothy Parker and Perry's Tot brands.)

The big breakthrough for rye whiskey came in 2010, when Bulleit Bourbon decided to sell a rye whiskey. With the marketing and sales weight of its parent company, international spirits conglomerate Diageo, rye suddenly was more widely available than it had been in decades. At the same time, thanks to the hundreds of craft distilleries and craft cocktail bars that had opened across the country, there was a veritable army of rye proselytizers popularizing the spirit with drinkers.

The story of rye's near death and rebirth was perfect for the sudden cultural obsession with authenticity and traditional drinks and food. One of the biggest rye fans I know is Wild Turkey brand ambassador Bruce Russell, the grandson of bourbon legend Jimmy Russell. Jimmy has worked at Wild

Turkey since 1954 (and has been master distiller since the '60s) and is definitely still captain of team bourbon. I can tell it hurts him a bit when Bruce drinks Wild Turkey Rye instead of the brand's bourbon. But the fact that a member of bourbon royalty is trumpeting the joys of rye whiskey just shows how much times have changed.

♦ THE FARM DISTILLERY AND THE CRAFT MOVEMENT

The massive growth in whiskey's popularity in the twenty-first century has been the result of a perfect storm of factors. These include the creation of small batch whiskies by the big whiskey conglomerates and the rebirth of cocktails. But another big contributor was the birth of the craft distilling movement, which brought whiskey making to communities around the United States.

At the beginning of this century, fewer than a dozen small distillers existed in the United States. If anything, the country had been steadily losing distilleries for decades. The major distillers—like Jim Beam and Brown-Forman—hadn't fared much better. Only a few of these giants remained and, having acquired the intellectual property of failed distilleries, they alone produced and sold nearly every American whiskey brand under a host of different names.

That all changed in 2001, when Ralph Erenzo scraped together enough money to buy a piece of rocky land in New York's Hudson Valley. He dreamed of creating a climbing center, having just operated a climbing wall in Manhattan a few blocks from Lincoln Center. But when he couldn't get the requisite permits, Erenzo drew inspiration from the ruins of an old distillery on his new property. That idea led Erenzo to open New York State's first new whiskey distillery since the beginning of Prohibition.

But first Erenzo had a minor feat to pull off: He had to convince the governor and the state assembly to create a new class of distilling license that didn't cost $50,000. His argument in favor of the change was that, by lowering the cost of setting up a distillery, it would encourage other entrepreneurs to follow Erenzo's lead. These new distilleries would then buy their grains from New York farmers.

The launch of Hudson Whiskey in 2005 ushered in a new era of small-scale whiskey making across the US.

Fortunately, Erenzo was successful, and in 2002 New York created a distilling license that cost just $1,450 and allowed a distiller to make 35,000 gallons (133,000 liters) of alcohol a year. In 2005, Erenzo fittingly snagged the first of these new licenses. Then, with

The Giant Distillery that Powered the Craft Whiskey Movement

While Prohibition was putting most American whiskey brands out of business, the story was very different for Canadian distilleries who remained open. The Bronfman family, who owned the Canadian spirits company Seagram's, put the time to good use.

After the repeal of Prohibition, the Bronfman family wasn't content just to sell Canadian whisky. Instead, Seagram's invested millions of dollars in building state-of-the-art distilleries and warehouses across the United States, including one in Lawrenceburg, Indiana, which would have an incredibly important second act.

Lawrenceburg, a city about 30 miles (48 kilometers) west of Cincinnati, sits on the banks of the Ohio River some 100 miles (161 kilometers) upstream from Louisville, Kentucky. It was an advantageous location given that the distillery could receive supplies from ships traveling along the river and then use the river to send out the finished whiskey to ports around the country. By 1979, Seagram's Lawrenceburg distillery was the largest in the world. According to a story in the *Indianapolis News*, the facility produced roughly 8 million cases of all kinds of spirits a year and was aging more than 1.4 million barrels.

In 2000, Seagram's liquor holdings were sold off, and the Indiana facility wound up in the hands of French spirits conglomerate Pernod Ricard. But by 2006, the giant, hulking facility and its incredible output was more of a liability than an asset, since it was still a struggle to increase sales of American whiskey. After studying its holdings, Pernod decided it just didn't need the facility and announced it would shut down completely. At the time, the company was very skeptical that anyone would want to buy it.

Fortunately, another company did see value in the distillery: Angostura. While famous for its eponymous bitters, which are commonly used for making a Manhattan or Old-Fashioned cocktail, the company also produces a line of rum. After Angostura acquired the old Seagram's distillery they renamed it Lawrenceburg Distillers Indiana (LDI) and used it to make spirits for a range of other companies.

Just three years later, the giant distillery was flipped again. MGP Ingredients Inc. bought it for $11 million from Angostura, which may be remembered as one of the best deals in spirits business history. At the time of the sale, it was reported that the distillery could produce 27 million gallons of spirits per year.

What happened next took the spirits industry completely by surprise.

The craft spirits movement took off and rye whiskey came back from the dead. Suddenly, MGP found itself at the nexus of a number of trends. Brands large and small, everyone from Templeton to Redemption to Dickel to Bulleit to High West to Smooth Ambler, were either contracting with the distillery to produce their rye and bourbon whiskies or buying finished whiskies from their warehouses.

The American craft whiskey movement likely wouldn't have been able to take off so rapidly without MGP supplying lots of brands with barrels of high-quality rye and bourbon that were ready to bottle immediately. (Most new whiskey brands don't have the luxury of waiting several years for their own whiskey to mature.) It should come as no surprise if one of your favorite American whiskies actually comes from MGP.

Some of MGP's customers have since built their own distilleries or have been acquired by large conglomerates, but they still depend on the Indiana facility for a huge amount of their supply. To be clear, there is nothing wrong or shameful about buying whiskey from a distillery and bottling it as your own, as long as you're up-front about its provenance.

After Prohibition, Seagram's built a large distillery in Lawrenceburg, Indiana, which is still open and continues to make whiskey for a range of large and small brands.

a still that arrived in pieces from China, Erenzo and his business partner, Brian Lee, opened the Tuthilltown Spirits distillery, which made bourbon, rye, and a range of other spirits. In 2010, for an undisclosed amount, they sold their flagship whiskey brand Hudson to William Grant & Sons, the historic Scotch company. (Then seven years later William Grant bought the actual distillery and the property.)

The success of Tuthilltown Spirits and the buzz that surrounded its opening led to a boom of upstate and downstate New York distilleries. What aided this growth was that in 2007 the state created an even more affordable "farm license" ($128), which stipulated that distillers use mostly locally grown grain. New York's sudden craft whiskey scene morphed into a domestic—and then an international—craft distilling movement that changed the way we all drink.

As of 2021, according to the American Craft Spirits Association (ACSA), there were 2,290 craft distilleries in the United States, many of which make whiskey. While there is no set definition for craft, ACSA defines their members as distilleries that make less than 750,000 gallons of alcohol per year, are transparent about their production method, and where investors own less than 49 percent of the company. Craft whiskies made in the United States proved especially popular in many overseas markets and inspired locals to build craft whiskey distilleries in England, Ireland, India, and Israel.

American Whiskey Family Tree

🌾 BRANCH: HEAVEN HILL

Heaven Hill, now a venerable American whiskey brand and distillery, was formed in 1933 in Bardstown, Kentucky. At the time, its chances of success were exceedingly slim.

Its story begins with Max L. Shapira, a Jewish immigrant from Lithuania, who started out as a peddler. He ultimately built a small chain of department stores in Kentucky called the Louisville Stores, which operated into the 1980s. He had five sons, each of whom ran a different location of the business.

As Prohibition was coming to an end, the family was approached by a group looking for money to open a distillery. Because there were so few operational facilities left after Prohibition's thirteen long years, there was an unusual number of parties trying to build new ones. But given that the US was still in the midst of the Great Depression, money was scarce—even for opportunities with great potential. Thanks to the Shapiras' successful chain of stores, the family had capital to invest in the project, which included several Beam family members, who, like today, were famous for their whiskey distilling skills.

Heaven Hill broke ground on its first distillery in 1935. Eventually, the Shapira

A Heaven Hill worker removes a barrel's so-called bung in order to pour out the whiskey for bottling.

A row of freshly bottled Elijah Craig bourbons get ready to be boxed up and sent out.

family bought out the company's other investors and continues to own and run the brand to this day. Heaven Hill now has more than 2 million barrels of whiskey aging in its seventy warehouses. (And those two numbers are surely going to rise as the company continues to expand production capacity.)

In 1996, a horrific fire completely destroyed Heaven Hill's distillery in Bardstown, Kentucky. Undeterred, the company was soon able to buy the Bernheim distillery from Diageo, in Louisville, which is located right next door to Brown-Forman's campus. As of writing this book, Heaven Hill is in the process of building a second distillery in Bardstown that will cost $135 million and open by the end of 2024. It will (at least) double the company's current distilling capacity.

Today, the company essentially makes two bourbon recipes and one rye whiskey recipe. So, the differences between its brands come down to how old the whiskey is and where in a warehouse it was aged—both of which play a huge role in how the finished whiskies taste. The distillery also makes three additional styles of whiskey: malt, corn, and wheat.

Heaven Hill's portfolio now includes many famous whiskies, including:

Elijah Craig Bourbon

This bestselling bourbon was inspired by the Baptist Reverend Elijah Craig, who lived in Kentucky in the late 1700s. Supposedly, he's responsible for whiskey's big epiphany: that aging spirit in a charred barrel would improve its flavor and turn it into whiskey. Unfortunately, the legend about Craig isn't true, since folks already knew about the benefits of barrel aging. And that's not to mention, as Gerald Carson points out in his fabulous book *The Social History of Bourbon*, that whiskey was sold unaged at the time. (But why let facts stand in the way of a good story?)

Regardless, Elijah Craig has become one of Heaven Hill's signature products and is currently distilled at its Louisville, Kentucky, distillery. The brand's cornerstone whiskey, Elijah Craig Small Batch Bourbon, is a robust 94 proof (47 percent alcohol by volume), is aged between eight and twelve years, and has a modest suggested retail price of $34. It's no wonder it has become a liquor store and bar standard. Meanwhile, the special-edition versions of Elijah Craig, including the 18-year-old, 20-year-old, and 21-year-old single barrel bottlings, have become sought-after by collectors and now often sell for thousands of dollars—if you can find them.

Evan Williams Bourbon

Evan Williams is a ubiquitous bourbon that has developed a reputation over the years for being a rich whiskey that won't break the bank. It's the second bestselling bourbon in the United States—with more than 3 million nine-liter cases of the whiskey sold in 2021. The standard Evan Williams Bourbon is 86 proof (43 percent alcohol by volume) and between four and five years old. There is also now the 90-proof (45 percent alcohol by volume) Evan Williams 1783 Small Batch, which is six to eight years old, as well as the acclaimed Evan Williams Single Barrel Vintage releases. No matter which variety you buy, they're now all made at Heaven Hill's main distillery in Louisville, Kentucky.

So, who was Evan Williams? Depending on whom you ask, he may have opened Kentucky's first commercial whiskey distillery in 1783. While I'd like to say this is true, it's quite doubtful. Regardless, he was a real person and an actual distiller.

Rittenhouse Straight Rye Whiskey

As you might imagine from its name—if you're familiar with Philadelphia, Pennsylvania, that is—Rittenhouse Rye was once actually distilled in Pennsylvania. In fact, the brand was originally named Rittenhouse Square, to honor the Philly landmark, when it was introduced in 1934 by Continental Distilling, then owned by Harry Publicker. The brand shut down for World War II and the name was shortened to Rittenhouse Rye when production began again in 1948 when it was sold as a 4-year-old bonded whiskey.

Rittenhouse was bought by Heaven Hill in 1999 and has now been produced in Kentucky for years. The whiskey was one of the few straight ryes still made in the early 2000s and is delicious, with a big punch of rye spice. It can hold its own in a cocktail—it's perfect for classic whiskey drinks such as the Manhattan, the Old-Fashioned, and the Sazerac—and mixes well with sweet vermouth and other ingredients. As a result, it became a favorite of pioneering craft bartenders who not only helped put Rittenhouse on the national spirits map, but played a central role in the rebirth of rye whiskey overall. (Its modest suggested retail price, $28, also makes it one of the best spirits deals of all time.) As required by US bottled-in-bond federal regulations, it is 100 proof (50 percent alcohol by volume) and at least four years old.

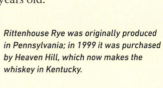

Rittenhouse Rye was originally produced in Pennsylvania; in 1999 it was purchased by Heaven Hill, which now makes the whiskey in Kentucky.

Pikesville Rye

Pikesville Rye started out as a classic Maryland whiskey first sold in 1895. After the rye whiskey distilling scene imploded in the second half of the twentieth century, Pikesville's distribution ultimately became

Pikesville Rye was historically a favorite of drinkers in Maryland and now Heaven Hill is trying to make it popular around the country.

limited to the Maryland area, and only some years after it joined Heaven Hill's portfolio in 1982 did this rye's availability expand across the country.

In 2016, Heaven Hill replaced the standard 80-proof (40 percent alcohol by volume) Pikesville Supreme with a 6-year-old whiskey with a potent 110 proof (55 percent alcohol by volume) version. The move helped elevate the whiskey and made it seem more premium.

Bernheim Original Wheat Whiskey

Isaac Wolfe Bernheim was a Jewish immigrant from Germany, who, along with his brother, built one of the largest American whiskey companies at the start of the twentieth century. His marquee brand was I.W. Harper, an amalgam of his initials and a gentile-sounding last name.

Heaven Hill introduced Bernheim Original Wheat Whiskey in 2005 to honor Bernheim, whose own surname had never before appeared on a liquor bottle label. Heaven Hill's Louisville, Kentucky, distillery actually stands on the site of Bernheim's distillery, which was rebuilt in the early 1990s. (For more on Bernheim, see pages 110–111.)

Bernheim Original Wheat is a unique whiskey in that its mix of grains is 51 percent winter wheat, plus 37 percent corn and 12 percent malted barley. (Keep in mind almost all straight American whiskies are made from a mash bill of at least 51 percent corn or rye.) This whiskey's special mash bill gives it a real spice, smoothness, and complexity. It is 90 proof (45 percent alcohol by volume) and aged for seven years.

Heaven Hill purchased the Bernheim distillery in Louisville, Kentucky, from Diageo in the late 1990s.

Old Fitzgerald Bourbon

While collectors and even, occasionally, drinkers will now pay a king's ransom to acquire a bottle of Pappy Van Winkle, it's less well known that Old Fitzgerald was actually Julian "Pappy" Van Winkle's signature whiskey. During Prohibition, Pappy and his partners acquired the brand for $10,000 from its owner S. C. Herbst and moved production to their brand-new Stitzel-Weller distillery in Louisville, Kentucky.

Heaven Hill acquired Old Fitzgerald in 1999 from Diageo, and now twice a year (in the spring and fall) the brand releases a statuesque decanter of Old Fitz. Each seasonal drop is eagerly awaited, and as a result the bottles are becoming ever more expensive and harder to find. As required by bottled-in-bond federal regulations, the whiskey is 100 proof (50 percent alcohol by volume) and is a minimum of four years old—the 2022 edition was a remarkable seventeen years old. No matter the vintage, Old Fitz is always a wheated bourbon, which means that it is made from a mix of corn, malted barley, and wheat, instead of the more common mix of corn, malted barley, and rye. The result is generally a creamier flavor without the unctuous rye flavor note.

Old Fitzgerald was Julian "Pappy" Van Winkle's signature whiskey when he ran the Stitzel-Weller Distillery. The brand was acquired by Heaven Hill in 1999.

passed away from amyotrophic lateral sclerosis (or ALS) in 2017 at the age of seventy-five. Each whiskey in the collection is incredibly special. Previous releases have included everything from a bourbon finished in a Cognac barrel to a 13-year-old wheat whiskey to a 27-year-old bourbon. Each fall Heaven Hill releases the latest addition to the collection.

Larceny Kentucky Straight Bourbon

Heaven Hill introduced Larceny Kentucky Straight Bourbon in 2012. Its name comes from a convoluted story about theft and John E. Fitzgerald, who was perhaps the founder and the original distiller of Old Fitzgerald Bourbon. (Some

Larceny Kentucky Straight Bourbon is a so-called wheated bourbon, since it's made from a mix of corn, malted barley, and wheat.

Parker's Heritage Collection

In 2007, Heaven Hill released the first edition of its Parker's Heritage Collection, which honors the company's former master distiller Parker Beam, who tragically

folks think Fitzgerald wasn't a whiskey maker at all but rather a treasury agent who liberally sampled barrels in warehouses that he had access to and that using his name was actually a joke.)

What I can say for sure about Larceny is that it's a wheated bourbon, like Old Fitzgerald, and that the standard bottling is six years old and is now made at the Bernheim distillery in Louisville, Kentucky. Heaven Hill has since added the higher proof Larceny Barrel Proof, which has racked up awards and accolades. Larceny whiskey tends to have a big hit of spice—ironically almost like a straight rye whiskey.

Henry McKenna Single Barrel Bourbon

For many years, Henry McKenna Single Barrel Bourbon was undervalued and underappreciated. Heaven Hill has recently begun to sell the 10-year-old bottled-in-bond, 100-proof (50 percent alcohol by volume) bourbon in more markets and McKenna has become a sleeper hit. (There is also a less expensive Henry McKenna Bourbon that is 80 proof/40 percent alcohol by volume.) The bourbon is named for an Irish immigrant who began making whiskey in the United States in the mid-1800s. Heaven Hill acquired Henry McKenna in 1989 when it bought ten liquor brands from Seagram's. The bourbon is now made at the Bernheim distillery in Louisville, Kentucky.

Mellow Corn

Mellow Corn is one of the few commercially available corn whiskies on the market. While its folksy label and funny name might make you think this whiskey is a joke, it has a devoted following of top bartenders and spirits experts. As required by bottled-in-bond federal regulations, it is 100 proof (50 percent alcohol by volume) and at least four years old. Mellow Corn is made from predominantly corn (80 percent) and aged in used bourbon barrels. Unlike bourbon or rye, corn whiskey can be aged in a used barrel, which means it has less vanilla and other flavors from the wood. I would argue that the mellowness in this whiskey's name is produced by the fact that it's not aged in a new barrel.

Few

In 2011, former intellectual property lawyer Paul Hletko started FEW in Evanston, Illinois. (It has been widely reported that the brand's name is a subtle nod to temperance activist Frances Elizabeth Willard, who lived in Evanston.) While he didn't

Attorney-turned-whiskey entrepreneur Paul Hletko started his craft distillery FEW in Evanston, Illinois.

have any distilling experience, he was inspired to open a distillery by his family's former beer business in Czechoslovakia, which was stolen from them during the Holocaust. FEW's square, apothecary-like bottles and intricately detailed labels look like turn-of-the-century World's Fair posters. The brand's lineup grew to include a number of different types of whiskies, including a straight bourbon, a straight rye, and a single malt. FEW has also pushed the envelope with its innovative Immortal Rye Whiskey, which includes Eight Immortals oolong tea, and its Cold Cut Bourbon, which includes cold brew coffee. FEW has also introduced an incredibly popular limited-edition series in collaboration with a number of famous bands, including the Flaming Lips, Alice in Chains, and Black Rebel Motorcycle Club. Heaven Hill acquired FEW in the winter of 2022, when it bought FEW's holding company, Samson & Surrey.

Widow Jane

When Heaven Hill bought the small spirits company Samson & Surrey, the deal included the American whiskey Widow Jane. While the brand is based in Red Hook, Brooklyn, it takes its name from a historic and famous limestone mine in the Hudson Valley town of Rosendale, New York. The brand's founder and original owner, Daniel Preston, got into some trouble because of how the whiskey had been labeled. Critics, along with a class-action lawsuit, alleged that the brand made it sound like the whiskey was made completely in New York, when in fact it was sourced from distilleries in Kentucky and later Indiana. Ultimately, the lawsuit was dismissed and the labels now accurately explain where the whiskey is produced. Currently, the brand buys barrels from different distilleries and also makes its own bourbon and rye in Brooklyn. Widow Jane's lineup includes its flagship 10-year-old bourbon plus the Widow Jane Decadence Bourbon, finished in barrels that previously held maple syrup. Their offerings also include the Widow Jane Lucky Thirteen, which is aged for thirteen years in an American oak barrel, and the Widow Jane The Vaults series, which features some of its oldest and rarest whiskies.

BRANCH: SUNTORY GLOBAL SPIRITS

What would American whiskey taste like if Johannes Jakob Boehm (aka Jacob Beam) never emigrated to the United States from Germany in the 1750s? There are many families that helped create the bourbon industry, but I would argue none has done more collectively than the Beams. Not only was the family involved in their own distillery, but the Beams worked making whiskey in countless other distilleries across Kentucky. The Beam family tree essentially tells the story of the growth of distilling in Kentucky.

The name Jim Beam is practically synonymous with American whiskey and members of the Beam family helped create countless brands across Kentucky.

Of course, the most famous Beam is James Beauregard Beam—better known as Jim Beam—who was born in 1864 and died in 1947. During Prohibition the family was forced out of the distilling business and basically lost everything, including the name of their original brand, Old Tub. Undeterred, Jim Beam partnered with investors in Deerfield, Illinois, to restart the family business after repeal, beginning with the construction of a new distillery just outside Louisville, Kentucky, in Clermont, Kentucky, where his eponymous brand was born. To expand their production capacity, in 1954, Beam bought the former Churchill Downs distillery in Boston, Kentucky. To this day, nearly all of Beam's whiskies are made at these two distilleries.

Jim's grandson, Booker Noe, later helped revive the bourbon industry, at the end of twentieth century, with his small batch collection of whiskey brands.

However, while the Beams were able to get back to work making whiskey, they never owned their own distillery or brand, which has been part of several conglomerates. In January 2014, the overall Jim Beam company was acquired by the Japanese giant Suntory for $16 billion. The newly formed spirits megacompany produces a vast selection of American whiskies, including:

Jim Beam White Label Bourbon

Jim Beam's signature whiskey is its famous White Label Bourbon. It is one of the biggest whiskey brands in the world, selling eleven million nine-liter cases a year. What makes it so popular? Besides name recognition, I would argue it delivers a lot of flavor for a modest price (the current suggested retail price is around $20). The bourbon is aged for four years and is 80 proof (40 percent alcohol by volume), which means it's perfect for sipping on the rocks, with a splash of soda, or in mixed drinks. It's a bar staple and one of my go-tos in a restaurant or bar with a limited or dubious drinks list.

Booker's Bourbon

Frederick Booker Noe was Jim Beam's grandson and created this groundbreaking bourbon when he was running the company's second distillery in Boston, Kentucky.

The launch of Booker's Bourbon was a watershed moment in the history of American whiskey and helped start its meteoric comeback.

(For the full history of the whiskey and Noe, see page 122.) Booker's Bourbon is cask strength, which means the proof varies from batch to batch, but is generally around 120 proof (60 percent alcohol by volume). Not only is the bourbon very potent, but it's also very tasty. (Alcohol carries flavor, so higher proof whiskies usually have more depth and complexity.) It can be sipped neat or with water and ice, which is how Noe would drink his eponymous whiskey. It also works well in classic cocktails, since it doesn't get lost when mixed with other ingredients, like sweet vermouth. Combined with seltzer, it makes a delicious Highball.

Knob Creek Bourbon

Knob Creek is one of the most successful bourbons launched in the modern era. After the success of Booker's, Jim Beam decided in 1992 to launch a whole collection of small batch whiskies, which looked and tasted different from what was then available in liquor stores and bars. Knob Creek's unique bottle shape—one part flask and one part pharmaceutical—caught people's eye and stood out on the shelf. The 9-year-old bourbon inside was also deliciously rich, with big notes of wood and vanilla. Knob Creek got so popular that Beam had to remove the age statement on the label in 2016, because it didn't have enough 9-year-old whiskey to keep up with demand. (Fortunately, the age was reinstated in 2020.) Knob Creek has also turned into its own microbrand, with a number of line extensions, including a Smoked Maple Bourbon, a Single Barrel Bourbon, and a 7-year-old straight rye.

Baker's Bourbon

Booker Noe wasn't the only descendant of Jim Beam to work at the distillery. Baker's Bourbon honors Baker Beam, who was Jim Beam's grandnephew and the son of Beam master distiller Carl Beam. The whiskey is at least seven years old and bottled at a robust 107 proof (53.5 percent alcohol by volume). Since Baker's is a single barrel bourbon, it also offers drinkers the unique opportunity to taste different barrels and see how each one is unique.

Basil Hayden Bourbon

The final bourbon that Booker Noe created for his small batch collection is Basil Hayden. It's an easy-drinking 80 proof (40 percent alcohol by volume) with much

In 1992, Booker Noe created a pioneering small batch collection of American whiskey, which included Basil Hayden Bourbon.

more rye in its mash bill (mix of base grains) than most of the other Jim Beam bourbons, making it a high-rye bourbon. It is also made with a different yeast strain from what Beam normally uses. This is because Basil Hayden is really an offshoot of the Old Grand-Dad family tree rather than the Beam family tree. The bourbon is named for a distiller in the 1700s (Basil Hayden) who was the actual granddad of R.B. Hayden, who started Old Grand-Dad (For more on how Beam acquired the brand, see the Old Grand-Dad entry on page 144.) The modern Basil Hayden brand also includes a 10-year-old bourbon and a Dark Rye Whiskey.

Devil's Cut Bourbon

According to Beam family lore, when Fred Noe (Booker's son) was a teenager in the 1970s, he was taught by a veteran distillery worker how to sweat a bourbon barrel.

Sweating is just a fancy term for collecting the whiskey contained in the wood cells of a barrel that has recently been emptied. What's the trick? Let it sit outside in the Kentucky sun and humidity and the whiskey starts dripping out.

The whiskey reclaimed from the barrel is particularly tannic and, as you can imagine, particularly woody tasting. It's something like the mouth-puckering liquid you get if you squeeze a used teabag. While you might not want to drink a big glass of this sweated bourbon, it is the secret ingredient in Devil's Cut. Beam created a proprietary process to extract this otherwise lost whiskey (which the company nicknamed the devil's cut), which is then blended with standard Jim Beam White Label. Thanks to Beam's innovative process, the finished bourbon has extra oaky notes and a bit of dryness.

Maker's Mark Bourbon

I think it would be pretty hard to find an adult who hasn't tasted or at least heard of Maker's Mark Bourbon. This American whiskey is incredibly important, as it helped bring the whole bourbon industry back to life. But this is not a brand that Jim Beam started, or that even involved a Beam family member—it was, in fact, created by Bill and Margie Samuels. (They were next-door neighbors of Booker Noe in Bardstown, Kentucky.) Bill's family had owned the well-known T.W. Samuels brand, which they were forced to sell a few years after Prohibition. For Maker's Mark, Bill famously decided to break with his family's historic bourbon recipe and swap wheat into the mash bill for the more common and spicier rye. Margie came up with the name for the brand, which was inspired by her collection of silver

In the 1950s, Maker's Mark Bourbon was created by spouses Margie and Bill Samuels. It has since become one of the most famous and popular American whiskies.

thimbles. She also came up with Maker's most signature and distinctive feature—the red wax dripping down the neck.

The whiskey went on sale in 1958, and for decades upon decades Maker's essentially made one type of bourbon at its Loretto, Kentucky, distillery. Then Margie and Bill Samuelses' son Bill Samuels Jr. came up with a new way to age their bourbon a second time by inserting toasted French oak barrel staves into barrels of their standard whiskey. This method produced the permanent line extension Maker's 46, which was introduced in 2010. It tastes similar to the brand's original bourbon, but has the added flavor notes of caramel and vanilla from the extra wood contact. Maker's 46 opened the door to unprecedented innovation for the brand, which now has a few versions to choose from, including a cask strength and a 101-proof (50.5 percent alcohol by volume) bourbon.

Legent

Legent bourbon is a special Beam whiskey that combines American whiskey-making expertise with Japanese blending know-how, which was introduced in 2019. Suntory's legendary and longtime chief blender, Shinji Fukuyo, traveled to Kentucky and selected barrels from the company's many warehouses with Jim Beam's master distiller, Fred Noe. Some of the whiskey was then aged for a second time in wine casks and some in sherry casks. Fukuyo blended together the three different types of whiskey to his exact specifications. The result has notes of vanilla from the American oak barrels as well as dried fruit notes from the sherry and wine casks.

Jim Beam Rye

Even though Jim Beam is best known for its bourbon, it produces one of the oldest rye whiskies of the recent revival, one of the few that have been available for several decades. When curious folks sought out straight rye during the late 1990s and early 2000s (aka the vodka years), Jim Beam Rye was one of the only bottles you could find (and its bright yellow label certainly stood out on shelves). Thanks to the rebirth of rye whiskey, in 2015 Beam replaced the yellow-label rye with its so-called Pre-Prohibition Style Rye 90 proof (45 percent alcohol by volume) that has a statelier dark-green label. While Jim Beam's rye is certainly more widely available than back in the day, it's still harder to find than Beam's more famous bourbons.

Old Crow Bourbon

This historic whiskey brand is holding on for dear life. It was started by Scottish immigrant Dr. James Crow, who is often credited with streamlining and modernizing whiskey production in the United States. (For a long time, it was said that he invented the sour mash process of fermentation, but there's evidence that it existed long before he began to use the method.) Old Crow Bourbon was a wildly successful brand and many liquor stores proudly displayed statues of its signature dapper bird complete with a monocle and a top hat. Glassware maker Libby even produced a small cocktail glass whose stem featured Old Crow's mascot.

But the downturn in whiskey drinking in the late 1970s really hurt Old Crow's sales. Beam acquired the brand in 1987 when it bought the liquor division of National Distillers and Chemical Corporation. After the acquisition, according to legendary whiskey writer Chuck Cowdery, Beam stopped using Old Crow's historic recipe and yeast strain and instead just subbed in its own bourbon. While you can occasionally still find Old Crow, it's usually relegated to the bottom shelf. The problem is that Beam has just too many historic and important whiskies in its portfolio. My hope is that one day Old Crow comes back to prominence.

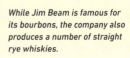

While Jim Beam is famous for its bourbons, the company also produces a number of straight rye whiskies.

Old Grand-Dad Bourbon

Old Grand-Dad Bourbon was once a powerhouse sought after by countless drinkers. It also was one of the whiskies that Beam acquired in the National Distillers and Chemical Corporation deal. There is an 80-proof (40 percent alcohol by volume) Old Grand-Dad bourbon as well as a 100-proof (50 percent alcohol by volume) bottled-in-bond, and a flavorful 114-proof (57 percent alcohol by volume) version. Old Grand-Dad is known for having a lot of rye grain in its mash bill, and also for being started by R.B. Hayden, who named the whiskey for his own old granddad, legendary whiskey maker Basil Hayden.

Old Grand-Dad is a brand that deserves to be saved, preserved, and marketed. Unfortunately, during the recent resurgence of American whiskey it has been largely forgotten. The one exception is the brand's potent 114-proof version, which is a cult favorite among craft cocktail bartenders. Thanks to its high proof and high rye quotient, it doesn't get lost in cocktails, and you can't beat its low price of about $30.

Old Overholt Rye Whiskey

Do you know what's the oldest continually operating whiskey brand in the United States? The answer is, of course, Old Overholt Rye Whiskey. It was started more than two hundred years ago by Abraham Overholt in West Overton, Pennsylvania. Overholt was the son of Henry Oberholtzer, who began making whiskey on his farm. Abraham's whiskey developed into the modern brand Old Overholt, which was made at a giant distillery in Connellsville, Pennsylvania.

The rye was originally produced in a three-chamber still and then possibly blended with rye whiskey made on a column still. Old Overholt was bought and sold several times before joining the Beam portfolio in 1987, in the National Distillers and Chemical Corporation

Old Grand-Dad is an incredibly historic whiskey brand that most people have never heard of or tasted.

The story of Old Overholt is arguably the story of American whiskey and goes back more than 200 years.

acquisition. The brand's production was moved to one of Beam's Kentucky distilleries. (Rye whiskey experts have suggested that the original recipe for the whiskey was changed when Overholt joined Beam.) Blame the overall waning interest in rye, or perhaps Beam's focus on bourbon, but Overholt was largely forgotten by the company's executives. The brand's glory days were long behind it and Overholt found itself at the end of a long line of other Beam spirits that needed marketing dollars and attention. Near the end, Overholt's signature 86-proof (43 percent alcohol by volume) 4-year-old was reduced to just three years of barrel aging.

For a moment, it seemed like the brand might become obsolete and possibly be discontinued by Beam, but then a small miracle occurred. Rye began to catch on with craft cocktail bartenders and whiskey drinkers, who discovered dusty bottles of Overholt in liquor stores. This new group of rye fanatics began to call for more attention to be paid to Overholt—and Beam answered. By 2022, the brand had restored the core 86-proof Overholt to four years of aging, and had also reintroduced a bonded whiskey and a 114-proof (57 percent alcohol by volume) version. It wouldn't surprise me if the brand's production was moved back to Pennsylvania one day. And it would be wonderful if Overholt once again included whiskey made on a three-chamber still. Fingers crossed!

BRANCH: BROWN-FORMAN

It's hard to overstate Brown-Forman's role in the American whiskey industry. But the company actually started out in the 1870s in a completely different and seemingly incongruous business—pharmaceuticals.

The "Brown" in Brown-Forman originally stood for George Garvin Brown and his half-brother, J.T.S. Brown Jr. They were in the drug business when they noticed a significant hole in the market. At the time, alcohol was seen as a cure-all and patients were often told by doctors to regularly take some. Besides the fact that alcohol is not actually a panacea, finding pure whiskey at the time, that wasn't full of harmful additives or cut with a range of fillers, was actually quite difficult. Much of what was passed off as whiskey was in reality just neutral grain spirit flavored and colored with things like creosote, burnt nutshells, and prune juice.

The Browns, who lived in Louisville, Kentucky, realized that patients needed pure pharmaceutical-grade whiskey. In 1870,

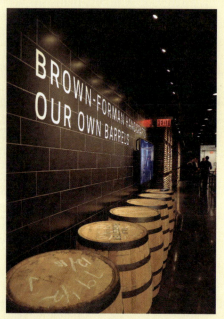

Brown-Forman is the only major American whiskey company to own its own cooperage.

did was effectively create a completely different system that ensured consistency, quality, and purity of the product. It is essentially how liquor is currently sold.

By the early nineteenth century, Brown-Forman had moved from medicinal whiskey to recreational whiskey. (Although during Prohibition, they were granted one of the few, lucrative federal licenses to supply pharmacies.) The company is still run today by descendants of George Garvin Brown and J.T.S. Brown Jr. Its portfolio has grown to include many famous and important whiskies, including:

Jack Daniel's Tennessee Whiskey

Jack Daniel's is one of the bestselling whiskies in the world. It was started after the Civil War by a man named, that's right, Jack Daniel. He lived in Lynchburg, Tennessee, which is where the brand's distillery is still located. Daniel hired distiller Nathan "Nearest" Green to make the whiskey. Green had been enslaved and worked making whiskey for Daniel's friend and former employer, Rev. Dan Call.

they introduced Old Forrester Bourbon, which originally contained whiskey from three well-known distilleries and was certified pure. (The company later removed one *r* from its name, giving us the Old Forester that's still sold today.)

Their idea doesn't sound all that earth-shattering now, as we usually buy whiskey bottled by the distiller. But keep in mind that nineteenth-century supply chains were much more circuitous. Most distillers sold their whiskey to brands who blended it and/or redistilled it. The brands then sold their barrels of whiskey to itinerant salespeople, who sold the casks to grocery stores or bars, which would finally sell the liquor by the glass or decanter to the end consumer. All of these steps in the supply chain meant that the whiskey that left the distillery was a far cry from what folks ultimately drank. What the Browns

Until the turn of the twentieth century, Jack Daniel's was made in a wooden chamber still, which was pretty standard equipment at the time. Today it is made in a number of giant column stills. Regardless of the still type, it has always been filtered through ground-up maple wood charcoal, which is called the Lincoln County Process. (See the Lincoln County Process, page 64.) Jack Daniel's, like the rest of the Tennessee liquor industry, was forced to shut down when the state essentially went dry in 1910 and remained so until 1933, with the repeal of Prohibition. But the brand truly came into its own after World

AMERICAN WHISKEY 147

Jack Daniel was an actual person who started his whiskey brand in the 1860s in Lynchburg, Tennessee.

War II, when Brown-Forman acquired it in the summer of 1956 from Jack Daniel's great-nephew, Lem Motlow, for a reported price of $20 million. At the time, Jack Daniel's made whiskey as well as other beverages, including applejack. (In 1924, Motlow somehow got off after killing a train conductor and seriously wounding a porter on a train in St. Louis, Missouri. He has since largely been written out of the brand's story.)

Under Brown-Forman, the brand prospered through the swinging '50s and '60s, and even became Frank Sinatra's signature drink. (Sinatra was actually buried with a bottle of Jack Daniel's.) While the rest of the whiskey industry crumbled during the last quarter of the twentieth century, Jack Daniel's prospered and was adopted by seemingly every generation, including the hair metal bands that partied along LA's notorious Sunset Strip. Today, the brand includes the standard Old No. 7 80-proof (40 percent alcohol by volume) whiskey along with many different line extensions, including Gentleman Jack (it goes through a second charcoal filtering after barrel aging), Single Barrel Select (there are currently four different whiskies in this subproduct line), and a Tennessee Rye (it is made from 70 percent rye grain and is charcoal filtered). The brand also introduced a 100-proof (50 percent alcohol by volume) bottled-in-bond version as well as a Triple Mash whose blend includes an American single malt. And don't forget the Sinatra Select in honor of Old Blue Eyes, which is aged in a special barrel that has been grooved to infuse the whiskey with even more charred wood flavor. Jack Daniel's sells more than 5 million nine-liter cases a year, making it one of the United States' biggest brands of any kind.

In 1956, Brown-Forman paid a reported $20 million for Jack Daniel's, which has become one of the country's biggest liquor brands.

Old Forester

While Jack Daniel's is Brown-Forman's largest whiskey brand, Old Forester was the company's first brand and can still be found in its portfolio. For many years, Old Forester lurked in the large shadow cast by Jack Daniel's, but Campbell Brown, George Garvin Brown's direct descendant and the current chairman of Brown-Forman's board of directors, made it his personal mission to celebrate the company's first brand. There is now an Old Forester distillery and tasting room in Louisville, Kentucky, which opened in the spring of 2018. It was built on the site of the company's original office, along what is known as Distillery Row, which it occupied from 1882 to 1919.

Currently, there is an 86-proof (43 percent alcohol by volume) Old Forester and a more potent 100-proof (50 percent alcohol by volume) bottled-in-bond version. There is also a series of throwback releases, including the Old Forester 1870 Original Batch whiskey and the Old Forester 1897 Bottle in Bond Whisky, which are inspired by historic whiskey-making methods. A few years ago, Old Forester introduced a straight rye that was a nod to a brand that Brown-Forman bought in 1940 and is made with a relatively large proportion of malted barley (20 percent). One of Old Forester's most highly coveted whiskies is its Birthday Bourbon, which is released every September 2nd, to commemorate George Garvin Brown's birthday. It comes in a unique decanter-like bottle and, while the whiskey could be purchased not that long ago at its modest suggested retail price of around $35, some stores now sell it for thousands.

Woodford Reserve Bourbon

Woodford Reserve is a relatively new addition to the Brown-Forman portfolio. It was introduced in 1996 and created to appeal to the new generation of connoisseur whiskey drinkers that was just developing at the time. Once the brand began to show promise, Brown-Forman built it a dedicated distillery in Versailles, Kentucky (an area famous for its Thoroughbred horse farms). Woodford Reserve is a blend of whiskey made in traditional, bulbous copper stills and whiskey made in efficient, modern column stills.

The brand's long-serving master distiller Chris Morris launched his pioneering Woodford Reserve Master's Collection in 2005, which has since included all manner of groundbreaking whiskies—some more delicious than others, but all nonetheless innovative and very interesting

Brown-Forman is one of the United States' biggest liquor companies, but back in 1870 it had just one brand: Old Forester.

Woodford Reserve Bourbon is one of the most successful modern brands to be created and was originally introduced in 1996.

to taste. The brand's lineup now includes the annual release of the limited-edition Double Oaked bourbon (aged for a second time in a toasted and charred barrel) as well as rye, malt, and wheat whiskies. Woodford Reserve also is one of the main sponsors of the Kentucky Derby, which is held on the first Saturday in May at the Churchill Downs Racetrack. To mark the occasion, the brand releases a commemorative bottle.

In 2020, Woodford Reserve sold more than 1 million nine-liter cases, which is quite a remarkable milestone for a relatively new brand. Reportedly, by 2026, the goal is to sell 2.5 million cases. A few years ago, Morris stepped down from his position and became the brand's master distiller emeritus. He was succeeded by his colleague, Elizabeth McCall, who assumed the title of master distiller.

BRANCH: DIAGEO

Diageo is one of the biggest spirits companies in the world, with an absurdly large number of Scotch brands including Johnnie Walker, Talisker, and Lagavulin. But when it comes to American whiskey its portfolio is fairly modest. This wasn't always the case, but the whiskey doldrums of the 1970s and 1980s convinced United Distillers (UD)—which was an integral part of the formation of Diageo in 1997—to slow down production and finally sell off most of its US holdings.

UD's most important asset was, arguably, the Stitzel-Weller distillery in Louisville, Kentucky, which opened in 1935 and had been the centerpiece of Julian "Pappy" Van Winkle's empire (yes, that Pappy). The distillery was shut down on January 28, 1993, and never reopened.

However, the barrel warehouses continue to be used to this day to age whiskey for a number of brands. (In 2015, Diageo renovated one of the buildings and added a very small still to produce experimental batches.)

By 1999, UD was part of Diageo, which decided to sell off its Old Fitzgerald brand and the giant Louisville Bernheim distillery to Heaven Hill. (As part of the deal, Sazerac purchased the W.L. Weller and Charter brands, and the David Sherman Corporation got Rebel Yell Bourbon.) The Bernheim distillery was a huge upgrade for Heaven Hill and an absolute necessity for them, since its own historic distillery in Bardstown, Kentucky, had burned down three years earlier.

But as American whiskey has become ever more popular during the past two decades, Diageo has put its considerable muscle behind building up its few historic and new brands. These efforts have included spending hundreds of millions on new distilleries and warehouses across Kentucky.

The conglomerate's portfolio now includes these whiskey brands:

Bulleit Bourbon

Diageo acquired Bulleit Bourbon thanks to the breakup of another liquor giant: Seagram's. The American whiskey brand was started by Vietnam War veteran and former tax lawyer Tom Bulleit. He

No one would blame you for thinking that Bulleit Bourbon dates back to the 1800s, but the brand was actually started in the late 1980s under the Thoroughbred name.

was inspired by his long-lost great-great-grandfather, Augustus Bulleit, a distiller and liquor salesman in the nineteenth century who disappeared on the road with a load of bourbon.

After dreaming for decades about starting a brand, Bulleit bought whiskey from the Leestown Company Inc. (the distillery would later become Buffalo Trace) in 1987 and sold it under the Thoroughbred brand name. In the mid-1990s, Seagram's heard about Bulleit and his bourbon, and acquired the brand in 1997 after a year of negotiations. As part of the deal, according to Bulleit's memoir, *Bulleit Proof*, he had to come up with a new name and direction for the whiskey. Bulleit and Seagram's settled on the name Bulleit Bourbon and the concept of frontier whiskey, which honors Augustus's story. Thanks to Seagram's, the brand also got a new package design—its now signature apothecary bottle, which was featured on episodes of HBO's popular Wild West TV show *Deadwood*.

Seagram's legendary distiller Jim Rutledge and master blender Art Peterson helped develop a formula for Bulleit Bourbon. The whiskey was produced at Seagram's Lawrenceburg, Kentucky, distillery. After the Seagram's breakup, that facility became home exclusively to Four Roses Bourbon, which for years continued to make Bulleit Bourbon under contract. That arrangement continued until 2017, when Diageo opened a $115 million distillery for Bulleit in Shelby County, Kentucky, outside of Louisville, Kentucky.

In 2011, Bulleit noticed the increasing interest of craft cocktail bartenders in rye whiskey, which had been largely forgotten. In response, they introduced Bulleit Rye, which became a runaway success and brought rye whiskey to the masses. It was spicy but not as unctuous or bold as other ryes and was made from a mash bill of 95 percent rye and 5 percent malted barley.

Bulleit has also introduced a 10-year-old bourbon and a Barrel Strength Bourbon.

While the brand rolls on, it does so without founder Tom Bulleit or his daughter Hollis, who formerly served as a brand ambassador. Hollis has made increasingly alarming allegations about her father's behavior, as well as claims that she was forced out of the company because of her sexual orientation. While Tom Bulleit denies these charges, both Bulleit family members are no longer affiliated with the brand.

George Dickel Tennessee Whisky

Famous for being Tennessee's *other* whiskey, George Dickel is often compared to its much better-known in-state rival Jack Daniel's. But Dickel has its own unique and interesting story. The company's founder, George Dickel, was a German immigrant who settled in Nashville, Tennessee. While an oversized bust of him proudly sits outside the brand's distillery in Tullahoma, Tennessee, he never actually owned the facility or made whiskey himself. Dickel was in fact a liquor wholesaler and retailer who passed away in June 1894. It was Victor Emmanuel Shwab who actually built the modern whiskey brand and bought the Cascade distillery in Tullahoma that supplied Dickel's store. He started out as an employee of Dickel and then became his business partner. Shwab also later married Dickel's sister-in-law, Emma Banzer.

All of his hard work was almost for naught, since right after the turn of the twentieth century Tennessee's own prohibitionary laws destroyed the state's whiskey industry. By 1910, Shwab had

George Dickel originally bought its whiskey from the Cascade Distillery in Tullahoma, Tennessee.

to move production out of Tennessee to Kentucky, where the brand was made at the A. Ph. Stitzel distillery (which would later become Stitzel-Weller). Like the rest of the American whiskey industry, Dickel had to shut down for national Prohibition in January 1920. After repeal, in 1936 or possibly early 1937, Dickel was acquired by Lewis Rosenstiel for, reportedly, $100,000 and added to his burgeoning Schenley empire. Until the late 1950s, Schenley was bottling whiskey made by its other distilleries across the country under the Dickel or Dickel's name. That practice ended once a dedicated Dickel distillery opened in Tullahoma in 1959, near the site of its original facility. It cost a reported $1 million and is still where the brand's whiskey is made. At the heart of the facility is a relatively short column still, which produces a heavy spirit and is perhaps what gives the whiskey its signature creaminess. Like its fellow Tennessee distillery Jack Daniel's, the whiskey is then filtered through homemade ground sugar maple charcoal before it is barrel aged. The filtration is able to lighten the spirit a bit and is an essential part of why Dickel tastes like Dickel.

In 1999, it appeared as if Dickel, once again, was in danger of disappearing for good. Diageo, which had acquired the brand, shut down the distillery for four years, but fortunately reopened it and has been running it ever since. Under the current general manager and head distiller, Nicole Austin, who came aboard in 2018, Dickel has recently enjoyed a new golden age, introducing a number of interesting and acclaimed whiskies, including a bourbon. In 2019, Dickel won *Whisky Advocate*'s Whiskey of the Year for its 13-year-old bottled-in-bond whiskey.

Austin also cocreated a collaboration bottling with Leopold Bros. in Denver, Colorado, which blends together rye produced at Dickel on its column still that is filtered through charcoal with rye produced at Leopold on its three-chamber still. The resulting whiskey is a fascinating chance to taste history and gives you a real sense of what rye was like before Prohibition.

Blade and Bow Bourbon

While the Stitzel-Weller distillery is no longer operating, in 2015 its history inspired the creation of Blade and Bow Bourbon. Each bottle of the whiskey comes adorned with one of five different actual keys. The keys pay homage to how, supposedly, the keys for the distillery were hung each day outside of the front door of the offices as a sign of hospitality.

While Louisville's historic Stitzel-Weller Distillery no longer makes any whiskey, Diageo continues to use its warehouses to age whiskey for its Blade and Bow Bourbon.

mostly sold outside the United States, but since 2015 it is once again available there. There is currently an I.W. Harper Kentucky Straight Bourbon Whiskey, a Kentucky Straight Bourbon 15-Year-Old, and a Cabernet Cask Reserve bottling, which is, as you might assume, bourbon finished in a cabernet wine cask.

Orphan Barrel Whiskey Distilling Co.

In 2014, Diageo launched the Orphan Barrel Whiskey Distilling Co. to feature unique and interesting whiskies that don't fit the style of any of its other brands. These are extremely limited bottlings and generally fetch a very high price. The first Orphan Barrel release featured two whiskies that had been aging at Stitzel-Weller: Old Blowhard, which was a 26-year-old Kentucky bourbon, and Barterhouse, a 20-year-old Kentucky bourbon. Since

The standard version of Blade and Bow is a blend of whiskies that go through a solera-like system, which ensures a consistency of flavor. There is also a special, limited-edition 22-year-old bourbon, which contains whiskey produced at other distilleries but aged in the Stitzel-Weller warehouses. Once the bottles of the 22-year-old are gone, they're gone forever.

I.W. Harper

I.W. Harper was once one of the most famous and important brands of American whiskey—but is now largely forgotten. It was started by Isaac Wolfe Bernheim in the late 1800s and grew to become a bestseller. Nearly a century later it found its way into Diageo's portfolio. (For more about Bernheim's incredible journey, see page 136.) For decades, I.W. Harper was

One of the great bourbon barons at the turn of the twentieth century was Isaac Wolfe Bernheim and his signature whiskey was I.W. Harper.

these first two offerings, there have been sixteen different releases in the Orphan Barrel series from across Diageo's portfolio of brands. While each Orphan Barrel is completely different, one of the few things that they share is that they're all bottled in square apothecary-like bottles, with whimsical names and labels to match.

Balcones

In 2009, master distiller Chip Tate started Balcones in an old Waco, Texas, welding shop that he converted into a distillery. This humble venture has since become one of the most successful and influential modern craft spirits brands. When Tate opened the business, the idea of aging whiskey in Texas was definitely untested. Despite early skepticism about the viability of the project, Balcones went on to win acclaim for not trying to make Kentucky bourbon or Maryland rye, but instead embracing its Texas identity and roots. Its Baby Blue Corn Whisky is made with only blue corn; its Brimstone whiskey is smoked with local Texas scrub oak; and its Lineage Single Malt Whisky is made with both Scottish and Texas barley. Not only did Balcones garner tons of awards and praise from spirits experts, but it also helped seed a thriving Texas whiskey scene, which now includes dozens of other brands.

Tate lost a fight with his investors and was forced out of the company in 2014. (He has since built his own distillery, Tate & Co., to make local brandies, and also started Tate & Co. Craft Copperworks.) Balcones was purchased by Diageo in November 2022 for an undisclosed amount.

When Balcones opened in 2009, it proved beyond a shadow of a doubt that you could make high-quality whiskey in Texas' famously hot climate.

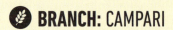 BRANCH: CAMPARI

You might be wondering what Campari, which is famous for the eponymous Italian bitter spirit, is doing in this section. Well, in 2009 it purchased legendary American whiskey brand Wild Turkey from Pernod Ricard for $575 million. Pernod had just bought Absolut Vodka for almost $9 billion and was trying to raise money for the acquisition by selling off some of its vast portfolio. Most of the brands it offloaded weren't big sellers—except Wild Turkey. I'd argue that it was a grave miscalculation by Pernod, which did not accurately predict the American whiskey boom and has been trying to replace Wild Turkey ever since. In 2022, Campari also bought craft American whiskey distillery Wilderness Trail. Read on to find out more about the company's growing whiskey portfolio.

Wild Turkey Bourbon

There are few whiskies better known than Wild Turkey Bourbon. It's a foundational brand that has helped prop up the whole American whiskey industry for decades. Its famous 101-proof (50.5 percent alcohol by volume) signature bottling is truly an icon. But Wild Turkey started out rather modestly—it was a house whiskey for Brooklyn-based liquor distributor and importer Austin, Nichols. (Austin, Nichols was first a very large grocery wholesaler and then changed its focus to the booze business.)

The bourbon was originally made for the company at the Ripy family's distillery in Lawrenceburg, Kentucky. According to lore, Thomas McCarthy, the president of Austin, Nichols, hosted a turkey hunt in 1940 and served some of his company's bourbon. After the trip his guests asked for some more of his wild turkey whiskey—and a new brand was suddenly born.

Ultimately, Austin, Nichols purchased the Ripys' distillery, and later Wild Turkey was sold to the Liggett Group. In order to fend off a hostile takeover by the British company Grand Metropolitan (which would later be one of the founding companies that would form Diageo), Liggett sold Wild Turkey to Pernod Ricard in 1980 for $97.5 million. But the plan didn't work as Grand Metropolitan took over Liggett. (A few years later, Pernod would once again outfox Grand Metropolitan for Irish Distillers—see page 337 for more.) In 2009, Campari bought Wild Turkey for $575 million and continues to run it today. For a number of years Austin, Nichols was the importer of Campari's eponymous bittersweet aperitif, so it seems fitting that Campari and Wild Turkey are back together.

Throughout all of these corporate moves, there has been one constant: the brand's master distiller, Jimmy Russell. He began working at the company on September 10, 1954, and was joined by his son Eddie on June 5, 1981. The Russells, both of whom have been inducted into the Kentucky Bourbon Hall of Fame, continue to work at the Lawrenceburg, Kentucky, distillery today. Eddie's son Bruce joined the company in 2015, and now works as a brand ambassador.

In 2011, Campari completed a $50 million expansion of the distillery, which reportedly increased its production capacity by 100 percent. The renovation also included a new visitor center. Then, in 2023, Campari announced that it was spending $161 million to build a second distillery for Wild Turkey, which would be built next to its original facility and increase the brand's annual production from 9 million proof gallons to 14 million

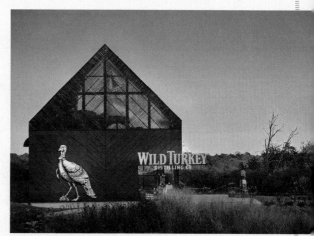

For decades, Wild Turkey 101 Bourbon has been one of the mainstays of the American whiskey industry.

While Wild Turkey keeps the proportions of its bourbon recipe a secret, it is produced from a mix of corn, malted barley, and rye.

proof gallons. This additional distillery is scheduled to open in summer 2025.

Wild Turkey is still best known for its 101-proof bourbon, as well as its 101-proof rye whiskey. Few whiskies can deliver that much flavor at such a modest price. At one point, the brand tried to discontinue the 101-proof rye, but bartenders, notably including the talented mixologist and podcast host Erick Castro, protested the change and saved the whiskey.

Starting in 1972, the brand began trying to appeal to a larger audience and introduced an 86.8-proof (43.4 percent alcohol by volume) bourbon. While that whiskey is no longer available, there is an 81-proof (40.5 percent alcohol by volume) bourbon and an 81-proof rye.

Jimmy Russell was best friends with Booker Noe, who created Jim Beam's pioneering small batch collection. So it's no surprise that Russell introduced his single barrel Kentucky Spirit a few years after Booker's Bourbon was launched. Kentucky Spirit is currently an 8-year-old whiskey that is 101 proof. To appeal to this new generation of drinkers, Wild Turkey also created Rare Breed, which is cask strength and a blend of 6-, 8-, and 12-year-old bourbon.

For collectors, Wild Turkey now offers a Master's Keep series of limited-edition bourbons and ryes. Recent additions have included a 17-year-old bourbon and a sherry cask finished bourbon.

Longbranch Bourbon

With the launch of Longbranch, Wild Turkey added a bit of Hollywood glamour to its brand. The whiskey was created in conjunction with movie star Matthew McConaughey, who for a number of years served as Wild Turkey's creative director. Longbranch, which was introduced in 2017, is definitely a departure for Wild Turkey, since it's filtered through both oak charcoal and mesquite charcoal—a nod to McConaughey's Texas roots. (In some

None other than Hollywood star Matthew McConaughey helped come up with Longbranch, which is filtered through two kinds of charcoal.

ways it's more of a mash-up of Kentucky and Tennessee than Kentucky and Texas, but I digress.) Admittedly, it's not a bourbon for all bourbon drinkers, but it does offer a new tool for brands to use as a way to attract new fans.

Wild Turkey's master distiller Jimmy Russell started working at the distillery in September of 1954 and Russell's Reserve was named in his honor.

Russell's Reserve

In the late 1990s, it seemed that Wild Turkey's famous master distiller, Jimmy Russell, was going to retire—he'd worked at the distillery for forty-five years at that point. To honor his years of service and his legacy, the brand created Russell's Reserve bourbon as a one-time limited edition. The delicious 10-year-old whiskey was picked by Jimmy's son, Eddie Russell. While the original reason for Russell's Reserve was a bust because, as of this writing, Jimmy is still working as the brand's master distiller, the product kicked off a successful second line of whiskey for Wild Turkey. (No matter when Jimmy retires, Russell's Reserve will be a tribute to him and his decades upon decades of employment at Wild Turkey.)

In 2001, the brand rolled out a wider release of this special bourbon, which was followed by a bottle and label redesign to make it more distinctive. The Russell's Reserve line now includes a 10-year-old bourbon, a 6-year-old rye, a single barrel bourbon, and a single barrel rye, as well as limited-edition releases.

Wild Turkey American Honey

The flavored bourbon craze was kicked off by Wild Turkey's launch of American Honey in 2006. While the idea seemed revolutionary when it debuted, Wild Turkey had first come out with a honey-and-whiskey liqueur back in 1976. It didn't really catch on, but the brand didn't give up and kept tinkering with the recipe for the next thirty years before it became a sensation. American Honey got so popular that just about every other major American whiskey producer at the time introduced a honey version, including Jim Beam, Evan Williams, and Jack Daniel's.

Wilderness Trail

The latest American whiskey brand to join Campari's portfolio is Wilderness Trail, which is located in Danville, Kentucky. It was started by friends Shane Baker and Pat Heist in 2006. Distilling was their backup plan after they gave up trying to be professional musicians.

The distillery does things a bit differently from most of its competitors. For one, Wilderness Trail employs a sweet mash process, which means each mash

Wilderness Trail is one of Kentucky's most innovative distilleries, but it's not in Louisville, Lexington, or Bardstown, but on the other side of the state in Danville.

is fermented with fresh yeast and doesn't use any of the previous run as a kind of starter. Its whiskey portfolio currently includes a wheated bourbon, a high-rye bourbon, and a rye whiskey, as well as 6-year-old and 8-year-old bourbons.

For a relatively new distillery it has a somewhat large capacity of 216 barrels a day, thanks to its three stills (two column stills and a hybrid pot-column). Its six warehouses are aging more than one hundred thousand barrels of whiskey. In the fall of 2022, Campari acquired a 70 percent stake in Wilderness Trail for $420 million.

BRANCH: PERNOD RICARD

Pernod Ricard started out as two French family businesses, which made Pernod and Ricard aperitifs, respectively. The businesses merged in 1975 and, thanks to a number of shrewd acquisitions in the twentieth century, it has become a giant spirits conglomerate with vast liquor holdings around the globe, including whiskey icons The Glenlivet and Jameson. At the end of the twentieth century, the company was similarly set up with American whiskey brands—it owned Wild Turkey and a giant distillery in Indiana that was originally built by Seagram's and would later become known as MGP.

Pernod didn't see a way to monetize its Indiana distillery and planned to completely close it down at first. Instead, it sold the facility to the holding company that owns Angostura bitters and Angostura rum. Then, in 2009, Pernod parted with Wild Turkey Bourbon in order to help pay for its nearly $9 billion purchase of Absolut Vodka and the rest of Swedish V&S Vin & Spirit AB.

Over the past few years, Pernod has made some moves to rebuild its portfolio of American whiskies. Read on for insight into its recent acquisitions.

Jefferson's Bourbon

Back in 1997, before bourbon was trendy, Trey Zoeller cofounded Jefferson's Bourbon with his father, Chet Zoeller.

Trey Zoeller, a Kentucky native, isn't a distiller, but rather a barrel hunter. He was buying barrels of unusually delicious whiskey before there was really a market for selling limited editions or small batch bourbons. Zoeller now admits that back in the late 1990s and early 2000s it didn't take much skill, since brands were focused on simply producing consistent signature whiskies. Anything that didn't fit the house style was blended away or could be bought by a savvy entrepreneur.

Jefferson's Ocean Bourbon is actually aged on the high seas aboard a cargo ship that crosses the equator two times.

Jefferson's was able to break through due to its high-quality bourbon and Zoeller's unflagging marketing of the brand. He even convinced *Esquire* magazine to co-create and co-brand a bottled Manhattan cocktail, which went on sale in 2015.

But Zoeller's greatest idea and marketing ploy was to age whiskey on boats. Not only did it make for great news stories but the exposure to sea air, wildly fluctuating temperatures, and the constant rocking had an actual effect on the whiskey—giving it a maritime note and unique complexity. This practice also had a historical precedent. Distillers really only began barrel aging their spirits once they saw how they were transformed during journeys to far-off ports.

Jefferson's Ocean is now the brand's signature product. Barrels of this whiskey go on a journey that usually crosses the equator twice, touches five continents, and visits at least twenty-five ports. There is now both a Jefferson's Ocean Aged at Sea Bourbon and a Jefferson's Ocean Rye. In addition, the brand's line of whiskies includes its Very Small Batch, which is a blend of up to four straight bourbons, and Jefferson's Reserve, which is a blend of older whiskies.

In 2006, Zoeller sold his company to Castle Brands for an undisclosed sum but

It's hard to miss Rabbit Hole's gleaming distillery, which is right in the heart of Louisville's NuLu neighborhood.

continued to run Jefferson's and be the face of the brand. In 2015, Castle Brands bought a stake in Kentucky Artisan distillery in Crestwood, Kentucky. This deal allowed Jefferson's to completely control the production of its own whiskey for the first time, a wise move considering how hard it is now to purchase barrels on the open market.

In 2019, Pernod Ricard acquired Jefferson's Bourbon when it bought its parent company, Castle Brands, for $223 million. Just as he did with his earlier deal, Zoeller stayed on and is still the brand's spokesperson and chief strategist. To further grow Jefferson's, Pernod announced in December 2022 that it was going to build the whiskey a $250 million distillery, visitor center, and three warehouses in Lebanon, Kentucky.

Rabbit Hole

If there is one brand built to capitalize on the Instagram age, it's Rabbit Hole. The whiskey is produced in a stunning glass-and-steel, $15 million distillery that has won architecture awards for its chic industrial design. At the heart of the building is a gleaming 48-foot (almost 15-meter) tall column still. Looking at this building you might assume it's located in downtown LA, or perhaps in Williamsburg, Brooklyn, but it's actually in the trendy Louisville, Kentucky, neighborhood of NuLu (New Louisville). The facility opened in 2018 and has become a local landmark, attracting other new businesses, such as the neighboring Hotel Genevieve.

Rabbit Hole came out of nowhere and beat the odds to become a success. The brand was founded by Kaveh Zamanian, who has a doctorate in clinical psychology and worked as a psychologist and psychoanalyst. His wife, Heather Bass, also has a doctorate in clinical psychology, is originally from Kentucky, and introduced Zamanian to bourbon. In 2012, he started the Rabbit Hole brand and began by buying whiskey as he planned his own distillery.

Rabbit Hole makes a range of whiskies, including a core four expressions: the four-grain Cavehill Kentucky Straight Bourbon Whiskey, the high-rye Heigold Bourbon, the sherry cask-finished Dareringer bourbon, and the Boxergrail rye whiskey. Rabbit Hole also has a Founder's Collection series of very limited and expensive whiskies.

In June 2019, Rabbit Hole was purchased by Pernod for an undisclosed price. Three years later, Zamanian was inducted into the Kentucky Distillers' Association's Bourbon Hall of Fame—an incredibly meteoric rise for a new brand.

TX Whiskey

As you likely guessed, TX Whiskey is from Texas. Thanks to the large population of the state, it's become a great market to get new spirits brands started. And TX definitely leans into its Lone Star State roots for its bourbon, by using only locally grown yellow dent corn and soft red winter wheat. Its yeast strain was collected from pecan trees growing in the state. And the bottle cap for the whiskey is covered in reclaimed leather from old cowboy boots—it doesn't get more Texas than that!

TX was originally distilled in a Fort Worth warehouse, which housed two hybrid pot-column stills manufactured by Louisville, Kentucky–based Vendome Copper & Brass Works. In 2014, TX bought

France's Pernod Ricard is hoping to use the notoriety of Texas to make its TX Whiskey a household name

the historic Glen Garden Country Club and built a vast Whiskey Ranch on the property. The new facility, which opened in 2017, not only includes a large distillery with a 50-foot (15-meter) copper column still, but also a tasting room, a giant gift shop, and event spaces. The brand claims it's the largest distillery west of the Mississippi. I guess everything in Texas is actually bigger.

TX was started by entrepreneurs Leonard Firestone and Troy Robertson. In 2012, they introduced their first product, TX Blended Whiskey, which is a combination of sourced whiskies. The brand has since introduced TX Bourbon, which it makes from local ingredients and ages for at least four years.

In 2019, Pernod acquired TX's parent company, Firestone & Robertson Distilling Co., for an undisclosed amount.

Smooth Ambler

The Smooth Ambler distillery sits in the shadows of West Virginia's picturesque Appalachian Mountains. It was founded in 2009 by John Little and his father-in-law, Tag Galyean. Reportedly, Galyean read about the craft spirits movement in *Time* magazine the year before and proposed that the family go into the liquor business.

Smooth Ambler has put West Virginia on the world whiskey map with its range of bourbons and ryes.

Unlike some of its craft competitors, Smooth Ambler has been honest about sourcing some of its whiskey from other distillers—in particular from the colossal MGP distillery in Indiana. The brand's Old Scout line exclusively features bourbon and rye it has bought from other companies. Its Contradiction Bourbon and Contradiction Rye include whiskies that Smooth Ambler has produced as well as sourced from others. If you want to try the bourbon or rye that Smooth Ambler has made itself, pick up bottles of its Founders' Cask Strength Series.

In 2016, Pernod bought the brand for an undisclosed sum. At the time of writing, John Little is still running the distillery but has stepped down as head distiller.

🌿 BRANCH: PROXIMO

Proximo is the American subsidiary of famous tequila maker Jose Cuervo. Cuervo is the world's biggest tequila brand and is owned by the Beckmann family, direct descendants of Jose Antonio de Cuervo y Valdes, who started the company back in 1758. Beginning in the early 2000s, the company decided to diversify their liquor holdings beyond agave spirits, and have since expanded significantly into whiskey. Read on to see which brands are now under the Cuervo umbrella.

Stranahan's Colorado Whiskey

Stranahan's Colorado Whiskey is the first whiskey distillery in Colorado since Prohibition to get a distilling license. The brand was started by Jess Graber and George Stranahan and released its first whiskey in 2006. Originally, the distillery was next door to the Flying Dog brewery in Denver, which was also started by George Stranahan. The whiskey was initially made by distilling some Flying Dog beer. But after Flying Dog moved to Maryland, Stranahan's began producing its whiskey from scratch, using a mash of only malted barley.

Fans of Stranahan's limited-edition Snowflake Whiskey start camping out on the street in front of the Denver distillery several days before its annual December release.

The distillery now makes several different whiskies. The Stranahan's Original is 94 proof (47 percent alcohol by volume) and aged for at least four years in new

American oak barrels. Alternatively, the distillery finishes the Original in used 500-liter (132-gallon) oloroso sherry casks, for its Stranahan's Sherry Cask single malt. There is also Stranahan's Blue Peak, which is 86 proof (43 percent alcohol by volume) and aged using a modified solera system (see page 39) where the whiskey is aged in various types of barrels. The brand's most sough-after single malt is its limited-edition Snowflake Whiskey, which varies from year to year—just as no two snowflakes are the same. It is now so popular that people start lining up outside the distillery days before the whiskey's fall release, camping out right on the street despite often freezing temperatures.

Stranahan's is arguably the first American single malt to catch on. It was acquired by Jose Cuervo in 2010.

Tincup Whiskey

It's hard to miss Tincup Whiskey's distinctive six-sided bottle, which comes topped with a stout metal shot glass. The package always reminds me of a vintage Thermos that you might imagine a Colorado miner carrying to work in the morning. Tincup now bottles several whiskies, including Original, which is a blend of bourbon made in Indiana and Colorado single malt; Tincup Rye, which is 90 proof (45 percent alcohol by volume) and is three years old; and finally Tincup 10 Year, a bourbon. The brand was created by Jess Graber and was first introduced in 2014.

For the first time since at least the beginning of Prohibition, Manhattan has its first (and legal) whiskey distillery, Great Jones.

Great Jones Distilling Co.

In 2021, Manhattan got its first whiskey distillery in at least a century. The Great Jones Distilling Co. is located in an elegant facility in the middle of the fashionable NoHo neighborhood. It includes a restaurant, bar, and event spaces. In the middle of the building, showcased like a piece of art behind a glass wall, are the copper pot still and the column still. The brand's signature Great Jones Straight Bourbon is made exclusively from grains grown in

The Tincup Original Whiskey is an easy-drinking blend of bourbon and single malt.

New York State. You can also purchase two other Great Jones offerings produced from local ingredients, a Four Grain bourbon and a rye.

🌾 BRANCH: RÉMY COINTREAU

Most of the spirits in Rémy Cointreau's portfolio date back at least a century and are so well known that they need no introduction. Among these famous names is one of the company's newest purchases, Westland Distillery, which makes American single malt and is still relatively unknown. Read on for more about this innovative distillery.

Westland Distillery

One of the leaders of the American single malt catgeory is the Seattle, Washington–based Westland Distillery. Founded by Emerson Lamb and Matt Hofmann in 2010, Westland has successfully developed its own spin on single malt by featuring local Pacific Northwest ingredients and resources. As a result, it has been able to carve out its own identity, distinct from bourbon, rye, and even Scotch. Westland works with Washington State University's Breadlab in Skagit Valley to identify and grow regional heirloom barley strains. The company even funds a fellowship to support a graduate student's research at the Breadlab.

Westland's signature single malt is made from a range of different types of malted barley and is aged for a minimum of forty months in a number of different types of barrels. It is not chill filtered and no color has been added to the 92-proof (46 percent alcohol by volume) whiskey.

Westland's Outpost Range line offers a number of cutting-edge whiskies, including the Garryana (aged in barrels made from the local Garry oak variety), Colere (made from heirloom varieties of barley), and Solum (made with local peat).

Spirits conglomerate Rémy Cointreau bought the brand in 2016 for an undisclosed amount. Lamb and Hofmann are no longer involved in the brand.

Seattle's Westland ages some of its whiskies in barrels made from regional American oak species.

🌾 BRANCH: SAZERAC/ BUFFALO TRACE

In a relatively short amount of time, Sazerac has grown from a fairly small spirits company into one of the most influential whiskey producers in the world, with some of the most sought-after bourbon and rye brands. But long before it was linked to such bestsellers as Pappy Van Winkle, W.L. Weller, and Blanton's, the company began hundreds of miles away from Kentucky, in Florida—and, in fact, had nothing to do with whiskey.

From the turn of the twentieth century to Prohibition, Newman Goldring distributed Schlitz beer across northwest Florida. (At the time, Schlitz was the best-selling beer in the world.) After repeal, the Pensacola, Florida–based distributor branched out from just beer to work across the liquor industry. To help him run the business, Newman brought on his son, Stephen.

About a decade later, a few important events took place, all set in motion by Newman's retirement. At that point Stephen decided to partner with Malcolm Woldenberg, and they renamed the family business Magnolia Marketing Company. Magnolia became one of the largest liquor distributors in the United States, and then a central part of the powerhouse distributor RNDC (Republic National Distributing Company).

Stephen and his wife, Mathilde, also decided to move back to her hometown of New Orleans, Louisiana. They'd barely settled in when Magnolia bought the local Sazerac Company in fall of 1948. Sazerac was a famous French Cognac house, which exported a lot of its spirits to the United States. On Exchange Alley in New Orleans

From Sazerac Rye to Weller to Pappy Van Winkle, the Buffalo Trace Distillery in Frankfort, Kentucky, is home to a range of bestselling whiskies.

there was even the famous Sazerac coffee house named for the Cognac brand, which also sold a line of bottled cocktails and spirits. Some also insist, despite the lack of evidence, that the Sazerac Coffee House is where the classic rye whiskey cocktail, the Sazerac, was created and popularized.

Ultimately, Stephen used the Sazerac name for his liquor company and began acquiring and creating spirits brands. You might assume this is where Sazerac got into the whiskey business, but the company's first big hit was with Taaka Vodka. The bottom-shelf brand can still be found around New Orleans and across the South. The modern Sazerac company really began to emerge in the early 1980s, right around the hiring of Peter Bordeaux and Mark Brown. The '80s where a tumultuous time in the liquor business, with some categories exploding in popularity while others suddenly and dramatically fell out of favor. These were the perfect economic conditions for a contrarian investor looking to scoop up well-established brands for a huge discount—and that's exactly what Sazerac started doing under the leadership of Bordeaux and later Brown. William Goldring, Stephen's son, who had become chairman of Sazerac, prefers to stay out of the press, but under his watch the company's portfolio has exploded and now includes more than 450 brands across the spirits industry.

One of their first key acquisitions was Dr. McGillicuddy's schnapps in 1989, which had been owned by Seagram's. (The company also got Eagle Rare and Benchmark bourbons in the same deal.) While schnapps was a good seller in a number of Midwestern markets, Sazerac eventually relaunched one of the Dr. McGillicuddy's flavors as Fireball, which became a national sensation.

But the company's most important acquisition took place in 1992, when it bought the George T. Stagg distillery in Frankfort, Kentucky. It was known then for producing Ancient Age whiskey, but the facility had an incredibly rich history and was once owned by legends Col. Edmund Haynes Taylor Jr. (aka E. H. Taylor) and George T. Stagg. Sazerac would later rename the distillery Buffalo Trace. Thanks to these acquisitions, by 1992 the company was four times bigger than it had been in 1981.

Over the past nearly thirty years, Buffalo Trace has been able to elevate its roster of American whiskies to the point where they routinely command hundreds or even thousands of dollars a bottle—that is, if you can find a store that has them in stock.

The company's rarest whiskies are reserved for its Antique Collection, which is released each fall with great fanfare. (The first edition of the Antique Collection came out in 2000.) The collection generally includes five whiskies: William Larue Weller bourbon, Thomas H. Handy Sazerac rye, George T. Stagg bourbon, Eagle Rare 17-Year-Old bourbon, and Sazerac Rye 18-Year-Old. To demarcate these truly special spirits from its regular portfolio, Buffalo Trace uses a simple yet elegant bottle design for each release, no matter the brand. The whiskies have a suggested retail price of $99 per bottle, but in actuality they usually sell for ten or twenty times that amount.

Read on to learn more about some of Sazerac's now-famous whiskies.

Blanton's Bourbon

As recently as the early 2010s, Blanton's Bourbon was fairly easy to find and sold for around $35. Those days are now long gone. I haven't seen a bottle of Blanton's on a store shelf in years, and when I last did it was going for many times the suggested retail price.

Whiskey fans, speculators, and collectors have driven up the demand for Blanton's Bourbon, which now sells for well over $100—that is if you can find it.

What's fascinating is that, for a long time, Americans had very little interest in Blanton's or higher-end bourbons. This deluxe whiskey was created by George T. Stagg's master distiller, Elmer T. Lee, in 1984 and was named for Albert Blanton, who'd been the president of the distillery for decades.

Besides the horse-shaped stopper, what made Blanton's Bourbon unique is that Lee hand-selected each single barrel and bottled them without blending them. While selling single barrels is now routine, this was a completely new idea in the 1980s. If anything, most liquor companies saw no future for American whiskey—the idea of making a premium whiskey seemed especially foolhardy. However, Blanton's wasn't originally for Americans but rather the Japanese market. At the time, the George T. Stagg distillery was owned by the Japanese company Takara Shuzo. (Takara Shuzo no longer owns the distillery but retained the Blanton's brand.) Sazerac now makes the whiskey and has the license to sell it in the United States.

If you look closely at a group of Blanton's bottles, you'll notice that there are actually eight versions of its signature jockey-and-horse stopper. Each one features the animal in a different position, like a strip of images taken by nineteenth-century photographer Eadweard Muybridge. Some people like to collect all of the stoppers, while others try to track down the Blanton's made for duty-free or various export markets with different proofs from the standard bottle sold in the US.

Buffalo Trace Bourbon

You might assume that Buffalo Trace Bourbon dates back to the 1800s, but it was actually first introduced in 1999 when Sazerac renamed its distillery in Frankfort, Kentucky. Most of the company's other whiskies have become collectors' items and are nearly impossible to buy, but for the time being you can still easily buy this bourbon, which sells for around $30. I fear that its price will also inevitably skyrocket, but in the meantime I suggest stocking up on this bourbon, which is delicious on its own or in mixed drinks.

Eagle Rare Bourbon

Sazerac's first premium bourbon was none other than Eagle Rare, which the company acquired from a 1989 deal with Seagram's for seven spirits brands. (Seagram's originally introduced the whiskey in 1975 with a potent 101 proof (50.5 percent alcohol by volume). According to Mark Brown, who served for years as Sazerac's president and CEO, Seagram's refused to continue to make Eagle Rare on a contract basis after the acquisition, so Sazerac was forced to find a different whiskey supplier. As a result, the bourbon tasted drastically different and letters started pouring in from angry customers—an important lesson for Sazerac.

Today, I don't think you'll find too many complaints about this whiskey, which has grown into a three-bottle line. The standard Eagle Rare is at least ten years old, the Double Eagle Very Rare is a 20-year-old bourbon and comes in an impressive crystal decanter, and possibly the most popular version is the Eagle Rare 17-Year-Old, which is part of the annual Antique Collection release. If you're lucky enough to get a bottle of the 17-year-old, it will come with a letter giving detailed stats and information about the whiskey's distillation and aging.

E. H. Taylor was not only an American whiskey legend but also fought for the US government to create distilling standards.

E.H. Taylor, Jr.

E.H. Taylor, Jr. is a fairly new brand with historic roots. The modern incarnation was launched by Sazerac in 2017, after it got the rights to the name from Jim Beam. (Beam had acquired the intellectual property for Old Taylor Whiskey when it bought National Distillers and Chemical Corporation in 1987, but by the 2000s wasn't actually using the name for a brand.)

Col. Edmund Haynes Taylor Jr. was an actual person, an important and influential distiller. (To read about his fight against dishonest distilling practices, see page 86.) In 1879, Taylor sold his O.F.C. (which likely stands for Old Fashioned Copper or Old Fire Copper) and Carlisle distilleries to George T. Stagg, and built his own distillery.

About a century later, the O.F.C. distillery would become Buffalo Trace distillery. It's ironic that Buffalo Trace produces a whiskey in Taylor's honor because, in the 1890s, Taylor sued Stagg for selling whiskey under the Taylor name. Not only did Taylor get an injunction preventing Stagg from using his name, but he was awarded $50,000 in damages and, reportedly, the profits from twenty-two thousand barrels of whiskey that were sold bearing his name.

When Sazerac decided to revive the brand, they based the modern label and packaging on an original bottle and tube that was in the collection of one of Taylor's descendants. The E.H. Taylor, Jr. Collection now offers several different whiskies, including Small Batch, Single Barrel, and even a rye. Almost every Taylor whiskey is bottled-in-bond (see page 86), which is a federal government classification and a guarantee of quality that Taylor championed when he was alive. Whiskey collectors particularly seem to prize this brand—a full lineup of the eleven Taylor releases was advertised by an online liquor store for $60,000.

Elmer T. Lee Single Barrel

In 1949, Elmer T. Lee began working at the distillery that would become Buffalo Trace. Thirty-six years later, he would retire after an illustrious career. Lee famously created Blanton's Bourbon, which helped kick off the rebirth of American whiskey. The single barrel Elmer T. Lee was introduced after Lee officially stepped down, but was still working as an ambassador for the distillery. Lee passed away in 2013 at the age of ninety-three.

Old Rip Van Winkle

There is arguably no American whiskey more famous than Pappy Van Winkle. The short version of the brand's backstory is that Julian "Pappy" Van Winkle was a famous whiskey executive in the twentieth

All hail Pappy Van Winkle! The mania for this whiskey only seems to reach new heights each year.

century. His Louisville, Kentucky, distillery, Stitzel-Weller, made some of the most respected whiskies of the time, including W.L. Weller and Old Fitzgerald.

After he passed away, the distillery was sold and passed through several hands, but hasn't been used in more than thirty years and is currently owned by Diageo. (For the full Pappy story, see page 98.)

The one brand that his family didn't sell was Old Rip Van Winkle, which they likely acquired the rights to after Prohibition but had never actually used. In October 1973, Pappy's son, Julian P. Van Winkle Jr., started a wheated bourbon company using the Old Rip Van Winkle name, whose whiskey is now usually simply referred to as Pappy. Since the Van Winkle family no longer owned a distillery, they had to buy whiskey for their new venture on the open market, which they continued to do for decades. In 2002, Buffalo Trace agreed to produce, age, and bottle their entire line of whiskies. The arrangement allowed the Van Winkles access to a consistent and regular supply of whiskey, and Buffalo Trace was really the perfect partner, since it already made a wheated whiskey—Pappy's old brand, W.L. Weller.

Years ago, you could fairly easily find the Van Winkle whiskies, but they have become nearly impossible to buy and cost hundreds if not thousands of dollars a bottle of late. At this point, buying Hermès's coveted Birkin bag might be easier (and less expensive)!

The Old Rip Van Winkle 10 Year and the Van Winkle Special Reserve 12 Year are usually easier to buy and relatively less expensive—about $1,000 a bottle. The more sought-after whiskies are the Pappy Van Winkle 15 Year, the Pappy Van Winkle 20 Year, and the Pappy Van Winkle 23 Year. The Van Winkle Family Reserve Rye 13 Year is in short supply and always has been, since it was originally produced for the Japanese market.

The fact that Buffalo Trace was producing Pappy Van Winkle was supposed to help increase the supply of the brand on store shelves and possibly lower the price. But given that the demand for Pappy seems to be limitless, I haven't seen any more bottles of the whiskey available. Maybe one day the prices will start to come down and you'll be able to just walk into any store and pick up a bottle—but I suspect that day won't come for a long time.

In the early 2000s, Sazerac Rye became incredibly sought after by cocktail bartenders and whiskey drinkers.

Sazerac Rye

Arguably, the first American whiskey to go viral was Sazerac Rye 18 Year, which became a sensation in the early 2000s. The whiskey, which is a core member of the Antique Collection, is still in very high demand and goes for around $2,000 a bottle. You'll have a much easier time finding the 6-year-old Sazerac Rye, which costs a fraction of the price—about $30— and makes an excellent Manhattan.

George T. Stagg

George T. Stagg is an uncut and unfiltered bourbon, which means the proof can, impressively, go above 130 (65 percent alcohol by volume). It is aged for at least fifteen years in a new charred American oak barrel. Unfortunately, the whiskey is part of Buffalo Trace's Antique Collection and comes out just once a year, in the fall. According to lore the idea for Stagg, named for the former owner of the Buffalo Trace distillery, came from a consumer.

To capitalize on the popularity of the brand and increase supply, Buffalo Trace introduced Stagg Jr. in 2013. Like George T. Stagg, Stagg Jr. is an uncut and unfiltered bourbon but is a bit younger (though usually at least eight years old) and fortunately comes out twice a year. While it originally was supposed to be a more affordable option, Stagg Jr. now sells for many times its $50 suggested retail price.

W.L. Weller

One of Sazerac's most historic brands is W.L. Weller. The whiskey goes back to the 1800s and is named for its founder, William Larue Weller. It is a wheated bourbon, which means it is made from a mix of corn, malted barley, and wheat instead of the more common rye. (Maker's Mark, Old Fitzgerald, Pappy Van Winkle, and Larceny are the other well-known wheated bourbon brands on the market today.) Sazerac acquired Weller in 1999 in a four-company deal that essentially divvied up most of Diageo's remaining American whiskey assets. One reason Weller has become very popular is that the whiskey uses the same mash bill (mix of grains) that Buffalo Trace uses for making the Pappy Van Winkle line. While using the same mash bill will produce similar whiskies, how the whiskey is distilled and how it is aged plays a major part in its final taste.

Historically, Weller was not easy to find and was primarily distributed in Texas, Oklahoma, and Kansas. There is a great anecdote that Pulitzer Prize–winning journalist Robert Caro tells in his memoir, *Working*, about how President Lyndon B. Johnson would send one of his staffers to go by "plane from city to city until three cases" of Weller were found to give as a gift to influential Georgia Senator Richard B. Russell.

Drinkers today may not have to fly around the country to put together a case of signature W.L. Weller Antique, but the whiskey is in high demand and is now quite expensive (generally a bottle goes for well over $100). In addition, there is the even more expensive Weller Full Proof, which is a powerful 114 proof (57 percent alcohol by volume), and the Weller 12 Year. The brand's rarest whiskey is the William Larue Weller, which is part of Sazerac's scarce Antique Collection. The most affordable Weller is the Special Reserve, which is 90 proof (45 percent alcohol by volume) and sells for about $65.

Early Times

One of Sazerac's newest acquisitions is Early Times. The brand was purchased for an undisclosed amount from Brown-Forman in 2020 as part of a deal that also included Canadian Mist and Collingwood. Early Times is one of America's oldest whiskies—started in the 1860s or possibly the 1870s by John Henry "Jack" Beam (Jim Beam's uncle). At first, it was marketed as Early Times 1776 to take advantage of the importance of the American Revolution and a nostalgia for the country's rustic roots. (The brand trademarked a logo in 1887 that even featured a log cabin.)

When Brown-Forman purchased Early Times in 1923, it was an established and respected brand that had fallen on hard times. Thanks to Prohibition in the US, it might have disappeared for good like so many other American whiskey brands that were no longer able to sell their product. Brown-Forman, on the other hand, had a license to bottle so-called medicinal whiskey, and bought Early Times and its warehouses of bourbon to shore up its dwindling supplies.

After repeal, Brown-Forman marketed Early Times as a quality bourbon for a "modest price." The plan worked, and for decades sales were robust in both the United States and Japan. After the downturn in whiskey sales in the 1980s, Early Times was turned into an 80-proof (40 percent alcohol by volume) "American Style Whiskey" (that is, a blended whiskey) for the domestic market, relegating it to the bottom shelf. But in Japan and other foreign markets, Early Times remained a straight bourbon and a bestseller. Even after whiskey sales began to pick up again in the US, Early Times languished in the Brown-Forman portfolio behind the better-known Jack Daniel's, Old Forester, and Woodford Reserve.

Early Times Whiskey really dates from an earlier time—it was started in the late 1800s by Jim Beam's uncle, John Henry "Jack" Beam.

A decade before selling the brand, Brown-Forman reintroduced Early Times as a straight bourbon in the US. Currently, you can buy both the blended American whiskey version and a bottled-in-bond bourbon. It will be interesting to see what Sazerac does with Early Times. Since the summer of 2021, it is now being made at Sazerac's Barton 1792 distillery in Kentucky, which is very close to where Early Times was originally produced.

BRANCH: WILLIAM GRANT & SONS

William Grant & Sons is world famous for its portfolio of Scotch superstars, including bestsellers Glenfiddich, Balvenie, and Monkey Shoulder. Over the past fifteen years, the company has also added a number of American whiskies to its growing spirits portfolios. Read on for more about these acquisitions.

Fistful of Bourbon

You might mistake Fistful of Bourbon for the name of a spaghetti western, but it's actually an American whiskey made by William Grant & Sons. It was introduced in 2018 and is a blend of five straight bourbons, an interesting way to apply Scotch blending techniques and skill to making American whiskey. While it seems like suggested retail prices for American whiskey are going up every day, I applaud William Grant for making this quaffable bourbon affordable (it costs less than $30 a bottle).

One of the watershed moments in the American craft whiskey scene was the launch of New York's Hudson Whiskey in 2005.

Hudson Whiskey

When Hudson Whiskey was introduced in 2005, it was the first whiskey to be produced in New York State since Prohibition. It is made in the pioneering Tuthilltown distillery, which is located in the Hudson Valley and helped kick off the craft distilling movement in the US and around the world. (For more on its history and founders, see page 129.) When the brand first started out, it used small barrels to try to speed up the aging process, and was sold in diminutive 375-milliliter bottles. Over time, Tuthilltown graduated to using full-size barrels and selling full-size bottles.

After getting a packaging refresh in 2020, replete with punny names, the brand now sells Bright Lights, Big Bourbon, a straight bourbon that is at least three years old; Do the Rye Thing, a straight rye that is at least three years old; Short Stack, a rye whiskey aged for a second time in a barrel that has held maple syrup; Back Room Deal, a rye whiskey aged for a second time in barrels that have held peaty Scotch; and Four Part Harmony, a four-grain bourbon that is at least seven years old. Almost all of the distillery's whiskies are certified kosher.

The brand was bought by William Grant & Sons in 2010 for an undisclosed sum.

🌾 BRANCH: BACARDI

While the name Bacardi is synonymous with rum, the company has established a relatively large portfolio of spirits over the past few decades. About ten years ago, it got into the American whiskey industry with the purchase of Angel's Envy, an innovative brand that has become Bacardi's signature bourbon.

Angel's Envy

When Lincoln Henderson created Angel's Envy in 2011, he was already a bourbon legend who had worked at Brown-Forman as a distiller for decades and helped create some of the company's signature whiskies. At the age of seventy-three, along with his son Wes, he released one final whiskey, Angel's Envy. Given that it was started from scratch, the brand didn't have its own distillery yet, so they needed to buy whiskey from other makers. To put their own spin on the bourbon, Henderson decided to age it for a second time in casks that previously held port. These "port pipes" gave the whiskey a fruity sweetness and a delicious softness. While many American whiskey makers have since tried finishing their whiskey in a second type

Bourbon Hall of Famer Lincoln Henderson's last project before he passed away was creating Angel's Envy bourbon.

of barrel, it was a fairly groundbreaking idea at the time that Angel's Envy rolled out, setting it apart from other brands. It didn't hurt that those first releases were absolutely delicious. What also helped the brand catch on was its distinctive bottle design featuring, of course, angel wings.

Lincoln passed away in 2013, and two years later the brand was sold to Bacardi for a reported $150 million. The brand then built a distillery inside a beautiful nineteenth-century red brick warehouse right in Louisville, Kentucky, opening in 2016. Six years later it completed an $8.2 million expansion and renovation of the facility, which added 13,000 square feet (1,200 square meters) of room and a new visitor center.

Besides its signature port-finished bourbon, the Angel's Envy line now includes a selection of American whiskies that have been aged for a second time in a range of flavorful barrels, including a rye finished in a Caribbean rum cask and a bourbon finished in an oloroso sherry cask. One of the most sought-after Angel's Envy whiskies is its limited-edition Cask Strength Bourbon, released each fall.

BRANCH: KIRIN

of whiskey and a glass of beer is the most classic pairings. So, it ense that popular Japanese beer Kirin bought the historic Four rbon brand in 2002. Read on bout this whiskey distiller that o the late nineteenth century.

es Bourbon

s an incredibly rich history dramatic twists and turns to fill an Agatha Christie novel. Since its founding in the 1880s by Paul Jones Jr., the brand has made all kinds of whiskey at different points, including a straight bourbon, a blend of straight bourbons, and a blended whiskey. As a result, the reputation of Four Roses has also fluctuated depending on who was making it at the time. Fortunately, you can now buy straight Four Roses Bourbon in the United States and it once again commands respect from bartenders and drinkers.

By 1888, Jones saw real potential in the brand and registered the name. Four Roses was originally not a bourbon, and for decades was marketed simply as "whiskey." What was it? Well, Four Roses likely started out as rye. A liquor store in Birmingham, Alabama, ran a series of advertisements in its local newspaper in 1889 that stated "I have now in stock a brand of whisky known as Four Roses, which I positively guarantee to be 1874 Rye, and I can honestly say that I believe it to be the oldest and finest whiskey sold in the US." It was sold for $0.20 per glass or $2 per quart (liter). A few years later, another store in Galveston, Texas, called it Four Roses Rye in its ads selling the Paul Jones portfolio of whiskies.

Because Four Roses was produced at a number of different facilities in the early days, it really could have been several types of whiskey that were bottled back then. In *Four Roses: The Return of a Whiskey Legend*, Al Young, the brand's longtime distiller and advocate, corroborates this theory. He writes that Jones started out buying whiskey from a number of distilleries and blending them together, a standard practice in the industry at the time. Regardless of who was making the whiskey, the brand was developing a reputation for quality. By 1889, it was being

While most whiskey distilleries have just one main yeast strain, Four Roses makes bourbon using an incredible five different yeast strains.

advertised in newspapers by liquor stores as "the best whiskey on earth."

In 1890, Jones tried to secure a consistent supply of whiskey for his brands by buying the J. Mattingly 1845 distillery in Louisville, Kentucky, for $125,000. Unfortunately, according to Young there was a large fire that severely damaged the facility and prompted Jones to sell it again.

Paul Jones passed away suddenly on February 1895 at the age of fifty-five, and left the very valuable company to his nephews, Saunders and Lawrence Jones. Later, Lawrence would take full control of the business.

In 1922, a few years into Prohibition, Lawrence Jones was able to buy the Frankfort Distilling Company, including its distillery. It was a shrewd move since the company was also one of the few brands to be able to bottle so-called medicinal whiskey, available in drugstores to people with a prescription from a doctor or dentist. As a result, Four Roses could be purchased in pharmacies across the country. Bottles of the 100-proof (50 percent alcohol by volume) whiskey were packaged in eye-catching bright yellow cardboard boxes featuring the brand's signature red roses (see page 97). In 1929, the handful of medicinal whiskey companies were even allowed to produce some whiskey, since the country's pre-Prohibition stocks of alcohol were running low. The medicinal whiskey business not only made sure no one would forget Four Roses, but also provided the company with an essential (and rare) revenue stream.

After repeal, the brand was a blend of straight whiskies made in the company's four distilleries located in Kentucky and Baltimore, Maryland. Thanks to its medicinal whiskey sales, it had the funds to run tons of advertisements in national magazines such as *Esquire*, which often touted Four Roses' history and explained how to properly make classic cocktails, including Eggnog, the Manhattan, and the Old-Fashioned.

In 1941, Lawrence Jones passed away at the age of eighty-one and his estate sold the company to liquor conglomerate Seagram's for a staggering $43 million. While that would be a huge amount today, at the time it was an unholy sum, particularly in the wake of the country still recovering from the Great Depression. But it was a reasonable amount given that Four Roses was a bestseller and had a large stockpile of valuable whiskey.

Until late 1946, Four Roses remained a blend of straight whiskies, but like most American brands it was ultimately forced to make a blended American whiskey. While there was huge demand for straight whiskey from consumers, distilleries had been shut down to support the World War II effort. To stretch their meager supplies of straight whiskey, they combined it with neutral grain spirit—basically vodka.

Many of the bourbon brands switched back to making straight whiskey as soon as possible after World War II, but Seagram's decided that Four Roses would remain a blended American whiskey in the United States and be a straight bourbon in export markets. It seemed like an odd move, given that it destroyed the brand's famous reputation and turned it into a cheap whiskey. (According to the brand's advertisements that ran in the 1950s, an outrageous 60 percent of the whiskey was neutral grain spirit.) And that's not to mention that the demand for bourbon abroad was fairly small at the time. The only explanation for this move is that Seagram's had too many other bourbon, rye, and Scotch brands and didn't need Four Roses competing against them.

For many years, it seemed like Four Roses might die an agonizingly slow death on the bottom shelf—largely forgotten by drinkers and bartenders. But then a series of small miracles occurred. In 2000 Seagram's merged with French media company Vivendi, which decided to sell off its newly acquired liquor assets, including Four Roses and the Frankfort distillery. Pernod Ricard and Diageo teamed up to buy all of Seagram's brands and as soon as this monster deal closed in 2002, they sold Four Roses and its accompanying distillery to Japan's Kirin Brewery Company, which is known for its eponymous beer brand. Fortunately, Kirin wanted to sell straight bourbon in the United States and fix Four Roses' reputation in the industry. And that is exactly what it did.

One of the advantages of buying the Frankfort distillery was that it used a number of different yeast strains and mash bills. Kirin was able to use these different recipes to rebuild the Four Roses brand and create unique flavor profiles. As of this writing, Four Roses has a standard bourbon mash bill as well as a high-rye mash bill, which includes 15 percent more rye grain. These two mashes are fermented using five different yeast strains, which produces ten different bourbons. This approach is unique, given that most brands make one or two basic whiskies from a single yeast strain and one or two mash bills.

Currently, Four Roses makes a straight bourbon whiskey, which is 80 proof (40 percent alcohol by volume) and combines all ten of its whiskies; a Small Batch Bourbon, which is 90 proof (45 percent alcohol by volume) and calls for four of its whiskies; a Single Barrel bourbon, which is 100 proof (50 percent alcohol by volume) and is made from the high-rye mash bill; and a Small Batch Select, which is 104 proof (52 percent alcohol by volume) and calls for six of its whiskies. The brand also releases limited editions of extremely rare and interesting whiskies.

🌾 BRANCH: CONSTELLATION BRANDS

One of the greatest success stories in the American liquor business is Constellation Brands, whose origins go back to 1945 when it was a bulk wine business in upstate New York. Over the last eighty years, the company has grown into a publicly traded behemoth with an impressive roster of beer, wine, and spirits brands. In 2016, it added Utah's acclaimed High West Whiskey. Read on for more about this pioneering distillery that started right in Park City, Utah.

High West Whiskey

One of the most popular ways to finish a day of skiing in Park City, Utah, is to take a trail that leads you right into this bougie town. Naturally, the name of the trail is Quit 'N Time, and it's also no wonder that David Perkins and his wife, Jane, built their High West Saloon right at the spot. What could be more perfect than ending a run and then having a celebratory whiskey? But the couple didn't just want to serve booze—they wanted to make it too. So they constructed a very small distillery with a 250-gallon (950-liter) still. No matter the size of the operation, it was a huge step for famously dry Utah, and was in fact the state's first legal distillery in 136 years.

In 2006, Dave began to make whiskey. Three years later the couple opened the saloon, which doubled as a tasting room and advertising billboard. But High West really became successful once it started buying high-quality bourbon and rye from a number of distilleries and combining them to make innovative blends. Part of what distinguished High West from other upstart craft whiskey brands was that it was always up-front about where its whiskey had been made—even listing provenance on the label of the bottle.

High West also introduced two delicious bottled cocktails, a barrel-aged Manhattan and a barrel-aged Old-Fashioned. While those beverages now do not seem particularly newsworthy, at the time bottled cocktails were pretty revolutionary because few other brands were selling them in the US. In 2015, High West built a very large distillery just outside of town in Wanship, Utah, which will allow the brand to make increasingly more of the whiskey it sells instead of buying it.

Park City, Utah, has long been famous for its ski slopes, but it's also now known for its local whiskey brand, High West.

When High West really began to take off, the founders decided to sell the company. Interest was high from a number of major spirits conglomerates, which reportedly resulted in a bidding war. After the dust settled, Constellation Brands bought High West in October 2016 for an estimated $160 million. High West continues to bottle Bourye (a mix of bourbon and rye, naturally) as well as its flagship bourbon, a blend of straight bourbons; its Double Rye, which combines pot still and column still rye; and its Campfire, a blend of bourbon and rye, plus some superpeaty Scotch.

High West also makes the limited-edition A Midwinter Night's Dram, which is a rye whiskey aged for a second time in used port casks. It was originally introduced in 2012 and is now a collector's item fetching hundreds of dollars more than its suggested retail price of $150.

🌾 BRANCH: ILLVA SARONNO

It's hard to find a liquor store that doesn't stock bestsellers Disaronno or Tia Maria. The brands' parent company, Illva Saronno, has also begun to build a collection of all kinds of spirits, including Baltimore, Maryland–based craft whiskey distiller Sagamore Spirit. Read on for more about how the brand has tried to revive Maryland's rye distilling industry.

Sagamore Spirit

For the better part of two centuries, Maryland was famous for its rye whiskey distillers. But thanks to a combination of major and minor events, there wasn't much left of the state's distilling industry by the 1970s. Any surviving brands, such as Pikesville Rye, were bought up by Kentucky bourbon makers and relocated to the Bluegrass State. So, whiskey drinkers, and rye lovers in particular, were happy when Sagamore Spirit opened its distillery in Baltimore, Maryland, in spring 2017. The company was launched just a few years earlier by Kevin Plank and Bill McDermond. Plank is one of Baltimore's biggest boosters and most famous residents, due to the success of the other local company he started, sports apparel brand Under Armour.

Sagamore produces a Core Collection, which includes a signature Rye Whiskey, a Cask Strength Rye Whiskey, a Double Oak Rye Whiskey, and also a Bottled-in-Bond Rye Whiskey. There is also a Reserve Series of limited-edition whiskies, which has included a rye whiskey finished in a rum cask and one finished in a port cask.

In 2023, the brand sold a majority stake to Italian spirits company Illva Saronno for an undisclosed price. Sagamore joins Disaronno and Tia Maria in Illva Saronno's portfolio.

🌾 BRANCH: DEUTSCH FAMILY WINE & SPIRITS

Since its founding in 1981, Deutsch Family Wine & Spirits has worked with some of the biggest wine brands in the world. While wine is still the main part of the company's business, it also has a small roster of spirits, including rye whiskey Redemption. Read on for more about this pioneering craft brand.

Redemption Whiskey

Looking at Redemption Whiskey's decanter-like bottle, you might assume it's been around for more than a century. The brand actually dates only to 2010, but it was one of the first new rye whiskies to come on the market in decades.

Redemption was founded by spirits entrepreneurs Dave Schmier and Michael Kandar, who bought the whiskey from the large MGP distillery in Lawrenceburg, Indiana. (MGP would soon become a source of whiskey for dozens and dozens of brands across the country.) Schmier and Kandar went on to sell the company to Deutsch Family Wine & Spirits in 2015 for an undisclosed amount, making it the first aged whiskey brand for Deutsch, which was more famous for its wine portfolio.

Redemption's signature whiskey is, of course, its rye. It's made from 95 percent

Redemption Rye was introduced in 2010 and helped re-establish the straight rye whiskey category in America.

taste the 18-year-old when it came out, and while I was super excited given the age of the whiskey, it was very tannic from so many years in the barrel. I would suggest skipping these vintage spirits and instead using your money to buy bottles of Redemption's signature rye.

🌾 BRANCH: HOTALING & CO.

In the second half of the nineteenth century, the most renowned liquor distributor in San Francisco was Hotaling & Co., which handled a number of famous brands, including sought-after American whiskey J.H. Cutter. Hotaling's notoriety only grew when its warehouse miraculously survived the devasting 1906 earthquake that destroyed most of the city.

In 2017, the Anchor Distilling Company, which originally had been founded by legendary entrepreneur Fritz Maytag, parted ways with Anchor Brewing, which was sold to the Japanese Sapporo Holdings. As a result of the sale, the spirits division had to rename itself and in early 2018 chose to resuscitate the Hotaling & Co. name. Its portfolio started with Maytag's truly old-school rye whiskey brand Old Potrero and gin brand Junipero, and has since grown to include spirits from around the world.

Find out more about Old Potrero and how it helped start the rebirth of rye in the United States and around the world.

Old Potrero

Fritz Maytag may well be the patron saint of lost causes. On a whim as a young man, he saved San Francisco's historic Anchor Brewery from closing down. If that wasn't enough to write him into beverage history, he went on to start a spirits company

rye grain, which is quite high and packs a spicy punch with a bit of oak sweetness. (The remaining 5 percent of the mash bill is malted barley.) This 92-proof (46 percent alcohol by volume) whiskey is still made at MGP. Redemption also bottes a Bourbon and a High Rye Bourbon. In recent years, Redemption has received a lot of attention for its Specialty Series, which includes a version of its standard rye that has been finished in Jamaican and Barbadian rum casks.

If you're looking for more mature spirits, there is a range of barrel proof bourbons and ryes that have been aged about ten years. Redemption also created a bit of buzz in 2017 by introducing six hundred bottles of an 18-year-old rye whiskey and eighteen bottles of an absolutely ancient 36-year-old rye. The original suggested retail price of the 36-year-old was $1,200 and by 2023 a bottle of it sold in a Sotheby's auction for $18,000. I got to

that would produce Junipero, an old-school type of gin, and Old Potrero, an old-school type of pot still rye whiskey.

To say Fritz was ahead of the curve is a massive understatement. When he started making spirits in 1993 there was, in fact, no curve to speak of. At the time, all of the other spirits companies were cutting rye whiskey production back to the bare minimum (one day a year) and contemplating getting rid of rye altogether. Fritz's Old Potrero was the first new rye whiskey to come out in years—and the market didn't really know what to make of it. It was so unusual and so different from bourbon or even Scotch that bartenders and drinkers weren't sure what it was or how to drink it. But Maytag persevered and slowly got the whiskey world to begin thinking and learning about straight rye—a major victory in itself. His brand in many ways laid the groundwork for the rebirth of rye whiskey as a whole.

Maytag ultimately sold his brewery and spirits business, but Old Potrero continues to be made and is currently in the Hotaling & Co. portfolio. I recently tasted it again, bracing myself for what I remembered as a heavy-handed dose of rye. But instead the whiskey was enjoyable and flavorful, with just enough rye. (While there's no doubt the whiskey has changed over the past three decades, so has my palate.) Perhaps Maytag was right all along?

In 1993, San Francisco entrepreneur Fritz Maytag revived one of the earliest styles of whiskey produced in the United States—straight rye whiskey made in copper pot stills.

BRANCH: EDRINGTON

From The Macallan to Highland Park to Glenrothes, the Scotches in Edrington's portfolio need no introduction. But among these brand titans is a relatively new upstart, Wyoming Whiskey. Read on for more about this pioneering distillery and its founders.

Wyoming Whiskey

Until 2009, there had not been a legal whiskey distillery in Wyoming since before Prohibition. Lawyers Kate and Brad Mead changed that when they built one on their cattle ranch in the small town of Kirby. With the help of their fellow attorney David DeFazio and some famed Kentucky distillers, including Lincoln Henderson and Steve Nally, they purchased a 35-foot-tall (11-meter) copper column still from Louisville, Kentucky–based Vendome Copper & Brass Works and began producing a Small Batch Bourbon Whiskey using local corn, barley, wheat, and water. The resulting whiskey is aged for at least five years on the property and is a unique 44 percent alcohol by volume, which was done intentionally because Wyoming was America's forty-fourth state.

The company has since introduced a range of different whiskies, including the Double Cask Bourbon Whiskey, which is aged for a second time in used sherry casks; the Single Barrel Bourbon Whiskey, which is by its very nature a limited edition; and a National Parks whiskey series that raises money for the National Park Foundation.

In 2018, Wyoming Whiskey sold a 35 percent stake in the company to the famous Scottish whisky company Edrington. In April 2023, Edrington increased its share of the company to 80 percent.

🌱 BRANCH: INDEPENDENTS

When I started writing about cocktails and spirits in the late 1990s, American whiskey was generally undervalued compared to other types of liquor, like pricey imported Scotch and vodka. At the time, stores and bars stocked just a handful of famous bourbons and Tennessee whiskies—and this selection of whiskies rarely changed. I wouldn't have believed you then if you told me that we were on the cusp of a new golden age for American whiskey. What helped breathe new life and energy into this historic category was the rise of craft distilleries, which started in the late 2000s. These independent operations had the freedom to make wildly new whiskies and take distilling risks. Most importantly they helped get drinkers and bartenders excited about American whiskey again. While a number of these pioneering brands have now been bought by large conglomerates, there are still plenty of independent distilleries around the United States that you should check out.

Blackened Whiskey

Blackened Whiskey was started by the Grammy Award–winning heavy metal band Metallica. It launched in 2018 with a blended American whiskey created by itinerant master distiller and spirits consultant Dave Pickerell. He was an obvious choice for Metallica, since he not only had

Famed heavy metal rock band Metallica teamed up with veteran distiller Dave Pickerell to create its whiskey brand, Blackened.

access to whiskey but also the know-how and ingenuity to create a unique brand. For this project, he decided to use a controversial sonic aging technique. The basic idea is that low-hertz sound waves help the whiskey go in and out of the wood cells within a barrel, which allows it to pick up ever more flavor and nuance. And, naturally, the sound waves that he would be blasting in the warehouse would be music from Metallica's catalog. In fact, the band members created playlists of their songs for each batch. (You could, conceivably, listen to those playlists as you drink the whiskey.)

Pickerell passed away just a few months after creating Blackened. He was succeeded by Rob Dietrich, previously the master distiller at Stranahan's in Denver, Colorado. (For more about Stranahan's, see page 162.) Blackened's signature whiskey is a blend of straight bourbons and ryes aged in a brandy cask. In 2022, Dietrich introduced the limited-edition Rye the Lightning, which is a straight Kentucky rye that has been aged again in madeira and rum barrels. (The whiskey's name is, of course, a play on the name of Metallica's second album, *Ride the Lightning*.)

Dietrich has also introduced a number of other special editions, including the Masters of Whiskey Series, which showcases collaborations between him and other well-known distillers. The first Masters of Whiskey release was a straight rye aged in madeira casks, which Dietrich produced with Willett's master distiller, Drew Kulsveen. (For more about Willett, see page 194.)

Castle & Key

Over the past decade, Castle & Key has risen from the ruins of bourbon legend E. H. Taylor's ornate Old Taylor distillery in Frankfort, Kentucky.

When the facility opened in 1886, it immediately became a landmark—the original design included a castlelike facade, a sunken garden, and other fanciful touches more befitting a European palace than a bourbon distillery.

Thanks to the crash of the American whiskey market, the distillery was shut down in 1972. Ultimately, Beam acquired Old Taylor and the distillery when it bought National Distillers and Chemical Corporation in 1987. Sazerac then was able to get the Taylor brand name from Beam and relaunch it in 2017. But the fate of the distillery looked pretty bleak. By 2010 when I visited the site, the buildings seemed too far gone to even offer a prayer that someone would rescue this piece of bourbon history before the vines and earth swallowed it up.

Fortunately, that is exactly what happened. In 2014, Will Arvin and Wes Murray heard about the distillery and decided to take on the Herculean challenge. The reported cost of the 83-acre (34-hectare) property and the remaining buildings was $950,000 and the initial budget forecast to get it back into working order was more than $6 million. Amazingly, many of the original structures were somehow saved and are once again being used.

Not only has the Old Taylor distillery been rebuilt, it is once again producing whiskey. Because Sazerac now makes Taylor whiskey at its own distillery, which is about 10 miles (16 kilometers) away, Arvin and Murray renamed their brand Castle & Key. (The "Castle" because of the building's famous design, the "Key" because the elegant springhouse has a keyhole-shaped water reservoir.) The original launch team included master distiller Marianne Eaves, the first woman in Kentucky ever to hold that title. (She left Castle & Key in 2019.)

In 2018, the newly revived distillery officially reopened, and two years later the aptly named Restoration Rye Whiskey was released. Castle & Key now sells a small-batch bourbon and a small batch wheated bourbon as well.

Frey Ranch Whiskey

While there are plenty of farm-to-table restaurants across the US, there aren't many American grain-to-glass spirits brands that grow their own grains. This is ironic, given that whiskey started out as something made by famers from their crops. Frey Ranch distillery in Fallon, Nevada, is one of the few modern distilleries to grow all of its own grains and distill and age all of its whiskey. The founders of the brand, Ashley and Colby Frey, grow corn, wheat,

Ashley and Colby Frey not only created their own eponymous Nevada whiskey brand, but also grow all the grains for it on their family's ranch.

rye, and barley on their family's 1,500-acre (600-hectare) ranch. In 2006, they decided to build a distillery and warehouse and begin producing a bourbon made from all four grains that they grow. Frey Ranch's line now also includes a bottled-in-bond rye, which is made completely from rye and is five years old. The company also has a single barrel program of bourbons and ryes.

High Wire Distilling

The first time I met Scott Blackwell he was talking at length about Southern folk art and I almost took him for a gallery owner before realizing he was cofounder of High Wire Distilling. But the distillery, which he started in 2013 in Charleston, South Carolina, with his wife, Ann Marshall, is just the latest project in a fascinating and diverse career. Blackwell has previously distributed ice cream, run a café, been a coffee roaster, and started the Immaculate Baking Company, which General Mills acquired in 2012. High Wire opened a year later and soon it established itself with a range of spirits that featured eye-catching labels that almost resemble vintage movie posters.

While Blackwell and Marshall could have played it safe, they decided to push the envelope with their Revival Rye, which is now completely made from the heirloom rye variety Wrens Abruzzi. Until recently, most rye whiskey brands bought the same commercially grown rye that weren't designed or particularly suited for

To make its signature Jimmy Red Bourbon, High Wire Distilling in Charleston, South Carolina, had to revive a lost heirloom strain of local corn.

making spirits. But historically, distillers would have used different types of rye, selected because they made a particularly flavorful whiskey.

The experience of making Revival Rye inspired another High Wire heirloom grain creation, Jimmy Red Straight Bourbon Whiskey, which is made with a type of corn that was historically grown on nearby James Island. By the time Blackwell and Marshall heard about it from heirloom grain legend Glenn Roberts, Jimmy Red was more lore than a viable crop, and no one was sure what whiskey made from it would taste like. Thanks to Blackwell's baking history, he had a hunch that the bright red and magenta kernels, which were as far as you can possibly get from common sweet yellow corn, would work for bourbon. But it wasn't easy to resuscitate Jimmy Red—it took six years to propagate the corn and have enough to make whiskey. But it was more than worth the effort. Now the brand harvests more than 1 million pounds (450,000 kilograms) of the special corn each year and produces a limited edition of highly sought-after bottles. The bourbon is aged for two years in heavily charred American oak barrels and is one of the most exciting additions to American whiskey.

Keeper's Heart Whiskey

It's not often that a brand introduces a completely new type of whiskey, but that's exactly what the Minneapolis, Minnesota–based Keeper's Heart has done with its Irish + American whiskey. For its signature product, the brand blends together Irish pot still whiskey, Irish grain whiskey, and American rye whiskey. There is also now

Running the stills at the O'Shaughnessy Distilling Co. in Minneapolis is Irish whiskey legend Brian Nation, who previously was the master distiller at the historic Midleton distillery in Cork.

an Irish + Bourbon, which combines bourbon with Irish pot still whiskey, and there is a 10-year-old Irish single malt.

Currently, all the whiskey the brand is selling has been bought from other distilleries. But the Keeper's Heart distillery is equipped with a range of different types of stills, including three copper pot stills, and they will soon be bottling whiskey made on site.

Keeper's Heart was created by members of the O'Shaughnessy family, which have deep roots in Minnesota. They built a modern distillery in St. Paul, Minnesota, that opened in the summer of 2021. Arguably, their most important achievement was getting Brian Nation, the former master distiller at Ireland's famous Midleton distillery, to move to Minnesota and make their whiskey. They also enlisted Dave Perkins, the founder of High West, to help with sourcing and blending the whiskies.

Keeper's Heart has been so successful that it inspired a few other brands to blend American and Irish whiskey together. Nation and Perkins make it look easy with their tasty and balanced whiskies, but it is actually quite difficult to do. Proceed with caution when trying some of the other international combos on the market.

Kings County Distillery

While it's often said that you can find anything in New York City if you look hard enough, from the start of Prohibition in 1920 until 2010, the Big Apple didn't have a single distillery. That changed when Colin Spoelman and David Haskell opened Kings County. (Kings County is an actual county in New York that is mostly made up of the borough of Brooklyn.) While the name of the distillery makes

When Kings County Distillery opened in 2010 it was making whiskey on tiny 24-liter stainless steel stills. It has since moved to a much larger space with three full-size copper pot stills.

it sound grandiose, its roots are very humble. It started in a tiny, 325-square-foot (30-square-meter) space in East Williamsburg. At the time, the whiskey was made in five 24-liter stainless steel stills. A couple of years later, the distillery moved to a much bigger space in the old Brooklyn Navy Yard. It also upgraded its equipment to three larger copper pot stills—two made by the Scottish company Forsyths and one by the American company Vendome.

It's easy to spot Kings County's whiskies because they come in a distinctive clear glass flask with a small paper label that looks like it was produced on a typewriter. The company's flagship line includes a straight bourbon, a blended bourbon, and a single malt. Its most distinctive whiskey is a peated bourbon, which is made with corn, rye, and some Scottish peated barley malt that gives it a good hint of smoke. Kings County also has a portfolio of unaged whiskies, including

Leopold Bros. in Denver, Colorado, is home to the only working three-chamber still in existence, which it uses to make its acclaimed rye whiskey.

a pretty good Chocolate Whiskey made with ground cacao bean husks.

Leopold Bros.

Leopold Bros. is the most important whiskey distillery that most folks have never heard of.

The Denver, Colorado–based company was started by two brothers, Todd and Scott Leopold, who continue to run it today. The pair grew up in Colorado but started out in the spirits industry by opening a brewery in Ann Arbor, Michigan. Todd went to the Siebel Institute of Technology in Chicago to learn about traditional and historic Germanic methods of beer brewing. (Scott went to Northwestern to study economics and environmental engineering, then to Stanford for a master's degree in environmental engineering.) Working in a brewery is a wonderful background for a whiskey distiller, since you first need to make beer in order to make whiskey.

Fortunately for whiskey drinkers, the Leopolds' days of brewing lagers and porters were curtailed fairly soon. A rent hike forced them to reconsider Ann Arbor, and they decided to relocate to an office park in Denver. They also decided to focus on making spirits.

Most importantly, Todd found a new passion: the three-chamber still. He discovered this piece of distilling technology in a 1907 study from the Bureau of Internal Revenue and became convinced that he needed to have one built. The still was an important innovation in American distilling history and a crucial step in the industry's move from pot stills to column stills. It created a style of whiskey that was distinct from what distillers were making in Scotland or Ireland.

Fortunately, his brother Scott signed off on the project and they somehow convinced Kentucky still maker Vendome Copper & Brass Works to build one of these expensive contraptions for them. The whiskey produced by the chamber still was even better than anyone could have imagined, with an incredible richness and complexity. (For more on how the three-chamber still works, see page 63.)

While Leopold Bros. still makes bourbon and Maryland Rye Whiskey in its pot stills, its focus is now on rye made in its three-chamber still, which is truly a taste of whiskey history. It is bottled on its own or blended with rye whiskey made by George Dickel for a special Collaboration Blend, which was inspired by Todd's research into late nineteenth century distilling practices. The Collaboration Blend is likely what American rye whiskey tasted like before Prohibition.

Lock Stock & Barrel

Spirits entrepreneur Rob Cooper launched Lock Stock & Barrel in 2013. He was one of the early proponents of rye and had a real talent for spotting and fostering trends. His family had been in the spirits business for a long time and he had created the popular St-Germain Elderflower Liqueur, which he sold to Bacardi for an undisclosed sum. (For more of Cooper's story, see page 127.)

At first, Cooper tried to buy rye from large American producers, but struck out because they didn't have much stock of the whiskey. He didn't give up and was able to find high-quality straight rye whiskey at a distillery in Alberta, Canada. The first edition of Lock Stock & Barrel was a 13-year-old whiskey. Over the years, the brand has released more of that whiskey as a 16-year-old, then as an 18-year-old, and finally as a 20-year-old offering.

Cooper also launched the related Hochstadter's Slow & Low Rock & Rye, which was essentially his attempt at bottling an Old-Fashioned. He released this historic whiskey-based liqueur (which had been touted as a cure for tuberculosis in the late nineteenth century) in full-size glass bottles and in small cans. Cooper created the formulation with well-known craft cocktail bartenders Chad Solomon and Christy Pope. The married couple, and later business partners, spent hours tweaking the cocktail recipe with Cooper, so it worked as a premade drink. Cooper launched the brand well before the modern canned and bottled cocktail boom. No surprise that he was once again on the forefront of a trend.

Cooper tragically passed away in 2016 at the age of just thirty-nine, but Lock Stock & Barrel and Hochstadter's Slow & Low Rock & Rye continue today and are run by his widow, Katie Cooper.

Michter's

Some of the most prized American whiskies today are made by Louisville, Kentucky–based Michter's. The brand's

One of the must-see attractions in Louisville, Kentucky, is Michter's Fort Nelson distillery, which includes a visitor center and a cocktail bar.

bourbons and ryes have a delicious richness and uncommon complexity that grabs your attention immediately. These are truly special whiskies.

While you might be tempted to think that Michter's is connected to one of the famous bourbon families, the modern iteration of the brand was in fact created by native New Yorker and Harvard Law School graduate Joe Magliocco. He first heard of Michter's while he was working for a local distributor during summers when he was off from college at Yale. At the time, the brand was located in Pennsylvania. The distillery's name, according to whiskey expert Lew Bryson, was dreamed up in 1950 by the owner at the time, Louis Forman, who mashed up the first names of his sons, Michael and Peter.

After the collapse of the American whiskey industry in the 1970s, Michter's fell on hard times and finally closed for good on Valentine's Day 1989. It seemed that the brand was destined to be lost to history, but in the 1990s Magliocco had the idea to bring the brand back. The prospects for Michter's were so bad that by that point the owners had walked away and abandoned the name and intellectual property. It was essentially Magliocco's for free, but he'd have to rebuild the company from the ground up. That would be no easy task, and was especially hard for someone who wasn't from Kentucky or related to one of the bourbon dynasties—but Magliocco was determined and focused.

The secret to the quality of his whiskey was that he hired

Michter's prides itself on not taking any shortcuts when it comes to making its whiskey—and you can certainly taste the difference.

industry veterans, such as master distiller Willie Pratt and his successor, Pam Heilmann, who had the freedom and authority to make the best whiskey they could. If the bourbon needed another six months of barrel aging, so be it. (This policy frustrated the sales force, who could hardly keep up with the demand, and earned Pratt the nickname "Dr. No" for denying their requests for more whiskey.) At the time of writing, Dan McKee, who was trained by Heilmann, is now the brand's master distiller.

When Michter's started, it made its whiskey in another distillery to Pratt's exacting standards. In 2015, the brand completed its own distillery in the Shivley neighborhood of Louisville. It uses old-school distilling and maturation practices, such as filling the barrels with alcohol at a lower proof and heating the warehouses, both of which are more expensive but yield delicious whiskey. Currently, Michter's produces a well-edited selection of whiskies: US 1 Kentucky Straight Rye, US 1 Kentucky Straight Bourbon, US 1 American Whiskey, and US 1 Sour Mash—all whiskies you have a shot at actually buying. The company also makes a 10-year-old straight bourbon, a 10-year-old straight rye, a 20-year-old straight bourbon, a 25-year-old Kentucky straight rye, and a 25-year-old straight bourbon. These are ever harder and more expensive to buy and some can fetch prices in the tens of thousands.

Visitors to Louisville should stop by Michter's Fort Nelson distillery, which is downtown and across the street from the

Louisville Slugger Museum & Factory. Not only did Magliocco save the Michter's name from disappearing, but he also saved the Fort Nelson building, which dates back nearly two centuries and was where Union soldiers in the Civil War gathered. Rebuilding Fort Nelson was a major job that took years, cost a small fortune, and involved many incredibly dramatic twists and turns before being completed. I dare say it was worth it. The gorgeous building, complete with a turret, now houses a small distillery, bar, and gift shop. The fermenters and copper pot still, which are used on a regular basis, are actually from the original Michter's distillery in Pennsylvania and link the brand's two historic chapters.

New Riff

New Riff, a relative newcomer to the American whiskey industry, has been in business only since 2014. It's located in Kentucky on the banks of the Ohio River, right across from Cincinnati, Ohio. While this might seem a bit far from the bourbon centers of Louisville, Kentucky, and Bardstown, Kentucky, during the 1900s the area was home to many distilleries. The company was started by Ken Lewis, who'd previously owned the liquor store The Party Source, which is located right across the street from New Riff.

Most of the whiskey the distillery produces qualifies for the bottled-in-bond designation, once the gold standard for bourbon and rye. (For more on the influential 1897 Bottled-in-Bond Act, see page 86.) Currently, New Riff has a flagship bourbon and rye as well as a series of limited-edition experimental whiskies, including one made from exclusively malted rye and another made from the heirloom grain called Turkey Red wheat.

New Riff is based in Newport, Kentucky, which is just across the Ohio River from Cincinnati.

New York Distilling Company

For years bartender, spirits educator, and consultant Allen Katz was on a personal mission to save American rye whiskey. Katz was one of a handful of rye whiskey evangelizers who shared the rich history and joys of drinking rye with bartenders, journalists, and just about anyone who would listen.

So, it was no surprise when Katz joined up with Tom Potter, the cofounder of the trailblazing Brooklyn Brewery, to start making rye whiskey. Their distillery, New York Distilling Company, opened in 2011 and was located inside an old corrugated steel warehouse in Williamsburg, Brooklyn. On a hybrid pot/column still built by the German manufacturer CARL, the company began producing Ragtime Rye and Mister Katz's Rock & Rye, a historic whiskey-based liqueur that is very similar to a bottled Old-Fashioned. Katz and Potter gained the respect of the industry by not selling any whiskey before it was at least several years old and using only full-size barrels to age their whiskey. They supported the operation by making a number of different gins, including their signature Dorothy Parker and Perry's Tot.

All of the New York Distilling Company's ryes are made from at least 75 percent New York State rye, and qualify for the Empire Rye designation as a result. The company also worked with the seed savers program at Cornell University to find an heirloom variety of rye grain. They settled on the Horton strain and had it propagated on an upstate New York farm. Now, all of the company's whiskies incorporate some of the historic grain in their mash bills.

In 2023, the New York Distilling Company moved its operation to a new facility several miles away in Bushwick, Brooklyn, which tripled its whiskey production capacity. At the same time, the company retired Ragtime Rye and introduced its new 92-proof (46 percent alcohol by volume) Jaywalk Straight Rye as well as the 100-proof (50 percent alcohol by volume) Jaywalk Bonded Rye that is aged seven years. The distillery's new signature is its 7-year-old Jaywalk Heirloom Rye that is bottled at cask strength at 114 to 116 proof (57 to 58 percent alcohol by volume) and is made from a mash of 75 percent heirloom Horton Rye and 25 percent organic Field Race Rye.

No matter which Jaywalk whiskey you try, you'll find an unusually rich and complex rye that is delicious in a cocktail or sipped neat.

Pinhook Bourbon

For seven years, Sean Josephs owned and ran Brooklyn's pioneering whiskey bar and restaurant Char No. 4. The establishment took its name from how American whiskey distillers used to specify the level of charring they wanted on the inside of their barrels. In 2010, Josephs launched Pinhook with a few friends by sourcing barrels from different distilleries and blending the whiskey together. By 2020, the brand found a permanent production partner in the Castle & Key distillery located in Frankfort, Kentucky, which had been built originally by legendary distiller E. H. Taylor. Josephs continues to serve as Pinhook's master blender and creates the formula for each whiskey himself.

Before starting Pinhook Bourbon, founder Sean Josephs ran acclaimed Brooklyn whiskey bar Char No. 4.

AMERICAN WHISKEY

If you look closely, you'll notice that the design of St. George's distillery was inspired by Alexandre Gustave Eiffel.

Pinhook releases a vintage of its Flagship Bourbon and its Flagship Rye each year, as well as a number of other special bottlings. Before Josephs got into the whiskey business, he worked as a sommelier at legendary Manhattan restaurant Chanterelle. His blending philosophy is that, just as wine changes from vintage to vintage, each Pinhook release should showcase its differences.

St. George Spirits

In an oversized former airplane hangar across the bay from San Francisco is one of the oldest craft distilleries in the United States, St. George Spirits. The brand was started in 1982 by German immigrant Jörg Rupf. And while the company has become well known for its line of gins that feature a range of unusual botanicals, when master distiller Lance Winters joined the company in 1996 he decided to make an American single malt. It was a questionable move, given that almost no whiskey distilleries outside of Scotland, Ireland, and Japan were making that style of whiskey at the time. Winters was ahead of the curve on American single malt and the perfect person to make this style of whiskey—the former US Navy nuclear submarine engineer brings an unusually high level of curiosity and old-fashioned Yankee know-how to creating and producing spirits. His first single malt vintage was introduced in 2000 and he continues to make the whiskey to this day.

In 2015, St. George began producing a whiskey for the local Oakland, California, restaurant Ramen Shop, which lead to the creation of the distillery's Japanese-inspired Baller American Single Malt Whiskey. The base spirit is made completely from malted barley in a pot still, which is then aged in American and French oak barrels before being charcoal filtered and finally finished in barrels that previously held the tart Japanese plum liqueur umeshu. And since it is St. George we're talking about here, the distillery naturally produces the umeshu itself from locally grown fruit. While Baller requires quite a few steps to make, I would argue it's more than worth the effort. The

Nathan "Nearest" Green was Jack Daniel's original master distiller and in 2016 his story inspired the creation of the Uncle Nearest Whiskey brand.

whiskey has almost tropical fruit notes and a whisper of smoke that work beautifully with the barley base notes. In addition to its single malt, the distillery also bottles an American whiskey called Breaking & Entering that it sources from Kentucky and Tennessee distilleries.

Uncle Nearest Premium Whiskey

Uncle Nearest is a modern brand with a fascinating history. Founder Fawn Weaver read a story by Clay Risen that ran in the *New York Times* in 2016 about the history of Jack Daniel's and the brand's original distiller, Nathan "Nearest" Green. Daniel had met Green when he was enslaved and making whiskey on Rev. Dan Call's farm in Lynchburg, Tennessee. In 1866, when Daniel decided to build his own nearby distillery, he hired Green to make his now famous whiskey. While many brands south of the Mason-Dixon Line were chiefly created and produced by enslaved people, we don't know much about them. Horrifically, but perhaps not surprisingly, their contributions have been falsely credited to the white plantation owners.

Despite living across the country in Los Angeles and having no distilling experience, Weaver decided that she would start a brand that honors Green. She not only succeeded but has been able to build a 323-acre (131-hectare) $50 million distillery in Shelbyville, Tennessee. To close the historic circle, Uncle Nearest's master blender is none other than Green's direct descendant, Victoria Eady Butler. (Emmy Award–winning actor Jeffrey Wright is also an investor in the company.)

Uncle Nearest launched in 2017 with its Uncle Nearest 1856 Premium Whiskey, which was made by another Tennessee whiskey distillery. The brand then released Uncle Nearest 1884 Small Batch Whiskey, which is aged, distilled, and bottled at its own facility.

Westward Whiskey

Christian Krogstad had always dreamed of being a brewer and winemaker. Fortunately for spirits drinkers, those careers didn't work out and he moved on to making hard liquor. Today, Krogstad is considered one of the creators of the craft spirits industry and helped kick-start the now global movement.

Using his beer-making experience, Krogstad started producing Westward American single malt in 2004 in his Portland, Oregon, distillery. The base of the whiskey is essentially a pale ale beer made from locally malted barley. It is then distilled twice in a custom-made hybrid

One of the brands you can thank for establishing the American single malt category is Westward Whiskey in Portland, Oregon.

pot still (made from both copper and stainless steel) and aged in lightly charred American oak barrels. The distillery offers a signature single malt that is 90 proof (45 percent alcohol by volume) as well as a cask strength version. Currently, you can also get Westward's whiskey finished in a pinot noir wine cask or in a stout beer cask.

Westward isn't just a pioneer in how spirits are made, but also in how they are marketed and sold. The brand has taken the tasting room out of the distillery, opening a bottle shop in downtown Portland as well as a store and a kiosk in the local airport. You can also join the Westward Whiskey Club to get special releases delivered to your house.

In fall 2022, Krogstad stepped down from his role at the company and was succeeded by head distiller Miles Munroe.

Vermont's WhistlePig was one of the brands that saved rye from completely disappearing and now bottles a range of whiskies made with the flavorful grain.

WhistlePig

In 2008, Raj Bhakta, a former contestant on Donald Trump's NBC TV show *The Apprentice*, started WhistlePig on an old dairy farm in southern Vermont.

Originally, the brand began by bottling whiskey that its master distiller, Dave Pickerell, purchased from a Canadian distillery. This created a bit of controversy, since the brand wasn't initially forthcoming about the origins of the rye. (At the time, the reputation of Canadian whisky was at a low point.) Despite this setback, the brand somehow managed to succeed and played a key role in helping to bring back rye whiskey. The brand then built its own distillery in Shoreham, Vermont, to Pickerell's specifications and began distilling whiskey in fall 2015.

Bhakta lost control of WhistlePig in 2016 and sold his stake back to the company in 2019. He then started an eponymous Armagnac brand. In 2018, WhistlePig took a sizable investment from luxury conglomerate Moët Hennessy Louis Vuitton (LVMH), which allowed it to expand its distillery and install a second still. WhistlePig now even grows some of its own grain, uses water from its own well, and has barrels constructed from local trees.

The brand's portfolio starts with the introductory 6-year-old PiggyBack 100% Rye and the matching 6-year-old PiggyBack 100 Proof Bourbon. The core collection includes the "bottled-in-barn" FarmStock Rye, which is made exclusively from Vermont ingredients; the Small Batch Rye Aged 10 Years; the Old World Rye Aged 12 Years and finished in madeira, port, and sauternes barrels;

and the Estate Oak Rye Aged 15 Years, which is aged in barrels made from oak harvested on WhistlePig's property. For collectors, the prize whiskey is the incredibly limited-edition Boss Hog. The series started in 2013 and has become ever more sought-after with each subsequent release.

Willett Distillery

After Prohibition was repealed, there was a huge distillery-building boom in the United States. While many of those brands are no longer made, Willett is one of the lucky few still in operation. Aloysius Lambert Thompson Willett opened the Bardstown, Kentucky, distillery in 1936, and on St. Patrick's Day 1937, the first barrel of whiskey was filled. Ultimately, the distillery was known for producing Old Bardstown Kentucky straight bourbon whiskey, which was introduced in the 1940s, and later for Johnny Drum, which was introduced in the 1960s.

The modern Willett distillery really began with the marriage of Even Kulsveen and Martha Harriet Willett in 1973. Martha is the granddaughter of the distillery's founder and Even is an immigrant from Norway who originally ran a spirits distribution business in Colorado. In July 1984, Even and Martha were able to buy the Willett brand name from the family. At the same time, the distillery, warehouses, and bottling facility were sold to other companies that were interested in making ethanol. It would take several years before Even and Martha could buy back the company's original facilities and property. Willett bottled bourbon and rye bought on the open market until January 2012, when it opened a completely new distillery in Bardstown, including a pot still made to Even's specifications. This marked the company's shift from buying whiskey to producing it. Even and Martha's son, Drew Kulsveen, is now the brand's master distiller. One of the things that differentiates Willett bourbon is that its mash bill contains more malted barley than many other brands, which gives the finished product a creamier texture.

Willett makes a robust portfolio of different bourbons, including its original brand, Old Bardstown, which is available at three different proofs. In the 1960s, the family added Johnny Drum bourbon, which is a robust 101 proof (50.5 percent alcohol by volume). I first heard about Willett when I was introduced to its small batch boutique bourbon collection, which debuted in the 1990s. It features four bourbons: Rowan's Creek, Noah's Mill, Kentucky Vintage, and Pure Kentucky. These whiskies first became popular in Japan and other foreign markets before catching on in the US.

The family later found success with its Willett Family Estate Bottled Bourbon and Willett Family Estate Bottled Rye, both introduced in 2008 and both highly sought-after and revered. Arguably, the distillery's most recognizable whiskey is the Willett Pot Still Reserve bourbon, which comes in an eye-catching glass bottle that itself looks like the family's original pot still. The brand has also worked on a number of collaborative whiskey projects with Blackened, as well as with the band Kings of Leon.

In December 2022, Willett announced that it was spending nearly $93 million to build a new distillery and warehouse.

SCOTCH WHISKY

SCOTLAND
Whisky Landmarks

Bill Lumsden

George Smith

Bonnie Prince Charlie

David Stewart

Robert Burns

John Johnston

Islands

Loch Ness

INVERNESS

Speyside

DUFFTOWN

River Spey

ABERDEEN

Highlands

Stirling Castle

Islay

GLASGOW

EDINBURGH

Edinburgh Castle

Lowlands

Campbeltown

STORES

Walker Grocery Store A

DISTILLERY

1. The Glenlivet Distillery, Ballindalloch
2. The Glenfiddich Distillery, Dufftown
3. The Macallan Distillery, Aberlour
4. Highland Park Distillery, Kirkwall, Orkney
5. Balvenie Distillery, Dufftown
6. Glenmorangie Distillery, Tain
7. Aberfeldy Whisky Distillery, Aberfeldy
8. Cameronbridge Distillery, Leven
9. Bowmore Distillery, Islay
10. Ardbeg Distillery, Islay
11. Laphroaig Distillery, Islay
12. Caol Ila Distillery, Islay
13. Talisker, Isle of Skye
14. Lagavulin, Islay

In the late 1990s, I found myself in Scotland. Few nongolfers in the United States had ever heard of St Andrews, the ancient Scottish university, or the nearby links course considered the spiritual home and actual birthplace of golf. Nevertheless, with a serious case of wanderlust and almost no aptitude for foreign languages, I decided to spend a semester of my junior year at the school, which is about 50 miles (80 kilometers) northeast of Edinburgh.

While my classes, the town, and the magnificent golf course were as impressive as I had imagined, the drinking culture was a bit of a disappointment, with almost no one drinking Scotch. The students knew as much about the whisky as I did at the time—which was to say, very little. Not that I was in danger of going thirsty—during my time there, the town's three main streets were home to a staggering thirty-five bars and pubs, most of them serving beer and very bad mixed drinks.

When the Cardhu Distillery in Speyside got its original distilling license in 1824, co-owner Helen Cumming was its master distiller.

At last count there were 145 whisky distilleries across Scotland, and a number of them, like Aberfeldy pictured above, date back to the nineteenth century.

Sometimes I ordered Scotch because it seemed appropriate to drink it while in Scotland. But it wasn't cheap, and you got exactly one small, measured shot. (I soon learned not to order it on the rocks, which translated to just a few tiny cubes that melted fast.) The selection of whisky was generally small and included only the largest producers. At the time, whisky had nothing on the beverage of the moment at St Andrews: Budweiser. Though this was imported and expensive, I guess the grass is always greener.

My timing was terrible. I was a few years shy of reaping the benefits of the whisky boom. A significant number of Scotch distilleries were still mothballed in the late '90s, having shuttered in the '80s when the international market for whisky cratered and demand dried up. The distilleries that remained were hanging on for dear life. Still, being in the country changed my connection to whisky and ultimately set me on a journey that landed me here, writing a doorstop of a book on the subject.

Wine people love to pontificate about the concept of terroir, which is just a fancy way of saying that a wine reflects the place where it was made. Oenophiles often focus on things like the amount of sunshine a vineyard gets or the type of soil the vines are planted in, but I would argue that, for Scotch, this sense of place translates differently. Once you experience "summer" in Scotland, which usually means a high of 13 to 16 degrees Celsius (55 to 60 degrees Fahrenheit), you get why Scots don't usually add ice to their whisky. And if you're ever lucky enough to find yourself on the Isle of Skye, you'll surely experience a bone-chilling sideways rain. Afterward, you might just want a dram of the island's signature whisky, Talisker, a peaty, smoky expression that feels like being wrapped in an old familiar quilt.

The simple act of drinking Scotch delivers a taste of where it was made. But while this may sound obvious, it's just a starting point. The country of Scotland was certainly my starting point for whisky—delivered via epiphany when I found myself there for the vaguest of youthful reasons. But my time there inspired me to understand its whisky on a much deeper level, and that led to understanding all whiskies on a deeper level.

At St Andrews, I struggled to find friends who shared my interest in whisky. And certainly none of us could have imagined that the spirit would experience an incredible rebirth followed by a meteoric rise over the next twenty-five years—beginning right after I left the spirit's spiritual homeland.

Today, the Scotch industry struggles to keep up with the thirst of drinkers. In the early 2000s, no one thought that—ten, twelve, or eighteen years later, when the whisky was fully mature—the demand for single malt would skyrocket and wildly outpace supply. In response, many of the biggest brands expanded their distilleries several times and now run them twenty-four hours a day, seven days a week. Any shuttered facility that could be reopened has returned to duty, and plenty of new ones have also been built. Now too, the Malt Whisky Trail has become a major attraction for folks visiting the country and the industry is once again a point of pride with Scottish people.

> ## Key Differences
>
> What makes Scotch, Scotch above all is that it can only be made and aged in Scotland.
>
> The other hallmarks of Scotch whisky are malted barley and pot stills, which you must use exclusively if you're making single malts. All Scotch must be aged for at least three years and most single malts are usually much older—at least ten years. This extended aging period is because of the country's famous temperate climate and the fact that the whisky is generally aged in a used barrel. While a number of Scotches are notoriously peaty and smoky, not all Scotch has these flavor notes—some are in fact smooth and fruity. While there are some Scotch-based cocktails, the whisky is generally drunk neat, with ice, water, or club soda.
>
> **Total Consumption:** Sales of Scotch whisky in the United States in 2023 totaled nearly 10 million nine-liter cases.

While my first time in Scotland might not have been ideal for a whisky drinker, it certainly speaks to the incredible journey that the spirit has taken over the past two centuries. It's been a roller coaster of extreme highs and dismal lows, but through it all Scotch has survived. It's an amazing history and one that will make you truly appreciate the dram in your glass.

Types of Scotch Whisky

There are three main types of Scotch: single malts, grain whisky, and blends. Here are the basics on these three historic categories.

♦ SINGLE MALTS

Arguably the most famous type of whisky on Earth, single malt Scotch can only be made, aged, and bottled in Scotland. A single malt is the production of a single distillery and must be made completely from malted barley. Single malt Scotch is distilled in a copper pot still. Generally, the spirit is distilled twice, but it can be distilled more times. For instance, the Lowland distillery Auchentoshan distills its whisky three times.

DEFINING SINGLE MALT SCOTCH

- A single malt must be made at a single distillery.
- It must be produced, aged, and bottled in Scotland.
- The mash (base grains) must be 100 percent malted barley.
- Only a pot still may be used to make the spirit.
- The whisky has to be aged in an oak barrel no larger than 700 liters (185 gallons).
- The finished whisky must be at least 80 proof (40 percent alcohol by volume).

Single malt Scotch must be aged for at least three years in an oak barrel but is usually at least ten years old when it's bottled.

In distilleries across Scotland, you'll find massive wooden or metal tanks called washbacks to ferment the so-called wort into a beer, which is then distilled.

Single malts must adhere to the specific regulations created by the Scotch Whisky Association (SWA), including that they must age for at least three years in an oak barrel. The cask can't be larger than 700 liters (185 gallons) and the finished whisky must be at least 80 proof (40 percent alcohol by volume). The only things a brand can add to the whisky are water and caramel coloring, the latter so it maintains a consistent color. If a bottle has a stated age on its label, that's the minimum age of the whisky it contains (meaning: it can be blended with older single malt from that same distillery).

There are currently more than 130 distilleries making single malt across Scotland. You absolutely can make single malt in other parts of the world, but under no circumstances can it be labeled Scotch. Even adding a term like "Glen" to your brand name will likely result in a cease and desist letter from the SWA.

DEFINING SCOTCH GRAIN WHISKY

- It must be produced and aged in Scotland.
- The mash (base grains) is generally corn and/or wheat with some malted barley.
- A column still is generally used to make the spirit.
- The whisky must be aged in an oak barrel no larger than 700 liters (185 gallons).
- The finished whisky must be at least 80 proof (40 percent alcohol by volume).

The Five Classic Regions of Scotch

If you start reading about Scotch, you'll no doubt soon encounter the five classic whisky-producing regions, each of which have their own style and flavor characteristics. Over the past century or so, many of these differences have disappeared, or in one case the area no longer is a major producer of whisky. While this spirited geography is not essential to know anymore, it helps show the foundations of the Scotch industry and how it has evolved over time.

The Lowlands

At your local liquor store, you're not going to find many Lowland single malts—if you're lucky they'll have a bottle of Auchentoshan. If you're really lucky you'll also find a bottle of Glenkinchie or Bladnoch. These three distilleries are located in southern Scotland, near Glasgow and Edinburgh. While the area was never known as a major center for single malt production, it is the home of Scotch grain whisky and continues to produce a staggeringly large amount of the spirit used by blenders. Dave Broom, in his excellent book *The World Atlas of Whisky* (2024), estimated that every year the Lowlands' six grain whisky distilleries produce nearly 80 million gallons (3 million hectoliters) of it.

Speyside

Speyside boasts dozens of distilleries, including stalwarts The Macallan, The Glenlivet, Glenfiddich, and Balvenie. For many, when they think of Scotch, what they are thinking about is the whisky produced in this region. Traditionally, this remote and rugged area in the country's northeast corner, hours and hours away from Edinburgh or Glasgow, was a favorite of single malt distillers, since it was too far away for tax collectors to bother making the trip. And if they did make the trip, they could be spotted with enough time to move the whisky and hide the stills.

When the Glenfiddich Distillery opened in 1887, the whisky was made on a still bought secondhand from rival Cardhu.

The majestic river Spey runs through this region, which boasts plenty of springs with soft water. Today, all the brands in Speyside have their own unique production styles and methods, which creates a huge range of malts. The word *glen* in Gaelic, in fact, means "valley," and many of the most famous whisky distilleries are named for their location.

The Highlands

The Highlands are the northern half of Scotland. Speyside is geographically within the Highlands but not considered part of it—it is a separate and distinct territory. Given how vast an area the Highlands encompasses, it's hard to say that there is a distinct style. It was a more useful designation before 1823, when it generally delineated the higher quality, smaller (and illegal) distilleries from the larger industrial ones in the southern part of the country, which is what we call the Lowlands. Today the Highlands includes an impressive array of famous distilleries.

Islay

There is a 239-square-mile (619-square-kilometer) rock 15 miles (24 kilometers) off the west coast of Scotland, called Islay, which is pronounced like eye-luh. Islay has been home to Scotch distilleries for hundreds of years. At last count there were nine distilleries: Ardbeg, Ardnahoe, Bowmore, Bruichladdich, Bunnahabhain, Caol Ila, Kilchoman, Laphroaig, and Lagavulin. It's not an easy place to live, with few creature comforts, amenities, or services—the roughly three thousand locals are connected to the mainland by ferry, or take their chances with the famously difficult weather and take a plane to and from the tiny airport.

As befits such a forbidding terrain, regularly lashed with high winds and sideways rain, the whisky is traditionally big and brawny. If you close your eyes, you can almost taste the salt and brine from the ocean, the minerals from the rock. And after a day walking through the moors of the island, you'll want to warm up in front of a roaring peat fire. The whisky has that element too. Using dried peat from the local, communal bog, the distilleries usually toast the malted barley over a smoky fire. That flavor is captured in the grain and becomes a signature element of Islay Scotch.

The Ardbeg distillery on the Scottish island of Islay dates back to 1815 and was shut down several times during its long history.

Campbeltown

If you look in a vintage whisky book or read old articles about the traditional Scotch regions, you'll often see Campbeltown mentioned. The area, which protrudes off the country's west coast, in the 1880s boasted so many important distilleries, including Hazelburn and Springbank, it was sometimes called Whiskyopolis. But the area fell on hard times and after World War I nearly all the distilleries closed. The region declined so dramatically that, for a while, the Scotch Whisky Association no longer recognized Campbeltown. Fortunately, the area is coming back, with several new distilleries open, including Dál Riata, Machrihanish, and Witchburn.

♦ GRAIN WHISKY

While whiskies are made from grain, the Scotch industry uses the term *grain whisky* to refer to a specific type of whisky typically made on a column still. (Technically, you could use a pot still, but it would be labor intensive and therefore expensive to produce.) The whisky can be made from any grain but is usually made from corn or wheat. However, grain whisky does need to contain some malted barley. Like all Scotch, it is aged in oak barrels for at least three years.

Grain whisky is rarely bottled on its own; it is primarily blended with single malts to make blended whisky. Grain whisky is usually quite smooth and quaffable as a result of being made on a column still, and is meant to balance out the flavorful single malts.

♦ BLENDED SCOTCH

Single malts may currently get most of the attention from drinkers, bartenders, and journalists, but the Scotch industry was built on the success of blends. A blended Scotch is made up of a number of single malts from different distilleries that are mixed together with grain whisky. About 90 percent of all the single malt produced in Scotland goes into a blend, such as Johnnie Walker, Dewar's, or Chivas Regal. A blend can contain dozens of single malts. Generally, the more expensive a blend, the higher percentage of single malt (versus grain whisky) it contains. And while the grain whisky component of blends is cheaper to produce—made from less expensive grain usually distilled in a column still and only aged for a few years—that doesn't mean blends are inferior to single malts, they're just a different experience. Think of a blend as an orchestra and a single malt as a soloist.

To make things more interesting (and complicated) there are also blended Scotches that include no grain whisky—just a combination of single malts from different distilleries—that are called blended malt Scotch whisky. This category is popular with some blenders trying to compete with single malts.

> **DEFINING BLENDED SCOTCH**
>
> - It must be produced and aged in Scotland.
> - It is a blend of usually multiple single malts and grain whisky.
> - The finished whisky must be at least 80 proof (40 percent alcohol by volume).

Making whisky in the nineteenth century was very labor-intensive and required a large number of workers, including this crew at Talisker on the Isle of Skye.

The History of Scotch

Scotch is the best-known whiskey in the world—it is also the most misunderstood.

The spirit has been made for hundreds of years in Scotland, but really only became widely available and a global bestseller in the second half of the nineteenth century. Thanks to a handful of expert brand builders and fortuitous opportunities, by the turn of the century, Scotch whisky was transformed into an affordable luxury enjoyed in bars and living rooms alike and became the gold standard for whiskey brands around the world. But because of Scotch's unprecedented growth and unrelenting marketing, a lot of the common knowledge about this whisky is, unfortunately, completely made up.

If you're familiar with the generally accepted version of Scotch history, you're going to be in for some surprises. So pour yourself a dram of single malt or blended Scotch, and enjoy the fascinating and dramatic journey that Scotch has gone on during the past few centuries.

During the 1800s, Scotch evolved from a farm product into an actual industry.

♦ WHAT WAS EARLY SCOTCH?

Irish distillers and historians have made a heartfelt argument for the Irish having created the original single malt (see page 314). But the great debate over whether it was Scotland or Ireland that first made whiskey is important only to a select few who market or sell whiskey—it doesn't matter all that much to the rest of us.

For one, our current ideas of borders and countries certainly didn't apply centuries ago. At the time, the Celts had spread across Northern Ireland and Scotland, which are separated by a channel that is, at its narrowest, only 12 miles (19 kilometers) wide. While we now think of Scotland and Northern Ireland as two distinct countries and a world apart, for the sake of talking about whiskey it is more accurate to see them as essentially one region.

More important to this mild debate, what these early whiskey distillers were making was a far cry from what we now know as Bushmills, Jameson, The Macallan, or The Glenlivet. In fact, in the 1300s, when the spirit was likely first produced, it was in many ways closer to gin than what we'd consider a whiskey today. It could be flavored with a range of botanicals and even sweetened with honey. And the base of the spirit wasn't made exclusively

We Made Whisky First

One of the longest-running spirited debates is whether the Scots or the Irish first made whisky.

If you ask a Scottish distiller, blender, or brand ambassador they'll tell you Scotland is the home of whisky. Case closed. If you deign to ask for evidence then you'll be told that in 1494 the official records of Scottish King James IV mention that he bought whisky from a distillery: "To Friar John Cor, by order of the King, to make aqua vitae VIII bolls of malt."

Essentially, that one note is what their case completely rests on that they made whisky earlier than anyone else. But if you notice it uses the Latin term *aqua vitae*, which means "water of life" and at the time was a catchall term for all kinds of alcohol, including brandy, wine, and eau-de-vie. So, we are not really sure what Friar John Cor was actually producing.

The Irish, naturally, have their own historical document, the "Red Book of Ossory," which is even older and dates back to the fourteenth century. But this document is, unfortunately, no more definitive and is problematic in its own way.

This means we are all still looking for a piece of hard evidence that will once and for all settle the debate of who made whisky first.

---

from malted barley but from all kinds of grains, including rye and oats, most likely mixed together.

No matter what these early spirits were made from, they were produced in simple, small pot stills made of clay or metal that were heated up over a fire. The alcohol was probably drunk immediately, like Irish moonshine, called poitín. And most likely this spirit was drunk by the distiller or their friends and neighbors. If it was poured into a barrel, it was done so for transportation and not for extended aging, which means it was clear like vodka, not a gorgeous amber color.

I once asked a group of Russian history scholars why they thought vodka was never aged in barrels. Their answer was that demand was so high that it got consumed shortly after it was made. This also speaks to the number of stills being used and their modest size, which could probably only make a small amount of liquor at one time.

Just as in the United States and Canada, the original Scottish distillers were farmers, so making whisky was a practical and logical decision, no different from turning milk into butter or apple juice into hard cider. What the distillers called draff, or the spent grain

Scotland's Taste for Sugar

One particularly striking, though buried, account in the final report of the UK Parliament's *Royal Commission on Whiskey and Other Potable Spirits* that was published in 1909, is the range of ingredients Scottish distillers used in the mid-nineteenth century. "In 1847 the Scotch pot still distillers produced 47,203 proof gallons made from sugar; and in the period between 1852 and 1864 they used some molasses and sugar in addition to malt." Clearly, the myth that pot still single malt Scotch has been made exclusively from barley is just that. Malted barley begins to be used exclusively for malts by the end of the nineteenth century, when it was written that "wherever the pot still process has been exclusively employed, malt only has been used."

left over after distilling, could be used to feed livestock, which was especially handy to have during Scotland's long, cold, and wet winters. (Even today the draff is usually sold as animal feed, either wet or dried in a giant oven.) The dung from the animals was then used to fertilize the land and make fields arable.

For hundreds of years, whisky was simply called by the Latin term for alcohol, *aqua vitae*, which means water of life—the original distillers were allegedly alchemists who sought this elixir for its magical properties. Many spirit terms we use today also mean water of life, including eau-de-vie and vodka. The Gaelic version of the term is *uisge beatha* (pronounced ISH-keh BA-ha), which is how whisky was referred to in Scotland and Ireland. Ultimately, the Gaelic mutated into the modern term *whisky*, which starts to show up with frequency only in the late 1700s. In fact, according to Dr. Nicholas Morgan's fascinating book *A Long Stride*, about the history of Johnnie Walker, in Scotland throughout the 1800s whisky was still often referred to as simply "aqua."

♦ LOWLAND VS HIGHLAND DISTILLERS

The history of distilling in Scotland can be split more or less into two distinct eras and two distinct locales.

The first era, the 1700s, was dominated by large producers in the Lowlands, near Glasgow and Edinburgh, that were making quite a bit of alcohol. While these distillers made whisky, which generally wasn't high quality, they also made a large amount of neutral grain spirit (basically vodka) that was sent to England and used as the base for gin. At the time, London was having its infamous and disastrous gin craze. This certainly helped Scottish distillers to dial in their distillation methods and create an actual industry—an advantage that later played a role in the production of whisky. These Lowland distillers were also able to get the government to tax alcohol production in a way that benefitted them, meaning brands that distilled spirits often and in large quantities.

But whisky was also distilled in the Highlands during the 1700s—just on a very small scale. It was also unregulated and illegal, since the distillers refused to pay the taxes, which were designed for high-volume distillers, or acquire an expensive license. Unlike the Lowland distillers, they weren't making enough volume to go legit. But they did have a few advantages over their southern neighbors. The remote Highlands boasted fresh spring water and copious amounts of barley, as well as another important and unique "ingredient"—protection from tax collectors, who rarely made the long and treacherous journey to the area. And being so far from the cities, Highland distillers developed their own techniques and styles for making whisky, including the fact that they used copper pot stills to produce small batches.

The Highlands were ultimately brought out of the tax shadows with the passage of the 1823 Excise Act, which lowered the cost of doing business for small distillers. Afterward, most of the single malt distilleries in the Highlands decided to get licensed and pay regular taxes. The Glenlivet was one of the first in Speyside to go legit when it got licensed in 1824. Not having to worry about being raided or attracting the attention of the Crown

Lagavulin single malt whisky from the island of Islay was historically a key ingredient of many famous Scotch blends.

The Summer Job of a Lifetime

At Elizabeth "Bessie" Williamson's graduation from Glasgow University in June of 1932, the lord rector of the school, Compton Mackenzie, reportedly urged the graduates "to live dangerously at this time, and not to put 'safety first' always in front of them. Let them go to the world and work with a will."

Williamson truly took these words to heart and accepted a temporary secretary job at the Laphroaig distillery on the island of Islay, which is off the west coast of Scotland. It was supposed to be a fun adventure before she found a permanent teaching position on the mainland. "I was always fond of country life, so I was glad to take it," she told the British newspaper *The Times* in 1967. Amazingly, she had never even tasted any alcohol before she arrived.

At the time, the distillery was run by Ian Hunter, a direct descendant of its founders, whose legal distilling history dates back to 1826. (They were no doubt illegally distilling for many years before that.) Hunter and Williamson got along very well, and ultimately she accepted a full-time position at Laphroaig.

When Hunter fell ill and was unable to work, Williamson led the distillery for years. In 1950, she was officially appointed managing director and given part of the business. Hunter passed away in 1954 and bequeathed her the rest of Laphroaig, which was then valued at £1 million. It was the first time a nonfamily member owned Laphroaig.

The second half of the twentieth century proved to be quite tumultuous for the Scotch industry, and in the early 1960s Williamson began to sell the company to some of its bigger customers, who were using Laphroaig's whisky in their blends. By 1972, she had officially retired and sold the rest of her shares. It was a shrewd time to exit the business—a few years later, the global whisky industry would crash.

Williamson passed away in 1982 at the age of seventy-one. She would no doubt be overjoyed that Laphroaig is not just still around, but thriving.

---

had distinct advantages, one of which was allowing these whisky distilleries to flourish and increase their production and distribution.

Most of the whisky made by these Highlands distilleries was sold by the barrel to grocery stores that doubled as bars and liquor stores. Many of these establishments would blend together the barrels they bought from different distilleries to make their own unique blends. These store owners had experience making proprietary blends, since they did more or less the same thing with tea. Johnnie Walker, one of the largest spirits brands on Earth, started out as the house blend of whiskies sold by the Walker family at their family store in Kilmarnock, Scotland. (Obviously, the family proved to have a knack for picking and blending whiskies together!)

♦ THE RISE OF THE BLENDERS

After the change in tax codes and licensing fees in 1823, it seemed as if the single malt distillers in the Highlands and along the west coast of Scotland might finally have a chance to succeed by coming out of the shadows and be able to produce whisky openly.

But the game would change again shortly, and in indelible fashion.

In 1830, an Irish tax official named Aeneas Coffey introduced his plans for a continuous column still. Until that point, whisky distillers primarily used pot stills all over the United Kingdom, which could produce a very flavorful spirit. But they took a long time for each distillation run, and were inefficient and incredibly labor intensive.

The column still, on the other hand, was a completely different technology. It essentially never needed to stop and could produce a staggering amount of spirit. You can use it to make whisky or a high proof neutral alcohol, like vodka, which was something that would take a lot of time and effort to do in a pot still. Critics (still!) argue that the column removes all the nuance and depth of flavor from a whisky. Coffey didn't come up with the idea for it, but his design perfected other people's previous attempts at creating one.

Coffey's still wasn't merely efficient, but flexible—you could easily make a lighter style of whisky from a range of grains. This grain whisky could then be aged and blended with a number of different single malts. The two types of whisky would then

William Hogarth's 1751 painting Gin Lane *depicts the consequences of Britain's failed attempt to increase grain sales by legalizing home distilling of gin.*

The Tax Collector Who Transformed Whiskey

Aeneas Coffey irrevocably changed the course of whiskey history. But for someone who played such a key role, we know precious little about him and what possessed him to design a new type of spirits still.

Even his birthplace is not certain. While it's generally believed he was born in Dublin in 1780, some historians place his birth in Calais, France, to Irish parents. But no matter where he came into this world, by 1818 Coffey was working in Ireland collecting taxes from distillers, and ultimately became the inspector general of excise. Given the nature of his job, Coffey developed an insider's understanding of the way whiskey was being produced and how the process could be made more efficient.

While the pot still's inefficiencies help it to make very rich whiskey by leaving in plenty of flavor compounds, it was very labor intensive to run. In the early 1800s, when the stills were heated directly over fires, they had to be maintained at a consistent heat for the duration of the distillation of each batch. This meant constant monitoring. And after each run the pot still had to be thoroughly cleaned inside before it could be used again. The biggest whiskey distillers had already installed a succession of ever larger pot stills and had a veritable army of workers tending them, but had essentially maxed out capacity. So a still that could work without stopping and needed fewer workers to run it was very appealing.

While Coffey usually gets sole credit for inventing the column still, there were several other inventors who had already created designs for continuous

balance each other out in terms of flavor. The smooth grain whisky would bring together all of the single malts and create a harmonious, consistent, and quaffable liquor. During the late 1800s this was particularly important, since some of the single malts could be overwhelming with huge flavors and fiery burn.

Single malt now must be made completely from malted barley, but Scottish distillers originally used other grains to make whisky. One key reason why barley became the de facto base was that it was grown locally and the government instituted Corn Laws in 1815 that made imported corn prohibitively expensive as a way to support local farmers. (These laws certainly made producing spirits more expensive and put British distillers at a disadvantage in competing against foreign-made spirits.) But in 1846, Parliament did away with the Corn Laws. The timing

stills, but none had really caught on. Robert Stein, who was from Scotland and patented his still design a few years before Coffey, came closest to success.

Ironically, Coffey's still was vilified in his homeland of Ireland, but was widely adopted and hailed as a major technological step forward in Scotland. The Scottish blenders truly saw the potential of Coffey's creation, and combined the grain whisky it produced with flavorful single malts. Coffey's original design consisted of two columns that later were simplified into one column.

Like Mary Shelley's Victor Frankenstein, Coffey could no longer control his powerful creation, which became popular with many distillers around the world. And while he wasn't run out of Dublin by torch-wielding villagers, Coffey and most of his immediate family moved to London to be closer to their clients.

Coffey passed away in 1852, but his name is still well known, and a version of his still design is widely used in many countries to make whiskey, including in Scotland, the United States, Canada, and now even in, yes, Ireland.

Aeneas Coffey changed the course of whiskey history when he patented his design for a continuous column still in 1830.

of the change couldn't have been more perfect for the column still to take off.

You could argue that the Crown should have learned its lesson about manipulating grain prices using the tool of distillation. In the 1700s, there was a scheme to increase domestic wheat demand by allowing folks to distill in their homes, which caused London to be awash in millions of gallons of gin. The disastrous effects of this economic policy on society, including a sizable increase in deaths and decrease in births, were captured in William Hogarth's infamous painting *Gin Lane*.

Once Lowland distillers could get cheaper corn and other grains in the mid-1800s, they began to use them in their new column stills, having abandoned their pot stills. Blenders could then add this grain whisky to their mix of single malts. The resulting whisky was easier to drink and less expensive to produce.

♦ **BUT IS IT SCOTCH?**

There was, however, a small problem with this plan: What would you call this blended whisky? Could you call it Scotch if it broke with tradition and wasn't produced in a pot still or made from malted barley? These questions became quite contentious and were ultimately the subject of Parliament's Royal Commission on Whiskey and Other Potable Spirits, which was undertaken in 1908 and involved 116 witnesses and thirty-seven sessions.

The report with the testimony runs for hundreds of pages and offers valuable insight into the history of Scotch and whiskey in general. Buried in it are a trove of fascinating facts that completely upend our modern view of whiskey history. (For one, it spells the term *whiskey* with an *e*, which undermines the idea that in the UK it has always been spelled without the letter.)

The overarching takeaway from the commission's findings is that there was never a consensus among whisky

The Original Whisky Writer

We can thank a tiny insect with a big appetite for grapevines for one of the most important spirits books of all time, *The Whisky Distilleries of the United Kingdom*, published in 1887.

In the second half of the 1800s, grape growers across Europe were in a hard-fought battle to save their vineyards from a tiny insect intruder named phylloxera. For years farmers and researchers frantically searched for a solution to end this epidemic, which made the incredibly popular beverages sherry, port, and Cognac virtually impossible to produce. As a result, British drinkers for the first time began to seriously contemplate drinking Scotch.

This in turn inspired Alfred Barnard to travel around the United Kingdom and Ireland visiting whisky distilleries and writing up his thoughts about each enterprise. Originally, his reports were published as distinct articles in the liquor industry publication *Harper's Weekly Gazette*; they were then collected and published shortly after as a book.

Some of his dispatches were long and detailed, while others were short and to the point. His writing tends to be on the flowery side, with great attention paid to the look and experience of each distillery's location, which lends it a travelogue feel.

Barnard was also very good at describing the production processes, which at the time must have seemed novel and fascinating to his readers. (These

makers in Scotland about what exactly constituted Scotch. The final report included this insightful opinion: "At first sight it seems strange that the definition of 'Whiskey,' a term now applied to a liquor which is so widely known, which for centuries past has been the national beverage in Scotland and Ireland, and which for some years has been very largely consumed in England, should give rise to such extreme differences of opinion. The explanation of these curiously divergent views is to be found in the uncertainty of the historical record relating to the subject."

For a spirit whose identity is inextricably connected to tradition and history, this is a shocking conclusion. A core part of what makes Scotch Scotch is its supposed connection to the past and a commitment to core practices and methods. And that's not to mention the superiority complex of Scotch drinkers, whose reverence for this classic whisky and its equally arcane drinking rules feels at times almost cultish.

detailed sections make me think of Mark Twain's *A Connecticut Yankee in King Arthur's Court* or Jules Verne's *Twenty Thousand Leagues Under the Sea* in their descriptions of the seemingly fantastical transformations taking place.)

However, what's truly fascinating is the fact that only few times does Barnard offer even a hint of how the whiskies tasted. I'm not sure why he consistently left out this key information, but it would certainly be interesting to read his descriptions of drinking the whiskies. While he passed away more than a century ago and folks are now quite familiar with whiskey, his book is still an incredibly helpful and important record of the industry at a critical period in its history.

"I wish to stimulate an interest in the art of distilling among those who trade in whisky, and to aid in demonstrating, what I am convinced is correct, that good whisky, as a beverage, is the most wholesome spirit in the world," wrote Barnard in the preface to his book. "Should I succeed in doing this, and my book proves of interest to my readers, I shall be gratified, and the publication of this volume will afford me pleasure to the end of my days."

I think Barnard can rest easy.

In 1887, Alfred Barnard published **The Whisky Distilleries of the United Kingdom,** *which contains a wealth of knowledge about the history of Scotch.*

The truth is a bit harder to swallow: Most of what we take for Scotch gospel today has been created fairly recently.

♦ SCOTCH FINDS ITS AUDIENCE

Before the 1800s, there just wasn't a huge demand for Scotch. The spirit trailed far behind brandy, gin, rum, port, and sherry. Remember, the Highland single malt distilleries didn't get licenses until after 1823, which meant that until then the bulk of the illicit production was sold and consumed in and around where it was made, in the community.

The invention of the column still meant that blenders could finally create a huge amount of whisky at a fairly low production cost, which allowed them to serve customers around the UK and beyond. The change in liquor regulations and tax codes in the UK, which made blending of whiskies on a large scale legal and profitable, also certainly helped make the liquor an international favorite.

But Scotch might not ever have become a global sensation without an unexpected boost from an American insect. In the 1870s, tiny phylloxera insects inadvertently imported on grapevines devoured every vineyard vine they could find across Europe, and in the process devastated grape brandy, sherry, and port production.

To woo converts from these well-established drinks, the industrious makers of Scotch blends such as Dewar's and Johnnie Walker created a mystique around the drink by dressing up the category with a more impressive backstory. This is when a lot of the supposed traditions and history surrounding Scotch whisky were first created. Early advertisements for these brands reinforced the idea that Scotch was a noble drink, sought out by kings and world leaders and on par with the finest Cognacs and the fanciest sherries.

These early ad campaigns were so successful because people, even in nearby England, didn't know much about Scotch or its history. In the 1880s, a British journalist named Alfred Barnard traveled around England, Scotland, and Ireland for an industry publication called *Harper's Weekly Gazette* to write about the burgeoning whisky distilling industry. In 1887, after a two-year tour, he produced his landmark book, *The Whisky Distilleries of the United Kingdom*, which included profiles for 161 different brands.

Barnard's description of The Glenlivet, which is currently the best-selling single malt in the United States, is exemplary of the growth of Scotch in the nineteenth century. After the founder of the distillery, George Smith, got a distilling license in 1824, the demand for the whisky rapidly grew. "From 50 gallons per week the output speedily increased to 1,500, until in 1859 a new and larger Distillery was built, and the output now exceeds 4,000 gallons per week."

Whisky from Ireland and Scotland became wildly popular in England through the 1890s. Despite having produced the spirit for hundreds of years and pioneered the single malt style, this was when the United Kingdom truly became a nation of whisky drinkers.

In 1899, the *Daily Telegraph* recounted how the House of Commons even installed a 700-gallon (2,650-liter) vat to hold Scotch whisky for its members' enjoyment (a second vat to hold Irish whiskey was planned). "It is a remarkable thing that in their increasing demands for whisky our legislators give a proof of how accurately they represent the national taste. The growth of whisky-drinking in England is extraordinary, and points to a great change in the habits of the people." The paper also included a year-by-year account of the staggering increase in the amount of whisky imported to England from Scotland and Ireland. In 1889, 2.8 million gallons (106,000 hectoliters) of Scotch was brought into England. By 1898, that figure increased to 6.1 million gallons (231,000 hectoliters). (Over that same time period, Irish whiskey imports increased from 2.2 million gallons [83,300 hectoliters] to 3.5 million gallons [132,500 hectoliters].)

While the distilleries were ramping up to meet this voracious new thirst, most folks still weren't drinking single malts but blends. Barnard wrote a small pamphlet called *How to Blend Scotch Whisky*, which was sponsored by Scotch brands and contained the description of three distilleries. He includes some interesting background on how Scotch's newfound popularity was changing its production methods.

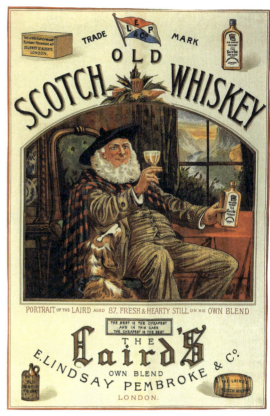

At the turn of the twentieth century, English companies were marketing a range of blended Scotch whiskies, like Laird's.

"The increasing demand on the part of the English people for good Highland whisky with a fair amount of flavour, has compelled the Scotch blenders to give higher quality and more age; and it is but fair to say that the large trade done in England direct by Scotch firms is simply the outcome of their being able to supply a want which the average English trader has hitherto ignored."

It's no wonder that the big blenders either began building their own single malt distilleries or began to buy them up. It's also why most of Scotland's distilleries are currently owned by big liquor conglomerates who use most of the single malt produced in their blends, including Johnnie Walker (Diageo), Dewar's (Bacardi), Buchanan's (Diageo), J&B (Diageo), and Chivas Regal (Pernod Ricard).

♦ GOLF & SCOTCH HIGHBALLS

While Scotch was finally taking hold in the UK, it was also gaining traction across the pond, in the United States. One reason this happened was a new American craze for golf. According to lore, the game was first played by shepherds who would stroll along the coast of Scotland and entertain themselves by hitting rocks with sticks. This developed into what are now called links courses, which tend to be shaped by geography, weather, and Mother Nature rather than bulldozers, backhoes, and Jack Nicklaus.

For Americans, the two Scottish pastimes were inseparable, and Scotch Highballs, specifically, became an important part of playing golf. "Scotch whiskey is as essential to a golf player as beer to a man at a clam bake," claimed a piece in the *New York Sun* that ran in 1899 under the very informative headline "Golf and Scotch Whiskey: The Growing Favor of the One Increases the Sales of the Other." The story quoted a "liquor dealer" who revealed, "The game of golf is responsible for an increase of almost 200 percent in the sale of Scotch whiskey in this country."

The liquor store Wood, Pollard & Co. even took out a small advertisement on the front page of the *Boston Globe* that same year touting the tight relationship between Scotch and golf. "Suppose you get a bottle from us, and the next time you come in from the golf links just try [a] whiskey and soda mixture and feel the gray matter under your hat tone up."

Dewar's went with a more aspirational approach in an ad that ran in the *New York Times* in 1905 that claimed, "Golfers Appreciate the refreshing Scotch High-Ball. Those who know the best order a Dewar's 'White Label' Scotch High-Ball." This was seemingly part of a larger strategy to tie the Dewar's brand to the popular carbonated cocktail. Earlier

At the turn of the century, golf was an essential part of early Scotch marketing in the US.

Americans Invade Scotland

The Scotch slump also led to a small and unexpected but historic consequence—the Dalwhinnie distillery, which is still making excellent whisky today, was sold to the American company Cook & Bernheimer. The Scottish facility was only a few years old, but having trouble staying open. This sale wouldn't be big news today, but in 1904 it was quite a milestone: the first time a Scotch distillery ended up in US hands. A breathless story in the *Atlanta Constitution* at the time crowed: "It is felt over here that no more daring attempt to capture a British industry has been made by the American invader than that which has just resulted in the transfer of a Scotch whisky distillery to an American firm."

that year, when Thomas "Tommy" Dewar was in the United States to watch the Ormond-Daytona automobile races in Florida, he gave an interview that was syndicated around the country in which he claimed that he discovered the Highball. The piece began with Dewar's account of visiting a dive bar on Broadway in New York in 1891 and making a joke that he needed a larger glass of whisky, which prompted the bartender to make him a Highball. "I have been told [that] was the first Scotch 'highball,'" he recounted. It surely made good copy, but the story doesn't really hold up. People had been drinking Highballs for decades and the term was already being used widely in the United Kingdom. *Ball* was a term that simply meant a measure of whisky.

The timing of Americans' twin interests in golf and Highballs was fortunate—as the century came to an end, it became painfully clear that Scotch distillers had widely overestimated how much whisky to produce. There was reportedly a surplus stock of 137.5 million gallons (5.2 million hectoliters) of Scotch aging in bonded warehouses. Scotland's building boom in distilleries helped create this so-called "whisky ocean." By 1899, there were 143 licensed distilleries in Scotland and another forty-one in the rest of the UK—an increase of 23 distillery facilities since Barnard's book was published twelve years before. "The distilleries are nearly all immense concerns, and production has been pushed to the utmost. Consequently, the supply has run far ahead of home consumption and the export trade combined. Under the impression that the market would expand with production, the distilleries have been kept running at full capacity," said a Wilkes-Barre, Pennsylvania *Sunday News* story. The US State Department had also received an alarming report from its Consul in Edinburgh about the seriousness of this crisis, given its potential for greatly decreased sales of American corn to Scottish distillers.

♦ LIQUID MEDICINE

The overproduction of Scotch at the turn of the century might have been a true disaster if not for a big save from an unlikely source—doctors. Just as modern reports of red wine's salutary effects on health and life expectancy have spurred sales of wine, the endorsement of whiskey consumption by doctors played a huge role in the spirit's popularity.

The phylloxera scourge (see page 10) once again played a part in bolstering whisky's profile. Because of the resulting shortage of wine and grape-based spirits, UK doctors could no longer prescribe their traditional alcoholic remedies (a small glass of Cognac). Just like drinkers, they looked to Scotland for an alternative.

"During the last twenty years doctors have recommended whiskey both as an ordinary dietetic beverage, chiefly on account of its low acidity as compared with wine and beer, and also as a medicine, chiefly because of the difficulty experienced a few years ago of getting good brandy and the price of the latter," claimed a 1908 article in *The Hospital: A Journal of the Medical Sciences and Hospital Administrations*. The piece went on to say "it must at once be emphasized that whiskey is one of the most convenient vehicles for the administration of alcohol in a pure form, and almost in any degree of dilution that may be required."

While it might now sound odd that the medical community would consider whiskey a cure, alcohol was considered a legitimate treatment for a number of health issues at the time. The healthcare industry accounted for a significant chunk of whiskey sales, and in the second half of the nineteenth century, Scotch was often advertised for medicinal purposes. The prescription of alcohol continued for decades, and famously, during US Prohibition, the huge loophole to legally buy booze was to get a doctor or dentist to give you a prescription for a bottle of "medicinal whiskey" that could be filled at a local pharmacy.

In the nineteenth century, Phylloxera insects ate their way across European vineyards and upended both the recreational and medicinal liquor industries.

♦ A NEW CENTURY FOR DISTILLERS

In the twentieth century, Scotch truly became an international bestseller and the whiskey category that distillers around the world tried to emulate. But this was far from a forgone conclusion as the calendar turned over into the new century. Scotland faced challenges from some familiar sources: Irish whiskey and its own regulations, as well as an identity crisis for the Scotch industry.

The first problem was at least a familiar one: Irish distillers, whose whiskey was very popular in the United States, particularly in New York. But the new century would prove cruel to the Irish whiskey industry, which would be almost completely destroyed by a combination of consequential events, including a war of independence and a trade war with England—among other major factors. What began as a threat to Scotch whisky ended up benefitting both Scottish and American distillers who were able to ultimately claim market share from their Irish rivals.

The true challenge for the Scotch industry around the turn of the century might have been more related to soul-searching. The Royal Commission on Whiskey and Other Potable Spirits, which was convened by Parliament, raised some serious issues. The most important of which was how Scottish distillers should make Scotch—in a pot still, column still, or both—and what it

Just after the turn of the twentieth century, Parliament convened a Royal Commission on Whiskey and Other Potable Spirits, which included exhaustive testimony from dozens of liquor experts.

should be made from—malted barley, unmalted barley, corn, or a blend of grains. It was understood that Scotch would never become a major player if the quality and production methods weren't consistent, but the conclusions of the Royal Commission ended up being impressive only in how lukewarm and noncommittal they were. Like just about any document produced by politicians, it went out of its way not to offend any of the major parties, who no doubt were lobbying hard for just such ambiguous findings.

After years of research and testimony, the Commission pronounced, "'whiskey' is a spirit obtained by distillation from a mash of cereal grains saccharified by the diastase of malt: that 'Scotch whiskey' is a whiskey, as above defined, distilled in Scotland." In effect, distillers could use whatever grain they chose to make the liquor. The only major development in the Commission's conclusion was that whisky should not be made from molasses or sugar.

The report also approved once and for all a distiller's right to use a pot still or a column still, or combine whisky produced on either of these pieces of equipment. And it did so in particularly well-wrought bureaucratic prose: "The claim for a prescriptive right of the pot still product alone to be called 'whisky,' as above stated, is based upon the fact that until about 1830 all whiskey was manufactured in pot stills. But a product does not lose its name because an improved or even altered mode of manufacture is employed. Similarly, before 1820 persons travelled in carriages or on horseback. But when railways were invented those who journeyed in them did not cease to be 'travelers.' It was not claimed that only those who continued to be conveyed by the old methods were 'travelers.'"

While the Royal Commission failed to establish definitive distilling standards, its work helped codify the rules of making whisky that ended up in the Immature Spirits (Restriction) Act 1915, which mandated that Scotch had to be aged for at least two years. The following year the aging minimum was extended to three years, which is still the minimum today. And the 1915 act ensured that neutral grain spirit mixed with coloring and flavoring could no longer be sold as whisky in the UK.

♦ **WHISKY & WAR**

World War I, the Great Depression, America's Prohibition, and World War II had a devastating effect on Scotch distillers, barley farmers, and all the industries adjacent to the whisky industry.

World War I started in April 1917 for the United States, but for the UK and the rest of Europe the fighting began in July 1914. The British government subsequently took control of the high-volume whisky column stills in Scotland, which, after being converted, were capable of producing high proof alcohol for use in explosives. The pot stills, which couldn't make a sufficiently high proof alcohol for munitions, were allowed to continue making whisky. To assuage concerns about the supply of Scotch, it was reported that Scottish distillers had a reserve of 130 million gallons (4.9 million hectoliters) of whisky aging, enough to satisfy drinkers for several years.

Scotch distillers were also under threat from another enemy, on the other side of the Atlantic: the temperance movement. Advocates for abolishing the sale of alcohol in the United States began gaining widespread influence in the late 1800s, with several states instituting some form of prohibition on their own. And with the US entry into World War I in 1917, the US government created the Food Administration, which instituted a food conservation program. This was all done to marshal resources for the war effort, but the regulations also required the shutdown of distilleries in the United States, and even, curiously, outlawed the importation of alcohol from other countries. Clearly, these wartime policies were used by the temperance movement as a test case for abolishing the sale and production of alcohol across the country.

During the first few years of World War I, the Scotch industry was desperate to sell whisky to US drinkers just to stay in business. So, before the American alcohol import ban went into effect, distillers sent convoys of steamships loaded with barrels and cases of whisky through dangerous waters patrolled by German submarines. In one of the last runs, the *Assyria* cargo ship, which had left Glasgow headed for New York, was sunk by a torpedo off the coast of Ireland. It was carrying thousands of gallons of whisky, which were lost at sea. The other fifteen ships in the convoy made it safely across the Atlantic.

♦ PROHIBITION AND REPEAL

After World War I, the temperance movement in the US took off, and the "drys" were able to get the National Prohibition Act passed, which went into effect in January 1920. But a significant amount of Scotch still found its way to the States, smuggled through Canada, Mexico, and the Caribbean. "And, take it from the enforcement faced, when a rum runner is captured with 500 cases of excellent Scotch aboard, it just means that nine other fast and staunch small boats have landed a like cargo," wrote Nelson Robins in Brooklyn's *Standard Union* newspaper in January 1930.

While the US was supposed to be bone dry, bootlegged whisky from Scottish distilleries was widely available.

For a time, despite the ban on selling, transporting, and serving booze, the US black market kept the distilleries in Scotland very, very busy. In the fall of 1922, the United Press International (UPI) wire service painted this evocative picture for its readers: "In the Highlands, the passengers on the night expresses flash past great lighted buildings, from whose tall chimneys the smoke belches nightlong, where the whirr of driving belts and the whizz of patent bottle stoppers is made on mass production principles in order that Mr. Jones of New York City or Mr. Brown of Detroit may have his 'Old Scotch' for the entertainment of himself and his friends."

But the illicit booze trade wasn't enough to sustain Scotland's distillers, because at the same time, in order to pay down World War I debts, the British government instituted an oppressive tax scheme on distilleries. Suddenly, taxes were due when the alcohol was put in the barrel, not when it was sold. "It costs 75 cents to produce a gallon of Scotch," explained the *Chicago Tribune* in 1932. "But as soon as it is made a government inspector appears and collects $17.50 in excise tax. Raw whisky cannot be served and the money sunk in taxes must lie idle for nearly a decade before the distillation is matured, when the product can be sold and the tax recollected."

On December 5, 1933, the Constitutional Amendment repealing Prohibition was ratified, and drinkers around the US celebrated.

If that wasn't bad enough, when the whisky was finally served in the UK, the government charged additional exorbitant taxes that ate most of the purchase price. This meant that bars had no incentive to sell Scotch, since the profits were so limited. The tax changes couldn't have come at a worse time—as the postwar economy slowed down drastically and the domestic demand for whisky waned.

It's no wonder that by 1932, just a few of Scotland's one hundred distilleries were open and producing Scotch. (The exact numbers of total distilleries and those that stayed opened varied in newspaper accounts, but essentially almost no whisky was produced that year.) Additionally, there were a number of stories of farmers who could not sell their barley to any distillery and had to leave it rotting in their barns.

When Prohibition was finally repealed in December 1933, New York Harbor was soon crowded with ships full of cases upon cases of Scotch. One can only imagine how good aged Scotch tasted after years of drinking the watered-down rotgut served during Prohibition. Almost immediately, fifty Scotch distillers reopened their doors in spite of the new tax, and began making whisky again. "The folk of the northeast are dour, canny people, but not given to over-optimism or exaggeration, but even they are smiling now and sometimes even rubbing their hands cautiously," reported a 1933 story in the *Ottawa Journal* that ran just two days before the repeal of Prohibition was ratified. The story went on to discuss how the distillers were buying up all the barley available, with some grain even coming from farms as far away as Australia and Denmark.

Despite producing relatively little whisky during Prohibition, the Scotch

Scotch Becomes Scottish

In a replay of turn-of-the-century worries, there was once again an intense debate about what exactly constituted Scotch. In late 1938, it was discovered that a firm called Henderson & Turnbull was using single malt made in Northern Ireland for its Scotch blend. The firm defended itself against charges of any wrongdoing by revealing that combining Irish grain whiskey with Scottish single malts was a common practice. Despite the exhaustive investigation undertaken for the Royal Commission in 1908, the question of where Scotch can be made wound up in a Scottish court.

Even the *Baltimore Sun* ran an editorial beseeching the UK to come up with a definition that could be defended. The editors worried that, just as California sparkling wine was labeled "champagne" at the time, so-called Scotch would soon be made around the world and consumers would be duped over and over again.

Interestingly, a similar court case occurred in the United States as well. The Federal Alcohol Administration had refused to allow a blend made from half Scottish and half Irish whiskey to be labeled Scotch. This case went all the way to the Supreme Court, which ultimately declined to weigh in on it.

Fortunately, a Scottish court ruled that all the ingredients in a Scotch blend needs to actually be made in Scotland. And on July 5, 1939, the court dismissed Henderson & Turnbull's appeal, which made the ruling final and set a precedent that still applies today.

brands had millions of gallons of it aging in their warehouses. Just a year before repeal, this enormous whisky supply was considered a huge problem. What would the Scottish distillers be able to do with all this whisky that seemingly no one wanted?

But the end of Prohibition turned this headache into a gold mine, one worth millions and millions of British pounds. In fact, thirsty Americans were draining Scottish warehouses at an alarming rate—in just the first six months of 1937, 2 million gallons (76,000 hectoliters) of Scotch were exported to the US, which, according to London's *Evening Standard*, was almost twice as much as was shipped during the same period the year before.

The situation for distillers on the American side of the Atlantic was quite a bit different. US brands struggled to restart up after years of being out of business. The lucky ones had barrels of either bourbon or rye made before Prohibition that somehow managed to survive. Despite being almost undrinkably woody, they were still sold by bars, restaurants, and liquor stores. On the other hand, there was also a lot of very young whiskey that had just been produced and was bottled as soon as possible. Given these less-than-ideal American whiskey options, you can understand the huge advantage Scottish distillers had, and why drinkers were craving Scotch.

I would argue that this was the moment the Scotch industry truly pulled ahead of American whiskey and established itself as the preeminent whiskey category in the world. Through the 1930s, many distillers across the United States struggled to get back on track and produce whiskey. As a result, the global demand for bourbon and rye dropped dramatically. In 1937, according to New Jersey's *Daily Record*, 45,000 gallons (1,700 hectoliters) of rye and bourbon were sold to foreign buyers, down from 230,000 gallons (8,700 hectoliters) the year before Prohibition started. It got so bad that, according to a 1938 column in the *Chattanooga Daily Times*, American whiskey brands lobbied Hollywood to replace the term "Scotch and soda" with "whiskey and soda" in film scripts in order to spur sales. "The top-hatted and tail-coated heroes who people the dreamland of high society in the movies have a powerful pull on buying habits, and the American distillers, no doubt, want their chance to prove that the same air of savoir faire and what-ho can be achieved with a highball made from rye or bourbon as with the drink which comes from over the water."

♦ SCOTCH JOINS THE WAR EFFORT

Just as things were looking up for Scotch distillers with the American market reopening, World War II started and the United Kingdom quickly shifted into survival mode. All of its resources were required for the fight against the Germans. While London was bombed relentlessly, Scotland was for the most part spared the Nazis' horrific blitzkrieg. The distilleries survived, but production of whisky became harder and harder as the war dragged on. Distillery workers were either on the front lines or supporting the war effort. Grain, and of course Scotch, were once again severely rationed.

Even when you were allowed to buy whisky there was often none to be had. This was particularly true in areas north of London, to which people had fled from the incessant air attacks. In 1941, it was reported by the UPI wire service that British pub owners were traveling up to 150 miles (241 kilometers) in search of bottles still for sale

British Prime Minister Winston Churchill was known for his prodigious consumption of liquor and in 1944 gave an important boost to the Scotch whisky industry.

in liquor stores that they could resell. "Distillers have cut the supplies to two-thirds of the 1939 consumption. There is an acute shortage in the evacuation areas in the country whose normal peace-time populations have been swollen by tens of thousands."

In 1944, Prime Minister Winston Churchill—who, according to his biographer William Manchester was fond of starting his day with several Johnnie Walker Red Label Highballs before moving on to champagne and brandy—made the decision to get distillers more grain, so they could start up production even before the war was officially over. Just as today, the Scotch whisky industry was a giant economic driver. If the country was to recover financially from the war, it needed Scotch to export.

But Scotch needs several years of barrel aging, so the revenue from the whisky's sale wouldn't come for some time, which is why Churchill wanted the industry to rev back up even before Victory Day. To help get the UK back on its feet, most of the Scotch produced was sold overseas for years after the war ended.

Other measures helped as well. To expedite production, for the first time in 1946, the government allowed whisky to be made on Sundays. Distilleries were also allowed to operate pretty much continuously. "The abolition of these Victorian restrictions effectively allowed all distilleries to more than double their production at a stroke, but at the same time fundamentally changed the pace and cycle of the whisky-making process," wrote Nicholas Morgan in his 2020 book *A Long Stride: The Story of the World's No. 1 Scotch Whisky*.

Churchill's decision to allocate grain to the whisky industry took a lot of courage and was certainly controversial. Across the Atlantic, US President Harry Truman, whose love of bourbon was well documented, was against using grain for distilling. "When millions face the threat of starvation, the use of grain for the production of whisky and other beverage spirits is a use which is clearly nonessential," he said in a speech to the United States Congress. After the war was over, he shut down US distilleries for months and redirected the grain they would have used to the Marshall Plan, which distributed it across the continent.

♦ **SCOTCH, AMERICAN STYLE**

With an assist from Churchill, Scotch was able to more than just get back on track—blended Scotch became one of the signature drinks of the *Mad Men* era. In January 1949, the Scotch industry also got a boost from the US federal government, which made it policy that American distillers could no longer label their whiskey as Scotch, or even use terms such as *Highlands* or *kilt* that subtly implied their whiskey was from Scotland. If US producers wanted to continue to make a Scotch style of whiskey, they could legally call it "Scotch type," which had obvious marketing disadvantages.

These US restrictions and Churchill's prescience helped trigger another Scotch boom. The number of whisky distilleries in Scotland nearly doubled between 1945 and 1960, to 106 facilities. To keep up with demand and maximize profits, some devious Scotch brands began selling whisky that was less than three years old in markets that didn't have a minimum aging requirement. (The United States, Canada, and Britain all required Scotch to be at least thirty-six months old.) Given the long fight over establishing what was and wasn't Scotch, this practice of selling very young whisky was obviously controversial. The Scotch Whisky Association (SWA) was adamant in its objections. On the other side, however, were more than three dozen brands who made millions selling this immature whisky around the world. "It is a fact that after some years of selling 18-month-old whisky to many lands, we have not had one complaint as to quality," insisted William Graham, the secretary of the Independent Scotch Whisky Association, which was an upstart rival to the SWA. Ultimately, the SWA won this fight thanks to an act of Parliament that mandated that to be labeled Scotch, the whisky would have to age for at least three years no matter where it would be sold. But the calm was short-lived—in the late 1950s, another threat to the quality and integrity of Scotch emerged. A number of brands began to stretch their blends by using more grain whisky and less single malt. "Veteran topers have a new charge to make against the United States. The flavor of Scotch whisky, they say, is gradually being altered to suit the American palate," wrote William H. Stoneman in the *Philadelphia Inquirer* in 1959. A lighter and smoother style of Scotch became increasingly popular with drinkers in the US. "It used to be common for a blender to use 50 or 55 percent of malt, to 50 or 45 percent of neutral grain whisky, the percentage is now often down to 45. One big blender who used to use 70 percent malt now uses 50 percent."

Not only did Dewar's White Label help establish the Scotch category, but it also helped create the template for marketing it.

By 1968, *Business Week* took a harsher tone toward the changes to the flavor of Scotch. "Distillers and importers have tailored blends to US tastes and pocketbooks. Scotch has become so light-spirited it's almost ghostly." Despite their clear disgust at what had happened to the whisky, the changes helped catapult Scotch sales in the United States to meteoric levels. Blended Scotch whisky was now an established international bestseller.

The other big change in the evolution of Scotch took place in the early 1960s, when spirits companies realized it would be much cheaper if they shipped whisky to the United States in barrels at 100 proof (50 percent alcohol by volume) and then added water and bottled it in the States. The result was a sudden surge of new blended Scotch brands on the shelves. "Now, one bottle of Scotch out of every five sold contains whisky shipped in the barrel," claimed a 1965 syndicated column from *Business Week*. "The big selling point of the bulks, of course, is price. They run $5 or less a bottle—a dollar or two below bottled-in-Scotland brands." Muirhead's Blended Scotch even ran an advertising campaign in American newspapers touting the practice, with the tagline, "We import by the barrel so you can save by the bottle." (The Scotch Whisky Association still allows blended Scotch to be sold in bulk and bottled in an export market. However, this practice isn't allowed with single malt Scotch whisky.)

In the early 1970s there was no question of Scotch's supremacy over

J&B Rare Blended Scotch Whisky takes its name from the initials of the London liquor shop Justerini & Brooks and became one of the most popular drinks of the 1960s.

whiskey produced in the United States. Sales of Scotch in the US grew from nearly 4.4 million nine-liter cases in 1952 to nearly 24 million nine-liter cases in 1975.

"The year 1970 was an indifferent one for most American companies, but you had no problems if you were selling Scotch whisky," wrote Milton Moskowitz in his 1971 syndicated column "Inside Marketing." "Americans' thirst for this smoky, malt beverage from the highlands of Scotland seems to grow year by year." Moskowitz went on to detail the great fortunes of the country's two top-selling Scotches, Cutty Sark and J&B, which each sold

From Fire to Steam

While Neil Armstrong was walking on the moon and Twiggy was strutting down Carnaby Street in an ultramodern miniskirt, a number of Scotch distilleries were still heating their pot stills over a coal fire. After World War II, the industry began moving away from these "direct fire" stills to those heated by steam jackets or steam pipes. This technology was hardly new—some companies, such as Glenmorangie, had embraced this technology as far back as the 1880s. The clear advantage of using steam is consistency—you can be sure that every batch of your whisky is made at the same temperature. Imagine trying to maintain a coal fire at a precise level for the duration of a distillation, which can take hours to complete. And while surely there were distillery workers who were expert at this task, some batch-to-batch variation using this imprecise style was inevitable.

Steam was also a lot safer because there was no open flame. In a room full of high proof alcohol, the threat of a catastrophic fire was no joke, and it did occasionally happen. (Modern distilleries go to great lengths to avoid fires by buying extremely expensive machinery and even light fixtures and switches that are sparkproof.) Another advantage of using steam was the ease of expanding by adding more stills, since distillers no longer needed to add more teams of workers to shovel coal and build fires.

Switching from direct fire to steam-heated stills was a major change that came with the potential to significantly alter the flavor of a brand's whisky. Think of making pizza in a wood-burning oven versus a gas-powered one—the finished product is going to be similar, but definitely tastes different.

While almost all Scotch distilleries switched over to steam by the end of the twentieth century, a few holdouts, including Glenfiddich and Glenfarclas, took a slightly different approach by installing gas-powered direct fire stills, which they continue to use today.

---

nearly 3 million cases in 1970. Dewar's was just behind, with nearly 2 million cases sold. Included in the column was reporting about the possible sale of Cutty for $120 million, which made sense because the brand was reportedly grossing $20 million a year.

♦ **FROM BOOM TO BUST**

As is often the case with boom times for whisky, Scotch's wild ride would soon come to an end. In June 1970, *Time* magazine was already reporting: "There has been a shift in Americans' taste, in the direction of 'lighter' drinks. The terms are vague, but light usually connotes lower proof, a less pronounced taste and lighter color, while heavy whiskies have a definite flavor, more aftertaste and more caramel color."

Sadly, *Time*'s forecast was spot-on for the next thirty-odd years of Scotch sales, which declined steeply as drinkers discovered the joys of rum, tequila, and most importantly, vodka. The latter not only ate whiskey's lunch but also its breakfast and dinner—and barely left any scraps in the pantry. By 2005, vodka sales in the United States were higher than sales of all types of whiskey combined.

Culturally speaking, it's no coincidence that Scotch consumption declined sharply in the 1970s. The decade may be remembered for disco and New York's Studio 54, but in many ways it was anything but a good time. The Vietnam War finally came to an end in 1975, after years of needless bloodshed and destruction. On the home front in the UK and the US, there was a serious recession. Between the global oil crisis, stagflation, and rampant unemployment, it seemed like the world was spinning dangerously out of control. The conservative surge that allowed Margaret Thatcher to became Great Britain's prime minister in 1979 and Ronald Reagan to ascend to the presidency of the United States in 1981 only further served to cleave the generations apart. Blended Scotch ended up on the less-cool side of the cultural divide, more the drink of British Conservatives and American Republicans than the younger generations that fed the zeitgeist. Just as they rejected the Rat Pack and the sugary

Famous British rocker Joe Cocker and friends enjoy some J&B blended Scotch at a recording studio in Macon, Georgia.

Ghost Distilleries

While there are surely stories about ghosts haunting distilleries across Scotland, the country's celebrated ghost distilleries don't involve any specters or apparitions. Rather, when the demand for Scotch dramatically declined in the late 1970s and early '80s, a significant number of the region's distillers were shut down. The idea was that the liquor business is cyclical, so when whisky drinking came back into vogue at some point in the future, these mothballed facilities would reopen and restart production.

But it took a long while before drinkers and bartenders rediscovered the joys of drinking Scotch. And this extreme lag before Scotch sales picked up meant that a number of these shuttered distilleries never opened again. However, because Scotch needs to age for years before it can be sold, a distillery may be long closed and yet there are sometimes still barrels of whisky from the defunct facility. Scotch from these ghost distilleries has become highly sought after, and bottlings from such gone-but-not-forgotten greats as Cambus (closed in 1993), St. Magdalene (closed in 1983), Ladyburn (closed in 1975), and Dallas Dhu (closed in 1983) have acquired an almost mythical status among Scotch fans. They might even *haunt* collectors who desperately want a taste of this liquid history and a trophy for their collection.

The most recent whisky boom has, implausibly, brought a number of these ghosts back to life, including a number of revered distilleries, like Port Ellen (reopened in 2024), Brora (reopened in 2021), and Rosebank (reopened in 2024).

In the 1970s and '80s, a number of distilleries around Scotland temporarily closed down, and others shut down for good, including Dallas Dhu, pictured above, which was shuttered from 1983 to 2025.

pop music of singers like Andy Williams (of "Moon River" fame) for grittier and edgier punk, new wave, hip-hop, and rap, they also wanted something other than their parents' whisky to drink.

The same shift was happening on the other side of the world in Japan, where domestic blends were rapidly falling out of favor with the new generation of drinkers. While this demonstrated how whiskey trends were truly international, there was also a very specific consequence for Scotch distillers. The Japanese whisky industry bought a huge volume of bulk Scotch whisky to mix into their blends. So, when the market for Japanese whisky collapsed in the 1980s, it meant Scotland lost one of its most important and valued customers. It was a huge blow that the Scotch industry really didn't need at the same moment that US consumers were also switching en masse to other types of liquor.

A health craze in the 1980s was the final nail in whisky's coffin. Evian-swigging yuppies who were whipped into shape by Jane Fonda's workout tapes insisted that whisky was somehow much worse for them than wine or clear spirits. This myth persists today with a number of vodka and tequila brands, which by law are not allowed to hype any real or perceived health benefits, but nonetheless sometimes capitalize on this misperception with whisper marketing campaigns.

With the rise of vodka and the cultural winds blowing in Scotch's face, blends, the backbone of the Scotch industry, weren't selling. This decline in demand meant that blenders didn't need as much single malt as they once did. And the single malt distillers disastrously had only one client—blenders.

For the first time in nearly a century, Scotch brands were in the position of having to figure out if their whisky was still relevant in the modern world. As painful as this reckoning process would be, Scotch needed to reinvent itself.

♦ THE "INVENTION" OF SINGLE MALT SCOTCH

Through the 1970s, '80s, and '90s, blended Scotch brands sold fewer and fewer bottles each year, which meant they soon had warehouses full of ever-older single malt.

An abundance of Scotch hardly sounds like a major problem, but with dwindling demand it was actually a disaster. For starters, distillers had to pay for warehousing the whisky as it aged, and they lost 2 percent on average every year to evaporation—the angel's share. And unlike in hotter, more humid climates, a Scotch whisky decreases in proof as a result of the alcohol's evaporation. The lower the proof, the less water can be added at bottling, which means fewer bottles to sell and less revenue. Between the angel's share and the reduced alcohol, profit margins get thinner and thinner. Plus, thanks to more years in the barrel, these older malts tasted different and would subsequently change the finished blend.

What could brands do?

The solution was to find a justification to charge more and create a demand for older whisky. Single malts and premium blends would allow brands to charge a lot more and cover the costs of the longer aging period. For the plan to work, consumers would have to be taught that the older the whisky, the better it tastes. That older whiskies weren't leftovers that no one wanted—they were in fact prized elixirs to be sought out and collected. Taking it a step further, distilling companies presented some of these bottlings as downright precious, a kind of liquid time capsule that was "misplaced" and only miraculously "rediscovered" in the warehouse. Old Scotch was thus rendered rare, not just a drink but a legitimate investment akin to a vintage Rolex watch or an original print of an Ansel Adams photo.

This wasn't a completely new idea. Chivas Regal had popularized the idea that older whisky was better when it introduced its incredibly successful 12-year-old blended Scotch back in 1951, which soon became a staple of the *Mad Men* set. (A few years later Chivas introduced an even ritzier 21-year-old whisky.) While there were other whiskies on the market that featured ages on their labels, Chivas 12 Year helped hammer home the connection between quality and age for consumers. (The whisky became so renowned that when Nikita Khrushchev visited the National Press Club in Washington, DC, he reportedly had a Chivas with water and one ice cube.)

But selling single malts as distinct products required a wholesale change in the way whisky was marketed, and a complete makeover for Scotch. Each malt was no longer just an unknown ingredient in a blend, but a distinct luxury product with a recognizable name. Every distillery suddenly needed its own flavor profile and a memorable backstory. The distillers were no longer unheralded managers of liquor plants or factories, but national treasures—the face of an international brand akin to the head designer at a French fashion house. (It's no wonder that luxury conglomerate Moët Hennessy Louis Vuitton [LVMH] now owns Glenmorangie and Ardbeg Scotches.)

Blends, like Chivas Regal, built the Scotch industry and are still in demand around the world.

♦ THE MYTH OF SINGLE MALT

A favorite trope of Scotch marketing is the brooding, kilt-wearing Scotsman drinking single malt on a majestic moor. But if you travel to Scotland, you'll be hard pressed to turn up many weather-hardened, white-bearded Highlanders opining about the spirit's inherent leather and tobacco notes—because those people never really existed. You might find such a character in a Highland Scotch bar that caters to tourists, but if you go to a locals' bar the scene is quite different. Beer and cider flow freely, and most folks drink blended whisky. It's telling that the bestselling Scotch in Scotland is the eminently quaffable blend the Famous Grouse. The brand's signature serve is the Low Flyer: a shot of whisky with a pint of beer. When it comes to Scotch, no one stands on ceremony in these bars.

So it's ironic that the savior of the Scotch industry was single malt, which very few at the time drank on its own, whether in America or in Scotland. An entertaining 1935 story in *Esquire*, "Smoke Gets in Your Nose," by Lawton Mackall, includes this passage about the dominance of blends (and the irrelevance of single malt at the time): "Virgin Scotch, technically known as 'self whisky,' went out of fashion in 1860. Here and there among the crags a horny-kneed ghillie may mutter through the burrs in his beard that he's an Auld Licht when it comes to liquor, and may still drink it unbalanced, but his kind are dwindling. The Scotch whisky the world knows and fondles between tongue and roof of mouth is a blend of blends, baffling to analyze but a cinch to swallow."

In the 1960s, William Grant and a few other distilleries started selling a small amount of single malt in America. "Charles Grant Gordon, a Scotsman whose family is known for its Grant's whisky, has a product he is struggling to make a mighty droplet in the torrent of scotch that flows from his native land to the United States," wrote Kenneth McKenna in a March 1969 edition of his advertising column in New York's *Daily News* newspaper. McKenna then introduces the concept of single malt to his readers. At the time, Americans were buying 14 million cases of blended Scotch and just ten thousand cases of single malt. "But product difference is what Gordon is selling, and he readily conceded that many people won't like his single-malt whisky. 'If I can annoy 90% of the market and have 10% that's all right with me,' he said with an honest Scottish laugh."

Tastes were also beginning to change. In response to the lighter blends that became popular after World War II, which were made with more grain whisky and less single malt, some drinkers who fancied themselves connoisseurs began looking for richer whiskies. This trend seems to have started in Europe. In 1963, the UPI news agency published a very small article titled "French Go For Straight Scotch," which detailed how the craze began. "Until about five years ago the French seemed to prefer blended whiskey—usually

What Does the Age on a Label Mean?

Most Scotch brands come in a few recognizable ages: 10, 12, 15, 18, 21, 25, and 30 years old. Distillers have used these age statements very effectively to broadcast the quality of their whisky and to get people to spend more and more on older whiskies.

So, what does the age of whisky actually mean? It's a bit more complex than you might think. Strictly speaking, the age refers to how long the whisky spent maturing in a barrel. Once that barrel is emptied and the whisky is bottled, the clock stops and its age is frozen. But there's one major caveat—if a distiller blends an older whisky with a younger whisky, the resulting mixture can only be labeled using the lower age. What that means is that there might be a touch of older whisky in your dram to give it more depth and nuance.

Given the vagaries of predicting supply and demand at least a decade in advance, brands have at times found themselves a bit short of stocks of the desired age. In that case, the company has three options: 1) announce that it has a temporary shortage and wait until it once again has the supply; 2) quietly remove the age from the bottle's label and give the whisky a new name; or 3) bottle an older whisky in place of the younger one, which is permitted. Over the years, brands have tried all three approaches with varying degrees of success.

40 percent single malt whisky and 60 percent grain spirits—but one Paris bar began serving straight whisky and the drink quickly became a status symbol."

Across the channel, a similar trend was taking hold in London. In 1964, an Associated Press story by Eddy Gilmore detailed how "in the high altitudes of snobbery, the whisky snob is replacing the wine snob." The piece goes on to explain that these drinkers go around the city looking for single malts and spouting off about how they're better than blends. Mind you, most people didn't really know what single malts were at the time. The story quotes British book publisher John Calder, who claims that single malt "is wasted on people who don't know the difference." He goes on to advise drinkers not to "dilute it with soda . . . Soda ruins a single malt. Just have it straight, or with a little water if you must. But no soda, please." This is the exact kind of nonsense you still hear today, from snobby drinkers as well as the occasional ill-informed brand ambassador or bartender.

A single malt can actually be a blend of whisky of different ages from the same distillery.

All of this begs the question: If a whisky is older, is it always better? Not exactly. Just because it's older doesn't mean you'll like it more than a younger version. A few more years of maturation may indeed transform your favorite whisky into a magical amber elixir. Or it could make it taste like a glass full of wood. The good news is that you're going to have to try it yourself to know if you like it.

By the early 1970s, the rise of single malts was in full effect, thanks to the message that they were the choice of people with discerning palates, and what the Scottish themselves drank.

Given that the Scotch industry was dominated by blends at the time, I can't imagine they would have chosen the narrative that single malts were the refined choice and blends were for rubes. But as the the decade marched on and sales of blended Scotch began to steadily decline, the industry was no doubt looking for any angle to bolster its fortunes. While blends had been the big business, it was clear that a new generation of drinkers was no longer impressed by them. To keep up with sexy Scandinavian vodka, something new and exciting had to be done.

It wasn't long before single malt brand ambassadors began to be quoted in articles that single malt Scotch whisky was supposedly the connoisseur's choice and what Scots themselves preferred, which lent credibility to this mostly revisionist history of Scotch drinking traditions. Neil McKerrow, then marketing

Starting in the late 1970s, the focus of the Scotch industry began to switch from blends to single malts.

director of Macdonald & Muir, which owned Glen Moray-Glenlivet and Glenmorangie in 1978, claimed in a *New York Daily News* story: "There is a definite consumer interest in prestige, premium-priced, single malt scotches," adding that he saw the popularity of single malt as "a definite maturation of taste."

To be fair, Johnnie Walker also seemed to understand the greater cultural shift that was happening, and began pushing its more deluxe Black Label and later its super premium Blue Label over the company's entry-level Red Label. Spirits marketing and innovations genius Tom Jago came up with the idea of renaming Johnnie Walker Oldest as Johnnie Walker Blue Label, which was relaunched in 1987. Even though it had a suggested retail price of $165 in America it was a hit with status-seeking customers, and by 1997, according to Nicholas Morgan's book *A Long Stride*, sales of Blue Label were up to nearly fifty thousand nine-liter cases a year.

By the winter holidays in 1988, Johnnie Walker decided not to promote Red Label at all; the move was a real statement about where the Scotch market was going. As a result of becoming ever more upscale, Johnnie Walker was arguably one of the few blended Scotch brands to remain relevant and carve out a significant space in a world dominated by single malts.

By the early 1990s, a sizable share of US liquor stores were carrying a small but impressive selection of single malts. It wasn't uncommon to find The Glenlivet 12 Year, Highland Park 12 Year, Laphroaig 15 Year, Lagavulin 16 Year, and The Macallan 12 Year on the shelves. At the time, the single malts were priced similarly to the first generation of small batch bourbons, but were significantly more expensive than the standard Scotch blends. It was easier to spot the difference, since the Scotch blends were often tellingly sold in 1.75-liter handles, while the more expensive single malt whiskies came in the standard 750-milliliter bottles.

In 1993, journalist Robert Lawrence Balzer put together a tasting of forty-two single malts (forty-one of them from Scotland, and a Bushmills bottling from Ireland) and wrote up the results for the *Los Angeles Times*. "Single-malt Scotch whiskey, once a well-kept secret of Scotland, is now the choice of many Americans," is how the story begins, and it includes a quote from noted British wine writer Hugh Johnson comparing single malts to the finest Bordeaux wines. Amazingly, most of the whisky brands Balzer included in his tasting are still available today. And their suggested retail prices would be screaming bargains today (like $28.99 for The Macallan 12 Year, which currently goes for at least twice that), but some bottles in the tasting were already selling for quite a bit, including a $260 bottle of Balblair distilled in 1965.

The uncertain whisky times likely led to the merger of liquor giants Grand Metropolitan and Guinness in 1997. The resulting powerhouse conglomerate was called Diageo, which is still one of the biggest liquor companies in the world. The combined portfolio was so mammoth and included so many different whisky brands, like Johnnie Walker and J&B, that Diageo had to sell Dewar's to Bacardi to assuage government concerns about a monopoly. "The driving force behind the surprise announcement today is the generational divide that has plagued the liquor business for years," wrote Youssef Ibrahim in the *New York Times* when the reported $22.27 billion deal closed. "Basically, distilled spirits are popular with people 60 and older, while younger drinkers tend to prefer wine, wine coolers, beer, or nonalcoholic drinks—a trend that does not bode well for future growth."

◆ **SINGLE MALT: THE GENUINE SCOTCH**

Despite the growing hype around single malts in the 1990s, the whisky didn't quite catch on for several years. It wasn't until around 2004 that Scotch sales finally began to increase, with single malts leading the way. The idea that malts were superior to blends and were what the Scots drank themselves, an idea first planted in the 1960s, finally came to fruition.

In truth, you couldn't have dreamed up a better product than single malt Scotch to entice hipsters in awe of all things heritage, who would pay a premium for so-called craft brands made by way of old-timey production methods. Accordingly, trendy stores in some of New York's and Los Angeles's fanciest neighborhoods were selling everything from letterpress greeting cards to hand-forged pots and pans.

In these environments, single malts seemed like an insider's secret. Knowing the different Glens was like passage into a deeply cool club. It was the perfect drink for an era that reveled in swing dancing, Johnny Cash, and everything mid-century modern. Malts even started being name-checked in movies as a means for characters to flex their sophistication.

In a memorable scene from the hit 1996 movie *Swingers*, Jon Favreau's character, Mike, is trying to act like a big-time gambler in a Las Vegas casino in order to get VIP treatment. To

Nineties hipsters fell hard for single malt Scotch, which began to show up in popular movies of the time, like *Swingers*.

The Perfect Finish

Look at the Scotch section of your favorite liquor store, and you'll see port, sherry, and even rum and beer prominently featured on labels. No one would blame you for being a little confused, but let me be the first to assure you that you're in the right place.

There's historical precedent for using a variety of barrels to age Scotch—for hundreds of years beverages and products were shipped in wooden barrels that were used over and over again. In the modern era, whisky producers employed either used bourbon barrels or casks that were seasoned with sherry. A number of Scotch brands (and several American whiskey brands) now "finish" their mature whiskey for a number of days, weeks, months, or even years in a second kind of barrel.

At its simplest, a whisky may first age in a former bourbon barrel or a sherry cask before then aging in a barrel that previously held anything from cabernet to port to rum to sauternes. Dewar's even recently aged its blended Scotch in barrels that had previously held mezcal.

This idea of finishing whisky dates back to when single malt brands were trying to reinvent themselves in the 1990s, and distance themselves from blends. Two Scotch distillers, Dr. Bill Lumsden from Glenmorangie and David Stewart MBE from Glenfiddich and Balvenie, decided to experiment with aging their whisky in different types of barrels. Their pioneering work in this area largely created this finishing method and a new type of whisky.

impress a crowd at a blackjack table he loudly orders what he imagines to be a high-roller drink. "A Scotch on the rocks, please. Any Scotch will do, as long as it's not a blend, of course. Single malt. Glenlivet, Glenfiddich perhaps . . . any Glen." After he loses $200 on the first hand, he's humiliated and forced to move to a lower-stakes table. Just as he cashes out his few remaining chips in anticipation of slinking back to his Los Angeles home, the server with his drink spots him. She complains that she walked around for an hour looking for him with his Scotch on her tray, but kindly offers to get him a new one. Mike then laments, "I didn't even want it. I just wanted to order it."

It's probably no coincidence that the rebirth of the classic cocktail also came around this time. An army of highly educated and highly motivated bartenders spread across the United

States, preaching the gospel of well-mixed drinks. Many of them were disciples of legendary bartender Dale DeGroff, who ran the bar at New York's famed Rainbow Room. While gin, rum, rye, bourbon, and even mezcal benefited directly from this movement, showing up in hundreds of drink recipes, single malt Scotch benefited too. The connoisseurship of classic cocktails and the deep knowledge of whisky come from a very similar place and require an appreciation of history, authenticity, and quality. On the other hand, if you don't know anything about drinks, a well-made cocktail or a glass of a complex single malt can still be mind-blowingly good.

It didn't matter that much if the common knowledge about the history and the proper way to consume Scotch wasn't accurate. If anything, these embellishments to Scotch history only served to give it more gravitas. And the supposed rules about how and how *not* to drink Scotch only served to make folks feel smart about liquor—perhaps for the first time in their lives.

We're Living in a Golden Age of Scotch Whisky

While the twentieth century was more of a roller coaster for Scotch distillers and brands than anyone could have predicted, the twenty-first century so far has been a golden age. Over the past twenty-odd years, Scotch has become so popular worldwide that the industry has had trouble keeping up with demand.

The popularity of single malts continues to grow each year, according to the Distilled Spirits Council of the United States. From 2002 to 2020, Scotch sales grew by a staggering 200 percent. Over the same time, sales of blended Scotch fell by nearly 14 percent. While that might not sound like much, it translates to a decrease of more than 1 million nine-liter cases of blended Scotch, which is significant. To be clear, the majority of Scotch sold is still blends but it's not hard to imagine that changing. During the decade

Caol Ila is the largest distillery on the island of Islay, and most of the whisky it produces goes into Scotch blends.

to come, sales of blended Scotch in the US and other major markets will continue to shrink, while those of single malts will keep growing exponentially.

In addition to the old chestnut that single malts are somehow more authentic than blends, and that the Scots themselves prefer single malts, another twist has been added to bolster the story that single malts are superior. According to this new argument, the blends were great to drink back in the day but are now not as good as they used to be, because they contain ever more grain whisky and ever less single malt. These claims aren't universally true and really depends on the brand and even sometimes the particular bottling. Blenders have been playing with the proportions of their blends for more than a century—it is not a recent development.

What can't be denied is that barrels of aged single malt have steeply risen in value. It's now hard to justify including them in a blend that sells for, say $25 a bottle, when bottling the single malt alone can bring twice or three times as much.

Some single malts have gotten so popular on their own that they're no longer used in blends at all. For instance, Diageo historically used Lagavulin's wonderful smoky and briny flavor notes to give Johnnie Walker Black Label its signature oomph and backbone. But Lagavulin, which is located on the revered island of Islay, has developed its own large following, and several years ago Diageo decided to bottle the distillery's production as a single malt. So what happened to Black Label? Don't worry—Diageo replaced the Lagavulin part of the blend with whisky from its distillery Caol Ila, which is also located on Islay. Problem solved. But—around the same time, Diageo also started marketing Caol Ila's single malt bottlings. These whiskies began to catch on with Scotch drinkers, who had never before tasted Caol Ila on its own. Diageo then wisely decided to pump the break on promoting Caol Ila as a single malt, before it got so popular the company wouldn't be able to use it in its blends.

The Future of Scotch

The reinvention of Scotch has almost worked too well. Single malts have become a revered luxury product and drinkers around the world are paying ever more for whiskies from their favorite distilleries. But because Scotch is an aged product, it can be hard to prepare for what the drinks market will be like in five years, let alone in ten or twenty. The industry has been rebuilt on selling 10-, 12-, 18-, and 21-year-old whisky, but if a distillery runs out of barrels of, say, their 18-year-old, there isn't much they can do until their other barrels reach that age. For this reason, in 2015, Laphroaig made the painful decision to discontinue its 18-year-old single malt for the foreseeable future. At the same time, the distillery introduced a number of other whiskies with no age statements, which gave it a bit more flexibility in terms of what barrels it could bottle.

Laphroaig wasn't alone in their approach—a number of other famous brands followed suit and pulled age designations off their labels. It was understandable. In the early 2000s, the industry's number-one concern was getting rid of its ocean of aged whisky—an abundance that was known as the whisky loch. No one had the time or the foresight to imagine future demand. And if someone had openly predicted that the global demand for single malt would explode

At first glance, The Macallan's distillery looks like a modern art museum, but it actually houses thirty-six copper pot stills.

in just a few years, it would've been treated like a cruel joke and dismissed as fantasy. But these so-called non age statement whiskies were incredibly confusing to consumers who didn't really understand why their favorite whisky was suddenly gone from the shelf and didn't know what to make of these new bottlings. Ultimately, distillers added ages back to the labels once they had enough mature stock.

An endemic problem in the Scotch business is that you have to make huge upfront investments to make the whisky, including buying all the barrels and paying to warehouse them. A Scotch whisky maker typically makes money only at the very end of the process. If you figure in all the amortized costs for the distillery and the facilities, you can understand why a brand doesn't want to significantly increase production if it can't be sure that the bet will ultimately pay out.

Hindsight is, as always, twenty-twenty. For the past several years, Scottish distilleries have been playing catch-up, running their operations nonstop to meet demand. Many of the biggest brands, including The Glenlivet and The Macallan, have significantly expanded or even built new, larger facilities. And for the first time in a long while, there is a generation of new distilleries opening in Scotland, including Aberargie in Perth and Arbikie distillery in Arbroath.

Some whisky experts are now worried that there is potentially too much whisky being produced, and that we may face a crisis in a few years. I'm more bullish (and perhaps foolish), but I think single malt brands won't have a problem selling the whisky they're producing today. At some point, single malt sales will plateau, and production and sales will fall into equilibrium, but I think we still have a long way to go until then.

Scotch Whisky Family Tree

BRANCH: DIAGEO

Diageo (DEE-ag-ee-OH) is one of the world's largest spirits companies. It owns all kinds of spirits brands produced around the world—from Casamigos tequila to Tanqueray gin to Guinness beer—but the heart of Diageo's business is Scotch. Currently, their vast whisky portfolio includes thirty single malt distilleries, plus grain distilleries, all across Scotland. By comparison, there are 145 total whisky distilleries in Scotland. (Diageo's Cameronbridge distillery in Scotland is currently one of the largest distilleries in the world, and is now carbon-neutral.)

While it has an impressive roster, Diageo was only formed relatively recently when Grand Metropolitan merged with Guinness in 1997 in a deal worth a reported $22.27 billion. Here are some of its most important Scotch whisky brands.

Johnnie Walker

The story of international bestseller Johnnie Walker really begins with a tragedy. In 1819, Alexander Walker passed away at the age of only thirty-nine, forcing his family to sell their farm. His son, John Walker, used the proceeds from the farm's sale to buy an upscale grocery store southwest of Glasgow in a village called Kilmarnock. The store sold food, wine, and most importantly, spirits.

Until the turn of the twentieth century, alcohol didn't come in a sealed bottle directly from a distillery. Distilleries (or

Before their name was synonymous with Scotch, the Walker family ran a luxury grocery store in Kilmarnock, Scotland.

their middlemen) delivered barrels to grocery stores, which doubled as liquor stores and bars. Customers would buy liquor by the glass from local stores or fill up a flask or decanter to take it home. These grocery stores would often create their own blends of tea, spices, and whisky. Johnnie Walker Scotch started as one of the house whiskies in the Walkers' family store. It was likely a combination of single malts and grain whisky that were bought from distillers across Scotland. The Walkers also, no doubt, sold single malts in their store.

In 1857, John passed away and his son Alexander took over the business. Alexander truly saw the potential in the family's house blend, which had simply been called Walker's Whisky by loyal patrons. He was responsible for introducing the brand's now iconic square bottle and signature slanted label.

Over the second half of the nineteenth century, the popularity of blended Scotch and Johnnie Walker grew dramatically, due in part to the phylloxera crisis (see page 10) that crippled Cognac, Armagnac, port, and sherry producers. As drinkers sought alternatives, Scotch became big business. To continue growing, the Johnnie Walker company realized it needed to start acquiring the single malt distilleries whose whisky they were buying. The first distillery Johnnie Walker bought was Cardhu (car-DEW), in 1893. The Speyside whisky became the official heart of the Walkers' blends, and Cardhu's whisky still goes into different Johnnie Walker whiskies. (See the Cardhu entry, page 258, for more.)

Until 1908, the brand was known as Old Highland Whisky, and at the time, the Walker family didn't like that its whiskies had developed the nickname "Johnnie Walker." According to Scotch authority Nicholas Morgan, who wrote the book *A Long Stride: The Story of the World's No. 1 Scotch Whisky*, it was the brand's marketing director, James Stevenson, who persuaded the family to officially rebrand the whisky as Johnnie Walker. Stevenson, whose father had run the Walkers' original Kilmarnock store, also developed the brand's now famous striding man logo.

Around the turn of the twentieth century, Scotch sales were further boosted by the popularity of the Highball in the United States, which led Walker to introduce its White, Red, and Black Label blends in 1906. Over the years, the brand's line up changed with the addition and subtraction of different colors, but in recent history it has always included Red and Black. The former is easy-drinking and known to be the world's bestselling Scotch, whereas the Black is aged for twelve years and has a

The heart of Johnnie Walker is whisky from the Cardhu distillery, which was built by John and Helen Cumming.

Johnnie Walker's famous logo, the so-called striding man, was dreamed up by the brand's marketing director, James Stevenson.

One of the most interesting Johnnie Walker whiskies is the High Rye bottling, which was launched in 2021 and includes a grain whiskey made from predominantly rye grain. It capitalized on the recent rebirth of rye whiskey started by craft bartenders and drinkers.

Dalwhinnie

At 1,185 feet (360 meters) above sea level, Dalwhinnie (doll-WINNIE) is Scotland's highest distillery, sitting at the base of the dramatic mountains in the Cairngorms National Park. Scotland is home to plenty of remote distilleries, but the otherworldly character of Dahlwhinnie's location can make you feel like an extra in a David Lynch film. It doesn't help that the facility feels deserted, and it now only requires a few people to run the whole place.

How does the elevation affect the taste of the whisky? I'm not sure, but I can say that it has the rare combination of depth, complexity, lightness, and drinkability. It's one of the whiskies I like to pour for folks who say they don't like Scotch. After tasting a wee bit of Dalwhinnie, their opinions usually change.

The distillery opened in 1897 but caused a stir only a few years later when it was bought by a group of Americans for £1,250. While Americans were rapidly developing a taste for Scotch and buying plenty of the whisky, the idea that they would actually buy a Scottish distillery didn't sit well in the UK. In 1925, Dalwhinnie safely returned to British hands when it was acquired by Distillers Company Limited (DCL), which would eventually evolve into the company known today as Diageo.

Currently, Dalwhinnie produces only a few different types of whisky. The easiest

smoky, peaty punch. In 2011, the brand introduced Double Black as a limited-edition bottling, which became part of the regular lineup a few years later. It's even smokier than the standard Black Label, with a higher quotient of maritime single malts from the west coast of Scotland.

Arguably Johnnie Walker's most famous whisky is Blue Label, which came out in 1987 and features rare and very old whiskies. (When it was first introduced, Blue was actually called Johnnie Walker Oldest.) I'm often asked if this is the brand's best whisky and if it's worth the price. While it is very pleasant to drink, I would honestly prefer to spend the money on several bottles of Black Label, which is a rich and versatile Scotch—but Blue has a cachet that few other whiskies can match.

The Dahlwhinnie distillery was built in the shadow of Scotland's Cairngorms National Park and dates back to 1897.

one to find is the honeyed 15-year-old, but there is also a Distillers Edition, which is aged for a second time in an unusually flavorful barrel. The most recent edition made use of an American oak barrel that had previously held oloroso sherry.

J&B Rare Blended Scotch Whisky

While today whisky drinkers tend to want rich and flavorful single malts, not too long ago what Americans wanted was an easy-drinking, light Scotch. J&B Rare was one of the most successful of these brands, with sales surging in the second half of the twentieth century.

It was created by the historic London wine and spirits merchant Justerini & Brooks, which opened its doors in 1749 and has held a royal warrant to supply the British monarchy since 1761. The company's store was forced to start selling whisky in the 1880s after the phylloxera crisis destroyed the wine, Cognac, port, and sherry industries. Justerini & Brooks created their first blended Scotch in 1884 and introduced J&B Rare in the 1930s.

After years of Prohibition, American drinkers were thirsty, and the quaffable J&B was a hit. But then the Scotch industry essentially shut down for World War II, and even after the distilleries were able to reopen, it took several years for the whisky to age. So it wasn't until the late 1950s that J&B really began to take off, and then sales absolutely exploded in the 1960s. In ten years, J&B sales went from half a million nine-liter cases to 2.5 million nine-liter cases per year. In fact, it got so popular that in 1969 six people were caught with a truck full of nearly nine hundred cases of J&B, stolen from the docks at Port Elizabeth, New Jersey.

By the 1980s, sales of J&B in the US began to slow down, but the Scotch continues to be popular around the world. In 2021, according to industry news website the *Spirits Business*, J&B was the tenth most popular Scotch brand in the world, selling 2.3 million nine-liter cases globally. The modern incarnation of J&B is a modestly priced blend of more than three dozen single malts and grain whisky.

Oban Single Malt Scotch Whisky

Oban is a gem of a whisky that doesn't get the attention it richly deserves. For years, most of the distillery's production disappeared into Diageo blends such as Johnnie Walker. But over the past two decades, more and more of the whisky has been bottled as a single malt. Located between Speyside and Islay, the distillery also produces a flavor profile in the middle of those two styles—heathered and very drinkable, with a whisper of briny air and peat. Oban's signature flavor, which is pleasantly lighter than many other maritime malts, may be due to its proximity to the sea, or the fact that it uses just two small pot stills to make its spirit.

The distillery was started in 1794 by Hugh and John Stevenson in the picturesque seaside town of Oban. It is on the west coast of Scotland, right across from the Isle of Mull. While I've heard the name pronounced many different ways, the former master distiller Kenny Gray insisted that it was simply oh-BEN.

The brand's most famous bottling is the 14-year-old Oban, which perfectly showcases its house style. But also look out for Oban Little Bay and the Oban Distillers Edition, both of which are aged in a range of barrels.

The port city of Oban along the west coast of Scotland is home to an acclaimed single malt distillery.

In an incredible twist of fate, after being closed for decades the Brora distillery reopened in 2021.

Brora

Until recently, folks in the whiskey industry talked about the Brora (B-roar-AHH) in reverential tones usually reserved for the deceased. The downfall and ultimate closure of the distillery in the 1980s became a cautionary tale about the changing tastes of consumers, specifically those who suddenly decide they don't want to drink Scotch anymore. For decades afterward, Brora was a so-called ghost distillery, the facility long gone but the remaining barrels of its single malt for sale. As the years passed, these barrels got rarer and ever more expensive. Bottles of Brora whisky can now go for thousands of dollars—if you can even find one to buy. Many of them have been snatched up by collectors.

The Brora story starts long before the infamous Scotch crash. The distillery was opened in the town of Brora by the Marquess of Stafford, the son of the Duke of Sutherland, in 1819. Through the nineteenth century, Brora was sought after as a single malt, unique because blended Scotch was much more widely available at the time. The distillery was originally named Clynelish (KLEIN-leash) and was called that until 1969. At the time, its owner, DCL (the predecessor to Diageo), decided to build a new Clynelish distillery right next door to the original facility. To distinguish the two distilleries, the old one was renamed Brora. (See the Clynelish entry, page 256, for more.)

The old facility suddenly became incredibly important, since Caol Ila, the busy Islay distillery, was being rebuilt at the time and wouldn't reopen until 1974. DCL, which owned both Brora and Caol Ila, needed heavily peated malts for its Scotch blends, so Brora was used to make that style of whisky. Ultimately, Brora was shut down in 1983 when global demand for whisky plummeted, seemingly dooming the whisky to slowly fade away.

But in a plot twist that I honestly didn't see coming, Brora was rebuilt by Diageo and reopened in 2021. The carbon-neutral facility now produces 800,000 liters (more than 211,000 gallons) of peated single malt, which I imagine will begin to hit the market as a single malt by the early 2030s. No doubt the mania created by collectors of the whisky produced before the 1983 shutdown influenced Diageo's decision to reopen the distillery. In the meantime, Diageo will continue to sell some of the vintage Brora whisky.

Haig Club Single Grain Whisky

The modern Haig Club Single Grain Whisky is loosely connected to the Haig (HAY-g) family who began making Scotch centuries ago. However, this new version was introduced in partnership with retired soccer star David Beckham and dates back only to December 2014. (The brand even hired movie director Guy Ritchie to create an ad announcing the new release.) It's not a single malt or a blend, but a grain whisky produced at Diageo's giant Cameronbridge distillery in Fife.

What does that mean? Well, that takes a bit of explaining. To make a Scotch blend you combine various single malts and tie it all together with so-called grain whisky, which is usually made on a high-volume column still and doesn't need to be created from exclusively malted barley. Over the past thirty years, spirits conglomerates have essentially taken the single malt out of blends and bottled the single malts separately. As a result, they've been left with plenty of aged grain whisky—and are trying to develop a market for it too.

The association with Beckham and the brand's unique, colognelike square blue bottle was, no doubt, Diageo's attempt to create a distinct identity for Haig Club apart from its other established Scotch whiskies. The jury is still out on whether this whole project was successful, but Beckham stepped away from Haig Club in 2023.

Though Beckham lent his star power to the brand, the whisky's namesake was a celebrity in his own right. The name is a nod to the legendary distiller John Haig and the brand Haig & Haig, which is also in Diageo's portfolio. The Haig family actually built the Cameronbridge distillery in 1824 and the family was a pioneer in the production of grain whisky. The modern facility, where Haig Club is made, was built on the site of the original one. Funnily enough, Haig is linked to another celebrity of sorts: In the eighteenth century, Irish whiskey distiller John Jameson married one of John Haig's daughters.

Talisker

Once you make the long, scenic trek to the Isle of Skye, off the west coast of Scotland, you may be greeted by ominous gray skies and cold sideways rain. That was my experience, anyway, when I visited Skye in the late 1990s. But once you find your bearings (and your way to the pub) you may begin to understand the flavor profile of the island's beloved whisky, Talisker (TAL-is-kerr). The muscular single malt has notes of sea brine and bright smoke. Like many foods and drinks, Talisker makes much more sense once you understand where it's produced and how it truly reflects that place.

The Talisker distillery was opened by Hugh and Kenneth MacAskill in 1830, after reportedly spending £3,000 to build the facility. For its first century in business, one of Talisker's defining characteristics was that it was distilled three times instead of the now standard two times. I imagine adding a third distillation made

Since 1830, the Isle of Skye has been home to the famous Talisker distillery.

the whisky lighter in both mouthfeel and flavor. Hopefully, Talisker will one day make a special batch that's distilled a third time, so we can see what its whisky tasted like when the distillery originally opened.

Talisker has plenty of smoke and peat flavor, but its house style is much more nuanced. There's a definite salty quality to it, as well as an inexplicable black pepper note, which is why the brand often serves fresh-shucked oysters with the whisky at events. It's also no wonder that Talisker is one of the secrets to Johnnie Walker Black Label's signature flavor, helping to provide its signature peaty backbone.

The 10-year-old version is the standard Talisker, and best exemplifies its unique mix of smoke, brine, and pepper. The brand has also introduced a range of single malts, including the brawnier Talisker Storm, which doesn't have a stated age, and a Distillers Edition, which is aged for a second time in an unusually flavorful barrel. The most recent edition made use of an oloroso sherry cask.

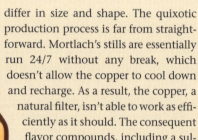

A dram of Talisker pairs beautifully with fresh-shucked oysters.

differ in size and shape. The quixotic production process is far from straightforward. Mortlach's stills are essentially run 24/7 without any break, which doesn't allow the copper to cool down and recharge. As a result, the copper, a natural filter, isn't able to work as efficiently as it should. The consequent flavor compounds, including a sulfur note, which would normally be extracted, are allowed to go through the still and can be found in the finished whisky. Although it might seem strange, this is actually a good thing, and responsible for Mortlach's distinctive flavor.

The distillery opened in 1823 and helped turn the charming Scottish village of Dufftown into a home for the single malt industry. Beginning in the 1860s, the distiller William Grant worked at Mortlach for more than twenty years before he opened his own distilleries, including the legendary Glenfiddich (GLEN-fidik) and Balvenie (BOL-venn-y). (See the entries on Glenfiddich, page 277, and Balvenie,

Mortlach

The Mortlach (MORT-lock) distillery is just down the road from Glenfiddich and Balvenie in Dufftown—but in terms of flavor, it's miles and miles away.

The distillery is famous for its big, unctuous whisky. One reason for Mortlach's uniquely heavy aroma and taste is that it is made in a range of stills that

While Mortlach has long been used by Scotch blenders, you can now find it bottled as a single malt.

Before starting his own distillery, William Grant worked at the nearby Mortlach distillery for years.

page 277, for more). In 1923, industry publication the *Wine and Spirit Trade Record* wrote of Dufftown, "What was once a sleepy Highland village has since become an important centre in a district justly celebrated for its fine Malt Whisky, and to-day Dufftown possesses seven Distilleries."

Mortlach has been a favorite of whisky blenders because the malt gives blends a solid base note. The Mortlach distillery was bought by bestselling Johnnie Walker in the 1920s, and while millions of drinkers have enjoyed Mortlach in Scotch blends, until recently few had ever had the whisky on its own as a single malt, or even heard of the distillery, for that matter. That all changed in 2014 when Diageo began releasing Mortlach as a single malt, and marketing it heavily in a number of key cities in North America, Europe, and Asia.

The brand now offers a standard line that includes a 12-year-old, a 16-year-old, a 20-year-old, and a 30-year-old whisky, plus additional limited editions. Unlike a standard Speyside single malt, the whisky is not accessible or approachable—Mortlach is proudly funky and weird. That's just how the whisky tastes. I would suggest trying it a few times to see if the whisky grows on you.

Caol Ila

On the east side of the Scottish island of Islay is a workhorse of a distillery, Caol Ila. It also has one of the hardest names for many non-Scots to pronounce (for the record it's coal-LEE-lah).

The vast distillery, which dates back to 1846, produces a river of supersmoky, peaty single malt. In the 1920s, it had one of the largest stills in Scotland, with a capacity of 6,567 gallons (249 hectoliters). After the distillery suffered a major fire in the early 1970s, it was rebuilt and expanded, increasing the number of stills from two to six.

In 2011, Diageo announced that it was going to spend $5.6 million to further increase the distillery's output to a staggering 6.4 million liters (1.69 million gallons) a year. Caol Ila is now by far the biggest distillery on Islay—nearly double the size of Laphroaig, the second largest distillery on the island.

Most of the facility's production goes into blends, and it's famously used as an ingredient in a number of Johnnie Walker's offerings. So if you like Johnnie Walker Black Label, then you will definitely love Caol Ila. In the United States, you can generally find a few different single malts from the distillery, including a 12-year-old and a Distillers Edition finished in a second type of barrel.

Every spring, the distillery blows the Scotch world's collective mind by releasing

One of the unsung heroes of the Scotch industry is Caol Ila, which produces peaty whisky that is primarily used in popular blends.

While the whisky might be readily available for the royals and their guests, it's traditionally been fairly hard to come by in the United States, which is a shame. Royal Lochnagar is a delightful and elegant whisky that can be drunk as an aperitif before dinner, or even as a nightcap. If you look hard enough you can find the 12-year-old, which has a regal blue label with white-and-gold lettering that, fittingly, almost resembles a knight's shield.

a limited-edition whisky that—contrary to the brand's style—isn't smoky. When I first heard about this special malt I thought it was a joke, but I can assure you it's no prank. The Unpeated Style Natural Cask Strength 15-Year-Old is highly sought-after by collectors because it gives you a rare sense of what the iconic whisky tastes like without its signature smoke.

Royal Lochnagar

There are neighbors . . . and then there is the King of England. The Royal Lochnagar (LOCK-nee-GAR) distillery is less than a mile from King Charles's pastoral summer home of Balmoral Castle in Aberdeenshire, Scotland. Along with the close proximity, there is definitely a special relationship between the whisky brand and the royal family. The distillery opened in 1825 and was visited by Queen Victoria and Prince Albert in 1848. Queen Elizabeth II was also a fan of Royal Lochnagar and granted it a sought-after royal warrant in 2021 to supply the royal households with Scotch.

Clynelish

Clynelish (KLINE-leash) is a relatively new distillery with a surprisingly long history. The modern Clynelish distillery opened in 1969 and was built by Distillers Company Limited (the predecessor to Diageo) right next door to one of its other distilleries, Brora (B-roar-AHH). The two distilleries are in the village of Brora, which is on the northeast coast of Scotland. The two distilleries don't just share a location and owner, but also a lineage. Brora was originally called Clynelish when it opened in 1819, and was renamed when the modern Clynelish distillery was built. (See the Brora entry, page 252, for more.)

Royal Lochnagar is practically next door to King Charles' Balmoral Castle in Aberdeenshire, Scotland.

Islay distillery Lagavulin dates back to the early 1800s, and its whisky has developed a loyal following.

While you can sometimes find the 14-year-old Clynelish Single Malt Scotch Whisky sold in the US, most of the distillery's production goes into Scotch blends. Drinkers and blenders like the whisky for its signature velvety, waxy note.

Lagavulin

I'm sure that John Johnston, the founder in the early nineteenth century of the Islay distillery that would become Lagavulin (LAG-a-vous-LIN), could never have imagined that his whisky would one day be the toast of twenty-first-century celebrities.

But Lagavulin is adored by actor Nick Offerman, who first tasted the single malt when he was starting his career in Chicago in the late 1990s. In fact, he insists

The first Scotch actor Nick Offerman ever tried was Lagavulin. Today he works with the distillery to create signature releases.

that it was the first Scotch he ever tried. Offerman later famously drank the whisky on the NBC television show *Parks and Recreation*, when he played the cantankerous character Ron Swanson. (The whisky is also a favorite of *Parks and Recreation* creator Michael Schur.) Offerman has since been able to convince Lagavulin to work with him—first on a couple of viral internet videos and then on some limited-edition whiskies.

The roots of the distillery are humbler than its modern Hollywood connections, going back to 1816. Originally, there were two small neighboring distilleries, which essentially merged together by 1837. By 1878, the combined distillery had established itself in the industry and was producing 75,000 gallons (2,800 hectoliters) of whisky a year.

Like many single malt distilleries, it was acquired by a blended whisky brand—in this case by White Horse in 1856. White Horse, whose eponymous blended Scotch brand is still sold today, was later itself acquired by Distillers Company Limited (DCL) in 1927. DCL would then become part of Diageo, which still owns Lagavulin today.

Over the past twenty-five years, Lagavulin has become a popular single malt, so much so that it is now bottled exclusively as a single malt and is not usually used in any blends. That shouldn't come as a total surprise, since even during the late nineteenth century when Scotch blends were the norm, Lagavulin was one of the few distilleries whose single malt was well known and sought-after by drinkers.

The standard Lagavulin is a 16-year-old whisky, a relatively advanced age at which the massive smoke notes have mellowed just enough to reveal the spirit's inherent dark fruit notes and a hint of brine and soap. In 2016, the brand also introduced an 8-year-old to celebrate the centennial of the distillery's founding. Not since the late 1880s had Lagavulin sold an 8-year-old whisky, one that Alfred Barnard called "exceptionally fine" in *The Whiskey Distilleries of the United Kingdom.* You can also find a Distillers Edition, which is aged for a second time in an unusually flavorful barrel. The most recent edition made use of an American oak barrel that had previously held Pedro Ximénez Sherry.

And let's not forget the above-mentioned Offerman editions. As of this writing, there were four of these collaborations—the most recent, spring 2024 release was an 11-year-old whisky finished for nearly a year in a barrel that previously held rum.

Linkwood

Diageo occasionally bottles Linkwood as a single malt, but usually the whisky goes into its blended whisky brands. Fortunately, over the years Linkwood has sold barrels of its whisky to independent bottlers who have released them as single malts. (It's no coincidence that Linkwood and the famous independent bottler Gordon & MacPhail are both based in the same small town of Elgin, Scotland.) These limited-edition bottlings can usually be bought in specialty liquor stores and from online retailers. Given that Linkwood has gained a cult following over the years, it wouldn't surprise me if Diageo one day decides to bottle and market the whisky on its own. But unfortunately for now, the historic distillery, whose roots go back to 1820, sits waiting for attention at the end of a long line with plenty of bestselling whiskies ahead of it.

Cardhu

The Cardhu (car-DEW) distillery legally opened in 1824, but probably was in business before it got its official license. Its name was originally Cardow and then Cardoor before it finally became Cardhu. No matter how you spell it, the name is Gaelic for "black rock."

While you can buy Cardhu as a single malt, most of the distillery's whisky is used by Johnnie Walker for blends.

It was founded by husband-and-wife team John and Helen Cumming and, by most accounts, Helen was the brand's original distiller. In 1885, the distillery was rebuilt and the old equipment was sold to William Grant for his new Glenfiddich distillery.

Cardhu was purchased by John Walker & Sons in 1893 for £20,500 and became the heart of the family's famous blended Scotch. The distillery's single malt played a key role in the rise of Johnnie Walker. Amazingly, Cardhu has stayed in the hands of the Walker family and is still used in a variety of Johnnie Walker blends today.

In 2003, Diageo was running out of its stock of Cardhu and decided to come up with an innovative solution—it transformed the brand from a single malt to a combination of single malts from several distilleries, which it labelled "pure malt." This change created a firestorm of criticism from consumers and other whisky producers alike, and not even a year later, Diageo decided to make Cardhu a single malt once again. Fortunately, you can usually find the honeyed Cardhu 12 Year in the US with ease.

Cragganmore

The Cragganmore (CRAG-en-more) distillery is located just south on the River Spey from some of the world's most famous Scotch distilleries.

While it's certainly less well known than some of its neighbors, the distillery dates back to 1869, and was founded by John Smith, who ran Glenfarclas for several years beforehand (see the Glenfarclas entry, page 303, for more). Smith had the benefit of both great timing and a great location, opting to build the distillery along a brand-new railroad and adjacent to one of its stations. The train was of course the most expeditious means of getting finished whisky to the market.

Cragganmore is featured in Diageo's heavily promoted Classic Malts of Scotland, which also includes Dalwhinnie, Glenkinchie, Lagavulin, Oban, and Talisker. In the United States, you'll most commonly find the Cragganmore 12 Year and a special Distillers Edition, which is aged for a second time in an unusually flavorful barrel. The most recent edition made use of a port barrel.

Glenkinchie

Today, most of the Scotch industry is located in Speyside, the Highlands, and on the west coast of Scotland, but in the nineteenth century there were also a number of whisky distilleries in the Lowlands of southern Scotland. By the early 2000s, just a few distilleries were open in the Lowlands, including Glenkinchie, near Edinburgh, and Auchentoshan, near Glasgow. (See the Auchentoshan entry, page 288, for more.)

Glenkinchie (GLEN-kin-SHE), which opened in the 1830s, makes a deliciously light single malt—almost an aperitif-style whisky that's perfect before a meal or for summer soirees. By the time I visited nearly twenty years ago, there wasn't much of the distillery left and a number of its buildings had been turned into apartment houses.

Fortunately, the distillery's giant still continues to produce plenty of single malt. Unfortunately, most of it doesn't come to the United States. It might take some effort, but you can find a bottle of the Glenkinchie 12 Year in the States, and also the Distillers Edition, which is aged for a second time in a flavorful barrel, the most recent edition of which used barrels that once held amontillado sherry.

Port Ellen

The ghost of the Port Ellen distillery has been haunting the Scotch industry for decades. The legendary Islay brand opened in 1825 and then closed in 1929. In 1967, it was renovated, expanded, and went on to produce peated whisky until 1983, when it was shut down for good. The most likely culprit for Port Ellen's (second) dramatic downfall? I blame changing tastes and vodka's sudden popularity.

Over the past two decades, the remaining barrels of Port Ellen single malt have become incredibly valuable. Diageo has stoked these fires with special releases of ever-older vintages that sell for thousands of dollars. In 2019, Diageo released a 39-year-old bottling that had a suggested retail price of nearly $6,000. Part of what makes these single malts so expensive is that there's a finite amount of whisky left from this so-called ghost distillery—it's an amazing story that plays particularly well with collectors, and journalists too.

In 2017, Diageo shocked the whisky world when it shared its plans to rebuild Port Ellen, as well as its Brora distillery, for a total cost of £35 million. (Brora was another ghost distillery; see page 252 for more.) The new Port Ellen facility opened in 2024 and makes 800,000 liters (211,000 gallons) a year of peaty whisky. We'll see if the new Port Ellen whisky has the same cachet as what came from the original facility—sadly, we won't know the answer to that question until about 2034.

BRANCH: PERNOD RICARD

Through a series of shrewd mergers and acquisitions beginning in 1988, Pernod Ricard has grown to become one of the largest spirits companies in the world. It's quite a meteoric rise, given that the modern company dates only to 1975, when the historic French brand Pernod, founded in 1805, merged with rival Ricard, started in 1932. While the brands' eponymous spirits, Pernod and Ricard, are anise-flavored liqueurs traditionally served as aperitifs, the combined company has vast Scotch holdings, including its crown jewels, The Glenlivet and Chivas Regal. Read on for more about these and other Pernod Ricard Scotch brands.

The Glenlivet

It doesn't take much effort to find a liquor store in the United States selling bottles of The Glenlivet (GLENN-live-ET). The brand is the bestselling single malt Scotch in America, with drinkers buying nearly 450,000 cases a year. But visiting its distillery in the Scottish Highlands is quite a bit more difficult than grabbing a bottle at the store.

In 1983, the Port Ellen distillery shut down. In 2024, it miraculously reopened and is once again producing whisky.

The Glenlivet is the bestselling single malt Scotch in the United States.

In fact, one of the reasons its remote location was originally chosen was that it would be hard for royal tax agents to reach. "There is not a village or a town anywhere near the place; the nearest railway station is about seven miles distant—a more lonely spot in winter, or a more delightful one in summer, could not be found for those who like quietude and rest," wrote Alfred Barnard in his landmark 1887 book, *The Whisky Distilleries of the United Kingdom*.

Besides being isolated, the distillery's site also had an excellent water source, the Livet spring, which is the origin of the whisky's name. An ideal setting for whisky making, the area was once home to many talented distillers, and all the delicious whisky made

In 1824, George Smith licensed his Speyside distillery, The Glenlivet, which was one of the first in the area to go legit.

there was originally known as "Glenlivet."

The Glenlivet as we know it came into existence in 1824. At the time, the royal tax rules changed and licensing costs were lowered, so the brand's founder, George Smith, decided to go legit and build a proper distillery. The Glenlivet was among the first distilleries in Speyside to get a license. Smith's decision was quite controversial because many of the distillers in the region preferred to keep on bootlegging, given how profitable it was. New, legitimate distilleries were a threat to their illicit production.

But Smith persevered, even if it meant carrying a weapon for protection and competing with the illegal whisky being sold in the area. His success can be seen in the sales: When he started the distillery in 1824, it made just 2,600 gallons (98 hectoliters) of whisky annually; by the end of the nineteenth century, it was cranking out 200,000 gallons (about 7,600 hectoliters) annually while quickly developing an international reputation.

To box out the other distillers in the area, George Smith and his son, John Gordon Smith, were able to trademark the name Glenlivet in the early 1870s. This power move meant that the region's reputation for excellent whisky would now be associated primarily with the Smiths' brand. To understand the magnitude of this development, imagine if one of the distillers on Islay legally owned the name Islay, and prevented all the other distillers from using it.

Once the Smiths secured the trademark, they took the other nine distilleries in the area to court to get them to stop using the name Glenlivet. In 1884, the Smiths and their competitors finally reached a settlement. The Smiths would pay court costs for all the parties involved and be able to call their whisky The Glenlivet exclusively, while the rest of the distillers would have to add a second name to their brand, like Aberlour-Glenlivet. Ultimately, the other brands dropped "Glenlivet" from their names.

Even after the industry switched to essentially only blended Scotch, The Glenlivet was still sought-after because its deliciously heathered single malt adds a wonderful note and a roundness to a blend. By 1923, it was arguably the best-known Highland single malt distillery in the world.

In the 1870s, the Smith family shrewdly trademarked the name The Glenlivet.

In the 1970s, there was a fight over control of the distillery by its owners, including Suntory, which was reportedly using The Glenlivet single malt in some of its blends (for more about this, see page 438). Ultimately, Seagram's bought the distillery and ran it for decades, until the company merged with Vivendi in 2000 and sold off its spirits holdings in a blockbuster deal that resulted in Pernod Ricard acquiring The Glenlivet and a number of other major brands.

Pernod Ricard grew The Glenlivet into one of the biggest whisky brands in the world, expanding the distillery several times. It now makes a wide range of whiskies, including its signature The Glenlivet 12 Year, which, to me, defines what a single malt from Speyside should taste like: highly quaffable, with notes of baking spices, toasted barley, and a bit of woody sweetness. In addition, the brand has a range of other single malts, including the very drinkable Founder's Reserve, which doesn't have a stated age; the rich and delicious 15-year-old, which is aged for a second time in a barrel made from French Limousin oak; and the pricey 25-year-old, which is finished in both Pedro Ximénez Sherry and Tronçais oak Cognac casks.

Chivas Regal

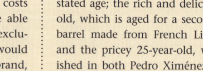

For decades, Chivas Regal 12 Year Blended Scotch Whisky was the epitome of luxury. It was the type of bottle kept at the back of your grandparents' liquor cabinet, only to be pulled out for special occasions and visiting dignitaries. Yet despite its lofty reputation, Chivas Regal was created by a

Chivas Regal continues to put out ever older whiskies, like the XV, which is finished in Cognac casks.

impressive debossed metallic cardboard box, the brand practically exuded status and wealth—it was the perfect drink for the Eisenhower years. According to an advertisement that appeared in the *New York Times* when it launched, the whisky was "for the few who can appreciate the difference." Even Nikita Khrushchev, who infamously restricted the sale of alcohol in the Soviet Union, couldn't resist Chivas. The Communist Party leader supposedly drank the whisky at the National Press Club when he visited Washington, DC, in the summer of 1959.

Above all, the whisky was smooth but with plenty of flavor provided by the dozens of single malts in its blend, both sourced from Seagram's giant portfolio of distilleries and bought from other companies. Chivas is also versatile—it can be drunk neat, on the rocks, or with a splash of club soda. According to the brand's early marketing campaigns, the reason for the creation of this deluxe 12-year-old whisky—and why it was exported to the US in 1951—was to celebrate the brand's 150th anniversary. While that certainly makes great ad copy, it's not quite accurate. What the anniversary actually celebrates is the founding of William Edward's original store in Aberdeen—James Chivas wouldn't join the enterprise for another thirty-five years! Throughout the decade, Seagram's spent tens of millions to promote its portfolio of spirits and a good amount of

grocer—just like a number of the world's most iconic whisky brands.

In 1836, James Chivas began working at William Edward's store in Aberdeen, which sold spirits and wines. Eventually, Chivas took over the store and was joined by his brother John for five years. The pair naturally renamed the business Chivas Brothers. By 1909, Chivas was exporting a blended Scotch to the US and Canada. A turning point for the brand came in 1949, when Seagram's bought Chivas Brothers for £85,070. A year later, the company paid £71,000 to acquire the Strathisla distillery in Keith, which not only provided Chivas with single malt, but also became the blended Scotch brand's honorific home.

These moves, along with the introduction of Chivas's now signature 12-year-old in 1951, made the brand a global sensation. From its deluxe bulbous bottle to its mature age and its

Scotch reached new luxury heights when Chivas Regal 12 Year Old was originally rolled out in 1951.

that budget was spent on ads for Chivas in national newspapers.

Another big factor in making Chivas a household name was its long association with the British monarchy and its royal warrant to supply their residences with whisky. To celebrate Queen Elizabeth II's coronation in 1953, Chivas Brothers created the Royal Salute—named for the ceremonial twenty-one-gun salute fired from the Tower of London to mark the occasion, it includes whiskies that are at least twenty-one years old. To this day, the company produces Royal Salute, as well as limited editions that celebrate monarchy milestones.

Seagram's ownership of Chivas ended in 2000, when Seagram's merged with Vivendi and sold off its liquor business. Pernod Ricard bought many of the Seagram's whiskey brands, including their bestseller, Chivas. Although the Scotch industry now focuses largely on single malts, as of 2023 the blended Chivas was the third most popular Scotch whisky brand in the world, selling nearly 5 million cases a year.

Aberlour

People in the spirits trade often talk about the effects a place can have on a whisky, but the village of Aberlour (A-burr-lauer) is a perfect example of a whisky's effect on a place.

The Aberlour distillery was built in 1826 by James Gordon and then sold in 1879 to James Fleming, who updated it and created the modern brand. Fleming went on to become immensely wealthy and left a lasting legacy beyond his whisky. When he died in 1895, his will stipulated that £500 of his fortune was to be used to construct an elegant suspension bridge over the nearby Spey River, a dangerous waterway that had claimed a number of lives. (The final cost of the project would be about twice as much as the estimate, but Fleming's widow, Margaret Stewart, provided the extra funds to finish the bridge.) Since then, countless locals and visitors have crossed the so-called Penny Bridge, which is still used today. Fleming also earmarked £9,000 of his estate for the creation of a local hospital, which continues to serve the community.

The Glenlivet casts a giant shadow in Pernod's portfolio, which means Aberlour, its smaller Speyside distillery, hasn't gotten its fair share of attention. (Aberlour was acquired by Pernod in 1974.) While Aberlour's understated status certainly makes it an easier find in stores, it's a shame that more folks aren't enjoying its deeply rich single malt.

The brand's signature and pioneering single malt, A'bunadh (ah-BOO-nah), was first released in 1998. It is aged completely in casks that previously held oloroso sherry and is bottled at cask strength without chill filtering. While these techniques now seem somewhat mundane, in the late 1990s the whisky was truly cutting edge. A'bunadh has an almost jammy richness that still stands out today. The brand now also offers A'bunadh Alba, which is aged in American bourbon barrels. (Try sipping the two versions next to each other to see the impact the wood can have on a whisky.)

A'bunadh Single Malt put the Aberlour distillery on the modern whisky map.

The Fleming family, who bought Aberlour in 1879, paid for the area's hospital and a bridge over the nearby Spey River.

Scapa

Scapa (scap-AHH) is one of the most northerly Scotch distilleries, so far north that it's almost in Scandinavia. It's located in Orkney, an archipelago of islands that sits in the North Sea at nearly the latitude of Oslo, Norway. The area's heritage is both Scottish and Scandinavian, thanks to the Vikings who colonized the area and used it as a staging point for their marauding trips to England and Ireland.

The Scapa distillery doesn't date back to Viking times, but to 1885, when it was built on Scapa Bay by whisky blender Macfarlane & Townsend. Scapa was later bought by Canadian conglomerate Hiram Walker in 1954, and then was owned by Allied Domecq when it acquired Hiram Walker in 1999. By the late 1990s, the distillery was producing whisky part-time and required extensive repairs. Fortunately, Allied Domecq decided to fix the facility and it returned to a full production schedule.

Just six years later, Allied Domecq was broken up and Scapa suddenly found itself in Pernod Ricard's portfolio. While the spirits company Edrington has promoted Orkney's other distillery, Highland Park, Scapa's honeyed whisky has not yet been a major priority for Pernod (with most of Scapa's output going into Pernod's blended Scotch brands). Currently, you can find a 16-year Scapa single malt as well as some duty-free expressions. If you're game enough to make it all the way up to Orkney, Scapa has a visitor center for tastings and tours.

BRANCH: EDRINGTON

Like a well-edited whisky list in a superb bar, Edrington has a relatively small Scotch portfolio, but the brands in it are all-stars. The company's roots stretch back to the late 1800s, beginning with the Robertson & Baxter company in Glasgow. But the modern incarnation of the company was really formed in the late 1990s when Edrington, now owned by the charitable The Robertson Trust, teamed up with William Grant to buy Highland Distillers. Edrington already owned a stake in Highland Distillers at the time, but buying out the rest of its investors insured that it would be able to own the sought-after The Macallan, and several other acclaimed distilleries. Read on for more about Edrington's portfolio of famous brands.

The Macallan

There are few Scotch brands as well known or revered by the general public as The Macallan (MA-cal-lan). In fact, the single malt has done what no other Scotch brand has been able to do—transcend the

In 2018, The Macallan opened a new distillery that cost £140 million and includes thirty-six copper pot stills.

Scotch world and become a member of the exclusive club of luxury goods makers, alongside icons such as Valentino, Baccarat, and Tiffany & Co.

Today, if you visit The Macallan in Speyside, you'll find a vast modern distillery that opened in 2018, with an undulating roof planted with eco-friendly grass. Looking at The Macallan's futuristic £140 million facility, you might not be surprised to learn that the same architects also designed a terminal at Heathrow Airport. The distillery includes a sea of thirty-six copper pot stills that are famously short, which is perhaps the key to the brand's unique rich and heavy flavor.

Certainly, no one would have foretold such an incredible future for the distillery, given its humble roots. Alfred Barnard barely mentions The Macallan in his pioneering and exhaustive 1887 book, *The Whisky Distilleries of the United Kingdom*. From Barnard's short entry it sounds like The Macallan is fairly uninteresting. So how did it become so famous?

The distillery was started back in 1824 by Alexander Reid, when the first wave of Scotch distillers began to get licenses and agree to pay taxes. But it would take decades for The Macallan to develop a reputation. The brand really began to take off in the 1960s, when interest in single malt was slowly starting to grow, and The Macallan was one of the few options available to drinkers in the US. In March 1965, *GQ* magazine ran a landmark story about drinking Scotch, written by well-known liquor writer Emanuel Greenberg, which names The Macallan as a single malt that all whisky lovers should track down and taste.

The brand also got a big boost when Seagram's began to name-check The Macallan (as well as The Glenlivet) in nationwide advertisements as an ingredient in its 100 Pipers Blended Scotch. The resulting demand for The Macallan was such that the brand expanded its distillery several times, going from six stills in the early 1960s to twenty-one in 1975.

Thanks to the crash of the blended Scotch market in the late 1970s and 1980s, The Macallan had to create a new brand identity solely as a single malt—a transition it was able to make quite successfully. "My list leads with Macallan Highland malt whisky, my Drink of the Year (also of last year) and widely regarded in the trade as the king of malts," wrote Kingsley Amis in his 1983 book *Everyday Drinking*. "Over Christmas I'll be staying off of it until comparatively late in the day, because the only drink you want after some of it is more of it."

In order to attract more attention in the US, The Macallan began exporting ever more expensive and rare whiskies. In 1989, legendary bartender Gary Regan reportedly sold $20 pours of The Macallan 25 Year at the North Star Pub in New York's South Street Seaport, while most of the bar's other Scotches cost between $4 and $6.50. The Macallan also began to hype its unique whisky-aging process—it used barrels previously seasoned with sherry—which set it apart from most other brands that used old bourbon barrels.

Although overall demand for whisky was still declining in the 1990s, industry players remained interested in owning The Macallan. In 1991, the Japanese conglomerate Suntory, which owned 10 percent of The Macallan at the time, increased its holdings to just over a quarter of the company. Then in January 1996, Highland Distillers bought Rémy Cointreau's 26 percent stake in The Macallan for nearly £47 million, before buying up the rest of the shares not owned by Suntory for an additional £88 million that same year.

Just three years later, Edrington and William Grant joined together to buy Highland Distillers, including The Macallan, for £601 million. (Edrington originally owned 70 percent of this new company and William Grant owned the rest.) Despite these deals, Suntory was able to hold on to its quarter of The Macallan, which it still owns today. (To make things even more confusing, in 2020, Suntory bought a 10 percent stake in Edrington.)

In 1997, The Macallan's stated goal was to increase the brand's annual sales of 150,000 cases a year to 900,000 cases a year. While that might have seemed ridiculously optimistic at the time, by 2018 The Macallan was reportedly close to breaking the million-case mark (with US sales of about 250,000 cases a year).

Thanks to its new owners at Edrington, the late 1990s was when The Macallan really became a breakout star. The brand started spending millions on

In 1824 Alexander Reid started The Macallan, which has become one of the world's most famous whiskies.

advertising campaigns and truly leaned into its claim of being the Rolls-Royce of single malts. To back this new identity, The Macallan began releasing whiskies with truly stunning prices. In 1999, it started selling a 50-year-old Scotch in the United States that came in a special crystal decanter and cost $3,300. While that may now sound like a bargain of sorts, it was jaw-droppingly high at the time.

The Macallan also introduced its Fine & Rare Collection of thirty-eight whiskies in 2002, which included single malts made from 1926 to 1973. The set originally cost $170,000. The first Collection sold in the US was reportedly bought by the Borgata Casino in Atlantic City, New Jersey. That set would have become a winning investment if the Borgata had held on to it: A 60-year-old bottle of the 1926 single malt from the Collection went for a record-shattering $1.9 million at a 2019 Sotheby's auction in London.

The Macallan has arguably introduced more collectible bottlings than any other distillery, deftly using the halo effect to raise the profile of its standard range of whiskies. As a result, The Macallan 18 Year currently sells for about $450. (It sold for a comparably measly sum of $150 in 2009.)

To keep up with the stratospheric demand for its single malt, The Macallan made some changes over the last decade, including to the barrels seasoned with sherry that it famously uses to age its whisky in. The brand formerly used only casks made from European oak staves, but now it employs casks made from American oak staves as well. Speaking of aging, in 2023, The Macallan made some moves to ensure that it will have a consistent supply of sherry-seasoned barrels. It bought the Spanish cooperage Vasyma and also half of the Spanish sherry producer Grupo Estévez. The Macallan's new distillery should also help increase supply, but it will take time for this whisky to age—it will be mature starting around 2030.

Highland Park Single Malt Scotch Whisky

You can't go much farther north than Orkney and still be in Scotland. The archipelago looks like it broke off from Scotland and is on its way to the nearby Norwegian coast. Orkney is home to the famous whisky distillery Highland Park, which proudly boasts of its links with nearby Scandinavia and Viking culture (see also the Scapa entry, page 265).

Orkney is at Scotland's northern tip and is home to acclaimed distillery Highland Park.

The locals like to say the trees grow sideways on Orkney, due to the extreme weather conditions. Despite its forbidding climate, the area has been home to Highland Park since about 1798, when it was founded in the town of Kirkwall by David Robertson. Robertson sold it in 1826 to Robert Borwick, who relaunched the distillery and ran it until he died in 1840. He left the distillery to his son George who, like his father, led the distillery until his death, in 1869. Ownership of Highland Park passed to George's younger brother, Rev. James Borwick. The reverend, who wasn't in the whisky business, decided to sell the distillery for £450. In 1895, its new owner, James Grant, expanded the distillery, which went from two stills to four. (The modern distillery still has the same configuration.) Grant's descendants sold Highland Park to Highland Distillers in 1937 for £185,000 and £35,000 in stock in the company. With the global depression still raging and a world war on the horizon, that considerable price was a testament to Highland Park's reputation and high quality.

Highland Park celebrates not only its Scottish heritage but also its Viking heritage.

The distillery and its twenty-three warehouses and other buildings are sturdily built from locally quarried stone designed to withstand the climate. The facility includes two historic kilns for drying floor malted barley over fires of coal or locally sourced peat. Highland Park is one of the few distilleries in Scotland that still floor malts, and its mash bill includes 20 percent of its own floor malted barley.

In 1999, Highland Park joined Edrington's portfolio of famous whiskies. The association with Edrington has helped the brand in many ways, including a £750,000 renovation in 2009. But, truth be told, Highland Park will always be the company's second priority behind The Macallan—a shame in my opinion, as I think Highland Park is a star that truly deserves top billing.

Currently, Highland Park makes a highly respected line of single malts, including a 10-year-old, a 12-year-old, an 18-year-old, a 21-year-old, and a 25-year-old. Like The Macallan, the whiskies are now aged in barrels that previously held sherry. For big spenders, Highland Park also bottles a 30-year-old and a 40-year-old whisky, along with limited editions.

The Glenrothes

While Scotch brands often tout romantic origins, The Glenrothes (GLENN-roth-es) has a pretty prosaic backstory.

In 1878, James Stuart & Co., which owned The Macallan at the time, began to build a second distillery in Rothes, Scotland. But when the local Caledonian Bank was forced to shut down temporarily, the distiller's financing fell through and construction of The Glenrothes was halted. The project was taken over by a new group of investors, including local lawyer John Cruikshank, Robert Dick, who worked for the Rothes branch of the Caledonian Bank, and William Grant, who worked for the Caledonian Bank branch in nearby Elgin. (This Grant, not to be confused with a different William Grant who started Glenfiddich, was involved in the financing of a number of distilleries in the area.) Together, the group was able to obtain a loan from the Caledonian Bank to build The Glenrothes distillery, which finally opened in May 1879.

Just a few years later, in 1887, The Glenrothes became a founding member of Highland Distillers, which owned whisky makers all across Scotland. The Glenrothes, which at different times was known as Glen Rothes and Glenrothes-Glenlivet, stayed in Highland Distillers' portfolio for decades.

At the end of the nineteenth century, The Glenrothes went through a massive renovation, which doubled the distillery's output from 150,000 gallons (5,700 hectoliters) of spirit a year to 300,000 gallons (11,400 hectoliters) a year. This was only the first of a number of expansions. In 1963, an additional two stills were added to The Glenrothes's original four stills. In 1980, four additional stills were added and in 1989, the still count increased by another two for a grand total of twelve stills. These expansions were necessary, since The Glenrothes was the heart of the bestselling blended Scotch Cutty Sark, which sold 20 million cases a year at the height of its popularity in the mid-twentieth century. Cutty was created by the famous London wine and liquor store Berry Bros. & Rudd, which first opened its doors in the seventeenth century and famously stocks the liquor cabinets at Buckingham Palace. (See the Cutty Sark entry, page 300, for more.)

The modern history of The Glenrothes is inextricably intertwined with the history of Cutty Sark, Berry Bros. & Rudd, and Edrington. In 2010, Edrington and Berry Bros. & Rudd decided to swap brands. Berry Bros. & Rudd would get The Glenrothes brand, while Edrington would get Cutty Sark and retain ownership of The Glenrothes distillery (and would continue to produce whisky for The Glenrothes). While Cutty was certainly not as popular as it once was, the whisky was still selling and there was a possibility that the brand could be resuscitated.

At the same time, The Glenrothes was just building its reputation. Originally, it tried to distance itself from other single malts by focusing on releasing single vintages from a specific year. (While you might not be able to get, say, a 12-year-old, you could get a bottle of whisky that was made in 1978.) By focusing on these rare lots, The Glenrothes could immediately charge more, as there was a built-in scarcity for these limited-edition releases. To bolster its own identity as a brand, The Glenrothes originally was packaged in a distinctive globe-like bottle, which somehow looked both modern and historical at the same time. (The brand has since elongated its signature bottle design.)

It took seven years for Edrington to realize its mistake in selling The Glenrothes. While sales of the whisky reportedly doubled during the period that it was owned by Berry Bros. & Rudd, Cutty Sark proved to be an increasingly hard sell in a Scotch market that continued to shift away from blends in favor of single malts. Edrington eventually bought back The Glenrothes from Berry Bros. & Rudd for an undisclosed price, then sold Cutty Sark to La Martiniquaise-Bardinet soon afterward.

Nearly a century ago, the GlenDronach distillery opened in Aberdeenshire.

While The Glenrothes still releases limited-edition whiskies, such as its 42-year-old, the brand has caved to market pressure and now offers a core line of single malts, including a 15-year-old, an 18-year-old, and a 25-year-old. Like its sister distilleries, The Macallan and Highland Park, most of The Glenrothes's whiskies are aged in sherry casks. But the flavor profile of The Glenrothes tends to be very rich, with plenty of delicious raisin and prune notes. Having once tasted dozens and dozens of its barrels to pick an "Editor's Cask," I can attest to the fact that The Glenrothes has plenty of interesting and unusual whiskies that it will surely release as limited editions.

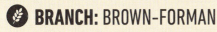

BRANCH: BROWN-FORMAN

If you take a trip along Scotland's whisky trail, at many of the distilleries you'll see used barrels from Jack Daniel's. How on earth did they get there from Lynchburg, Tennessee? Well, Jack Daniel's only uses new charred American oak barrels, and once they're emptied the casks are sold to distillers around the world, which reuse them to age a range of spirits.

The boatloads of gently used barrels from Jack Daniel's and the other American whiskey brands in the portfolio of its parent company, Brown-Forman, are essential for the Scotch industry to make Scotch.

But Brown-Forman doesn't just provide Scotland with barrels; since 2016 it also makes its own single malt. It bought Benriach (BEN-ri-ock) for about $410 million from Scotch veteran Billy Walker and his South African investors, Geoff Bell and Wayne Keiswetter. The purchase included not just the Benriach distillery but also the GlenDronach (Glenn-DRON-ick) and Glenglassaugh (Glenn-GAS-sow) distilleries. (Six months before the acquisition, Brown-Forman sold two of its brand, Southern Comfort and Tuaca, to Sazerac for $544 million. I imagine the timing of the two transactions was not random.)

Through a series of shrewd moves, Walker had built a small but well-respected whisky company, and breathed new life into distilleries jettisoned by larger Scotch

Rachel Barrie is now the master blender for Brown-Forman but for decades played key roles at a range of famous distilleries.

companies. Almost exactly a year after completing the sale to Brown-Forman, Walker and a new group of partners bought the largely unknown GlenAllachie (Glenn-AL-a-key) distillery from French conglomerate Pernod Ricard, with an eye to rebuilding that brand.

To run its new distilleries, in 2017 Brown-Forman hired Scotch legend Rachel Barrie. She honed her skills at Glenmorangie, where she worked for sixteen years as a master blender and whisky maker. She then moved to Morrison Bowmore Distillers (now part of Suntory Global Spirits), where she blended a number of brands including Bowmore, Auchentoshan, and Laphroaig. If you are a Scotch fan, you have tasted her work.

Read on for more about Brown-Forman's portfolio of single malts.

Benriach

At the height of the Scotch boom in the late nineteenth century, John Duff built the Benriach (BEN-ri-ock) distillery in Elgin, Scotland. Sadly, his timing could not have been worse: Just as the distillery was getting on its feet, the overheated whisky industry imploded. Benriach closed in 1900 after only two years in business.

While its closing was not unusual, what's fascinating is how the distillery sat mothballed for decades and decades. All the while, Benriach continued to floor malt barley the old-fashioned way for its neighbor, Longmorn. Finally, in 1965, The Glenlivet Distillers Ltd. bought the facility and began making whisky there again.

In 1977, Seagram's acquired the distillery and began to add the single malt to its blended Scotch brands, including Chivas

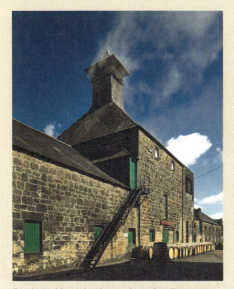

Benriach's history has been a dramatic roller coaster, but it beat the odds to remain in business today.

Regal. Seagram's would notoriously go on to merge with Vivendi and then shockingly sell off its liquor portfolio in 2000. One of the beneficiaries would be Pernod Ricard, which acquired quite a few brands from Seagram's, including Benriach.

This megadeal happened just as the whiskey renaissance was getting started around the world—but it wasn't yet in full swing. Pernod soon realized that Seagram's had underreported how many bottles of Chivas and Martell Cognac were in its warehouses. While today that would be great news, in 2002 the market could not yet absorb the overstock. Pernod was able to get Seagram's to refund £20 million of the selling price and immediately scaled back production of Chivas, which meant the mothballing of four Scotch distilleries, including Benriach. The closed distilleries were put up for sale.

This was the perfect opportunity for Billy Walker and his partners to approach Pernod about buying Benriach. In 2004, Pernod agreed to sell the distillery to Walker for a reported £5.4 million.

Almost immediately the new owners began trying to raise the profile of Benriach by releasing a line of single malts. Given that drinkers and bartenders had no preconceived notions about what the whisky should taste like, the brand had license to experiment. The distillery's current lineup reflects this creative freedom, including even peated malts, which are pretty rare for a Speyside brand to produce. Benriach sells whiskies from ten years old to forty years old. In 2012, the distillery started floor malting some of its barley again, so look out for special releases made exclusively with this homemade malt.

In 2016, Walker and his partners sold Benriach along with GlenDronach and Glenglassaugh to the Louisville, Kentucky–based Brown-Forman for $410 million.

Only a handful of Scotch distilleries, including Benriach, continue to floor malt their barley the old-fashioned way.

For decades, GlenDronach was the main malt in Teacher's Highland Cream Blended Scotch.

GlenDronach

GlenDronach opened in 1826 and was built by a group led by James Allardice. In 1920, the distillery was bought at auction by Captain Charles Grant for £9,000. Whisky was in his blood—he was the son of William Grant, who founded Glenfiddich and Balvenie.

The Grants owned GlenDronach until 1960, when it was sold to the popular blended Scotch brand Teacher's. For the next thirty years, the distillery pumped out whisky that was primarily used in blends. Ultimately, the drop in global blended Scotch sales forced then-owner Allied Domecq to close the distillery in 1996.

It reopened in 2002, reportedly to supply blenders across the Scotch industry with single malt. But there was one small problem: Modern EU regulations required that the distillery's historic coal-fired stills be replaced with those that were heated with safer steam. Thankfully, Allied Domecq announced in 2004 that it would make the necessary changes to the stills.

Just as it looked like things might actually work out for GlenDronach, Allied Domecq was bought by a few of its competitors in 2005. The distillery suddenly found itself in Pernod Ricard's portfolio, but Pernod wasn't done making big deals. Just three years later, it bought the Swedish company Vin & Spirit for $8.34 billion to land its star brand, Absolut Vodka. To assuage investor fears that it might be carrying too much debt, Pernod immediately pledged to sell off $1 billion worth of brands already in its portfolio. One of the brands that was put up for sale was GlenDronach.

Almost immediately Billy Walker and his partners snapped up the distillery for a reported £15 million, and then spent £250,000 to reopen it. The new owners began to promote the fact that the whiskies were aged in sherry casks, which give the drink its signature rich fruit and baking spice notes.

GlenDronach and its sister distilleries, Benriach and Glenglassaugh, were then sold to Brown-Forman in 2016. Given that international sales of the brand's whisky have reportedly tripled since the acquisition, it seems like this move might be GlenDronach's last for a while. Particularly in light of Brown-Forman's decision in 2022 to embark on a $30 million expansion of the distillery.

The distillery's lineup now focuses on whiskies that have been aged in casks seasoned with either Pedro Ximénez or oloroso sherry, including a 12-year-old, a 15-year-old, an 18-year-old, and a 21-year-old, as well as limited editions and special releases for duty free.

Glenglassaugh Coastal Single Malt Scotch Whisky

Glenglassaugh (Glen-GAS-sow) was closed for much of the twentieth century, so it's a small miracle that the coastal distillery is open and thriving today.

James Moir and his two nephews, Alexander and William Morrison, along with local coppersmith Thomas Wilson, spent £10,000 to build the northern Highlands distillery in 1875. The distillery, which overlooks the North Sea, sits proudly near the beach on a gorse-covered hill, like a lighthouse guiding whisky drinkers into a safe harbor. Nearly twenty years after its founding, Highland Distillers bought Glenglassaugh for £15,000. The new owners ran it for all of sixteen years before shutting it down. The facility wasn't really put back to full use until it was rebuilt in 1959, after which it made whisky until closing once again in 1986.

In 2008, the distillery was owned by Edrington and, while defunct, was far from worthless. Several times it looked like Glenglassaugh might be sold before finally the Dutch-based Scaent Group paid £5 million for it and set about reopening the facility. The deal also included a

In 1875, the Glenglassaugh distillery opened on the northern Highland coast overlooking the North Sea.

Thanks to a range of local and international factors, Glenglassaugh has shut down several times.

reported five hundred casks of rare whisky, which the brand began to bottle and sell for quite a price. Given the infrequencies of production at Glenglassaugh, by 2013 when Billy Walker and his partners bought the brand from Scaent, few people had ever heard of it.

Glenglassaugh no longer flies below the radar, and you can easily find its single malts. A few years ago, the brand revamped its lineup and released a core collection of three main bottlings that are each aged in a different type of cask—a 12-year-old, the Sandend, and the Portsoy.

BRANCH: WILLIAM GRANT & SONS

William Grant & Sons has played a major role in turning single malt from a largely overlooked ingredient to an international bestseller—primarily by pushing the industry to innovate and modernize. As a result, you might be tempted to think that it's a relatively new company, but in fact its roots go back to the mid-1800s.

Many histories of William Grant & Sons start with the construction of its signature Glenfiddich (GLENN-fid-dick) distillery in Dufftown, Scotland. As it's told, William Grant and his children built the facility by hand and then started distilling on Christmas Day in 1887. But that of course begs the question of what the family was doing before 1887. It turns out William Grant was working not too far away, at the Mortlach distillery in Dufftown. He started out in 1866 as a bookkeeper and ultimately became the distiller for that brand, which is still in operation today. The Glenfiddich distillery cost £775 to construct, including the stills and other equipment that Grant bought from the

Glenfiddich's name comes from the Gaelic term for "valley of the deer."

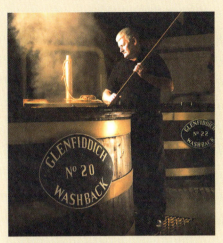

On Christmas Day 1887, William Grant and his family started making the whisky that would become the bestselling brand Glenfiddich.

Cardhu distillery in Knockando for £129, which included delivery.

In the 1960s, Glenfiddich began to bottle single malt Scotch and promote it in the United States. It was a bold move because very little single malt was sold as a distinct product at the time, going instead into blends like Grant's (made by William Grant & Sons), Chivas Regal, Johnnie Walker, and Dewar's. William Grant's single malt whisky was far from an overnight success, but it did lay the groundwork for the single malt's eventual widespread distribution and meteoric rise in popularity.

William Grant is still family owned and has its own cooperage, so it can afford to be more innovative and take chances, whether that be by popularizing single malt, opening the industry's first visitor center at the Glenfiddich distillery in 1969, or creating a new technique for aging Scotch. Read on to find out more about some of the Scotch brands in the company's impressive portfolio.

Glenfiddich

The Glenfiddich (GLENN-fid-dick) distillery is still located in the center of bucolic Dufftown, Scotland. The brand's name is derived from a Gaelic expression meaning "valley of the deer," and, fittingly, it looks exactly as you might imagine the archetypal Scottish whisky distillery to be built.

On that first fateful Christmas in 1887 when the distillery opened, the Grants, according to records, produced 223 gallons (844 liters) of alcohol there. Today, the distillery is a wee bit bigger, after several expansions, in order to keep up with the incredibly high demand for its single malt. A recent £30 million renovation equipped it with forty-three copper pot stills that run 24/7 most of the year. Glenfiddich sells nearly 200,000 nine-liter cases per year in the US alone. In addition to its ubiquitous 12-year-old, Glenfiddich has many other single malts of all ages and styles. Its 14 Year Old Bourbon Barrel Reserve, which is aged in both used and new American oak barrels, is steadily becoming a bestseller.

The Balvenie Single Malt Scotch Whisky

The Balvenie (BAL-ven-KNEE) distillery sits across the road from Glenfiddich and was built in 1892 for the grand total of £2,000. One of its original stills came from the Lagavulin distillery on Islay, and the other came from the Glen Albyn distillery in Inverness. While the distillery started producing alcohol in 1893, it wouldn't play a key role in the Scotch industry for more than a century.

In the 1970s, drinkers turned to vodka and other beverages and the

Just across the road from Scotch giant Glenfiddich is its sister distillery The Balvenie.

whiskey market crashed; blended Scotch began to seemingly lose more customers and market share by the minute. Single malt distillers, whose only real customers were whisky blenders, needed a new game plan. David Stewart, who started working at William Grant in 1962, began experimenting with the idea of aging whisky a second time in a different kind of cask—a technique now known as finishing.

While it was common knowledge that the cask imbues whisky with lots of flavor, distillers generally looked to make a consistent spirit in lieu of special releases. But now that brands were suddenly forced to market their whisky directly to consumers, every single malt needed to stand out and offer a distinct character and backstory. So, Stewart took mature Balvenie whisky aged in a used American whiskey barrel and aged it a second time in a used sherry cask. The two different types of barrels each contributed something different to the whisky. The first resulting product was called The Balvenie Classic. In 1993, Stewart used the same process to create the now legendary The Balvenie DoubleWood 12, which not only put the distillery on the international spirits map but popularized the technique of wood finishes.

Stewart surely did not invent the idea of finishing whisky in a second barrel. In fact, The Balvenie had even previously released the 10-year Founder's Reserve, which was a whisky that had been aged in a number of different kinds of barrels. But it was Stewart and Glenmorangie's master distiller, Bill Lumsden, who really championed the technique. Thanks to whisky finishing, we have a whole new range of whisky flavors. Stewart's significant contributions to the Scotch industry were recognized by Queen Elizabeth II, who in 2016 made him a Member of the Order of the British Empire.

In addition to the DoubleWood 12, The Balvenie sells a huge range of other single malts in different markets, including the very popular Caribbean Cask, which is fourteen years old and finished in a rum cask.

Grant's Scotch Whisky

These days Glenfiddich and The Balvenie tend to hog the marketing spotlight, but Grant's Scotch Whisky is actually a giant brand. It sold 4.4 million nine-liter cases around the globe in 2023, making it the fourth-bestselling Scotch brand in the world.

Grant's was first launched in 1898 and is currently a mix of single malts and grain whisky produced at William Grant's Girvan distillery. The most common variety you'll encounter is the modestly priced Triple Wood, which, as you might imagine, involves aging the whisky in three different kinds of barrels: one made from virgin oak, one used American bourbon barrel, and one bourbon barrel that has also previously held Scotch. The brand also offers older and more expensive versions.

Monkey Shoulder Blended Scotch Whisky

"Monkey shoulder" is the cheeky name for an occupational hazard that once afflicted Scotch distillery workers. Traditionally, in Scotland barley was floor malted, which is a process that turns the starch in the grain into more easily fermentable sugar. The barley would be wetted down with water and then spread out over a screen. To avoid mold, the barley had to be turned by hand with a flat shovel. The workers who turned the barley would develop a muscular shoulder, which was colloquially called a monkey shoulder.

In 2005, William Grant used the term as the name for its new blend of single malts, which was originally available only in the UK. Technically, the whisky is a malt Scotch, which is different from a blended Scotch because it doesn't include any grain whisky, just single malts. It is made from a combination of single malts from the Glenfiddich, The Balvenie, and Kininvie distilleries, which are then "married" in barrels for three to six months. In 2012, Monkey Shoulder was launched in the United States. Currently, there is only one version of it available in the US, but the brand also sells a peated Smokey Monkey version in London and Paris, which it introduced in 2017.

Taking a cue from its name, William Grant has marketed Monkey Shoulder as a fun, "mischievous" alternative to straight-laced single malt, which can be drunk in a range of cocktails. Monkey Shoulder's brand ambassador Seb Derbomez even came up with the idea of turning a cement truck into a giant cocktail shaker. Dubbed "The Monkey Mixer," it comes complete with a chromed drum that can hold 2,400 gallons (more than 9,000 liters) and actually dispenses drinks from the machine's chute.

While Monkey Shoulder Scotch might have a playful name, the whisky itself is no joke.

Drambuie

The history of Drambuie reads like a Hollywood movie script, including a dramatic battle, an epic chase scene, and even a secret formula for a magical elixir.

The abridged version of the story is that Prince Charles Edward Stuart, aka Bonnie Prince Charlie, believed he should be the King of England and led an army of mostly Scotsmen to overthrow the monarchy. His plan came to an end in 1746, when he lost the Battle of Culloden, near Inverness. He was forced to run for his life and found a sympathetic supporter on the remote Isle of Skye. John MacKinnon sheltered Bonnie Prince Charlie until he could escape to France. According to legend, the would-be monarch was so grateful that he gave MacKinnon the recipe for his personal tincture.

More than a century later, MacKinnon's descendants shared the recipe with fellow Isle of Skye resident John Ross, who started to commercially bottle the liqueur, which would later be called Drambuie. While this story seems to have it all, the one thing missing might be the truth. What we can say for sure is that Bonnie Prince Charlie did have a personal liqueur that he drank for medicinal reasons. Did he or perhaps an aide give it to the MacKinnon family? Quite possibly.

The modern version of the liqueur has a base of Scotch and is flavored with honey and a range of herbs and spices. Some have speculated that Bonnie Prince Charlie's recipe would have used the more widely available brandy rather than whisky. Regardless, Drambuie went on to become a huge hit in the 1950s, primarily thanks to the iconic Rusty Nail cocktail (see the entry, page 512, for more info and recipe). The two-ingredient drink calls for Drambuie and blended Scotch. Just as the Rat Pack was eclipsed by new acts, so was the Rusty Nail, which has largely been forgotten.

William Grant, who bought the brand in 2014, has tried to revive Drambuie, as well as the Rusty Nail.

The Famous Grouse

Some might say that the ultimate measure of the quality of a Scotch is how well it sells in Scotland. For decades, no Scotch has outsold The Famous Grouse in its home market.

The quaffable blended whisky was created back in 1895 by Perthshire spirits and wine importer Matthew Gloag. According to legend, he named the brand after the grouse bird because the city of Perth was a popular spot for bird hunters. He only sold the Scotch in his shop and by mail order. (Gloag would ship the whisky via railroad, and customers would pay the station agent when they picked up their delivery.)

To market his Grouse brand whisky, Gloag frequently took out advertisements in newspapers across Britain—the earliest that I can find is a Christmas promotion that ran in London in December 1899. By 1906, Gloag was running ads touting deals for "Two bottles famous 'Grouse' brand," which cost seven shillings and six pennies. A few years later, "famous" went from being a descriptor to part of the whisky's official name. The modern brand likes to say the name change happened

From revolutionaries to the Rat Pack, the Scotch-based liqueur Drambuie has an incredibly colorful history.

The most popular Scotch in Scotland is the modestly priced blend Famous Grouse.

because Grouse became so well known. While that's possible, it wouldn't surprise me if Gloag simply realized the power of calling it The Famous Grouse—which definitely has a ring to it.

And Gloag certainly knew a thing or two about marketing. In fact, The Famous Grouse wasn't the first whisky brand Gloag sold or even created. In the 1880s, he ran ads in British newspapers for his Monopole Scotch whisky, which was made from the "finest home-grown barley" and aged in sherry casks. Gloag no doubt applied some of the lessons he learned working on Monopole to The Famous Grouse. Regardless, what he did worked—sales of The Famous Grouse grew in the UK.

One reason for The Famous Grouse's early local popularity was its local focus; until relatively recently, the brand did not concentrate its efforts on the export market. The Famous Grouse wasn't even available in the US until the early 1970s. The decision to sell it in the States was made by Highland Distillers, which bought the brand from Gloag's descendants in 1970 for £545,000, along with 350,000 shares of Highland Distillers stock.

"If you have never heard of this brand, we're not surprised," wrote the *New York Times* in August 1975. "It is a well-established name in Scotland, but only recently introduced to America." Even a decade later, the brand was still largely unknown, running ads in American newspapers to introduce itself to drinkers. "Until recently most Americans couldn't lay hands on a bottle of The Famous Grouse. Visitors to Scotland learned in a sip or two why this deluxe Scotch ranks first in the land of Scotch."

The brand's new owners were able to boost worldwide sales, according to whisky writer Ian Buxton, from 40,000 cases in 1970 to more than 1 million cases by 1979. In 1999, Edrington bought Highland Distillers, including The Famous Grouse and its portfolio of all-star single malts. To this day, The Famous Grouse continues to be the bestselling Scotch in Scotland.

Over the past twenty years, Edrington has tried to make the brand relevant to modern, US-based drinkers by introducing a number of new The Famous Grouse variations that have had mostly mixed results. The standard The Famous Grouse blended Scotch remains a highly underrated buy and is a bargain. It is ideal for sipping on the rocks, or making Highballs and other Scotch cocktails. You can also now get Smoky Black, which includes—you guessed it—more peaty single malts in the blend. It's a great deal and brings a bit more flavor to the party, adding a pleasant smoky note to mixed drinks. In 2024, Edrington sold Famous Grouse to its Scottish rival William Grant for an undisclosed sum.

Craigellachie's whisky was primarily used for Scotch blends, but you can now find it bottled as a single malt.

🌾 BRANCH: BACARDI

Bacardi Rum is one of the most popular spirits brands on Earth, and its success has allowed its owners, the Bacardi family, to diversify into a range of other alcoholic beverages. Ironically, the deal that really transformed Bacardi from a relatively small rum company into a major player in the global alcohol industry was the formation of its rival Diageo in 1997. To convince regulators that Diageo wouldn't have a monopoly, the newly formed conglomerate agreed to divest itself of Dewar's Scotch and four single malt Scotch distilleries (Aberfeldy, Aultmore, Craigellachie, and Royal Brackla), as well as Bombay Gin. Seizing this opportunity, Bacardi paid $1.9 billion for all of these brands in 1998.

It was an interesting time to get into the Scotch business, as blends began to fade and single malts really began to take off. It understandably took some years for Bacardi to figure out what it wanted to do with Dewar's, and how to handle its four new whisky distilleries, which were not household names—their production primarily went into blends.

In 2014, Bacardi decided to introduce the Last Great Malts collection, which was the first time many drinkers were able to taste whiskies from Aberfeldy (AH-BURR-fell-day), Aultmore (AULT-more), Craigellachie (CRAIG-al-a-KEY), The Deveron (DEV-er-RON) and Royal Brackla (Ba-RACK-lah) as single malts.

Read on to find out more about Dewar's and Bacardi's single malt Scotch distilleries.

Dewar's Blended Scotch Whisky

Dewar's is one of the most famous Scotch brands of all time, with roots that stretch back nearly two centuries.

The company was started by John Dewar, who was born in Aberfeldy, Scotland, and originally trained as a carpenter. Instead of following that career path or going into farming like his family, he decided to move to the city of Perth and began working at a wine store. In 1846, Dewar opened his own store in the area, where he ultimately created his own Scotch blends.

While John Dewar's name is emblazoned on millions of bottles of Scotch, it wasn't he who built the brand into an international bestseller, but his two sons, Thomas "Tommy" Dewar and John Alexander Dewar. The brothers only officially became part of the family business right around the end of their father's life in 1880, and John Dewar never saw the celestial heights that his eponymous

John Dewar started out as a liquor store owner in Perth, where he made his own whisky blends.

Dewar's White Label Blended Scotch became ubiquitous in the twentieth century.

brand would reach. "Up to about ten years ago our name was little known south of the Border," Tommy admitted to the *Westminster Budget* in 1895.

Like many small Scotch blenders, Dewar's benefited from the whisky boom at the end of the nineteenth century, but the secret to its phenomenal success was the Dewar brothers' combination of savvy and talent. John Alexander had real business and whisky-blending skills, while Tommy was a master marketer and a shameless self-promotor. In 1892, Tommy became an international celebrity and arguably the first brand ambassador when he went on an epic trip that included stops in twenty-six countries. Each destination would generate media buzz both there and back home in the UK. The trip also allowed him to introduce the whisky to new markets and set up a sales network. "Our name is known now in almost every corner of the civilized globe," Tommy told the *Westminster Budget* in 1895. "It is just as easy to get a 'John Dewar' on the top of the Rocky Mountains as it is at the Gaiety Restaurant, Strand."

If that wasn't enough, Tommy published an account of his travels called *A Ramble Round the Globe*. (If you're looking for any insights on whisky or Tommy's legendary marketing skills, you'll be sorely disappointed. What you will find instead is a travelogue.) And while Tommy's marketing tactics are now commonplace, they were downright cutting edge at the time, and helped shape how whiskies are still promoted.

At the turn of the century, Dewar's began marketing its now ubiquitous White Label Scotch. An advertisement that ran in the *New York Times* in 1903 touts it as "The most popular OLD Scotch Whisky in the world." Notably, White Label came out several years before Johnnie Walker introduced its own iconic color-coded line of blended Scotches.

Originally, the only Scotch you could buy in the United States was fiery single malts that were consumed in so-called Hot Scotches. "The whisky was white as gin and was not popular with New Yorkers of those days," wrote bartender Patrick J. Duffy in a letter to the editors of the *New York Times*. Dewar's and other leading blends offered a more refined whisky, which had been barrel aged and blended back in Scotland. The grain whisky gave it smoothness and the single malts contributed plenty of flavor.

What helped make Dewar's even more famous in the US was the Highball craze sweeping the country in the early 1900s, which Dewar's was quick to capitalize on.

While Scotch is now often sipped neat, in the early 1900s Dewar's used the Highball to establish itself in the United States.

Some even credit Tommy Dewar for introducing the drink to Americans. While I'm doubtful of that claim, the drink really caught on and was boosted by people's interest in another Scottish export—golf. It's hard to overestimate the importance of the Highball in terms of how it changed the perception of Scotch.

To keep up with demand for their brand, Dewar's opened the Aberfeldy (AH-BURR-fell-day) distillery at the end of the century, adding to the brand's incredible growth and also closing the circle on an astounding success story. John Dewar left his hometown as a poor young man, but his sons returned to the area as practically nobility. In fact, both Tommy and John Alexander became actual barons. Adding another chapter to the family lore, John Alexander's philanthropy was legendary, and he served in parliament for sixteen years as a member of the Liberal party.

In 1925, Dewar's joined forces with several of its rivals, including Johnnie Walker, Haig, and Buchanan's, when it merged with Distillers Company Limited (which became one of the core components of modern-day Diageo). This consolidation became necessary because of the giant shift in the Scotch market as sales fell in the UK but took off in the United States during Prohibition, when Scotch was smuggled in through the country's porous borders and slaked the thirst of countless Americans.

By the time John Alexander (aka Lord Forteviot) passed away in 1929 and Tommy (aka Lord Dewar) in 1930, they had both become fabulously wealthy and truly celebrities. Through most of the twentieth century, Dewar's was a staple that you could find at just about any bar or liquor store. It was like an old friend whom you could depend on to reliably show up for a drink on a rainy night or meet you for a Scotch & Soda at an airport lounge.

But along with the rest of blended Scotch, Dewar's increasingly found itself being replaced by single malts on the top shelf. Critics charged that Bacardi was maximizing its profits by using less single malt and more grain whisky in the brand's blends. We may never know if that was actually going on, but Bacardi is now on a mission to restore Dewar's to its former glory. (And John Alexander and Tommy would be happy to know that Aberfeldy whisky is still the core of the brand's blends.)

In addition to the easy-drinking White Label, Dewar's has recently introduced a number of award-winning whiskies, and master blender Stephanie Macleod has reworked some of its legacy bottlings, including its famous 12-year-old. For some limited releases, Dewar's has been finishing its blended Scotch in a range of flavorful and unusual barrels, such as casks that once held smoky Ilegal Mezcal.

Bacardi's strategy seems to be working, as sales of the brand continue to climb. In 2023, Dewar's reportedly sold more than 3 million nine-liter cases around the world. One reason for its continued popularity is that the brand's range is undervalued and therefore a great bargain. I imagine sales will only continue to increase as a new generation of whisky drinkers discovers an old classic.

Aberfeldy Single Malt Scotch Whisky

If you like Dewar's, then you'll probably love Aberfeldy. The distillery was built in the late 1890s with the express purpose of supplying Dewar's with single malt for its blended Scotch whisky. It's no coincidence that Aberfeldy opened during the first

The Dewar family constructed the Aberfeldy distillery at the end of the nineteenth century, and its whisky became the heart of their eponymous blend.

Scotch boom, at the time when Dewar's became an international bestseller. This unprecedented growth drove Dewar's to secure a very large and consistent supplier of single malt. Naturally, the easiest way to accomplish this was to build its own distillery. Within twenty years, Aberfeldy was aging 500,000 gallons (19,000 hectoliters) of whisky in its warehouses. What's really interesting is that the distillery mainly used casks that had formerly held sherry to age its whisky. And there was no better place to build the distillery than Perthshire, where John Dewar, the founder of Dewar's, was born. The facility was built by his sons, John Alexander and Tommy Dewar, and served as a monument of sorts that celebrated their father, who had passed away in 1880.

While you could find special Aberfeldy single malt releases in duty-free stores until fairly recently, it wasn't widely available in the US. However, in 2015, Bacardi relaunched the brand and you can now find an Aberfeldy 12 Year, a 16-year-old, and a 21-year-old in liquor stores across the country.

Craigellachie Single Malt

There are just a few famous landmarks in the tiny Scottish town of Craigellachie (CRAIG-al-a-KEY): The historic Craigellachie Hotel and its legendary Quaich Bar, the Highlander Inn and its vast whisky selection, and the Speyside Cooperage, which supplies or fixes barrels for many distilleries that no longer have their own coopers. And since 1891, the town has also boasted an eponymous distillery whose shining copper stills are clearly visible to all who have the pleasure to walk or drive by it.

The original investors in the distillery were a group of whisky blenders and store owners. At the time, Scotch was booming and both blenders and store owners were trying to make sure they had a supply of whisky to sell. In 1919, Mackie & Co., the makers of White Horse blended Scotch, bought out the rest of their fellow investors in the distillery. Not even ten years later, Mackie & Co. would be bought by Distillers Company Limited, which eventually helped form Diageo.

Since 2014, Bacardi has released a range of ever older vintages of Craigellachie single malts, including a 33-year-old, a 39-year-old, and a 51-year-old. There is also a core range of whiskies, including its signature 13-year-old, 17-year-old, and 23-year-old.

Spare barrel hoops, like these hanging at the Craigellachie distillery, are a necessity—as the whisky ages, so do the casks, which sometimes need to be fixed and repaired.

Royal Brackla Highland Single Malt Scotch Whisky

Royal Brackla (Ba-RACK-lah) might not yet be a household name, but one of the most important scenes in William Shakespeare's *Macbeth* supposedly takes place at Cawdor Castle, which is right near where the distillery would be built centuries later. As a result, the Highland town of Nairn and the surrounding Scottish countryside have been enjoying reflected glory and attention for centuries.

From Shakespeare's Macbeth to actual royalty, Royal Brackla has a colorful and long history.

No offense to Shakespeare, but the Royal Brackla distillery has an interesting and important history of its own that deserves attention. Captain William Fraser built the distillery back in 1812, and unlike most of his contemporaries, he actually got a proper license and paid the required taxes. No one can be sure why, but given that Nairn is located right on the Moray Firth, he may have figured that he could ship out tons of whisky by sea, making it hard for him to get away with anything. A profile of the distillery from 1924 in the *Wine and Spirit Trade Record* speculated that perhaps Brackla and other legitimate distillers also were distilling whiskey on which they weren't paying taxes. Even if Fraser was breaking the law, it didn't prevent King William IV from giving the distillery a royal warrant in 1833. As a result, Brackla became Royal Brackla.

In 2015, Bacardi revamped Royal Brackla and launched a line of single malts that it now sells around the world, including a 12-year-old, a 16-year-old, and a 21-year-old. It's still arguably one of the lesser-known whiskies in Bacardi's portfolio, but it offers a beguiling mix of flavors given its signature slow distillation process and aging in casks that previously held sherry.

BRANCH: SUNTORY GLOBAL SPIRITS

In a merger of whiskey powerhouses, Suntory bought Jim Beam in 2014 to form the international conglomerate Suntory Global Spirits. While the heart of the new company's portfolio is American and Japanese whiskies, both companies had previously invested in Scotch distilleries. Suntory acquired Bowmore and Auchentoshan (OCH-en-TOSH-en) in 1994 and Beam acquired Laphroaig (LAH-froyg) and Ardmore (ARD-moor) in 2005.

While nearly all single malt Scotch is distilled twice, Auchentoshan is an exception to the rule and distills its whisky three times.

Read on for more about Suntory Global Spirits' important Scotch brands.

Auchentoshan Single Malt Scotch Whisky

Nothing about Auchentoshan is standard. Not only is it located just outside Glasgow (not up in the Highlands or on a remote island like most Scottish distilleries), but it also distills its whisky an extra time. Most Scottish single malt is distilled twice in a traditional copper pot still. Auchentoshan distills its whisky three times, as is more usual in Ireland. This extra step means the whisky is a bit smoother and lighter. But Auchentoshan is no lightweight—it has plenty of bold fruit flavor.

The distillery dates back to 1825, and has been rebuilt several times, including once after it was hit by bombs during World War II and suffered massive damage. Later it was a member of the first generation of single malts to be widely available in the US, during the late 1980s.

Over the past few years, Auchentoshan has experimented with a range of different types of barrels, including those made from new oak, which add big wood notes to its whiskies. Look out for the Auchentoshan Three Wood, which is aged in three different types of barrels: used bourbon barrels, oloroso sherry casks, and Pedro Ximénez sherry casks.

Ardmore Highland Single Malt Whisky

The Ardmore (ARD-moor) distillery was built in the late 1890s to produce the heart of William Teacher & Sons' famous Highland Cream. The facility, located about 30 miles (48 kilometers) northwest of Aberdeen, was designed to be a workhorse: It produces a certifiable river of single malt that is later combined with other malts and grain whisky. It was purposely built near a railroad line, which provided the necessary raw ingredients for its production and easy access to transport

Just north of Aberdeen, the Ardmore distillery produces and ages single malt whisky, which is mostly used in Teacher's Highland Cream Blended Scotch.

Bowmore has an incredibly long history that goes back to the late 1700s and is, in fact, the oldest distillery on the Scottish island of Islay.

the finished whisky to customers around the UK.

Thanks to the explosion in popularity of blended Scotch in the 1950s, the distillery was expanded from two stills to four. Production capacity increased again in the 1970s, when an additional four stills were installed, for a total of eight. Despite these renovations, the distillery, unbelievably, continued to use coal fires to heat its stills until 2001. This antiquated process also provided the brand's signature smoky note. Mercifully, even after it converted from coal to steam heat, the brand was able to figure out how to keep its famous flavor intact.

Most of Ardmore's yearly output of 5 million liters of spirit still goes into Teacher's Highland Cream, but you can also find Ardmore sold today as a delightful single malt. It's one of the few whiskies that will satisfy fans of heathered Highland malts as well as those who like more intensely peated Islay malts.

Bowmore Single Malt Scotch Whisky

Bowmore makes some of the most peaty and smoky Scotch on the market. I particularly like drinking the Islay-based brand's 15-year-old on a frigid winter evening when heavy, wet snowflakes slowly fall from the sky. The single malt is more than just a smoke bomb—thanks to aging in used bourbon barrels and finishing in oloroso sherry casks, it has a range of nuanced flavors that reveal themselves as I watch the snow build up on the windowsill.

But if Bowmore whisky is allowed to age undisturbed for decades and decades, something even more incredible happens—the whisky sheds its peaty character like a butterfly emerging from a cocoon and develops tropical fruit notes. And I don't mean you taste a hint of sweetness—it's full-on mango and papaya flavors. Why does this happen? I'm not exactly sure, but I have had the good fortune to taste several very old Bowmore whiskies that all have developed these unusual tropical notes. Unfortunately, very old bottles of Bowmore have now become rare collectors' items that sell for staggering prices. In 2017, the distillery released seventy-four bottles of a 50-year-old whisky made in 1966, with a suggested retail price of $30,000. (Yes, you read that correctly—$30,000 for one bottle.)

While that price is eye-catching, Bowmore has for decades succeeded in turning Scotch from a luxury product into a veritable investment vehicle. It started with the 1993 introduction of Black Bowmore, which was made in 1964 and had aged exclusively in sherry casks. As a result, the whisky was incredibly dark and had a dense flavor that was completely different from that of the Scotch blends popular at the time. Initially, it sold for about $200, but its value began to rise quickly; by 1999, it was selling for $700. If you can find one today, it would cost tens of thousands of dollars.

The distillery has a long and interesting history going back, reportedly, to 1779, which makes it the oldest licensed distillery on Islay. Over its nearly 250 years in business, the distillery has changed hands several times and was bought by Suntory in 1994, which owns it still. Most Scotch brands now purchase their malted barley from maltsters, but Bowmore continues to use the traditional technique of floor malting for some of the barley it uses to make its whisky. Without a doubt, this approach contributes to the brand's unique flavor.

Laphroaig

Laphroaig has been a sought-after whisky for more than two centuries. The distillery was founded by brothers Donald and Alexander Johnston at the turn of the nineteenth century, though the family was distilling illegally for years (they appear to have gotten a license and started paying taxes in 1826). Because of this, no one is exactly sure where the 1815 founding date on Laphroaig's bottle comes from, but I imagine it was a rough approximation of when the brothers decided to make whisky full time, sans license.

When journalist Alfred Barnard visited the Islay distillery in 1877 to do research for his book, the heavy and unctuous single malt was primarily used by Scotch blenders who prized its "peat reek" flavor and were willing to pay a premium for it. Without a doubt, the fact that the distillery only made a small amount of spirit kept its price high.

In 1923, Laphroaig was still using its small 760-gallon (2,900-liter) spirit still and only making 2,000 gallons (7,600 liters) a week. The style of the single malt didn't seem to have changed at all since its founding, but the *Wine and Spirit Trade Record* stated that it was using sherry casks to age the spirit for five years. (An interesting fact that shows just how long Scotch makers have been experimenting with aging their whisky in different types of barrels.) While the single malt was primarily still sold to blenders, the same publication noted that it was "second to none as a liqueur whisky, or for medicinal use." And they weren't alone in this opinion: Another fan of the distillery is the King of England, Charles III, who has visited the distillery several times and even bestowed his royal warrant on it in 1994.

One reason for Laphroaig's unique flavor is that it malts about 20 percent of its base barley the old-fashioned way, by floor malting. The barley is left soaking for forty-eight hours so the starches naturally

In the nineteenth century, peaty-and-rich Laphroaig single malt was a favorite ingredient of Scotch blenders.

turn to sugar. Then, right before the seeds begin to germinate, they're smoked over a fire of local peat for seventeen hours, which helps give the whisky its signature pungent flavor.

It's quite astounding that Laphroaig developed such a high-quality whisky and reputation, given the difficulties its founders faced during its first hundred years in business. Throughout the nineteenth century, a series of untimely and dramatic deaths in the Johnston family meant that several different people ran the distillery at different times, including the Johnstons' neighbor Walter Graham, who also ran the Lagavulin distillery. Lagavulin's owner, Mackie & Co., was also the agent of Laphroaig for many years. In 1908, after Laphroaig ended this arrangement, Mackie decided to build the Malt Mill distillery to directly compete with Laphroaig, and even used the same water source and the same still design. But the copycat distillery was unsuccessful, and ultimately closed.

Ian Hunter, a distant relative of the Johnstons, began working at the distillery in 1908 and is credited with turning Laphroaig into the modern brand we know today. Incredibly, the distillery stayed in family hands until 1950, when Hunter passed away and left it to Laphroaig's long-time manager, Bessie Williamson, who started working at the distillery in the summer of 1934 as a temporary typist and essentially never left. Williamson became the first woman in the twentieth century to own and run a Scottish distillery and

Scotch drinkers around the world are now very familiar with Laphroaig's iconic green-and-white label.

was a spokesperson of sorts for the industry; she went on tours of the United States and other countries promoting Scotch.

In the 1960s, Williamson sold the distillery to Seager Evans and Co. Several mergers and acquisitions later, Laphroaig passed into the portfolio of Allied-Lyons in 1990, which would ultimately become Allied Domecq. In 2005, Allied Domecq was bought by Fortune Brands (then the parent company of Jim Beam) and Pernod Ricard. In the complex deal, Beam got Laphroaig and has owned the brand ever since.

The Laphroaig 10 Year has become an industry staple, but my personal favorite is Laphroaig Quarter Cask, which is aged in a used bourbon barrel and then finished in a smaller cask. As a result of this unusual maturation, the whisky's pungent peat reek mellows a bit and the flavor of the spirit really comes through each sip.

BRANCH: MOËT HENNESSY LOUIS VUITTON (LVMH)

The Paris-based LVMH is famous for its French designer clothing brands and Champagne and Cognac houses, so you may be surprised to learn that it also owns several whisky brands. Despite competition from a number of other large spirits conglomerates, LVMH was able to buy Glenmorangie (GLENN-more-angie), Ardbeg (ARD-beg), and Glen Moray (MORE-ray) and their accompanying distilleries for £300 million in 2004. (They later sold off Glen Moray.) Read on for more about these two historic and important Scotch brands.

Glenmorangie

In 1843, William Matheson, a former distillery manager, converted a nearly century-old brewery in the Scottish town of Tain into the Glenmorangie distillery. By 1887, the facility was annually making 20,000 gallons (760 hectoliters) of whisky and was soon rebuilt to significantly increase production. It was likely during this renovation that Glenmorangie first installed its famously tall copper pot stills. The tallest in Scotland, these stills have long and elegant necks that are the same height as an adult giraffe. No doubt, they are partially responsible for the heathered and quaffable nature of the whisky. Because of its iconic stills, Glenmorangie has adopted the giraffe as a symbol of the brand and has partnered with nonprofits

Glenmorangie helped pioneer the technique of aging a whisky in two types of barrels.

that support giraffes.

In 1918, Glenmorangie was purchased by Macdonald & Muir and a business partner. After a few years, Macdonald & Muir was able to take complete control of the brand. The Macdonalds owned the distillery until 2004, when it was sold to LVMH.

Arguably, one of the most important events in the brand's history occurred when Dr. Bill Lumsden became the distillery manager in February 1995. One of the first graduate students at Heriot-Watt University in Edinburgh to study whisky making, Lumsden had worked in the industry for about a decade before joining Glenmorangie. He is a relentlessly creative person with seemingly limitless curiosity, but his ideas about how to revolutionize Scotch were so far ahead of the curve that they weren't understood or welcomed at first—even at Glenmorangie. Despite this, he remained stubborn and persevered. "The Glenmorangie distillery became my giant experimental laboratory," Lumsden told me. About four years later he became the master distiller running Glenmorangie, Ardbeg, and Glen Moray, allowing him to more or less shape the future of single malt Scotch.

By the 1990s, Glenmorangie was helping to lead the single malt revolution. In a bold move, the distillery decided to mostly stop selling its whisky to blenders and instead focused on creating a unique identity as a single malt. A lot of the brand's new profile revolved around Lumsden's experiments with aging whisky. Just like David Stewart at The Balvenie (see The Balvenie entry, page 277, for more), Lumsden realized that aging whisky in two different types of barrels could generate a range of exciting flavors. By 1997, Glenmorangie was selling whiskies that had been primarily aged in a used American oak bourbon barrel first, then finished for a few months in casks that had previously held either madeira, sherry, or port.

Even before Lumsden joined the company, Glenmorangie had been experimenting with aging whisky in different types of barrels. Its 1963 Vintage, which was released in 1987, was aged in a used

Dr. Bill Lumsden joined Glenmorangie in 1995 and not only breathed new life into the distillery but into the entire Scotch industry.

American oak bourbon barrel as well as in a used European oak sherry cask. And one of the first projects Lumsden worked on when he joined the company was aging its standard 12-year-old whisky—which had been aged initially in an American oak barrel that previously held bourbon—for a second time in a European oak cask that previously held port. The Glenmorangie 12 Year Port Wood Finish Scotch was released in October 1995 and had a suggested retail price of $40 a bottle, which was quite a bit of money at the time.

Over the past several decades, Lumsden and his team have rethought every aspect of making single malt, from the type of grain to the strain of yeast to where the oak for the barrels is grown. As a result, Glenmorangie has released one innovative whisky after another, which has pushed the envelope and added excitement to the entire industry.

Over the next ninety years, the distillery was bought and sold several times before winding up in Hiram Walker's portfolio in 1977, though at the time the brand's style of deeply peaty and smoky Scotch seemed to be the last thing folks wanted to drink. As the fortunes of imported vodka rose, the fortunes of Ardbeg and its fellow distilleries on Islay seemed to fall in response. The distillery closed and opened several times over the next decade before Hiram Walker was

Ardbeg dates back more than two centuries but almost closed for good in the late 1990s.

Ardbeg

Ardbeg (ARD-beg) is famous for producing some of the smokiest and peatiest whisky in Scotland. The distillery was built on the island of Islay, off the western coast of Scotland, in 1815 by the local Macdougall family. When Alfred Barnard visited Ardbeg in the course of writing his iconic 1887 book, *The Whisky Distilleries of the United Kingdom*, the brand was making a staggering 250,000 gallons (9,500 hectoliters) of whisky a year, which was sold to larger firms in Scotland for blending with other whiskies.

bought by Allied Domecq, which decided in 1996 to close and mothball Ardbeg—perhaps for good this time.

But just a few months later, Glenmorangie came to the rescue and bought Ardbeg and its distillery for £7 million. It took more than a year for the distillery to reopen and for production to begin again. Not only did Glenmorangie reopen it, but they also invested several million pounds to renovate and modernize it. This started a new era for Ardbeg as a single malt instead of a whisky to be sold exclusively to blenders. The brand's new owners made this clear by releasing a 17-year-old Ardbeg single malt and a vintage whisky from 1975. At the time, it seemed like a long shot that such peaty Scotch would ever catch on with drinkers, but the gamble paid off and Ardbeg is once again acclaimed for its smoky and nuanced whisky.

In 2000, the distillery introduced its now landmark 10-year-old whisky, which is incredibly peaty but also has an unmistakable sweetness. Three years later, Ardbeg released the nearly impossible-to-pronounce Uigeadail (OOG-a-doll) whisky, which combines whisky aged in used bourbon barrels with whisky aged in used sherry casks. Ardbeg has also introduced a tremendous number of limited-edition bottlings—many of which are chosen by its "Committee" of 180,000 drinkers and are only available to its members. Fortunately, you can join the Committee for free.

🌾 BRANCH: RÉMY COINTREAU

Rémy Cointreau is famous for its signature brands Cointreau and Rémy Martin, but more than a decade ago it branched into the world of whisky and purchased acclaimed Islay Scotch distillery Bruichladdich (BROOKE-laddie). Read on for the story of how this famous distillery almost closed for good and was then reborn.

Bruichladdich

The history of Bruichladdich (BROOKE-laddie) is split into two distinct eras—let's call them ancient history pre-2000, and modern history for everything afterward.

The dividing line is when American Brands sold the distillery in 2000 for just over $10 million to independent bottler Murray McDavid, which was founded by Mark Reynier, Simon Coughlin, and Gordon Wright.

Bruichladdich was originally built in 1881 by brothers Robert, William, and John Harvey. Their late father was in the whisky business and left them enough money to build the distillery on the west coast of the Scottish island of Islay. Bruichladdich joined such smoky icons as Laphroaig, Bowmore, and Ardbeg, which were all started decades earlier and helped put Islay on the whisky map. The Harveys shut down the distillery in 1929 and it remained dormant until 1937, when it was sold to Joseph Hobbs. It wouldn't be the last time Bruichladdich changed hands. In 1968, the distillery became part of the portfolio of Edinburgh-based Invergordon Distillers, which tried to promote Bruichladdich and its other single malt, Isle of Jura. This attempt failed to impress the *Economist*, which wrote in the summer of 1991 that these two brands "will never become top-sellers around the world." (Ouch.) So, it's understandable that a few years later, after

The Islay distillery Bruichladdich barely survived the twentieth century but has recently found success.

For fans of super peaty whisky, Bruichladdich offers Octomore and its Port Charlotte line of single malts.

Invergordon Distillers was taken over by its rival, Whyte & Mackay, that Bruichladdich was closed down. The fate of the distillery seemed dismal at best.

Just as it appeared Bruichladdich might crumble into the sea, Murray McDavid came along, bought the distillery, and, with the help of master distiller Jim McEwan, reopened it in 2001. (McEwan had previously worked at the famed Islay distillery Bowmore for almost four decades.) Harkening back for a moment to the brand's ancient history, the *Wine and Spirit Trade Record* wrote in 1923, "Bruichladdich Distillery is neither completely old-fashioned nor completely modern, and therein lies it attraction." Murray McDavid and McEwan took that sentiment, updated it for the modern Scotch fan, and introduced a range of whiskies that challenged what people expected from Islay, even Scotland as a whole. Many of the whiskies are in fact unpeated, including the acclaimed Classic Laddie bottling.

At the other end of the spectrum is Bruichladdich's incredibly dank and peaty Octomore, launched in 2008, which became a sensation with whisky collectors willing to pay a premium for this smoke bomb. (It also offers the heavily peated Port Charlotte line of whiskies.)

In 2011, Bruichladdich introduced The Botanist Island Dry Gin, which is also made at the Islay distillery. To connect the gin to Islay, the brand employs a local forager to harvest nearly two dozen types of wild botanicals across the island, such as bedstraw, mugwort, creeping thistle, and tansy, all used to flavor the gin. The idea is not as odd as it might seem at first. Scottish distillers in the 1600s and 1700s flavored their uisge beatha (ISH-keh BA-ha), an early form of distilled liquor that would lead to Scotch, with a range of botanicals and even honey.

Cofounder and managing director Reynier, who fancied himself a disrupter, clashed more than once with the Scotch Whisky Association, cementing his reputation in the industry. His notoriety also no doubt helped attract a buyer for the distillery. In 2012, Rémy Cointreau acquired Bruichladdich for $90.3 million. Reynier had not wanted to sell the business but was outvoted by his partners. He left Bruichladdich soon after the deal closed, but Rémy remains committed to turning Bruichladdich into a major player in the Scotch industry. Reynier went on to start Irish whiskey brand Waterford, focusing on the idea of where and how the grain is grown affects the flavor of the spirit. (See the Waterford entry, page 365, for more.)

🌾 BRANCH: WHYTE & MACKAY

In one form or another, the Glasgow-based Whyte & Mackay (WHITE & MAC-eye) has been in the Scotch business since 1881, when it was founded by James Whyte and Charles Mackay. The partners began by selling wine and spirits, then, during the Scotch boom at the end of the nineteenth century, began producing their eponymous blended whisky brand.

Over the next century the company would become a significant player in the Scotch industry, selling bulk whisky and bottling its own brands. By 2015, Whyte & Mackay was the fifth largest exporter of Scotch to the US.

Whyte & Mackay was also involved in some pivotal mergers and acquisitions. In 1988, Brent Walker bought Whyte & Mackay as part of a bigger $330.9 million purchase from Lonrho. Two years later, Brent Walker sold Whyte & Mackay for $270 million to American Brands, where it joined Jim Beam in the conglomerate's portfolio. A year later, Whyte & Mackay began its hostile takeover of its competitor, Invergordon Distillers. (The deal was far from easy to close, but after two years Whyte & Mackay finally prevailed.)

In 2007, Vijay Mallya, the Indian entrepreneur, bought Whyte & Mackay for £500 million. Five years later, Diageo acquired just over 50 percent of Mallya's company, United Spirits, for $2.05 billion. Thanks to Diageo's vast Scotch holdings, Diageo had to sell off Whyte & Mackay for regulators to approve the deal. Finally, in 2014, the Philippines-based company Emperador, which is owned by Alliance Global Group, paid $675 million for Whyte & Mackay, and still owns it today. Quite an impressive rise from Whyte & Mackay's humble roots as a wine and spirits merchant in Glasgow.

Read on for more about the company's main two brands.

The Dalmore Highland Single Malt Scotch Whisky

It is hard to talk about The Dalmore (DOLL-moor) without first mentioning the brand's larger-than-life master blender, Richard "The Nose" Paterson. He joined Whyte & Mackay in September 1970 and has essentially never left the company. Along the way, he became The Dalmore's biggest booster. Paterson is known for his strong mustache and dapper sense of style, favoring ties and pocket squares. His tastings are theatrical, with a flair for the memorable—he can come off as part Borscht Belt comedian and part Las Vegas, Nevada, magician. Arguably his greatest trick was turning The Dalmore into a true luxury brand. Some of the distillery's single malts now go for staggering sums, including two bottles of the 64-year-old Trinitas that each sold for £100,000 in 2010.

The distillery's history dates back to approximately 1839, when it was built on Alexander Matheson's pastoral estate in Alness, Scotland, on the east coast of the country just north of Inverness. The Dalmore sits directly above the Cromarty Firth, which leads right into the North Sea, an incredibly important location for both sourcing ingredients from afar and shipping out finished whisky. (A later railroad line was similarly helpful.) Matheson built the distillery with just two stills, not to run himself but to rent out to tenants. The first was the Sutherland family according to its 1860 license, with Margaret Sutherland listed as the distiller. Just seven years later, brothers Andrew and Charles Mackenzie rented the distillery. Their arrival would be a huge event in the history of The Dalmore—with their brother William, they were able to buy the distillery in 1891 from the Matheson family for £14,500, including 500 acres (200 hectares) of land. By the turn of the century, the distillery had four stills and, according to a promotional pamphlet that Alfred Barnard wrote, was ten times its original size.

The Mackenzie family owned the distillery until 1960, when they partnered with Whyte & Mackay to form a new company. Just a few years later The Dalmore doubled its capacity by adding another four stills.

Currently, The Dalmore offers the Principal Collection, which features a range of whisky between the ages of twelve and twenty-one years. Most of these single malts are aged in American oak bourbon barrels and finished in sherry casks. There are also Limited Editions, which can cost tens of thousands of dollars. These whiskies are either incredibly old or have been aged in unusual barrels. For instance, the Luminary No 1. 2022 Edition single malt whisky was aged in a number of different barrels, including one that was made from Scottish Tay oak, Japanese mizunara oak, and American white oak staves.

Jura Single Malt Scotch Whisky

While the Scottish island Islay and its famous Scotch distilleries get a ton of attention, just to the east is another lesser-known Scottish island, Jura, with its own distillery. The Jura (YOUR-rah) distillery first opened its doors in 1810 when there wasn't much else on the tiny, remote island. "The principal denizens of these weird rocks are eagles, red deer, and grouse," wrote whisky historian Alfred Barnard in 1887. Barnard goes on to talk about the sparse food selection on the island, so perhaps it's not a complete surprise that the distillery shut down in 1901. What *is* surprising is that it reopened in 1964 after being reconstructed. Jura then became part of the Scotch company Invergordon in 1985, as part of a bigger £17.8 million deal.

Invergordon was eventually taken over by rival Whyte & Mackay. And while The Dalmore has succeeded, Jura has yet to really break through with drinkers and bartenders. Part of the problem is that, unlike Islay, Jura has just one distillery, which makes it a bit more difficult to get attention. (It doesn't help that to get to Jura you first have to travel to Islay, which isn't itself easy to reach.)

You can now find a range of Jura offerings on store shelves that come in a distinctive bottle that has a pinched waist, including the core 10-year-old, 12-year-old, and 18-year-old. There is also a range of whiskies finished in a second barrel, such as the 14-year-old, which is aged in barrels that previously held bourbon as well as those that previously held rye whisky. The distillery manager (aka the master distiller), Graham Logan, began at Scapa as a trainee mashman in the fall of 1991 and has been with the brand for more than thirty years now.

BRANCH: CAMPARI

Italian spirits company Campari is a fairly new player in the Scotch industry. It acquired historic single malt maker The Glen Grant in 2005 from Pernod Ricard. Read on for more about the story of a distillery that dates back nearly two centuries.

The Glen Grant distillery in Rothes, Speyside, is famous for its lush surroundings and impressive garden.

The Glen Grant Speyside Single Malt Scotch Whisky

While The Glen Grant is very popular in Europe, it's just beginning to build a following in the United States. It didn't help that for decades the brand was deep in the shadow cast by its sister distilleries, Aberlour and The Glenlivet.

In 1840, brothers James and John Grant built The Glen Grant after owning Aberlour for several years. James Grant had personally fought for the Morayshire Railway to be built and, according to liquor historian Dave Broom, in 1858 contributed £4,500 toward the expansion of the line to Rothes, which is where the brothers had built their distillery. As a thank-you, there was even a train named after The Glen Grant. To capitalize on this development, the distillery expanded to produce more whisky. The Glen Grant was also one of the first distilleries in the area to install electric lights and use pneumatic malting drums.

Prized by blenders, The Glen Grant was ultimately purchased by The Glenlivet in 1953. This made sense because the two distilleries share a similar style—both are easy-drinking with plenty of flavor but not a ton of wood or smoke. "It is pure, mild and agreeable," read an advertisement that The Glen Grant ran in the *Wine Trade Review* back in 1868. "The essential oils and impurities, which render other whiskies harsh and disagreeable, are, in the Glen Grant Whisky, detected and separated from it in the process of manufacture."

To satisfy demand and perhaps to attract a buyer, The Glen Grant expanded several times in the 1970s, installing ten giant 20,000-gallon (760-hectoliter) washbacks (fermenting tanks) and adding six additional stills, bringing their total to ten. Despite these renovations, the stills continued to be tall and equipped with purifiers, which guaranteed that the spirit would be gentle. "We noticed a purifier attached to the head of each Still, consisting of a copper vessel with a water basin at the top, which effectually prevents anything but the purest steam from passing,

To attract whisky drinkers and collectors, The Glen Grant has released a series of incredibly old single malts, including a 70-year-old expression.

all impurities being sent back into the Still," wrote whisky historian Alfred Barnard in 1887.

The expanded The Glen Grant was eventually purchased by Seagram's in 1977 as part of its £48 million acquisition of The Glenlivet Group (the deal also included Longmorn). The whisky industry was on the precipice of a giant crash at the time, but Seagram's used The Glen Grant in its bestselling blend, Chivas Regal, which continued to be popular for decades despite falling sales of other whiskies.

But this wouldn't be the last time The Glen Grant was sold. Pernod Ricard bought The Glenlivet, Aberlour, Longmorn, and The Glen Grant from Seagram's in 2000. Then, in 2005, Pernod sold The Glen Grant to Campari for £80 million. Campari has worked hard to raise the distillery's profile in the US and around the world, releasing a series of ever-older The Glen Grant single malts, including a 60-year-old that honors its former master distiller, Dennis Malcolm's, sixty-year career, at a whopping suggested retail price of $30,000. The brand's standard line now includes a 10-, 12-, 15-, 18-, and 21-year-old. In addition, The Glen Grant offers a number of limited-edition whiskies, which change from year to year.

BRANCH: LA MARTINIQUAISE-BARDINET

While Pernod Ricard has evolved into a drinks behemoth, France also boasts another major liquor conglomerate: La Martiniquaise-Bardinet, which dates back to 1934. The company is known for its rum and port brands, including bestseller

Porto Cruz, but also owns a few whisky brands, including the historic Cutty Sark. Read on for more about this famous Scotch blend.

Cutty Sark Blended Scotch Whisky

Before there was a blended Scotch brand, the original *Cutty Sark* was a famous three-masted clipper ship built in Scotland in 1869. It was the FedEx of its time, hauling cargo from faraway ports to England in record times. And before there was a speedy clipper ship, the nickname Cutty Sark, an eighteenth-century Scottish term for a short undergarment, was given to the character Nannie in the epic poem "Tam o' Shanter," by Scotland's national bard, Robert Burns. The likeness of the character, a scantily clad witch, was even a figurehead on the famous ship.

So, when historic wine and spirits store Berry Bros. & Rudd wanted to launch an easy-drinking blended Scotch in 1923, it used this familiar name, which certainly would have resonated with customers in the UK. The store even put a clipper ship right on its distinctive yellow label. The name and image of the ship no doubt had a double meaning for many Americans, since plenty of bottles of the whisky were illegally transported to the country during Prohibition on fast boats.

For a time, Cutty was the bestselling Scotch brand in the US, with thirsty Americans buying 20 million nine-liter cases a year—a truly staggering amount of whisky. But the past forty years have not been kind to the brand, as blended Scotch has struggled to appeal to modern drinkers, who prefer single malts.

In 2010, Berry Bros. & Rudd traded Cutty to Edrington and in return got the acclaimed single malt Glenrothes. The two brands have a shared history because Glenrothes was the heart of Cutty Sark blend for decades. But during the past twenty years, it made financial sense to bottle increasingly more Glenrothes as a premium single malt than to use it in the modestly priced Cutty.

Unfortunately, Edrington had made a bad deal and should have kept Glenrothes, which was a better complement to the other famous single malts in its portfolio. So, in 2017, Edrington was able to convince Berry Bros. & Rudd to sell it back. Almost immediately, Edrington put Cutty up for sale, and it was ultimately bought by France's second largest spirits company, La Martiniquaise-Bardinet.

You can still find the standard Cutty Sark blended Scotch, made from a mix of single malts and grain whisky, on store shelves. There is also a higher proof Prohibition version at 100 proof (50 percent alcohol by volume), as well as a 12-year-old blended Scotch. True to its history, the modern brand continues to be easy-drinking and accessible.

BRANCH: INDEPENDENTS

The Scotch business is dominated by a few giant multinational conglomerates who own multiple brands. But this is actually nothing new—the rise in popularity of blended Scotch in the second half of the nineteenth century led to a wave of consolidation in the industry with blenders buying up scores of single malt distilleries. However, there are still several historic and modern brands that aren't owned by large corporations. Read on for more about a few of these independents.

Compass Box Scotch Whiskymakers

Back in 2000, when John Glaser started boutique whisky company Compass Box in his London apartment, he was light-years ahead of the rest of the spirits industry. It's perhaps no surprise given that the American-born Glaser has a deep curiosity about the world and a professorial demeanor.

Glaser realized that there was a hole in the market for unique and small batch whiskies that didn't fit into the portfolios of the huge conglomerates. So, he created his own range of fascinating blended whiskies, helping to usher in a new era for the industry, one that embraced innovation and wasn't fixated on consistency above all.

Entrepreneur and innovator John Glaser started his boutique blended Scotch company Compass Box Whisky in his London apartment in 2000.

Without a distillery of his own, Glaser bought barrels that he sourced from other brands. Why, you might ask, would these companies sell him whisky? Well, for many brands it's not worth it to release a random single barrel of whisky or even ten barrels of a whisky unless the resulting retail price covers the effort and cost associated with producing and marketing the bottling. And that's not to mention that these one-offs battle for shelf space with a company's standard line of whiskies. But for Glaser it was all about using these unusual casks as ingredients in his groundbreaking new creations—the whole is truly greater than the sum of its parts for this innovator.

Compass Box started with Hedonism, which is a mix of different Scottish grain whiskies. It's very rare to taste grain whisky on its own, since it's primarily produced as an essential component of blended Scotch. While you can't make a blended Scotch without grain whisky, it's generally never mentioned. Leave it to Glaser to realize that there would be a market for this largely overlooked whisky, which, like bourbon, is produced in a column still and aged for years in barrels. He blended the initial batch of Hedonism in his London apartment and he and his wife, Amy, delivered the first cases to stores in their Volkswagen Jetta.

Glaser first got the idea for his business when he was working in London for Scotch giant Johnnie Walker. And, for the record, he pitched his idea for Compass Box to Johnnie Walker and they passed, which is when he struck out on his own.

While Compass Box is widely hailed and has won numerous awards for its whiskies, the Scotch Whisky Association (SWA) has taken issue with some of its methods and innovations. Famously, the industry's governing body made Glaser

In addition to its core collection, Compass Box offers a range of limited-edition blended whiskies, like Art & Decadence.

take the first version of his Spice Tree off the market and forced him to find a way to produce it without violating the SWA's regulations.

Hedonism was just the start for Glaser. During the past twenty-five years, he introduced dozens of innovative and delicious whiskies. While many of the Compass Box releases are limited editions, there is now a core line that includes Spice Tree, which is aged in barrels made of both American and French oak, and The Peat Monster, an elegant and delicious smoke bomb. Glaser's Artist Blend and Glasgow Blend, (both initially called Great King Street), are some of the greatest spirits bargains around and should be in everyone's home bar.

In 2022, private equity company Caelum Capital bought a controlling interest in Compass Box and not even two years later Glaser resigned. He is reportedly still a minority shareholder in the business.

Glenfarclas

Glenfarclas (GLENN-FARK-lass) was built on a cattle farm in the shadow of the towering Scottish mountain Ben Rinnes. At the time, there wasn't much else nearby. The exact date when the distillery originally opened is hard to pin down, but Glenfarclas and whisky historian Alfred Barnard cite the date of 1836, when it got its first license. No matter when whisky was first made on the site, the most important moment in the brand's history was arguably in 1865, when John Grant bought the distillery from Robert Hay for £511.95.

At the end of the century, the Grants sold half of the business to Pattison, Elder & Co., then used some of the money to completely refurbish the distillery and add a pair of giant copper stills. A few years later when Pattison went bankrupt, the Grant family was able to take back complete control of Glenfarclas. While the distillery has undergone several expansions, amazingly it has remained independent and is still owned by the Grant family five generations later.

Glenfarclas Scotch is particularly rich and complex, which is in great part due to the distillery's dedication to using barrels that previously held oloroso sherry. Perhaps because it isn't owned by a large conglomerate, Glenfarclas can also take risks that might not make sense from a conglomerate's perspective but *do* make sense from a flavor point of view. While Glenfarclas is less well known than many of its bigger Speyside neighbors, such as The Glenlivet and The Macallan, it's a hidden gem worth seeking out.

Kilchoman Islay Single Malt Scotch Whisky

It takes a lot of courage to open a new distillery on Islay, as you'll inevitably be compared to the island's other incredible distilleries, including Ardbeg, Bowmore, and Laphroaig. But that's just what Anthony and Kathy Wills did in 2005, when the couple opened Kilchoman (Kill-HOME-man). Not only has the distillery succeeded, but it even grows some of the barley it uses to make its Scotch. Kilchoman doesn't take any shortcuts in the whisky production process, which means every year it floor malts about 6 tons (5.4 metric tons) of its barley—a truly backbreaking effort.

Although the malted barley is smoked over a peat fire, the whisky isn't a smoke bomb and has elegant citrus notes and an unexpected lightness. Its 100% Islay whisky is truly barley-to-bottle, made using grains grown at the brand's farm. Each edition of the 100% Islay is different and usually includes barley from several harvests. Also, look out for the Machir Bay bottling, which includes whiskies that have been aged either in used bourbon barrels or former sherry casks.

Glenfarclas dates back to the early nineteenth century and is renowned for its single malt aged in sherry seasoned barrels.

IRISH WHISKEY

IRELAND
Whiskey Landmarks

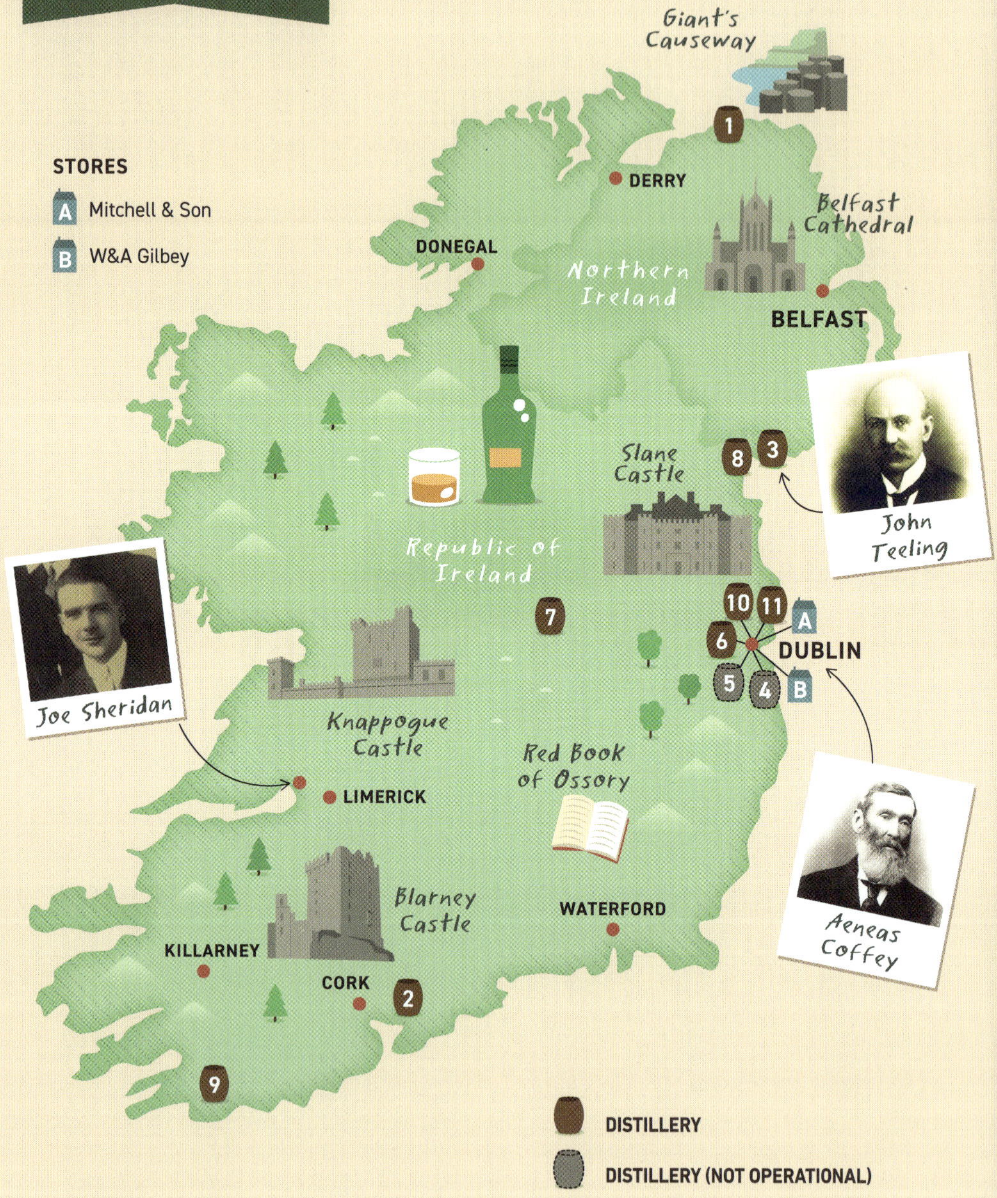

STORES
- A: Mitchell & Son
- B: W&A Gilbey

Giant's Causeway

DERRY

DONEGAL

Northern Ireland

Belfast Cathedral

BELFAST

Slane Castle

John Teeling

Republic of Ireland

Joe Sheridan

DUBLIN

Knappogue Castle

LIMERICK

Red Book of Ossory

Aeneas Coffey

Blarney Castle

KILLARNEY

CORK

WATERFORD

DISTILLERY

DISTILLERY (NOT OPERATIONAL)

1. Bushmills distillery, County Antrim, Northern Ireland
2. Midleton distillery, County Cork
3. Cooley distillery, County Louth
4. Power's defunct John's Lane distillery, Dublin
5. Jameson's defunct Bow Street distillery, Dublin
6. Teeling distillery, Dublin
7. Kilbeggan distillery, County Westmeath
8. Great Northern distillery, County Louth
9. West Cork distillery, Skibbereen, County Cork
10. Tullamore D.E.W. distillery, County Offaly
11. Roe & Coe distillery, Dublin

Most of the clichés Americans learn about Ireland are completely and utterly incorrect.

First, no one eats corned beef and cabbage. Seriously, don't try to order it in Dublin or Belfast. You'll just be laughed at by the entire restaurant. (Irish immigrants began to make it only when they got to New York and were introduced to the joys of corned beef by the city's Jewish immigrants.)

Second, St. Patrick's Day is not a major holiday back in the old country. It's another tradition that Irish Americans really created after they settled in the United States. (No, they don't dye Dublin's River Liffey green—and don't ever ask for a green beer.) I found all this out the hard way when I showed up at a deserted Irish pub in Scotland on March 17. The Irish bartender took one look at me and my friends and said "Americans?" Guilty as charged.

Third and most important, not all Irish whiskies taste like Jameson. And modern Jameson was not the whiskey that was historically made on the island—our Jameson would not have been considered drinkable

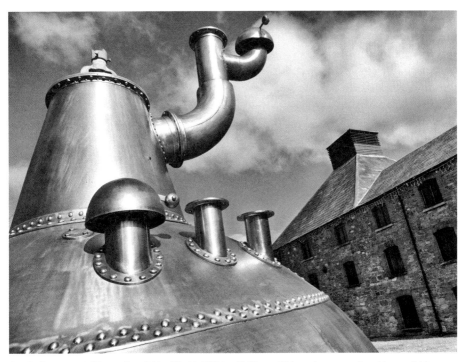

A retired copper pot still now sits outside of Cork's Midleton distillery, which produces a number of famous Irish whiskies.

Key Differences

For a long time, if you asked a bartender what Irish whiskey tasted like they would essentially describe Jameson—honeyed and easy drinking. To be fair, Jameson for all intents and purposes *was* Irish whiskey for a number of years, and continues to be phenomenally popular.

But in fact, Irish whiskey includes a range of different styles. Above all, it must be produced and aged somewhere on the island to be considered Irish whiskey. Irish distillers may make their whiskey from a mash that includes both malted and unmalted grain—only single malt has to be 100 percent malted barley. (This is one key distinguishing point from Scottish single malt, which is made completely from malted barley.) Usually, Irish whiskey is distilled three times, which is one more distillation than is normal in Scotland. It is aged for at least three years in a wooden barrel not exceeding 700 liters (185 gallons) in size.

Total Consumption: Sales of Irish whiskey in the United States in 2023 totaled nearly 5 million nine-liter cases.

---

by the Jameson family at the turn of the twentieth century. I say this with all the love and respect in the world, since I do like to drink Jameson, but it's very different from what the brand and the Irish whiskey industry produced throughout the 1800s.

This change in Irish whiskey came about because of a huge battle in the early 1900s that pitted Irish distillers against their Scottish rivals over the very definition of whiskey. While not geographically distant, they couldn't have been farther apart in their approach to making whiskey. (Spoiler alert: The Scots won and it almost destroyed the Irish whiskey industry.)

So why do Americans know so little about actual Irish drinking culture and history? The short answer is that Irish whiskey faced one major crisis after another during the twentieth century. At the dawn of the twenty-first century, it was incredible that there were any Irish distillers still operating. In order to survive, distillers essentially had to reinvent how they produced and marketed their whiskey.

The fact that we're currently experiencing a prolonged Irish whiskey boom, and a larger renaissance of distilling around the island, is frankly miraculous. For the past twenty-five or so years, Irish whiskey has been unstoppable, and once again has taken its rightful place on the backbar alongside Scotch and American whiskey.

To understand this modern boom, we have to go back to the beginning, all the way to the dawn of whiskey. Whiskey history is full of twists and triumphs and struggle—and the Irish story might be a standard bearer in terms of drama. So, pour yourself a dram of your favorite Irish whiskey. As they say on the Emerald Isle, sláinte!

The town of Bushmills in Northern Ireland got its first distilling license in 1608.

Types of Irish Whiskey

There are four main types of Irish whiskey: single malt, pot still, grain, and blended. No matter which kind you buy, it has to be distilled and aged somewhere on the island to be considered Irish whiskey. Here's a cheat sheet for the different categories.

♦ SINGLE MALTS

Single malts are predominantly made by Bushmills, in Northern Ireland, from malted barley in a classic copper pot still. The process is very similar to how Scotch is produced, except Irish single malt whiskey is usually distilled three times, while Scotch is typically distilled only twice. Most Irish whiskey

DEFINING IRISH SINGLE MALT

- It must be produced and aged in the Republic of Ireland or in Northern Ireland.
- The mash (base grains) has to be 100 percent malted barley.
- The whiskey must be made using a copper pot still.
- It is usually distilled two or three times.
- It has to age for at least three years in a new or used wooden barrel.
- The finished whiskey must be at least 80 proof (40 percent alcohol by volume).

While single malt is now identified with Scotland, Ireland was likely making the style of whiskey first.

DEFINING IRISH POT STILL WHISKEY

- It must be produced and aged in the Republic of Ireland or Northern Ireland.
- The mash (base grains) must contain at least 30 percent malted barley and at least 30 percent unmalted barley.
- Up to 5 percent of the mash may be made up of other unmalted grains, such as oats or rye.
- The whiskey is made using a copper pot still.
- It is usually distilled two or three times.
- It has to age for at least three years in a new or used wooden barrel.
- The finished whiskey has to be at least 80 proof (40 percent alcohol by volume).

is no longer peated. However, there are a few Irish brands that do offer smoky or peaty expressions, and the style was certainly more common in the nineteenth century. Irish single malt must be aged for at least three years in a wooden cask no larger than 700 liters (185 gallons)—usually a used bourbon barrel. Some single malts are finished in a range of other types of casks, including sherry, port, Cognac, and wine. After at least three years of aging, it can be called Irish whiskey. Spirit caramel may be added to fix or improve the color of the whiskey.

♦ POT STILL WHISKEY

Irish whiskey has a unique category, referred to as pot still. The acclaimed Redbreast, Yellow Spot, and Midleton Very Rare are all pot still whiskies. The major difference between pot still and single malt whiskies is that single malt is made from 100 percent malted barley, while pot still whiskey is made from malted and unmalted barley and may also contain up to 5 percent of other cereal grains, such as oats and rye. Pot still whiskey is often made in a larger still than those used to produce single malt. Three distillations is generally the standard, and the spirit must be aged for at least three years in a wooden cask no larger than 700 liters (185 gallons)—usually a used bourbon barrel. Some pot still whiskies are finished in a range of other types of casks, including sherry, port, Cognac, and wine. Spirit caramel may be added to fix or improve the color of the whiskey.

♦ GRAIN WHISKEY

Just like in Scotland, Irish distillers can make grain whiskey. This is very different from single malt or pot still whiskey because it is made using a column still, also known as a patent still or Coffey still. The mash for grain whiskey is also different from that for single malt or pot still whiskey in that it contains some malted barley (up to 30 percent), but the majority is usually unmalted grains, such as corn, wheat, or barley. The spirit must be aged for at least three years in a wooden cask no larger than 700 liters (185 gallons)—usually a used bourbon barrel.

♦ BLENDED WHISKEY

Most Irish whiskey consumed today is a blend, including of course the Irish whiskey bestseller Jameson, which makes up more than half of sales in the United States and worldwide. Irish blends are a mix of pot still and/or single malt with grain whiskey. A number of brands, including Tullamore D.E.W., Paddy's, and Lost Irish make their blends from all three kinds of whiskey.

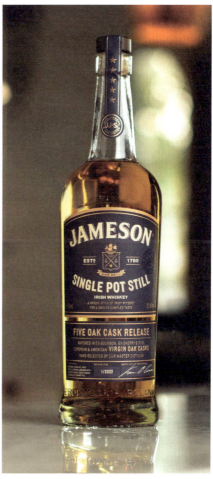

Most Irish whiskey sold today is a blend but some brands still bottle single pot still whiskey.

DEFINING IRISH BLENDED WHISKEY

- It is a mix of grain whiskey with single malt and/or pot still whiskey.
- All the elements must be produced and aged in the Republic of Ireland or in Northern Ireland.
- The finished whiskey has to be at least 80 proof (40 percent alcohol by volume).

DEFINING IRISH GRAIN WHISKEY

- It must be produced and aged in the Republic of Ireland or in Northern Ireland.
- The mash has to contain malted barley, but it has to make up less than 30 percent of the overall base grain mix. The rest of the mash is usually unmalted wheat, corn, barley, or a combination of these grains.
- The whiskey is made using a column still.
- It is distilled two or three times.
- It has to age for at least three years in a new or used wooden barrel.
- The finished whiskey must be at least 80 proof (40 percent alcohol by volume).

This so-called mash tun was used at Jameson's historic distillery on Bow Street in Dublin.

Distilleries across Ireland, including the Jameson facility on Bow Street, had coopers onsite who would build and repair wooden barrels.

The History of Irish Whiskey

Irish distillers were arguably the first people in the world to produce whiskey. Over hundreds of years, they helped to refine the spirit and create a bona fide industry whose success seemed virtually unstoppable. In bars both near and far, Irish whiskey was a bestseller and thirsty patrons asked for brands, like Bushmills, by name. In spite of its long history, though, the Irish whiskey industry almost completely died after World War II. Of the hundreds of distilleries operating in the 1800s, ultimately there were just three left: Bushmills, at the top of the island in Northern Ireland; Cooley, near Dublin; and Midleton, in the south, in Cork.

During the twentieth century, a number of calamitous events made it ever harder to produce and sell Irish whiskey, and drinkers around the globe lost their taste for the spirit—opting instead to buy a river of blended Scotch.

Fortunately, like the plot from a lost Frank Capra movie, just at the brink of Irish whiskey's complete destruction, an improbable rebirth happened around the year 2000, which led to a distilling boom. Suddenly, Irish whiskey was on fire with bartenders and drinkers around the world, who extolled the virtues of the category and its rich distilling history.

♦ WHO WAS FIRST?

Whiskey distillers like to speak in grandiose terms. Their whiskey isn't just good, it's the best. And their ancestors didn't just make whiskey, they practically invented the art of distilling. This is certainly true for Scotch.

Since the turn of the century, Scottish brands have done a masterful job marketing their whiskies around the world. So much so that the other major whiskey-making countries have been playing a game of catch-up. But the Scotch industry didn't just excel at promoting its whiskies—it created a convincing backstory about how the Scottish created whiskey and could call the shots as a result. (This narrative was flexible enough to bend and suit the evolving portfolio of Scotch whiskies.)

There is just this one small problem with this narrative: There is a very high probability that whiskey was invented in Ireland and only then made its way across the Irish Sea to Scotland. (At the channel's narrowest point, the two coastlines are just 12 miles [19 kilometers] apart.) While the Scotch industry bitterly disputes whiskey's Irish origins, the earliest reference anyone has found—yet—about *possible* whiskey distillation is in the *Red Book of Ossory*, which dates to the fourteenth century and is thought to have been started by Bishop Richard de Ledrede, who was based in Kilkenny, Ireland. The tome's dramatic name, which sounds like something from *Game of Thrones*, is simply a nod to its red leather covers, which protect the portfolio of vellum pages.

But this is far from an open-and-shut case. Why does a book of religious holiday hymns written in Latin and Anglo-Norman contain a recipe for making liquor? The short answer is we don't know. But regardless, in an aside about "aqua vini" (wine) there are directions for how to turn it into aqua-vitae via distillation. You may be wondering what any of this has to do

The town of Bushmills has been making single malt whiskey longer than any other place on Earth.

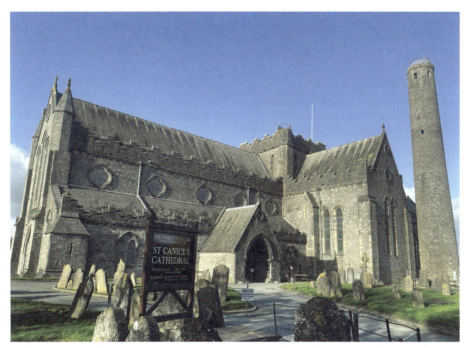

The Irish whiskey industry cites a passage in the fourteenth-century Red Book of Ossory as proof that the island was distilling whiskey before Scotland. It's now on display at St. Canice's Cathedral in Kilkenny, shown here.

with making whiskey. The text seems to prove that folks in Ireland were familiar with the basics of distilling. Given that most people didn't have easy access to grapes or wine, it's assumed that they would instead use beer as a base, which was readily available and made from malted oats or other grains. The term *aqua vitae* was used for all kinds of distilled spirits, made from all kinds of ingredients. Some experts also point out that the name *aqua vitae* wasn't commonly used in Scotland until several hundred years later, which may indicate that the Irish were far ahead in the art of distilling.

We don't know who wrote the exact entry that refers to distilling in the *Red Book of Ossory*. The "pages of the book were used over many years for a succession of widely varied entries in at least thirty-six hands, the latest items being of the reign of Queen Elizabeth I," wrote Richard Leighton Greene in the introduction to his 1974 translation, *The Lyrics of the Red Book of Ossory*. But no matter who wrote the recipe, it was no doubt an Englishman. "After Dublin, Kilkenny was the most important centre of English power in Ireland and was surrounded by a wall of legal privilege, outside of which the native Irish were zealously kept," wrote Greene. In fact, the bishop himself was from Leatherhead, in Surrey. So was this actually an English liquor recipe?

That is certainly possible and, if true, would completely blow up our theories about who first created whiskey.

Here's what we do know: The roots of whiskey distilling in Ireland go back centuries, to when alcohol was essentially a farm product. Folks would use simple stills to turn their excess grain into a shelf-stable product whose value was significantly higher than that of its base ingredients. The town of Bushmills got a distilling license in 1608, which was more than 150 years before the official brand was established. This certainly means that the area's residents were serious about distilling for their own needs.

♦ THE RISE OF THE MODERN WHISKEY INDUSTRY

Regardless of whether Ireland was the first place where whiskey was made, the island's distillers were able to create a serious industry for themselves rather quickly. Many of the most famous distilleries were founded and licensed back in the late 1700s (see the Irish Family Tree, page 000), including John Jameson's Bow St. distillery (1780) and his rival John Power's John's Lane distillery (1791).

This production gave Ireland a head start for its whiskey industry, while at the time Scotland's best single malt distilleries were far from

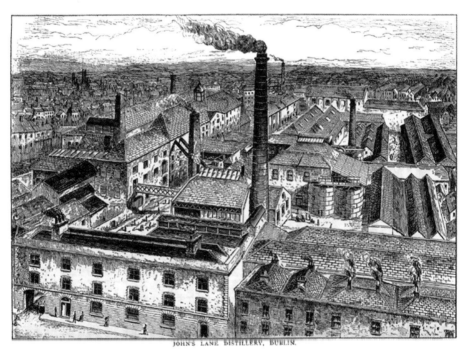

The town of Bushmills has been making single malt whiskey longer than any other place on Earth.

What is Poitín?

Often when I lead an Irish whiskey tasting, someone will ask about the Irish alcohol poitín (PO-cheen), and how it's connected to what we're tasting. Well, just as American whiskey has an outlaw cousin, moonshine, Irish whiskey has the much-mythologized poitín. Historically, this illicit and unaged liquor was made from potatoes or grain by folks who didn't have a distilling license but hopefully knew what they were doing. But to be clear, Irish whiskey didn't evolve from poitín—the two types of alcohol developed separately. And, really, over the last several hundred years a very small amount of poitín has been made as farmer-distillers drastically decreased in numbers.

What helps keep people talking about poitín is that, in recent years a handful of distilleries have begun to sell upscale legal poitín as an alternative to vodka or gin. Belfast's acclaimed BAR 1661 even makes their Irish coffee with poitín. Their coffee drink has become a sensation and has certainly helped raise the profile of this old-style spirit.

---

professional commercial endeavors. Most were tiny, illegal operations hiding in the Highlands.

Since the whole island of Ireland was part of the United Kingdom, thanks to the 1823 Excise Act, it became both advantageous and a lot easier for Irish distillers to get a license instead of bootlegging their whiskey. (The act had a similar effect in Scotland.) By the end of that year, there were forty licensed distillers on the island. And their numbers grew as cutting-edge steam power, instead of wood, coal, or peat, helped the brands run ever larger pot stills. (Conversely, the number of illegal distilleries fell dramatically.)

Irish whiskey also had a place of prominence in the United States. The horrific Irish Potato Famine of the late 1840s sent massive waves of immigrants to the States and other countries in search of a better life. These transplants brought with them their rich drinking culture and a love of whiskey, which irrevocably shaped their new homelands.

A few decades later, Irish whiskey imports (along with whisky from Canada) would become essential, as the bloody US Civil War derailed much of the country's distilling industry. Pot still whiskey from Ireland slaked the thirst of countless drinkers.

Thanks to its now global reputation and exports to a number of markets around the world, Ireland's distilleries were no longer small upstarts, and by the late nineteenth century had grown into giant facilities that covered acres and acres of Dublin. These distilleries used very large pot stills, which produced consistently high-quality whiskey.

Running parallel to the legitimate whiskey trade was a large-scale and well-organized bootlegging business in Ireland. As in Scotland, there is a long tradition of Irish distillers doing things off the books. Some of these early whiskey makers supplied smugglers who sailed to Scotland and sold or traded pot still whiskey for other products, such as rum and tobacco. Through the early 1800s, there were also thousands and thousands of small, illegal farm stills across Ireland making whiskey or the local moonshine, poitín.

♦ IRELAND'S SIGNATURE STYLE

Until 1830, whiskey was fairly similar in Scotland and Ireland, produced in traditional bulbous copper pot stills. But there were some significant differences between the two spirits as well. In Scotland, distillers primarily used malted barley as the base of the whisky, and sometimes toasted the grains over peat fires. In Ireland, most distillers used a mix of malted and unmalted barley, plus oats, rye, or corn.

The reason the Irish don't use only malted barley like the Scots isn't romantic or complicated, but economic—it cost more. In 1785, the tax a distiller had to pay was based on how much malted barley they used. Adding unmalted barley and other grains greatly lowered a distiller's tax bill. It

If you visit Bushmills today, you'll still find this four-story stone warehouse full of barrels of aging whiskey.

also changed how the whiskey tasted, and inadvertently gave Irish whiskey its creaminess and an inherent spice. This difference in the mash bill became a signature for Irish distillers, and even today many of them still use a mix of malted and unmalted barley. (Over time, Irish distillers stopped adding the other grains to their pot still whiskey, although the regulations still allow them to do so if they want.)

Bushmills, in Northern Ireland, is the famous exception to the rule, and makes incredible single malt from a mash of 100 percent malted barley. Today, in Ireland, the difference between single malt and pot still whiskey comes down to whether the mash is completely malted barley or if it includes unmalted barley and possibly other grains. Why didn't the Scotch distillers make a similar money-saving move? Well, the single malt distillers refused to pay any taxes, which is why they were located in the Highlands away from the Crown's tax collectors.

Irish distillers also generally favored very large stills. These big apparatuses had the advantage of producing a lot of spirit, but the compelling reason they were used was the Distilling Act of 1779. "It introduced a complicated system of imposing a minimum payment on every still, calculated on size and capacity," wrote Malachy Magee in his 1980 book *1000 Years of Irish Whiskey*. "It was based on the assumption that each still, fully loaded, could be worked a minimum number of times over each period of 28 days." This tax scheme meant that if distillers had any hope of making a profit, they needed to build an oversized still and use it often.

When Alfred Barnard visited the Power's mammoth John's Lane distillery in Dublin for his groundbreaking 1887 book, *The Whisky Distilleries of the United Kingdom*, he was impressed by the brand's giant still house and its humongous pair of 25,000-gallon (946-hectoliter) pot stills, which were "said to be the largest Pot Stills ever made."

No matter the size of the stills, Irish distillers triple-distilled their whiskey, while Scottish distillers usually limited it to two times through the still. The extra distillation tends to give Irish whiskey additional smoothness and drinkability.

♦ REJECTING THE COFFEY STILL, REJECTING WHISKEY BLENDS

In 1830, Aeneas Coffey, an Irishman, patented his plans for a continuous column still. The whiskey world would never be the same—particularly in Ireland.

While there had been other attempts at modernizing the traditional distilling process, including Robert Stein's pioneering 1827 design, Coffey's invention essentially splits the history of whiskey into two epochs, life before the column still and life after it.

A pot still is wonderfully inefficient and eventually produces a big, bold spirit. On the other hand, a column still, also known as a patent still or a Coffey still, is a well-oiled machine that efficiently and systematically

Catholics vs Protestants

John Jameson was Scottish and a Protestant.

Just as the myth of the worm in tequila has largely been debunked, it's time to retire the notion that Protestants drink Bushmills and Catholics drink Jameson.

Ask a barfly in an American dive about Irish whiskey and they'll no doubt bring up this supposed fact. For example, Dominic West's character, the hard-drinking detective Jimmy McNulty, on an episode of the critically acclaimed TV series *The Wire*, calls Bushmills "Protestant whiskey" when the bartender tells him he only has that brand, and not Jameson. (Despite the remark, McNulty quickly drains a glass of Bushmills anyway.)

This notion of a religious division of Irish whiskey is complete barroom BS.

If you don't believe me, ask someone who grew up on the Emerald Isle—you'll usually get a bewildered look. Irish expats who have spent significant time in the States say that they heard this only when they got to the US, never back home.

While this nonsense doesn't deserve a further look, note that the long-serving master distiller at Bushmills in Northern Ireland, Colum Egan, is Catholic. Irish whiskey icon John Jameson, whose whiskey is now famous around the world, was Protestant (and Scottish!). Furthermore, Bushmills is now owned by a Mexican company, Jose Cuervo, and Jameson is owned by the French company Pernod Ricard. (For decades, Jameson and Bushmills were even owned by the same company.)

So where did this idea come from? No one is sure exactly. There have been some jokes in both Irish and American newspapers over the years about a religious drinking divide, but nothing concrete. The one theory that makes the most sense is that this idea was created by someone selling Jameson on the East Coast of the US in the 1980s or 1990s when Irish Catholics far outnumbered Irish Protestants.

Bushmills is now owned by the Beckmann family, which started and still runs Jose Cuervo Tequila.

produces a river of alcohol—every hour. (For more on how the Coffey still works, see the description on page 32.)

In Scotland, this new distilling technology was adopted in the mid-1800s by pioneering entrepreneurs who saw its potential to revolutionize the way Scotch was produced. While stores and other establishments had been blending together single malts from across the country for many years, thanks to Coffey's design and some changes in liquor regulations, brands began adding copious amounts of grain whisky made on a column still to these blends.

The grain whisky could be made from just a little malted barley, with less expensive corn or wheat making up the balance. The inherent smoothness of the grain whisky could offset the roughness of the single malts. This blending also allowed the Scotch industry to become much more profitable and scalable, since it was a way to produce a consistent whisky from many different single malts that all tasted different. And stretching the single malts this way meant the brands would have enough product to sell not just in their home market of the UK, but also in the British colonies and around the world.

In Ireland, however, most of the distillers had a completely different opinion of whiskey produced on a column still: In short, they didn't like it—and they didn't want to debase their pure pot still whiskey by blending with it. As a result, most whiskey sold in Ireland continued to be made in a pot still. At the time, Irish whiskey was a bestseller domestically and in a number of export markets including England and the US. It seemed foolhardy to mess with its flavor, and unnecessary to change how the spirit was produced. Irish distillers nobly believed that quality and tradition would ultimately win out over the blends.

While a few Irish distillers installed column stills, the grain whiskey they made was used in very cheap blends. Ironically, Aeneas Coffey, a Dubliner who'd been the Inspector General of Excise in Ireland, would inadvertently become the nemesis of Irish whiskey. (For more on Coffey read the profile of him on page 212.)

♦ THE FALL OF IRISH WHISKEY

One of the great mysteries of whiskey history is why people stopped drinking Irish whiskey in the twentieth century. How did it come to pass that whiskey distillers in the United States, Canada, and Scotland thrived during much of the 1900s, especially after World War II, while their Irish counterparts struggled just to stay in business? Given Irish whiskey's prominence and popularity in the 1800s, this reversal of fortune was both unpredictable and difficult to fathom.

Irish whiskey's struggle may sound exaggerated, given that there are now dozens of distilleries across Ireland putting out a range of whiskey styles. There are so many new products that there is practically no more room in liquor stores and bars to contain the

For decades, Irish distillers insisted that whiskey should only be made using copper pot stills.

number of different bottles coming from the Emerald Isle. But Irish whiskey's amazing growth only started at the beginning of the twenty-first century, long after just about every other type of whiskey had risen to prominence. (In truth, it took so long for Irish whiskey to come back that most of the world's other great whiskies had already become wildly popular, crashed back to Earth, and were on their way up once again.)

After thinking for a long time about the reason for Irish whiskey's struggle and almost disappearance, the only reasonable answer I can conjure is a near deadly combination of incredibly bad timing, changing tastes, and a stubbornness to change.

♦ THE WAR OVER STILLS

Irish whiskey's fall from grace really began at the turn of the twentieth century. It was around then that it became clear that the column still had the potential to completely disrupt the Irish whiskey industry, prompting most Irish distillers to fight like hell against its adoption.

What made this brawl particularly bruising was that no one could agree on how you should and should *not* make whiskey. The debate got so heated that it went all the way to Parliament, which in 1908 convened a Royal Commission on Whiskey and Other Potable Spirits. (Ireland was still a part of Britain until 1921.) In order to settle this matter once and for all, witnesses from different parts of the liquor business were called to testify about what was traditional, what was safe to drink, what tasted best, and what whiskey drinkers expected.

Some of the most interesting testimony is from the Irish distillers, who were very honest and vocal in their detestation of column still whiskey and the making of blends with it. On the fourth day of the hearings, the commission called Andrew Jameson, the managing director and co-owner of Dublin's famed John Jameson & Son distillery. Asked for his definition of Irish whiskey, he responded: "It is a spirit distilled in a pot still, which should go through at least two or three distillations, and made from a mash that comes from cereals grown in Ireland." The chairman of the proceedings, Lord James of Hereford, followed up by asking "Will you give your reasons to the commission, please, why you excommunicate the patent still?" To which Jameson responded, "Because the patent still excommunicates the flavor; the pot still keeps the natural flavor of the grain used."

Jameson goes on to elaborate his opinion about how whiskey should be made, and insists that alcohol made in a column still should not even be called whiskey, since he believed that name should belong only to spirits made in a pot still. "If I asked for a glass of whiskey and I got a glass of patent still spirit, I would be very much displeased, and I would have a flavorless thing which would not in any way give me an idea of a glass of whiskey or anything compared to it."

The next expert witness called was Jameson's rival, James Talbot Power, the chairman and principal of one of Dublin's other famed brands, John Power & Son. Power didn't have a very high opinion of whiskey made on a column still either: "It would not be accepted by any Irishman as whiskey."

While the testimony and opinions of Jameson, Power, and others were admirable, they failed to convince the commission. The column still, the pot still, and the spirits they produced were essentially given equal status by Parliament. A nearly identical event took place in the United States a year later, when President William Howard Taft settled a similar debate, basically deciding that whiskey was whiskey no matter how it was made. Parliament's ruling, of course, greatly benefitted the Scotch blenders—they were now free to market their whisky as whisky around the world. It also proved to be an almost knockout punch for Irish distillers.

♦ **AN UNFAIR COMPETITION**

What ultimately doomed Irish whiskey was that it just couldn't keep pace with blended Scotch, which flooded England and other important markets with affordable and tasty booze. No matter how large the Irish distillers built their pot stills nor how many they had, it was impossible to compete with the output of the Scottish column stills. It didn't help that at the turn of the twentieth century there was a massive building boom of distilleries in Scotland.

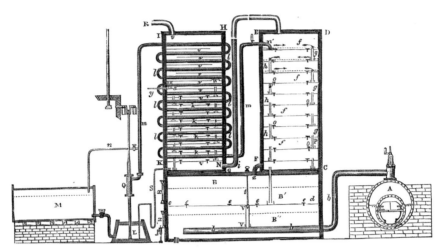

In 1830, Aeneas Coffey patented his design for a continuous column still that revolutionized the whiskey industry far beyond Ireland's borders.

To give you a sense of the disparity in output, in 1906 there were twenty-two column stills in Scotland and Ireland combined, compared to 165 pot stills. But all of those pot stills made just 14 million gallons (530,000 hectoliters) of 100-proof (50 percent alcohol by volume) spirit compared to 22 million gallons (833,000 hectoliters) of 100-proof (50 percent alcohol by volume) spirit from not even two dozen column stills. (For his 1887 book, Alfred Barnard visited a whiskey distillery in Belfast, which employed a pair of Coffey stills—each could distill 4,000 gallons [151 hectoliters] of spirit per hour.)

While whiskey drinkers today might have sided with Ireland's decision to make whiskey the old-fashioned way, a hundred years ago things were different—selling blends was a lot easier than selling pot still whiskey. So, making blends gave Scotland a huge advantage over Ireland.

These were just the first major blows to Ireland's whiskey industry. By the winter of 1916, according to a piece that ran in the *Irish Times*, around half of the Irish whiskey distilleries had already closed for good. And things for Irish distillers would only get worse: The cumulative effects of a number of major domestic and international events that came in rapid succession—World War I, the Spanish flu pandemic, the Irish War of Independence, the Great Depression, US Prohibition, and, finally, World War II—would be devastating.

♦ THE MYTH OF THE POTATO

By the mid-1930s, the Irish whiskey industry was understandably a wreck. Of the hundreds of distilleries in operation in the 1800s, there were now just a few left that had been able to hold on through all of the cataclysmic changes. The survivors, of course, stubbornly continued to produce traditional single malt or pot still whiskey. But their dedication didn't come without a cost. In the fall of 1935, *Esquire* magazine's resident drinks writer, Lawton Mackall, wrote a column extolling the virtues of Irish whiskey and debunking a number of myths, which was really quite an endorsement given that he himself was of Scottish descent.

One of the points Mackall made was that Irish whiskey had an identity crisis, because many drinkers believed it was made from potatoes. "Bluntly, it's the junk. Yet throughout America one bumps into this notion continually, even bartenders declaring Irish Whiskey to be of mashed-potato parentage—which is about as reliable as would be a statement that absinthe was a product of eggplant."

Oh, how the mighty had fallen.

Mackall went on to explain what Irish whiskey actually was, and that it was made in the most traditional way. He even referenced the island's low opinion of whiskey made on a column still and the distillers' steadfast refusal to change. The Irish whiskey advertising running in American magazines at the time certainly supports Mackall's message. In the mid-1930s, Jameson ran a campaign touting its flagship 7-year-old pot still whiskey as "the sportsmen's whiskey," which was tied to fly-fishing and hunting. The ads also hammered home the spirit's long heritage. "We've made it by the traditional pot still method for 150 years because we think it's the best way to make whiskey. It's aged 7 years in wood and never 'hurried' by so much as a day. It's a hearty, honest whiskey."

♦ **ADDING INSULT TO INJURY**

While the Irish whiskey advertising campaigns and the positive press were a valiant try, nothing the Irish whiskey brands did to grow sales really worked, putting the Irish further and further behind the other major whiskies. The drink of choice in the postwar world was the affordable and easy-to-drink blended whiskey, whether it came from Scotland, the United States, or Canada. In an era obsessed with space travel, futuristic car designs, and jet airplanes, the old-school whiskey being made in Ireland seemed ever more like a relic from another time.

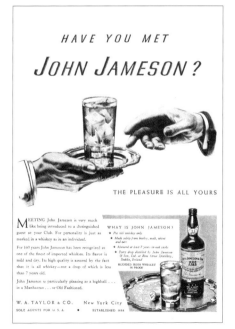

Jameson's signature whiskey used to be a pure pot still whiskey and the brand touted the fact that "not a drop of which is less than 7 years old."

By 1952, things were looking so grim that Irish whiskey was dangerously close to dying out altogether. At that time there were just six distilleries left in Ireland producing whiskey. In that year, just 17,000 nine-liter cases of Irish whiskey were sold in the US. To put that in perspective, American, Canadian, and Scotch whiskies collectively sold nearly 65 million nine-liter cases in the US in that same year. The sad state of affairs for Irish whiskey was particularly hard to fathom given the huge numbers of Irish Americans and Irish-themed bars across the US.

Things were so bad that Irish distilleries began contemplating the unthinkable: making blends. Irish pot still whiskey and single malts were somehow considered too flavorful on their own, especially compared to blended Scotch.

By 1955, Irish whiskey had more or less hit rock bottom.

♦ A CAFFEINATED SAVIOR

Help finally came from an unlikely source: the Irish Coffee. The drink, calling for coffee, whiskey, sugar, and whipped cream, became the signature beverage of Shannon Airport in southern Ireland, which played a small but important role in the launch of intercontinental air travel. Shannon was the perfect refueling spot for planes traveling between the Americas and destinations across Europe. As a result, the drink introduced Irish whiskey to the jet-set crowd, which we would now call influencers.

One of the people who tried the drink in Ireland was *San Francisco Chronicle* travel columnist Stanton Delaplane, whose championing of Irish Coffee in the early 1950s helped it become one of the hottest cocktails in the United States (see The Myth and Legend of the Irish Coffee, opposite).

Suddenly, bars across the US were finally selling tons of Irish whiskey again. The demand puzzled brands and importers at first, who couldn't understand why orders were pouring in out of the blue. According to a *Time* magazine story about Irish Coffee's meteoric rise, shortly after Delaplane's *Chronicle* story was published in 1953 ". . . came a startled cable from Ireland to a San Francisco liquor importer: WHAT'S HAPPENING? The answer: Delaplane had touched off a craze for Irish coffee."

Newspaper travel columnist Stanton Delaplane kicked off the Irish Coffee craze in the United States with the help of the Buena Vista Cafe in San Francisco.

The Myth and Legend of the Irish Coffee

Irish Coffee is one of the world's most famous cocktails—right up there with the Manhattan, the Martini, and the Daiquiri. This is quite a feat, because there aren't many other popular drinks that require Irish whiskey. Moreover, Irish Coffee isn't actually that popular in Ireland. For starters, Ireland is an island of tea drinkers—at least before the recent Starbucks invasion. All of this begs the question of how this coffee cocktail came to be created in Ireland. The story starts with Pan Am and the birth of intercontinental commercial flight.

The Wright brothers famously flew their biplane along a beach in North Carolina in 1903, but it wasn't until the 1930s that the dream of passenger plane travel became a reality. Thanks to the cutting-edge Yankee Clipper seaplane, Pan Am and other pioneering airlines could finally offer service from the US to the UK and Europe. The one catch was that these planes would have to refuel at the southern tip of Ireland, at Foynes Airport, which is now called Shannon. (Originally, the seaplanes would actually take off and land on the River Shannon.) This area made sense because it was the nearest point and closest gas station to the United States. After fueling up, the planes would drop off passengers at airports all across Europe.

While the Irish Coffee was created in Ireland, it became super popular in the United States.

One popular theory suggests that the Irish Coffee was hastily thrown together in 1939 to pacify chilly and cantankerous passengers on just such a refueling stopover. The creator was Joe Sheridan, the chef at the airport. More likely, according to historian David Wondrich, Sheridan first served the drink in 1944 or 1945 to VIPs who were touring the newly constructed Shannon Airport.

Coffee and spirits are old friends, of course, having been paired up in drinks around the world—from Caffè Corretto in Italy to Café Brûlot in New Orleans, Louisiana—long before Shannon Airport existed. So it made sense on some level that Sheridan's drink was a hit, a fresh addition to the coffee cocktail repertoire. Soon all the travelers passing through the airport were offered a freshly made "Gaelic Coffee," which over time became known as Irish Coffee.

The recipe for the Buena Vista Cafe's Irish Coffee is very simple: whiskey, sugar, coffee and freshly whipped cream.

One of the people to try this concoction was the Pulitzer Prize–winning *San Francisco Chronicle* travel writer Stanton Delaplane, who was known for his "Postcards" column. Delaplane became so enamored of the Irish Coffee that he recounted the history of the drink in a piece he wrote in 1953. He also went to the Buena Vista Cafe in San Francisco to see if they could make it for him. (For the record, the Buena Vista wasn't an Irish bar at all; despite its Spanish name it began life as a German tavern.)

Thanks to Delaplane's column and promotion, the drink quickly became a smash success for the Buena Vista Cafe, which made the drink the same way Sheridan did at Shannon Airport, with hot coffee, an appropriate amount of Irish whiskey, rich sugar syrup, and a dollop of fresh whipped cream. Mixed this way, it's an incredibly satisfying beverage that tastes good with brunch, or after dinner with dessert.

San Francisco's Buena Vista Cafe is still going strong today and claims to serve up to 2,000 Irish Coffees every day.

Sheridan and Delaplane unwittingly created a monster of a cocktail whose popularity just kept growing. In 1956, Marilyn Monroe and Arthur Miller were photographed enjoying an Irish Coffee at Shannon Airport. In March of that year, Irish Coffee was *Esquire* magazine's Classic Drink #6. The magazine's headnote to the recipe read like a Gaelic poem: "Here's a mighty brew that'll warm the soul of the diabal or, like the harp music of Trogain, heal the sick and make sad hearts merry."

The Irish Coffee was no longer being served only at the Buena Vista and the Shannon Airport, but all over the United States. A story from that era in Dublin's *Irish Times* reported that it had even become a sensation in Las Vegas, Nevada, where a hotel was serving a thousand Irish Coffees a week, and that the famous actor and comedian Danny Kaye had supposedly quipped, "There's nothing funny about this drink—it's nectar." A bar in the popular Irish pavilion at the 1964 World's Fair in Queens, New York, sold a reported eight hundred Irish Coffees a day to thirsty visitors.

While it seemed like the Irish Coffee was unstoppable, its momentum finally began to slow in the 1970s. It became a kind of kitschy drink that, while still well known, could be found exclusively in Irish pubs or chain bars in New York or Boston, Massachusetts.

With each passing decade, the Irish Coffee was becoming ever more irrelevant, drunk on St. Patrick's Day by shamrock-bedecked revelers who paired it with green bagels and chased it with pints of green beer. But despite its declining reputation, the drink never fully disappeared from the collective consciousness of drinkers.

New York's award-winning bar the Dead Rabbit has introduced a new generation of drinkers to the joys of the Irish Coffee.

Then, in 2012, the Irish Coffee was adopted as the signature drink of the brand-new lower Manhattan bar, the Dead Rabbit, which was one of New York's most heralded bar openings and went on to win a slew of prestigious awards. The establishment's version of the classic is delicious, with high-quality coffee, fresh whipped cream, a demerara sugar syrup, and, of course, Irish whiskey. This has given the cocktail a second act, and a new set of fans. The best part? You no longer have to fly to Ireland to enjoy it.

The Buena Vista Cafe in San Francisco, which was where Delaplane and owner Jack Koeppler started the craze, was soon selling nearly a quarter of a million Irish Coffees a year, using one thousand cases of Irish whiskey. (Before Delaplane's "discovery," the bar went through just two cases of Irish whiskey a year.)

The drink was an incredible ambassador for Irish whiskey. Many of the Irish whiskey brands soon were running advertisements in US newspapers and magazines promoting Irish Coffee, which of course included the basic recipe that anyone could make. One ad from 1956 read: "Thousands of travel-weary passengers have tried and loved Irish Coffee at the famous Shannon Airport. Now Power's Irish Whiskey lets you make this wonderful discovery right in your own home. Now you can enjoy a unique experience in delightful refreshment."

It wasn't a surprise that Irish distillers jumped on this marketing plan, given their long track record of failing to attract new fans despite trying just about every angle to move bottles. Such was their dedication that in the winter of 1957, Dublin's first Jewish mayor, Robert Briscoe, was coming to the United States on a promotional tour and made a point of promising Irish distillers that he would tell American Jews all about the joys of his city's pot still whiskey. (A small story about his upcoming trip ran in the *Vancouver Sun* with the hilarious headline, "Jews Will Be Urged to Drink Irish Whisky.") Another interesting marketing ploy was used by the brand Irish Whiskey, which tugged at the heartstrings with newspaper advertisements that claimed it was only "for *men* who are proud of their *Irish blood*."

Irish whiskey brands sold 40,000 nine-liter cases in the United States in 1960, more than double the figure of just five years earlier. This jump was definitely helped by the sudden popularity of Irish Coffee, which continued to be popular throughout the decade.

In 1961, Irish distillers and the Irish trade board (called Córas Tráchtála) set up the Irish Coffee corner inside the popular midtown Manhattan restaurant Jim Downey's Steak House. This special pop-up bar served a number of beers and spirits made in Ireland, but Irish Coffee was the star of the show, naturally served in a fancy Waterford Irish Coffee glass. This pop-up event was part of a larger push that the Irish trade board and distillers undertook in the late 1950s and early '60s, with about half a million pounds dedicated to the effort. (Although that was still a fraction of what Scotch distillers were spending on marketing—reportedly an incredible £3 million a year.)

But while sales were up, Irish whiskey was now primarily seen as an ingredient for this sweet-and-caffeinated cocktail. Business was finally moving in the right direction, but the spirit was now pigeonholed. Brands were no doubt hoping for a halo effect, where folks who liked Irish Coffee would start drinking the whiskey on its own or in other cocktails. Sadly, that would take a while to finally happen. But it certainly wasn't for a lack of trying—in the early '60s, Bushmills ran an advertising campaign with the tagline "makes any whiskey drink taste better" with an illustration of an Irish Coffee, plus five other recommended drinks, including Irish whiskey on the rocks and in a Highball.

♦ DON'T CALL IT A COMEBACK

The key to truly growing sales of Irish whiskey wasn't the Irish Coffee. Solid success resulted when distillers finally gave up after more than a hundred years of steely resistance, and pivoted to blended whiskey.

After years of American distributors pleading and begging Irish distillers to make whiskey more like blended Scotch, they finally conceded. "In an attempt to get in on the profitable American market, two big Dublin distilleries are going to produce a lighter type whisky," announced a small story in Ontario's *Windsor Daily Star* in July 1953. "It will be a blend of pure pot still and patents still whiskey. We don't know what the Irish will think of this departure from their favorite brands—or even what people on this continent will think as they sip the new flavor. But the Irish want to export something more than emigrants, fine linens and sweepstake tickets."

Dublin-based W&A Gilbey was one of the Irish distillers that produced a new blend for export. As reported in the *Irish Times* in 1956, the company spent two and a half years creating and market testing eighty-seven different blends before rolling out its Crock o' Gold Whiskey. Crock o' Gold was meant to compete with the best Scottish blends and came in a flasklike bottle packed in a drawstring tweed bag.

In an insightful 1962 *GQ* story, "Have a Drop O' Irish," Emanuel Greenberg credits the Irish Coffee and a subsequent marketing campaign by

The impressive copper stills may get all of the attention, but a range of tanks is necessary for the fermentation and distillation processes, including these washbacks at Slane Castle.

the Irish government for helping to get people drinking Irish whiskey again. But "third, and most important, is the introduction of lighter, blended Irish whiskies, much as the Scotch distillers have done years before." He explains that these *"blended* Irish whiskies are made by mixing twenty-five to thirty-five per cent of this rich, malty pot still whiskey with sixty-five to seventy-five per cent of lighter grain whiskies, which are distilled at higher temperatures in the patent or 'continuous' still. The tang of the pot and the zest of the malt remain in these lighter Irish blends, but they do not overwhelm."

Reading that last sentence, you can imagine generations of Irish distillers turning over in their graves—it is exactly what they didn't want happening. Greenberg at least mentions that pot still and single malt whiskies still outsold these blends in Ireland.

Lowering their historic resistance to blends did seem to help. In 1965, sales of Irish whiskey reached 87,000 cases, more than double what was sold in 1960. The Irish industry also gained undeniable energy and a sense of purpose in 1966, when three of the remaining four brands of Irish whiskey—Jameson, Power's, and Cork distilleries—joined forces to create one company, the Irish Distillers Limited. This was an enormous deal, made from extreme necessity—it was the equivalent of mortal enemies Coke, Pepsi, and Dr Pepper merging to form one company.

The tone of the advertising took a more proactive turn around this time.

In 1966, Jameson started running advertisements in newspapers that were brutally honest about the Irish distilleries' frustrations. "Psychologists say it's better not to repress strong emotions. And we have a strong emotion. It's about Irish whiskey. And Scotch. Scotch is a fine beverage and deserves its popularity. But enough is enough already. The truth is, Scotch has obscured a drink that richly deserves its own place in the sun."

With the change to producing and marketing blends having a positive effect on sales, Irish whiskey suddenly and miraculously had a heartbeat. "The only way out, from Ireland to the United States market, was compromises," wrote star *St. Louis Post-Dispatch* columnist Jack Rice in the fall of 1974. "Blend it, soften the taste, range it somewhere between the smoke of Scotch and the gentle hearth fire of bourbon."

In 1969, the requirement that Irish whiskey be aged for five years before it could be sold also reverted back to the earlier standard of three years, which is what the Scotch industry had used since 1916. The Irish distillers had instituted the mandatory extended aging period in 1926 as a means to distinguish pot still whiskey from generally younger Scottish blended whisky. Unfortunately, the reality of making Irish distillers age their whiskey for an extra two years only made the spirit more expensive to produce, which, of course, aided cheaper Scotch brands. So, permitting modern Irish brands to sell younger whiskies in America and other export markets, helped to level

When the Midleton Distillery opened in 1975, it was set up with a range of equipment in order to be able to make a number of famous Irish whiskey brands.

the playing field and allowed them to be competitively priced.

There was one last key step in the contraction and consolidation of the Irish whiskey industry, a move that seemed to prime Irish whiskey for a proper renaissance. Giant Canadian liquor conglomerate Seagram's bought Bushmills in 1972 for a reported $9.7 million, then bought a 15 percent stake of Irish Distillers for a reported $8 million. As part of the deal, Seagram's sold Irish Distillers a 25 percent stake in Bushmills for $2.4 million. While certainly a confusing transaction, it meant that all of the remaining distilleries on the island were now financially tied together and would rise or fall together.

In 1973, Irish Distillers embarked on its most ambitious project yet—building a new, mammoth £9 million distillery, Midleton, located at the bottom of the island. It would be the first new Irish distillery built in at least a century. The facility, which opened in the summer of 1975, effectively created a new chapter for Irish whiskey. Not only was it state of the art, but the production of all of Irish Distillers' brands (save Bushmills, which remained at its historic distillery at the top of the island) moved to Midleton.

According to a story in the *Irish Times*, "Part of the cost was caused by the insistence of the directors that their new distillery should be capable of producing all the famous whiskies

To keep up with the global demand for Irish whiskey, distilleries, like Bushmills, continue to expand.

in exactly the way they have always been made, and to ensure that their unique flavours and characteristics are preserved. In this sense, Midleton is perhaps best viewed as a complex of distilleries rather than as one large distillery."

This also meant the painful closing of several large, historic distilleries, including Power's John's Lane facility, which covered six acres (2.4 hectares) of Dublin and dated back 185 years. (Several artifacts, including the antique spirit safe, were saved and moved to Irish Distillers Museum in Cork. There was also a reported 80 tons [73 tonnes] of scrap copper that would be sold.) These changes were much more than just a question of logistics and efficiency, but truly changed the identity and geography of Ireland's most famous city, which was practically synonymous with making beer and whiskey.

♦ **THE BIRTH OF A NEW JAMESON**

Irish Distillers essentially bet the whole future of Irish whiskey on Jameson and, to a lesser extent, Bushmills. The main point of this strategy was to give Jameson a makeover: In the early 1970s, it became a blend, after having been a proud pot still whiskey for nearly two centuries. This move seems like an obvious decision now, but at the time it was a crazy long shot that Irish whiskey would ever be a bestseller again. It helped that this new Jameson became part of Seagram's portfolio in the US—and the powerful conglomerate put its marketing muscle behind the brand.

To promote Jameson, it was reported that in 1977 Irish Distillers spent $3.5 million on marketing, which was an especially large sum given that it had spent a measly $80,000 in 1972. "Realizing that America is the world's prime market, we launched a three-year research project into the American taste and the overall US liquor scene," Jack McGowan, the export development manager for Irish Distillers told the *Los Angeles Times*. "So we can really boast that the Irish whiskey in the market now is specifically tailored to the American taste for lightness. It is blended and it is extremely mixable. We make no secret of the fact that our target in this country is the US Scotch drinker."

In 1974, Irish Distillers bought 55 percent of Bushmills from Seagram's, raising its stake to 80 percent. Four years later, it bought the remaining 20 percent to wholly own the brand, which meant that now just a single company owned the only two operating distilleries on the entire island and produced every drop of Irish whiskey made no matter what name was on the label. It was a deeply radical transformation for such a vibrant industry, one that was once composed of hundreds of independent distilleries and even more brands. While this monopoly was not ideal, Irish whiskey was fighting for its life and its fate was far from certain.

♦ IRISH GETS HIP

Through the 1970s and '80s, Irish whiskey sales continued to grow, even as the fate of whiskey overall was beginning to look doubtful. Clear spirits were the hot trend with the new generation of drinkers, and most whiskey was already feeling the lack of love. But not Irish. The year 1985 wasn't a great year for American whiskey or Scotch, but Irish brands moved a record 330,000 cases in the States. That number is even more impressive given that at the time drinkers in the US had a choice of just Murphy, Dunphy, Bushmills, Jameson, and Power's, all of which were, of course, owned and made by Irish Distillers. The news of the day was the introduction of Bushmills Black Bush (a blend aged in oloroso sherry casks) and the 12-year-old Jameson 1780, which replaced both Jameson's 12 Year and 15 Year bottlings. These were more premium whiskies, designed to compete head-to-head with the high-end blended Scotch Chivas Regal. What was going on? Was the US finally developing a taste for blended Irish whiskey?

The new generation of American drinkers had resoundingly rejected the blended Scotch and rye whiskey favored by their parents, and instead started ordering something completely different—imported vodka.

While Irish whiskey and vodka couldn't be farther apart on the spirit spectrum, Irish whiskey was also fairly unknown at the time, and different from the other whiskies out there. It was definitely a whiskey your parents didn't drink, and so had a kind of outsider cool factor. Bushmills' early 1980s

Establishing a New Top Shelf

In December 1985, Irish Distillers introduced a brand-new whiskey, Midleton Very Rare, which cost an unheard-of sum—£40. (The suggested retail price in 2023 was around $200.) The original plan was to sell just 20,000 bottles each year of this classic pot still whiskey. "There won't however be all that many of the younger generation purchasing Midleton Very Rare," reported the *Irish Times*. "At £40 a bottle it will hardly be seen in pubs and will function almost entirely as an ultra-exclusive, well-packaged premium product to be given as a present to whiskey connoisseurs who would appreciate a tipple which is a class apart." It was a very interesting move given that the Irish distilling industry was just starting to come back to life and made little business sense. But it was truly indicative of the kind of whiskey that Irish Distillers actually wanted to make—pot still, not blends. The introduction of this super premium and expensive Midleton Very Rare was meant to show the world what real Irish whiskey should taste like and ensured that, for the time being, pot still whiskey would still be made. The bottling was almost like a whiskey time capsule to be opened at some uncertain date in the future so folks would understand what the world was like before Irish blends.

Midleton Very Rare established a new high-end watermark for the Irish whiskey industry.

magazine advertising campaign hammered this point home. Each of the full-page, full-color ads featured a striking woman in the middle of what looks to be a swinging cocktail party of well-dressed yuppies pregaming before they went to Studio 54 (everyone is, naturally, drinking glasses of the whiskey). The tagline of the ad campaign was: "Old Bushmills. It's changing people's minds about Irish Whiskey."

For the first time in nearly a century, being different from Scotch was an asset to Irish whiskey. If you were drinking Irish whiskey in the 1980s, it was a decisive choice. "On the one hand is Scotch whisky, the brash and lordly one, with its characteristic smokiness and aggressive flavor (not to mention the prominent advertising of its manufacturers), a beverage well known to imbibers of both dilettante and well-cultivated tastes," wrote Bruce Weber in a 1983 edition of *Esquire* magazine. "On the other hand is brother Irish whiskey, a spirit unpomped, uncircumstanced."

For a rapidly gentrifying generation of yuppies attracted to anything that connoted status, Irish whiskey had the perfect set of attributes and the right pedigree. Blended Scotch was for everyone, Irish whiskey was for those in the know. This is basically the same strategy that Scotch single malt distillers employed in the 1980s and 1990s, when they made a switch from just supplying blenders to bottling their own single malts.

♦ THE BIRTH OF CRAFT DISTILLING

In 1987, the monopoly on Irish whiskey enjoyed by Irish Distillers was broken when the Cooley distillery opened in the middle of the island. It was started by the academic and serial entrepreneur Dr. John Teeling, who saw a huge opportunity in Irish whiskey. "I believe it is unique in that it is specifically Irish and tied up with our history and mythology," he told Olive Keogh for a 1991 profile for the *Irish Times*. "It's the sort of product which will go on forever, no matter who owns the companies producing it."

While Cooley never made as much whiskey as Bushmills or Midleton, in some ways it provided the blueprint for the recent craft spirits explosion in Ireland. Cooley produced a range of interesting whiskies, from the peated single malt Connemara to the double distilled Tyrconnell Single Malt to the blended Kilbeggan, which challenged people's perceptions of Irish whiskey. Cooley also provided contract whiskey for a number of upstarts who didn't have their own distilleries, which helped create an influx of new brands. (Ultimately, Dr. Teeling sold his distillery and its brands to Jim Beam in 2011 for €71 million. A few years later, he started the Great Northern distillery in a former Harp brewery in Dundalk, Ireland, which supplies a new generation of start-up brands with whiskey.)

The success of Irish whiskey didn't go unnoticed. In 1988, the conglomerate London-based Grand Metropolitan, which owned a range of single malt distilleries and major blended Scotch brands and would later become Diageo, made it known that it would like to acquire Irish Distillers, including its two distilleries and all of its brands. For most of the Irish whiskey industry to be in English hands was just too horrible an outcome to contemplate. So Irish Distillers did the only thing it could—it found a different buyer in France, Pernod Ricard.

It wasn't an obvious solution, since Pernod's portfolio at the time centered on historic French spirits, including its anise-flavored namesakes Pernod and Ricard. While Pernod could only offer £247 million for Irish Distillers, compared to Grand Metropolitan's £275 million, it was enough to complete the acquisition. This move, naturally, shocked and outraged Grand Met's executives.

The deal couldn't have worked out better for Pernod. Ireland was suddenly picking up momentum and beginning to have its long-overdue moment. Arguably, the international success of rock band U2, which in the 1980s and 1990s put out hit record after hit record, certainly helped the country's image. Then the historic 1998 Good Friday Agreement brought peace to Northern Ireland and the so-called Celtic Tiger economic boom brought unprecedented opportunities and enriched the Republic of Ireland. Finally, it seemed like the island had the world's attention and was the place to be. What better time for the rebirth of Irish whiskey?

After a slight dip in sales in the late 1980s, Irish whiskey caught fire and became one of the fastest growing types of spirits in the United States. Sales of Irish whiskey shot up from 282,000 cases in 1995 to 600,000 cases in 2005. It took just three more years for Irish whiskey to break the million-case mark. But it wasn't done growing. By 2012, it crossed 2 million case sales and by 2015 3 million case sales. As of this writing, Irish whiskey is selling nearly 5 million cases annually in the US.

Without question, Irish whiskey is back.

Teeling Bros. offers a range of different styles of whiskies, including single malt, single pot still, and blends.

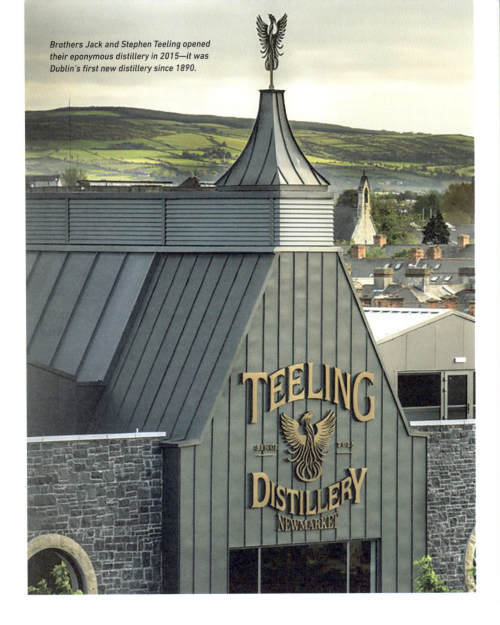

Brothers Jack and Stephen Teeling opened their eponymous distillery in 2015—it was Dublin's first new distillery since 1890.

♦ JAMESON IS KING

To be very clear, most of Irish whiskey's unbelievable growth in the late twentieth and early twenty-first centuries came from one brand—Jameson.

Irish Distillers' risky plan in the early 1970s of rebuilding the category around the newly formulated Jameson blend actually worked incredibly well. They invested heavily in marketing and also in upgrading the barrels in which the whiskey aged.

It certainly helped that during the past twenty-odd years the Scotch category has completely focused on high-priced bottlings. Gone are the days of modestly priced blends in extra-large bottles. Scotch is now all about ever more expensive single malts with big, bold flavors. If blended Scotch was for everyone, then single malt is exclusively for connoisseurs.

In the twenty-first century the traditional whiskey roles have essentially flipped. The Scotch industry preaches to drinkers about the wonders of old-school straight whisky made in a copper pot still the way it was done hundreds of years ago. And the Irish whiskey industry promotes easy drinking and extra-smooth blends that have no pretensions and are as delicious sipped neat as they are mixed with ginger ale. The more serious and stuffier the Scotch marketing, the looser and more fun became Jameson's attitude.

At a certain point in the early 2000s, Jameson realized that there was no point competing with the Scotch brands, and that it would actually be beneficial not to be grouped with Scotch on store shelves or in bars. Instead, Irish Distillers went after American whiskey's customers. Irish whiskey bottles were literally moved in liquor stores from their traditional spot next to Scotch to sit side by side with bourbon, rye, and Tennessee whiskey. It was an ingenious idea, since the two types of whiskey had a similar price at the time and Irish whiskey still seemed novel to many American whiskey drinkers.

Jameson also built an army of brand ambassadors, usually men and women who had grown up in Ireland, to evangelize and educate bartenders across the country about the joys of Irish whiskey, while dispelling any myths along the way. Given the reasonable price of most Irish whiskies, both professional and amateur bartenders felt comfortable combining it with a range of mixers. Unlike Scotch, there were no set "rules" for drinking Irish whiskey—which helped people feel confident about drinking it any way they wanted, free of judgment.

♦ THE RETURN OF POT STILL WHISKEY

For decades, the only widely available Irish whiskey was blended whiskey and that was the case whether or not you were in Ireland, Europe, or the US. The pot still whiskey made by the giant Midleton distillery was primarily used for blending with grain whiskey. (A token amount of the historic whiskey was bottled every year as the incredibly pricey Midleton Very Rare.) Even Redbreast, the famed Dublin pot still whiskey stopped selling its whiskey in the 1980s. The brand was only revived in the early 1990s after a columnist for the *Irish Times* wrote a piece pleading for its return. For a few dark years, it seemed like pot still whiskey might completely disappear as Ireland became synonymous with easy drinking blends.

To create its complex Black Barrel, Jameson ages its whiskey in a deeply charred cask.

The Truth About Irish Single Malt

Blended Irish whiskey is now a big seller in the US and around the world. But some of the most expensive and sought-after Irish whiskies are actually single malts. These rich and complex spirits generally range in age from ten up to thirty years old. And, while you can buy single malts from a number of different brands, many of these bottlings have something very important in common—they were all likely produced by Bushmills in Northern Ireland.

The Bushmills distillery and eponymous brand was officially started in 1784 by Hugh Anderson and its malts were soon famous in Ireland, Europe, and the US. Unlike the large southern Irish distillers, Bushmills never started adding unmalted barley to its mash bill. (Perhaps it was too famous to switch to making pot still whiskey.) So as a result, for decades, it was stubbornly the only distillery on the whole island keeping single malt alive. Given how hard it was to sell Irish whiskey in the second half of the twentieth century, Bushmills didn't have much competition until the 1990s when the Cooley distillery introduced its own single malt, Tyrconnell.

It's perfectly legal for another Irish distillery to buy whiskey from Bushmills and bottle it under its own name, though I have to admit the practice does bother me a bit. These single malts are not cheap (the older age statement whiskies can now go for a couple of thousand dollars), and it seems pretty disingenuous to charge that much and take credit for a whiskey you didn't actually create. I'd be more comfortable with this practice if the brands were transparent about the process and told drinkers and collectors upfront that they didn't make the whiskey, but in fact picked a really special barrel.

This situation reminds me of the early days of the American craft spirits movement, when many brands weren't actually making their bourbon or rye but instead were buying it from the giant MGP distillery in Lawrenceburg, Indiana. A number of these upstarts who were sourcing spirits really laid it on thick when it came to their brand stories and how they supposedly made their own whiskies. This was a dirty little (well-known) secret in the spirits industry that created quite the ugly backlash when it went public.

I fear that something similar will happen in the Irish whiskey industry when drinkers realize that the bottle that they just paid $3,000 for was actually made by a completely different distillery than the label might imply. What's the easiest way to avoid this situation? Buy your single malt from Bushmills. Then you don't need to worry about it being sourced from someone else.

The Pickleback

For a few years, one of the most popular drinks in craft cocktail bars was one of the most unlikely, the Pickleback—a shot of Jameson followed by a shot of pickle brine. Some of the world's finest bartenders would happily enjoy this potent duo with a knowing grin.

While the whole mini craze now seems so absurd that it couldn't have possibly happened, I can assure you that it did. In 2006 specifically, when a Brooklyn establishment called the Bushwick Country Club began offering a shot of Old Crow Bourbon with a shot of brine from the craft pickle brand McClure's, which at the time had a factory in the same neighborhood. The bar served the pickles and had a ton of leftover brine. According to legend, one night the pickle juice was served to a patron paired with a shot of American whiskey, by bartender Reggie Cunningham. It was so odd and fun that it caught on with the local hipsters. While it's certainly bizarre, there is a similar tradition of eating pickled veggies and taking shots of vodka in Russia and Eastern Europe, which gave the silly Pickleback a bit of historical gravitas.

The change to Jameson instead of American whiskey was thanks to Chris Patino, who for many years worked for Pernod Ricard building the company's relationship with the bartending trade and creating fun and educational events for them. While bourbon or rye might stand up better to the brine, Jameson worked surprisingly well in this combination.

The Pickleback is no longer common, but it was quite significant in the modern history of Irish whiskey. The Pickleback made Irish whiskey seem fun and deserving of a second look. It helped Jameson to truly shake up its image, and galvanized the point that Irish whiskey was not the same as Scotch in terms of stuffy drinking decorum.

In the early 2000s, Brooklyn hipsters made Irish whiskey cool by drinking shots of it with pickle brine.

But by the 2000s, things had miraculously turned around so definitively that Irish Distillers began to cautiously sell more pot still whiskey in Ireland as well as export a small sampling of it to the United States and other markets, including the aforementioned Redbreast, which went on sale in the US in 2008. Redbreast was almost a test case, reminiscent of what William Grant & Sons did in the 1960s when it started selling some of its Glenfiddich Scotch in the US to see if selling single malt was a viable option.

The success of Redbreast encouraged Pernod to introduce some of its other pot still whiskies, including the acclaimed Spot line, which now includes Blue Spot, Green Spot, Red Spot, and Yellow Spot. In 2023, the company even brought out a limited-edition pot still version of Jameson, which harkens back to the brand's origins. Over the next several years, I imagine Pernod will continue trying to move more drinkers from modestly priced blends to pricier and more flavorful pot still whiskies.

Redbreast is a taste of Irish whiskey's past, when pure pot still was the dominant style.

♦ THE IRISH CRAFT EXPLOSION

Not long ago, it was easy to count the number of distilleries in all of Ireland, and to generalize about what Irish whiskey was and what it was not. You could generally say that Irish whiskey

Dozens of new craft distilleries have recently opened around the island, which has led to a huge increase in the number of Irish whiskey brands being bottled.

was triple distilled and incredibly smooth, with a honeyed flavor on the palate. That was the common description used for years by drinks writers, liquor store clerks, and bartenders. And it's no coincidence that it's essentially the opposite of what was commonly said about single malt Scotch.

Those days are over.

Now, it is quite a bit harder to generalize about Irish whiskey, given the sheer number of distilleries across the island and the wide variety of styles and types of Irish whiskies that they produce. At last count, there were thirty-eight Irish whiskey distilleries operating in greater

Ireland, according to the industry group Drinks Ireland, and another two dozen in the works. This is a staggering jump from 2010, when there were just four distilleries (Midleton, Bushmills, Cooley, and Kilbeggan).

Some new brands now even peat their barley for some of their whiskies, including Teeling's Blackpitts Peated Single Malt, which is more like the Scotch made on the island of Islay than a traditional Irish pot still. Waterford, which released its first bottles in 2020 and was started by Mark Reynier (whose previous project was reestablishing the famous Scotch distillery Bruichladdich), is all about the terroir of Irish whiskey and how the spirit reflects the place where the grain was grown. And that's not to mention the proliferation of brands using different types of barrels to age their whiskey. Lost Irish, which was started in 2021, alone ages its blended Irish whiskey in six kinds of barrels, including those that previously held South African brandy, Caribbean rum, and Japanese shōchū. Some distillers are even abandoning Irish staple barley altogether, like Power's, which in 2023 introduced a whiskey made completely from rye grain.

There are even whiskey distilleries operating in Dublin again. Teeling, which was started by Jack and Stephen Teeling, whose father founded Cooley, was the first to open in 2015, followed a few years later by the Pearse Lyons distillery, Diageo's Roe & Co distillery, and the Dublin Liberties distillery. I imagine we'll see more opening in the city, as well as in many towns and villages around the island.

Compared to those of Scotch, the rules for making Irish whiskey are relatively loose, which has spurred a lot of creativity and innovation. The recent explosion of whiskey styles and techniques once again begs the age-old question: What exactly is Irish whiskey? Just as in 1908, I can see a clear divide between the traditionalists and the innovators, which could lead to a possible clash—and a reckoning—down the road.

But in the meantime, Irish whiskey's future looks very rosy. Jameson is still the face of the industry and one of the most important spirits in the world, but it can no longer define Irish whiskey on its own. With other large brands such as Bushmills, Tullamore D.E.W., and Cooley, and the proliferation of creative, smaller craft Irish distilleries, the hope is that one day Jameson drinkers will graduate to other styles of Irish whiskey. The jury remains out about whether that will actually happen, but I'd bet that Irish pot still and single malt are the future of Irish whiskey, and may be the next big spirits craze. (Stock up now while you can still easily find these bottles!)

What's absolutely certain is that, after waiting for nearly a century in the wings, Irish whiskey is ready to be the star of the show.

Irish Whiskey Family Tree

🌾 BRANCH: PROXIMO

In 1758, José Antonio de Cuervo y Valdés was granted a parcel of land in Mexico by the king of Spain and soon began making tequila. Over the next several centuries, his descendants turned the family's eponymous tequila business into a multinational conglomerate, which now includes several Irish whiskey brands. (Its American holding company is called Proximo, but it's wholly owned by Cuervo.) One of its key acquisitions was the historic Northern Irish distillery Bushmills. Read on for more about Bushmills and Proximo's other Irish whiskey brands.

Bushmills

In 1608, the Northern Irish town of Bushmills got one of the earliest known distilling licenses. The modern brand was started a bit later—in 1784—but Bushmills is still the oldest continually operated whiskey distillery on the island. The brand was a bestseller almost immediately and was advertised by name in the United States as far back as the nineteenth century. While that might not sound impressive today, at the time it was far from a common practice—most liquor ads in newspapers just touted the type of alcohol for sale, but didn't mention the distiller's name. The fact that Bushmills

The secret ingredient in whiskey is water, and Bushmills' water source is the River Bush.

was featured prominently meant that American drinkers knew the brand and were impressed by it. It certainly didn't hurt that the distillery is just a couple of miles from the incredible Giant's Causeway—a huge series of interlocking rock columns caused by an ancient volcanic eruption—which has been attracting tourists since the 1700s.

While the most popular style of Irish whiskey today is a blend of pot still and column still whiskies, Bushmills is unique in that it became famous for its single malt. Its whiskey is made entirely from malted barley, which is distilled three times in a copper pot still. The process is very similar to how Scottish single malt is produced (the key exception being that most single malt made in Scotland is distilled just twice).

Northern Ireland may very well be the first place in the world where single malt was produced. The Irish now insist that this style of whiskey—their style—made the incredibly short trip to Scotland and not the other way around.

There are now a number of other Irish distilleries that make single malt, but Bushmills was the only brand on the whole island to produce it for decades. With just a few exceptions from after World War II to around 2010, regardless of the brand name listed on the bottle, all the Irish single malt sold around the globe was actually produced by Bushmills. By continuing to make this historic spirit—regardless of demand by drinkers—Bushmills ensured that the world would not lose this incredible piece of liquid history.

For a number of years, there were only two operating Irish distilleries, Bushmills at the top (northern end) of the island and Midleton at the bottom (southern end) of the island. At one point, the industry had contracted to such an extent that both facilities were actually owned by the same company: Irish Distillers.

Irish Distillers was eventually acquired by Pernod Ricard in 1988. Pernod then sold Bushmills to Diageo, which ultimately flipped the distillery to Proximo for the remaining part of Don Julio Tequila that Diageo didn't already own, plus $408 million. No matter who owned Bushmills, however, master distiller Colum Egan has made the whiskey since 2002.

Bushmills now makes a delicious 10-year-old, a 16-year-old, and a 20-year-old. In recent years, the brand has put more marketing muscle behind promoting these whiskies, which are as good as if not better than most Scottish single malts.

Bushmills is now best known for its Original. Ironically, this easy-drinking whiskey is not a single malt, but a blend of 45 percent single malt and 55 percent grain whiskey. I imagine the term "Original" was

While Bushmills is inextricably connected to single malt, to survive it created a blend called the Original.

To keep up with demand, in 2023 Bushmills opened a second distillery with ten copper pot stills.

chosen to refer to Bushmills as Ireland's original brand and not because the specific whiskey was the distillery's original product—either way it's a bit of a confusing name.

Original was introduced in the late 1960s, most likely to compete with blended Scotch, which was wildly popular around the world. (Incredibly, there wasn't much of a demand for Scottish single malts at the time.) The handful of surviving Irish distilleries all finally introduced blends after decades of refusing to make them.

In the late 1970s, Bushmills introduced the acclaimed Black Bush to the US, which is 80 percent single malt and 20 percent grain whiskey. The secret to the smooth, full-bodied whiskey is that it is aged for up to eight years in barrels that previously held sherry and those that previously held bourbon.

In spring 2023, Bushmills added a second distillery, which is aptly named the Causeway distillery. The new facility cost $46 million and opened with ten stills, which doubled the brand's capacity.

The Sexton Irish Whiskey

The Sexton comes in a squat, black, hexagonal medicinal-style bottle, like something that might show up on *Antiques Roadshow* (or in a BBC show about a church elder who solves crimes in a small Irish seaside town).

Despite its old-timey packaging and branding, The Sexton is actually relatively new—it was introduced by Proximo in

In 2017, Proximo built another distillery in the town of Bushmills, and the whiskey it produces there is sold under the Sexton name.

In 2023, Proper No. Twelve expanded its product line with a 70-proof (35 percent alcohol by volume) apple-flavored whiskey.

2017. The whiskey is made from malted barley and aged for up to five years in barrels that previously held sherry. The distillery is a newly constructed facility just down the road from the iconic Bushmills distillery.

Proper No. Twelve Irish Whiskey

Serial celebrity spirits entrepreneur Ken Austin started Proper No. Twelve Irish Whiskey with the controversial Irish UFC fighter Conor McGregor in 2017. (Austin also started the bottled cocktail brand Delola with actress and musician Jennifer Lopez and Teremana Tequila with wrestler turned actor Dwayne "The Rock" Johnson.)

McGregor's celebrity was enough to rocket the whiskey brand to immediate success. In its first few months alone, Proper No. Twelve's owners claimed that they had sold "hundreds of thousands" of bottles. While sales continued to grow over the next few years, McGregor proved to be a less than ideal face for the brand and has had several serious brushes with the law in both Ireland and the United States.

In 2021, Proximo decided to buy out Proper No. Twelve's founders in a deal that reportedly could be worth as much as $600 million. (Proximo started out with a 20 percent stake in Proper No. Twelve and then increased it to 49 percent before buying the rest of the brand.)

In 2024, McGregor was held liable for sexual assault by a Dublin jury and Proximo announced that the brand would no longer be associated with him.

Proximo continues to make the original Proper No. Twelve Whiskey, which is a mix of grain whiskey and Bushmills single malt. Proximo has since also introduced Proper No. Twelve Irish Apple, which is a light 70 proof (35 percent alcohol by volume) and combines apple flavor with its whiskey.

🌾 BRANCH: PERNOD RICARD

Irish whiskey helped turn Pernod Ricard from a fairly small, family-owned French liquor company into a giant conglomerate.

In the 1980s, British liquor company Diageo was interested in taking over Irish Distillers, which for many years had a monopoly on Irish whiskey. To avoid falling into English hands, Irish Distillers was able to successfully sell itself to Pernod instead—a deal that turned out to be one of the shrewdest in spirits industry history.

Jameson and Irish whiskey in general were poised for an epic comeback—and Irish has indeed exploded over the past several decades. According to the Distilled Spirits Council of the US, sales of Irish whiskey climbed by more than 1,100 percent between 2003 and 2022. It was Jameson's whiskey that accounted for much of this incredible growth. Read on for more about Jameson and the other Pernod Irish whiskey brands.

Jameson

You may want to sit down for this. . . . John Jameson was, deep breath, actually Scottish and Protestant. In fact, he married Margaret Haig, the daughter of famed Scotch whisky maker John Haig. The couple moved to Ireland and started making whiskey there in 1784. Ultimately, Jameson started his own Dublin distillery, which became well known for its pot still whiskey. By the turn of the century the brand was one of Ireland's most famous.

The Jameson family, like most of the Irish whiskey industry, refused to embrace

With sales of nearly 47 million bottles in 2023, Jameson is the biggest Irish whiskey brand in the US.

the column still when it was introduced in the 1830s. During the famous Royal Commission on Whiskey and Other Potable Spirits, convened in 1907, Andrew Jameson, the managing director and co-owner of the company, testified that Irish whiskey needed to be made in a pot still. And the family refused to make anything but traditional pot still whiskey from a base of malted and unmalted barley. In fact, through the 1960s the only Jameson you could buy was a 7-year-old pot still whiskey. But this seemingly noble decision almost doomed the brand. In the 1960s, Jameson finally relented and started to make a blend of pot still and column still whiskies, which was exported to the US. This blended whiskey is essentially the Jameson that modern drinkers know. And while John Jameson might not have agreed with the decision, it ultimately saved both the Jameson brand and the Irish whiskey industry as a whole.

In desperation, Jameson was also forced to merge with several of its competitors to form Irish Distillers. To take

Jameson, like all Irish whiskey, has to be aged in a wooden barrel for at least three years.

advantage of economies of scale, the distilling was centralized at one facility, Midleton, which was constructed in Cork.

It's hard to find a store that doesn't stock the standard Jameson, which is a blend of triple distilled pot still whiskey and grain whiskey. It has not only become the most popular Irish whiskey, but also one of the bestselling whiskies of any kind. Thanks to its success, Jameson now offers a small portfolio of different variations, including the rich and almost smoky Black Barrel. While I never thought we'd see a pure pot still Jameson, the brand introduced the limited-edition Single Pot Still Whiskey in 2022.

Power's Irish Whiskey

One of the most important Irish whiskey brands has gotten somewhat lost during the spirit's tumultuous modern history. During the nineteenth century, Dublin-based John Power & Son was incredibly popular and as famous as its crosstown rival, John Jameson.

The company's history goes back to the eighteenth century and starts with innkeeper James Power. At the time, inns played an important role in the liquor trade because many of them also housed pubs and de facto liquor stores. So, it's not surprising that Power decided to close his inn and build a small distillery in 1791. According to Alfred Barnard's 1887 book *The Whisky Distilleries of the United Kingdom*, Power's facility initially produced about 6,000 gallons (23,000 liters) of liquor a year, with "its chief motive power being a horse mill." Over the next century, the Irish whiskey boom transformed the distillery, which took up more than 6 acres (2.4 hectares) of the city by the end of the century. The heart of this John's Lane distillery were five giant copper pot stills—some of which could hold 25,000 gallons (950 hectoliters). The brand was famous in Ireland and the United States for its pure pot still whisky, which was made from malted and unmalted barley.

Like the rest of the Irish whiskey industry, Power's was humbled by the events of the twentieth century. In 1966, Power's merged with its competitors John Jameson and Cork distilleries. The new company, the Irish Distillers Group, decided to leave Dublin and build one giant distillery in Cork to produce all of its different whiskey brands. Jameson became a blended whiskey and was promoted as the company's core product in the US. This move arguably saved Irish whiskey, but Power's became increasingly irrelevant.

I would like nothing more than to say that Power's has finally found its way, including an audience that appreciates it. But, if anything, the brand seems to be more lost than ever. It drastically redesigned its label and bottle, giving it a kind of hipster apothecary look that feels a bit off. In an attempt to capitalize on the recent success of American whiskey, Power's also introduced a 100 percent rye whiskey, which I would argue is the last thing it should be making. Fortunately, the brand still makes two pure pot still whiskies, Three Swallow and the 12-year-old John's Lane, which are worth your attention.

Redbreast

For decades, some of the best Irish whiskey quietly aged beneath the streets of Dublin in W&A Gilbey's subterranean bonded warehouse. The pure pot still whiskey was produced by Jameson and, after aging in Gilbey's cellar for twelve years, was sold as Redbreast. The whiskey was made from a

Redbreast is made from a mix of malted and unmalted barley and distilled in a large copper pot still.

The modern version of Redbreast is still a single pot still whiskey, now aged in two kinds of barrels, those that formerly held bourbon and those that formerly held sherry. It is a rich and elegant offering that I like to serve to folks who claim they don't like Irish whiskey. The Redbreast line has now grown to include a 15-year-old, a 21-year-old, and a 27-year-old, among other bottlings. The secret to the brand's success has been veteran master blender Billy Leighton, who played a major role in rebuilding it.

Blue Spot, Green Spot, Red Spot & Yellow Spot

Green Spot Irish Whiskey dates back more than a century and was created by famed Dublin wine merchants Mitchell & Son, which is still open today. The store would buy unaged pot still whiskey made by Jameson, which at the time was also located in the city, and age the spirit for years in its own cool cellar before bottling it and selling it under its own name.

mash of malted and unmalted barley and distilled three times in Jameson's oversized copper pot stills. The earliest advertisement I could find for the brand ran in the *Irish Times* in the summer of 1912 and touts "Redbreast J.J. Liqueur Whiskey," which lists John Jameson & Son as the producer.

Redbreast was able to catch on because it was older than most of its competitors, including Jameson's signature 7-year-old whiskey. But even a brand as beloved as Redbreast fell victim to the global whiskey bust and was discontinued in the mid-1980s. It might have been gone at the time, but it wasn't forgotten. "It was a delight, a limousine amongst whiskeys," wrote Kevin Myers in the *Irish Times* in 1990. Fortunately, others felt the same—not even a year later Redbreast was once again available in Ireland. But it wouldn't be until 2008 that the whiskey was introduced to the US. By that time Redbreast (and for that matter, Jameson) was owned by Pernod Ricard.

The Mitchell & Son liquor store in Dublin differentiated the whiskey barrels aging in its cellar with a dab of paint, which inadvertently led to its line of Spot Irish whiskies.

Given that the store sold a range of different types of alcohol, the Jameson barrels were given a large distinguishing green paint dot to identify them so they would be easy to keep track of.

Originally Mitchell & Son sold this Irish whiskey as Old Pat, but in the early 1900s they decided to rebrand it as Green Spot. By the mid-1920s, the company's ad stated, "Connoisseurs will appreciate Mitchell's 10-year-old Whisky (Green Spot)." Around the same time, it was also selling a 7-year-old whiskey that was then called Blue Seal, which I believe became what we know today as Blue Spot. These whiskies were ultimately joined by the Yellow Spot 12 Year and Red Spot 15 Year. According to acclaimed writer Lew Bryson, Mitchell & Son sold the full line of Spots through the early 1950s. But by the end of the century just Green Spot was still being bottled, and it could be found only at the Mitchell & Son store in Dublin.

Today, Green Spot is a pot still whiskey that is aged for up to a decade in a variety of barrels including casks that have previously held bourbon and ones that previously held sherry. In addition to Green Spot, Pernod now has a whole Spot line of pot still whiskies that was created with the help of Mitchell & Son. In 2011, it first released Yellow Spot, which is aged for at least twelve years in three kinds of barrels that previously held bourbon, sherry, or the sweet fortified wine malaga.

Pernod then added Red Spot, which is aged for at least fifteen years in three kinds of barrels that previously held bourbon, sherry, or marsala. Red Spot was introduced in 2018.

The last Spot to be reintroduced was the Blue Spot 7 Year, which debuted in the spring of 2021. It's aged in three kinds of barrels that previously held bourbon, madeira, or oloroso sherry.

Midleton Very Rare is the original luxury Irish whiskey and is still sought after by drinkers and collectors.

Midleton Very Rare

Since it was introduced in December of 1985, Midleton Very Rare has been considered the gold standard of Irish whiskey. As you might have surmised from its name, the pure pot still whisky is produced at the Midleton distillery in Cork. (The name echoes the Cork Distilleries Company's Midleton Whiskey brand, which was discontinued in 1970.) The first edition was selected in 1984 by Midleton's legendary master distiller Barry Crockett and released the following year. It was a 12-year-old pot still whiskey that cost more than £40—a staggering amount at the time.

Very Rare was a bold gamble by Irish Distillers, who were desperate to change the perception of Irish whiskey. Specifically, there was no shortage of skeptics who believed that Irish whiskey couldn't be considered a luxury product. A 1985 article about the introduction of

Midleton Very Rare in the *Irish Times* was even titled "Whiskey launch could backfire." And to be fair, this wasn't the first time Irish Distillers tried to do this: In 1971, it introduced a high-end blended whiskey called Midleton Reserve, which didn't catch on.

But Crockett was undeterred. For Very Rare, he used the best barrels in the company's warehouse. What was also unusual about the whiskey is that from the start Irish Distillers planned to sell an annual edition of the liquor and the company has actually done just that—it has dutifully released a vintage of the whiskey each year. While the original Very Rare was completely pot still whiskey (made from a mash of malted and unmalted barley), some of the future editions combined pot still and aged grain whiskey.

It took several decades, but amazingly a luxury market did develop for Irish whiskey. Oddly, Midleton Very Rare is still relatively unknown by drinkers and definitely worth seeking out. Pernod now also releases some truly rare and expensive special editions of the brand, including a 46-year-old pot still whiskey with a suggested retail price of $45,000 a bottle when it went on sale in 2021.

Knappogue Castle Irish Whiskey

In the mid-1960s, Mark Edwin Andrews and his wife, Lavone Dickensheets Andrews, were on vacation in Ireland when they spotted Knappogue (NAH-pogue) Castle in County Clare. The impressive stone structure dates back to the fifteenth century, but was in desperate need of saving. Despite its sorry state, the couple fell in love with the castle. Although they lived in Houston, Texas, they bought the building anyway and set about restoring it.

In some ways they were the perfect stewards for the structure, as Lavone had an architecture degree from Rice Architecture. (She was the only woman in her graduating class of 1935.) She later worked for the well-known Houston architect John Staub before starting her own practice. Mark had been assistant secretary of the navy before entering the oil industry. He was the founder of Ancon Oil & Gas, which he ran for thirty-five years.

Not only did the couple rebuild the castle, but it became a tourist attraction famous for its so-called medieval banquets. Around the time they bought the

Knappogue Castle made a splash in the late 1990s by introducing an Irish whiskey made in 1951.

castle, Mark also bought a number of barrels of Irish whiskey, which had been made by the B. Daly distillery in Tullamore. (The same distillery was the original home to Tullamore D.E.W.) In 1987, he began bottling and selling it as Knappogue Castle Irish Whiskey. The family eventually parted ways with the castle, which is still open today for medieval banquets, but kept the whiskey brand.

In 1999, Mark and Lavone's son, Mark Andrews III, relaunched the brand and introduced a 1951 vintage of Knappogue Castle Irish Whiskey (bottled in 1987) which sold for a suggested retail price of $600 a bottle. While the '51 was out of reach for most drinkers at the time, its rarity and price tag garnered plenty of press for the brand. It also helped launch Knappogue's line of modern (and more affordable) single malt whiskies, made at the Cooley distillery.

Mark was able to use the success of Knappogue Castle Irish Whiskey to build a small portfolio of different spirits, including Jefferson's Bourbon and Goslings Rum. He called this company Castle Brands, and sold it to the giant spirits conglomerate Pernod Ricard for $223 million in 2019. Knappogue whiskey continues to be sold today, and while there aren't many bottles of the vintage '51 left, you can certainly find the brand's incredibly smooth 12-year-old, 14-year-old, and 16-year-old single malts on store shelves. Fans of Speyside Scotches will certainly enjoy these elegant whiskies.

BRANCH: DIAGEO

International booze conglomerate Diageo seemingly has every kind of alcohol in its deep portfolio, but for a number of years, incredibly, it didn't have an Irish whiskey. Read on to find out how the company created one in central Dublin, as well as about the history of its Irish whiskey cream liqueur, Baileys.

Baileys

As odd as this may sound today, there was a whiskey-based cream liqueur craze in the late 1970s. It was of course started by Baileys, which first hit the market in Ireland in 1974 and was exported to the Netherlands and then around the world the following year. (It became available in the US in 1979.)

The popular story goes like this: In the early 1970s, the board of directors at the spirits company W&A Gilbey was desperately looking for a new product to sell abroad, which would be entitled to a newly created fifteen-year tax exemption designed by the Irish government to spur exports. Since Gilbey's already had a successful eponymous gin brand and

Baileys was dreamed up by two British drinks consultants in the 1970s and quickly became an international bestseller.

Redbreast Whiskey, it needed something completely new. (See the Redbreast entry, page 350, for more about its history and the history of W&A Gilbey.)

The Baileys' origin story so far is not in dispute, but who actually came up with the idea to combine Irish whiskey, Irish cream, and chocolate? That's a bit contentious. In an interview with the *Irish Times* in the mid-1980s, David Dand, the managing director of Gilbey's, insisted that Baileys was created in his company's boardroom. While this is certainly plausible, I think there's a more credible creation story.

Tom Jago, who was then the head of innovations at Gilbey's parent company, International Distillers & Vintners (IDV), hired London consultants David Gluckman and Hugh Reade Seymour-Davies to come up with a new product for the company. According to Gluckman's 2017 memoir, *That S*it Will Never Sell*, he and Seymour-Davies were the ones who actually came up with the idea and first combined Jameson Irish Whiskey, Cadbury's Powdered Drinking Chocolate, sugar, and Irish cream in their office. "Hugh and I were taken by surprise," wrote Gluckman. "It tasted really good. Not only this, but the cream seemed to have the effect of making the drink taste stronger, like full-strength spirit. It was extraordinary." The whole thing came together in a fit of creativity that took a total of forty-five minutes. Gluckman shared their test batch with Jago, who was impressed enough to present it to the Gilbey's executives, including Dand. What helped get Baileys green lit was that IDV had been bought by the conglomerate Grand Metropolitan, which also happened to own a large Irish dairy.

Which leaves only the question of where the brand's name came from.

The creamy Brandy Alexander was a popular cocktail in the 1970s and was enjoyed in hip clubs and bars.

There was a restaurant near Gluckman and Seymour-Davies's Soho office that was called Baileys Bistro, and the name felt somehow perfect to adopt for the Irish cream. At first, they called their concoction Baileys Irish Cream Chocolate Liqueur, but this eventually morphed into Baileys Original Irish Cream. Adding "Original" was a stroke of genius, since it gave the product a halo of authenticity and history even though it was a new creation. The old-timey Baileys bottle design also gave the brand a gravitas, even though it was essentially the same bottle used by its sister brand Redbreast.

No matter what it was called or who invented it, Baileys was a perfect drink for the disco age, which featured a range of sweet and creamy cocktails. In fact, the recipe for Baileys is very close to the formula for the classic Brandy Alexander cocktail, which was quite popular at the time. (In 1974, John Lennon infamously drank an excessive number of them one night with Harry Nilsson at the Troubadour club in LA.)

By 1982, Baileys was an unexpected smash hit, selling more than 2 million cases a year in one hundred markets. The brand's international sales were so significant that they made up 1 percent of all Irish exports and a whopping 60 percent of Irish liquor exports at the time. These stats were particularly impressive given that Gilbey's was dubious Baileys would ever find an audience after it sold just eighteen thousand cases when it launched in 1975.

Baileys was so successful that, by the end of the '80s, there were dozens of other brands creating cream liqueurs in Ireland and abroad that used all kinds of base spirits, including Martell Cognac, DeKuyper Peachtree Schnapps, Myers's Rum, and Grand Marnier Orange Liqueur. (In the early 2000s, Jago, who went on to have an incredible career in the liquor industry, even introduced his own vodka-based vanilla cream liqueur, which he named after himself.)

While most of these copycat products are long gone, every few years a liquor brand will launch a new cream liqueur in an attempt to steal Baileys' thunder. (RumChata has arguably been the only creamy competitor to actually catch on.) But overall, Baileys is still the cream liqueur king, with a firm ownership on the holiday season. It's particularly popular served over ice cream and paired with other decadent desserts. You can still find the 34-proof (17 percent alcohol by volume) Baileys Original, as well as many different versions, including a dairy-free Baileys and a light Baileys.

One of the biggest questions about Baileys is whether it should be refrigerated. Through the magic of chemistry, the liqueur is shelf-stable and you can store it at room temperature in your liquor cabinet. The Original lasts up to twenty-four

The modern Roe & Co distillery in Dublin was inspired by the city's Roe distillery that was in operation in the eighteenth century.

months from the date printed on the back label—whether or not the bottle has been opened. Some of the other Baileys variants have a slightly shorter life expectancy of eighteen months.

Roe & Co

The new Roe & Co brand was launched in 2017, with its Dublin distillery opening in 2019. Roe & Co pays tribute to a very famous and historic Irish whiskey that has been out of business for decades.

The original company got its start back in 1757 when Peter Roe purchased the Thomas Street distillery. By the time famous whiskey writer Alfred Barnard wrote about the facility in 1887, it took up 17 acres (7 hectares) of Dublin and produced almost 2 million gallons (76,000 hectoliters) of whiskey that was exported to markets around the globe. Like most of the major

Irish whiskey brands at the time, the distillery used giant copper pot stills exclusively. "The Whisky is Dublin Pot Still of the finest quality," wrote Barnard. He added that the Roe's whiskey was exported to many foreign markets, including the Unites States, Canada, and Australia, "and is well known and appreciated everywhere."

A few years after Barnard's visit, George Roe merged his family's company with William Jameson and the Dublin Whiskey Distillery Company to form the Dublin Distillers Company Ltd. But even a combined entity wouldn't be able to handle the calamitous twentieth century and, like many of their Irish whiskey competitors, they were forced to close in the late 1940s.

The new Roe & Co distillery cost €25 million to build and is located very close to the original distillery on Thomas Street in the Liberties neighborhood of Dublin. Diageo repurposed an old power station that had for years served its iconic beer brand, Guinness. What makes the location perfect was that the Roe family and the Guinness family were originally neighbors.

Unlike the whiskey produced by the Roe family, however, the modern version is a blend of single malt and column still whiskey, which is aged in used bourbon barrels.

BRANCH: WILLIAM GRANT & SONS

William Grant & Sons is one of the major players in the Scotch industry that expanded into Irish whiskey when it acquired Tullamore D.E.W. in 2010 from Irish beverage company Cantrell & Cochrane (C&C Group). Ever since, William Grant has worked hard to rebuild the brand. Read on about the history of Tullamore D.E.W.

Tullamore D.E.W.

Tullamore D.E.W. is, hands down, one of the most famous Irish whiskies of all time. It dates back to 1829, when it was founded

Famous Scotch company William Grant bought Tullamore D.E.W. in 2010, and a few years later built the brand its own distillery.

by Michael Molloy. The Williams family bought a stake in the business in 1903 and, according to E. B. McGuire's excellent book *Irish Whiskey: A History of Distilling, the Spirit Trade, and Excise Controls in Ireland*, controlled all of it by 1931.

Despite its history, there wasn't much left of Tullamore D.E.W. by the early 2000s—though its downfall really started long before then. The brand's distillery closed in 1954 and the whiskey was made for years afterward at other Irish distilleries. Originally, Tullamore D.E.W. was a pure pot still whiskey distilled three times, but by the mid-1950s it was making one of the first lighter-style blended Irish whiskies, which combined 7-year-old single malt with 7-year-old grain whiskey. This new, easier-drinking whiskey would become the dominant style among Irish distillers in the second half of the twentieth century.

In 1964, the Williams family sold the brand to its rival John Power & Son, which a couple of years later merged with John Jameson and Cork Distilleries to form Irish Distillers. Unfortunately, Tullamore D.E.W. found itself buried in a portfolio of bestsellers, seemingly destined slowly to become irrelevant. In the 1980s, the whiskey wasn't even available in the US. But in 1993 things finally changed for the brand when C&C Group was able to buy it from Pernod Ricard. (The purchase price was never disclosed, but it was part of the deal where Pernod also got the whisky brand Royal Canadian.)

In 2010, William Grant gained control of Tullamore D.E.W. when it bought C&C Group's spirits division for nearly $367 million. (A few months later, William Grant sold Campari the rest of the brands it got in the C&C deal for $167.6 million—so the price for Tullamore D.E.W. was essentially $200 million.) After much speculation, William Grant spent $45 million to build Tullamore D.E.W. a new whiskey distillery in the town of Tullamore, which opened in 2014. It has the capacity to make 1.5 million nine-liter cases of whiskey per year, which gives you a sense of how big William Grant wants Tullamore D.E.W. to grow in the next few years. The facility makes both pot still Irish whiskey and single malt, which will allow Tullamore D.E.W. to continue to sell its current lineup, including both a blended Irish whiskey as well as a single malt.

The brand's signature Tullamore D.E.W. Original Irish Whiskey actually combines three kinds of whiskey: single malt, pot still, and grain. It is then aged in three types of barrels: used bourbon barrels, used sherry casks, and barrels that previously held Tullamore D.E.W.

A note on the brand's name: When William Grant bought Tullamore D.E.W., it capitalized the "D.E.W." in the whiskey's name as a way to honor the brand's nineteenth-century distiller Daniel E. Williams. But did Williams actually add his own initials to the brand's name? Doubtful. For one, I haven't found any reference to this unique trademark mentioned

When peaty Conamara was introduced in the 1990s it challenged the accepted honeyed flavor profile of Irish whiskey.

before William Grant's purchase of the brand. D.E.W. may also refer to alcohol, as in Mountain D.E.W., which is actually a cheeky reference to moonshine.

🌾 BRANCH: SUNTORY GLOBAL SPIRITS

When I started writing about drinks in the late 1990s, Cooley was producing some of the most interesting Irish whiskies. The distillery, located in the middle of the island, started out as a government-owned alcohol plant that was then bought in 1987 by Dr. John Teeling, a professor and entrepreneur. The one thing Teeling wasn't, however, was a distiller—and that's perhaps why he came up with some really unusual whiskies.

Just six years after Teeling opened Cooley, Irish Distillers tried to buy Cooley distillery for £9.5 million in order to close it down. Reportedly, Irish Distillers didn't believe Teeling's whiskies were up to their standards and would hurt Irish whiskey overall. Some have speculated that Dr. Teeling's plan all along was for his company to be acquired by the conglomerate. Unfortunately, the Irish government didn't approve the sale. The rationale was that Irish Distillers already owned the only other two whiskey distilleries on the island, so it didn't need Cooley as well—especially if it was only buying it to close the facility.

As a result of this failed bid, Teeling was forced to run the company for years. During that time, he not only produced whiskey for his own brands, but also provided whiskey in bulk to many other companies, which bottled the spirit under their own names. In 2011, Teeling finally sold his distillery and the brands

When Dr. John Teeling opened Cooley in 1987, it was only the third distillery operating in Ireland.

he started to American whiskey company Jim Beam for €71 million.

Beam made it clear that it wanted to focus on just Cooley's own brands and would no longer supply other companies with whiskey. Overnight, this helped shrink the industry and reduced the number of Cooley's competitors. Three years later, Beam itself was acquired by Suntory in a megadeal. Read on for more about Cooley's whiskies.

Connemara

Connemara broke all the supposed rules of Irish whiskey. While most of the industry was touting its easy-drinking and honeyed blends, Connemara was proudly peated and, even odder, a single malt. Irish whiskey is usually triple distilled, but not Connemara, which is just double distilled.

Of course, peat and single malts are not just the provenance of Scotland. There is plenty of historical precedent for making a smoky whiskey from malted barley on the Emerald Isle. When Connemara debuted in the late 1990s, most folks had no idea what to make of it—many just assumed it was some kind of Islay Scotch knockoff. Thankfully, the Irish whiskey world is quite a bit larger and more diverse today and, as a result, Connemara is not quite as polarizing. (There are even other Irish whiskey brands that have released peated expressions.)

It seems like poetic justice that the brand is now in the same portfolio as the legendary smoky whiskies Bowmore and Laphroaig.

Tyrconnell

When Tyrconnell (tur-CON-nell) debuted in the early 1990s, it challenged the Bushmills monopoly on producing Irish single malt whiskey. But the whiskey wasn't just a copycat—it blazed its own trail. For one, Tyrconnell owes as much to Scotland as it does to Ireland. It is distilled two times, as is usually done in Scotland, not Ireland, and many of the Tyrconnell expressions available today are finished (aged for a second time) in port, sherry, or madeira casks, a technique pioneered by Scotch distillers.

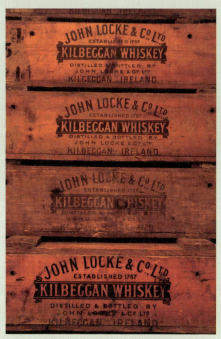

Kilbeggan claims that its distillery dates back to 1757, and the modern brand was introduced in the 1990s.

Tyrconnell is a revival of a "famous" Irish whiskey brand made by Andrew Alexander Watt at his Abbey Street distillery in Londonderry. According to lore, the brand was inspired by, and named for, a swift racehorse. While it's hard to find much mention of the original brand at all in historic records, what I can say is that Watt famously produced grain whiskey on a column still at the Londonderry distillery in Northern Ireland. Thankfully, Dr. Teeling chose to make the modern version of the whiskey a single malt.

Traditionally, Irish whiskey has been distilled three times, but Tyrconnell is distilled twice.

Kilbeggan

Kilbeggan (KILL-beg-inn) proudly touts that its distillery was constructed back in 1757, which would make it the oldest in Ireland. And while there certainly was distilling in the area, according to E. B. McGuire in his exhaustive *Irish Whiskey: A History of Distilling, the Spirit Trade, and Excise Controls in Ireland*, he didn't find any supporting evidence of the brand's claim. But no matter when the distillery was first built, it was clearly long ago.

What we know for certain is that the distillery shut down in 1953 and fell into disrepair. The townspeople started making repairs to the structure to ensure that it didn't fall down completely. Teeling began making whiskey under the Kilbeggan name in the early 1990s at his Cooley distillery, but moved production to the original Kilbeggan facility in 2007, which has been its home ever since.

In addition to its signature blended Irish whiskey, Kilbeggan has introduced a line of special small batch whiskies to great acclaim, including a rye and a pot still whiskey.

BRANCH: SAZERAC

Sazerac has built a veritable empire of insanely popular American whiskey brands produced at its Kentucky distillery Buffalo Trace. The company also has hundreds of other spirits brands in its portfolio, produced around the world. A few years ago, it added the historic Irish whiskey Paddy's. Read on for more of its story.

Paddy's Old Irish Whiskey

Paddy's Old Irish Whiskey (formerly called Paddy) is one of the last vestiges of the venerable Cork Distilleries Company, which dates back to 1867. According to lore, the brand was named for Cork's industrious and charismatic salesman

Paddy's Old Irish Whiskey goes back to 1913, when it was introduced by the Cork Distilleries Company.

Patrick J. O'Flaherty, and introduced in 1913. (Paddy is of course the traditional Irish nickname for Patrick.) In 1966, Cork Distilleries merged with its competitors John Jameson and John Power & Son to form Irish Distillers. In 1973, the company moved production of Paddy's to Irish Distillers' brand-new Midleton facility.

The modern version of Paddy's is a blend of the three kinds of Irish whiskey: single malt, pot still, and grain. The next change for Paddy's came in 2016, when the New Orleans, Louisiana-based company Sazerac bought the brand from Irish Distillers for an undisclosed amount. However, Irish Distillers still creates the easy-drinking whiskey for its new owner. Under Sazerac, the name of the brand has changed slightly from "Paddy" to "Paddy's." (For Sazerac's full story, see page 165.)

🌿 BRANCH: BROWN-FORMAN

It's hard to go anywhere in Louisville, Kentucky, and not be reminded of the Brown family. Not only did they play a major role in building the American whiskey industry, but they also helped grow the city. Over the years, the company has expanded into other spirits far beyond rye, bourbon, and Tennessee whiskey, including gin, tequila, Scotch, and now Irish whiskey. Read on for the story of its foray into Irish whiskey.

Slane Irish Whiskey

There are few pairings as perfect as whiskey and rock and roll. So it's only fitting that Slane Castle, an actual castle famous for hosting major rock concerts, including performances by the Rolling Stones, Bob Dylan, and the Red Hot Chili Peppers, is now also home to a whiskey distillery.

The idea for Slane Irish Whiskey was conjured up by Alex Conyngham and his father, Lord Henry Mountcharles, whose ancestors have lived at Slane Castle since 1703. Naturally, they would launch the brand at a 2009 Oasis concert that took place at the Castle. Lacking their own distillery, they bottled whiskey made at the Cooley distillery. The family might never have begun distilling if Jim Beam hadn't bought Cooley in 2012. In a move that shocked the spirits industry, Beam decided to stop selling whiskey made at the Cooley distillery to other brands, which forced a number of them out of business. Slane was nearly one of these casualties.

Without Cooley's whiskey, Conyngham and Lord Mountcharles announced their plans to build a £12 million distillery on their estate. That facility was never built; instead they decided to sell their brand in 2015 for an undisclosed amount to Louisville, Kentucky-based liquor company Brown-Forman. The brand's new owners followed through on the plan to build a distillery on the Slane Castle grounds, erecting a $50 million facility in the castle's former stables. Conyngham remains involved with the brand as its chief ambassador. It's

In 2015, American whiskey giant Brown-Forman bought the Slane Irish Whiskey brand and built a distillery in Ireland.

Ireland's Slane Castle is famous for hosting rock concerts and is now home to a whiskey distillery.

the first distillery Brown-Forman ever built from scratch outside the US.

While the first batches of Slane Irish Whiskey aged, the brand bought stock from other distilleries, producing first its Triple Casked Blend, aged in three types of barrels: new barrels, those that previously held Tennessee whiskey, and those that previously held sherry. The long-range plan for the brand is to make all the whiskey on-site from locally grown grains.

BRANCH: BACARDI

While the spirits industry is a thoroughly modern business, a number of the largest companies are still family run, including Bacardi. The Bacardi family has turned their eponymous rum brand into one of the bestselling spirits in the world and has built a portfolio of other all-stars, including Dewar's Scotch and Grey Goose Vodka. Given that Teeling Whiskey was started by two brothers and was very much a family-run company, it only made sense that Bacardi invested in it and ultimately acquired it. Read on about this impressive new Irish brand.

Teeling Whiskey

Brothers Jack and Stephen Teeling grew up in the whiskey business. They watched as their father, Dr. John Teeling, transformed a mothballed alcohol plant into the Cooley distillery. Their family then built a business that became so popular that Jim Beam purchased the facility and all their brands in 2011.

So, Jack and Stephen took the next logical step and started their own whiskey company in 2012, called simply Teeling Whiskey. In order to have something to sell immediately, they were able to buy barrels of whiskey from Cooley and other distilleries on the island. Then they set about building a distillery in the Liberties area of Dublin, which opened in 2015, making it the city's first new distillery in 125 years. To make the whiskey they hired American distiller Alex Chasko, who had a background producing craft beer. (Remember, the first step in making whiskey is making beer, so Chasko's experience was actually perfect for the job.)

Teeling Whiskey has attracted a following for its incredibly old single malts, which are sourced from another distiller, as well as for its whiskies finished in a range of different types of barrels. As the whiskey made by Chasko reaches maturity, more of what the brand sells will have been produced at its own distillery. Its signature Small Batch whiskey is a blend of single malt and grain whiskey aged in barrels that

Running the copper stills at Dublin's Teeling Bros. is American Alex Chasko.

previously held rum. They also sell a number of other whiskies, including a single pot still, a single malt, a single grain, and even a peated single malt.

In 2017, the brothers reportedly sold an 8 percent stake in their company to Bacardi for $4.8 million. Shortly afterward, Bacardi increased its investment in the company to 40 percent and then in December of 2023 took control of it.

🌿 BRANCH: MARK ANTHONY BRANDS

While Mark Anthony Brands isn't itself a household name, the company's signature brand is the bestselling hard seltzer

Glendalough is one of the leaders of the craft distilling movement in Ireland.

White Claw. Over the last decade it's also been building a whiskey portfolio, including the Irish Glendalough. Read on for more about this brand.

Glendalough Irish Whiskey

Recently, it feels like practically every Irish town and neighborhood has opened or reopened a distillery. One of the most successful of these new ventures is Glendalough (GLEN-dull-ah), which was started by Donal O'Gallachoir and a few partners in 2011.

Originally, the distillery made an upscale version of the Irish moonshine poitín as well as gin before moving on to whiskey, which first arrived in 2013. In 2016, the founders sold a minority stake in the company to Mark Anthony Brands for €5.5 million. Three years later, Mark Anthony, owner of White Claw Hard Seltzer, bought the rest of Glendalough for an undisclosed amount.

Glendalough currently sells a few different kinds of whiskey, including single malt, pot still, and single grain. It tries to use both local ingredients, such as Irish oak barrels, as well as more far-flung ones, such as Japanese mizunara oak barrels.

🌿 BRANCH: INDEPENDENTS

While Irish Distillers and Bushmills still make the majority of Irish whiskey sold today, starting around 2010 a new generation of independent distillers began making whiskey around the island. Read on for more about a few of these craft brands.

Over the last 15 years, dozens of new independent Irish whiskey distilleries have opened.

Dingle Irish Whiskey

Many craft distillers in the United States followed the same basic business plan when they launched: They sold vodka and gin to pay their bills while their whiskey aged. It makes a lot of sense because white spirits can be made today and sold tomorrow. This plan proved so successful that distillers around the world are now using it, and Dingle is a prime example. The distillery became well known for its vodka and range of gins when it opened in 2012. Three years later, it released its first batch of single malt whiskey.

Dingle was started by Oliver Hughes, Liam LaHart, and Peter Mosley, who previously opened the wildly successful craft brewery, the Porterhouse Brewing Company, in 1996.

Great Northern Distillery

There may not be second acts in the United States, but F. Scott Fitzgerald would be happy to know there are apparently second acts in Ireland. Four years after selling his Cooley distillery to Jim Beam for €71 million in 2011, Dr. John Teeling opened his Great Northern distillery in an old Harp beer brewery. His new facility is equipped with both column and pot stills, which allows him to make a number of different whiskies: grain, single malt, and pot still. But Teeling doesn't bottle and market these whiskies himself; he instead sells his spirits to other companies. Thanks to the supply from Great Northern, a number of new Irish whiskey brands have been able to launch over the past few years.

Lost Irish Whiskey

Lost Irish is a well-traveled whiskey. The brand was launched in 2020 by former Tullamore D.E.W. brand ambassador Tim Herlihy and Neil Sands. Its signature spirit is a blend of three kinds of whiskey: pot still, grain, and single malt. The whiskey is then aged in six kinds of barrels that have each previously held something different and hail from six continents, including barrels from South African brandy, Caribbean rum, and American bourbon.

Waterford Whisky

After reviving the historic Islay Scotch distillery Bruichladdich and selling it to Rémy Cointreau for $90.3 million in 2012, no one would blame Mark Reynier for taking a break. (See the Bruichladdich entry, page 295, for more.) But that's not how Reynier is wired. Instead, he took on a new project starting an Irish distillery, Waterford, which makes only single malt whiskey. And because we're talking about Reynier, an entrepreneur and visionary, the brand has a completely unique approach and philosophy: It is the self-proclaimed largest producer of organic and biodynamic whiskies in the world.

Waterford centers on the idea of terroir—that each whiskey reflects the place where it's made, in particular the place where the grains are grown. The brand uses only Irish barley and it waxes poetic about the grains in the same way a hipster sommelier in Brooklyn extols the virtues of their obscure natural wine. In fact, Waterford's Single Farm Origin line proudly states on the label the name of the farm that grew the barley.

For years, the large whiskey distillers would tell me that where they got their grain didn't matter as long as it had the right starch and moisture content. While production on a grand scale definitely mitigates differences in the barley, corn, or rye, when you're making truly small batch whiskey like Waterford you will absolutely get differences from batch to batch and from farm to farm. And you'll be able to taste this terroir in a dram of the finished whiskey.

West Cork Distillers

It's hard now to imagine the sad state of the spirits world back when West Cork Distillers was founded in 2003 by friends John O'Connell, Denis McCarthy, and Ger McCarthy. Classic cocktails were just coming back to life after several decades of decline and the craft distilling movement was more of a concept than a reality. The whiskey industry was dominated by legacy distillers who had somehow managed to survive the lean years. Undeterred, the West Cork Distillers trio bought a couple of Swiss schnapps stills and began making a small amount of alcohol. With the odds firmly against them, somehow the distillery not only survived but prospered. In 2014, West Cork moved into a proper distillery, which is now equipped with eight copper pot stills and two column stills. (It has an additional three stills to make gin.)

West Cork's signature product is an easy-drinking blend of single malt (25 percent) and grain whiskey (75 percent) aged in used bourbon barrels. The distillery also makes single pot still whiskies from malted and unmalted barley, as well as single malts. West Cork further produces a line of whiskies finished in a range of different types of barrels—everything from casks that have held rum to barrels that have held calvados or IPA beer. Last but certainly not least, they also produce a whiskey for a brand owned by the famous Celtic punk band The Pogues.

Mark Reynier made his name resuscitating Scotch distillery Bruichladdich. His next act was starting Irish whiskey distillery Waterford.

CANADIAN WHISKY

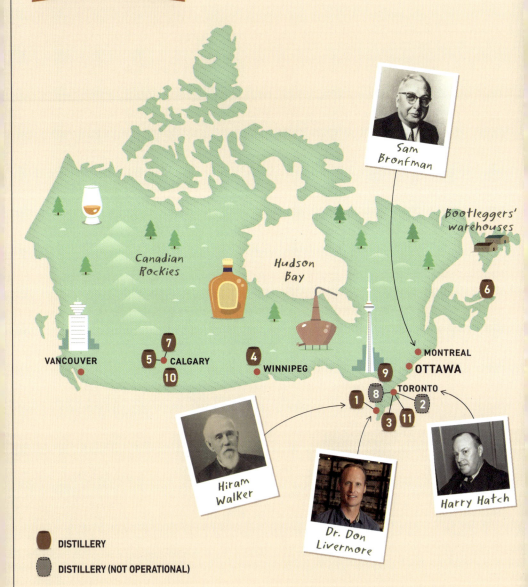

The journey to the top of the old concrete grain elevators at the Hiram Walker & Sons distillery in Windsor, Ontario, is not for the faint of heart.

It's 85 feet (26 meters) straight up an old, enclosed, rusty steel staircase. But the view from the top is worth the workout. Stretching before you on the opposite riverbank is a postcard view of downtown Detroit, Michigan. On a clear day, it almost feels like you can see all the way to Chicago and beyond.

The sheer height of the grain elevators gives you a sense of the massive scale of the distillery and how much whisky it produces. Consider, for starters, that every year 120,000 metric tons (132,000 tons) of corn, 10,000 metric tons (11,000 tons) of rye, and hundreds of tons of barley and wheat are delivered by a seemingly never-ending parade of oversized trucks. Each load is carefully inspected to ensure that the grain meets rigorous standards.

While this isn't Canada's only distillery, it is by far the country's largest. In fact, it is one of the largest distilleries in all of North America. But it wasn't until I made the trip across the Detroit River to visit the Hiram Walker distillery that I truly understood the magnitude of Canada's whisky industry. Nor did I understand, until I began writing this book, the incredibly important role that Canada's whisky industry played in shaping American whiskey after Prohibition.

While the trip from Detroit to the Hiram Walker facility (now owned by French spirits conglomerate Pernod Ricard) is less than 4 miles (6 kilometers),

> ## Key Differences
> The rules for making Canadian whisky are pretty loose compared to those of many other countries.
>
> - Essentially, the overarching regulation is that the whisky must be made and aged in Canada.
> - It must be aged for at least three years in a wooden barrel (new or used) no larger than 700 liters (185 gallons).
> - Spirit caramel and flavorings may be added.
> - Most Canadian whisky is a smooth blend intended to be drunk as you like it—neat, on the rocks, or in a mixed drink.
>
> **Total Consumption:** Sales of Canadian whisky in the United States in 2023 totaled nearly 18 million nine-liter cases.

it's a world away from the United States in terms of how the company makes whisky.

Hiram Walker's distillery on the banks of the Detroit River was a fairly modest affair when he bought it in 1858. The facility has since grown into one of the largest distilleries in North America.

Canada is famous for its easy-drinking blends. A Canadian blend starts with a base whisky (usually made from corn, wheat, or rye) that doesn't have a ton of flavor and is typically made on a column still. The base whisky is then blended with a large range of "flavoring whiskies," including straight rye, bourbonlike whisky, or Scotch-like single malt. In a sense, for most Canadian distillers the base whisky is the canvas and these mature flavoring whiskies are the colorful paints. What separates Canadian blended whisky from other kinds of blends made around the world is the breadth and depth of its components.

Although Canadian whisky often doesn't get the same respect as Scotch or bourbon, it is certainly popular, and is currently bolstered by a new generation of brands that deserve your attention.

Seagram's produced a range of Canadian whiskies. Here, an inspector checks a Seagram's whisky for color.

Types of Canadian Whisky

While the country's industry was once dominated by just eight gigantic distillers primarily producing blends, there are now dozens of craft brands, which are helping to push Canadian whisky in new directions.

Here are the basic requirements for each type of whisky.

♦ (JUST) CANADIAN WHISKY

Most whisky made in Canada falls under the catchall term *Canadian whisky*, including the bestsellers Canadian Club and Crown Royal. This whisky can be made from any kind of grain and can be a straight whisky or a blend of different whiskies. It can also be made on a highly efficient column still or a traditional pot still. Brands may add spirit caramel to change or improve a whisky's color, and they can also add flavoring. (Crown Royal hit it big with its Regal Apple Whisky, which has become a huge seller.) This kind of whisky tends to be a blend of corn whisky and four to six mature flavoring whiskies.

♦ CANADIAN RYE WHISKY

One signature of many Canadian whisky blends is a spicy rye note, which has led to quite a bit of confusion over the years. At the end of the twentieth century, when American straight rye whiskey was in short supply, Canadian blends were often used as a substitute by bartenders. If you asked for a rye Manhattan, for example, it would no doubt be made with Canadian Club. As

---

DEFINING CANADIAN WHISKY

- It must be produced and aged in Canada.
- The spirit must be aged for at least three years in a wooden barrel no larger than 700 liters (185 gallons).
- The finished whisky has to be at least 80 proof (40 percent alcohol by volume).
- It can be bottled as a straight whisky or as a blend.
- Distillers may add spirit caramel and flavoring.

DEFINING CANADIAN RYE WHISKY

- It must be produced and aged in Canada.
- The spirit must be aged for at least three years in a wooden barrel no larger than 700 liters (185 gallons).
- The finished whisky has to be at least 80 proof (40 percent alcohol by volume).
- It can be bottled as a straight whisky or as a blend.
- Distillers may add spirit caramel and flavoring.

The award-winning rye whisky, Lot No. 40, is changing the overall perception of Canadian whisky.

The Canadian government requirements for producing rye whisky are exactly the same as for the overall Canadian whisky category. Bizarrely, there are no requirements for how much (if any) rye grain needs to be used in its production. The amount of rye grain in a mash bill or the amount of finished rye whisky in a blend is up to the particular brand.

♦ CANADIAN MALT WHISKY

Historically, Canadian distillers have made a single malt-style whisky from barley, which was used as a flavoring whisky in blends. A number of brands, such as Glen Breton, are now bottling and selling these single malts.

DEFINING CANADIAN MALT WHISKY

- It must be produced and aged in Canada.
- The spirit must be aged for at least three years in a wooden barrel no larger than 700 liters (185 gallons).
- The finished whisky has to be at least 80 proof (40 percent alcohol by volume).
- The whisky must be made from a mash of exclusively malted grains.
- It can be bottled as a straight whisky or as a blend.
- Distillers may add spirit caramel and flavoring.

a result, Canadian whisky and straight rye erroneously became synonymous. Fortunately, that misconception has been largely debunked—but some Canadian distillers are now bottling straight rye whisky to great acclaim, adding another wrinkle to this historic confusion.

The 9.09 Percent Rule

If you ask self-proclaimed liquor experts about Canadian whisky, they will no doubt bring up the 9.09 percent rule. This innocuous-sounding regulation allows a Canadian distiller to add to their whisky up to 9.09 percent of an unaged wine or another spirit that is at least two years old.

According to Canadian whisky authority Davin de Kergommeaux, this practice became popular in the 1980s so that low-priced Canadian brands could compete with less expensive American blends (which were traditionally a mix of unaged, cheap neutral grain spirit and straight whiskey). While the more expensive Canadian whiskies don't usually make use of this loophole, a few have made interesting, higher-quality offerings that include a small amount of bourbon or sherry.

The craft distillery Eau Claire in Alberta uses a range of different types of barrels to age its whiskies.

The History of Canadian Whisky

Although the United States and Canada share a nearly 4,000-mile (6,400-kilometer) border that stretches from the Atlantic Ocean to the Pacific Ocean, the two countries created completely different styles of whisky. They even spell whiskey differently—generally with an *e* in the US and without it in Canada.

Despite their different approaches to how the spirit should be made and aged, the whiskey heritage of the two countries is undeniably interwoven. Over and over again, the neighbors have played important roles in each other's whisky history. In fact, Americans started a number of Canada's most famous whisky brands. And without Canada during Prohibition, the United States would have come much closer to being a completely dry country (and a far less culturally rich one). So it should come as little surprise that you'll find a lot about Canada in the chapter on American whiskey, and a fair amount on the United States in the pages that follow.

♦ ORIGINS OF CANADIAN WHISKY

For many years, the origins of the Canadian whisky industry were credited to Scottish and Irish immigrants arriving in the late 1700s. And that made sense: After the American Revolution ended, many of the Tory loyalists to the crown fled north across the border to try their luck in what would become Canada, rather than live in the new experiment in democracy. This migration supposedly led to the birth of the country's distilling industry.

But while many families indeed moved north to escape George Washington's new government, distillers already existed in Canada. Near Quebec, many farmers used small stills to turn the local bounty into a range of spirits. "Exactly who made the first Canadian whisky, and where or when they made it, will never be known," wrote Davin de Kergommeaux in his excellent book *Canadian Whisky: The New Portable Expert*. "Canada's original inhabitants did not distill alcohol, but when European immigrants began arriving en masse, whisky and whisky stills arrived with them."

♦ INDUSTRIALIZATION AND THE RISE OF CANADIAN CLUB

While the whiskey industry in the United States started essentially because the country broke away from the United Kingdom, Canada's whisky industry really got its start because it was tied to the old country. Some of Canada's first major distillers, including breakout star Molson, began exporting boatloads of whisky to England in the 1820s.

But what Canadian distillers were making in the early nineteenth century is very different from what we associate with the country today. A national style of whisky had yet to develop and the spirit was made from a range of grains—some companies used wheat, others used malted barley or even a

CANADIAN WHISKY 375

By the early 1900s, Hiram Walker and its signature brand Canadian Club had grown into a huge venture with warehouses full of whisky barrels.

One of the brands that built the Canadian whisky industry was Toronto's Gooderham & Worts, which was started in the 1830s.

mix of grains as a base. No matter what the whisky was made from, brands generally used pot stills and distilled their whisky once, twice, or even three times. Kergommeaux points out that some of these early whiskies were often very weak, about 40 proof (20 percent alcohol by volume) and were sometimes charcoal filtered and/or flavored. Just as in America or Scotland, the distilling was usually part of a bigger and vertically integrated enterprise. Mill owners at the time would sometimes be paid by customers with grain. The mill owner would then turn their grain into whisky, which was a way to increase its value. The leftovers from the distilling process would then be used to feed livestock.

Thanks to English drinkers, Canadian whisky was able to increasingly industrialize, with the leading distillers building impressive facilities. In the late 1850s, Gooderham & Worts Ltd. installed a nearly four-story, steam-powered wooden still in its state-of-the-art Toronto distillery, which was luxuriously built from limestone. Combined with its pot stills the company could make more than 2 million gallons a year, which was a staggering sum at the time. These wooden chamber stills were also used in the US (Jack Daniel's produced its famous Tennessee whiskey on one through the nineteenth century) and the technology allowed North American distillers to establish a distinct and different style of whisky from what Scottish and Irish distillers were making. The UK remained a loyal customer of Canada's whisky distillers until Scotland's blended whisky industry really took off in the second half of the nineteenth century.

Fortunately, Canada's distillers found another large export market for their whisky that was significantly closer: the United States. In the 1860s, the Civil War shut down many US distilleries, but Americans were, naturally, still thirsty. Canadian distillers benefitted from their neighbor's internecine struggle and were only too happy to send a river of whisky across the border. And the Canadian liquor industry boomed massively as a result.

One of the folks to directly benefit was Hiram Walker, who had just gotten into the distilling business a few years before the Civil War started.

He was born in Massachusetts in 1816 and moved to Detroit, Michigan, in 1838, where he went into the grocery business. Later, he bought a flour mill and a distillery in Ontario across the river from Detroit. While this might seem like an odd background for a whisky baron, you can't make whisky without first milling grain. Historically, the relationship between distillers and millers has always been close. Walker's time working as a grocer was also important, considering that people often bought and drank liquor at a grocery store. His combination of experience led to a calling in the spirits industry—one that blossomed into a vast whisky empire.

Given that Walker was from the northeast of the US, it makes sense that he began making a bourbonlike whisky made from a mash of mostly corn with some rye, malted barley, and oats. He also installed a wooden steam-powered three-chamber still, which evolved from the single chamber wooden still used by Gooderham & Worts Ltd. (For more on the history of the chamber, see page 63.) Walker would then take the alcohol coming off the chamber still and redistill it in a copper pot still, a very standard process at the time. The second distillation increased its proof and smoothed out its flavor. He also produced a second type of whisky that was almost entirely made from rye and had more flavor. He then combined these two different styles of whisky, more or less establishing the origins of Canada's trademark blending style. (Walker also produced and sold a number of other types of whiskies.)

According to Kergommeaux, by 1871 Walker had installed a cutting-edge continuous column still made of copper that could easily and quickly produce whisky. His still was made by the American firm of Hoffman, Ahlers & Co., which at the time was located in Cincinnati, Ohio, and later moved to Louisville, Kentucky.

The column still was a revolutionary piece of technology and was adopted by distillers in Scotland around the same time, using it to make grain whisky that was then blended with more flavorful single malt pot still whiskies, which is how blended Scotch is still made today. Walker essentially did the same thing with a similar blend of Canadian whiskies.

Over time, several of Canada's other distillers also began to use continuous stills to produce a base whisky, which they blended with a number of different types of other whiskies.

Walker's defining creation—and sensation—was Canadian Club. It was the first whisky in the country to come from a distillery in a sealed glass bottle—a major innovation that ensured the alcohol hadn't been adulterated. In the mid- to late-1800s, distilleries sold whisky only by the barrel

While Hiram Walker's most famous creation is Canadian Club, the distillery made a range of other whiskies, including Walker's Deluxe Straight Rye.

with broad name recognition. Walker, a master promoter, began running frequent newspaper ads for his whisky across Canada—from Nova Scotia to British Columbia. "The fame of the whiskey distilled in Walkerville did not spread over the world of its own accord," wrote the *Montreal Daily Star* in the obituary it ran for Walker in 1899.

Canadian Club was made and bottled in Ontario at the Hiram Walker distillery, originally a straight rye whisky as advertised in 1879. Over time, however, it turned into a blend. And that wasn't the only change—Canadian Club was originally known as Walker's Club. Several theories exist about why the name was changed, but according to Gerald Carson's excellent 1963 book *The Social History of Bourbon*, Walker was forced to add where the whisky was produced by the US government. Apparently, American bourbon producers were very worried by the brand's popularity in the 1880s and thought adding "Canadian" to the label would hurt its reputation. "They pulled on their Congress gaiters, packed their valises, and took off for Washington to argue that people who enjoyed Walker's Club Whisky might think they were drinking the national drink, made in Kentucky," wrote Carson. While Walker was supposedly forced to change his brand's name, the Kentuckians' plan backfired—it turned out Canadian Club became an even more distinctive and more powerful name.

As a result of Walker's PR efforts and even the scuffle over adding its location, Canadian Club was one of

to stores, which essentially doubled as bars (producing glass bottles at the time was labor intensive and expensive). The liquor would then be parceled out to customers by the glass or decanter. By the time the whisky crossed a customer's lips, it was likely to have been mixed with a range of substances—many of which you wouldn't want to put in your body.

While the health of consumers certainly benefitted from Walker's whisky coming in a sealed bottle, it also benefitted him immensely, as he could market it as a distinct brand, a novel concept at the time. There were relatively few whiskies in the late nineteenth century

the first North American whiskies to become truly a brand name, not only in its home market, but also in the United States, where it was also available. So much so that it publicly battled a wave of imitators looking to cash in on its reputation. In 1892, industry trade publication *Bonfort's Wine and Spirit Circular* ran a small story about Canadian Club attempting to stop the sale of Montreal Club, which had an incredibly similar look and, to boot, wasn't even made in Montreal.

Three years later, Canadian Club ran a series of advertisements in US newspapers, including in the *Chicago Tribune*, warning consumers of another knockoff. This "spurious whisky" was called Canadian Rye Whisky, made by a mysterious company called W.G. Smith & Bros., which, according to the ad, didn't actually exist. "The very high reputation enjoyed by our 'Canadian Club' Whisky has led to a number of more or less dangerous imitations in outward appearance . . . which we have built up by several years of effort and very large expenditures of money." These ads only served to bolster Canadian Club's reputation because, if other companies were trying to imitate the brand, the whisky must be very good.

♦ A NEW CHALLENGE TO CANADIAN CLUB

At the beginning of the twentieth century, Canadian Club suddenly found itself on the other side of US law. Dr. Harvey Wiley, chief chemist of the US Department of Agriculture (predecessor to the modern Food and Drug Administration) was appalled by the state of the whiskey industry in the US and in Canada. According to Wiley's research, most brands in both countries were basically blending straight whiskey with neutral grain spirits (essentially vodka) or worse, coloring and flavoring neutral grain spirit with a range of awful additives and calling it whisky (making some of these concoctions downright dangerous to drink).

Wiley insisted that only straight whiskey—unblended, uncut, and barrel aged—should be called whiskey; anything else was a fraudulent imposter.

What made Wiley particularly passionate (and indignant) about the

At the turn of the twentieth century, the United States and Canada got into a vicious fight about how whiskey should be made.

In the early 1900s, Corby proudly made straight rye whiskey and advertised that fact to consumers.

issue, was that he enjoyed drinking straight rye whiskey. So he knew what the real stuff should look, smell, and taste like. He also thought that whiskey should retain a large amount of flavor, including the fusel oil, a flavorful but controversial substance produced during fermentation.

To be fair, what Wiley demanded from distillers and whiskey brands is essentially what modern drinkers expect from a premium bourbon or rye. Thanks to his efforts, along with the support of President Theodore Roosevelt and Attorney General Charles Bonaparte, the Pure Food and Drug Act was passed on June 30, 1906. Wiley used that legislation to prevent whiskies not made according to his standards from calling themselves whiskey in the US.

A number of distillers were overjoyed, particularly those who already made their whiskey according to Wiley's standards, including the H. Corby distillery in Canada. For them, the legislation was an opportunity to promote their brands. Corby began touting its process of making straight rye whisky and the fact that "we have always matured our whisky in the good old-fashioned way—ripening it in charred oak barrels." The company was so confident that its whisky was superior that it offered readers a free sample of its "Special Selected" rye whisky if they returned the coupon in the ad.

Wiley's ideas about whisky were of course not shared by other Canadian distillers—even many of the reputable ones. The problem was that some of them, like they do today, made a base spirit in a column still that had relatively little flavor and blended it with more flavorful whiskies made in a pot still. While this method was economical and highly efficient, in Wiley's mind it was a shortcut and no substitute for straight whisky that had been aged in a wooden barrel.

Hiram Walker soon found its distilling methods a target of Wiley and the United States federal government. The brand even printed and distributed a book detailing its fight with Wiley, dramatically titled *A Plot Against the People: A History of the Audacious Attempt by Certain Kentucky Straight Whisky Interests to Pervert the Pure Food Law in Order to Create a Monopoly for Their Fusel Oil Whiskies and to Outlaw All Refined Whiskies*.

In the book, Hiram Walker defends itself against Wiley's charges and explains that Canadian Club makes "two distillates of opposite character—one, having grain flavors and a very small amount of fusel oil; another, having practically neither. When these two distillates are combined in such proportions as [to] give the desired flavor, the small amount of fusel oil in the one is so distributed that it becomes a negligible quantity: the mixture is reduced to the proper strength with water, and put away in oak casks to mature for at least five years."

Essentially, the brand mixed a small amount of what Wiley would consider whisky with a much lighter and more neutral spirit before allowing the mixture to age in a barrel for several years. The obvious advantage of this method is that it's much cheaper and quicker than making straight whisky. It also produces an easy-drinking whisky, which has a wide appeal.

In June 1908, US federal marshals confiscated 5,405 cases of Canadian Club sitting in a warehouse in Detroit, Michigan. "The contention is that, instead of being labeled simply 'Canadian Club whisky,' it should be branded 'Canadian Club whisky, a compound of pure grain distillates,'" wrote the *Detroit Free Press*, reporting on the seizure. "In other words, the agricultural department insists that it shall be labeled a 'compound,' which, the Walkers believe, would practically kill their export business into this country, besides having a damaging effect on their trade elsewhere."

So Canadian Club, which billed itself as "by far the most widely sold Whisky in the whole world," went on the offensive against Wiley, of the Department of Agriculture, attacking his opinions and insisting that he had a sinister agenda. In 1908, the brand launched an attack like one you'd see in a bitter political campaign, running newspaper ads in large, bold fonts that established so-called "Important Facts," which naturally supported its whisky.

♦ WHISKY IS WHISKY?

For a while, things looked grim for Canadian Club and other distillers in both the United States and Canada who didn't make straight whiskey. Would they be forced to cave in and change their production methods, or put "imitation" or "Compound" on their labels?

After several years, the fight between Wiley and these distillers escalated, and ultimately reached the White House. However, by that point, Wiley's supporter Teddy Roosevelt was

In 1909, US President William Howard Taft defined what constitutes whiskey, which vindicated Canadian distillers.

their whisky," the ad continued, "they should use Kentucky 'Straight Whisky:' Canadian Club will not suit them."

Having survived Wiley's challenge, Canadian Club would soon have to deal with another potentially devastating piece of US legislation: the one that codified Prohibition.

♦ THE CROSS-BORDER EFFECT OF AMERICA'S PROHIBITION

Given Canada's proximity to the United States, it's no surprise that major US events have helped shape Canada's liquor industry—Prohibition being exhibit A.

Thanks to a loophole during the famously dry period that lasted thirteen years (1920–33), plenty of booze that ended up in the States was made by, or passed through, Canadian hands. At the heart of this story are two tiny islands, Saint-Pierre and Miquelon, located 12 miles (19 kilometers) off the coast of Nova Scotia in the Gulf of

no longer president. William Howard Taft was, and he wasted no time ending the whiskey debate. In April 1909, he convened a panel to hear testimony from a range of distillers and experts. By December, Taft ruled in favor of Canadian Club, concluding more or less that whiskey had traditionally been made in a number of different ways, so its definition shouldn't be narrowed by the Pure Food and Drug Act.

Canadian Club began running newspaper ads trumpeting that Taft had ruled in their favor and exonerated their production practices: "Now the Attorney-General has decided that the Pure Food Law does not require our label to be changed by a single letter. If any consumers really want fusel oil in

Prohibition in the US helped Canadian distillers who found many ways to get their whisky to thirsty drinkers across the border.

Bootleggers used different modes of transportation to smuggle Canadian whisky into the US.

Saint Lawrence. While, geographically, they appear to be part of Canada, they are technically still territories governed by France (a holdover from France's colonial days, when it ruled a sprawling empire). These lovely but otherwise inconsequential and isolated rocky outcroppings provided an incredibly important loophole for bootleggers. Wayne Curtis, in his excellent 2007 story "Bootleg Paradise" for *American Heritage* magazine, described it best: "They're just 93 square miles—slightly smaller than the borough of Queens, New York—but these tiny islands were to Prohibition what Iwo Jima was to the Pacific Theater in World War II, dots on a map whose history far surpassed their humble geography."

During America's Prohibition, Canadian and European distillers could legally ship their products to these then sparsely populated islands, given their French ownership. After the booze arrived on Saint-Pierre and Miquelon, it was no longer the concern of the brand—so where it went next was, naturally, out of their control. The brands, of course, knew that their booze would then be smuggled into the US by a sophisticated and far-reaching bootlegging syndicate made up of crooks, gangsters, and middlemen, who would sell the alcohol for an incredible profit. This ridiculously roundabout piece of bureaucracy allowed distillers to technically abide by the Canadian law forbidding them to ship alcohol directly to their dry neighbor. In 1954, the *New York Times* went as far as calling the town of Saint-Pierre, "the liquor warehouse of a nation."

It was obvious that the small populations living on Saint-Pierre and Miquelon islands—many of whom spent their days fishing the area's icy waters—weren't consuming all the alcohol suddenly landing on their shores. It of course made its way illegally into the United States, where it was widely sold to eager drinkers. "The islanders look on prohibition in America as a godsend, for it has brought them out of bankruptcy, permitted their harbors and towns to be improved, and made citizens generally prosperous," noted the *New York Times* in a story about the pavilion Saint-Pierre and Miquelon erected for the 1931 International Colonial Exposition in Paris. (The headline of this piece, "Bootleggers' Gold Builds Display Pavilion for St. Pierre and Miquelon at Vincennes Fair," made it clear that it was no secret what was happening on these islands.)

Business was so brisk on the islands that a car dealership opened on Saint-Pierre despite there being nowhere to drive and few roads. If you visit today, you can see evidence of the Prohibition boom times—industrious residents used some of the many discarded wooden liquor crates to build fences and portions of their homes.

But Saint-Pierre and Miquelon weren't the only routes Canadian whisky took to the United States. During wintertime, under the cover of darkness, an army of sturdy Model Ts filled with crates of whisky drove over the frozen-solid Detroit River, which separates the two countries. Windsor, Ontario, which was home to Hiram Walker's giant distillery, is located directly across from the Motor City. The facility sits right on the shore, tantalizingly close to the United States. (According to lore, a number of sunken wrecks along the riverbed are still packed with ancient bottles of bootleg booze.)

Liquor was also sent via boats that docked off the coast of the United States. These buoyant whisky warehouses were serviced by a flotilla of smaller boats that would ferry the booze ashore. It was part of a constant game of cat and mouse with US authorities, who tried mightily to catch the bootleggers and break up the various smuggling rings.

♦ THE RISE OF THE BRONFMANS AND SEAGRAM'S

There is a common misconception that Prohibition was a start-to-finish boom time for all of Canada's distillers. In reality, the Canadian whisky industry suffered greatly during Prohibition. The United States, after all, had been a huge buyer of Canadian whisky, so staying in business meant you'd have to work with a group of enterprising entrepreneurs to get your whisky across the border. For some distillers, this was a proverbial bridge too far, and they were happy to sell their distilleries at a premium to people who were willing to take these extreme risks.

Naturally, the smugglers of Canadian whisky were the biggest winners during US Prohibition. And a number of companies found ever more creative ways to clandestinely supply the United States with their whisky, while making a fortune in doing so. These bootleggers would dominate both the Canadian and international liquor business during Prohibition, and for decades to come.

One of the major players in this game was the Bronfman family. Jewish immigrants from Bessarabia, an area now in southwest Ukraine and Moldova, they settled in Montreal in 1899. Yechiel and Mindel Bronfman, who had four sons (Sam, Harry, Abe, and Allan) headed the family. They worked themselves up from running hotels and bars to owning

Sam Bronfman led his family's giant liquor business, Seagram's, which ultimately included whiskey distilleries around the world.

Seagram's was famous for its exacting quality control and had labs that routinely double checked the work of its distillers.

distilleries, which they built into a vast liquor empire with holdings stretching around the globe.

The Bronfmans have always insisted that they weren't bootleggers, yet a river of their alcohol flowed through the Saint-Pierre and Miquelon islands, and they were somehow able to raise a tremendous amount of capital during Prohibition. So much so that, in 1928, the family acquired the historic Joseph E. Seagram & Sons brand. Perhaps fearing the rampant anti-Semitism at the time, the Bronfmans decided to use the patrician-sounding Seagram name for their growing company. The profits from the family's illegal sales allowed them to stockpile mature whisky that would immediately go on sale across the border the moment Prohibition ended.

With the ratification of repeal in December 1933, Seagram's quickly spent millions building distilleries around the United States and buying up other brands, which allowed them

American law enforcement had trouble stopping the fleet of fast ships coming from Canada loaded with cases of whisky.

to produce a variety of whiskies and control a huge share of the whiskey market in the United States.

But repeal also created a logistical headache for the Bronfmans that morphed into a nightmare. When Prohibition ended, the alcohol in their warehouses on the islands of Saint-Pierre and Miquelon suddenly became trapped in a tax limbo. If Seagram's legally shipped the alcohol to the United States or back to Canada, they would have to pay taxes on it. (Since the liquor was for export, Canadian tax authorities didn't require the company to pay taxes on it originally, when it left the country.) So what did the Bronfmans, who were allegedly quite skilled in the art of wheeling and dealing, do? They and other bootleggers decided to try to sneak all their booze back into Canada. The risks were high—the Canadian government was much stricter about liquor entering the country than leaving it. But the reward was also high—if they were successful, the bottles could be sold for full price and they wouldn't have to pay any taxes on them.

Unfortunately, the plan didn't quite pan out.

The Canadian government arrested the four Bronfman brothers and more than fifty others, then slapped the family with a $5 million tax bill. The siblings had to put up $400,000 in bail just to get out of jail. "Smuggling liquor INTO Canada? You thought it worked the other way, didn't you? Well, repeal in the United States upset a lot of apple carts in the liquor-running business," reported a wire service story in January 1935 that ran in papers across the US. "Of course this was just as illegal as 'running' it into the United States, and a lot more dangerous, as it turned out."

Although the Canadian government knew about the Saint-Pierre and Miquelon scheme during Prohibition, they didn't shut it down. The jobs and revenue it generated during the Great Depression were much needed, which likely led the government to look the other way. But bootlegging alcohol *into* Canada was a much different story, as it threatened to take money out of government coffers. Incredibly (but not surprisingly) the Bronfmans were able to beat the bootlegging rap, with some newspapers at the time chalking it up to the convenient disappearance of company records. In June 1935, Canadian Judge Jules Desmarais ruled that the government failed to make its case.

The Bronfmans weren't as lucky with the American federal government. Henry Morgenthau Jr., secretary of the US Treasury at the time, pursued Seagram's in an attempt to get the company to pay taxes on all of the booze it illegally exported to the United States. In 1936, the Bronfmans ultimately paid a fine of $1.5 million, but didn't have to admit any wrongdoing. It was an enormous sum of money at the time, and spoke to the volume of alcohol they produced and sold to buyers in the US.

The family's activities and arrest earned them an illicit reputation, which continues to this day. (They have tried to change the public's perception of their family through extensive philanthropy.) Beginning in the late 1920s, Harry Bronfman was even referred to in Canadian newspapers and political debates as "king bootlegger." Modern writers and social critics have pointed out that while the family most definitely broke the law and made plenty of money doing so, they were scapegoated by Canadian media and society because they were Jewish immigrants. Bootlegging, after all, was widespread and they were hardly the only ones who engaged in it.

♦ HARRY HATCH MAKES GOOD

On the other hand was Harry Hatch, who also made plenty of money during Prohibition selling whisky destined for the US, but somehow avoided association with this unsavory activity.

Thanks to Prohibition in the US, Harry Hatch was able to buy up several distilleries and form the powerful Hiram Walker-Gooderham & Worts Ltd.

Entrepreneur Harry Hatch began building his distilling empire by buying Toronto's venerable Gooderham and Worts in 1923.

Hatch started out with a single liquor store in Whitby, Ontario, that he bought in 1911 for $2,500, and thanks to his bootlegging activities during America's Prohibition ultimately acquired a number of major distilleries to form the Hiram Walker-Gooderham & Worts Ltd. conglomerate. His first major success was the Corby distillery, which he bought a stake in, and with his help went from producing a reported 500 gallons (1,890 liters) a month to pumping out 50,000 gallons (1,890 hectoliters) a month. Most of that increase in production and sales was of whisky destined for drinkers across the border, which, thanks to US distilleries being shut down for World War I and then Prohibition, were desperate for liquor. Since he was a part owner he benefitted directly from this increase in sales. He took his share of the profits and then bought Toronto's historic Gooderham & Worts Ltd. distillery in 1923 for $1.5 million. While the company had been around for nearly a century and played an incredibly important role in Canada's distilling history, at that point the Gooderham family was ready to get out of the business.

Under Hatch's direction Gooderham & Worts Ltd. distillery reportedly sold nearly 100,000 cases of whisky to bootleggers in 1926 alone. It was certainly no coincidence that he paid $14 million for the huge Hiram Walker distillery in Windsor, Ontario, that same year. According to Hiram Walker's *Outline of the Distilled Spirits Business* published in 1946: "Five million dollars was for tangible assets including whiskey in storage. The $9,000,000 was for the good will attached to the trademark 'Canadian Club.'" The potential to make a fortune during Prohibition surely figured into that sky-high valuation for the company. Hatch used some of his ill-gotten gains from his Gooderham & Worts Ltd. and Corby distilleries to buy the massive Hiram Walker. By owning major Canadian distilleries and a number of popular brands, Hatch had vast power in the Canadian whisky business, and played an outsized role in supplying the United States with bootlegged whisky.

Yet when he died in 1946, his obituary in the *New York Times* didn't mention him benefitting from Prohibition at all. It credits his financial success to a seemingly masterful business acumen and a magical ability to grow sales astronomically. In fact, Prohibition isn't mentioned once. His obit in Ontario's *Windsor Daily Star* goes even further, characterizing him as a heroic Horatio Alger–like character. "Starting modestly as a liquor retailer, he rose rapidly to a ranking as one of the world's leading distillers and along the way became one of Canada's most successful breeders of racehorses."

♦ LIFE AFTER REPEAL

After the repeal of Prohibition, Canadian whisky distillers had a pair of huge advantages over their American competitors—they had plenty of delicious whisky to sell and large cash reserves from their Prohibition profits. This allowed them to expand exponentially across North America and exert tremendous influence on how whiskey was made in the United States. It was sweet revenge: Just a few decades before, these same Canadian distillers were at the mercy of the American federal government over what could be labeled whisky. At the time, Canadian distillers had to fight simply to get their brands back on US store shelves.

Now these Canadian companies were running some of the largest distilleries in the United States, and were getting Americans to drink what they termed a lighter version of straight bourbon or straight rye—essentially making the signature spirits of the United States taste more like Canadian whisky. And it was the perfect moment to make a power move. Thanks to Prohibition, many Americans had no idea what real bourbon or rye should taste like—they were just happy for unadulterated whiskey. In terms of market dominance by Canadian distillers, the US federal government would normally have monopolistic concerns, but

Canadian distillers were ready for the Repeal of America's Prohibition in 1933 and had warehouses full of mature whisky ready to bottle.

it was preoccupied with ending the Depression and the potential for another world war on the horizon. The great Canadian expansion into the American whiskey market was less about who was building these new mammoth distilleries around the country or the style of the whiskey being produced, but how many jobs they were producing and the positive economic news they represented.

But the scale and pace of the expansion was nonetheless staggering. In 1938, Seagram's had two distilleries. By 1939, it had five in the United States and Canada that were pumping out all kinds of liquor. In that one year, the company went from the ability to age 321,000 barrels to being able to age 1.65 million barrels. Its stock of spirits grew similarly, from nearly 17 million gallons (643,500 hectoliters) to nearly 83 million gallons (3.14 million hectoliters), with a staff that swelled from 529 employees to 4,009. By comparison, American bourbon and rye producers were struggling to scrape together enough money to rebuild and put anything drinkable on store shelves. (Seagram's continued to lead the industry until the year 2000, when the family sold its company for roughly $30 billion to Vivendi, which then sold off the liquor brands and distilleries to a range of spirits rivals.)

These Canadian distillers didn't limit their influence to just North America. They went after spirits and producers around the globe. Hiram Walker went on a tear in Scotland, buying up Ballantine's stock of whisky and then single malt distilleries Glenburgie in Forres and Miltonduff in Elgin. In the fall of 1938, Hiram Walker opened "the largest distillery in Europe" in Dumbarton, Scotland, which according to the company's *Outline of the Distilled Spirits Business* was constructed to make grain whisky for its Scotch blends. The following year it opened the Lowland Inverleven single malt distillery. At the end of 1943, the company acquired the tremendous Mattaldi-Simon grain distillery in Buenos Aires, Argentina.

♦ EVERYONE WANTS BLENDS

Just as in the United States, Canadian distillers switched over on November 1, 1942, to making war goods to support the Allies. But right after World War II ended, the Canadian whisky industry continued its meteoric rise and helped to popularize alcoholic beverages that were easy to drink. What certainly helped was that the United States limited and then paused whiskey distilling in order to provide grains to hungry people around the world. Canadian distillers, on the other hand, were working overtime stocking their warehouses. In the 1950s, blended whiskey, whether made in Scotland, the United States, or Canada, was the dominant seller. During the same time, the proof of straight whiskies was coming down from a potent 100 proof (50 percent alcohol by volume) to a more manageable (and profitable) 86 proof (43 percent alcohol by volume). For the most part classic cocktails were out, and the "smoothness" of whiskey was a prized characteristic—one

After Prohibition, Canadian brands became famous for their easy drinking blended whisky.

that was historically synonymous with Canadian whiskies.

Because supplies of whiskey had been limited or nonexistent going back to World War I, it wasn't hard to redefine what it should actually taste like. It's also understandable why people would choose something designed to be quaffable and easy to mix with ginger ale or club soda. (Just pour some peaty Islay single malt for someone who has never had whisky before, and you'll quickly understand why a blend is a much easier sell.) Finally, when you factor in the post-Prohibition marketing muscle of Seagram's and Hiram Walker, it's no surprise that Canadian whisky became a staple around the world. (The big Canadian whisky companies also had American-made straight bourbons and ryes in their portfolios, should tastes change and the market for spirits with more flavor grow.)

But all whiskey blends are not equal, nor are they made in the same way. In Scotland, blenders combine a selection of single malts with aged grain whisky. In the United States, blenders generally combine straight bourbon or rye with a much cheaper, unaged neutral grain spirit, which can be made from any grain. In Canada, blenders combine flavorful wheat, rye, single malt, or bourbonlike whisky with a base of aged corn, wheat, or rye whisky that intentionally doesn't have

From 1960 to 1980 sales of Canadian whisky in the US grew by a meteoric 345 percent.

much flavor. These particular Canadian combinations create a smooth whisky with what was historically known as a "lighter" flavor, which distillers around the world tried to emulate. The secret to Canada's success was the mellow base whisky, which was combined with bigger and bolder flavoring whiskies. It was more or less the formula Canadian Club used at the turn of the century to become an international sensation.

The Canadian practice of using corn or wheat whisky in their blends is definitely an improvement over the preference for a base of neutral grain spirit in the US. But keep in mind that Canada doesn't require distillers to use new or charred barrels, just barrels that are 700 liters (185 gallons) or less. And the more times a barrel has been used, the less flavor and color it gives a spirit as it ages. So while Canadian whisky, by law, must be aged for at least three years, it might not pick up much flavor if it's been aged in a heavily used cask. Of course, a number of premium Canadian brands age their whisky in new charred oak barrels or, like many single malt Scotch brands, in used bourbon barrels, which give a spirit a lot of rich flavors.

Blends also made business sense. By combining straight flavoring whiskies with a base of either aged grain whisky or corn whisky, you lower production costs and increase supply. A new, heartier strain of corn, one that could withstand the country's cold temperatures, was also propagated in the 1950s. And because corn was cheaper than wheat or rye, the former soon replaced the latter as the grain Canadian distillers preferred for their base blending whisky.

From 1960 to 1980, sales of Canadian whisky in the US, by far its biggest market, grew by an astronomical 345 percent! In the 1970s, as Scotch and American whiskey sales began to falter, Canadian whisky continued to be popular. By the early 1980s, sales of Canadian whisky in the United States first surpassed those of Scotch and then beat the combined tally for bourbon and American rye. Canadian whisky hit its zenith in 1985, selling more than 23 million nine-liter cases.

Over the next couple of decades, sales began to taper off. Surprisingly, Canadian whisky never completely crashed like American whiskey and Scotch did. For many years, even at the height of the vodka boom, you could still count on just about any bar having at least one bottle of Canadian whisky on the shelf.

In the 1950s, blended Canadian whisky was a favorite of the man in the grey flannel suit and was featured prominently on the hit TV show Mad Men.

Canada Stays the Course

Following decades of dominance, and then quiet persistence, by the late 1990s Canadian whisky frequently ended up as the punchline of a bad bar joke.

Brands like Canadian Club and Crown Royal are perennial bestsellers, but their success came from being relatively easy to drink and blending perfectly with cola and other mixers. Those qualities suddenly became liabilities compared to the bold and brash Scottish single malts, bourbon, and rye that became prized near the beginning of this century.

Like Scottish blends, Canadian whisky appeared to lose relevance to the modern drinker. The whisky may have defined the *Mad Men* era, but by the twenty-first century it felt thoroughly outdated. The Canadian whisky industry needed a makeover and a new product to sell—the answer to their prayers was, fortunately, already aging in their warehouses.

For many years, as the American rye industry crumbled and faded out of sight, many bars substituted Canadian Club or Crown Royal in a classic rye Manhattan. It sort of made sense, given that Canadian whisky distillers used rye in their whiskies, and Canada is also a major producer of the grain.

All of the whisky made at Hiram Walker's Windsor, Ontario distillery is fermented in one of its thirty-nine giant tanks.

(To be fair, most bourbon distillers also use rye to make their whiskey, though it would make zero sense to use bourbon in a supposed rye Manhattan.)

When tastes began to migrate from blends back toward straight whiskey, Canadian distillers had one major advantage over their American counterparts—they distill and age each grain separately and then combine the different, fully matured whiskies to create a blend. This makes for a ton of needless work—just keeping track of all of the different grain whiskies is a major commitment. You have to wonder why they don't just grind up all the grains at the same time and distill them together. But, as a result of this unique production process, Canadian distillers were sitting on barrels and barrels of straight rye whisky when the sales of their blends began to tank in the mid-1980s. And while all that straight rye was originally destined to be mixed with other types of whisky, a number of clever Americans saw the potential for bottling it on its own.

Two iconic entrepreneurs (now sadly not with us) had the same idea around the same time. Around 2010, Rob Cooper, creator of the ubiquitous elderflower liqueur St-Germain, and Dave Pickerell, former head distiller at Maker's Mark, who later set up countless craft distilleries around the United States, both found their way to Suntory Global Spirits' Alberta Distillers Limited in Calgary. Each wanted to buy casks of straight Canadian rye and bottle it for the US market, which was once again beginning to develop a taste for it.

Spirits entrepreneur Rob Cooper's first hit was St-Germain Elderflower Liqueur. His next venture was selling straight Canadian rye whiskey.

Rye had almost completely disappeared from the United States, despite being arguably the country's native spirit. Before discovering the mother lode in Canada, Cooper and Pickerell tried in vain to find an American source of aged rye whiskey. But no US distillers at the time were making rye in great quantities. The few distilleries that produced the flavorful whiskey made it just one day a year.

Cooper used the barrels he purchased from Alberta to form his new brand Lock Stock & Barrel; Pickerell used his whisky as the base for a number of the craft whiskey projects he was working on, including Hillrock and WhistlePig. There was

Dr. Don Livermore is the master blender at the Hiram Walker distillery and has worked incredibly hard to push Canadian whisky in new directions.

just one problem: No one understood that Canada made some of the finest straight rye whisky in the world. This was a time when it wasn't unusual to overhear bartenders cruelly and unfairly disparaging Canadian whisky as brown-colored vodka.

So, Cooper and Pickerell did what they thought best: They didn't go out of their way to mention the fact that their whisky hailed from Canada. The strategy worked. By the time word got out that their whiskies originated across the border, they were already in demand and widely praised.

Cooper's and Pickerell's success benefitted the Canadian whisky industry overall. Some Canadian distilleries introduced their own straight rye whiskies. Corby, the behemoth producer once owned by Hiram Walker in Windsor, Ontario, is now part of spirits conglomerate Pernod Ricard, and produces the majority of Canadian whisky. In 2012, it revived Lot No. 40, a 100 percent rye whisky made in a giant pot still.

Around the same time, Canada developed a craft spirits movement whose products quickly exploded in popularity. Canadian whisky expert Davin de Kergommeaux estimates that, in 2007, there were just two or three craft distilleries in the whole country. By 2022, there were 250. Canada's whisky industry, which had been essentially made up of eight giant distilleries, now includes a range of brands across its provinces.

The large distillers also began to look through their warehouses and pull out not just aged straight rye whisky, but also straight corn whisky. Canadian Club has released a number of acclaimed whiskies in its Chronicles series that are all corn based and at least forty years old.

All of these developments have helped to change the perception of Canadian whisky and boost sales in the United States and around the world. Canadian distillers have bottled a dizzying array of different types of whisky over the past decade—everything from straight rye to single malt to four grain whisky. Look out for this new generation of Canadian whiskies—they're a far cry from the blends of old.

Canadian Whisky Family Tree

BRANCH: CAMPARI

Gaspare Campari started his Milan-based liquor company back in the 1850s, building on the success of his eponymous bitter red aperitif. Fast forward nearly 170 years and his business, now known as Campari Group, has grown to include a large portfolio of all kinds of spirits, including one Canadian whisky, Forty Creek. Here is its story.

Forty Creek

Before there was a craft distilling movement in Canada there was Forty Creek, which opened back in 1972. While it's common to find craft distilleries across Canada's ten provinces and three territories now, at the time Forty Creek was founded the country's distilling industry was made up of eight giant facilities. Despite this intimidating atmosphere of behemoths, Otto Rieder was undeterred. And perhaps he was willing to challenge the status quo because distilling was in his blood—his grandfather made fruit-based eau-de-vie (unaged brandy) in Switzerland. With fruit brandy in mind, Rieder built his distillery in Grimsby, about 30 miles (48 kilometers) west of Niagara Falls, because it was close to farmers who could provide an excellent source of fruit.

The focus for the distillery—originally called the Rieder distillery—switched to whisky when John Hall bought the business in 1992 and renamed it Kittling Ridge Estate Wines and Spirits. Hall and the long-serving master blender Bill Ashburn, who was hired by Rieder in 1987 to produce wine and spirits, started to make some exciting and innovative whiskies. An encouraging sign that they were on the right track came via one of their earliest whisky releases, Pure Gold Whisky, which became an unexpected bestseller in Taiwan of all places.

But the real game changer for Forty Creek was its Barrel Select Whisky, which was introduced in 2000. It's a flavorful blend of rye, corn, and barley whiskies each separately distilled in copper pot stills.

Originally, Ashburn even seasoned the barrels the whisky aged in with his homemade sherry-style wine.

"I'm still a winemaker, but making whisky is thrilling," Hall told the *Toronto Star* in 2000. "From the creativity standpoint, it's a whole new canvas to paint on, but you have to be more patient to see the results. You can produce wine and get it to market within a couple of years. With whisky, you must wait six, eight, 12 years before you can sell your product."

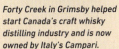

Forty Creek in Grimsby helped start Canada's craft whisky distilling industry and is now owned by Italy's Campari.

In 2013, Hall sold Kittling Ridge Estate Wines to rival Magnotta Winery. A year later, he turned around and sold Forty Creek Whisky and the distillery to Campari, reportedly for $167.2 million. The brand currently sells its Barrel Select bottling as well as almost ten other whiskies.

BRANCH: SUNTORY GLOBAL SPIRITS

When Japanese liquor conglomerate Suntory merged with Jim Beam in 2014, it acquired two incredibly significant Canadian whisky assets, Canadian Club and Alberta Distillers.

Read on for more about these two important brands.

Canadian Club is not only the country's first breakout star spirit, it was one of the world's first international bestsellers.

Canadian Club

Ironically, the quintessential Canadian whisky, Canadian Club, was actually created by an American, liquor legend Hiram Walker. Born in Massachusetts, Walker moved to Detroit in 1838 when he was twenty-two. At first he worked in the grocery business and then in a tannery, but Walker's life took a momentous and fortuitous turn in 1857 when he bought a flour mill across the river in Canada and then, a year later, a nearby distillery.

It was the perfect time to get into the whisky business. The US Civil War started just a few years later, leading to skyrocketing demand from US customers. Walker's liquor business expanded rapidly and suddenly, growing the once sparsely populated area around his facility. "For years before the town was incorporated Hiram Walker was a unique municipal figure, being practically the mayor, common council, board of public works, fire department, lighting and water works manager, etc.," recounted his obituary in the *Detroit Free Press* in 1899. It's little wonder that the part of Ontario where his facilities were located was officially named Walkerville.

The whisky made there was originally called Walker's Club or Club Whisky, but the brand was renamed in the 1880s, when it became Canadian Club. Hiram Walker's training manual from 1946 claims that the brand was forced to make this change because rival American distillers successfully lobbied the US government to require whiskey makers to include where their products were produced on the label, which they thought would limit the appeal of Walker's whisky. (Spoiler alert: Their ploy didn't work.)

In the 1880s, Walker's Club was also the first Canadian whisky to be bottled at the distillery, a huge and important innovation, since whisky in Canada (and in the US) at the time often contained all kinds of dangerous ingredients added by distillers, blenders, distributors, and bar owners. By 1894, Canadian Club was touting its purity, advertising in newspapers like the *New York Times* that it was perfect for "medicinal use." This was no small claim because doctors often instructed their patients to take whisky as a cure for myriad medical conditions.

By the 1890s, before Walker passed away, he was running a huge distillery with a reported 3,000,000 gallons (113,600 hectoliters) of whisky aging in his warehouses. After his death the Walker family ran the business until December 1926, when it was sold to enterprising liquor salesman Harry Hatch for $15 million. (Hatch had already bought the large Gooderham & Worts Ltd. distillery a few years before.) Canadian Club would become a Prohibition-era staple in speakeasies around the US, smuggled across America's porous borders, even sometimes being driven over the frozen Detroit River. After repeal, Canadian Club grew to become an even bigger seller. By 1940, it was exported to nearly a hundred countries around the world.

While the whiskey industry as a whole collapsed during the second half of the twentieth century, Canadian Club was still widely available and continued to be one of the biggest liquor brands. It was often enjoyed with cola (CC & Coke) or with other mixers. In 2004, the brand announced an incredible milestone: It had sold its 300 millionth nine-liter case of whisky. Following a number of mergers and acquisitions, Canadian Club is now in the Suntory Global portfolio. And while most of its line is still produced at the giant Hiram Walker distillery in Ontario, the facility is now owned by rival liquor company Pernod Ricard. According to the *Spirits Business*, Canadian Club sold 6.5 million nine-liter cases in 2022, making it the fifth bestselling whiskey in the world.

Canadian Club continues to be an easy-drinking blend of three types of

In the late 1800s, the Hiram Walker distillery had grown into a veritable municipality.

whisky: a 100 percent corn whisky made on a column still; a 100 percent rye whisky made on a column still; and a whisky made from a mash of rye, malted rye, and malted barley, which is distilled on a column still and then in a pot still. Each type of whisky is then aged either in a former bourbon barrel or in one that previously held Canadian whisky. (The exact proportions of each whisky in the blend is a trade secret.)

Currently, the brand has its standard Canadian Club 80-proof (40 percent alcohol by volume), 1858 Original Whisky, which has been aged for five years, the 80-proof Reserve 9 Year, and the 80-proof Classic 12 Year. To capitalize on the modern rye trend, Canadian Club introduced a whisky made from 100 percent rye in 2016, which is made at the Suntory Global distillery in Alberta. But keeping with Canadian Club traditions, the whisky is a blend of a 100 percent rye whisky made on a column still and a 100 percent rye whisky distilled on a column still and then in a pot still. The whiskies are each aged in new barrels, in used bourbon barrels, and in used Canadian barrels. So, this version of Canadian Club is a 100 percent rye whisky, but it's also a blend.

Alberta Distillers

Alberta Distillers is the most important Canadian whisky distiller you've probably never heard of.

The company was started in 1946 by industrialists Frank McMahon and Max Bell. The partners built their distillery in Alberta, whose farms would grow the grain they would turn into alcohol.

The distillery produced a range of different kinds of spirits, but when it was acquired by Beam in 2010 it was known for

Whisky drinkers have discovered the delicious Alberta Rye Whisky Dark Batch, which is made at North America's largest rye distillery.

its straight rye whisky. Canadian whisky is often erroneously called "rye" no matter what it's made from, but Alberta Distillers was actually making whisky exclusively from the grain. A lot of Alberta Distillers' business at that point was selling its rye and other whiskies in bulk quantities to other brands around the world.

Some barrels of the company's straight rye were bought by pioneering craft distiller Dave Pickerell, which he used in a number of projects, including Vermont's WhistlePig (see page 193). Spirits entrepreneur Rob Cooper was another customer of Alberta Distillers, using the distillery's whisky to start his Slow & Low and Lock Stock & Barrel brands.

What further helped the distillery capitalize on the sudden interest in rye was its Alberta Rye Whisky Dark Batch, which was introduced in 2014. Unexpectedly, the spirit isn't completely rye whisky but a blend made up of 91 percent rye whisky, 8 percent bourbon, and 1 percent sherry. "Don't make that face: the stuff is delicious in a Manhattan," wrote Lew Bryson in the *Daily Beast* in 2016, "where that little bit of sherry grabs the vermouth and runs wild." Dark Batch has drawn a lot of attention and helped the distillery develop a reputation with craft bartenders and connoisseurs.

Bulk sales are still a huge part of Alberta Distillers' business, but it's Alberta Premium Rye Whisky that has become a big hit. The whisky is made completely from Canadian rye grain and is aged for at least five years. In fact, Alberta Premium is the most popular rye whisky in the world—selling more than 340,000 nine-liter cases a year. You may be asking yourself why you don't know about it. Well, it only became available in the United States in 2022. (In 2021, the distillery released a small allotment of its more premium Cask Strength version of the whisky in the US for the first time, which was very well received.)

Alberta Distillers claims to be the largest producer of rye whisky in North America, with 450,000 barrels of the whisky currently aging in its warehouses.

🌾 BRANCH: PERNOD RICARD

In 2005, French liquor company Pernod Ricard teamed up with Beam to buy the assets of their rival, Allied Domecq. In that monster $14 billion deal, Pernod added the giant Hiram Walker distillery in Windsor, Ontario, to its portfolio, as well as a majority stake in Corby, which owns a number of acclaimed Canadian whisky brands. Overseeing the distillery and all of these whiskies is Hiram Walker's visionary master blender Dr. Don Livermore, who has a PhD in brewing and distilling from Heriot-Watt University in Edinburgh, Scotland.

Since becoming the distillery's master blender in 2012, Livermore has produced an array of innovative whiskies that have challenged the common misconception that Canadian whisky is supposed to be a bland and inoffensive spirit. Livermore has proven beyond a shadow of a doubt that Canadian whisky deserves to be taken seriously and appreciated.

Here are some of Pernod's most important Canadian whisky brands.

Lot No. 40 Canadian Rye Whisky

While it's hard to talk about Canadian whisky without focusing on rye, until recently the country bottled almost no straight rye whisky. But the success of Lot

Since it was reintroduced in 2012, Lot No. 40 Rye Whisky has developed a devoted following of bartenders and drinkers.

No. 40 changed all that. The whisky, produced at the Hiram Walker distillery in Windsor, Ontario, has a 100 percent rye mash and is distilled in a column still, and then once again in a large 8,000-liter cylindrical pot still. The spirit is aged in new oak barrels and as a result is full of spicy rye flavor. "It's almost like the single malt of Canadian whisky," said Hiram Walker's master blender, Don Livermore, in the *Globe and Mail* a few months after the rye was relaunched in 2012. Hiram Walker had first tried to sell Lot No. 40 in the late 1990s, but the timing was terrible because the rye whiskey industry was almost completely dead. But the second time around, however, Lot No. 40 quickly developed a following and has since won a slew of awards.

Also look out for the even bolder Lot No. 40 Dark Oak, which is very similar to the standard Lot No. 40, but is aged for a second time in heavily charred casks and is bottled at a potent 96 proof (48 percent alcohol by volume).

J.P. Wiser's Canadian Whisky

Like his fellow Canadian whisky baron Hiram Walker, John Philip Wiser was actually American. Born in 1825, in Trenton, New York, Wiser moved to Prescott, Ontario, as an adult, where he managed the Egert and Averell distillery, co-owned by a relative (possibly his uncle). Wiser then bought the facility in 1862, which was a good time to be making whisky because the US Civil War had shut down many of that country's distilleries, creating a huge opportunity for Canadian distillers.

Wiser's name is now associated with whisky around the world, but during his lifetime he was more famous for being a

J.P. Wiser's produces a range of different Canadian whiskies at its Ontario distillery.

rancher. The two businesses were actually interconnected, since the leftovers from making whisky were used as animal feed. When Wiser passed away in 1911, a story in Ontario's *Owen Sound Sun Times* newspaper mentioned that the distillery's spent grain could sustain a thousand head of cattle—a statistic that demonstrated the huge amount of whisky Wiser was making at the time.

Today, J.P. Wiser's is made at the Hiram Walker distillery in Ontario. The heart of the brand's portfolio is the bestselling J.P. Wiser's Deluxe (a corn whisky aged in Canadian whisky barrels for at least four years) and J.P. Wiser's 10 Year (a blend of corn whisky and a large percentage of rye whisky, aged in three types of barrels: new barrels, used bourbon barrels, and used Canadian whisky barrels). The distillery also regularly releases a number of significantly older editions, including a 15-year-old (a blend of corn whisky, rye whisky, and a touch of sherry) and an 18-year-old corn whisky aged exclusively in used Canadian whisky barrels.

The modern Gooderham & Worts brand pays tribute to one of the founders of the Canadian whisky industry.

Gooderham & Worts Ltd.

William Gooderham, a self-made industrialist who emigrated from Britain in 1832, not only helped build the Canadian whisky industry, but Canada itself.

Gooderham was a foot solider in the British army before leaving the service to join his sister, Elizabeth, and brother-in-law, James Worts, in York, Canada (York would be renamed Toronto a few years later). Worts had built a wind-powered mill before Gooderham joined his business. But just two years later, disaster struck when Worts's wife, Elizabeth, died giving birth. According to Davin de Kergommeaux's *Canadian Whisky*, Worts was overcome with grief and drowned in the company's well a few weeks later.

Gooderham carried on the business himself and soon started distilling whisky. Over the next two decades, his nascent distillery evolved into an impressive limestone facility, which was equipped with a nearly four-story, steam-powered wooden still. He was the president of the Bank of Toronto as well as a co-owner of the Toronto & Nipissing Railway. Gooderham naturally used the train line to bring grain and other whiskey-making resources to Toronto. When Gooderham passed away in 1881 at the age of ninety, he left a vast fortune reportedly worth $10 million.

By the time US Prohibition arrived, however, the Gooderham & Worts Ltd. distillery had fallen on hard times. Industrious liquor salesman Harry Hatch then bought the facility in 1923, and its whisky was soon being smuggled across the border to the supposedly dry United States. Hatch was selling a reported 100,000 cases of whisky a year, and in 1926 was able to buy Gooderham & Worts Ltd. rival, Hiram Walker, in Ontario, for $15 million.

Today, the Gooderham & Worts Ltd. name is not as well known as some of its competitors, and its whisky isn't as widely available. But Pernod Ricard continues to keep it alive and you can currently buy Gooderham & Worts Four Grain Whisky, which is a blend of corn, wheat, barley, and rye whiskies.

Pike Creek Canadian Whisky

Just a short drive from the Hiram Walker distillery is Pike Creek, which is home to sixteen vast, unheated warehouses that currently house 1.6 million barrels. The name of the area is now used for this whisky brand, a blend of corn and rye whiskies aged for ten years in American oak barrels that previously held bourbon, and a second time in casks that previously held rum.

BRANCH: JOSE CUERVO

Over the past fifteen years, famous tequila producer Jose Cuervo has built up an impressive selection of whiskies, including Ireland's landmark Bushmills and Colorado's pioneering American single malt Stranahan's. In 2017, it added the Canadian whisky Pendleton to its portfolio.

Pendleton

Before there was a Pendleton Whisky, there was a rodeo. In the early 2000s, Hood River Distillers in Oregon came up with the idea to partner with the historic Pendleton Round-Up and use the event's name and bucking horse logo for a premium 10-year-old Canadian whisky brand. The whisky was introduced in 2003 with a suggested retail price of $26 a bottle, which made it a splurge. A percentage of the brand's sales went to the Pendleton Round-Up Association, which runs the rodeo. While you might assume that Hood River Distillers made this whisky, it was actually purchased from an undisclosed Canadian distiller.

Pendleton Whisky quickly became a big hit with the attendees of the rodeo as well as with other drinkers. In 2017, the brand sold 250,000 nine-liter cases and in December of that year it was bought by Jose Cuervo for $205 million.

Pike Creek is a blended Canadian whisky that is aged in used bourbon barrels and then aged in barrels that previously held rum.

Pendleton Whisky is named for the Pendleton Round-Up, which is a rodeo that takes place each fall in Oregon.

The brand now sells four main whiskies, which are all made in Canada and are still bottled by Hood River Distillers. Fresh spring water from Mount Hood is added to the whisky right before being bottled in order to bring the proof down to a specific alcohol level. You can choose from the 80-proof (40 percent alcohol by volume) Original, which doesn't have a stated age; the 90-proof (45 percent alcohol by volume) Midnight, which is a blend that includes whisky aged in a barrel that previously held American brandy; the 80-proof 1910, which is made completely from a rye mash and is aged twelve years; and the 80-proof Directors' Reserve, which is twenty years old and was aged exclusively in American oak barrels.

BRANCH: DIAGEO

When it comes to Scotch, no company can rival Diageo's breadth and depth of whiskies. But the international spirits giant has just one Canadian whisky—the biggest one, Crown Royal. Crown Royal was one of the key assets Diageo acquired when it bought half of Seagram's spirits and wine division in 2001.

Crown Royal

The late 1930s were incredibly stressful times for the British monarchy. King George VI was thrust onto the world's stage when his older brother abdicated the throne to marry American Wallis Simpson—not to mention there was a global depression afoot and a potentially devastating world war on the horizon. The new king and his wife, Queen Elizabeth, decided to go on a goodwill tour of Canada at the time, to see their loyal subjects and build support. They embarked on a monthlong journey that would take them from Quebec to Halifax. According to lore, during one of the royal couple's stops, Seagram's owner Samuel Bronfman presented them with special bottles of his blended Crown Whisky, each packed in a cloth bag. (A different version of this story has Seagram's providing cases of this special whisky for the royals' train journey.)

Decades later this story was the basis for creating the Crown Royal brand, and certainly inspired its regal packaging, which includes a crownlike stopper. At first, the whisky was only available in Canada in limited quantities, but in 1963 Seagram's decided to make it more widely available and introduced it to the United States. The release included a major newspaper advertising campaign across the US that touted Crown Royal as "perhaps the *rarest* whisky in the world." The price was also eye-catching, at $8.70 a fifth,

Crown Royal's distinctive bottle shape and purple cloth sack are famous around the world.

Famous Canadian whisky Crown Royal was originally created in honor of King George VI and Queen Elizabeth's visit to Canada in the late 1930s.

which was several dollars more than other Canadian whiskies at the time and in line with premium blended Scotch. Seagram's actually used this price difference as proof of the brand's quality in some of its ads that ran in the late 1960s. "First, Crown Royal costs you more than other whiskies. Second, it tastes better than other whiskies."

Because of its premium price, its rich flavor, or its distinctive deep purple cloth bag—or all three—Crown Royal became a bestseller. In fact, it's the biggest Canadian whisky brand today. According to the *Spirits Business*, it sold 9 million nine-liter cases in 2021, which made it the fifth most popular whiskey in the world.

A series of innovative releases has helped Crown Royal stay relevant and popular. The first one to really catch on was Crown Royal Maple, which hit the market in 2013. It was followed by a range of other flavors, including the incredibly popular Crown Royal Regal Apple. Another hit was its Crown Royal Northern Harvest Rye, which was introduced in 2015. While it was technically a blend, it was almost completely straight rye whisky, which accounted for its distinctive hit of spice.

To keep up with sales, Diageo announced in 2022 its plan for a new $245 million distillery and warehouse complex in St. Clair Township, Ontario, which, when it opens in 2025, will be carbon neutral and powered by renewable energy. It has the capacity to produce 66.3 million bottles of whisky per year. Currently, Crown Royal is produced at three other distilleries across Canada, including Diageo's giant facility in Gimli, Manitoba.

BRANCH: SAZERAC

A series of shrewd acquisitions by the Goldring family over the past century has transformed their family business, now called Sazerac, from a regional distributor into one of the United States' largest liquor companies, with a vast portfolio of brands. Sazerac's knack for buying undervalued brands from other companies and turning them into bestsellers is the secret to their success.

Starting in the mid-1990s, Sazerac began quietly buying whisky brands and production and bottling facilities from its Canadian rivals, including the Old Montreal distillery in Quebec. The hiring of master blender Drew Mayville in 2004 also helped. A Quebec native, Mayville had previously been the master blender at Crown Royal. With his experience and expertise Sazerac has been able to produce some interesting and acclaimed Canadian whiskies. See below for more on some of the most important Sazerac Canadian whisky brands.

Caribou Crossing Single Barrel Canadian Whisky

One of the crown jewels in Sazerac's whisky portfolio is Blanton's Single Barrel Bourbon, so it's not a huge surprise that the company introduced a single barrel Canadian whisky, Caribou Crossing, in 2010. However, Sazerac won't offer any details about how Caribou Crossing Whisky is made and whether it's a straight whisky or a blend of whiskies. All the brand will say is that it bottles one barrel at a time, which means there are significant deviations from barrel to barrel and bottle to bottle—no matter what kind of whisky it is.

Collingwood Canadian Whisky

In 2011, Brown-Forman rolled out triple distilled Collingwood Canadian Whisky, packaging it in a slick decanter-like bottle. What was inside the bottle was also unusual—a whisky aged in new oak barrels and then aged again in a giant tank with pieces of charred maplewood. While this method might sound cutting-edge, there's historical precedent for it. Some of Canada's earliest distillers filtered their whisky through charcoal, which is similar to the

Sazerac has helped make American whiskey a luxury product and is now trying to do that for Canadian Whisky with Caribou Crossing.

Lincoln County Process (see page 64) that Brown-Forman employs in the production of its international bestseller, Jack Daniel's Tennessee Whiskey. Collingwood is made at the Canadian Mist distillery in Collingwood, Ontario.

Despite the synergy between Jack Daniel's and Collingwood, Brown-Forman sold the Canadian whisky, along with Canadian Mist, to Sazerac in 2020 for an undisclosed amount.

Canadian Mist

Since the Canadian Mist distillery opened in 1967 it has been pumping out an ocean of modestly priced, triple-distilled Canadian whisky, which is perfect for mixing with cola. The brand has no aspirations to become a darling of bartenders and spirits connoisseurs. Currently, one of its taglines is, "When your party's too big for small-batch," which basically says it all. While it might not be fancy, Americans have bought a ton of Canadian Mist, making it the most popular Canadian whisky in the US for a number of years.

In 2020, Canadian Mist and its distillery were sold by its owner, Louisville, Kentucky-based Brown-Forman, to New Orleans, Louisiana–based Sazerac as part of a larger deal.

Fireball Cinnamon Whisky

Seemingly, it happened overnight: The sickly sweet and uncomfortably spicy Fireball Cinnamon Whisky became a sensation. However, the actual story of this flavored whisky is quite a bit longer and far more fascinating than you might suspect.

It all started back in May 1989, when Seagram's decided to sell off seventeen

For decades, the modestly priced Canadian Mist has been a staple of bars and liquor stores

different brands from its vast portfolio of spirits. It was a decidedly mixed bag that included everything from Eagle Rare Bourbon to Burnett's Gin and Nikolai Vodka. Heaven Hill and Sazerac teamed up to buy the lot of them at an undisclosed price, which they then split up between them.

As part of the deal Sazerac wound up with Dr. McGillicuddy's schnapps, which at the time came in one flavor, menthol mint. No one could have possibly foretold how significant the acquisition would be.

Over the next few years, Sazerac began to introduce new versions of the

Bestselling cinnamon whisky Fireball started out as a spin-off of Seagram's Dr. McGillicuddy's schnapps.

schnapps, including a vanilla-flavored one and a 66-proof (33 percent alcohol by volume) cinnamon one, which had a Canadian whisky base and a catchy name. After first testing the brand in Canada, in 2001 Sazerac launched Dr. McGillicuddy's Fireball in the United States. The name was soon shortened to just Fireball.

During its first few years in existence, Fireball's sales were relatively modest. But then Wild Turkey American Honey was relaunched in 2006 and became an instant bestseller, giving the nascent flavored whiskey category a huge boost. American Honey's success led to a range of other whiskey brands rolling out their own honey-flavored concoctions. Suddenly, store shelves were packed with whiskies flavored with everything from cherry to apple to peanut butter.

As a result, Fireball took off and has grown exponentially ever since. According to industry publication *Market Watch*, sales of Fireball in the United States alone totaled nearly 7 million nine-liter cases in 2021, accounting for almost half of all flavored whiskey sales in the US.

Seagram's VO Canadian Whisky

The nearly ubiquitous Seagram's VO was one of the most popular Canadian whiskies for decades. The brand was started in the 1910s, which might be why no one knows exactly what "VO" stands for. There are two theories: one that it simply means "very old," and another that it stands for "very own," since it may have been first blended exclusively for the brand's owners on the occasion of the wedding of Thomas Seagram.

Regardless of the name's origin, the brand became very popular in the United States after Prohibition, when it was a 6-year-old blended whisky. In the early 1940s, Seagram's even increased VO's age to seven years. But after World War II, it once again became a 6-year-old and rocketed to success as an easy-drinking whisky. By 1981, it was reportedly selling 3.5 million nine-liter cases a year, but the brand would stagnate in the same decade and then finally decline. In a blockbuster deal, Diageo acquired Seagram's VO when it bought half of Seagram's spirits portfolio in late 2000.

By the time Diageo sold Seagram's VO to Sazerac in 2018 as part of a $550 million, nineteen-brand deal, the whisky had lost quite a bit of its luster. Instead of being stocked on the top shelf at liquor stores, you can now usually find it at the bottom, with no stated age. Quite a fall from grace for one of the brands that helped establish Canadian whisky around the world.

Black Velvet

For decades, the easy-drinking value brand Black Velvet has been one of Canadian whisky's mainstays, albeit one that has been passed around a bit.

Over the past twenty-five years, Black Velvet has had quite a few owners. In 1999, Diageo sold it along with several other Canadian whiskies for $185.5 million to Canandaigua Brands. (Canandaigua Brands would later change its name to Constellation Brands.) Then in 2019, Black Velvet was flipped to the Kentucky-based Heaven Hill as part of a $266 million deal that included the brand's Alberta distillery.

While you can still easily find the Black Velvet Original 3 Year and the Black Velvet Reserve 8 Year, there are now also three flavored versions of the whisky: caramel, apple, and peach.

BRANCH: MARK ANTHONY GROUP

Hard seltzer has become a huge part of the spirits business. And there are few bigger players in hard seltzer than White Claw, which is part of the innovative Canadian spirits company Mark Anthony Group. (The company's first product was the sensation Mike's Hard Lemonade.) In 2018, it introduced the Canadian whisky Bearface—read on for its story.

Bearface Canadian Whisky

Given the Mark Anthony Group's track record of creating some of the most innovative and successful alcohol beverages of the twenty-first century, there were

While the Seagram's corporation is no longer around, its signature VO has continued to be produced and sold by Sazerac.

BRANCH: HEAVEN HILL

Heaven Hill is the largest independent, family-owned spirits producer in the United States. It started back in 1935, producing just bourbon, but through a series of shrewd and prescient acquisitions it has grown its portfolio to include a range of different kinds of spirits, including one Canadian whisky: Black Velvet.

The Mark Antony Group introduced Canadian Bearface Whisky in 2018.

great expectations when the company announced its new Canadian whisky brand, Bearface, in 2018. Its first release was the 7-year-old Triple Oak corn whisky, which is aged in used bourbon barrels and then finished in a French oak cask that formerly held red wine, and then in a new Hungarian oak cask.

Bearface's One Eleven Oaxaca Edition is even more innovative, combining Canadian whisky with Mexican mezcal. If you're wondering how that's possible, it's because Canadian distillers are allowed to add to their whisky up to 9.09 percent of a different spirit or an unaged wine (for more on the 9.09 rule, see page 373). Most brands add a bit of sherry, but this is the only Canadian whisky I know of that uses mezcal.

If you think the One Eleven Oaxaca Edition pushes boundaries, you should check out Bearface's limited-edition Wilderness Series, which is really out there. The whiskies have incorporated everything from matsutake mushrooms to seawater. I'd expect nothing less from the Mark Anthony Group.

BRANCH: INDEPENDENTS

While most Canadian whisky brands are owned by large international spirits conglomerates, since the 1990s a number of small independent craft distilleries have opened up across the country. Read on for more about a few of these upstarts.

Eau Claire Distillery

While a lot of brands talk about farm-to-glass distilling, few go as far as Eau Claire distillery in Alberta, which grows 20 acres (8 hectares) of barley and harvests it using draft horses and equipment that honestly belongs in a museum. The brand was started by former beer executive David Farran in 2013 and its distillery was built in the shadows of the Canadian Rockies, at 4,000 feet (1,200 meters) above sea level.

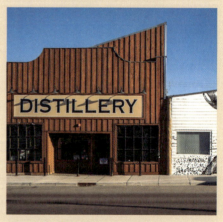

Alberta's Eau Claire has an impressive speakeasy-style bar and event space next to its distillery.

Eau Claire uses horses and antique farm equipment to harvest barley for one of its special whisky expressions.

Eau Claire now makes a number of different whiskies, including its signature single malt, which is made from its own barley and released in specially numbered batches as well as Stampede Canadian Rye Whisky and Rupert's Exceptional Canadian Whisky.

Found North

There is a long history of independent bottlers in Scotland, who buy casks from distillers and then bottle and release the whiskies under their own brands. A new company, called Found North and started by brothers Nick and Zach Taylor, is trying the same thing with Canadian whisky. They buy barrels from unnamed sources and combine them to create new blends. So far, the company has put out an interesting selection, including Batch 008, which combines an 18-year-old rye aged in a former madeira cask with a 19-year-old rye and four corn whiskies that were aged for between twenty-two and twenty-six years.

Glenora

While you can now get single malts made around the world, one of the first of these

Found North is one of the new craft whisky brands that have opened across Canada.

all-barley whiskies to be produced outside of Scotland and Ireland was Glen Breton, which is made at the Glenora distillery in Nova Scotia. The pioneering distillery was started in 1990 by Bruce Jardine, who sadly passed away before the first batch of his whisky was sold in 2000.

While the whisky was an immediate hit with Canadian drinkers who loved the novel concept of a local single malt, the distillery had to deal with the Scotch Whisky Association (SWA), which demanded that the single malt change its name in 2004. The SWA claimed that folks would see "Glen" and erroneously assume the whisky was from Scotland. (After a nine-year saga, the Canadian courts finally decided, drum roll, in favor of Glen Breton.) While certainly unpleasant, the court battle attracted a certain notoriety for the distillery, which helped it develop a loyal fan base.

Glenora now produces a range of different single malts—from a peated expression to one aged in a barrel that previously held ice wine.

Still Waters

When Barry Stein and Barry Bernstein opened their tiny Still Waters distillery north of Toronto in 2009, the odds that they would succeed were against them. The global craft distilling movement was just starting and the Canadian whisky industry was dominated by a few very large players, which weren't particularly interested in changing things up at the time. But not only have Stein and Bernstein been able to stay open by producing a range of spirits, they have successfully launched the standalone Stalk & Barrel brand, which now includes single malt, rye, and a blended whisky.

JAPANESE WHISKY

When I tell people what I do for a living, the first thing they usually want to talk about is the sought-after and pricey bourbon Pappy Van Winkle. The second topic is less predictable: They want to know about Japanese whisky.

Until 2009, Japan's spirits industry was fairly small, with most of its production consumed domestically. To many outsiders, Japanese whisky seemed like a novelty.

How times have changed. Over the past sixteen years, Japanese whisky has become one of the biggest success stories of the recent whiskey boom, with bottles coveted by bartenders, collectors, curious drinkers, celebrities, and status seekers. Prices of Japanese whisky have skyrocketed as a result. The selection of Japanese whisky available has also exploded in many export markets, including the US and the UK, making Japanese whisky a novelty no more.

But in the immortal words of hip-hop legend Biggie Smalls, "Mo money, mo problems." A scandal erupted in 2020 over Japan's lax whisky regulations, which allowed some brands to bottle whisky made outside of the country and call it Japanese whisky. The problem threatened to undermine the country's entire industry. Fortunately, that loophole has largely been closed.

Like many of the other foundational whisky cultures, Japan's comes with a compelling origin story. That story is also far tidier than others, involving essentially one Japanese distillery that not only launched the whole whisky culture in Japan but also enshrined its founders in the pantheon of whisky greats.

One of the most interesting features of Nikka's Yoichi distillery is its direct-fired stills.

Key Differences

Across a bit more than a century, Japanese whisky has evolved from a Scotch copycat to a dynamic and unique industry. For decades there were just a handful of distillers in Japan, each producing a number of different styles of whiskies using both column and pot stills as well as all kinds of barrels. In Japan, each whisky brand distills and ages every component of their blends, as opposed to Scotland, where rival companies buy and sell barrels of whisky to one another.

Up until recently, Japan had relatively few regulations that producers had to follow—essentially it just had to be bottled in the country. But as of March 31, 2024, members of the Japan Spirits & Liqueurs Makers Association, which is the governing body for the industry, must follow a tighter set of regulations. Essentially, all types of Japanese whisky must be produced and aged in the country. The base of the whisky now must include malted grains and the spirit has to mature for at least three years in a wooden barrel (new or used) that is smaller than 700 liters (185 gallons). The finished product must be at least 80 proof (40 alcohol by volume) and spirit caramel may be added to adjust the color of the whisky. (Keep in mind these regulations also only apply to members of the association.)

Japan has carved out a niche for itself in the international whisky market by adding local flavors, such as a sandalwood note from aging whisky in casks made from locally grown mizunara oak.

Total Consumption: In 2023, the United States imported more than $81 million worth of Japanese whisky.

Types of Japanese Whisky

Thanks to the country's historically lax regulations, Japanese distillers had the freedom to experiment widely with the way they produce and blend whisky. Keep in mind that until the early aughts, most of the whisky was consumed domestically, which allowed it to be tailored to local tastes. Like other big whisky-making countries, Japanese whiskies are divided into a handful of different categories. Here is a cheat sheet for each.

♦ JAPANESE MALT WHISKY

The first Japanese whisky was created based on the process at the Hazelburn distillery in Scotland. So it should come as no surprise that Japanese malt, like Scottish single malt, is made from malted barley, is produced at one distillery, and is generally distilled twice in a copper pot still. While these whiskies should now be completely produced and not just bottled in Japan—even the water should be locally sourced—the malted barley grain may still be obtained overseas. When it comes to aging, a distiller has lots of freedom to use different kinds of barrels. But no

DEFINING JAPANESE MALT WHISKY

- Malt whisky is required by the Japan Spirits & Liqueurs Makers Association's regulations to be produced, aged, and bottled in Japan.
- The mash (base grains) must contain malted grains and may also contain unmalted grains.
- The whisky must be aged for at least three years in Japan in a barrel no larger than 700 liters (185 gallons).
- The finished whisky has to be at least 80 proof (40 percent alcohol by volume).
- Spirit caramel coloring may be added.

Suntory opened its Yamazaki distillery outside of Kyoto more than a century ago, and it is still in use today.

DEFINING JAPANESE GRAIN WHISKY

- Grain whisky is required by the Japan Spirits & Liqueurs Makers Association's regulations to be produced, aged, and bottled in Japan.
- The mash (base grains) must contain malted barley and may also contain unmalted grains.
- The whisky must be aged for at least three years in Japan in a barrel no larger than 700 liters (185 gallons).
- The finished whisky has to be at least 80 proof (40 percent alcohol by volume).
- Spirit caramel coloring may be added.

matter what kind of cask is used, the whisky has to be at least three years old before it can be bottled.

♦ JAPANESE GRAIN WHISKY

Just like malt, Japanese grain whisky takes many of its cues from Scotland. Similar to its Scottish counterpart, this type of Japanese whisky includes some malted barley but is likely mostly made from corn, wheat, or rye, and is usually the product of a giant column still. Interestingly, some grain distilleries, such as Suntory's Chita facility in the Aichi Prefecture, make several kinds of grain whisky, each with different levels of flavor and intensity. This allows a blender many options instead of being limited to one universal grain whisky. Some brands also bottle a "single grain whisky," which is the product of one distillery. The name of this subcategory is very confusing, because *single* seems

Shinji Fukuyo is only the fifth person to hold the position of chief blender at Suntory.

to mean just one type of grain, but the whisky is in fact generally made from several types of grain.

♦ JAPANESE BLENDED WHISKY

Historically, the Japanese whisky industry was all about blends, since the industry was originally based upon Scotch blends—expressed as a combination of mature malts and/or grain whisky. While there is now significant competition from other styles, Japanese blends are still incredibly popular both domestically and abroad. But there are a few subcategories you should know about, including the "single blend," which is a combination of malt and grain whiskies produced by only one distillery. There is also "pure malt," which is a blend of 100 percent malts (no grain whisky) that are produced at a number of different distilleries.

DEFINING JAPANESE BLENDED WHISKY

- Blended whisky is required by the Japan Spirits & Liqueurs Makers Association's regulations to be produced, aged, and bottled in Japan.
- The whisky must be aged for at least three years in Japan in a barrel no larger than 700 liters (185 gallons).
- The finished whisky has to be at least 80 proof (40 percent alcohol by volume).
- Spirit caramel coloring may be added.

The History of Japanese Whisky

The history of whisky making in Japan is fairly short. In fact, of all the major whiskey-producing countries, Japan's backstory is the briefest—by far. That isn't to say that people in Japan haven't been producing or drinking alcohol for ages, it just wasn't typically whisky. Historically, fermented rice-based sake and distilled rice-based soju were the most popular alcoholic beverages across the country. It wasn't until about a century ago that Japanese whisky was born, thanks largely to two people: Masataka Taketsuru and Shinjiro Torii.

This story really begins with Taketsuru and his quest to learn how to make Scotch. His journey to do this would take him nearly 6,000 miles (9,700 kilometers) away from home and land him in one of the great centers of whisky making: Campbeltown, Scotland.

Born in Hiroshima at the end of the nineteenth century, Taketsuru was quite knowledgeable about making liquor from an early age—his family was involved in the sake business going back to 1733 and he'd studied it in high school. Taketsuru later worked for the Settsu Shuzo liquor company, which sent him to Scotland in 1918 to learn how the Scots made whisky, so that when he came home, he could set up a distillery. For the two years that he was in Scotland he was an eager student and took copious notes. An English translation of his diary from his time in Scotland was recently published, and is aptly titled: *On the Production Methods of Pot Still Whisky*. (One veteran of the Scottish whisky trade likened the experience of reading the book to glimpsing a rival spy's notes.)

Even though Taketsuru's plan to learn how to make Scotch faced several major challenges—including how he would get there right after the end of World War I, and the fact that the Scots likely wouldn't share their whisky secrets with a random visitor—he was undeterred. And while Taketsuru wasn't always welcomed with open arms and often faced overt racism, including that a number of hotels wouldn't rent him a room, he not only spent almost two weeks in

Nika's Yoichi distillery was built in Hokkaido in 1934 and includes traditional Scotch-style copper pot stills.

While many brands now make Japanese whisky, the industry was really created by two people: Shinjiro Torii (left) and Masataka Taketsuru (right).

Speyside at the Longmorn distillery but also made it to Campbeltown, where he worked for five months at the Hazelburn distillery.

Arguably, Taketsuru's most formative experience was at Hazelburn, where he found a mentor in Peter Innes, the distillery manager, who showed him how they produced their famous single malt. "What is intriguing and important is the way in which Taketsuru was transformed from the chemist who could, by using his specialist knowledge, make up to order any type of 'spirit,' to the man who regarded himself as above all a whisky distiller—and indeed as a whisky blender—as meticulous as the Scots," wrote Olive Checkland in her 1998 book, *Japanese Whisky, Scotch Blend*. In his notebooks, Taketsuru carefully recorded all the knowledge he picked up at Hazelburn and at other distilleries.

During the course of his time in Scotland, Taketsuru also met his future wife, Glaswegian Jessie Roberta Cowan, who was later known as Rita. "Masataka and Rita's marriage, initially without the approval of either family, lasted a lifetime," wrote acclaimed drinks writer Michael Jackson in London's newspaper the *Independent* in 2002. "So did his determination to make a Japanese whisky as good as Scotch. What had been a project became his life's mission."

When Taketsuru got back to Japan, despite his successful fact-finding mission to Scotland and his new passion for Scotch, his original employer, Settsu Shuzo, decided against building a whisky distillery. No doubt the onset of a global depression helped inform that decision. Taketsuru was instead hired in 1923 by Shinjiro Torii.

At the time Torii ran Kotobukiya Limited, which included a liquor shop, an importing business, and his line of Akadama Wine. His company would ultimately grow from those humble beginnings into the giant multinational liquor conglomerate Suntory Global Spirits. (In 1963, the name was changed from Kotobukiya Limited to Suntory.) Torii also wanted to build Japan's first whisky distillery and start a Scotch-like brand, according to a 1934 story in the *Japan Times*. He too had made a tour of Scottish distilleries, in the late nineteenth century.

Taketsuru was, of course, the perfect person for Torii to hire, and their partnership lasted for a decade, resulting in the building of the Yamazaki distillery in Kyoto, which was completed in 1924. To create their single malt they had propagated a strain of barley that was a favorite of Scotch makers, then floor malted the grain and smoked it with imported peat. The spirit was produced in copper pot stills and aged in casks that had been first seasoned with sherry. Hazelburn's distiller, Innes, even supposedly tasted and advised on the first spirits produced by Torii and Taketsuru.

It would be a huge understatement to say that Yamazaki's first

On Masataka Taketsuru's trip to Scotland, he learned about whisky and met his future wife, Jessie Roberta Cowan.

Suntory's first attempt at whisky flopped with Japanese drinkers.

whisky—Shirofuda (White Label), released in 1929—wasn't popular. The whisky was basically a flat-out failure. Taketsuru and Torii had made a smoky, peaty Scotch in Japan—and drinkers didn't like it. It's understandable that it was a hard sell, since the country didn't have much of a whisky drinking culture, and an Islay-like Scotch is definitely an acquired taste.

I imagine this first flop spurred the two fathers of Japanese whisky to part ways, which is what happened in 1933. Torii decided to change his company's whisky to make it easier to drink and ultimately introduced the quaffable Kakubin in 1937, which is still very popular today and available across Japan. The success of Kakubin, according to Brian Ashcraft, author of *Japanese Whisky*, was due to the fact that it was less peaty, lower proof, and lighter than Shirofuda. And I would argue that without the introduction of Kakubin there might not have been a Japanese whisky industry at all. (Over the years, Kakubin evolved into a blend of whiskies produced at Suntory's three distilleries: Yamazaki, Hakushu, and Chita.)

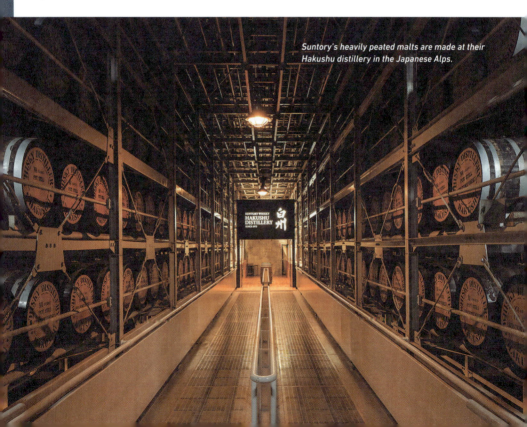

Suntory's heavily peated malts are made at their Hakushu distillery in the Japanese Alps.

A Unique Blending System

For many decades, Suntory and Nikka were essentially the entire Japanese whisky industry.

However, Japanese whisky was modeled on blended Scotch, which presented a major problem. Blended Scotch is a mix of grain whisky and single malts from across Scotland, each with vastly different flavor profiles. To replicate Scotch, Japanese distillers would need to make a range of different malts—some smoky and rich, some light and ethereal, others floral and fruity.

One obvious solution would have been for Suntory, Nikka, and their rivals to exchange barrels. The idea might sound ridiculous, but it's fairly standard for competitors in Scotland to buy and sell barrels with one another.

Because of the rivalry between Japan's two major whisky companies, that kind of cooperation wasn't a real possibility. So what could the distillers do? They certainly could have bottled their single malts as a distinct product, but there wasn't much of a market for that kind of whisky at the time—even for Scotch. If Japanese distillers were going to be successful and stay in business, they needed to make blends.

Suntory and Nikka did the only thing they could in lieu of cooperating: Each company built several distilleries across Japan, capable of producing a portfolio of different kinds of malts and grain whiskies. They did this by using several varieties of grains and stills to make the spirit, as well as a range of wooden barrels to age it in. To provide a sense of the scope, at its three Japanese distilleries, Suntory alone currently creates more than a hundred different whiskies for its blenders to use.

Historically, Japanese brands have made all the components of their whisky blends themselves instead of buying barrels from other distillers.

Taketsuru left to start his own whisky company, which was originally called Dai Nippon Kaju and would ultimately become known as Nikka. His Yoichi distillery, which he designed entirely, including the stills, was built in remote Hokkaido, which reminded him of Scotland. The first product from Taketsuru's new company, Nikka Kakubin (Square Bottle), came out in 1940. While the whisky's bottle looked vaguely like Suntory's similarly named Kakubin, the flavor of Nikka's whisky was in line with the smoky Shirofuda in terms of its flavor profile.

♦ THE BOOM YEARS

Just as World War II irrevocably transformed the American whiskey industry, it similarly altered the course of Japanese whisky. But perhaps not in the way most would expect: Without the war, Japanese whisky might not have ever been able to catch on and prosper.

For one thing, World War II led to a shortage of Japan's preferred alcoholic beverage, sake, which no doubt helped increase sales of its nascent whisky. One of the major buyers of said whisky was the Japanese military, which kept both Suntory and Nikka busy throughout the war. Their distilleries were

After World War II, Suntory whisky grew in popularity in Japan and in several other countries.

considered essential to the war effort, which allowed them to remain open to make both whisky and war goods. (Reportedly, in order to increase the amount of whisky available for soldiers to drink, the Japanese military administration ruling Java began using a distillery there in 1942 to make a whiskylike alcohol from potatoes.)

After the end of World War II, Japanese distillers got another boost from soldiers, only this time they were American. US troops stationed in Japan and around the Pacific became great customers of the Japanese whisky industry. At that point, American GIs were happy to get their hands on any whisky, as bourbon and rye from the US and Scotch were in short supply during and right after the war.

As Japan began to rebuild postwar, many Japanese industries sought growth by exporting goods around the world. In 1949, the first Japanese whisky exported since the mid-1930s was sent to Bangkok, Hong Kong, and Hawaii. These represented the first salvo of Japanese whisky to sell globally.

"Like toys, tankers and textiles, whisky with a 'Made in Japan' label is becoming popular abroad," said an AP story that ran in American newspapers during the summer of 1958. "In fact, Scotland's whisky makers are even complaining that Frenchmen are drinking more Japanese scotch than Scotch scotch."

Japanese distillers didn't have immediate success in the US. That was because, until 1962, Japanese whisky wasn't a recognizable category in the United States—only Scottish, Irish, and Canadian distillers were allowed to sell whiskey there. (The situation was the same in Canada, which also initially banned the importation of Japanese whisky.) It took three years before Suntory's application to change US rules was finally approved.

The company wasted no time in publicizing its whiskies. In the fall of 1962, Suntory began selling its 6-year-old Pure Malt Whisky in the San Francisco Bay area and in Philadelphia, Pennsylvania, to test the viability of the American market. This initial foray was likely successful, because the following year Suntory's president, Keizo Saji, son of the company's founder, Shinjiro Torii, was in Los Angeles promoting his family's whisky. The company also hired advertising agency Botsford, Constantine & Gardner to create the first Japanese whisky promotional campaign in the United States.

One of those first Suntory ads ran in 1963 in the *Los Angeles Times*. It was undeniably eye-catching, designed with a huge amount of white space and a simple but decorative border—quite a departure from the busy ad that ran next to it for a chain of hardware stores, overstuffed with prices, illustrations, and text in a carnival of fonts. Under a stylized image of a bottle of Old Suntory and a glass filled with whisky and ice, the copy said, in almost all lowercase letters: "perhaps you are ready for refreshingly superior taste in whisky. join those who are discovering the pleasure of pouring something quite unique. Suntory, the classic

Suntory Royal was a blended whisky aimed at Scotch drinkers.

whisky of Japan." Underneath the text, the ad gave a brief history of the brand, how the whisky was made, and the way to drink it. ("*Bon vivants* in the know can tell you this: Suntory is fine as whisky-and-splash, goes well in cocktails and tall mixes, and quietly proves itself in a glass neat.") While the ad made some comparisons to Canadian whisky and Scotch, it emphatically stated: "Suntory borrows nobody's colors—is a whisky all its own."

Not to be outdone, Nikka ran a full-page ad in the *New York Times* a few years later, featuring a sponsored interview with its founder, Masataka Taketsuru. It focused on the history and success of the brand—and claimed that Nikka sold 3.5 million cases of whisky in 1968.

Arguably, Nikka and Suntory had the most success changing Japan into a nation of whisky drinkers. But how did they do it? "The increase of Japan's whiskey-drinking population is chiefly attributed to the improvement in the economic status of the middle-class," wrote the *Japan Times* in November 1961. "Urban salaried-men and high-class factory workers are now often found stopping 'for a short one.'" In addition, the article cited several other supporting trends, including the recent popularity of home bars and the explosive growth of Suntory's chain of Torys Bars across Japan, which in 1954 numbered around thirty and in 1961 numbered around 20,000.

♦ SCOTCH, OR NOT-SCOTCH?

By the late 1960s, Japan had become a major whisky market for both domestic and imported brands. In the decade that followed, Japanese drinkers consumed more whisky than any other country in the world except the United States. Japanese distillers ultimately found success by creating their own signature style, which involved using domestic barley strains, barrels built from domestic oak, and seasoned with house-made sherry, rather than importing ingredients and just trying to copy what had been done in Scotland. What helped Suntory and Nikka differentiate their various brands of blended whiskies was that they both built additional distilleries in different parts of Japan. These new facilities produced a range of different styles of whiskies with a wide variety of flavors, which allowed both companies to create unique blends.

"When I first came here 32 years ago, we were trying to imitate Scotch whisky," explained Suntory's distillery plant manager Tadeo Onishi in the *New York Times* in 1969. "We did everything we could to capture the Scotch taste, even importing sherry barrels from Spain. We import peat from Scotland and some malt from Germany, Australia, Czechoslovakia, and other countries. We also import barrel staves from America. But this is a Japanese product. We use our own sherry to age the barrels and our own water from the mountains behind the plant. The taste is distinctively our own." In the summer of 1970, Suntory even erected a giant billboard above New York's Queens Midtown Tunnel, which proudly proclaimed that in Japan Suntory makes great whisky.

Distinguishing a unique identity for Japanese whisky and moving away from traditional Scotch production methods might now sound like an obvious step, but it took courage for distillers to create an unorthodox business plan, one that many other countries would later follow to establish their own whisky industries. In many ways, it was the success of Japanese whisky that legitimized the distilling aspirations of other countries, proving that the spirit doesn't need to be made (or taste like it's made) in Scotland, Kentucky, or Ontario.

By the end of the 1970s, Suntory offered thirteen different whiskies in Japan and sold a reported 10.8 million bottles of its blended Old Suntory Whisky globally, becoming the best-selling whisky in the world for a time.

What helped make Suntory and Nikka popular was that both companies employed celebrities to pitch their whiskies on Japanese television— Orson Welles and Alfred Hitchcock for Nikka, and Sammy Davis Jr. and Sean Connery for Suntory. (This history of using American stars to sell whisky in Japan provides the setup for the 2003 movie *Lost in Translation*, starring Bill Murray and Scarlett Johansson. In the film, Murray is in Japan to record a commercial whose famous tagline is

Bill Murray's character in Lost In Translation *is in Japan to record a TV commercial for Suntory. The plot was inspired by the history of Japanese liquor brands featuring celebrities in advertisements.*

Built outside of Kyoto in the 1920s, Suntory's Yamazaki Distillery has evolved into a modern facility.

"For relaxing times, make it Suntory time.")

Inspired by the success of Suntory and Nikka, several other companies built distilleries in Japan, including the Mt. Fuji distillery in 1973, which was a joint venture between beer maker Kirin, blended Scotch makers Chivas Brothers, and international spirits conglomerate Seagram's. Whisky was so popular in Japan at the time that even the consumption of sake had declined steeply.

Suntory was also courting international tourists around that time, offering distillery tours and even opening a whisky museum. In addition, the company ran large advertisements in American newspapers. During the 1977 holiday season, Suntory touted its Royal, which at the time cost $10 a bottle. According to the ad, "It is a fine blended whisky, made with barley malt, like most Scotch." In the same ad, the company also publicized its Suntory Signature, which cost $60 a bottle and bore the signature of the distillery's president, Keizo Saji—"Probably the most expensive whisky in the world."

It's interesting that the ad didn't mention anything about what made Japanese whisky special. If anything, it went out of its way to reinforce a connection to Scotch, with the unsubtle tagline "Slightly East of Scotch."

Another ad in the same series presents a bottle of Suntory Royal next to a bottle of Chivas Regal. In large block letters it details Suntory's production method: "Just the way the very best of Scotches are made." It ends with: "Although it is made the very same way, from the very same ingredients, it still retains a unique character all its own. Smoother, lighter and more distinctive. Suntory Royal may be close to Scotch,

but it's still about 10,000 miles apart."

The ad hammered home the idea that Japanese whisky was incredibly similar to Scotch. The concept of highlighting the brand's smoothness and lightness was nothing new—it had been used for years by whiskey distillers around the world, including by those pushing Scotch and Canadian blends.

Sadly, none of these ads really worked—by the 1980s, Americans weren't much interested in drinking whiskey, no matter where it came from.

♦ THE COLLAPSE OF JAPANESE WHISKY

While the whiskey industry in the United States and Scotland peaked—and then disastrously crashed—in the 1970s, it would be another ten years or so before Japanese distillers experienced the same fall, which was no less dramatic or painful. It didn't help that in 1984 the government raised the rate of taxes that liquor companies had to pay, which pushed retail prices up and drove drinkers to switch to lower-priced shōchū, which suddenly boomed. (Shōchū is usually made from rice, sweet potato, or barley, and is fermented with the mold koji and distilled.) As a result, Suntory saw sales of its then flagship Suntory Old blended Scotch fall from 10 million cases in 1983 to 6.5 million cases in 1984.

Adding insult to injury, the remaining Japanese whisky drinkers in the 1980s weren't going for domestic blends, but increasingly turning to Scotch, bourbon, and rye. Even in the home market, sales of Japanese whisky were a fraction of what they'd been just a few years before.

The Japanese whisky slowdown couldn't have come at a worse time. Several Japanese liquor brands in the late 1970s and early '80s had expanded their distilleries exponentially or built completely new facilities based on the erroneous belief that a big increase in demand was on its way. Just as in Scotland and the United States, a number of Japanese whisky distilleries were forced to shut down in response, leaving the industry on the verge of complete extinction.

"Many of the newer international converts to Japanese whisky will have no idea of how precarious the situation was for close to 25 years," wrote Dave Broom in his insightful and lavishly illustrated book *The Way of Whisky*. "They have only known it in the good times, when Japanese whisky began to appear in export markets."

One of the unintended consequences of the foreign whiskey boom in Japan is that it helped save American whiskey. As Americans couldn't get enough Screwdrivers, Greyhounds, and Cosmos—basically anything and everything made with vodka—American whiskey sales were drying up. But not in Japan, where demand for bourbon and rye kept many US brands in business.

The Japanese thirst for American whiskey got to the point where, in 1992, the historic Japanese liquor company Takara Shuzo bought the American bourbon brands Ancient Age and Blanton's. The company still owns both whiskies today, although the brands are produced and marketed by the American company Buffalo Trace. (Shuzo had some experience with foreign brands, having teamed up with another Japanese company called Okura to buy the large Scottish distillery Tomatin in 1984.) The giant Japanese brewer Kirin purchased legendary American whiskey brand Four Roses in 2000 and subsequently brought it back to prominence. As a result, Four Roses was once again sold in the United States as a straight bourbon and not as a low-priced blended whiskey, reversing a decision made by Seagram's, the brand's previous owner.

The Japanese demand for American whiskey would only become more crucial to the fortunes of US distillers in the 1980s and '90s, as domestic demand for bourbon and rye continued to fall. During this period, some brands, like historic Kentucky bourbon Early Times, were essentially only available in Japan. According to Brown-Forman's 1988 annual stock report for investors, Japanese drinkers were buying almost as much whiskey as drinkers in the United States, which is why the company was selling increasingly more of its brands in Japan.

I remember Julian Van Winkle telling me not to write about his then largely unheralded Pappy Van Winkle Rye Whiskey in the early 2000s, because he had created it for a Japanese client who bought most of it. While it was nominally available in the United States, the whiskey was really only available in Asia—Van Winkle was concerned that my readers at the time would be upset if they couldn't find it in American liquor stores.

The Modern Era

The Japanese whisky industry began in the 1920s during a particularly tough period, when the world teetered on the edge of a global economic depression and another world war loomed. What ultimately put the country's distillers on the map was largely easy-drinking blends. However, by the 1980s, the country's distillers would need whisky with more character to save them.

Japanese distillers were hoping for a transformation similar to what was already underway with Scotch drinkers, who were turning away from ubiquitous, quaffable blends and warming to more expensive and, ostensibly, more sophisticated single malts. In 1984, Suntory launched its single malt Yamazaki. A decade later, it added the peaty single malt Hakushu to its portfolio. These two whiskies brought the company full circle. They were, in many ways, similar to the company's first, failed attempt to sell whisky: Shirofuda. Arguably, this whisky flopped because it was too much like Scotch, with too much flavor. While those characteristics weren't right for the 1920s, they would soon be prized by drinkers and collectors in the first decades of the twenty-first century.

While the Japanese whisky industry had attempted to launch in foreign markets, including Brazil, the UK, and the US, the home market was historically its most important one. But in the

Since 2012, the selection of Japanese whiskies has exploded with new releases from both established and upstart brands.

1980s, when tastes changed and Japan fell into a decades-long economic depression, the industry was forced to look outside of Asia and court whisky drinkers in other parts of the world.

♦ FROM NOVELTY TO NECESSITY

When I started writing about spirits more than twenty-five years ago, Japanese whisky was literally hiding in plain sight, gathering dust on store shelves.

Yamazaki's launch in 1984 helped introduce Japanese whisky to modern bartenders and drinkers, but it was Hibiki 12 Year, which Suntory introduced in the United States in 2009, that changed everything. Its elegant, fluted cylindrical decanter—unique among other bottles—looked more like a large perfume atomizer than a whisky bottle, driving interest and therefore demand.

The whisky inside the bottle was equally impressive and unexpected. The blend called for more than twenty whiskies, including single malts from the Yamazaki distillery and from the Hakushu distillery. In some ways it tasted more like Cognac than whisky, with rich fruit notes (think apple and pear). The key to this flavor was the fact that one of the whiskies in the blend had been aged in a barrel previously used for the Japanese sour plum brandy umeshu. (Umeshu has an almost candylike combination of sweet and tart.) Interestingly, the Hibiki blend for the United States didn't include any whisky aged in the very rare and expensive mizunara oak barrels, which imparts a sandalwood note that is highly desirable in Japan (see The Mystique of Mizunara sidebar, page 442). Perhaps the company was unwilling to use any of the precious mizunara oak for a product that might not find a zealous audience? Or maybe it was a way to get rid of the umeshu cask whisky? Or an attempt to create a whisky for the American palate? Regardless of why the blend was created, Hibiki was an immediate hit with whisky writers, bartenders, and aficionados—all of whom began to rave about it.

The success of Hibiki 12 Year led the way for American whiskey lovers to discover Suntory's full range of offerings. It also created an opening for its rival Nikka, which, after being

American bartenders and whisky lovers fell in love with Hibiki 12 when it was released in the United States in 2009.

absent from the US market for many years, introduced its Single Malt Yoichi 15 Year and Taketsuru Pure Malt 12 Year in 2012. A number of other distilleries that were largely unknown in the United States at the time, including Mars Iwai and later Chichibu and Fuji, were also able to ride the new wave of popularity. A near obsession with Japanese bartending, bars, and barware among American craft bartenders helped further fuel the popularity of Japanese whisky.

In 2011, the Tales of the Cocktail conference named Kenta Goto the American bartender of the year. Goto had grown up in Japan and moved to the United States as an adult, where he became the head bartender of New York's famous bar Pegu Club. His elegant bartending style introduced many of his colleagues and customers to Japanese customs and traditions of hospitality, including the idea of omotenashi, which involves anticipating your guest's needs even before they do. Adding to the new obsession with all things Japanese in the bartending world, the famous Japanese mixologist Kazuo Uyeda's book, *Cocktail Techniques*, was translated and published in the United States for the first time in 2010. (Many of the best cocktail bars in the US still use Japanese or Japanese-inspired shakers, mixing glasses, jiggers, and spoons exclusively.)

Seemingly overnight, hipsters from New York to LA were drinking Japanese whisky. The spirit became a status symbol and a trendy alternative to the popular and much better

Thanks to talented bartenders like Kenta Goto, Japanese hospitality has influenced bar culture around the world.

known small batch bourbon or single malt Scotch. Then, in 2014, Suntory bought Jim Beam for $16 billion. The move not only combined two spirits powerhouses but, thanks to Beam's army of ambassadors and industry connections, the deal also opened many doors for Suntory's Japanese whisky portfolio.

All of these developments plus a limited supply came together to transform Japanese whisky from a curious oddity into the holy grail. Starting around the time of the merger, if you could find a liquor store that still had Japanese whisky in stock, the prices were shocking. A bottle of Yamazaki 18 Year was suddenly going for $1,000—ten times its suggested retail price. (Caution: These whiskies still cost that much and prices probably won't come down anytime soon!)

Suntory and Nikka, as well as a host of other brands, began introducing Japanese whiskies to the US market

Core Philosophies of Japanese Whisky Making

If you talk to a Japanese distiller or blender, they will at some point bring up the idea of monozukuri. While the term roughly translates to "making things," it has a much broader meaning in Japan—something akin to the western idea of craftsmanship. No matter what you're making or doing, you should do it with intention and with an almost obsessive goal of refining the process and improving your skill set. Whisky benefits from distillers having this core belief. In order to produce a consistent product, you need an exacting and disciplined approach.

On the other hand, you'll sometimes hear distillers and blenders talk about the idea of wabi-sabi, which is the appreciation of the imperfections in an object or product.

While at first these two principles might seem contradictory, I see monozukuri and wabi-sabi working in tandem. In fact, they perfectly encapsulate what it's like to make whisky. You can control many of the factors and elements of producing spirits, but there is part of the process that is still unpredictable and can generate unexpected yet delicious results. And no matter how perfect you make your whisky, once the bottle is open and its contents exposed to the air and to dilution in the glass by ice or water, its flavor, aroma, and color are going to change. So, try to be in the moment and appreciate the whisky in your glass and toast all the hard work that was required to make it.

Master distillers and blenders in Japan are guided by certain key philosophies, including monozukuri and wabi-sabi.

In 2020, it was revealed that some Japanese distilleries sourced their whiskey from overseas, prompting changes to Japanese industry standards.

with astounding speed, winning honor after honor at spirits competitions. Some of the bottlings were delicious, like Suntory's heavily peated malts from its Hakushu distillery, which was a revelation for folks who generally associated that assertive flavor profile exclusively with Scotland's Islay distilleries. After the immense popularity of single malt Scotch, US drinkers were finally primed for smoky and peaty Japanese whisky similar to what Taketsuru and Torii originally produced in the 1920s.

♦ THE FALL FROM GRACE

It seemed like nothing would stop Japanese whisky from joining the revered ranks of Scotch and bourbon—or perhaps even surpassing them—until the unthinkable happened in May 2020.

The world of Japanese whisky was embroiled in a giant scandal that threatened to undermine the legitimacy of the entire industry and its supposed devotion to craft and tradition.

It was an open secret that some Japanese distillers were sourcing whiskey by the tankerful from Scotland and North America. They would bottle it or blend it with their own whisky and, under Japan's incredibly loose liquor laws, label the resulting spirit Japanese whisky. Yes, simply bottling a Scotch or

Canadian whisky in Japan was enough to call it Japanese whisky. As you can imagine, there was a global outcry about this practice. Drinkers, bartenders, writers, and collectors felt duped and betrayed. Could their favorite Japanese whisky really just be rebottled Scotch?

To repair the industry's reputation, the Japan Spirits & Liqueurs Makers Association agreed to pass new standards in February 2021, which ensures that going forward Japanese whisky would actually be produced, aged, and bottled in Japan. Japanese companies would have three years to update their labels. Some brands chose immediately to clarify what they were bottling, which revealed a number of whiskies that included spirits produced overseas or otherwise didn't meet the new regulations.

Even before the scandal broke, the Japanese whisky industry's rapid growth and the lack of liquor laws had caused speculation from some spirits industry insiders that something like this was happening. For one, it was hard to rationalize how the country's distillers could suddenly increase their whisky production so quickly to satisfy this sudden meteoric rise in global demand in the 2010s.

But Japan's incorporation of foreign whiskey in its products is neither a new practice nor a trade secret. In fact, it was a core practice of the industry for many years to blend Japanese whisky with Scotch.

In 1977, Seagram's, a minority shareholder in the famous Scotch brand The Glenlivet, wanted to buy the rest of the company. So, in December of that year, it paid £47 million for the iconic distillery. One of the other major shareholders in The Glenlivet before this sale was the Japanese liquor giant Suntory, which owned 11 percent of the distillery. It turned out that Suntory not only handled sales of The Glenlivet in Japan but was also a big customer of the distillery, buying a lot of its bulk single malt. Suntory "has built its success so far on buying whisky from Scotland and mixing it with the Japanese product," wrote Nicholas Hills, at the time for Southam news services. He quoted an unnamed Scotch distiller who was worried about selling malt to the Japanese brands, thereby helping them improve their product. "In the year 2000, we

Throughout the 1970s, many Scottish distillers became increasingly dependent on Japanese brands for sales.

may look back and say what on earth did we think we were doing supplying the Japanese with our malt." While the unnamed distiller was off by about ten years, their prediction was prophetic.

Suntory's use of The Glenlivet was certainly well known. A piece by Christopher Wilkins in the *Times of London* even outlined where Suntory could buy whisky if, after Seagram's acquisition, it suddenly lost access to the distillery's single malt. "It already buys from other companies, including, it is understood, Tomatin and Hiram Walker which produces Ballantines," wrote Wilkins, who ended his story by hypothesizing that Suntory might just buy a Scottish distillery, so it could be assured of a consistent whisky supply.

This plan might sound a bit too obvious, but one of Suntory's rivals, Takara Shuzo, did just that in 1986, when it acquired the gigantic Tomatin distillery with another Japanese company, Okura. According to the history of Tomatin on the brand's website, it went from selling its single malt to Scottish blenders to supplying it to Japanese ones. Its biggest customer for two decades before the sale? Takara Shuzo. In 1989, Nikka bought the Ben Nevis distillery, and in 1994, Suntory bought Morrison Bowmore, which owned three historic Scottish single malt distilleries, Bowmore, Auchentoshan, and Glen Garioch. Suntory has also owned a large stake in The Macallan for decades.

Perhaps one reason why Seagram's was so interested in acquiring The Glenlivet was that it had entered into a partnership with the Japanese brewing

Suntory owns a stake in Scotland's iconic The Macallan brand.

giant Kirin and legendary blended Scotch producers Chivas Brothers to build the Mt. Fuji whisky distillery in Gotemba, Japan. The facility opened in 1974 and produced a traditional peated pot still whisky that was the heart of its two brands, Robert Brown and Dunbar.

"The company also buys a variety of Scottish single malt whiskies to add to that produced locally," reported Tracy Dahlby, in a 1977 *New York Times* article about the Gotemba distillery. For centuries, Scotch blenders have sought out The Glenlivet's single malts, and I imagine Seagram's may have wanted it for these two Japanese brands as well as for its bestseller, Chivas Regal, and other Scotch brands.

While Scotland would rather have sold Japanese customers bottles of its finished whisky, at the time Japan had very high duties. Selling bulk whisky was a way for the Scottish distillers to avoid these tariffs and maximize their profits. According to a 1968 newspaper advertisement from Scotch giant Distillers Company Limited (DCL), most of the Scotch exports to Japan were bulk whisky that was destined to be used "by the Japanese domestic industry to improve the flavour of some of their brands of Japanese whisky." A few years later, in 1973, DCL became one of the most vocal critics of selling bulk whisky to Japan: ". . . for we do not believe that this type of business is in the long term interest of the Scotch Whisky industry."

Nevertheless, throughout the 1970s, many Scottish distillers became increasingly dependent on Japanese brands for sales. (The large Japanese chain of Seikyo grocery stores announced in 1977 that it was rolling out three affordable whiskies made from Scottish single malts blended with domestic grain whisky.) Scottish bulk malt whisky exports to Japan, as reported in Reuters, grew from 3 million liters (790,000 gallons) in 1970 to 23 million liters (6.1 million gallons) in 1976. (And Japan wasn't alone in importing bulk Scotch—Portugal and other countries did the same.)

This meant that the 1980s crash of the Japanese whisky industry was also a major blow for Scotland. "Exports of Scotch to Japan—its third largest overseas market—fell by nearly one third last year, almost entirely due to the decline in demand for bulk Highland malt whisky to blend with local product," wrote Alan Hamilton in a piece aptly titled "Scotch on the Rocks?" that ran in the *Times of London* in February 1986. It also may have been why Scottish distillers suddenly turned their attention to the US market to sell this surplus of single malt as a distinct product.

So, why did Japanese distillers use imported whisky in their blends? It was an easy way to expand supply and also solved the problem of finding a range of flavorful ingredients for blends without having to buy barrels from a rival. And adding some of The Glenlivet's whisky certainly improved the taste of a blend.

Japanese Whisky's Second Act

In considering the future of Japanese whisky after this damage to its reputation, I'd argue that the industry got off fairly easy. For one, it's hard to say which brands actually used the legal but deceptive practices. It doesn't help that the companies were given three years to quietly fix the situation without having to admit to any wrongdoing.

Most commentators also wrote this off as a one-time episode caused by the sudden explosion in popularity of Japanese whisky around the world. As the narrative goes, Japanese whisky became too popular for its own good and the distillers just couldn't keep up with the orders flooding in. Fortunately for Japanese distillers, the historic use of bulk Scotch in Japanese blends hadn't been discussed or written about recently and wasn't widely known by modern journalists or experts.

However, this isn't the first time the Japanese whisky industry's practices have been called into question. In 1976, the US Fair Trade Commission (FTC) wanted the country's distillers to be more transparent about their production methods and to create standardized regulations and definitions. One major issue was that some Japanese whisky blends were a mix of single malts and alcohol made from potato, sweet potato, or molasses. Essentially, they were made more like low-quality American blended whiskey, which is a blend of unaged neutral grain spirit and straight whiskies, and less like blended Scotch or blended Canadian whisky, which are made completely from aged whiskies. It's not clear when or if the use of non-grain alcohol was discontinued.

So far, this modern scandal hasn't slowed the sale of Japanese whisky much or damaged its reputation as a luxury product. I haven't seen retail prices for acclaimed Japanese whiskies coming down, and many bottles are still treated as status symbols. In fact, many drinkers seem to have missed this whole controversy. While some brands had to discontinue whiskies or launch bottlings as "world blends," thanks to a growing fascination with whiskies made outside of the US, Scotland and Canada, I imagine sales of Japanese whisky will continue to increase and we'll see even more distilleries open around the country.

The Mystique of Mizunara Oak

Forget used bourbon barrels, port pipes, or sherry butts. The world's most sought after whiskey barrels are made of mizunara oak, which imparts sandalwood-like aromas to a whisky. Don't feel bad if you've never heard of this oak variety. It's rare and has only become widely known outside of Japan somewhat recently.

While American white oak (*Quercus alba*) is generally the standard for making barrels used by the whiskey industry—many brands are desperate to get their hands on mizunara casks.

These Japanese oak trees (*Quercus crispula*) grow incredibly slowly, with trunks that take beautiful twists and turns. So while these trees may be aesthetically pleasing, they certainly wouldn't be a cooper's first choice for making barrels.

In fact, brands started using mizunara oak because after World War II, importing American oak or European sherry-seasoned casks was too expensive and difficult. (As far back as 1939, Japanese distillers were reportedly having a hard time getting sherry-seasoned barrels.) According to Suntory lore, at first their mizunara casks were disappointing, expensive to produce, and not exactly watertight. In the 1950s, the brand was once again able to get foreign casks and the mizunara casks were left to age in the warehouse. But just as the tree takes a long time to grow, it takes decades for mizunara barrels to impart their unique flavor to a whisky.

In the 1980s, it must have been quite a shock to taste the fully matured whiskies aged in mizunara oak. This whisky convinced Suntory to continue to make and use mizunara oak barrels, even though they no longer had to. The company is the largest proponent of aging whisky in Japanese oak, but, according to Brian Ashcroft's fascinating book *Japanese Whisky*, Suntory is only able to source a supply of the wood that yields about 150 barrels a year.

I remember the first time I tried one of Suntory's mizunara offerings, the 18-year-old Yamazaki Mizunara Cask 2017 Edition. It had a suggested retail price of $1,000 a bottle. (In 2024, it was selling for about $10,000.) Before the tasting, I imagined it would taste similar to the brand's other whiskies aged in other types of barrels, or similar to Scotch or American whiskey. I couldn't have been more wrong. The sandalwood note is subtle but powerful. The whisky's profile was unique—unlike any other spirit I had ever tried before.

Until a few years ago, most of the whiskies aged in mizunara casks were sold in Asia. But since they've become available in the US and the UK, they've become a sensation. It's not often that whisky makers discover a tool to create a completely new flavor, so you can understand why brands from Angel's Envy Bourbon (US) to Dewar's (Scotland) to Glendalough (Ireland) have come out with special mizunara oak editions.

Japanese Whisky Family Tree

🌾 BRANCH: SUNTORY

It's hard to overemphasize the role that Suntory played in creating the Japanese whisky industry—it remains the biggest distiller of the spirit in Japan by far. But when the company's founder, Shinjiro Torii, decided to make whisky in the 1920s it was far from a sure thing. In fact, Torii's venture was a huge gamble. He was betting not only that Japanese people would want to drink whisky when it was by no means popular, but that drinkers outside of Japan would take his whisky seriously.

It helped that Torii knew a lot about the Japanese alcohol business—he ran a liquor store and also created the Akadama Port Wine brand. He also got a lucky break early on: In 1923, he was able to hire Masataka Taketsuru as his master distiller. Taketsuru had recently come back from Scotland, where he'd worked at several Scotch distilleries and studied chemistry.

Suntory started the Japanese whisky industry more than a century ago and continues to lead it today.

In order to increase the range of whiskies it makes, Suntory opened the Hakushu distillery in 1973.

When he got back home, the company that sent him, Settsu Shuzo, didn't have the finances to build a distillery. So Taketsuru began working for Torii and together they built the Yamazaki distillery in Kyoto, which opened in 1924. In 1929, Suntory (known as Kotobukiya until 1961) released its first whisky, Shirofuda (White Label). And it was a tremendous failure. It tasted too much like peaty Scotch, which wasn't popular in the country at the time. A few years later, Taketsuru left Torii's company to start his own distillery, which would ultimately become Nikka.

Undeterred, Torii continued, and in 1937 introduced the lighter, easy-drinking Kakubin (Square Bottle), which was much more successful than Suntory's first release and remains very popular today.

While Suntory was undeniably successful in growing the Japanese market for whisky, the company was less effective for quite a long time at getting drinkers in the United States and Europe to buy their spirits. Although it wasn't for a lack of trying—Suntory advertised via a giant neon billboard in New York City's Times Square in the 1990s. But it wasn't until the launch of Hibiki 12 Year, created exclusively for the American drinker and released in 2009, that Japanese whisky truly blew up in popularity.

Today, Suntory is led by Torii's grandson, Nobutada Saji, and produces whiskies at three facilities: single malt at its original Yamazaki distillery, which has been expanded multiple times; single malt at the Hakushu distillery located in the country's Southern Alps region since 1973; and Scotch-like grain whisky at the Chita distillery, which opened in 1972 in the Port of Nagoya. Collectively, the distilleries make more than one hundred different types of whisky—everything from heavily peated single malt to light and floral grain whisky. This diversity gives Suntory's legendary chief blender, Shinji Fukuyo, a wide spectrum of flavors to employ in his whisky blends.

Read on for more on some of Suntory's whiskies.

Kakubin

Suntory has been making Kakubin (KAH-coo-bin) for more than a century, and a river of the affordable blended whisky is drunk in Japan, where it's usually served in Highballs. More than 6 million nine-liter cases of Kakubin were sold in 2022, which made it the sixth bestselling whiskey in the world. It's a mix of whiskies produced at Suntory's three different distilleries, Yamazaki, Hakushu (HOCK-shoe), and Chita, which are located around Japan.

Yamazaki

At the heart of Suntory's historic Yamazaki distillery are its rows of copper pot stills.

The founder of Suntory, Shinjiro Torii, was succeeded by his son, Keizo Saji, who oversaw the release of many of the company's now signature whiskies, including the award-winning Yamazaki Single Malt. It is made from malted barley in copper stills at Suntory's original distillery, which opened back in 1923 and is located just outside the ancient city of Kyoto. The Yamazaki line currently includes a 12-year-old, an 18-year-old, a 25-year-old, and a Distiller's Reserve edition. Each of these malts includes whiskies that have been aged in a range of barrels, including expressions aged in American, Spanish, or Japanese Mizunara oak. Suntory has also released some incredibly old and wildly expensive limited-edition Yamazaki whiskies, including the Yamazaki 55 Year, which was distilled in 1960 and introduced in 2021 with a suggested retail price of $60,000.

Toki

One of the key elements in making any whisky is time, so it's fitting that this quaffable whisky is named Toki (TOE-key), the Japanese word for time. Primarily created for the American and Canadian markets, Toki was introduced in 2016. It's a blend of whiskies from all three of Suntory's distilleries, but the stars of the show are the single malt made at Hakushu and the grain whisky from Chita, which is quite flavorful and has a rich mouthfeel.

In 2016, Suntory introduced the quaffable Toki, which is designed to be used in cocktails.

Hakushu

While peaty and smoky single malt is now most associated with the Scottish island of Islay, Suntory also makes this style at its Hakushu (HOCK-shoe) distillery. The facility opened in 1973 and is located in Japan's Southern Alps, not too far from the Nagano prefecture. Whisky made at Hakushu has been used in a number of the brand's blends for decades but starting in 1989 Suntory has also bottled it as a single malt. The Hakushu line currently includes a 12-year-old, an 18-year-old, a 25-year-old, and a Distiller's Reserve edition.

Hibiki

While Shinjiro Torii started to make whisky in 1924, he'd already been in the liquor business importing sweet wine since 1899. To honor the ninetieth anniversary of Torii's start, his son, master blender Keizo Saji, introduced Hibiki (HE-be-key) in 1989. Saji came up with the original formula for this special whisky, which called for thirty single malts and grain whiskies, with the company's then chief blender, Koichi Inatomi. Its twenty-four-faceted decanter-like bottle is hard to miss and was famously featured in Sofia Coppola's 2003 movie *Lost in Translation*. (Subsequent Hibiki bottlings have had different blends of single malts and grain whiskies.)

In 2009, Suntory introduced Hibiki 12 Year, a special version of the whisky designed specifically for the US market. It was the first time Hibiki was available in the States, and it became a sensation with bartenders and whisky connoisseurs. The Hibiki line, which is all a blend of single malts and grain whiskies, currently includes the 86-proof (43 percent alcohol by volume) Japanese Harmony that doesn't have an age statement, as well as the older and rarer 21-year-old and a 30-year-old edition.

BRANCH: NIKKA

Masataka Taketsuru's mission in life was to make high-quality whisky in Japan that could compete with Scotch.

Taketsuru's quest began while he was working for the Japanese liquor company Settsu Shuzo. He was sent to Scotland in 1918 to learn as much as he could from the country's famous distillers. This was quite a challenge, given that he had no contacts in Scotland and essentially had to talk his way into distilleries. However, Taketsuru did have a background in making alcohol, since his family had been making sake for centuries in Hiroshima. Against all odds, Taketsuru was able to work at several

Nikka offers a large variety of whiskies in Japan, including its Clear Black Blended Whisky.

distilleries and found a mentor in Peter March Innes, the manager of the Hazelburn distillery in Campbeltown at the time. Taketsuru took copious notes from his time in Scotland, with the aim of going home and building a distillery. While he was learning about whisky, he also met Jessie Roberta Cowan (Rita). The couple decided to get married and headed back to Japan in 1920.

While Taketsuru's two-year trip was a huge success, when he returned to Japan Settsu Shuzo didn't have the means to build a distillery. But Taketsuru was soon hired by Shinjiro Torii, who was also very interested in making whisky in Japan. The two quickly set to work building the Yamazaki distillery outside of Kyoto, which opened in 1923 (Torii's business would ultimately become the international conglomerate Suntory).

Taketsuru worked for Torii for ten years before setting out to create his own whisky company, Dai Nippon Kaju, which would become known around the world as Nikka (KNEE-kah) Whisky in 1952. In 1934, he built the Yoichi distillery in Hokkaido to make single malt in traditional copper pot stills, which are heated by coal fires to this day. This design is based on what Taketsuru saw used in the Longmorn distillery in Speyside, Scotland, when he briefly worked there in 1919. "In fact, I chose my first location in Hokkaido because it looked so much like the Scotch Highlands—mountains, clean air, pure spring water, and a good supply of peat," Taketsuru told the New York Times for

Nikka'a founder, Masataka Taketsuru, built the Yoichi distillery in 1934 because the location reminded him of the Scottish Highlands.

an advertorial he ran in 1969 about his brand.

A couple of years later in 1954, Japanese beer company Asahi bought a significant stake in Nikka, though Taketsuru continued to run the company, and Nikka's popularity in Japan soon began to grow significantly. To help satisfy the brand's customers and increase the variety of whiskies it bottled, Taketsuru added the Miyagikyo distillery in 1969 in the Sendai area, which reminded him of the Scottish Lowlands. The facility was designed to be quite different from Yoichi and was originally used to make single malt—one difference is that the stills are heated with steam and are much larger than at Yoichi. As a result, the whisky produced here has a much lighter and more ethereal flavor and mouthfeel. Nearly thirty years later, continuous stills based on Aeneas Coffey's original designs from 1830 were added to the distillery in order to produce grain whisky from corn.

Taketsuru passed away in 1979, but his company continued on without him and weathered a number of challenges, including the crash of the whisky market in Japan in the 1980s. In 2000, Asahi bought the 42 percent of Nikka that it didn't already own in a stock swap.

During the second half of the twentieth century, Nikka tried to crack the US market without much success. Finally, in 2012, thanks to the explosion of interest in Japanese whiskies, it reintroduced several of its expressions, which were finally appreciated.

Here are some of Nikka's whisky brands to look out for.

Yoichi Single Malt Whisky

As you might have guessed from its name, the Yoichi (yo-CHI) Single Malt Whisky is made at Nikka's original distillery of the same name in Hokkaido. The barley is generally peated and the whisky is made in copper pot stills that are heated directly over a coal fire. Nikka bottles a range of Yoichi single malts and most of them have a peaty note.

Miyagikyo Single Malt Whisky

Just as Nikka releases a range of single malts from its Yoichi distillery, it also produces a range of single malts at its Miyagikyo (ME-ya-gi-KEY-yo) distillery, which is located near Sendai. If Yoichi is meant to be the company's equivalent of a Scottish Highlands distillery, then Miyagikyo is

The design for Nikka's Yoichi distillery was inspired by Scotland's Longmorn Distillery.

supposed to be the company's equivalent of a Scottish Lowlands distillery. Along this line of reasoning, Miyagikyo's whiskies tend to be on the more delicate side.

Coffey Grain & Coffey Malt Whiskies

In Scotland, grain whisky made on a continuous still is generally not bottled on its own, but combined with single malts to make blended Scotch. So, it's a unique opportunity to try Nikka's grain whisky made on a continuous still that is closely based on Aeneas Coffey's pioneering original 1830 design. The whisky has a base of mostly corn.

Nikka also uses these stills to make a whisky from malted barley. For a while, Nikka did blend single malt from its Scottish distillery, Ben Nevis, with Japanese single malt to make this Coffey Malt Whisky. The brand says those "experiments" are now over.

Both the Coffey grain and malt whiskies are aged in American oak casks that have been used several times before and don't contribute much to the finished whisky, which allows the flavor from the grain to shine.

Nikka Days Blended Whisky

Nikka Days is an easy-drinking 80-proof (40 percent alcohol by volume) blend of the brand's grain whisky and peaty single malts, which is designed to be used in Highballs and other cocktails. It was created for American drinkers and introduced in the summer of 2020.

The easy drinking Nikka Days is perfect for mixing with club soda.

Nikka Taketsuru Pure Malt Whisky

In 2020, Nikka celebrated its founder, Masataka Taketsuru, with this pure malt whisky, which, fittingly, is a blend of single malts produced at both the Yoichi and the Miyagikyo distilleries.

Nikka From the Barrel Blended Whisky

One of the most sought-after Nikka whiskies is the From the Barrel expression, which was originally produced in 1985 and calls for more than one hundred single malts and grain whiskies. The blend is then married (allowed to come together) for several months in a used barrel. Nikka releases the blend in distinctive squat, square bottles at a robust proof of 102.8 (51.4 percent alcohol by volume).

BRANCH: FUJI

In the shadow of Mount Fuji, three spirits giants—Kirin Brewery, Seagram's, and Chivas Brothers—decided to partner and build a state-of-the-art distillery in Gotemba, Japan, outfitted with several types of stills that could make a wide range of whisky styles.

While you might assume that this facility opened somewhat recently, it actually dates back to 1973. There was a boom in Japanese whisky at the time, which seemed poised to finally break through in a number of foreign markets. Unfortunately, the demand for whisky in Japan and in the rest of the world soon collapsed.

Fuji Whisky dates back to 1973 when it was started in Gotemba by a trio of major liquor companies.

Fast forward to the early 2000s when Seagram's portfolio of spirits were sold off. After the dust settled, the Gotemba distillery was co-owned by Kirin and Pernod Ricard, which had acquired Chivas Brothers and its stake in this Japanese venture. In spring 2003, Kirin bought out Pernod and continues to run the facility today. The Fuji Whisky produced at the distillery is now available in five markets (Japan, Australia, the US, Singapore, and France) and the brand has announced a goal of rapidly growing its sales tenfold.

You can find a number of different Fuji expressions in its current markets. The brand is arguably best known for its Fuji Single Grain, which combines three of its own grain whiskies. Fuji also produces a Single Blended Japanese Whisky. (In the US, this product is simply labeled Fuji Japanese Whisky.) The terms *single grain* and *single blended* are a bit confusing, but they just mean that all the whisky in each blend were produced at a single distillery, in this case Fuji's distillery.

 BRANCH: KANOSUKE

The recent interest in Japanese whisky has spurred the founding of a number of completely new craft brands. One of these is Kanosuke (can-NO-ski), which opened in 2018 and was built along a picturesque beach on Japan's southernmost main island of Kyushu. As a result of its location, similar to the distilleries on Scotland's western islands, Kanosuke's warehouses are exposed to the briny ocean air and the whiskies pick up subtle maritime notes.

At the heart of the distillery are three copper pot stills, which each have a unique shape. Kanosuke makes single malt from malted barley, and its different stills allow the brand to produce whiskies that taste different from one another other, which can later be blended together or bottled separately. Kanosuke also makes pot still whisky from a mash of malted and unmalted barley at the nearby Hioki (He-oh-key) Distillery.

Each year Kanosuke releases a new edition of its single malt. The first several have been aged in a range of different kinds of barrels, which run the gamut from casks that have previously held bourbon to those seasoned with shochu. Kanosuke has also produced a whisky from a mash of unmalted barley, which was called New Born.

Kanosuke, which is located on the island of Kyushu, is part of a new generation of craft Japanese brands.

BRANCH: MARS

While Kiichiro Iwai is often left out of the retelling of Japanese whisky history, he actually played an incredibly important role in the spirit's creation in Japan. When Iwai worked at the Settsu Shuzo liquor company, he was the one who sent Masataka Taketsuru to Scotland to learn everything he could about making whisky. By the time Taketsuru came back to Japan, the country was suffering under the global depression, forcing Settsu Shuzo to cancel its distillery project. Taketsuru then built the Yamazaki distillery for Suntory's founder, Shinjiro Torii, and later started his own whisky company, Nikka.

Decades later, Iwai finally got his whisky distillery. He partnered with the Hombo family, which had been making the distilled spirit shochu since 1909. Then in 1960 they decided to make whisky—later known as Mars—at their facility in Yamanashi, which is about 70 miles (112 kilometers) west of Tokyo. "Using Taketsuru's notes and Iwai's expertise the whisky was in the big, smoky, old style," wrote Dave Broom in his excellent book *The Way of Whisky*. "It was too old-fashioned for Japan, and nine years later it closed. The jinx had struck again."

After Iwai passed away, in the 1970s and 1980s Hombo made whisky a few more times in a few different locations around Japan, without much success. Each of these experiments ended with the company stopping its production of whisky. While it seemed that the story of this brand might end there, thanks to the recent explosion in popularity of Japanese whisky, Hombo gave it one more try in 2011 and has finally found success.

The brand, which is now known as Mars, makes its whisky in the mountainous

Nagano region in the middle of the country. Its distillery, now called Komagatake, is 2,600 feet (790 meters) above sea level—higher than any other distillery in Japan. At this altitude, according to Mars, the aging process slows down, so you get less wood flavor in the whisky and more of the spirit's inherent flavor.

In the late 1970s and early '80s, Mars had used the Tsunuki distillery in Kyushu to make a bit of whisky. The facility was recently refurbished and Mars began making whisky there again in 2016. It is currently the country's southernmost whisky distillery. Mars also constructed warehouses on Yakushima island, a portion of which is a UNESCO Natural World Heritage site.

During the past few years, Mars's line of Iwai Whisky has become widely available in the United States. You can now find several varieties, including blends, single malts, and special editions.

Iwai is named for one of the industry's founders Kiichiro Iwai.

Iwai Japanese Whisky

Mars's signature expression is Iwai (EE-way) Whisky, which features a deep blue label. It is the distillery's version of bourbon and is made from a mash of 70 percent corn and 30 percent malted barley. The easy-drinking whisky is aged for at least two years in used bourbon barrels.

Iwai 45 Japanese Whisky

The Iwai 45 is a higher proof version of the standard Iwai Whisky. As you might guess from its name, it's 45 percent alcohol by volume, which makes it ideal for cocktails as well as when served on the rocks, or with club soda.

Iwai Tradition Japanese Whisky

The Tradition bottling is made from a mash bill of 30 percent corn and 70 percent malted barley, and features a whisper of peat—kind of like blending corn whisky with some Islay Scotch. It is aged in used bourbon barrels as well as in sherry and other wine casks.

Komagatake Single Malt Japanese Whisky

I imagine that Komagatake (co-MA-gat-a-kay) Single Malt is the type of big and bold whisky that Kiichiro Iwai dreamed would become popular in Japan when he sent Masataka Taketsuru to Scotland. It is made in copper pot stills at Mars's Nagano distillery. Each edition of the single malt has been slightly different, but all are made from barley that is peated—some years heavily, other years lightly. It is then aged in a variety of barrels. The 2021 release was aged in the company's warehouses on the island of Yakushima.

BRANCH: AKASHI

Akashi (AH-ka-she) might not have the name recognition of its bigger rivals, but the family-run company that produces it, Eigashima Shuzo, actually has a very long history of making sake and other types of liquor in Japan—its roots stretch back to 1679.

Eigashima Shuzo has a long history of producing a range of different alcohols.

Some innovative distillers like Kikori are using rice to make whisky.

In fact, Eigashima Shuzo claims that it was awarded Japan's first whisky distilling license in 1919, though it didn't actually make whisky until the mid-1960s, when it built the White Oak distillery near Osaka Bay. The facility was originally equipped with two small copper pot stills. While Eigashima Shuzo continues to make a range of different types of alcohol, it built a larger whisky distillery in 1984 that it still uses today. Akashi currently produces single malt as well as blends, which are aged in a range of flavorful casks.

BRANCH: KIKORI RICE WHISKY

Japanese alcohol makers have long used rice as the base for making sake and shochu. Now some industrious brands are using the grain to make whisky. One of these is Kikori (KEY-core-ee), which was started in 2015 by American entrepreneur Ann Soh Woods. The brand's whisky is distilled completely from a base of rice and is aged for at least three years in a range of different types of barrels.

BRANCH: HATOZAKI

The Kaikyō distillery in Hyogo, Japan, started producing shochu in 1917 and exactly a century later began producing whisky. Although it took quite a while, the move makes sense as the production of both spirits is similar. Currently, the brand's lineup includes Hatozaki (HA-toe-zak-ee) Finest Whisky, an easy-drinking 80-proof (40 percent alcohol by volume) blend that includes 40 percent single malt and 60 percent grain whisky. The brand recommends this whisky be enjoyed in Highballs and other cocktails. Hatozaki's other permanent expression is the Hatozaki Small Batch Pure Malt Whisky (in the United

States it is simply called Hatozaki Small Batch Whisky), which combines different single malts that are around five years old and aged in various kinds of barrels. Also, keep a look out for Hatozaki's limited-edition releases of rare whiskies under the Omakase name.

🌾 BRANCH: HAKATA

For more than a century, whiskey distillers around the world have been experimenting with fermenting grains using the Japanese mold koji instead of yeast. It's an interesting idea as koji is used to make sake, shochu, miso, and some types of soy sauce. The bacteria is particularly prized because it creates rich, savory flavors. At the Hikari distillery in Fukuoka, master distiller Naomi Mitsuya used this technique to ferment part of the barley for his Hakata (HA-kah-tah) single malt whisky. He then aged the whisky in casks that had been seasoned with sherry. Mitsuya is now retired, but Hikari still makes its Hakata whisky using his unique production methods. Currently, the brand sells single malts aged for ten, twelve, sixteen, and eighteen years.

🌾 BRANCH: CHICHIBU

One of the famous faces in Japanese whisky today is Ichiro Akuto, who built the Chichibu (CHI-chi-boo) distillery in 2007 and remains its head blender. The facility is located about 60 miles (100 kilometers) northwest of Tokyo. As with many modern whisky makers, Akuto's ancestors had been producing liquor for centuries—in his case, brewing sake. After World War II, the family began to also produce a small amount of whisky, but without much

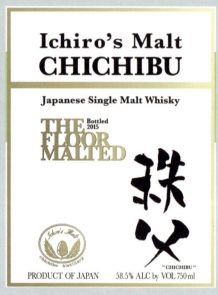

Japanese aficionados and collectors prize bottles from Ichiro Akuto's distillery Chichibu.

success. Ultimately, his family sold their liquor business, including their Hanyo distillery, but Akuto was fortunately able to buy its stock of aging whisky. In 2007, he built his own distillery, Chichibu, and was soon producing his own whisky. In an incredible twist of events, the whisky from the Hanyo distillery has become a highly sought-after collector's item and established Akuto's distilling credibility.

The Chichibu distillery has made a name for itself with its single malts and by releasing very limited editions that are aged in a variety of different kinds of barrels—everything from casks that previously held red wine to those that once held imperial stout beer. Akuto has also experimented with blending his whisky with others from around the world to create a global blend.

WORLD WHISKEY

WORLD
Whiskey Landmarks

DISTILLERY

1. Stauning distillery, Skjern, Denmark
2. Mackmyra distillery, Gävle, Sweden
3. Lark distillery, Hobart, Tasmania, Australia
4. Sullivans Cove distillery, Hobart, Tasmania, Australia
5. Starward distillery, Port Melbourne, Australia
6. The Chuan Whisky distillery, Sichuan Province, China
7. Eryuan distillery, Yunnan Province, China
8. Cotswolds distillery, Warwickshire, UK
9. The English distillery, Norfolk, UK
10. The Lakes distillery, Cumbria, UK
11. Armorik distillery, Brittany, France
12. Domaine Des Hautes Glaces distilleries, French Alps, France
13. Amrut distillery, Bangalore, India
14. Paul John distillery, Bangalore, India
15. Milk & Honey, Tel Aviv, Israel
16. Riachi distillery, Khenchara, Lebanon
17. Abasolo distillery, Jilotepec de Abasolo, Mexico
18. Sierra Norte distillery, Oaxaca, Mexico

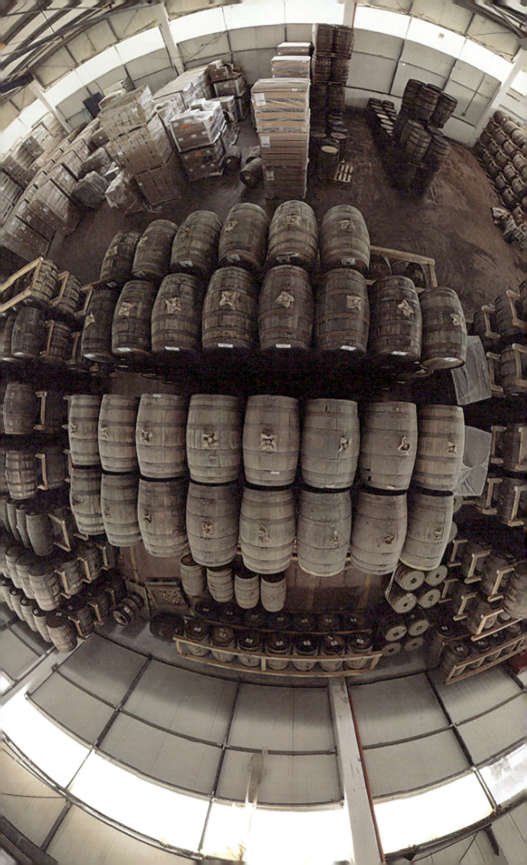

From Mexico to Israel, Australia, and seemingly everywhere in between, there are now distilleries producing a wide variety of whiskey.

It's frankly an amazing transformation for a spirit that was once made in just a handful of regions. Whiskey has now gone both global and viral—and I don't expect this trend to slow down anytime soon, with no doubt many more distilleries yet to open around the world.

Some of these upstart regions are already challenging the old guard, both by producing classic styles as well as by breaking new ground with creative whiskies that disrupt traditional categories. Unencumbered by history or tight regulations, they are often able to push the envelope and truly rethink and reinvent whiskey distilling methods. In future editions of *The Whiskey Bible*, don't be surprised to see some of these whiskey-producing countries or regions become stand-alone chapters.

Read on for some of the most interesting and unique whiskey regions around the world.

Whiskey has gone global as impressive new distilleries have opened up around the world, challenging the supremacy of traditional whiskey powerhouses.

Australia

From Penfolds to Foster's, you don't have to look too hard to find Australian-made alcoholic beverages. But while the land down under is famous for its wineries and breweries, until recently it didn't have much of a domestic distilling industry. Australians drink plenty of whiskey, but historically it's been mostly imported from Scotland and the United States.

This began to change in the 1990s, when pioneering Tasmanian whisky maker Bill Lark began a nascent craft distilling movement by getting the government to create a new class of licenses for small distillers. Today, there are more than a hundred distilleries across Australia making a range of whiskies. What has helped spur creativity and innovation in Australian distilling is that the rules for making whisky there are minimal. Essentially, whisky has only to be distilled from a mash of grains and aged for at least two years in a wooden barrel.

Over the past few years, some of these Australian brands have begun to be exported to Europe and the United States. I imagine in the coming years you'll see even more of them showing up on liquor store shelves. Here are a few to look for now.

♦ AUSTRALIAN WHISKY BRANDS TO KNOW

Lark Distillery

When the global whiskey industry hit rock bottom in the 1980s, Australia certainly wasn't immune. According to the Australian Distillers Association, there were no whisky distilleries operating in the country during that time. And while the country never had a huge number of distillers, the absence of them at the time was still quite a shock.

Who knows how long that drought might have persisted if Bill and Lyn Lark hadn't decided that they wanted to make whisky in Tasmania. The couple started out modestly, distilling a minuscule amount of spirit in a tiny 5-gallon (20-liter) pot still. At first, they were doing this illegally—they couldn't qualify for a proper distilling license because it was designed for large-scale production. The Larks were fortunately able to get the government to give distilling licenses to folks like themselves who were just

Bill and Lyn Lark got the Australian government to create a craft distilling license so they could open their Tasmanian distillery.

getting started by making a small amount of whiskey. In 1992, they officially and legally launched their distillery, and six years later introduced their initial single malt, which was made from local barley smoked over fires of local peat.

Today, Lark produces a large range of whiskies, including Classic Cask Single Malt, which is double distilled and aged in both port- and sherry-seasoned casks, and Symphony Nº1, a blend of the distillery's different single malts.

Tasmania's Sullivans Cove is one of the most highly awarded single malt whiskies in the world.

Sullivans Cove

In an incredible upset, Sullivans Cove's French Oak Single Cask Whisky took home the title of world's best single malt at the World Whiskies Awards in 2014, beating out stalwarts from Scotland and other legacy producers located around the globe. It was a stunning achievement for the Tasmanian distillery founded just two decades earlier. The award not only established the bona fides of Sullivans Cove, but the reputation of the entire island state of Tasmania.

The result of this attention is that Sullivans Cove has become the Pappy Van Winkle of Australia—meaning: Good luck getting your hands on a bottle, and if you do, be prepared to pay top dollar for it!

Even more fascinating than the success of Sullivans Cove is the distillery's unique production methods. For starters, it works with a brewery to make the distiller's beer (also known as wash) from Tasmanian malted barley instead of producing it itself, which is then distilled twice in a unique-shaped copper pot still. The whisky is then typically aged for between nine and eighteen years in either American oak barrels that previously held bourbon or French oak casks that previously held port.

Another key difference to the brand's production process is that most of Sullivans Cove's expressions, including the famed French Oak Single Cask, are bottled from just one barrel at a time. As a result, there will be significant variation from bottle to bottle, and production is very limited.

Starward Whisky

Starward is arguably the most famous and widely available Australian whisky. In 2022, it captured more medals than any other spirits brand at the San Francisco World Spirits Competition, which was quite a coup given that the brand was founded in just 2007 in a former Qantas Airways hangar in the shadow of Melbourne's airport. And that's not to mention that its founder, Dave Vitale, originally worked in the financial planning industry before becoming the business manager for Bill Lark's pioneering Lark distillery in Tasmania.

Starward uses only locally grown ingredients to make its whiskies. Its signature bottling is the single malt Nova, which is made from malted barley distilled twice in copper pot stills, then aged in barrels of various sizes that formerly held shiraz, cabernet sauvignon, and pinot noir from wineries in the Yarra and Barossa Valleys. In addition, the brand makes a number of other expressions, including Two-Fold Double Grain Whisky, which is an easy-drinking blend of wheat whisky and single malt, also aged in wine barrels.

Vitale told the *Australian* newspaper that he started using red wine barrels because the price of casks that had previously held the locally made sherry-like wine Apera had dramatically increased in cost—from A$80 to A$120 a barrel. While pragmatism may have driven the switch, it immediately differentiated Starward from its competitors and added a welcome rich, fruity note to the whisky.

In 2015, Diageo's venture capital fund Distill Ventures reportedly invested $7.2 million in Starward, which helped the brand to export its whisky to a wider number of markets that now include the United States and thirteen other countries. The investment also allowed Starward to move from its humble hangar to an impressive facility in Port Melbourne.

Morris Australian Single Malt Whisky

It seems only fitting that Morris Single Malt Whisky is made in Rutherglen, Victoria, a town that takes its name from a place in Scotland. While the brand has been making fortified wines since 1859, only in 2016 did it begin producing whisky on its antique copper pot/column hybrid still, which dates to the 1930s. Morris currently makes a single malt that was aged in a range of its own wine barrels for at least three years, as well as an expression finished in muscat fortified wine barrels.

Australia's Starward ages its whisky in casks from nearby vineyards that previously held red wine in order to create its signature flavor.

China now boasts several whisky distilleries, including The Chuan in the Sichuan province.

EAST ASIA

East Asia has an incredibly long history of producing alcohol, one that goes back for centuries. Today, you can find several grain-based and clear spirits, including baijiu, which is extremely popular—Moutai baijiu is, in fact, the most valuable spirits brand of any kind in the world.

Given the region's enormous population of more than 1.7 billion people, its growing demand for luxury goods, and its small-but-burgeoning appetite for whisky, it should come as no surprise that a handful of whisky distilleries have opened, plus there are dozens and dozens of other ones in the works. That figure includes distilleries from a range of major players in the international spirits industry, all of them betting that they can get East Asian drinkers to increasingly switch from local spirits to whisky in the next few years. (Note: Given the size and sophistication of Japan's whisky industry, it has its own chapter in this book, which outlines its specific production regulations.)

As of the time of publication, these whiskies needs to be aged for at least two years in oak barrels, but otherwise there aren't specific rules for its production. It will be fascinating to watch how this market develops and how distillers integrate local twists to making whisky.

♦ **EAST ASIAN WHISKY BRANDS TO KNOW**

The Chuan Whisky

In August 2019, French liquor conglomerate Pernod Ricard announced

Diageo built a distillery in China's Yunnan province to make single malt whisky.

that it had invested in expanding its portfolio of legacy whiskies by adding stalwarts Jefferson's Bourbon and Knappogue Castle Whiskey. A few days later it also announced that it was making a $150 million investment in the future of whiskey—by building a distillery in China's Sichuan province to produce single malt.

The picturesque distillery and attached visitor center in Emeishan City officially opened at the end of 2023 when its Pure Malt Whisky was introduced. This whisky is made by master distiller, Yang Tao, from both European and Chinese barley and aged in a variety of barrels: ex-bourbon, seasoned with Spanish sherry, and others made from oak harvested from China's Changbai Mountains. According to a story in the *Financial Times*, the initial release was a blend of Chinese and Scotch whisky. Ultimately, the distillery is planning to bottle a single malt made exclusively in China.

Eryuan Malt Whisky

From Scotland to Ireland to Tennessee, international spirits conglomerate Diageo owns dozens of whiskey distilleries around the world. A new entry to their geographic portfolio is now China's Yunnan province. In 2022, the company began construction of a $75 million, 710,000-square-foot (66,000-square-meter) distillery to produce Eryuan single malt whisky. The plan, as of publication, is to use domestic ingredients, including water from

The Chinese Chuan distillery, built by international conglomerate Pernod Ricard, features traditional copper pot stills.

nearby Erhai Lake. The distillery and visitor center was forecasted to open in December 2024.

Kavalan

Thanks to the hot and humid summers, which cause alarmingly high levels of evaporation and accelerated maturation, there are plenty of good reasons why you wouldn't want to make single malt whisky in Taipei, but Tien-tsai Lee wasn't interested in any of them.

Lee is the founder of King Car Group, which owns the very popular Mr. Brown canned iced coffee and other nonalcoholic beverage brands, In the early 2000s, Lee and his son, Yu-ting, enlisted the help of the famous whisky consultant Dr. Jim Swan—who was often called the Einstein of whisky—to help them plan their Kavalan distillery. In 2005, over the course of nine months, it was built in the mountainous Yilan area south of Taipei. The following March it began producing whisky.

The distillery buys malted barley from Scotland and double distills the spirit in traditional copper pot stills. It uses a range of different barrels to age its whisky. Given the climate, the maturation process takes only a few years—most of the Kavalan whiskies are aged from two to three years. To get the most out of the aging process, some of the barrels are sanded down

For nearly twenty years, Kavalan has been producing a number of award-winning single malt whiskies.

inside, toasted, and finally recharred. The process gives the barrels new life and was one of Dr. Swan's signature techniques, which he later employed at a number of pioneering distilleries around the world, including Milk & Honey in Israel.

"Our strategy as a latecomer is simple. We can't compare with 12-, 15- or 21-year-aged whiskies in terms of age. Where we can compete is in terms of quality. We need to produce the best, best, best quality to be able to compare," Yu-ting Lee told the *Financial Times* in 2016. While that was certainly an ambitious goal, Kavalan has been able to deliver on it, producing a range of whiskies that have developed a loyal following. In 2015, its Solist Vinho Barrique whisky was crowned World's Best Single Malt at the World Whiskies Awards. The following year its Solist Amontillado Sherry Single Cask Strength took home the title of World's Best Single Cask Single Malt Whisky at the same contest.

Given all of the attention and increasing demand for the whisky, in 2016 Kavalan doubled its distilling capacity by installing an additional ten pot stills, and in 2023 added a third warehouse. I imagine this won't be the distillery's last expansion.

Omar Single Malt Whisky

In 2009, a whisky distillery opened about two hours south of Taipei in Nantou and four years later began releasing Omar Single Malt. The name of the whisky is derived from the Gaelic word for amber, *ómra*. The brand now offers a range of whiskies that are aged either in used bourbon barrels or in sherry-seasoned casks.

Some of Omar's releases are finished in some unusual and exciting barrels, such as those that previously held lychee liqueur or green plum liqueur. Omar also makes a peated single malt whisky.

The Lakes distillery was built by Scotch veteran Paul Currie on a converted dairy farm and now makes a range of whiskies.

England

Historically, England left whiskey distilling to Scotland and Ireland, choosing instead to produce gin. In fact, from 1901 to 2006 there were no registered whisky distilleries in the entirety of England. So, it's somewhat amazing that there's now a flourishing English craft whisky scene with forty-five distilleries across the country, according to the English Whisky Guild. These brands are currently aging an estimated 50,000 barrels of whisky. To make whisky in England it must be aged for a minimum of three years and, if you're making single malt, it needs to be made from malted barley. The recently formed English Whisky Guild is trying to create a standard that would add other production specifications as well.

It will be interesting to see how the English whisky industry develops and ultimately distinguishes itself from its long-established neighbors in Scotland and Ireland.

♦ **ENGLISH WHISKY BRANDS TO KNOW**

Cooper King Distillery

Cooper King is one of the newest English whisky distilleries. What sets it apart is that it doesn't follow the traditional Scottish or even American game

Cooper Kings makes a truly global spirit, blending techniques and methods from distillers around the world.

plan for distilling. The production process, a combination of traditional and thoroughly modern techniques, is based on what the founders, Dr. Abbie Neilson and Christopher Jaume, saw in Tasmania, which is home to many of Australia's best craft whisky distilleries.

Cooper King starts by floor malting the English heritage barley called Maris Otter. After a lengthy fermentation, the wash is distilled twice in a 238-gallon (900-liter) Australian-built copper pot still named Neilson and finally the spirit is aged in small 100-liter (26-gallon) barrels that come from the United States and/or France. The brand's first single malt was aged for four years and released in 2023.

Cotswolds Distillery

For thirty years, American Daniel Szor experienced the highs and lows of working in global finance. By 2014, he was living in England's beautiful Cotswolds and contemplating his next move. But instead of spending his time relaxing and enjoying the area's famously charming towns and historic homes, he decided to turn his love of whisky into a business: the Cotswolds distillery. The company began producing single malt from local barley in a renovated barn, selling its first bottles in 2017. It later expanded and built a larger distillery. According to the *Spirits Business*, Cotswolds distillery was producing 132,000 gallons (500,000 liters) of whisky and gin per year by 2022. You can now buy a range of the distillery's single malts aged in a variety of different barrels.

In 2023, historic London liquor shop and spirits company Berry Bros. & Rudd invested an undisclosed amount in the Cotswolds distillery.

People on holiday in the Cotswolds can now drink whiskey named for the picturesque area.

The English Distillery

In 2006, English single malt whisky sounded like the punch line to a bad joke. It had been more than a century, after all, since the last drop of whisky had been made in the country. But that didn't stop James Nelstrop from building a distillery in his hometown of Norfolk and beginning to make single malt in copper pot stills. It certainly helped that he could buy locally grown barley from farms run by his extended family. Given that he was the only English distillery in existence, he aptly named his business The English distillery and, fittingly enough, the then Prince Charles was on hand for the company's opening in 2007.

Nelstrop not only showed that you could make fine whisky in England, but inadvertently started a craft distilling craze across the nation. In 2014, he passed away and was succeeded by his son, Andrew Nelstrop, who is currently chairman of the business. I imagine James would be quite proud of the company he built: In an amazing twist of events, The English distillery's Sherry Cask Matured was named best single malt in the world at the 2024 World Whiskies Awards. It is an accomplishment that I suspect no one could have predicted back in 2006.

In addition to its major award winner, the Sherry Cask Matured, The English distillery makes a range of different single malts aged in a variety of barrels, from new oak to those that have previously held rum.

King Charles (then Prince) celebrated the opening of the pioneering English Distilling Company in 2006.

The Lakes Distillery

While whisky making is often called an art form, I'm not sure I know of any other brands besides The Lakes distillery that were inspired by the arts. The founder of the company, Paul Currie, often visited the picturesque Lake District, which was famously the muse and home of many creatives, including English Romantic poet William Wordsworth. In 2013, Currie bought an old stone dairy farm near the town of Keswick and set about converting it into a whisky distillery. He no doubt drew upon his years of experience working for Scotch brands, as well as the lessons he learned starting the Arran distillery on the Scottish Isle of Arran with his father and brother. The Lakes distillery currently releases a range of its single malt and also bottles blends, which combine Lakes's own single malt with Scottish single malts and grain whisky.

France

Between the wine, the Cognac, and the Armagnac, you'll never go thirsty in France. But what's incredible and not at all well known is that the French also drink a river of whiskey. In fact, France is one of Scotland's best customers every year.

Given the French thirst for whiskey it should come as no surprise that there are now dozens of distillers all around France making it. Most of the whisky currently produced by these brands isn't widely exported, but if its production in France continues to evolve and grow, it won't be too long before you start seeing more French whiskies available around the world.

♦ FRENCH WHISKY BRANDS TO KNOW

Armorik Whisky Breton Single Malt

In 1993, France went from just drinking single malt to actually producing it. That year is when Armorik opened a distillery in Brittany equipped with two copper pot stills to exclusively make whisky. The facility was soon producing the country's first single malt. Five years later, Armorik began selling bottles of its inaugural release and ultimately put the region on the international whiskey map. The brand was instrumental in coming up with a standard for making so-called Brittany whisky (Whisky de Bretagne), which guarantees that a spirit was actually made and aged in the area.

Today, Armorik makes a range of single malts from barley grown in France and ages it in a variety of barrels, including ones made by a local cooper from oak grown in the nearby Cranou and Brocéliande forests. In 2020, Armorik even started selling a peated version of its single malt. While Armorik was a new endeavor, its parent company, Warenghem distillery, began producing a range of liqueurs in 1900.

Brenne Single Malt

Brenne Single Malt was launched in 2012 and hails from Cognac. It is made completely from local barley and produced in a traditional alembic Charente still, which the distillery usually uses for making fruit brandy. After two distillations, the whisky is aged in new French Limousin oak barrels and finished in used Cognac casks. Brenne's signature product is its Estate Cask, which is aged for a minimum of six years and is 80 proof (40 percent alcohol by volume). There is also the small batch Brenne Ten, which is aged for a decade and is 96 proof (48 percent alcohol by volume).

France, long famous for its Cognac distilleries, started producing single malt whisky in 1993 with the opening of Amorik.

Brenne, started in 2012 by Allison Parc, merges Cognac distilling traditions with single malt whiskey distilling traditions.

Domaine des Hautes Glaces

Looking at the square glass bottle of Hautes Glaces you might mistake it for cologne for Brooklyn hipsters or perhaps the final MFA project of a glass-blowing student. But the brand, which is located in the French Alps and was started in 2009, is intentionally trying to create a new creative identity and direction for whisky making that involves using fewer natural resources. For one, it controls every aspect of production, from growing its organic grain to harvesting wild yeasts to distilling the whisky. Its single malt, Indigène, is made from its own malted barley and tries to tie the whisky to the land. It's distilled twice in a wood-fired pot still and aged in different kinds of barrels. The final whisky is a blend of one hundred single malts that matured in a variety of casks. Hautes Glaces also makes a number of "exploratory" whiskies that are produced from the harvest of just a single plot of its land, including a malted rye whisky.

In 2017, the distillery was bought by large spirits company Rémy Cointreau, which also owns single malt whiskies, Bruichladdich (Scotland) and Westland (Seattle, Washington), for an undisclosed sum.

Domaine des Hautes Glaces, located in the French Alps, uses locally grown grain and wild yeasts.

India

With a population of 1.4 billion people, it's no surprise that India is now one of the largest whiskey markets in the world. Thanks to changing attitudes about alcohol among adults coming of age who are now often interested in drinking, and the tremendous business opportunity they represent, the biggest liquor companies in the world are now paying ever more attention to India.

However, because of extremely high tariffs, a patchwork of regional alcohol regulations, and dry states, just a tiny amount of whiskey is imported to India. Scotch currently makes up a measly 2 percent of the country's overall whiskey sales, according to the Scotch Whisky Association.

While some Indian brands blend cheap imported bulk Scotch with locally made whisky, or worse, make so-called whisky from molasses, there is also now a thriving high-end single malt distilling scene that has gotten the attention of drinkers in Europe and the US. (Just as in Scotland, single malt in India needs to be aged for at least three years in oak barrels.)

Over the next few years, you'll be seeing ever more of these bottles on store shelves and bar menus.

♦ INDIAN WHISKY BRANDS TO KNOW

Amrut

If you want to be the best you have to beat the best, and that's exactly what the Bengaluru-based Amrut Distilleries did in 2004 when it launched the first Indian-made single malt in Glasgow, Scotland.

It was a bold move: If its whisky caught on in Scotland, it would be a tremendous marketing coup, but if it failed it would be a disaster that the brand

Amrut challenged Scotland's dominance in the single malt category and inadvertently created a premium Indian whisky industry.

India is one of the biggest alcohol markets in the world, and a number of the country's whisky brands, including Paul John, are now available far outside its borders.

would have a hard time living down. Fortunately, Amrut impressed drinkers, bartenders, and critics and developed a devoted following. A few years later, in 2010, Amrut introduced its single malts to India and the United States.

While Amrut had never sold a single malt before 2004, it had been distilling a huge range of other spirits since the 1960s and in the 1980s started making whisky blends. "India has always been a huge whisky market, but at the lower end. We wanted to move from quantity to quality, and the biggest challenge was to gain acceptance from the luxury whisky market in Europe," the late Neelakanta Rao Jagdale, then chairman of Amrut, told the *Economic Times* in 2012.

Amrut currently makes about twenty different kinds of single malts. Given the tropical climate of Bengaluru and Amrut's location 3,000 feet (910 meters) above sea level, the brand claims its whiskies age about three-and-a-half times faster than whisky in Scotland. Currently, most of its whiskies are aged for about five years.

Its signature and bestselling whisky, Fusion, was introduced in 2009 and combines a nonpeated single malt with a peated single malt. Arguably its most innovative release to date is the Naarangi, which is finished in a barrel that was first filled with oloroso sherry and orange peels. Thanks to its sweet and fruity notes, the whisky almost tastes like a bottled Old-Fashioned.

Paul John

The New Orleans, Louisiana–based Sazerac company has built an impressive portfolio of star whiskey brands, including Pappy Van Winkle, Blanton's, Buffalo Trace, Weller, and E.H. Taylor. So, it was a real milestone in 2017 when it bought a 43 percent stake in Paul John Single Malt's parent company, John Distilleries, based in Bengaluru. (And yes, the founder of the company is named Paul P. John.)

While John Distilleries makes a range of spirits, in 2012 it began producing single malt from Himalayan six-row barley at its distillery in Goa, on the west coast of India. The spirit is double distilled in Indian-made copper pot stills that are designed to produce a lighter style of whisky. The whisky is aged in used American oak bourbon barrels or sherry-seasoned casks for at least five years. The core of the brand's portfolio are the nonpeated Brilliance, the lightly peated Edited, and the heavily peated Bold.

Thanks to both domestic and international demand for the whisky, since 2021 Paul John has significantly ramped up its production of single malts.

Israel

While Jews were instrumental in building the American whiskey industry, until recently there was no distillery in Israel making the spirit. Whiskey is, generally speaking, inherently kosher, which increases the probability that the country's nascent whisky industry will succeed. And, unlike wine, there are just a few biblical rules concerning its making.

Milk & Honey

In the Torah, Israel is referred to as the land of milk and honey, so it's only fitting that the country's first and only single malt whiskey distillery is called, yes, Milk & Honey. The facility, which opened in 2016, is located in the seaside town of Jaffa and was set up with the help of legendary whisky consultant Dr. Jim Swan. One of his ideas for the brand was to age its whisky in an STR wine barrel, which stands for shaved, toasted, and recharred. Essentially, the inside of a used wine barrel is scraped and then heated before it is finally charred—a process designed to give new life to a used barrel.

Currently, the brand makes a number of different types of single malt whisky, including its signature M&H Classic, which is aged in both used bourbon and its special STR barrels. It also produces the APEX line of limited-edition single malts, which are finished in a range of interesting barrels, such as those that previously held pomegranate wine.

Israel's Milk & Honey uses a few different types of barrels to age its single malt whiskey.

Lebanon

Arak, the national drink of Lebanon, is arguably one of the world's oldest spirits, dating back centuries. The country also boasts a significant number of breweries and wineries. We can now also add a single malt whisky to that list, the Athyr, made by the Riachi distillery, located in the village of Khenchara.

Athyr Single Malt

In 2019, the historic Riachi distillery introduced the first single malt whisky ever to be distilled in Lebanon. It is made from local ingredients, including barley, and aged in barrels made from Lebanese oak (*Quercus libani*). So far, the brand has released several limited editions, including malts that have been finished in cedar barrels or aged in clay amphorae.

With Athyr, Lebanon joins a growing group of nations producing and selling single malt whisky.

Mexico

Thanks to the popularity of the Margarita, the Paloma, the Mezcal Negroni, the Batanga, and countless other drinks, brands can't keep up with a surge in global demand for tequila and mezcal, which are two of the fastest growing spirits in the world.

But in the shadow of agave-based liquor, there is another Mexican spirit with huge potential: whisky. The country doesn't have a very long history of making whisky, but it does have something very important going for it—corn, which is indigenous to the region. While Kentucky might claim to be the home of bourbon, Mexico is the home of corn.

Mexico produced a significant amount of whisky when the United States enacted Prohibition and distilleries in the US were forced to shut down. Along the shared border of the two countries, a number of Mexican-made bourbon brands popped up (at the time, you could still legally call your whiskey bourbon even if it wasn't produced in the United States). Most of these distilleries closed down once Prohibition was repealed.

Recently, a new type of Mexican whisky has been created by entrepreneurs not looking to create bourbon-like brands, but instead whiskies that reflect the area where they are made and that have a sense of place. These spirits generally are made from heirloom corn varieties and celebrate Mexico's connection to the grain.

Abasolo's corn whisky is the latest chapter in Mexico's long history with the indigenous grain.

According to the *New York Times*, as of January 2024, there are more than ten distilleries making whisky in Mexico. This is the beginning of a real trend and one that over the next decade could get very big.

♦ MEXICAN WHISKY BRANDS TO KNOW

Abasolo El Whisky De Mexico

The name of Dr. Iván Saldaña should be familiar to mezcal lovers, since he is one of the world's top agave experts and the creator, in 2010, of Montelobos Mezcal, which was later bought by Campari. He was also the cocreator of the Mexican chile liqueur Ancho Reyes. Saldaña is relentlessly curious and in 2020 decided to turn his attention to another indigenous Mexican grain: corn. He figured out that you could make whisky out of the historic Cacahuazintle variety, which is normally used for making tortillas and other traditional foods. He then built the country's first dedicated whisky distillery about 60 miles (100 kilometers) north of Mexico City, in Jilotepec de Abasolo.

The sleek facility would look at home in the Hollywood Hills, but inside it uses the historic and traditional nixtamalization method of heating the corn in an alkaline solution. The kernels are then dried, roasted, milled, and mashed with some malted corn. After fermentation, the spirit is double distilled in copper pot stills and aged for two years in toasted new and used oak barrels.

The Abasolo warehouse is unique—it is essentially open to the elements, with no walls, which ensures plenty of temperature fluctuations, which is essential for maturation. "We wanted to figure out a process that truly honors Mexican corn, which has been culturally important here since before the Spaniards arrived," Saldaña told the *Washington Post* in 2021. Given his track record, it didn't take long to get the attention of liquor conglomerate Pernod Ricard, which bought a minority stake in Abasolo in 2021.

Sierra Norte Single Barrel Whiskey

While Oaxaca is synonymous with agave-based mezcal, it's now also home to Sierra Norte. The brand was started by veteran mezcal master distiller Doug French, who makes the whiskey using a base of 85 percent local heirloom Criollo corn and 15 percent malted barley. Producing corn-based whiskey in Oaxaca actually makes quite a bit of sense, given that grain was likely first farmed in the area thousands of years ago.

Move over tequila and mezcal—there's a new generation of Mexican whiskey distillers, including Sierra Norte in Oaxaca.

The brand's spirit is double distilled in copper pot stills and aged for two to three years in French oak barrels that previously held red Bordeaux and Burgundy wine. What's fascinating is that the corn the brand uses comes in a range of colors, which Sierra Norte distills and bottles separately. So you can compare Sierra Norte Whiskey made from red, purple, white, black, yellow, or rainbow corn.

The brand bottles only single barrels of its whiskey, which means there are differences from batch to batch.

The Stauning distillery in Denmark combines innovation with old-school distilling techniques.

Scandinavia

When you think about Scandinavian drinking culture, aquavit, vodka, and perhaps glögg first come to mind. But since the late 1990s, the area has developed a red-hot whisky scene, with a number of influential and innovative distilleries that have earned international reputations.

While this development might seem a bit odd at first, Scandinavia is just across the North Sea from Scotland. During the Middle Ages, marauding Vikings would famously make the short trip by boat and raid Scotland and Ireland. Some of the northern Scotch brands, including Highland Park, now lean heavily into this period of history and their connection to the Vikings. Read on for some of the brands making history today in Scandinavia.

♦ SCANDINAVIAN WHISKY BRANDS TO KNOW

Stauning Danish Whisky

Stauning has an old soul. While that might sound like a strange thing to say about a brand founded in 2005, its distillery in Skjern, Denmark, employs some of the most traditional and archaic methods to make its whisky, including floor malting the barley and heating its rows of copper pot stills over a direct flame. But Stauning isn't a museum—the brand is able to deftly walk a tightrope between authenticity and innovation.

The distillery has certainly come a long way since it was founded by nine friends in an old butcher shop, which they fitted with two small pot stills. Ultimately, their whisky was good enough to garner attention from Diageo's venture capital arm, Distill Ventures, which in 2015 invested £10 million in the business. Stauning used some of that money to build a striking distillery that opened in 2018, equipped with a staggering twenty-four copper pot stills, all heated over direct flame.

Stauning currently makes many different styles of whisky—everything from smoky single malt to a straight rye to a blend of three malts. There is also a line of even more experimental whiskies that have been finished in a range of unusual barrels, such as one that previously held mezcal.

Mackmyra Swedish Single Malt Whisky

Nearly twenty thousand Mackmyra whisky barrels are slowly maturing at the bottom of an old 160-foot-deep (50-meter) mine shaft in Bodås, Sweden. While this location is certainly unique, it's only one of the brand's surprising whisky aging sites, which also include a barge on the Seine in France and the top of a Swedish ski resort.

But unusual is the norm for Mackmyra, in northern Sweden, which was started by eight civil engineers in 1999. According to lore, they got the idea to open Sweden's first whisky distillery while they were on a skiing trip. I imagine they were drinking whisky when they had this sudden epiphany. Rikard Lundborg, one of the founders, told the *Wall Street Journal* in 2011: "We had no money, no experience and no credibility."

The distillery has made a name for itself with a range of single malts that combine local ingredients with traditional production methods. Some of its whisky is aged in a proprietary barrel that combines heads made from Swedish oak

Sweden's Mackmyra put Scandinavia on the global drinks map and inspired a new generation of whiskey brands.

Mackmyra ages its whiskies in a range of unique and innovative sites across Sweden.

with staves from an old bourbon barrel. And its Svensk Ek Whisky is completely aged in barrels that are made from Swedish oak. For its peated expressions, Mackmyra even uses locally harvested peat and juniper fronds.

In 2011, Mackmyra had an IPO on the Nasdaq OMX stock exchange. It used the infusion of capital to help build a larger, state-of-the-art distillery, which was designed to have as little environmental impact as possible.

ENJOYING WHISKEY

While I love writing and talking about whiskey, what I love most is drinking it with friends and loved ones.

Let's start with what I think should be the primary consideration when drinking whiskey: It should be enjoyable. However, I've found that for far too many people the experience is fraught with anxiety about looking foolish or making a wrong choice. I firmly believe that you should proudly drink what makes you happy. I despise whiskey snobbery, and it saddens me that adults drink things they don't like because it's the safe choice, one that won't engender any discussion (or embarrassment).

When it comes to whiskey, I also believe that there are no stupid questions. If you're wondering about something whiskey-related, it's likely that many other folks have the same question but are too self-conscious to ask. In this chapter, I've answered the questions I'm most frequently asked about drinking and buying whiskey. I've also addressed some of the biggest misconceptions I encounter regularly. And I've included all manner of advice on storing bottles, the type of glass to use, notes on the history of some of the most famous whiskey cocktails, and quite a bit more.

My hope is that by offering my take on some of whiskey's fundamental and not-so-easy questions and concepts, you can—in the judgment free safety of your own home—find your own answers, but also gain the confidence to not only choose a whiskey that truly suits you, but also talk about it confidently. After all, talking about and sharing whiskey is one of the great pleasures of drinking it, and will lead you to new experiences and your next bottle to try.

Finding Your Go-To Dram

I often hear stories from people who tried a pungent whiskey as a young adult, when they first started drinking spirits and cocktails, and hated it. As a result, they have gone out of their way to avoid whiskies of all kinds ever since.

Before heading to the bar or liquor store, answer the questions below to help you find a whiskey you'll enjoy drinking.

There are many versions of this sad tale, with the initial, offending dram identified as one of dozens of whiskies from around the world. And I understand why it happens—whiskey can be overwhelming to the inexperienced palate. It can taste like nothing else you've ever tasted before. If you don't know what to expect from a peaty, briny Scotch, that first sip can be a real shock to the system.

It's not the fault of the whiskey, but rather of the person who decided to throw a novice into the deep end without a life preserver. The universe of whiskey is vast—if you don't have a favorite whiskey or don't like whiskey in general, I honestly believe it's only because you haven't tasted the right one yet. Fortunately, many of those who've had a bad seminal experience find their way back to whiskey only to discover they really enjoy drinking it.

So there's no shame if you're still figuring out your favorite whiskies. It just takes a bit of exploration. To find your go-to dram, you should ask yourself a series of questions. But keep in mind there are no wrong answers, and the more honest you are with yourself, the easier this process will be. Here are some initial thought starters to get you going on your journey:

- How do you like to drink whiskey? (Neat, on the rocks, with a mixer, etc.)

- How often do you drink whiskey? (Every evening, once a week, only at a bar, etc.)

- What are you willing to spend on whiskey?

- What flavors do you gravitate toward? (Sweet, bitter, sour, spicy, smoky, etc.)

- What flavors do you avoid? (Sweet, bitter, sour, spicy, smoky, etc.)

Once you've got your answers, visit a favorite liquor store or whiskey bar and explain what you're looking for. (If they aren't particularly helpful, go to a different establishment.) Keep an open mind and be willing to try whiskies from all over the world. And remember above all that this should be a fun exercise, one that will introduce you to whiskies that you haven't tried before.

The Evolving Palate

Think of drinking whiskey like eating chocolate. Most people start with milk chocolate and as they indulge their sweet tooth, they gradually shift to increasingly darker and more complex chocolate with less sugar and more cacao flavor. Whiskey is similar in that most people start out with sweeter, smoother whiskies and, as their palate becomes more experienced, turn to whiskies that have notes of tannic wood, spice, smoke, or even brine.

This usually means folks who like American whiskey start out with an easy-drinking bourbon like the quaffable, wheated bourbon Maker's Mark and then, as they get more experienced, start ordering whiskies with a higher percentage of rye grain that adds spiciness and a more astringent mouthfeel. With Scotch, people may start with an easy-drinking blended Scotch or a Speyside malt like The Glenlivet before moving on to peaty maritime whiskies, such as those from the Scottish island of Islay.

This is an oversimplification, of course, but it gives you a sense of how the human palate works. There is no prize for drinking extremely smoky whiskey or superspicy rye. Learning to appreciate whiskey is a never-ending journey and it's also okay to revisit some early stops. Just as I find myself often craving a milk chocolate bar, I still like a glass of Maker's Mark or The Glenlivet.

♦ HOW MUCH DO YOU NEED TO SPEND ON WHISKEY?

One of the hardest things for someone getting into whiskey to figure out is how much to spend on a bottle. While I would like to say that there is a minimum or maximum price you need to pay for a decent dram, it is far from that straightforward of a transaction. Some of my favorite whiskies cost less than $25 a bottle, while other favorites cost hundreds, or even thousands. The truth is you can find a delicious whiskey at just about any budget—how much you spend really depends upon your own flavor and brand preferences.

So even though I can't give you an exact price for what you should pay, I can give you some general advice that will hopefully help you find a bottle in your price range.

The secret to Maker's Mark's approachable signature flavor is a mash bill that includes wheat instead of rye.

Don't sleep on legacy distilleries, which tend to produce consistently good whiskies.

Generally, whiskies from legacy producers that have been around for decades (or centuries) are a much better deal than whiskies from a new craft distillery. This is a question of economies of scale, which gives large producers a huge advantage over smaller upstarts, since it lowers their overall production costs.

The established distillers also produce a huge number of bottles each year that are incredibly consistent and widely available. Which leads to my second point: Don't be scared of whiskey that doesn't break the bank or that you can easily find at any liquor store. Some of these ubiquitous whiskies are indeed ubiquitous because they are incredibly good. Scarcity or a bank account–busting price tag doesn't make a whiskey taste any better. In fact, it takes an incredible amount of skill and talent to make a consistent whiskey in large volumes.

If you are getting into Scotch, don't forget about blends, which combine single malts with grain whisky. Blends, like Chivas Regal, Dewar's, and Johnnie Walker are designed to be easy-drinking and to be drunk with ice, water, or mixers. They were wildly popular for most of the twentieth century and it's only since the 1980s that many drinkers have begun to buy single malts instead of blends. And that's not to mention that blends are generally much cheaper compared to single malts. In fact, the bestselling Scotch sold in Scotland is Famous Grouse, which is a blend and is an incredible bargain.

One of the best ways to figure out what you like on a fairly tight budget is to buy 50 ml minibottles, which are also sometimes called nips or

Mini bottles are a great way to taste a lot of different whiskies without breaking the bank.

miniatures. Many brands make these diminutive bottles that contain just enough to give you a sense of what the whiskey tastes like and whether you want to buy a full-size bottle.

♦ ARE THE MOST EXPENSIVE WHISKIES THE BEST?

Many people believe the oldest and most expensive whiskey is the best. If the fanciest cars and finest clothes cost more, shouldn't the very best whiskey? After all, whiskey has become a well-established global luxury product.

Well, maybe not so fast. While there are reasons why a $10,000 bottle of Scotch costs that much, it doesn't mean you'll like it any more than a $50 Scotch, or even a $30 one for that matter. But how could that be?

When you buy an expensive bottle, you're paying for the privilege of drinking whiskey from a so-called unicorn barrel that beat the odds and was special enough never to be bottled.

It's important also to understand the basic economics for distillers, which go something like this: Every day a barrel ages in a warehouse, it costs them money. Not only is there the expense of building and maintaining a warehouse, but there are the taxes that have to be paid on the alcohol when it's bottled or even sometimes when it's aging in the warehouse. Compounding matters is that over time, a significant volume of the whiskey in a barrel evaporates (depending on the climate, that loss could be up to 10 percent a year). Then there's the cost of the bottle and packaging. For special bottles, this can be significant—rare whiskies tend to come in packaging special and eye-catching enough to befit such a unique spirit. A handblown decanter and a presentation box can take months to produce and cost hundreds of dollars each. So brands quite rightly want to recoup their investment. Keep in mind that they don't see any financial return until the whiskey is finally bottled and sold. And even then, if it's sold in the

The price you pay for a bottle of whiskey includes a range of costs incurred by the distiller, the distributor, and the retailer.

United States the distiller usually has to share a significant portion of its profits with a distributor and a retailer.

To truly understand why some of these whiskies are superexpensive, it's helpful to think of it as paying for a taste of liquid history. Distilling techniques, equipment, and methods change over time. For instance, in the twentieth century most Scotch distillers switched from heating their stills

Aging whiskey in a barrel is an incredibly expensive process, and to make matters worse, you are continually losing a bit of the alcohol to evaporation.

over actual fires to using more consistent and less dangerous steam coils or steam jackets. This change—made for the sake of safety and efficiency—saved countless still houses as well as the very lives of untold workers. But it also altered the flavor of the whiskey. Whiskey made before this switch is now sought after by collectors, since it's a finite quantity. The same goes for whiskey that was produced by a distillery no longer in operation. The output from these so-called ghost distillers is particularly prized and valuable (see page 232).

You might have noted that I've said almost nothing about the taste of these rare whiskies. With certain brands the flavor is almost irrelevant. This might sound bizarre, but keep in mind that many of these pricey bottles will never be opened—they're often bought instead as trophies or as investments. Others will go to casinos or steak house around the world, where they'll be poured for high rollers and big shots and fetch hundreds or thousands of dollars per glass. At that price, the expectation that it will be the greatest whiskey ever to touch your lips overrides the actual flavor for many people—the experience is a self-fulfilling prophecy.

I've been very fortunate to have tasted many old whiskies without actually spending my own money to do it. This has allowed me to drink some astounding and divine spirits, but it has also meant choking down some truly mouth-puckering, over-oaked drams that should have been bottled decades ago. A few years ago one very old rye actually turned my stomach, forcing me to flee from the tasting as soon as possible to recover.

So, is the most expensive whiskey the one you'll like the best? Probably not. With super high-end whiskies, you're essentially paying a premium for a chance to travel back in time to taste what whiskey was like decades ago. Is that experience worth $20,000 a bottle? Well, that's your decision, but for that sum you could buy a river of whiskey made more recently.

♦ ARE WHISKIES FROM CRAFT DISTILLERIES INHERENTLY BETTER?

Buying eggs used to be a fairly straightforward proposition. The only real decisions you had to make were what size egg you wanted and whether you preferred brown or white ones. Now, go into a typical Whole Foods and you're faced with a wall of choices, including free-range, hormone-free, organic, and even vitamin-enriched eggs. Those eggs also cost a lot more, with a dozen sometimes going for more than $10. (Yes, I live in New York City.)

For many people, spending more for better-quality eggs makes complete sense. Over the past twenty or so years, artisanal and heritage products have become increasingly popular and seem healthier than other options. At the same time, industrial food production techniques have become more familiar and highly scrutinized. (Reading about how pigs are raised on commodity farms will likely ensure you never eat most supermarket bacon again.) As a result of these shifts in consumer habits, many big food and drink brands have found themselves scrambling to stay relevant while holding onto market share. That sometimes means sunsetting certain products or completely reworking their recipes.

For whiskey, this begs the question: Are craft whiskey brands inherently better than traditional legacy brands because they purport to be made on a smaller scale? The answer may surprise you. Here's the truth: Unlike producers

The equipment and methods for making whiskey are fairly standard across the industry for both large and small distillers.

of eggs, cheese, or meat, craft distillers have almost no advantages over larger brands.

For starters, big whiskies have economies of scale, so they can often offer their products at lower prices. With a product like eggs, the higher price for the artisanal brand may well be worth it to you given how the hens are treated. But it's not quite the same with spirits. For one thing, despite their folksy packaging and charming backstory, many craft brands are actually buying their whiskey from giant industrial producers. Yes, they're essentially bottling someone else's booze.

To get a clear sense of the advantages between big and small whiskey makers, it's helpful to consider all the factors going for each:

Equipment
All whiskey distillers purchase their stills and other equipment from just a handful of manufacturers. Usually, craft brands use small stills because that's what they can afford. If they had a bigger budget, they would buy bigger stills. *Advantage*: Big distillers.

Ingredients
Big distillers generally have long-standing contracts with farmers and get the first pick of grains. What they reject is then offered to smaller brands. However, there are some pioneering craft brands that are either growing their own grains or partnering with farms to propagate heritage strains. But for the time being, most distillers—no matter their size—are still buying commodity grains. *Advantage*: Big distillers.

Barrels
Once the grains are turned into a spirit, that spirit needs to be aged to be called whiskey. Again, the big distillers either own their own cooperages or have long-standing contracts with coopers. They also have the budgets to buy the best barrels. Meanwhile,

The type of barrel a whiskey ages in is incredibly important, since the alcohol picks up plenty of flavor and color from the wood.

some craft brands either use smaller barrels to try to speed up the aging process (spoiler alert: it doesn't work) or they're forced to buy barrels that aren't as well made, since those are the only ones that are available. It doesn't sound like a big deal, but bad barrels can ruin even the best-made whiskey. Big distillers—well established and well capitalized—can often wait longer for their whiskies to age, while craft upstarts need to sell their whiskies earlier to recoup their investment. *Advantage*: Big distillers.

Innovation

When it comes to innovation, small craft brands can try all sorts of new techniques and ingredients. If an experiment goes south, a company loses a barrel or blends it into another product. For a big brand to do anything innovative, it needs to be on a much grander scale, since it immediately needs to sell tens of thousands of cases to justify its investment.

Additionally, most small producers will not face a huge backlash if one of its products fails to take off. Many craft distillers start by producing entire portfolios of spirits and eventually begin to focus on producing only the bestsellers. Some of the techniques, ingredients, and flavors that have been championed by smaller brands are often later picked up by the bigger brands once they see their potential. *Advantage*: Craft distillers.

Ultimately, if a craft brand succeeds against the long odds it faces, its reward is now to be considered a big producer, leading to a slew of other considerations.

Craft distillers around the world often start new trends by producing innovative and creative whiskies.

Tasting Whiskey

Tasting a whiskey can be a transportive experience—a sip or two can take you across the world.

One of the biggest misconceptions I encounter is that many people conflate tasting whiskey and drinking whiskey. But there is actually a huge difference between the two.

When experts or distillers are tasting a dram, they usually make an almost clinical evaluation. The whiskey is generally kept at room temperature and sometimes water is added with a pipette to lower the proof. It's then sniffed, tasted, and scored. Next sample, please.

I have, of course, attended and led many whiskey tastings for connoisseurs and the curious drinker and we generally start by carefully evaluating the color of the spirit, dissecting its aromas, analyzing its many flavors on the palate, and, finally, commenting on the length of its finish.

Thankfully, drinking whiskey is much more of an enjoyable experience than that and, for most of us, involves a bit of contemplation, lots of good conversation, and hopefully a few laughs.

As your interest and experience with whiskey grows, you'll find a happy medium between tasting and drinking. No matter if I'm at a distillery or in a friend's kitchen, I still like to take a minute or two to think about what I'm smelling and tasting. A good whiskey is designed to be savored after all—it is specifically made to be full of flavors that have developed over years or even decades.

In time, some whiskies will become like old friends, their flavors and aromas so familiar that you could easily recognize them blindfolded. Other whiskies, new to you, will occasionally

Take a moment to look at the color of the spirit—it can sometimes reveal information about the barrel the whiskey was aged in.

A Bad Taste in Your Mouth

I spend most of my time talking about the full range of whiskey's delicious flavors and beautiful aromas. But if I'm being honest, not all whiskies are created equal, and sometimes I taste some really gross drams. How the hell does that happen?

Basically, at every step of the whiskey-making process, there's a chance for things to go astray, which can result in what are called off notes. Beginning with the grain, if it's moldy for example, those musty flavors (think: damp basement) will only intensify as the grain is turned into alcohol.

The fermentation stage is also potentially fraught. If the yeast has mutated or a rogue strain has muscled out a brand's desired one, you'll get a rainbow of funky and unexpected flavors in the finished whiskey.

Even when the spirit enters the barrel, it's not out of harm's way. If the wood is too green, which means it hasn't been dried properly before being turned into a barrel, it will possibly ruin the whiskey by adding herbal or wintergreen notes. (This sometimes shows up in very old whiskey from the 1800s, when barrel-construction practices and methods were different.) Conversely, if a whiskey is aged too long in a barrel, all you'll taste is bitter wood notes, which I can assure you is not enjoyable no matter how prestigious or expensive the whiskey.

While all of these deleterious outcomes are possible, there are many safeguards in place to prevent a flawed whiskey from being bottled. But some brands are better than others when it comes to quality control. And financial constraints sometimes mean that a distiller will release a whiskey that's not their best effort. If you think there is something actually wrong with the whiskey you bought (not simply that you don't like it), I recommend that you contact the distillery directly. Any reputable brand will want to know if the whiskey they're selling is flawed.

---

jolt you out of your everyday life and demand your immediate attention and respect. These rare finds have the ability to transport you around the world and remind you that life can still surprise you no matter how many whiskies you've tried in the past.

What sometimes strikes me the most is how a whiskey's flavor changes as it gradually evolves in my glass or is diluted by melting ice. What also fascinates me is when a whiskey smells one way but tastes completely different. I like to ponder how the whiskey was made and how that affected what I'm getting in the glass. (Can I taste the port barrel finish? The heirloom rye grain? The sweet mash?)

What follows is some general advice on identifying and enjoying the aromas

Tasting a whiskey actually starts by first sniffing its aromas.

and flavors of whiskey. The process of identification might seem like a frustrating exercise at first, but it's a skill like any other and requires practice. Thankfully, it doesn't really feel like practice most of the time.

♦ FOLLOW YOUR NOSE

The first step to appreciating a whiskey is smelling it. Keep your mouth slightly open, which helps you draw in all the aroma notes and prevents your olfactory senses from becoming overwhelmed. (If your nose does get overwhelmed, don't worry, just give it a few minutes away from the whiskey to recover.)

Slowly lower your nose into the glass. Sometimes, you can find different aromas slightly above the glass as opposed to in it. Give it a swirl and a small sniff. Do you pick up a hint of smoke? A pear or apple note? A bit of hot sawdust? Remember there are no wrong answers—it's your nose!

Another consideration is how much aroma you're getting. There are some whiskies that will perfume your whole house if you leave a glass of it on your counter. Others will make you work hard to pick up any hint of scent or just offer a tantalizing tease of what's to come on the tongue.

If you're having a very hard time picking up any aromas on the nose, there's an old trick that might help. Pour a tiny bit of whiskey on your palms and then rub them together back and forth quickly. Then smell your palms. The heat from the friction helps the spirit release some of its aromas.

♦ TAKE A SIP

Now the moment we've all been waiting for—take a small sip. For me, the first taste is like a primer coat of paint for my mouth. Rarely am I able to form a full impression right off the bat, so I like to take a second sip in quick succession.

Some folks recommend kind of chewing your sips of whiskey like you would a morsel of steak. While this might sound very strange at first, it helps to work some air into the whiskey and distribute it around your mouth, both of which help release the spirit's flavor compounds.

After you've tried a few sips and taken a minute to ponder what flavors you're getting from your dram, it's time to add a small amount of water

Take a small sip of whiskey and roll it around your palate. Once it's sufficiently coated, take a second sip.

The last step in tasting is reflecting on a whiskey's finish and aftertaste.

(less than a teaspoon to two ounces of whiskey) and taste it again. Thanks to a chemical reaction that occurs, a spirit will often open up as you add water, which also brings down the proof.

♦ MOUTHFEEL AND FINISH

While most of your whiskey appreciation is based on how it smells and tastes, you'll also want to keep mouthfeel (the texture of the spirit on your tongue) and finish in mind.

The mouthfeel of a whiskey is kind of an X factor that works in harmony with the aromas and flavors you get from your nose and palate. Does a whiskey feel thin or thick? Overpowering or delicate? Factors that affect mouthfeel are the base grains and the way a whiskey is distilled, as well as how many times it's distilled.

The very last thing to consider is how long the whiskey's flavor lingers on your palate after you swallowed your sip. Does it disappear without a trace

Dialing in Your Palate

Finding the right words to describe what you're smelling and tasting in a dram of whiskey takes experience and practice. At first you might recognize a flavor but not be able to identify it out of context. It's like running into a former neighbor in a foreign city. You know you know this person, but you struggle to remember your exact connection to them or even their name. It's kind of the same thing with identifying flavors. You might taste, say, banana or vanilla, but it can be hard to pinpoint what that familiar note is exactly.

The more you taste, the easier it will become to identify aromas and flavors. Here are the most common flavors that show up in many whiskies, which you should look out for as you taste.

- Vanilla
- Baking spice
- Corn
- Barley
- Banana
- Black pepper
- Dill pickle

- Apple
- Pear
- Mango
- Papaya
- Raisin
- Cedar
- Honey

- Walnut
- Pecan
- Peanut
- Hot sawdust
- Burning rubber
- Smoke
- Salinity

This list is by no means exhaustive. What makes whiskey distilling and drinking so much fun is that you never know exactly what you'll discover in your glass!

like a ghost? Or does it stick around for an uncomfortably long time, like a chatty coworker who doesn't seem to get how busy you are? Ideally, there's a middle ground—the flavor is meaty enough that you can appreciate the aftertaste, but it shows itself out after an enjoyable amount of time.

♦ **THE CASE FOR ADDING ICE OR WATER TO YOUR DRAM**

Can you keep a secret?

Many of the whiskey experts I've met in my more than two decades writing about drinks like to add ice and/or water or club soda to their whiskey when they're relaxing after a long day. Is that blasphemous?

Adding water or ice doesn't hurt the whiskey—it actually helps it to open a bit.

Only if you believe the bartenders, store clerks, friends, and family members who have been telling you for decades that you can't possibly add anything to a dram or it will ruin the whiskey. As an avowed believer in drinking what you like, how you like it, I say if that means you actually want to drink whiskey neat at room temperature, go for it. But if you're willing to broaden your mind a bit, give whiskey with ice, water, or club soda a try. Whiskey drinkers often treat dilution as a dirty word, something to be avoided at all costs, but a little water actually is a good thing—it helps open up the whiskey a bit and releases aromas and flavors. It should tell you something that whisky blenders in Scotland dilute the barrel samples to about 40 proof (20 percent alcohol by volume) when they're making selections.

Still unconvinced? Consider that Scotch really only became popular in the United States at the turn of the twentieth century because of the Highball (whiskey with club soda) craze. In fact, I'd argue that the Highball is as important to the enduring popularity of whiskey as is the Manhattan and the Old-Fashioned. It was really only during the past thirty-odd years, with the rise of single malts and investment-grade bottlings, that these strict "rules for drinking whiskey" emerged.

Liquor legend and Jim Beam's grandson, Booker Noe, used to drink bourbon in what he called Kentucky Iced Tea, which he made in a tall glass that he filled with ice cubes, high proof whiskey, and spring water. Depending on how strong he wanted the drink, he would add more or less water. I think Noe's approach serves as a good ground rule for all drinkers: Bring the proof down to whatever tastes good and feels comfortable to you—whiskey shouldn't overwhelm all your senses, and you should never feel like you're struggling to drink it.

In the United States, whiskey has to be at least 80 proof (40 percent alcohol by volume) and many whiskies are bottled at that strength. I'd suggest drinking these whiskies closer to neat, since alcohol (like fat in food) carries flavor, and if you dilute the spirit too much there won't be much whiskey flavor left. Higher proof whiskies, or brawnier ones, like the smoky, peaty malts from the Scottish island of Islay, or cask strength bourbons, can usually better stand up to water, ice, or use in cocktails. But the bigger the whiskey the more skill it often takes to find things that complement it.

No matter the whiskey, make sure that the water you're adding is fairly soft (low in mineral content) and neutral. In some parts of the world, the water has a very specific taste and even a smell. This should not be used in whiskey—if your water is flavorful, use bottled water instead. The same goes for water used to make ice.

And when it comes to ice, I find that simpler is better. Some folks insist on using giant ice cubes the size of baseballs, but that isn't required or necessary. I personally like a few 1-inch-by-1-inch (2.5-by-2.5-centimeter) cubes (that I make in a silicone mold), which cool my whiskey but also melt only a bit.

But let's not fall into that oh-so-whiskey trap of overcomplicating things. There is no right way. Drinking whiskey is kind of like buying a cup of coffee. You can have it black, with a splash of milk, a bit of sweetener, or you can add a ton of milk, sugar, chocolate syrup, pumpkin spice, or whipped cream.

You wouldn't listen to a random stranger telling you how to order your coffee at Starbucks, so don't let one tell you how to drink your whiskey.

Large and very cold cubes are ideal because they melt slowly and don't overly dilute your glass of whiskey.

Glasses

Years ago, I had lunch in Manhattan with Richard Geoffroy, who was then the cellar master of the famed Dom Pérignon champagne house. The plan was to taste several special glasses of his bubbly. A squad of servers approached our table with trays of gleaming, empty glass flutes, but Geoffroy immediately requested bulbous red wineglasses instead.

I was more than a little puzzled. Sparkling wine is generally served in statuesque flutes or retro-looking coups. Why would we drink champagne out of oversized red wineglasses? Geoffroy's answer was simple: You can't stick your nose into a flute. The larger opening of a wineglass allows you to really sniff a wine's aromas.

I think the same is true when it comes to the ideal whiskey glass. A number of companies make crystal glasses designed for tasting whiskey. The most famous is Glencairn, which usually supplies the major whiskey festivals and tasting events with glassware. I have certainly drunk my share of whiskey from these glasses, whose design is no accident and is meant to capture and direct aromas to your nose. If you don't have one of these glasses, you can use a sherry glass, a brandy snifter, or just a small wineglass instead.

Perhaps it's the shape of my nose, but like Geoffroy, I prefer to use a glass with a wider opening. Whiskey can taste different in subtle ways depending on the shape and size of the glass you're using. To help find your ideal

Professional whiskey tasters often use a specialized tasing glass, which helps them to sniff out all the nuances in the spirit.

glass, pour an ounce of the same whiskey into a few different kinds of glasses and see if you can detect any variations or determine if you prefer one type of vessel over another.

A traditional Old-Fashioned or rocks glass is generally not used for professional tastings, since they don't channel aromas to your nose in quite the same way as a curved glass. But given that most whiskey is probably drunk out of one of these designs, if that's all you have, so be it. You can do basic tasting in one of these glasses (and easily fit your nose inside of it). And if you're so moved, there's more than enough room for adding water, ice, or even club soda. Then, finally, the drinking can begin!

Collecting whiskey has become more popular in recent years; as a result, the price of many bottles have rapidly increased.

Collecting Whiskey

People have been collecting wine for centuries. Auctions of rare bottles now regularly take place in major cities around the world, to say nothing of the countless wine stores with amazing selections of vintages they've been quietly cellaring for years.

Until recently, however, if you wanted to build a spirits collection your options were fairly limited to scooping up new releases and limited editions that many brands offer each year. For example, New York State held its first spirits auction since Prohibition in 2005, at a Christie's location in Rockefeller Plaza. Many states still forbid the auction of spirits, but the rules for selling vintage hard alcohol have fortunately loosened a bit over the years (though they're still fairly restrictive). Before buying and selling whiskey in your area, check with your state liquor authority about local laws. In many places, it's still illegal for individuals to buy and sell bottles from one another or for an individual to sell bottles to a liquor store or bar.

However, bartenders and aficionados have found a legal and fun way to build collections in recent years—scouring off-the-beaten-path liquor stores in search of rare vintage bottles forgotten on dusty shelves or in cardboard boxes disintegrating in basements. These whiskey treasure hunters have turned up all kinds of rarities, from sought-after ryes and bourbons from the 1970s to first-generation Scottish single malts from the 1980s and '90s.

There's also a thriving whiskey trade on social media, facilitated by online whiskey-collecting groups. While you may be tempted to buy some of these bottles, be warned that this trade is illegal in most parts of the United States and is completely unregulated. Sadly, it's not uncommon to be tricked into purchasing a fake whiskey. Buyer beware.

♦ STORING WHISKEY

An unopened bottle of whiskey can essentially last indefinitely. However, there are a few best practices to follow that should help ensure a bottle's incredible life expectancy, and facts to know if you ever decide to open it.

Once the whiskey goes into the bottle, it stops aging and should not change significantly. It is ready to drink immediately and does not need to sit in a cellar for years before you should open it. (Unlike fine wine, which continues to mature and improve in the bottle for years, if not decades.) This is also why a 10-year-old bottle of whiskey will always be a 10-year-old bottle of whiskey, regardless of whether or not you open it today or in a century—the ten years of aging took place in the barrel, not the bottle.

If a bottle has never been opened, or is open but almost full, it has a better chance of remaining good. The problem is that air in the bottle causes alcohol to evaporate. According to Doug Frost's excellent entry in *The Oxford Companion to Spirits & Cocktails*, "once sufficient ethanol has evaporated, what is left in the bottle loses its antibacterial properties and becomes vulnerable to decay." The general rule of thumb is, the more air in the bottle the quicker you need to drink it.

It's also a very bad sign if the amount of whiskey in a bottle is going down (without your participation)—this means the cap no longer seals and is allowing in air and allowing the alcohol to evaporate. Needless to say, the flavor of the whiskey is beginning to change. For this same reason, if I was decanting my whiskey, I would use a decanter with a stopper that formed a tight seal, for a whiskey that I planned to drink in the next two to three months.

A bottle of whiskey should always be stored standing straight up, not on its side like a prized Bordeaux wine. Spirits do best away from direct sunlight and exposure to UVA light—the back of a liquor cabinet in your living room or inside a closet is a good place. You should also keep your booze at a comfortable and consistent room temperature (68–72°F/20–22°C) or, if possible, a few degrees cooler than room temperature. Whiskey can weather normal fluctuation of temperature, but keeping your booze above your stove, next to the oven, or in a small room with a clothes dryer is a recipe for disaster—you'll essentially cook the spirits.

Even if a bottle has been properly stored, don't be surprised if the cork breaks when you're opening the bottle. This is a common occurrence, because

When stored properly, bottles of whiskey can last for decades.

the bottle has been standing up and the cork has dried out. If this happens, use a sharp skewer or a garnish pick to extract the cork from the neck of the bottle. (To reseal the bottle, use a so-called wine stopper. I like the silicone ones made by OXO that expand in a bottle's neck.) If some of the cork falls into the bottle, pour the whiskey though a strainer into a clean bottle or decanter.

How to Drink It

I can't say this enough: You should drink whiskey any way that makes you happy. Full stop. And no matter what anyone says, you should feel empowered to add a bit of water, ice, or even ginger ale or ginger beer. The ratio of whiskey to mixers (or ice) really depends on your personal preference. I'd suggest adding a little at a time until you find the right balance for you.

There are a few classic cocktail recipes that work with many different types of whiskey, including the Old-Fashioned, the Highball, the Julep, the Sour, and the Manhattan. I'm including some of these recipes here, sorted by the type of whiskey that is usually used, but feel free to experiment. While you might prefer to alter the recipe ratios slightly depending on the type of whiskey you're using, the general formulas are pretty universal. The cocktail recipes here also appear, along with many others, in the Cocktails appendix (see page 553).

♦ AMERICAN WHISKEY

While you can always drink your whiskey neat, on the rocks, or with soda, it was practically designed for cocktails. The drink we now think of as the first modern cocktail, the Old-Fashioned, was often originally made with rye whiskey. (It's a delicious combination of spirits, bitters, sugar, and ice.) The earliest description found in print ran in an 1806 newspaper in Hudson, New York. A reader had written in because the previous week the editor had used the word *cock-tale* and hadn't defined the term. All of the other fancy and imaginative drinks recipes essentially grew out of that one simple recipe.

One of the reasons American whiskey is such a popular ingredient is that it's generally been widely available and affordable. I also think it has never really been perceived as a precious commodity that needs to be handled with extra special care or spoken about in hushed and reverential tones. This was a spirit not for pontificating but for drinking, and it's been used in just about every possible combination you can think of. Here are a few recipes that deserve to be mentioned, and help tell the story of how the cocktail evolved in the United States.

While it's wonderful to sip a dram of whiskey neat and contemplate the state of the world, you should also feel empowered to add ice or mixers.

Old-Fashioned

INGREDIENTS

1 teaspoon sugar

2 dashes Angostura bitters

Splash of water

2 ounces (60 ml) bourbon or rye whiskey

GLASS: Old-Fashioned

GARNISH: Orange peel and/or brandied cherry

DIRECTIONS

Add the sugar, the bitters, and the water to an Old-Fashioned glass and muddle them. Then add the whiskey and fill the glass with ice. Stir, and garnish if you like with an orange peel and/or brandied cherry.

(Note: This recipe also appears on page 562.)

The Manhattan

From the Old-Fashioned came the megahit, the Manhattan, which now consists of whiskey, sweet vermouth, and bitters. The history and evolution of the drink is representative of how a lot of cocktail recipes are created. Bartenders are curious by nature, and are often bored in between periods of insane activity. During those down times, they often take classic concoctions and tinker with ratios and ingredients. Vermouth, in the late 1800s, was the new hip ingredient. It's no wonder that folks started adding it to cocktails like the Old-Fashioned.

Who first created the drink is still a mystery. What we do know is that it developed over time. A number of the earlier recipes called for either sweet or dry vermouth (some bartenders even used both types). Other early versions used more vermouth than whiskey, which we now call a Reverse Manhattan (see page 564 for recipe). From this experimentation also came another famed cocktail, the Martini, which at its essence is very similar to the Manhattan.

Today, the Manhattan is often made in craft cocktail bars with rye, but it can certainly be made with bourbon, which produces a delicious, slightly sweeter version of the drink.

The Mint Julep

Forget apple pie, what could be more American than enjoying a freshly made Mint Julep while watching the Kentucky Derby on the first Saturday in May? Well, it turns out the drink's roots are quite a bit more international than that—and have little to do with bourbon. For starters, its name comes from the Persian word *julap* and it was originally made with rosewater. It was prized by the English in the 1700s for its supposed medicinal properties. When it got to the United States, it became a recreational beverage with plenty of crushed ice and the rosewater was ultimately jettisoned.

The Mint Julep was elevated to a work of art by a number of Black bartenders working across the American South, including the talented Tom Bullock, author of the 1917 cocktail book *The Ideal Bartender*. His version of the Mint Julep was so famous that it even played a role in a libel court case involving former president Theodore Roosevelt.

The Sazerac

There are few drinks with a history as contentious as the Sazerac's. But thankfully, the recipe is not up for debate—it's very similar to an Old-Fashioned, the key difference being that you first coat the inside of your glass with absinthe. The anise flavor of the absinthe is the perfect foil for the spice of the rye whiskey.

The debate around the Sazerac centers on the origins of its name. Until fairly recently, it was believed that the drink was invented at the famous New Orleans, Louisiana, cocktail bar the Sazerac House, and originally featured Cognac instead of whiskey.

Manhattan

INGREDIENTS

- 2 ounces (60 ml) rye whiskey or bourbon
- 1 ounce (30 ml) sweet vermouth
- 2 dashes Angostura bitters

GLASS: Cocktail
GARNISH: Brandied cherry

DIRECTIONS

Combine all of the ingredients in a mixing glass and fill it with ice. Stir, then strain into a chilled cocktail glass. Garnish with a brandied cherry.

(Note: This recipe also appears on page 560.)

Teddy Roosevelt and the Mint Julep

Could trust-busting, cavalry-leading Teddy Roosevelt actually resist finishing a delicious Mint Julep?

The former president's drinking habits were at the heart of a $10,000 libel lawsuit he filed in 1912 against George A. Newett, the editor of the *Iron Ore* newspaper in Ishpeming, Michigan. Newett ran a story in the paper that referred to Roosevelt as "not infrequently drunk"—a charge that Roosevelt vehemently disputed. Given that the temperance movement was at the height of its power, being labeled as a heavy drinker was career ending for a national politician.

It was so important that Roosevelt refute the accusation that he took the stand to defend himself. He quickly admitted, "I am not a total abstainer," but then testified that he didn't drink most types of alcohol, unless he was directed to by the surgeon general for his health. The one thing he admitted to drinking? Mint Juleps.

"There was a fine mint bed at the White House and I may have drunk half a dozen Mint Juleps there in a year." And since leaving office, "I think I have tasted Mint Juleps twice, part of a glass at St. Louis and a sip from a loving cup at Little Rock, Arkansas."

While Roosevelt ultimately was vindicated, winning a settlement of six cents plus an apology, you have to wonder if he lied under oath. The Mint Julep Teddy claimed that he only had "part of" was made by the famous Black bartender Tom Bullock who at the time worked at the St. Louis Country Club. The *St. Louis Post-Dispatch* was so incredulous of Roosevelt's claim that it ran an op-ed that asked: "Who was ever known to drink just a part of one of Tom's?" The paper concluded that when Roosevelt "says that he consumed just a part of one he doubtless meant that he did not swallow the mint itself, munch the ice and devour the very cup."

Personally, I think there was a perjury case to be made, though charges were never pressed.

Amazingly, until recently the Mint Julep wasn't made with bourbon. Through the nineteenth century, you were more likely to find a Julep made with rum and brandy than whiskey. In the first cocktail book, *How to Mix Drinks*, from 1862, pioneering bartender Jerry Thomas lists several recipes for the drink, with only one calling for whiskey. In Bullock's book, he features both the familiar "Mint Julep—Kentucky Style" as well as the "Mint Julep—St. Louis Style," which calls for rye whiskey, gin, grenadine, lime and lemon juices, and club soda.

As for the Kentucky Derby, the Mint Julep was loosely associated with the race when it began in the late 1800s. At the time the Julep was a very popular drink, and the version served at Churchill Downs Racetrack, no doubt, was made with bourbon. However, by 1919, the last Derby before Prohibition, the link between the race and the drink was well established. "And the historic and famous 'mint julep' will pass with this year's race," ran a story in newspapers across the country. "It long has been an institution at Churchill Downs where 75 feet of bar and an army of bartenders catered to the thirsty."

Right after repeal, the connection seems a bit more tenuous. Brown-Forman put out a pamphlet called *How to Make Old Kentucky Famed Drinks*, the purpose of which was to remind drinkers who'd just weathered thirteen long years of Prohibition what good whiskey was and how to make proper cocktails with it. The first drink mentioned was none other than the Mint Julep, which was credited to Martin Cueno, the head bartender at the Louisville, Kentucky, private Pendennis Club. While his recipe for the drink is the one we use now, there's no mention of a connection to the Derby. But the race is mentioned a few drinks later in the write-up for the Kentucky Derby Fizz, a mix of whiskey, powdered sugar, an egg, curaçao, and lemon juice. The directions end with this comment: "A very smooth drink, popular with old-time Derby crowds."

Eventually, the Fizz . . . fizzled out, and the Mint Julep became intrinsically tied to the Derby. Now, on race day, you can find delicious Juleps made with fresh mint and high-end bourbon at restaurants and bars around the country. The one place you can't easily get one made from scratch? Churchill Downs. Most of what's sold at the track is a bottled premade version produced by Brown-Forman's historic brand Old Forester.

President Teddy Roosevelt swore under oath that the only alcohol he indulged in was the occasional Mint Julep.

Mint Julep

INGREDIENTS
- 2 ounces (60 ml) bourbon
- ½ ounce (15 ml) simple syrup (1 part sugar, 1 part water)
- 6 to 8 mint leaves

GLASS: Julep cup or rocks
GARNISH: Mint leaves

DIRECTIONS

Put the mint leaves and the syrup in a Julep cup or rocks glass and muddle them lightly. Add the bourbon and fill the cup or glass with crushed ice. Stir until the glass is nicely frosted. Mound some more crushed ice on top and garnish with mint leaves.

(Note: This recipe also appears on page 560.)

Thanks to the phylloxera epidemic and its effect on the world's brandy supply (see page 10), savvy bartenders supposedly replaced the French spirit with widely available rye whiskey.

It's a beautiful story, which has been repeated many times in print. The only problem is that, according to drinks historian David Wondrich, there is no definitive proof to support this story. Yes, there was a Sazerac House in New Orleans that was known for its drinks. Yes, phylloxera allowed whiskey to steal the spotlight and the market share of Cognac. And yes, a version of the Old-Fashioned calling for an absinthe rinse was popular in NOLA. But the trail grows cold beyond that. There just isn't any solid proof that it was first mixed at the Sazerac House.

Regardless of whether the story is truth or myth, there are few pleasures as fine as sipping a Sazerac on a steamy afternoon in a historic New Orleans bar.

♦ SCOTCH

One of the dumbest whiskey debates by far is how to "properly" drink Scotch. The answer should, of course, be however you damn well like it.

Seriously. A lot of the reverence that prevents people from adding water, ice, club soda, or other mixers to Scotch is completely made up for the sake of marketing. The supposed sanctity of single malts, which shouldn't be diluted or altered under any circumstances, helps justify the high price of the whisky and supports the idea that it's for incredibly discerning palates. The idea behind this "thinking" is basically that what pours out of the bottle in a golden ribbon is like a perfect work of art that just needs to be appreciated in silent reverence. So, please keep your voice down as I gently swirl my 25-year-old Scotch in my special crystal whisky glass. I hope you're laughing, because what's being peddled to you by a number of brands is largely a joke.

A great part of the reason marketers were able to trick us all into believing this nonsense is that up until the 1980s there wasn't really a tradition of drinking single malt even in Scotland, so they essentially created a backstory for this style of whisky.

The earliest Scotch mixed drink was the Toddy, which came into vogue in the 1840s and calls for Scotch, hot water, sugar, and a piece of lemon peel. Dr. Nicholas Morgan, in his book *A Long Stride*, postulates that the first Scotch blends created in the early 1850s were explicitly produced for drinking in a

Sazerac

Contributed by Neal Bodenheimer

INGREDIENTS

- 4 spritzes Herbsaint
- 2 ounces (60 ml) Sazerac Rye
- 4 dashes Peychaud's Bitters
- ¼ ounce (10 ml) demerara syrup (1 part demerara sugar, 1 part water)

GLASS: Double Old-Fashioned
GARNISH: Lemon peel

DIRECTIONS

Using an atomizer, spritz the interior of a chilled double Old-Fashioned glass with the Herbsaint and set the glass aside. Combine the rest of the ingredients in a mixing glass and fill it with ice. Stir, then strain into the prepared glass. Garnish with a lemon peel.

(Note: This recipe also appears on page 566.)

While single malt Scotch should be tasted neat and at room temperature, it also works surprisingly well in cocktails.

One of the original and bestselling whisky drinks is the Highball, which was traditionally made with a mix of Scotch and club soda or ginger ale. In the 1800s, the term *ball* was used for a dram of whiskey, and the *high* meant it was being stretched out with a mixer.

One reason this combination may have taken off is that English drinkers could no longer easily find a high-quality brandy and soda because of the phylloxera epidemic—so they subbed in Scotch for this drink.

"Scotch and soda became the English gentleman's drink and eventually the elite nightcap of the American drinker," wrote Suzanne Hamlin in 1979 in a *New York Daily News* story about the rise of single malts in the US. This carbonated concoction Toddy. But before blends came along, folks were using single malts in their Toddy recipes, and it's still a wonderful drink made with a big, brawny whisky.

Hot Toddy

INGREDIENTS

2 ounces (60 ml) Scotch
2 ounces (60 ml) boiling water
1 teaspoon sugar

GLASS: Mug
GARNISH: Lemon peel or wedge

DIRECTIONS

Fill a mug with the boiling water and let it warm up for about 90 seconds. Discard the water. Combine all the ingredients in the heated mug and stir. Garnish with a lemon peel or wedge.

(Note: This recipe also appears on page 558.)

Rob Roy

INGREDIENTS
- 2 ounces (60 ml) Scotch
- 1 ounce (30 ml) sweet vermouth
- 2 dashes Angostura bitters

GLASS: Cocktail
GARNISH: Brandied cherry

DIRECTIONS

Combine all of the ingredients in a mixing glass and fill it with ice. Stir, then strain into a chilled cocktail glass. Garnish with a brandied cherry.

(Note: This recipe also appears on page 565.)

became so popular that even famed sparkling water Perrier was marketed in the early 1900s as a mixer for whisky.

With the introduction of proper cocktails, Scotch found its way into a few famous recipes, including the Manhattan variant of the Rob Roy (Scotch, sweet vermouth, and bitters; see above) and the incredibly popular Rusty Nail (blended Scotch and Scotch-based liqueur Drambuie; also on the next page).

The truth is that Scotch, even single malt, can be used in a range of cocktails. Certainly, one could make a tasty Scotch Old-Fashioned or a Scotch Julep. The spirit also pairs very well with ingredients such as honey and citrus. I once heard about a brand ambassador for the super peaty and smoky Scotch Ardbeg who would order Margaritas made with the distillery's pricey Uigeadail Single Malt Whisky instead of tequila. The bartender on duty, veteran New York mixologist Toby Cecchini, first thought the order for this cocktail was a joke, since, after all, who would use Uigeadail in a Margarita? After double-checking that, yes, this was what the guest wanted and she was okay with the higher price of the drink, he made a round of these Ardbeg Margaritas. And guess what? They tasted pretty good (Toby later made me one). So, if you like a mezcal Margarita or a mezcal Paloma, you might want to try swapping in a smoky Scotch, like Ardbeg or Bowmore.

The hardest part of making cocktails with Scotch is working up the courage to use an expensive bottle of, say, Uigeadail that sells for around $85. Working with a $20 bottle of Tito's

Rusty Nail

INGREDIENTS
1 ounce (30 ml) blended Scotch
½ ounce (15 ml) Drambuie

GLASS: Rocks

DIRECTIONS
Combine all of the ingredients in a rocks glass. Fill the glass with ice, then stir.

(Note: This recipe also appears on page 565.)

Vodka is a lot less intimidating. Make a mistake? Just start over. Don't like what you created? Just pour it down the sink.

Fortunately, you can still find a whole range of blended Scotches that sell for a reasonable price, like Dewar's, Chivas Regal, and Johnnie Walker Black Label, all of which will bring a lot to a mixed drink. In fact, until fairly recently the whole Scotch market was blends that were specifically made to be quaffed and enjoyed in mixed drinks. If anybody asks what the hell you're doing making drinks with Scotch, just tell them that's how the Scots originally took their whisky.

And no matter how you choose to drink your Scotch, instead of saying cheers use the Gaelic sláinte (SLAWN-cha)!

♦ IRISH WHISKEY

Given that Ireland has been making whiskey for centuries and there are tons of Irish pubs around the world, you might expect there to be countless cocktails calling for the spirit. The truth is, people in Ireland usually drink their whiskey on the rocks, neat, with a splash of soda, or deliciously paired with a fresh pint of Guinness.

You can certainly use Irish whiskey in classic American whiskey cocktails like an Old-Fashioned or a version of the Manhattan—but there really aren't many popular classic or modern drinks that explicitly call for Irish whiskey. Usually, the recipe cited is Cameron's Kick (see page 557), which isn't exactly a famous drink, and calls for both Irish whiskey and Scotch.

Of course, there is one famous Irish whiskey cocktail that most people know: the Irish Coffee. It's almost ironic that such a majestic and historic spirit would be connected with a modern drink that was only dreamed up in the late 1930 or early '40s. And unless you order one at the handful of establishments known for making the cocktail properly—such as the Buena Vista Cafe in San Francisco and the Dead Rabbit in New York—it's often a monstrosity composed of an unholy mix of stale coffee, cheap booze, and overly sweet canned whipped cream. Another reason the Irish Coffee is an odd ambassador for Irish whiskey: While the drink is known in Ireland, it's not very popular among the Irish, and never has been. This makes sense when you consider that it was originally mixed up for travelers on layovers—first possibly at the Foynes Flying Boat Station and later definitely at the adjoining modern Shannon Airport—as they made their

Irish whiskey is typically drunk neat or on the rocks in Ireland—but some cocktails (modern and historic) call for the spirit.

Irish Coffee

Contributed by the Dead Rabbit

INGREDIENTS

- 1 ounce (30 ml) Bushmills Original Irish Whiskey
- 1¼ tablespoons (20 ml) demerara syrup (2 parts demerara sugar, 1 part water)
- 3½ ounces (100 ml) hot coffee

GLASS: 6-ounce (200 ml) glass
GARNISH: Whipped cream

DIRECTIONS

Combine the whiskey and demerara syrup in a 6-ounce (200 ml) glass. Add the coffee (there should be an index finger's worth of space at the top). Top with freshly whipped cream.

(Note: This recipe also appears on page 559.)

Cameron's Kick
Created by Harry McElhone

INGREDIENTS

1 ounce (30 ml) Scotch
1 ounce (30 ml) Irish whiskey
½ ounce (15 ml) lemon juice
½ ounce (15 ml) orgeat syrup

GLASS: Cocktail

DIRECTIONS

Combine all of the ingredients in a shaker and fill it with ice. Shake, then strain into a chilled cocktail glass.

(Note: This recipe also appears on page 557.)

way to other UK and European destinations (see The Myth and Legend of Irish Coffee, page 327).

Arguably, the next most famous Irish whiskey cocktail in the US is the Big Ginger (Irish whiskey, ginger ale, a squeeze of lemon, and one of lime.) This is the house drink at a bar in downtown Minneapolis, Minnesota, called the Local, where this simple yet refreshing idea was so popular that the bar sold more Jameson than any other establishment in the world for three years straight in the late 2000s. (And that includes pubs in Dublin.)

The Big Ginger doesn't have to be made exclusively with Irish whiskey, but it certainly tastes good with it. And if you leave out the citrus, you've got a classic Highball, which has been popular for decades and was one of the drinks that put Scotch whisky on the map. This drink is generally called a Whiskey Ginger and tastes especially good if you use a high-quality ginger ale or a spicy nonalcoholic ginger beer. (The British Fever-Tree, the Bermudan Goslings, and the Jamaican Reed's all make great carbonated ginger beers.)

Given its long history, you might ask why aren't there more drink recipes that call for Irish whiskey? It's a good question and one that has puzzled me for years. One theory is that Irish whiskey gets lost in a cocktail, so bartenders prefer to use a spirit with bigger flavors that are a better match for, say, vermouth or liqueurs. But this theory fails to account for the fact that Irish whiskey was primarily pot still or single malt until the 1950s, both of which are more rich and brawny than a lot of the competition.

The corollary theory is that Irish whiskey is so delicious it doesn't need to be improved on with the addition of other ingredients. I respect both arguments, but note that vanishing into a mixed drink definitely hasn't slowed down vodka's success, and being delicious hasn't slowed down bourbon's either.

Perhaps the reason for the dearth of cocktails tied to Irish whiskey is because, up until the late 1800s, whiskey wasn't a popular cocktail ingredient, lagging far behind the bartender favorites of gin, brandy, and rum. And when the phylloxera outbreak catapulted other whiskies into the starting lineup, Irish distillers were facing one challenge after another and missed out on a golden age of mixology.

With all that said, somewhere on Earth I think there's a bartender or two working on an Irish whiskey cocktail that will become a modern classic. Until then, I'll have mine on the rocks with perhaps a splash of club soda.

♦ CANADIAN WHISKY

I know it sounds ridiculous, but basically the only famous Canadian cocktail is a version of the Blood Mary—the Bloody Caesar—made with vodka and the tomato-and-clam-broth concoction Clamato.

So you can imagine when it comes to drink recipes calling for some of the country's local whisky, there really aren't any notable creations or signature serves. Perhaps Canada's notoriously polite populous would never deign to tell you how you should drink whisky.

Canada is now famous for its blended whisky, which generally combines several different types of whiskies.

More likely, I think the lack of signature cocktails made with Canadian whisky might have to do with the fact that Canadian distillers produce a wide variety of whiskies—everything from affordable blends to full-flavored straight rye whiskies and everything in between. Many of these new whiskies, like Forty Creek Barrel Select or straight rye Lot No. 40, are now used by top bars in classic American whiskey cocktails like the Old-Fashioned and the Manhattan.

The only drink that comes close to being a Canadian whisky cocktail is the 7 & 7 (Seagram's 7 and 7UP soda). It was a simple, two-ingredient drink that, for a time, seemingly every establishment in the Western hemisphere could make, no matter how crappy the bar or bartender. The only hitch is that, while Seagram's was a Canadian company, Seagram's 7 is a blend of American whiskey. This cocktail also works beautifully with a traditional Canadian blend like Crown Royal or Canadian Club. It's also quite close to the other dive-bar stalwart, Canadian Club & cola.

♦ JAPANESE WHISKY

Traditionally, if you were at a bar in Japan, you'd often hear patrons ordering a Mizuwari (lots of still water with some whisky) or possibly a whisky served in a glass with a single crystal-clear, hand-carved, tennis ball-size ice cube.

Today, you'll still find folks drinking Japanese whisky in those ways, but another similar drink has grown even more popular: the Highball. The simple, refreshing mix of club soda and whisky in a tall glass filled with ice has become a sensation across the country—and a signature of modern Japanese bar culture. In Japan, the drink generally is made with a lot more club soda than whisky, which turns into an easy-drinking and low alcohol cocktail.

Over the last fifteen years or so, the giant conglomerate Suntory put its vast marketing might behind making the cocktail ubiquitous. The company even installed eight thousand Highball machines in casual izakaya restaurants (think: a Japanese pub with complimentary pub grub) and in some cocktail bars across the country. At the touch of a button, these automated bartenders produce a highly carbonated, icy cold Highball made, of course, with one of Suntory's whiskies—usually Kakubin or with the American Jim Beam White Label. (For these two whiskies, the machines are set to a ratio of one part whiskey to four parts club soda.) The company is beginning to introduce these machines in the United States, though the US machines usually use one part of Suntory's Toki Whisky with three parts club soda.

This isn't the first time the Highball has become either a sensation or a vehicle to promote whiskey. The Highball is the drink that helped make blended Scotch popular in the United States at the beginning of the twentieth century. That's when the cocktail became a classic, and it's the reason so many people kept soda siphons in their home bars. If you're a fan of old black-and-white films from the 1930s, you'll often see characters fixing themselves a drink by pouring a dram of

Japanese whisky has become a sensation in Japan as well as in the US and Europe.

whiskey and topping it was a squirt of soda water from a siphon. For decades, the Highball was popular in Japan and America but, like most classic drinks, fell out of favor in the 1970s and '80s.

For the most part—except in dive bars and old-school establishments—the Highball was forgotten. If you happened to order a "whiskey with soda," you'd get a glass filled mostly with whiskey, crappy ice, and a stingy splash of club soda that was mixed with a plastic red stir straw. After one or two songs blaring from the jukebox, the small ice cubes would have completely melted and the soda lost its snap—resulting in a watery mess. And, seemingly, a very sad end for an otherwise dignified concoction.

Fortunately, the drink has made a comeback, which began in Japan in 2008. According to Dave Broom's book, *The Way of Whisky*, the Highball's rebirth was in large part because of the aforementioned marketing campaign by Suntory. A less trumpeted fact is that it was born of necessity. The company's whisky sales, following sales in the rest of the industry, had fallen precipitously. Suntory noticed that the two establishments in Japan still selling high volumes of its whisky both served Highballs. Using this intel, over the next few years the company made an effort to reintroduce the drink, creating a program for mostly izakaya-style restaurants and some cocktail bars around the country. Fortunately, the plan worked, reviving not just the Highball but helping to bring back the Japanese whisky industry.

The Highball's return from obscurity lifted the fortunes of the Japanese whisky industry.

When I visited Japan in 2018, Suntory had opened dedicated Highball bars. I drank at one in Tokyo that served Maker's Mark Bourbon (see page 142) exclusively, but you can find the drink in all types of establishments across the country. Highballs are particularly popular at what's called a tachinomi (TA-she-no-me), essentially a bar for commuters where patrons stand. The idea is to have a quick drink or two with perhaps a bit of food and then be on your way. If you prefer a drink while riding your shinkansen (bullet train), you can enjoy a canned Suntory Highball.

Some izakayas also serve the incredible 10-ounce Mega Highball (roughly 2 ounces/60 ml of whisky to 8 ounces/240 ml of club soda), which comes in a giant glass that looks like an Oktoberfest-size beer stein. Given that the drink is mostly club soda, even the Mega Highball has a relatively low alcohol content and pairs remarkably well with yakitori and other delicious small delicacies.

Highball

Contributed by Kenta Goto

INGREDIENTS

1 ¼ ounces (40 ml) Japanese whisky

4 ounces (120 ml) club soda

GLASS: Highball

DIRECTIONS

Combine all of the ingredients in a Highball glass and fill it with ice. Stir lightly.

(Note: This recipe also appears on page 558.)

You can, of course, find some of the best cocktail bars in the world in Japan, which serve all the classic whisky drinks. And just like in Scotland, the rise of single malts has changed Japanese drinking culture. While most Japanese whisky is still a blend and used in mixed drinks, single malts and pricier blended offerings are generally sipped neat or over a beautifully carved ice cube.

♦ WORLD WHISKEY

What makes writing about the world of whiskey exciting and engaging is that it's always changing and evolving. And one of the biggest recent developments for the spirit is that it's now being made outside the traditional whiskey-producing regions. Most of the distillers in these areas start out by releasing familiar and historic styles, like single malt or straight rye, and then over time begin to use local ingredients or innovative techniques. Melbourne's Starward (see page 461), for instance, uses freshly emptied wine barrels from local Australian wineries to age its whisky.

I think the same is true for how people drink whiskey in these areas—they start by enjoying it neat, on the rocks, or in classic cocktails, and then over time begin to create their own drinking customs and traditions. In China, for example, the combination of whisky and cold green tea has become a huge trend. Over the next few years, I imagine we'll see more of these new and innovative ways to drink whiskey. And in the meantime if you get a bottle from one of these upstart whiskey regions, I would start by trying it neat first and then begin experimenting with different mixers.

A WHISKEY TIMELINE

1300s
"The Red Book of Ossory" from Kilkenny, Ireland, likely dates to this period and includes a possible tangential reference to distilling. Irish whiskey brands claim this is proof that Ireland made whiskey before Scotland.

1494
The first description of possible whisky making in Scotland appears in the Exchequer Rolls (official records) of the Scottish king, James IV: "To Friar John Cor, by order of the King, to make aqua vitae VIII bolls of malt."

1608
The town of Bushmills, in what is now Northern Ireland, is granted a license by the king of England to make whiskey.

1640
The US distilling industry begins on Staten Island. Willem Kieft, director-general of the Dutch colony of New Netherland, makes some kind of spirit there from rye and corn.

1648
A letter from Emanuel Downing to his brother-in-law, John Winthrop, former governor of the Massachusetts Bay Colony, includes the first reference to making a spirit specifically from rye grain in the North American colonies.

1757
Peter Roe begins making whiskey in a Dublin distillery that he bought. Under the direction of his descendant George Roe, the business will ultimately be called Roe & Co and become one of Ireland's largest whiskey distilleries.

1776
The American colonies declare their independence from Great Britain—one of the key moments that changes the US from a territory that produces and primarily drinks rum to a country that produces and drinks whiskey.

1779
Bowmore claims that it first opens on the Scottish island of Islay and begins producing peated whisky.

1780

John Jameson and his partners get a license for his original Bow Street distillery in Dublin, Ireland. By 1805, the family will have complete control over the facility and its whiskey brand.

1785

Irish distillers are now taxed by how much malted barley they use to make their whiskey. In protest of this tax, and to lower their costs, distillers begin to use a mix of malted and unmalted barley (as well as some other grains) instead of primarily malt. This mixed mash bill (the spirit's base ingredients) becomes a signature of Irish whiskey, one that is still in use today.

1791

James Power gets a license for his John's Lane distillery in Dublin, Ireland. Power's will become one of the cornerstones of the Irish whiskey industry.

1791

To help the US government pay back debts incurred during the American Revolution, Treasury Secretary Alexander Hamilton institutes a tax on distillers, which is met with outrage and open resistance in Pennsylvania. Hamilton ultimately sends troops to quell this insurrection in an incident now known as the Whiskey Rebellion.

1792

Kentucky officially joins the United States, becoming the fifteenth state in the Union. Its influence on whiskey making and the eventual rise of bourbon will be immense.

1797

George Washington opens a distillery on his Mount Vernon plantation in Virginia. The facility makes rye whiskey and other spirits. It is quite successful but after Washington's death in December 1799, the distillery is shut down and eventually falls into disrepair.

1806

On May 13, the upstate New York newspaper the *Balance, and Columbian Repository* publishes a definition for the term *cock-tail*. A "Cock-tail, then, is a stimulating liquor, composed of spirits of any kind sugar, water, and bitters." This is the first time the term is defined in print and is essentially the makings of the recipe for what we now call an Old-Fashioned.

1806
John Dewar is born in Aberfeldy, Scotland. After training as a carpenter, he moves to Perth and works in a wine store. Ultimately, he opens his own store, which is where he begins to sell his blended Scotch whiskies. He will live until 1880.

1810
Abraham Overholt gets control of his family's small western Pennsylvania distillery and slowly transforms it into a brand, which becomes the legendary rye whiskey Old Overholt. More than two hundred years later, the whiskey is still on store shelves and is now America's oldest continually operated whiskey brand.

1817
New York gets its very first Irish bar. According to cocktail historian David Wondrich, this pioneering establishment, the Fly Market Hotel, is founded by recent immigrants Murtagh and Alicia Byrne.

1820
John Walker uses his inheritance to buy a small gourmet grocery store in Kilmarnock, Scotland, which sells food, wine, and spirits. The house whisky blend sold there will ultimately be known as Johnnie Walker Blended Scotch Whisky.

1823
The United Kingdom passes an Excise Act that lowers taxes and entices distillers in the Scottish Highlands to get licensed and give up making illicit spirits.

1824
The Glenlivet gets a proper distilling license and becomes one of the first Highland single malt makers to go legit.

1824
The Macallan distillery is opened in Speyside, Scotland, by Alexander Reid.

1830
Aeneas Coffey submits his patent application for his revolutionary continuous column still, also known as a Coffey still, a beer still, or a patent still. This incredibly efficient new piece of equipment will quickly and irrevocably transform the whiskey industry around the globe.

1830
Colonel E. H. Taylor is born in Kentucky. He goes on to be one of the most important and influential distillers of American whiskey, running the O.F.C., Carlisle, and Old Taylor distilleries. In the late nineteenth century, he relentlessly fought to ban the imitation whiskey being peddled by unscrupulous companies.

1832

William Gooderham emigrates from Great Britain to York, Canada (later to be known as Toronto). There he first runs a flour mill and then starts the Gooderham & Worts Ltd. distillery, which becomes Canada's largest whisky producer for a time.

1846

British Parliament repeals the Corn Laws, which makes foreign grains much cheaper to import to the UK. This significantly lowers the cost of producing grain whisky in a column still, allowing blended Scotch to be an economically viable product to sell.

1853

Commodore Matthew C. Perry of the US Navy forces his way into Tokyo Harbor and, in the process, brings whiskey to Japan for the first time.

1853

Andrew Usher starts selling his eponymous Green Stripe blended Scotch, a mix of single malts and grain whisky made on a column still. This combination of spirits becomes the most popular whiskey in the world.

1857

Scottish grocer and whisky blender John Walker passes away. His son Alexander Walker inherits his store and its house whisky brand, Old Highland Whisky, whose popularity grows exponentially under Alexander's direction.

1858

Hiram Walker buys a distillery in Windsor, Ontario, after purchasing a flour mill in the area the previous year. It is the start of what will become a giant liquor empire that helps to establish the Canadian whisky industry.

1860s
Johnnie Walker first uses its now iconic square bottle for its Scotch whisky.

1861
The American Civil War begins in the middle of the night on April 12 and will continue for almost exactly four years. It will not only shut down many American whiskey distilleries but also help their counterparts in Ireland and Canada, who will satisfy the thirst of drinkers in the US.

1862
The New York celebrity bartender Jerry Thomas publishes the first-ever bartenders guide, *How to Mix Drinks or, The Bon-Vivant's Companion*. It proves so popular that the recipes are copied far and wide and featured in a range of other drinks books. Thomas's book will go through many editions and is still in print today.

1863
The Strathspey Railway opens up, which ultimately connects the Speyside region of Scotland with Perth and the rest of the world. It is a huge event for the Scotch whisky industry, allowing for easier access to raw ingredients and much easier and more economical shipping for finished whisky.

1863
Phylloxera is first discovered in European vineyards. Over the next several decades, the tiny insect will topple the bestsellers Cognac, sherry, and port and all but end production of wine in general. This provides the perfect opportunity for whiskey from Ireland, Scotland, and the US to step into the spotlight for a starring role.

1866
Jack Daniel gets a license for his distillery in Lynchburg, Tennessee, which is still open today.

1870
George Smith and his son John Gordon Smith begin the process of trademarking the name *Glenlivet*. After the family receives the trademark a few years later, they effectively own the term, which had previously been used by all of the distillers in this part of northern Speyside.

1870
Old Forester begins selling the first American whiskey to come in a sealed bottle. It is intended for doctors to prescribe as a cure-all for their patients, a common practice in the nineteenth century. Unfortunately, whiskey is often watered down at the time, or worse, made from neutral grain spirit and all kinds of deleterious ingredients. Old Forester whiskey immediately becomes a safer alternative for patients to take.

1871
George Smith, founder of The Glenlivet, passes away.

1874
Julian "Pappy" Van Winkle, the future dean of Kentucky distillers, is born in Danville, Kentucky. At nineteen years old, he leaves college and becomes a whiskey salesman, the beginning of his long and illustrious career. He will not retire until 1964.

1875
The Trade Marks Registration Act goes into effect in the UK, allowing brands, including The Glenlivet, to claim and protect their intellectual property.

1879
George T. Stagg buys Colonel E. H. Taylor's O.F.C. and Carlisle distilleries in Frankfort, Kentucky. Taylor stays on for another seven years before leaving to open his Old Taylor distillery, located less than 10 miles (16 kilometers) away.

1880
The Kentucky Distillers' Association forms in Louisville and to this day represents most of the Bluegrass State's whiskey producers.

1887
British journalist Alfred Barnard publishes his seminal book, *The Whisky Distilleries of the United Kingdom*, which includes detailed descriptions of 161 distilleries in England, Scotland, and Ireland.

1887
On December 25, William Grant opens the Glenfiddich distillery in Dufftown, Scotland. The facility is built with the help of his children, and the company is still owned by his descendants today.

1892
William Grant builds a second distillery, The Balvenie, located very close to his Glenfiddich distillery.

1897
The Bottled-in-Bond Act establishes a new production standard for whiskey in the United States. To qualify for the designation a spirit must now comply with a number of strict regulations, including that it be 100 proof (50 percent alcohol by volume), aged for at least four years in a bonded warehouse, be produced in a single season, and the distillery where it's made must be identified on its label.

1899
The Bronfman family leaves Bessarabia and arrives in Montreal, where they begin to build an empire that will one day become known as Seagram's and control much of the world's spirits industry.

1899
Famous American spirits magnate and distiller Hiram Walker passes away. During the late nineteenth century he helped to lead the Canadian whisky industry.

1903
Michael J. Owens patents a machine in the US to produce glass bottles, which quickly revolutionizes a number of industries, including how whiskey is marketed and sold.

1903
Englishman Sir John Harmsworth buys a French spring whose carbonated water is thought to be medicinal. He soon begins marketing his sparkling water brand, Perrier, as a mixer for whiskey

1904
The Dalwhinnie distillery is purchased by US company Cook & Bernheimer. This is the first time a Scotch distillery is owned by an American firm and is a big deal in the UK. To this day, Dalwhinnie still makes very fine single malt Scotch but is back in British hands as part of the spirits conglomerate Diageo.

1906
The US Pure Food and Drug Act passes, which revolutionizes the way that not only food but alcohol can be produced and labeled in the US. The legislation has vast consequences for the liquor industry. It ensures that customers are actually getting what they pay for, not imitation whiskey.

1906
Johnnie Walker introduces its now ubiquitous White, Red, and Black Label whiskies. According to Scotch expert Dr. Nick Morgan, this is done in response to a spike in demand from the popularity of the Highball (a cocktail of spirits and soda water).

1907

Charles Albert Crampton and Lucius Moody Tolman submit their nine-year study of whiskey aging, conducted for the US Bureau of Internal Revenue. It offers a wealth of information on the effectiveness of different common distilling practices, while also proving that many of the best rye whiskies sold in the US are made on a three-chamber still.

1908

British Parliament creates a Royal Commission on Whiskey and Other Potable Spirits to establish a definition for whisky and standards for its production. The conclusion of the Commission is, disappointingly, quite vague but the lengthy report and testimony reveal much about the liquor industry in Scotland and Ireland.

1908

Historic Tennessee whiskey brand Jack Daniel's trademarks the mysterious designation "Old No. 7," which is still featured prominently on its bottles and in its current advertisements. No one can agree on what it refers to but there are many colorful theories.

1908

Johnnie Walker introduces the "striding man" logo, which is still in use today on its bottles and in its advertisements. The blended Scotch brand finally embraces the nickname Johnnie Walker in place of its official name, Old Highland Whisky.

1909

President William Howard Taft issues his landmark "whiskey is whiskey" ruling in December. This effectively ends a war between Dr. Harvey W. Wiley, the chief chemist of the Department of Agriculture, and a number of brands in the US and Canada, including bestseller Canadian Club.

1909

The American temperance movement is gaining traction and able to get Tennessee to go dry. The state's whiskey brands are forced to shut down or move their production to other states. It will be decades before distillers in the state are allowed to reopen.

1911

Famed Tennessee whiskey distiller Jack Daniel passes away. No one can agree on his birthday, but Daniel was reportedly sixty-five when he died. A few years before his death, Daniel's nephew Lem Motlow takes control of the distillery and goes on to run it for decades.

1915

The Immature Spirits (Restriction) Act passes in the UK, mandating that Scotch needs to be aged for at least two years. In 1916, that minimum is increased to three years.

1917

Tom Bullock publishes *The Ideal Bartender*, the first cocktail book written by an African American. It includes a short introduction by one of his customers at the St. Louis Country Club, George Herbert Walker, two of whose descendants (the Bushes) would become president of the US. Bullock's bourbon Mint Juleps are so famous they prominently figure in a court case involving Teddy Roosevelt and his alleged drinking habits.

1918

Masataka Taketsuru is sent by his employer, the Settsu Shuzo liquor company, to Scotland to learn as much as he can about whisky making. His trip is more or less the starting point for the Japanese whisky industry.

1920

Prohibition begins in the US and will irrevocably change the liquor business in America. No one can legally manufacture, transport, or sell hard alcohol countrywide for general consumption. Only a few companies are given licenses to bottle so-called medicinal whiskey, sold in pharmacies.

1923

Famed whiskey distiller Col. E. H. Taylor passes away at the age of ninety-three. His legacy includes the landmark brands and distilleries Old Taylor, Heritage, Carlisle and O.F.C. A vocal supporter of Dr. Harvey W. Wiley of the Department of Agriculture, Taylor helped to ensure that American whiskey was safe and delicious to drink.

1923

Brown-Forman buys famous American bourbon Early Times, originally founded by John Henry "Jack" Beam in the 1860s or 1870s.

1923

Masataka Taketsuru is hired by Shinjiro Torii to help his company, Kotobukiya Limited (later known as Suntory), build the Yamazaki distillery in Kyoto and make whisky. The facility opens the following year.

1923

Liquor entrepreneur and bootlegger Harry Hatch buys the Gooderham & Worts Ltd. distillery in Canada, whose whisky is used to slake the thirst of Americans during Prohibition.

1925

Lewis Rosenstiel, betting that US Prohibition will end soon, buys the Pennsylvania distillery Schenley. After repeal, he turns Schenley into one of the largest liquor companies in the world.

1925

Top blended Scotch brands Johnnie Walker, Dewar's, and Buchanan's unite to create the powerful Distillers Company Limited. An odd set of circumstances forces the move, including sales rapidly declining in the UK while Prohibition in the US meant a shortage of whisky to drink across the Atlantic.

1926

Well-known Dublin whiskey distillery Roe & Co closes its doors and will not reopen for almost a century.

1926

Harry Hatch is so successful bootlegging whisky during US Prohibition that he pays $15 million for the giant Hiram Walker distillery in Windsor, Ontario. The acquisition allows him to increase his supply of whisky by several million barrels.

1928

The Bronfman family buys the Montreal firm of Joseph E. Seagram & Sons. Afterward, their company is known by the patrician-sounding name, Seagram's.

1929

Kotobukiya Limited (later known as Suntory) introduces the first proper Japanese whisky, Shirofuda (White Label). Unfortunately, it tastes too much like Scotch; it's even peated and doesn't catch on with Japanese drinkers. It nearly dooms the Japanese whisky industry before it even starts.

1929

The US stock market crashes, which begins the country's Great Depression. The tax revenue that is lost from the liquor industry due to Prohibition becomes harder and harder for the federal government to do without.

1930

Dr. Harvey W. Wiley passes away at the age of eighty-five. As the chief chemist of the US Department of Agriculture he fought for years against distillers and brands that took shortcuts and adulterated their whiskies. He advocated for the use of traditional methods and for whiskey to be full-flavored. While President Taft ultimately undermined many of Wiley's efforts, he left a significant legacy that endures today in the widely available range of high-quality whiskies.

1933

The repeal of US Prohibition is finally ratified, making it once again legal to manufacture, transport, and sell hard alcohol in the States. While the American whiskey industry tries to restart, the country is flooded with mature booze from Canada, Ireland, and Scotland.

1933

Masataka Taketsuru leaves Kotobukiya Limited (later known as Suntory) to start his own whisky brand, which will ultimately be known as Nikka. The following year, he builds his own distillery in Yoichi, Hokkaido.

1934

The five Shapira brothers pool their money to fund the construction of the Heaven Hill distillery in Bardstown, Kentucky. Heaven Hill's distillery remains open to this day and continues to be owned by the Shapira family. Their portfolio includes bestsellers Evan Williams Bourbon, Elijah Craig Bourbon, Rittenhouse Rye, and Pikesville Rye.

1934

Right after the repeal of Prohibition, Seagram's constructs a giant distillery in Lawrenceburg, Indiana, along the Ohio River. This distillery will change hands several times and ultimately become MGP Ingredients Inc. In the early 2000s, the facility will play a crucial role supplying many start-up craft whiskey brands across the country with its rye and bourbon.

1935

Julian "Pappy" Van Winkle and his partners, Alex T. Farnsley and Arthur Phillip Stitzel, open the new Stitzel-Weller distillery in the Shively neighborhood of Louisville, Kentucky. The distillery is home to such bestsellers as Old Fitzgerald, W.L. Weller, Cabin Still, and Rebel Yell. The facility officially opens for business on Saturday, May 4, the same day as that year's Kentucky Derby.

1936

To regulate the reborn American liquor industry, the Federal Alcohol Administration (FAA) is established and starts creating category standards.

1937

Kotobukiya Limited (later known as Suntory) reevaluates its whisky strategy and introduces a second product, Kakubin, a hit that is still sold today in Japan.

1938

For the first time since 1909, whiskey is officially being made in Tennessee again when the Lem Motlow distillery begins making its signature brand, Jack Daniel's.

1939

A Scottish court refuses to overturn a lower court's ruling that Scotch must be made in Scotland and can't contain whiskey made in Ireland or anywhere else.

1939

According to lore, Crown Royal is created by Seagram's for a tour of Canada by the new British king and queen, King George VI and Queen Elizabeth. The regal-looking whisky is then introduced after World War II as a permanent part of the Seagram's lineup.

1940

Nikka releases its first Japanese whisky and is able to stay open through World War II by selling whisky and war goods to the Japanese military.

1942

In the middle of World War II, the British Wine & Spirit Brand Association decides to become the Scotch Whisky Association (SWA), which is still Scotch's governing body. In addition to creating policies and rules, which the SWA strictly enforces, it also advocates for Scotch in markets around the world.

1945

Legendary American whiskey magnate Isaac Wolfe Bernheim passes away at the age of ninety-six. He and his brother, Bernard, emigrated from Germany and were able to build one of the largest American spirits companies. His flagship brand, I.W. Harper Whiskey, became a bestseller and is still available today. Bernheim also created an eponymous 13,000-acre (5,260-hectare) arboretum south of Louisville, which is still a treasured landmark in Kentucky.

1946

Enterprising entrepreneurs Frank McMahon and Max Bell open Alberta Distillers, which will become known for producing straight rye whisky.

1948

New Orleans, Louisiana,–based liquor distributor Magnolia Marketing Co. buys the famous Sazerac name and its business of bottled cocktails and spirits. It is the beginning of the modern Sazerac company, which will ultimately become a titan of the American whiskey industry.

1949

American distillers can no longer call a whiskey made in the US Scotch. They can still make a similar product, but it has to be called "Scotch type." This really starts the idea of creating a so-called designation of origin for a whiskey, essentially linking a specific country or region to a specific type of whiskey. This will become a very effective sales and marketing tool.

1951

Seagram's comes out with Chivas Regal 12-Year-Old Blended Scotch, which helps establish the super-premium whisky category and creates the idea that older spirits are better and more valuable.

1952

San Francisco Chronicle travel writer Stanton Delaplane writes about the Irish Coffee in his column and gets his local bar, the Buena Vista Cafe, to start making the concoction. The drink becomes a huge hit and helps reintroduce Irish whiskey to America, essentially saving the Irish industry.

1954

Wild Turkey's long-serving master distiller, Jimmy Russell, begins working at the distillery on September 10. He is not even twenty years old when he starts and remains with the brand today.

1956

Historic Tennessee whiskey brand Jack Daniel's is bought by Brown-Forman for a reported $20 million.

1958

President Dwight D. Eisenhower signs the Forand Bill, which extends the length of time whiskey can age from eight years to twenty before it is considered fully mature and taxes  are due. This small but significant change in tax regulations saves giant liquor company Schenley millions of dollars and helps start the marketing of extra-old whiskies.

1958

Lewis Rosenstiel, the head of Schenley, announces plans to form the Bourbon Institute, which seeks to establish bourbon as a protected product of the United States. The organization tries to ensure that distillers in other countries can't call their whiskey bourbon.

1958

Bill Samuels Sr. and his wife, Margie Samuels, release the first bottles of their Maker's Mark Bourbon, which is made with corn, malted barley, and wheat (instead of the more common rye). It will go on to become one of the most popular bourbons in the world.

1958

After being out of business for almost fifty years, George Dickel begins construction of a $1 million new distillery in Tullahoma, Tennessee. Less than a year later it opens and begins producing a 4-year-old sour mash whiskey. The distillery was built on or close to the location of its original facility, which closed in the early 1900s.

1962

Sir David Stewart is hired by William Grant as a clerk and ultimately becomes the malt master and master blender of both Glenfiddich and The Balvenie single malt Scotches in 1974. As of this writing, he was still working for William Grant some sixty-plus years later.

1962

Thanks to Suntory's lobbying, the US recognizes the Japanese whisky designation for the first time, which allows Japanese brands to start selling their bottles in US stores and bars.

1963

The regal-looking Crown Royal whisky is introduced to the US as a permanent part of the Seagram's lineup and becomes a bestseller.

1964

A congressional resolution on May 4 makes it official that bourbon can be made only in the United States: "Whereas Bourbon whiskey has achieved recognition and acceptance throughout the world as a distinctive product of the United States: Now, therefore, be it." The passage of the legislation is due in great part to Lewis Rosenstiel and his Bourbon Institute.

1965

Julian "Pappy" Van Winkle passes away at the age of ninety-one. The "Kentucky Dean of Distillers" leaves behind a very large whiskey legacy. Decades later, his grandson will make Pappy famous once again with whiskey drinkers around the globe.

1966

In a desperate move to survive, three major Irish whiskey producers John Jameson, Powers, and Cork Distilleries merge to form the Irish Distillers Limited. This new company will reshape Irish whiskey and help save it.

1969

Glenfiddich opens a visitor center and starts the Scotch tourism trend, which will eventually attract millions of visitors each year.

1970

Sales of American whiskey in the US reach an all-time high, followed by a spectacular crash of the category. Over the next thirty years or so, sales of the whiskey continue to decline.

1970

Richard "The Nose" Paterson starts working at Scotch company Whyte & Mackay. He remains with the company for more than fifty years and today is famously the master blender of its The Dalmore Single Malt Whisky.

1971

The Irish Distillers Limited relaunches Jameson as an Irish whiskey blend for the US market. Traditionally made as a 7-year-old pot still whiskey, it is a huge gamble for Jameson, with the fate of the Irish whiskey industry hanging in the balance. Thankfully, the blended whiskey is a hit.

1972
Suntory opens its grain whisky distillery, Chita, in the Port of Nagoya. It produces a range of different grain whiskies that are key components of Suntory's blends.

1972
Norton Simon pays $20 million in stock for Pappy Van Winkle's distillery, Stitzel-Weller, and all of its brands, including Old Fitzgerald. The Van Winkle family keeps just one brand, Old Rip Van Winkle, which they use to start a new company.

1972
National Distilling shuts down the historic Old Taylor distillery in Frankfort, Kentucky, originally built by legendary distiller E. H. Taylor. For the next four decades, it will slowly fall into complete disrepair and come close to disappearing for good.

1972
Otto Rieder opens an eponymous distillery in Grimsby, Ontario, to make fruit brandies. Over the next several decades, his company will evolve into the pioneering Canadian craft whisky distillery Forty Creek.

1973
Suntory opens its third whisky distillery, Hakushu, in Japan's Southern Alps region. It makes heavily peated single malt whisky.

1973
Despite no longer having the Stitzel-Weller distillery, Julian P. Van Winkle Jr. (Pappy's son) decides to start the Old Rip Van Winkle distillery.

1973
The Irish Distillers Limited begins construction on its giant £9 million Midleton distillery in Cork, at the southern tip of Ireland. When the facility opens two years later, it produces every single Irish whiskey on the market, except Bushmills. As a result, Dublin's historic John's Lane distillery (which made Power's) and Bow Street distillery (which made Jameson's) are closed and dismantled.

1973
The Bourbon Institute, the Distilled Spirits Institute, and Licensed Beverage Industries, Inc. join together and create the Distilled Spirits Council of the United States (DISCUS), which still represents the industry today.

1975
Historic French spirits companies Pernod and Ricard merge to form the new conglomerate Pernod Ricard.

1975
Sales of Scotch in the US reach an all-time high and then fall off a cliff. It will take three decades for Scottish distillers to rebuild their industry, which involves switching from making blends to bottling and marketing single malts.

1977
Seagram's becomes the sole owner of the legendary Scotch The Glenlivet. They pay £47 million to buy out their co-owners, including Suntory, which owned an 11 percent stake.

1978
Irish Distillers buys from Seagram's the remaining 20 percent of Bushmills that it doesn't already own. This gives the company a total Irish whiskey monopoly. The industry, once made up of dozens and dozens of distilleries, is now down to two remaining facilities, Midleton and Bushmills.

1978
The Glenlivet opens a visitor center at its distillery. For the first time, the brand's fans can see where the single malt is made.

1980
Pernod Ricard buys Austin, Nichols, the makers of Wild Turkey, from the Liggett Group. This move is reportedly made to foil rival Grand Metropolitan's attempt to acquire Liggett.

1983
Thanks to the downturn in Scotch sales and changing tastes, legendary distilleries Brora and Port Ellen are both shut down. The whisky aging in the distilleries' warehouses will become increasingly valuable.

1984
Suntory introduces the Japanese single malt Yamazaki, named for the company's original distillery in Kyoto, which opened in 1924.

1984
In an attempt to revitalize the American whiskey industry, George T. Stagg's legendary master distiller Elmer T. Lee creates the single barrel bourbon Blanton's. He names it for Col. Albert B. Blanton, the former president of the distillery. It is sold in both the United States and Japan, where it quickly becomes a bestseller.

1985
The Japanese whisky industry crashes, thanks to changing tastes in Japan. It will take about twenty years for it to rebound.

1986
The first edition of Booker's Bourbon is sent out as a holiday gift to distributors and retail store owners. This present essentially kicks off the rebirth of bourbon and American whiskey.

1987
Johnnie Walker Oldest is given a makeover and a new name, Johnnie Walker Blue Label. The whisky is a hit and helps the blended Scotch brand stay relevant in an increasingly single malt–obsessed world.

1987
National Distillers and Chemical Corporation sells its American whiskey portfolio to Jim Beam for $545 million. In the deal, Beam gets mainstays Old Crow, Old Grand-Dad, Old Overholt, and Old Taylor, as well as warehouses overflowing with mature whiskey, which is repurposed as part of Beam's Small Batch Collection.

1987
Dr. John Teeling and a group of partners open the Cooley distillery, Ireland's first independent whiskey distillery. (The rest of the industry is owned entirely by Irish Distillers at the time.)

1988
French spirits firm Pernod Ricard is improbably able to beat out spirits giant Grand Metropolitan to buy the historic Irish Distillers Limited. The £247 million deal includes the whole Irish whiskey industry, except for Cooley, and helps transform Pernod Ricard into a major player in the liquor industry.

1989
Suntory introduces its whisky Hibiki, a blend of thirty single malts and grain whiskies, in Japan. It is created to honor the ninetieth anniversary of Suntory's founder Shinjiro Torii, starting his original liquor business in 1899.

1989
Sazerac gets into the premium bourbon business when it buys Eagle Rare and Benchmark from Seagram's. As part of the deal, Sazerac gets fifteen other brands, including Dr. McGillicuddy's schnapps. In 2001, Dr. McGillicuddy's extends its line with a new spin-off, Fireball.

1989
Japanese whisky company Nikka buys Scottish distillery Ben Nevis.

1989
Famed Pennsylvania whiskey brand Michter's shuts down on Valentine's Day. Its roots stretched back to 1753. (It was America's oldest distillery.)

1990
The Glenora distillery opens in Nova Scotia and produces Canada's first modern single malt whisky.

1990
In Tasmania, Bill Lark begins his quest to get the Australian government to create a distilling license for small craft distillers. Two years later, he receives the first of these licenses and formally sets up the Lark distillery to make single malt whisky.

1992
Historic whiskey brands Ancient Age and Blanton's Bourbon are sold to Japanese liquor company Takara Shuzo. The sale includes the historic George T. Stagg distillery in Frankfort, Kentucky, which is put back on the market and purchased by Sazerac. As part of the deal the distillery will continue to produce Blanton's Bourbon for Takara Shuzo, and Sazerac also secures the rights to market the brand in North America. Seven years later, Sazerac renames the facility the Buffalo Trace distillery.

1993
Trailblazer and visionary Fritz Maytag starts Anchor Distilling Company and begins to make Old Potrero Straight Rye Whiskey in San Francisco. He helps kick off the craft distilling movement and gives life to the moribund rye whiskey category that was on life support at the time.

1993
On January 28, United Distillers (UD) shuts down Pappy Van Winkle's famous Stitzel-Weller distillery in Louisville, Kentucky.

While the facility is used for aging whiskey, it will never again reopen and, as of this writing, is still closed. UD shifts the production of its American whiskies to its nearby Bernheim distillery. In a few years, UD will be part of the merger to create giant liquor conglomerate Diageo.

1993

The Balvenie introduces its pioneering and influential 12-year-old DoubleWood whisky. It is created by malt master Sir David Stewart and popularizes the now ubiquitous technique of barrel finishing Scotch.

1993

Bowmore introduces a 1964 single malt aged exclusively in sherry casks, the first of its "Black Bowmore" bottlings. The whisky originally carries a suggested retail price of nearly $200  in the US. At the time the price seems exorbitantly high, but the bottles now go for tens of thousands of dollars on the secondary market.

1994

Julian Van Winkle III begins to release bottles of the Pappy Van Winkle Family Reserve series of whiskies, which ultimately cause an international sensation that makes the bottles highly sought after by drinkers, bartenders, and collectors. (Good luck finding one now!)

1994

Giant Japanese whisky company Suntory buys Bowmore, Auchentoshan, and Glen Garioch single malt Scotches.

1995

The Bruichladdich distillery, located on Islay in Scotland, shuts down and is mothballed.

1995

Dr. Bill Lumsden is hired by Glenmorangie to be the distillery's manager. He spends the rest of his career working on the brand.

1996

Around two in the morning on November 7, a horrific fire destroys Heaven Hill's Bardstown, Kentucky, distillery and seven of its warehouses, containing one hundred thousand barrels of whiskey. It takes all night for a reported 150 firefighters to put out the flames.

1996
Making an American single malt is one of the first projects that distiller Lance Winters undertakes when he joins the pioneering San Francisco Bay Area distillery St. George Spirits. He had previously worked in the US Navy as a nuclear engineer.

1996
The Ardbeg distillery, located on Islay in Scotland, shuts down and is mothballed. This is one of many times the distillery closes and reopens since the early 1980s.

1997
Not even a year after closing, Ardbeg is bought by Glenmorangie for £7 million from its owner, Allied Domecq.

1997
Diageo is formed through a $22.27 billion merger of Grand Metropolitan and Guinness. This new company has a vast portfolio of bestselling whiskies and beers from around the world. To get regulators to approve the merger, the company is forced to sell Dewar's to Bacardi.

1997
Joe Magliocco decides to relaunch famous American whiskey brand Michter's. He moves it from Pennsylvania to Kentucky and eventually builds a distillery in Louisville as well as a home for the brand in the city's historic Fort Nelson building. The Michter's name is once again synonymous with quality whiskey.

1998

On June 6, the hit HBO TV show *Sex and the City* debuts. The show and later motion pictures are a major catalyst for making cocktails cool and sexy again. The Manhattan cocktail gets plenty of attention from Carrie Bradshaw and her friends, which introduces it to a whole new generation of drinkers.

1999
To help spur tourism, the Kentucky Distillers' Association designates an official Bourbon Trail, which originally includes seven distillery stops. In 2012, the organization adds a Kentucky Bourbon Trail Craft Tour. According to the latest statistics, the two trails combined have 1.7 million visitors a year.

1999
Mackmyra begins to make single malt whisky in Sweden. Dreamed up by eight friends who met studying engineering, the distillery's opening eventually spurs a Scandinavian whiskey-making boom.

1999

Diageo sells off most of its American whiskey holdings in a four-company deal valued at $171 million. According to the terms of the agreement, Sazerac gets the W.L. Weller and Charter brands; the David Sherman Corporation gets Arrow Cordials and Rebel Yell Bourbon; and Heaven Hill gets the Bernheim distillery in Louisville, Kentucky, as well as the Old Fitzgerald and Christian Brothers Brandy brands. The new distillery is key for Heaven Hill's survival because three years prior a fire had destroyed its distillery in Bardstown, Kentucky.

1999

Sazerac announces that, as of June 1, its Ancient Age distillery in Frankfort, Kentucky, will now be known as the Buffalo Trace distillery. (For the previous seven years, it was technically called the Leestown.) This is not just a name change, but a key shift in how the company approaches the bourbon business, meaning that there will now be a focus on tourism as well as education. The company also introduces its signature Buffalo Trace Bourbon.

2000

Japanese beer maker Kirin buys historic American whiskey brand Four Roses. The new owners decide, fortunately, to produce only straight bourbon. (Its previous owner, Seagram's, had turned it into a blended American whiskey.) Thanks to this decision, Four Roses once again is proudly poured by bartenders across the US and becomes a darling of whiskey writers.

2000

The Bronfman family decides to get out of the liquor business and sells its whole company to Vivendi for $30 billion. Vivendi in turn disposes of Seagram's vast empire of spirits brands and distilleries, which are bought by Diageo and Pernod Ricard for more than $8 billion. It is a disastrous decision by the Bronfmans, as their liquor business will soon be worth exponentially more than what it was sold for.

2000
The Triple Eight distillery, located on the tony Massachusetts island of Nantucket, releases its first American single malt whiskey, Notch. (Triple Eight is owned by Cisco Brewers and Nantucket Vineyard.)

2000
Peaty Scotch distillery Ardbeg introduces its now signature 10-year-old whisky.

2000
A group of investors led by Mark Reynier buys the mothballed Islay, Scotland, distillery Bruichladdich for $10.1 million from Connecticut-based American Brands.

2000
John Glaser quits his job at Johnnie Walker and starts his own boutique blended whisky company, Compass Box, in his London apartment.

2001
Ralph Erenzo kicks off New York's influential craft spirits movement when he builds Tuthilltown, the state's first whiskey distillery since before the start of Prohibition.

2001
The Kentucky Distillers' Association creates the Kentucky Bourbon Hall of Fame. The first class inducted includes American whiskey legends Parker Beam, Elmer T. Lee, Booker Noe, Jimmy Russell, and Bill Samuels Jr.

2001
Sazerac introduces the Canadian whisky–based Dr. McGillicuddy's Fireball in the US. The cinnamon-flavored spirit becomes the international megahit called simply Fireball.

2002
On October 15, master mixologist and father of the rebirth of the cocktail Dale DeGroff publishes his seminal book, *The Craft of the Cocktail*. It includes not only DeGroff's personal and tested drink recipes, but also his advice and historical information. It immediately becomes an essential reference for both professional and amateur bartenders around the world.

2002
Famed Scottish distillery The Macallan launches its Fine & Rare Collection, which originally includes thirty-eight single malts produced between 1926 and 1973. These releases immediately help convince consumers and collectors that whiskey could be a serious investment.

2002

Julian P. Van Winkle III strikes a deal with the Buffalo Trace distillery to produce whiskey for his family's brand, Old Rip Van Winkle.

2003

On September 9, movie director Sofia Coppola releases her hit film *Lost in Translation*. In one memorable scene, Bill Murray films a television advertisement for Suntory whisky. It helps give the brand a coolness and introduces it to a whole new generation of hipster American drinkers.

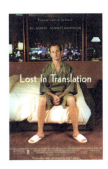

2004

French luxury fashion conglomerate Moët Hennessy Louis Vuitton (LVMH) buys Glenmorangie, Ardbeg, and Glen Moray for a reported £300 million.

2004

At the age of seventy-four, Frederick Booker Noe passes away. The eponymous bourbon brand he created continues on and helps to usher in a new era of American whiskey drinking and connoisseurship.

2004

Heaven Hill opens its Bourbon Heritage Center in Bardstown, Kentucky. The attraction helps create the trend of bourbon tourism and leads other whiskey brands to open their doors and offer tours and experiences to consumers.

2004

Amrut Distilleries releases the first Indian single malt, in of all markets Glasgow, Scotland. The brand's international success leads to a high-end Indian whisky industry and an appreciation for whisky made in India.

2005

Fortune Brands and Pernod Ricard team up to buy rival Allied Domecq for a reported $14 billion. Fortune Brands, which will later become Beam, gets a number of famous whiskey brands, including Maker's Mark, Laphroaig, and Canadian Club. Pernod gets mainstays Ballantine's Scotch and the colossal Hiram Walker distillery in Ontario in their share of the deal.

2005

Pernod Ricard sells the historic Northern Ireland distillery Bushmills to rival spirits company Diageo. Pernod then focuses its efforts on Jameson.

2005

Bartender Sam Ross develops the Penicillin cocktail while working at landmark New York establishment Milk & Honey. The drink calls for two kinds of Scotch as well as sweetened ginger syrup, honey syrup, and lemon juice. It becomes a modern classic, showing up on bar menus around the world, and inspires other bartenders to make Scotch cocktails.

2005

Nine Danish friends start Stauning Danish Whisky. In 2018, the brand moves into a new distillery in West Jutland that features two dozen direct-fire stills. It now produces a range of different styles of rye and single malt whiskies.

2006

Thanks to a grant from the Distilled Spirits Council of the United States, George Washington's distillery is rebuilt on his Virginia plantation, Mount Vernon, and visitors are invited to tour the facility.

2006

The Pickleback is first created in a Brooklyn bar. The combination of a shot of whiskey followed by a shot of pickle brine is quickly adopted by hipsters and the craft cocktail bartender community. Jameson becomes the whiskey of choice in a Pickleback, helping to boost the brand's reputation within the liquor trade

2007

The Local, an Irish pub and restaurant in Minneapolis, Minnesota, is recognized by Jameson as its best account in the world. In 2006, the establishment goes through nearly five thousand bottles of the whiskey, more than any other bar on earth.

2007

On July 19, hit AMC television show *Mad Men* debuts and helps bring back the most essential whiskey cocktail the Old-Fashioned. In one memorable scene, Don Draper (played by Jon Hamm) even teaches hotel magnate Conrad Hilton how to make the drink.

2007

Pioneering whiskey writer and book author Michael James Jackson passes away.

2007

A congressional resolution makes September National Bourbon Heritage Month in the United States. It "recognizes bourbon as 'America's Native Spirit' and reinforces its heritage and tradition and its place in the history of the United States."

2007

In Melbourne, Australia, David Vitale starts his whisky brand, Starward, in an old Qantas Airways hangar.

2008

Suntory begins installing Highball machines across Japan in izakaya-style restaurants and some bars in an attempt to boost sales of its whisky. Fortunately, the classic mix of whisky and club soda in these machines becomes a sensation.

2008

Pernod Ricard pays $8.3 billion to acquire the Swedish company Vin & Spirit. The deal centers on getting international bestseller Absolut Vodka as well as several other smaller brands, such as Plymouth Gin. To help pay for the purchase, Pernod sells off a number of brands, including Wild Turkey bourbon, which is bought by Gruppo Campari for $575 million. This sale will haunt Pernod for years, as American whiskey explodes in popularity.

2009

Suntory creates the Hibiki 12 Year blend for the US market, which takes off, becoming a favorite of bartenders and whiskey connoisseurs.

2010

Maker's Mark shocks the spirits world by finally introducing a second whiskey, Maker's 46. The innovative bourbon, aged with a range of flavorful staves, is created by Bill Samuels Jr., the son of the founders of the brand, Margie and Bill Samuels.

2010

Kings County distillery opens a tiny facility in East Williamsburg, becoming New York City's first whiskey distillery since the beginning of Prohibition.

2010

Scottish distillery The Dalmore sells not one but two bottles of its 64-year-old single malt Trinitas for £100,000 each.

2010
William Grant buys Cantrell & Cochrane's C&C Group liquor division for $367 million to gain control of Tullamore D.E.W. Irish whiskey.

2011
Jim Beam pays €71 million for Ireland's only independent Irish whiskey distillery, Cooley. The deal includes the Connemara, Kilbeggan, and Tyrconnell brands. It also allows Beam to cancel the production contracts of many small Irish whiskey brands.

2012
Rémy Cointreau buys the innovative Islay distillery Bruichladdich for $90.3 million. The deal includes The Botanist Gin, which uses locally foraged botanicals. Bruichladdich's visionary managing director, Mark Reynier, leaves the company.

2012

Jack McGarry and Sean Muldoon open their long-awaited Irish pub-cum-cocktail bar, The Dead Rabbit, in lower Manhattan. The pair had previously run the bar in the superdeluxe Belfast hotel The Merchant. Their New York establishment doesn't disappoint, winning award after award while gaining a loyal following.

2012
The 100-percent-rye whisky Lot 40 is reintroduced, which helps to kick off a Canadian rye whisky trend. The whisky was originally launched in the late 1990s but failed to catch on with drinkers.

2012
Dr. Don Livermore is appointed master blender at the massive Hiram Walker distillery in Ontario. In his post, he revolutionizes the distillery's portfolio of whiskies,  bringing acclaim and attention to the Canadian whisky industry as a whole.

2013
Bourbon Hall of Famer and former George T. Stagg master distiller Elmer T. Lee passes away at the age of ninety-three. Nearly thirty years prior, he creates Blanton's Bourbon, which helps start the rebirth of American whiskey.

2014
Diageo sells the famed Irish whiskey distillery Bushmills to Proximo (the parent company of Jose Cuervo Tequila) for a reported $408 million. A major part of the deal is that Diageo also gets the other half of Don Julio Tequila that it didn't already own from Proximo.

2014

Suntory acquires Jim Beam for $13.6 billion. The transaction combines two historic and powerful spirits companies into the newly formed Beam Suntory. The deal naturally helps Suntory sell its portfolio of Japanese spirits in the US, and similarly helps Beam sell its portfolio of North American whiskies in Japan.

2014

William Grant opens the new Tullamore D.E.W. distillery, which cost $45 million to  build and can produce up to 1.5 million nine-liter cases a year. It's the first time since 1954 that the brand has its own, dedicated distillery.

2014

Gruppo Campari buys pioneering Canadian craft distillery Forty Creek for a reported $167.2 million.

2014

Tasmanian distillery Sullivans Cove's French Oak single malt improbably wins the coveted title of world's best single malt at the World Whiskies Awards, beating out entries from around the globe. The whisky becomes an immediate sensation.

2016

Brown-Forman enters the Scotch business by buying Benriach, GlenDronach, and Glenglassaugh for about $410 million. The three distilleries were previously bought and revitalized by whisky industry veteran Billy Walker and investors Geoff Bell and Wayne Keiswetter.

2016

High West distillery is bought by Constellation Brands for an estimated $160 million. The company's sale helps spur the acquisition of a number of American craft  whiskey brands by large conglomerates, demonstrating how valuable some new brands have become.

2016

The Balvenie malt master, David Stewart, is knighted by Queen Elizabeth II for contributions to the Scotch industry.

2017

Diageo pledges to spend £35 million to rebuild Scottish ghost distilleries Brora and Port Ellen. Closed since 1983, both facilities have since developed cult followings for their remaining stocks of so-called ghost whiskies.

2017

Inspired by a 2016 story in the *New York Times* by Clay Risen, entrepreneur Fawn Weaver starts the whiskey brand Uncle Nearest. It honors Nathan "Nearest" Green, who worked in Tennessee as a distiller when he was enslaved. He later became Jack Daniel's first distiller and helped to create the bestselling whiskey.

2017

Ralph Erenzo sells his Tuthilltown distillery and its Hudson line of whiskies to Scottish company William Grant & Sons. It one of the first major acquisitions of a craft brand by a major legacy producer.

2018

Brown-Forman opens up a distillery and visitor center for its Old Forester brand in downtown Louisville, Kentucky, on historic Whiskey Row, for a reported cost of $45 million. The address of the facility is significant, as the building once housed the offices of Brown-Forman's founder, George Garvin Brown.

2018

After an extensive reconstruction, Frankfort, Kentucky's historic Old Taylor distillery reopens as Castle & Key and begins to produce American whiskey again. Originally constructed in the 1880s by distilling legend E. H. Taylor, the facility has been closed since 1972.

2018

Itinerant distiller Dave Pickerell passes away at the age of sixty-two. The former master distiller at Maker's Mark helped kick off the craft-distilling boom in the United States by consulting on brands across the country, as well as serving as the master distiller or distiller for WhistlePig, Blackened Whiskey, and Hillrock Estate.

2019

Diageo launches the historic Roe & Co Irish whiskey brand in the heart of Dublin. The original Roe distillery went out of business in 1926. The new one is housed in a former power station that once served the Guinness brewery.

2019

French spirits company Pernod Ricard buys Castle Brands for $223 million, adding Knappogue Castle and Jefferson's Bourbon to its vast portfolio.

2020

The international whiskey world is rocked when it is revealed that some Japanese brands have been buying whiskey from other countries and clandestinely blending it into their own whiskies. As a result, the Japan Spirits & Liqueurs Makers Association introduces new standards for its members to follow.

2021

Leopold Bros. distillery in Denver, Colorado, begins to release its long-awaited Three Chamber Rye, which quickly sells out. It's the first time in decades that whiskey in the US has been made in a three-chamber still, which was standard for rye producers in mid-Atlantic states before World War II. It gives drinkers a real taste of history and an idea of what rye might have tasted like before Prohibition.

2021

The Scottish ghost distillery Brora reopens and begins to make whisky again after being closed for thirty-eight years.

2022

In order to keep up with demand for its signature Canadian whisky, Crown Royal, Diageo announces that it is building a new $245 million distillery in St. Clair Township, Ontario, which will produce 66.3 million bottles of whisky per year.

2023

After being closed for forty years, the legendary Scottish ghost distillery Port Ellen on Islay once again starts making single malt.

2023

Liquor conglomerate Pernod Ricard introduces its The Chuan pure malt single malt whisky. The distillery that makes it is located in China's mountainous Emeishan City in the province of Sichuan.

CLASSIC AND MODERN WHISKEY COCKTAIL RECIPES

30 Classic Whiskey Cocktails

ALL RECIPES MAKE ONE COCKTAIL UNLESS OTHERWISE NOTED.

Blue Blazer

Contributed by Jerry Thomas

It goes without saying that pouring ribbons of flaming alcohol between metal mugs is incredibly dangerous and there should be at least several fire extinguishers at the ready, if not a whole company of firefighters. "The novice in mixing this beverage should be careful not to scald himself," wrote Jerry Thomas in his pioneering 1862 book, *How to Mix Drinks or the Bon Vivant's Companion*. Supposedly, he was prone to tossing the liquid over his head and catching it behind his back, which not only mixed the drink but was no doubt a real showstopper. "To become proficient in throwing the liquid from one mug to the other, it will be necessary to practise [sic] for some time with cold water."

Pyrotechnics aside, what's interesting about this recipe is that the Scotch must have been incredibly high proof if it could be lit on fire after having been mixed with boiling water. Truly fire water! Cocktail experts who dare make a Blue Blazer, such as Dale DeGroff and David Wondrich, suggest using a cask strength whisky, which is quite flammable.

INGREDIENTS
- 1 teaspoon confectioners' sugar
- 1½ ounces (45 ml) boiling water
- 2 ounces (60 ml) Scotch

GLASS: Heatproof tumbler
GARNISH: Twist of lemon peel

DIRECTIONS

Add the sugar to a heatproof tumbler and set aside. Combine the boiling water and Scotch in a flameproof 1-pint metal tankard with a handle and thin lip, which makes it easy to pour. (You will need two of these tankards.) Carefully light the mixture on fire with an extra-long match. With extreme caution pour the flaming liquid back and forth between two flameproof 1-pint metal tankards. Wondrich suggests pouring the flaming liquid from the side of the cup, so the flames don't go up your arm. "If well done this will have the appearance of a continued stream of liquid fire," wrote Thomas. Snuff out the flames by putting the empty mug on top of the full mug. Pour the drink into the prepared heatproof tumbler and garnish with a lemon peel.

Blood and Sand

Contributed by Harry Craddock

Harry Craddock was the head bartender of the American Bar at the Savoy Hotel in London. In 1930, he published *The Savoy Cocktail Book*, which includes the recipe for this Scotch-based cocktail. The drink may take its name from the 1922 silent film *Blood and Sand*, in which Rudolph Valentino stars as a young Spanish bullfighter. Craddock's recipe calls for cherry brandy, which is now fairly hard to find, so usually the drink made with Heering cherry liqueur. Fruity and rich, it's a polarizing drink that some love and others can't stand, but at least all can agree it doesn't taste like blood or sand.

INGREDIENTS

¾ ounce (20 ml) blended Scotch
¾ ounce (20 ml) cherry brandy
¾ ounce (20 ml) (45 ml) sweet vermouth
¾ ounce (20 ml) (45 ml) freshly squeezed orange juice

GLASS: Cocktail
GARNISH: Brandied cherry

DIRECTIONS

Combine all of the ingredients in a mixing glass and fill it with ice. Stir, then strain into a chilled cocktail glass. Garnish with a brandied cherry.

Bobby Burns

Contributed by Hugo R. Ensslin

There aren't many countries that I know of where poetry is taken as seriously as Scotland. The national bard, Robert Burns, died on July 21, 1796, yet the country still celebrates his birthday each January. (A proper Burns Night dinner includes recitations of his poems, glasses of Scotch, and, of course, a serving of some of the country's famous haggis.) So it's no surprise that Burns should have a Scotch cocktail named for him.

The earliest recipe found, which appears in Hugo Ensslin's 1916 edition of *Recipes for Mixed Drinks*, is basically a Manhattan variant, but includes a couple of dashes of the French herbal liqueur Bénédictine. Depending on your taste, you may want to adjust Ensslin's proportions to 2 ounces Scotch and 1 ounce sweet vermouth.

INGREDIENTS

1 ounce (30 ml) Scotch
1 ounce (30 ml) Italian vermouth
2 dashes Bénédictine

GLASS: Cocktail
GARNISH: Lemon twist

DIRECTIONS

Combine all of the ingredients in a mixing glass and fill it with ice. Stir, then strain into a chilled cocktail glass. Garnish with a lemon twist.

Boilermaker

The pairing of a glass of booze and a glass of beer is a favorite in many cultures around the globe. Depending on where you are in the world, the spirit and the type of beer will vary greatly—sometimes the spirit is even dropped into the pint of beer. In the United States, a Boilermaker is traditionally a shot of American whiskey and a glass of lager beer, but many bars have now created their own signature pairings.

INGREDIENTS

  2 ounces (60 ml) Wild Turkey 101 Bourbon
  12 ounces (330 ml) Miller High Life Beer

GLASS: Shot, pint

DIRECTIONS

Pour the whiskey into the shot glass and the beer into the pint glass. Shoot or sip the whiskey and then drink the beer.

The Boulevardier

Contributed by Toby Cecchini

This drink is essentially a whiskey twist on the classic Italian Negroni cocktail. The Boulevardier substitutes whiskey for gin in the famous triumvirate of equal parts gin, sweet vermouth, and bitter Campari. American socialite Erskine Gwynne, who ran a magazine named *Boulevardier*, popularized the drink in 1920s Paris. The recipe for the cocktail (calling for bourbon) even shows up in Harry McElhone's 1927 *Barflies and Cocktails* book. This modern take from famed Brooklyn bartender Toby Cecchini ups the whiskey to two parts. He also uses rye instead of the more common bourbon, which gives the drink a note of savory spice.

INGREDIENTS

  1 ounce (30 ml) Old Overholt 86-Proof Rye
  1 ounce (30 ml) Old Forester 100-Proof Rye
  1 ounce (30 ml) Campari
  1 ounce (30 ml) sweet vermouth (2 parts Cinzano Rosso, 1 part Carpano Antica Formula)

GLASS: Coupe
GARNISH: Lemon twist

DIRECTIONS

Combine all of the ingredients in a mixing glass and fill it with ice. Stir, then strain into a chilled coupe. Garnish with a lemon twist.

Bourbon Rickey

This refreshing bourbon drink is essentially a Highball with a squeeze of lime. While the Bourbon Rickey caught on first, the later gin version became even more popular—especially in Washington, D.C. Col. Joseph Kerr "Joe" Rickey is credited with introducing the Bourbon Rickey to the city, where it became the specialty of Shoomaker's bar. The carbonated combination was named in his honor.

INGREDIENTS

- 2 ounces (60 ml) bourbon
- Half a lime
- Club soda

GLASS: Highball

DIRECTIONS

Pour the bourbon into a Highball glass and fill it with ice. Squeeze the lime half into the glass and drop it in. Top with club soda. You can vary the strength of the drink by how much club soda you add.

Brown Derby

Contributed by Eric Alperin

The Brown Derby cocktail may or may not be related to the historic Los Angeles restaurant of the same name, which, in fact, looked kind of like a giant mud-colored hat. The recipe is included in the 1933 book *Hollywood Cocktails* by George Buzza Jr. The one problem, according to spirit historian David Wondrich, is that he hasn't been able to find any link between the Brown Derby drink and the Brown Derby restaurant. Buzza likely found the recipe in Harry Craddock's *The Savoy Cocktail Book*, an iconic art deco bartending manual, and simply gave its de rigueur drink a different name—the classic Hollywood star treatment.

INGREDIENTS

- 2 ounces (60 ml) bourbon
- 1 ounce (30 ml) freshly squeezed grapefruit juice
- ½ ounce (15 ml) honey syrup*

GLASS: Coupe

DIRECTIONS

Combine all of the ingredients in a shaker and fill it with ice. Shake, then strain into a chilled coupe glass.

*Honey syrup

Combine 3 parts orange blossom honey with 1 part hot water in a heatproof tumbler. Stir thoroughly and store in a glass bottle in the refrigerator.

Bourbon Milk Punch

Contributed by Commander's Palace

For hundreds of years, professional and amateur bartenders have been mixing whiskey with milk. To clarify these concoctions, the dairy was curdled by adding acidic citrus juice. While the process may be somewhat stomach turning, the finished (and miraculously clear) product is absolutely quaffable and was shelf-stable before refrigeration. Thankfully, once refrigeration became more ubiquitous and cheaper, folks began serving an unclarified Milk Punch, which has become a staple in New Orleans, Louisiana. In the 1950s, famed NOLA restaurateurs the Brennan family began to promote the drink as part of their decadent breakfast menu at their eponymous establishment. To this day it's still served at the family's award-winning restaurants Brennan's and Commander's Palace.

INGREDIENTS
- 2 ounces (60 ml) bourbon
- 1½ ounces (45 ml) heavy (whipping) cream
- 1 ounce (30 ml) simple syrup (1 part sugar, 1 part water)
- ½ teaspoon pure vanilla extract

GLASS: Rocks
GARNISH: Freshly grated nutmeg

DIRECTIONS
Combine all of the ingredients in a shaker and fill it with ice. Shake, then strain into a rocks glass filled with ice. Garnish with a light dusting of freshly grated nutmeg.

Cameron's Kick

Created by Harry McElhone

David Wondrich found this drink in the first edition of Harry McElhone's *ABC of Mixing Cocktails*, which came out in 1922. Despite Wondrich's best efforts at championing the drink, it's still fairly unknown. What makes the recipe very special is that it calls not only for Scotch but also Irish whiskey, as well as the almond-based orgeat syrup. While it's an odd combination of ingredients, it somehow works.

INGREDIENTS
- 1 ounce (30 ml) Scotch
- 1 ounce (30 ml) Irish whiskey
- ½ ounce (15 ml) lemon juice
- ½ ounce (15 ml) orgeat syrup

GLASS: Cocktail

DIRECTIONS
Combine all of the ingredients in a shaker and fill it with ice. Shake, then strain into a chilled cocktail glass.

Highball

Contributed by Kenta Goto

While there is currently a Highball craze in many American bars, the drink is far from new. The original Highball craze took place at the start of the twentieth century and helped establish Scotch in the United States. In fact, the "ball" in the name was a measurement term for an amount of whiskey, as in "I'll have a ball of Scotch." About a century later this carbonated concoction would help Japanese whisky distillers attract a new generation of domestic drinkers. As a result, the Highball has now become synonymous with Japanese drinking culture. You can even buy canned versions of the drink on the wickedly fast shinkansen bullet trains that crisscross the country.

INGREDIENTS

1¼ ounces (35 ml) Japanese whisky
4 ounces (120 ml) club soda

GLASS: Highball

DIRECTIONS

Combine all of the ingredients in a Highball glass and fill it with ice. Stir lightly.

Hot Toddy

These days the Hot Toddy has become a catchall for any hot drink festooned with a gaudy garnish (think candy canes) and featuring a ridiculous number of ingredients, including every spice you can carry and then some. The original drink, which was also known by the unfortunate moniker Whiskey Skin, is a very, very simple recipe. No matter what you call it, the Hot Toddy works best with a big, bold Scotch, like an Islay single malt (such as Laphroaig or Ardbeg) or a Scotch blend that has a lot of Islay whisky in it (such as Johnnie Walker Black Label). One of the secrets of the elixir is to warm the mug before adding the ingredients, which helps ensure that it doesn't cool too quickly.

INGREDIENTS

2 ounces (60 ml) Scotch
2 ounces (60 ml) boiling water
1 teaspoon sugar

GLASS: Mug
GARNISH: Lemon peel or wedge

DIRECTIONS

Fill a mug with boiling water and let it warm up for about 90 seconds. Discard the water. Combine all the ingredients in the heated mug and stir. Garnish with a lemon peel or wedge.

Irish Coffee

Contributed by The Dead Rabbit

Made wrong, the Irish Coffee is an undrinkable mess. But when made in the right proportions, it's easy to see how the drink became a viral sensation in the 1950s and helped save the Irish whiskey industry. This recipe comes from the award-winning New York bar The Dead Rabbit, which has made the Irish Coffee its signature drink.

INGREDIENTS

- 1 ounce (30 ml) Bushmills Original Irish Whiskey
- 1¼ tablespoons (20 ml) demerara syrup (2 parts demerara sugar, 1 part water)
- 3½ ounces (100 ml) hot coffee

GLASS: 6-ounce (200 ml) glass
GARNISH: Whipped cream

DIRECTIONS

Combine the whiskey and demerara syrup in a 6-ounce (200 ml) glass. Add the coffee (there should be an index finger's worth of space at the top). Top with freshly whipped cream.

Mamie Taylor

One of my favorite fundamental bartending formulas calls for the combination of a spirit with fresh lime juice and ginger ale or ginger beer. If you use Goslings rum you get a Dark 'n Stormy. If you use vodka, you get a Moscow Mule. And if you use blended Scotch, you get a Mamie Taylor. The drink was supposedly created by a Rochester, New York bartender in 1898 and was named for singer and actress Mayme Taylor. No one is sure why the drink's name is spelled slightly differently from the performer's name.

INGREDIENTS

- 2 ounces (60 ml) blended Scotch
- Half a lime
- Ginger ale or ginger beer

GLASS: Highball

DIRECTIONS

Pour the blended Scotch into a Highball glass and fill it with ice. Squeeze the lime half into the glass and drop it in. Top with ginger ale or ginger beer. You can vary the strength of the drink by how much soda you add.

Manhattan

Arguably, the most famous whiskey cocktail is the Manhattan. The drink is as elegant as the borough's art deco masterpiece, the Chrysler Building, and is a memorable combination of rye or bourbon with sweet vermouth and Angostura bitters. The modern proportions of ingredients in the recipe, 2:1:2, are incredibly easy to remember, since 212 is the original area code for Manhattan. Given how famous the cocktail is, it's a shock that we have no idea who created it or even at what bar it was first served. What we can say is that it probably was initially mixed in the late 1880s, when Italian vermouth first became available in the US.

INGREDIENTS

2 ounces (60 ml) rye whiskey or bourbon
1 ounce (30 ml) sweet vermouth
2 dashes Angostura bitters

GLASS: Cocktail
GARNISH: Brandied cherry

DIRECTIONS

Combine all of the ingredients in a mixing glass and fill it with ice. Stir, then strain into a chilled cocktail glass. Garnish with a brandied cherry.

Mint Julep

These days the Mint Julep is inextricably tied to the Kentucky Derby and bourbon. However, through the 1860s the drink wasn't usually made with whiskey but with a range of other types of spirits, including rum, gin, and brandy. The original version of the concoction was thought to be medicinal, and over centuries has been reinvented several times. The term *julep* comes from the Persian term for rose water, *gûl-ab*, which is fascinating because there is no rose water in the standard Mint Julep recipe. While today ice is readily available, in the 1800s using so much of it to make one drink must have seemed like a ludicrous waste of money, and made the Mint Julep a true luxury.

One note about making this drink: Some folks really crush the mint when you only need to lightly muddle it. What's the problem? If it's pulverized,

the mint can make your drink taste bitter. Legendary bartender Tom Bullock, who was world-famous for his Juleps, warns in his landmark 1917 cocktail book *The Ideal Bartender*, "Be careful and not bruise the Mint." It still holds true today. For a change of pace, try making a Mint Julep with rum or brandy.

INGREDIENTS
- 2 ounces (60 ml) bourbon
- ½ ounce (15 ml) simple syrup (1 part sugar, 1 part water)
- 6 to 8 mint leaves

GLASS: Julep cup or rocks
GARNISH: Mint leaves

DIRECTIONS

Put the mint leaves and simple syrup in a Julep cup or rocks glass and muddle them lightly. Add the bourbon and fill the cup or glass with crushed ice. Stir until the glass is nicely frosted. Mound some more crushed ice on top and garnish with mint leaves.

Modern

Created by John E. Haas

There are forgotten whiskey cocktails and then there is the Modern. Rarely is this drink ever mentioned or found on menus. It does, however, appear in the *Hoffman House Bartender's Guide* from 1905, which says a lot about its past, since the hotel's bar was one of New York's most popular and influential establishments. Cocktail sleuths David Wondrich and Doug Stailey were able to track down a bit more info on the creator of the drink, who turns out to have been a Pennsylvania bartender named John E. Haas. Unfortunately, not much is known about Haas, but he leaves this very interesting and creative recipe.

While sloe gin at first blush seems like an odd choice, real sloe gin is delicious—look out for one from Plymouth Gin or Fords Gin—and is sweetened with sugar and infused with sloe berries, which are kind of like a cross between a cranberry and a cherry. As a result, the finished cocktail is almost like mixing a Rob Roy with a Sazerac.

INGREDIENTS
- 1¼ ounces (35 ml) Scotch
- 1¼ ounces (35 ml) sloe gin
- 1 dash absinthe
- 4 dashes orange bitters
- ½ ounce (15 ml) lemon juice
- 1 teaspoon rich simple syrup (2 parts sugar, 1 part water)

GLASS: Cocktail
GARNISH: Cherry

DIRECTIONS

Combine all of the ingredients in a shaker and fill it with ice. Shake, then strain into a chilled cocktail glass and garnish with a cherry.

New York Sour

The key ingredient in this historic variation on the traditional Whiskey Sour is a splash of dry red wine. While it may sound like an odd combination, the vino adds a delicious note to the cocktail and really works well with a flavorful rye whiskey. The drink dates back to the 1880s and had several other names before the name New York Sour stuck.

INGREDIENTS

   2 ounces (60 ml) rye whiskey
   ¾ ounce (20 ml) lemon juice
   ¾ ounce (20 ml) simple syrup
      (1 part sugar, 1 part water)

   GLASS: Cocktail
   GARNISH: ½ ounce (15 ml) dry red wine and a brandied cherry

DIRECTIONS

Combine all of the ingredients in a shaker and fill it with ice. Shake, then strain into a chilled cocktail glass. Float the dry red wine on top of the drink by pouring it over the back of a spoon. Garnish with a brandied cherry.

Old-Fashioned

The Old-Fashioned is the quintessential cocktail: spirits, sugar, bitters, and water. In the mid-1800s, bartenders started adding newly available ingredients to the mix, including absinthe and later sweet and/or dry vermouth. This experimentation led to the creation of a number of other standards, including the Manhattan and the Sazerac. While the recipe below is the *original* standard, many professional and amateur bartenders like to include muddled cherries and oranges. And if you're in Wisconsin, you'll find a bewildering array of bizarre ingredients added to your Old-Fashioned, including celery stalks and a significant splash of 7UP or Sprite soda. And the drink will usually be made with brandy instead of whiskey! While I don't mind a brandied cherry in my Old-Fashioned, I can do without the other additions.

INGREDIENTS

   1 teaspoon sugar
   2 dashes Angostura bitters
   Splash of water
   2 ounces (60 ml) bourbon or rye whiskey

   GLASS: Old-Fashioned
   GARNISH: Orange peel and/or brandied cherry

DIRECTIONS

Add the sugar, bitters, and water to an Old-Fashioned glass and muddle them. Then add the whiskey and fill the glass with ice. Stir, and garnish if you like with an orange peel and/or brandied cherry.

Old Pal

Thanks to the recent Negroni and Boulevardier hype, the related Old Pal has once again started to show up on craft cocktail bar menus. But what separates the Old Pal from those other Campari drinks is that it has an innate dryness from the dry vermouth (instead of sweet) and the inherent spice of the rye. We know from Arthur Moss's section in Harry McElhone's 1927 book *Barflies and Cocktails* that the recipe was created by William "Sparrow" Robertson, a Paris-based sports writer for the *Herald Tribune*. But Robertson's recipe for the drink, which was technically called My Old Pal, calls for Canadian Club and sweet Italian vermouth. By 1930, it had evolved into a mix of rye whiskey, dry vermouth, and Campari, which is how it is still usually served.

INGREDIENTS

1 ounce (30 ml) rye whiskey
1 ounce (30 ml) Campari
1 ounce (30 ml) dry vermouth

GLASS: Cocktail
GARNISH: Lemon peel

DIRECTIONS

Combine all of the ingredients in a mixing glass and fill it with ice. Stir, then strain into a cocktail glass. Garnish with a lemon peel.

Presbyterian

The Presbyterian is not only a refreshing mixed drink but also solved an important problem for many. Because it's basically a Highball with both ginger ale and club soda, the drink is fairly low in alcohol and looks a lot like a glass of soda. Both are important attributes when you don't want to bring attention to what you're imbibing. According to legend, many teetotaling members of the Presbyterian church didn't want to be seen enjoying hard liquor, so a nondescript beverage was ideal. No matter your motives, this is a great sipper for a hot day and, given its low proof, is very sessionable.

INGREDIENTS

2 ounces (60 ml) bourbon
2½ ounces (75 ml) ginger ale or ginger beer
2½ ounces (75 ml) club soda

GLASS: Highball

DIRECTIONS

Combine all of the ingredients in a Highball glass and fill it with ice. Stir.

Remember the Maine

Contributed by St. John Frizell & Garret Richard

Charles H. Baker was a notorious bon vivant who traveled the world in the 1920s. He ultimately wrote about his adventures in the grandiosely titled travelogue *The Gentleman's Companion*, which was published on January 1, 1946. This cocktail takes its name from the US Navy battleship *USS Maine*, whose sinking in Havana Harbor in 1898 was a catalyst for the Spanish–American War. But despite the drink's name, in Baker's book he recalls having it in Cuba when the country's dictator Gerardo Machado was toppled. Baker wrote of the experience: "a Hazy Memory of a Night in Havana during the Unpleasantness of 1933, when Each Swallow Was Punctuated with Bombs Going off on the Prado."

INGREDIENTS

- 3 spritzes St. George Absinthe
- 2 ounces (60 ml) Wild Turkey 101 Rye
- ¾ ounce (20 ml) Carpano Antica Sweet Vermouth
- ¾ tablespoon (10 ml) Heering cherry liqueur
- 3 drops saline (1 part kosher salt, 4 parts water)

GLASS: Coupe
GARNISH: Lemon twist

DIRECTIONS

Using an atomizer, spritz a chilled coupe glass three times with the absinthe and set the glass aside. Combine the rest of the ingredients in a mixing glass and fill it with ice. Stir, then strain into the prepared coupe. Express a lemon twist over the top of the drink and discard the twist.

Reverse Manhattan

In the late 1800s, the recipe for the Manhattan was far from standardized. In fact, bartenders tried many different formulas before settling on the recipe we know today. Some of these alternative recipes called for more sweet vermouth than whiskey. These "inverted" drinks are now referred to as a Reverse Manhattan. Since you're using less whiskey, the Reverse Manhattan is naturally lower in proof and more of the vermouth flavor comes through in the finished cocktail. If you've never had one of these, it's worth mixing one up.

INGREDIENTS

- 1 ounce (30 ml) rye whiskey or bourbon
- 2 ounces (60 ml) sweet vermouth
- 2 dashes Angostura bitters

GLASS: Cocktail
GARNISH: Brandied cherry

DIRECTIONS

Combine all of the ingredients in a mixing glass and fill it with ice. Stir, then strain into a chilled cocktail glass. Garnish with a brandied cherry.

Rob Roy

It would be easy to dismiss the Rob Roy as just a takeoff on the Manhattan, but thanks to the Scotch it becomes a completely different drink, with a well-honed smoothness. So, who was Rob Roy anyway? Rob Roy MacGregor was a Scottish folk hero who was born in 1671 and died in 1734. Often compared to Robin Hood, he became known for standing up to authority. His story has been told in books, plays, and several movies, including a 1995 film starring Liam Neeson.

INGREDIENTS
- 2 ounces (60 ml) Scotch
- 1 ounce (30 ml) sweet vermouth
- 2 dashes Angostura bitters

GLASS: Cocktail
GARNISH: Brandied cherry

DIRECTIONS

Combine all of the ingredients in a mixing glass and fill it with ice. Stir, then strain into a chilled cocktail glass. Garnish with a brandied cherry.

Rusty Nail

The Rusty Nail is the quintessential example of midcentury modern bartending: It is simple to make and features blended Scotch. But don't dismiss this drink as schlocky kitsch before you try it—it's actually a tasty combination. It probably works so well because Drambuie is a historic Scotch-based liqueur flavored with honey, herbs, and spices. Think of this drink like a Gaelic Old-Fashioned.

INGREDIENTS
- 1 ounce (30 ml) blended Scotch
- ½ ounce (15 ml) Drambuie

GLASS: Rocks
GARNISH: Lemon peel

DIRECTIONS

Combine all of the ingredients in a rocks glass. Fill the glass with ice, then stir. Garnish with a lemon peel.

Sazerac

Contributed by Neal Bodenheimer

At least once in your life you should experience the joy of having a well-made Sazerac in New Orleans, Louisiana. While many stories and theories connect the cocktail's origins to NOLA and its legendary Sazerac House, the drink's history is complicated to say the least. What I can say for sure is that the cocktail is essentially an Old-Fashioned whose glass is washed with absinthe.

The drink became synonymous with New Orleans, in part because authentic absinthe was banned in the United States for many years. In its absence, the absinthelike liqueur Herbsaint, created in the Crescent City, became the substitute of choice. And Peychaud's Bitters—another essential ingredient for making the cocktail—was not widely available outside Louisiana until recently. So if you wanted to make the drink, you pretty much had to go to New Orleans. Fortunately, you can now find absinthe and Peychaud's Bitters across the US and, as a result, can get the drink in most craft cocktail bars.

INGREDIENTS

- 4 spritzes Herbsaint
- 2 ounces (60 ml) Sazerac Rye
- 4 dashes Peychaud's Bitters
- ¼ ounce (5 ml) demerara syrup (1 part demerara sugar, 1 part water)

GLASS: Double Old-Fashioned
GARNISH: Lemon peel

DIRECTIONS

Using an atomizer, spritz the interior of a chilled double Old-Fashioned glass with Herbsaint and set the glass aside. Combine the rest of the ingredients in a mixing glass and fill it with ice. Stir, then strain into the prepared glass. Garnish with a lemon peel.

Uncle Angelo's Eggnog

Contributed by Dale DeGroff

You either love Eggnog or hate it. I haven't found too many folks who don't have an opinion about the creamy holiday drink. While variations of Eggnog have been made for hundreds of years with a combination of dairy, eggs, and liquor (some of the earliest recipes call for rum), bourbon is now the most popular booze to use in this festive drink.

This is the personal recipe of legendary bartender Dale DeGroff, which calls for both bourbon and spiced rum. It was created in the 1950s by DeGroff's great uncle Angelo, who won an Eggnog contest sponsored by Four Roses Bourbon. For several years, Angelo's recipe even appeared on the Four Roses label. DeGroff included his family's recipe in his seminal book *The Craft of the Cocktail*.

This recipe makes eight six-ounce servings.

INGREDIENTS

6 large eggs, separated
¾ cup (150 g) sugar
1 quart (1 l) milk
1 pint (5.7 dl) heavy (whipping) cream
8 ounces (2.4 dl) Four Roses Bourbon
6 ounces (1.8 dl) spiced rum

GLASS: Punch
GARNISH: Freshly grated nutmeg

DIRECTIONS

In a large bowl, use an electric mixer to beat the egg yolks well, slowly adding ½ cup (100 g) of the sugar as you beat, until the mixture turns light in color. Add the milk, cream, bourbon, and rum, then refrigerate until well chilled. Just before serving, beat the egg whites with the remaining sugar until they hold stiff peaks. Fold the whites into the Eggnog mixture. Serve cold in punch glasses, with freshly grated nutmeg sprinkled over the drink.

Vieux Carré

Contributed by Neal Bodenheimer

Forget the Hurricane and the Hand Grenade, it doesn't get more New Orleans, Louisiana, than the Vieux Carré. The drink was created in the 1930s by bartender Walter Bergeron right in the middle of the French Quarter at the Hotel Monteleone, which is still open today. The first recipe for the drink that anyone can find is in Stanley Clisby Arthur's 1937 book *Famous New Orleans Drinks and How to Mix 'Em*. While the book is not the most reliable source for information, award-winning NOLA bar owner Neal Bodenheimer believes Arthur's history of this drink, which credits Bergeron, is correct.

INGREDIENTS

¾ ounce (20 ml) Sazerac Rye Whiskey
¾ ounce (20 ml) Cinzano Rosso Vermouth
¾ ounce (20 ml) Pierre Ferrand 1840 Cognac
¼ ounce (5 ml) Bénédictine
2 drops Angostura bitters
2 drops Peychaud's Bitters

GLASS: Double Old-Fashioned
GARNISH: Lemon peel

DIRECTIONS

Combine all of the ingredients in a double Old-Fashioned glass and then add one large ice cube. Stir, and garnish with a lemon peel.

Waldorf

Contributed by Frank Caiafa

I think of the signature drink of New York's historic Waldorf Astoria hotel as a cross between a Manhattan and a Sazerac. This recipe comes from Frank Caiafa, the former bar manager of the hotel's famous Peacock Alley bar—the birthplace of many classic cocktails—and author of *The Waldorf Astoria Bar Book*. According to Caiafa, the original recipe included much more absinthe, which was too overwhelming for most of his customers. For the version he served at the hotel, he dialed back the absinthe as well as the vermouth to create a much more drinkable cocktail. If you're shocked that he would change the proportions of the hotel's eponymous cocktail, you should know that the *The Old Waldorf-Astoria Bar Book* from 1931 featured several versions of the drink.

INGREDIENTS

- 2 ounces (60 ml) Rittenhouse Bottled-in-Bond Rye Whiskey
- 1 ounce (30 ml) Martini & Rossi Sweet Vermouth
- ¼ ounce (5 ml) Pernod Original Recipe Absinthe or Pernod Pastis
- 2 dashes Angostura bitters

GLASS: Cocktail
GARNISH: Lemon peel

DIRECTIONS

Combine all of the ingredients in a mixing glass and fill it with ice. Stir, then strain into a chilled cocktail glass. Garnish with a lemon peel.

Ward Eight

Contributed by Eric Alperin

The Ward Eight is a fascinating cocktail because it includes orange juice and grenadine, which you don't often see mixed with whiskey. This recipe is in fact very close to the version of the Tequila Sunrise that the Rolling Stones turned into a sensation. But long before Mick and Keith came along, Bostonians were drinking the Ward Eight around the turn of the twentieth century. The secret to this drink is to use artisanal grenadine if you can find it.

INGREDIENTS

- 2 ounces (60 ml) rye whiskey
- ½ ounce (15 ml) lemon juice
- ½ ounce (15 ml) freshly squeezed orange juice
- ½ ounce (15 ml) grenadine

GLASS: Coupe
GARNISH: Lemon peel

DIRECTIONS

Combine all of the ingredients in a shaker and fill it with ice. Shake, then strain into a chilled coupe. Garnish with a lemon peel.

Whiskey Sour

For about a century—from the 1840s to the 1950s—the Whiskey Sour was one of the most popular whiskey drinks in America. When the Tequila Sour (aka the Margarita) took off in the second half of the twentieth century, the Whiskey Sour got pushed to the wayside and was ultimately forgotten by modern bartenders and drinkers. But don't sleep on this tasty mix of rye whiskey, fresh lemon juice, and simple syrup. After tasting one, you'll wonder why it took you so long to discover it.

INGREDIENTS

2 ounces (60 ml) rye whiskey

¾ ounce (20 ml) lemon juice

¾ ounce (20 ml) simple syrup (1 part sugar, 1 part water)

¾ ounce (20 ml) liquid egg white (optional)

GLASS: Cocktail

GARNISH: Brandied cherry and orange wheel

DIRECTIONS

Combine all of the ingredients in a shaker and fill it with ice. Shake, then strain into a chilled cocktail glass. Garnish with a brandied cherry and an orange wheel.

30 Modern Whiskey Cocktail Classics

Bensonhurst

Created by Chad Solomon

The best bartenders are perfectionists who are curious by nature, which means they endlessly tinker and refine their recipes. Even a classic like the Manhattan is not exempt—its formula serves as inspiration for a seemingly endless number of new variations. One of my favorites is from veteran bartender Chad Solomon, which includes a drop of Italian Luxardo Maraschino Liqueur and artichoke-based Cynar 70. Naturally, he named his creation for the traditionally Italian American neighborhood of Bensonhurst, in southwest Brooklyn.

INGREDIENTS

2 ounces (60 ml) Lock Stock & Barrel Vatted Rye Whiskey

¾ ounce (20 ml) Noilly Prat Extra Dry Vermouth

¼ ounce (5 ml) Luxardo Maraschino Liqueur

¼ ounce (5 ml) Cynar 70

2 drops mineral saline (by weight, 1 part kosher salt, 9 parts water)

GLASS: Nick & Nora

DIRECTIONS

Combine all of the ingredients in a mixing glass and fill it with ice. Stir, then strain into a chilled Nick & Nora glass.

Benton's Old-Fashioned

Created by Don Lee

In 2008, the Benton's Old-Fashioned took bartending to a new level of cool. It was created by bartender Don Lee when he was working at New York's modern speakeasy PDT (Please Don't Tell), which helped kick off the neo-speakeasy trend around the world. For many years, it was a major accomplishment to score a reservation at the establishment. Lee took the Old-Fashioned, which at the time was the humblest of drinks and had largely been forgotten, and gave it a trendy makeover. He used the molecular bartending technique of fat-washing, which is a fancy way of saying he added clarified bacon fat to the alcohol. And it wasn't just any old bacon he used, but bacon from Tennessee's prized Benton's Smoky Mountain Country Hams, a favorite among celebrity chefs across the country.

While bacon certainly made the drink buzzworthy, it became a standard because of its taste. Bourbon and barbecue are old friends, and the Benton's Old-Fashioned certainly showcases why that pairing works so well. The

smoke and sweetness of the pork is the perfect foil for the wood and vanilla of the whiskey. Lee also replaced the standard sugar in an Old-Fashioned with dark maple syrup, which adds a richness that complements both the bacon and the bourbon.

INGREDIENTS

2 ounces (60 ml) Benton's Bacon-Infused Four Roses Yellow Label Bourbon*
¼ ounce (5 ml) Grade B maple syrup
2 dashes Angostura bitters

GLASS: Rocks
GARNISH: Orange twist

DIRECTIONS

Combine all of the ingredients in a mixing glass and fill it with ice. Stir, and strain into a chilled rocks glass with no ice. Garnish with an orange twist.

*Benton's Bacon-Infused Four Roses Yellow Label Bourbon

If Benton's bacon fat is unavailable, substitute another intensely smoked artisanal bacon.

INGREDIENTS
- 1 bottle (750 ml) Four Roses Yellow Label Bourbon
- 1½ ounces (43 g) Benton's bacon fat (warmed until liquid)

DIRECTIONS

Cook one pound of sliced Benton's Bacon and reserve the fat. Pour the bottle of bourbon and warm bacon fat into a 1-quart (1 l) freezer-proof plastic or glass container with a cover. Set aside at room temperature for 12 hours. Freeze the infusion for 4 hours, then with a spoon scoop out and discard the solidified fat.

Blinker

Created by Toby Maloney

Some readers might be wondering if this recipe is in this chapter by mistake, since there is a historic recipe of the same name that dates to the 1930s. But this is a modern version of the Blinker that Toby Maloney created in 2007 for his award-winning Chicago bar, The Violet Hour. Instead of the traditional grenadine syrup, he substituted raspberries and lemon juice.

"This is without a doubt the greatest brunch drink of all time," Maloney wrote in his James Beard Award–winning book *The Bartender's Manifesto: How to Think, Drink & Create Cocktails Like a Pro*. Once you try it, I'm sure you'll agree with him.

INGREDIENTS
- ¾ ounce (20 ml) simple syrup (1 part sugar, 1 part water)
- 3 dashes Peychaud's Bitters
- 5 fresh raspberries
- 2 ounces (60 ml) rye whiskey
- 1½ ounces (45 ml) freshly squeezed ruby red grapefruit juice
- ¾ ounce (20 ml) lemon juice

GLASS: Collins
GARNISH: Grapefruit peel and skewered raspberries

DIRECTIONS

Combine the simple syrup, bitters, and raspberries in a shaker and muddle them. Add the rest of the ingredients and fill the shaker with ice. Shake, then strain into a collins glass filled with ice. Garnish with a grapefruit peel and a skewer of raspberries.

Bourbon Renewal

Created by Jeffrey Morgenthaler

Ask most professional or amateur bartenders to make you a drink with crème de cassis and you'll likely get a sparkling Kir Royale. Leave it to the immensely talented Jeffrey Morgenthaler to mix the black current liqueur with bourbon and lemon juice. His Bourbon Renewal is one of the most successful modern whiskey cocktails.

INGREDIENTS

- 1½ ounces (45 ml) bourbon
- ½ ounce (15 ml) crème de cassis
- 1 dash Angostura bitters
- ¾ ounce (20 ml) lemon juice
- 2 teaspoons simple syrup (2 parts sugar, 1 part water)

GLASS: Old-Fashioned
GARNISH: Lemon wheel

DIRECTIONS

Combine all of the ingredients in a shaker and fill it with ice. Shake, then strain into an Old-Fashioned glass filled with ice. Garnish with a lemon wheel.

Brownstoner

Contributed by the Red Rooster Harlem

In 2010, celebrity chef Marcus Samuelsson opened his Harlem restaurant, the Red Rooster, and the Brownstoner cocktail soon became one of the establishment's signature drinks. While it was supposedly inspired by the Old-Fashioned, I would argue that it's so far removed from the classic that it is a wholly new creation.

The genius of this drink lies in infusing the bourbon with nutmeg. It really reminds me of Samuelsson's time running New York's acclaimed Scandinavian restaurant Aquavit, which always had a wide selection of infused aquavits on its menu. The Brownstoner's other essential ingredients also have a Nordic connection: Heering cherry liqueur is from Denmark, and elderflower is a popular flavor in Sweden, where Samuelsson grew up.

INGREDIENTS

- 2 ounces (60 ml) Nutmeg-Infused Bourbon*
- ¾ ounce (20 ml) Heering cherry liqueur
- ¾ ounce (20 ml) St-Germain Elderflower Liqueur

GLASS: Cocktail
GARNISH: Orange wedge

DIRECTIONS

Combine all of the ingredients in a mixing glass and fill it with ice. Stir, then strain into a chilled cocktail glass. Garnish with an orange wedge.

*Nutmeg-Infused Bourbon

INGREDIENTS

- 1 bottle (1 l) bourbon, such as Bulleit
- 5 whole nutmegs

DIRECTIONS

Combine the bourbon and whole nutmegs in a pitcher. Cover and infuse at room temperature for 48 to 72 hours—after the first two days, taste it every few hours to see if you want an even deeper flavor or if it's to your liking. Once done, strain the infused whiskey into a clean bottle.

Cab Calloway

Created by Tiffanie Barriere

Whiskey and sherry are old friends. In fact, many Scotch brands use barrels that are first seasoned with sherry to age their single malts. But what I find fascinating about Atlanta, Georgia-based bartender Tiffanie Barriere's recipe is that it calls for just half an ounce of rye whiskey, which supports the actual star of the show, the oloroso sherry. In many ways, this drink is similar to a Reverse Manhattan, which inverts the standard proportions of the classic and shifts the focus from the whiskey to the sweet vermouth. So put on a Cab Calloway record and mix up one of these delicious drinks.

INGREDIENTS

1½ ounces (45 ml) oloroso sherry
½ ounce (15 ml) rye whiskey
¼ ounce (5 ml) apricot liqueur
¼ ounce (5 ml) dry vermouth
2 dashes Angostura bitters
2 dashes orange bitters

GLASS: Rocks
GARNISH: Lemon twist

DIRECTIONS

Combine all of the ingredients in a mixing glass and fill it with ice. Stir, then strain into a rocks glass filled with ice. Garnish with a lemon twist.

DuBoudreau Cocktail

Created by Jamie Boudreau

Not that long ago, if you were looking to try a vintage whiskey, one of the few places that might have a bottle of it was Jamie Boudreau's landmark Seattle, Washington, bar Canon, which he opened in 2011. The establishment inspired many collectors and drinkers to search for old and dusty bottles of booze that had been forgotten on store shelves and in liquor cabinets. At Canon, not only could you sample a rare dram, but you could also enjoy a fine mixed drink, including Boudreau's signature DuBoudreau Cocktail. There is a lot going on in the drink, with spicy rye, herbaceous Italian amaro Fernet-Branca, bitter French aperitif Dubonnet, and sweet and flowery St-Germain. Somehow, all of its flavors work in concert to make a perfect aperitif.

INGREDIENTS

1½ ounces (45 ml) bonded rye whiskey
¾ ounce (20 ml) Dubonnet Rouge
¼ ounce (5 ml) Fernet-Branca
¼ ounce (5 ml) St-Germain Elderflower Liqueur

GLASS: Coupe
GARNISH: Lemon zest

DIRECTIONS

Combine all of the ingredients in a mixing glass and fill it with ice. Stir, then strain into a chilled coupe glass. Garnish with lemon zest.

Emerald Old-Fashioned

Created by Joaquín Simó

Don't be fooled by this cocktail's name! It is a far cry from the standard Old-Fashioned recipe. It combines a delightful single malt Irish whiskey with honey and two historic herbal liqueurs from France. It really showcases the floral notes in Irish whiskey. I would expect nothing less from Joaquín Simó, who has been at the forefront of the craft cocktail scene for years.

INGREDIENTS
- 2 ounces (60 ml) Knappogue 12-Year-Old Single Malt Irish Whiskey
- 1 teaspoon green Chartreuse
- 1 teaspoon Dolin Génépy
- 1 teaspoon honey syrup (2 parts wildflower honey, 1 part water)

GLASS: Rocks
GARNISH: Mint sprig

DIRECTIONS

Combine all of the ingredients in a rocks glass and fill it with ice. Stir, then garnish with a mint sprig.

Flannel Shirt

Created by Jeffrey Morgenthaler

At the heart of this delicious drink is a traditional pairing: bourbon and apple cider. To take it to the next level, top bartender Jeffrey Morgenthaler adds some lemon juice to brighten up the mix, a bit of amaro to give it a base note, and some demerara syrup and allspice dram to bring the cocktail together.

INGREDIENTS
- 1¾ ounces (50 ml) blended Scotch
- ½ ounce (15 ml) Averna Amaro
- ½ teaspoon St. Elizabeth Allspice Dram
- 2 dashes Angostura bitters
- 1½ ounces (45 ml) fresh apple cider
- ¼ ounce (5 ml) lemon juice
- 1 teaspoon demerara syrup (2 parts demerara sugar, 1 part water)

GLASS: Rocks
GARNISH: Orange twist

DIRECTIONS

Combine all of the ingredients in a shaker and fill it with ice. Shake, then strain into a rocks glass filled with ice. Garnish with an orange twist.

Fitzgerald Fizz

Created by Lynn House

While you might be tempted to assume that famed author and gadfly F. Scott Fitzgerald was the inspiration for this drink, it is actually named for John E. Fitzgerald, a distiller who lived in the late 1800s. He was well known for his Old Fitzgerald whiskey, which is one of the few wheated bourbons on the market. (A wheated bourbon is made from corn, malted barley, and wheat instead of the more common rye.) Old Fitz is now produced by Heaven Hill, for which Lynn House works as a brand ambassador.

INGREDIENTS

1½ ounces (45 ml) wheated bourbon
1½ ounces (45 ml) hibiscus tea
¼ ounce (5 ml) lime juice
¼ ounce (5 ml) lemon juice
½ ounce (15 ml) simple syrup
  (1 part sugar, 1 part water)
1 egg white
1½ ounces (45 ml) soda water

GLASS: Collins
GARNISH: Edible hibiscus flower

DIRECTIONS

Combine all of the ingredients except the soda water in a shaker and shake. Fill with ice, then shake again. Strain into a collins glass filled with ice. Top with soda water and garnish with an edible hibiscus flower.

Gold Rush

Created by T.J. Siegal

The Gold Rush is essentially a Whiskey Sour made with honey instead of the standard sugar, which adds sweetness and a richness that complements the baking spice notes in the bourbon. The recipe is so simple that I'm amazed it has not become a standard sooner. The backstory of the Gold Rush also shows that good ideas can come from anywhere. This drink wasn't created by a rock star bartender but a patron at the landmark New York bar Milk & Honey. Customer T.J. Siegal came up with the basic idea while sitting at the bar, and the establishment's owner, legendary bartender Sasha Petraske, came up with the exact measurements and created the specifications for the honey syrup. It soon caught on at Milk & Honey, then at other bars around the city, and finally in establishments around the country.

INGREDIENTS

2 ounces (60 ml) Elijah Craig Bourbon
¾ ounce (20 ml) lemon juice
¾ ounce (20 ml) honey syrup
  (3 parts honey, 1 part water)

GLASS: Rocks

DIRECTIONS

Combine all of the ingredients in a shaker and fill it with ice. Shake, then strain into a frozen rocks glass with a single large ice cube in it.

Good Night, Irene

Created by Audrey Saunders

I like to think of this drink as a grown-up Mint Julep. But instead of muddling fresh mint, expert bartender Audrey Saunders adds Branca Menta, which is the mint version of the Italian amaro and bartender favorite Fernet-Branca. Branca Menta always tastes slightly medicinal to me, which actually is perfect for this cocktail, since the Julep was originally considered a cure-all.

INGREDIENTS

2 ounces (60 ml) Maker's Mark Bourbon
1 ounce (30 ml) Branca Menta

GLASS: Double Old-Fashioned
GARNISH: Mint sprig

DIRECTIONS

Combine all of the ingredients in a shaker and fill it with ice. Shake, then strain into a double Old-Fashioned glass filled with cracked ice. Garnish with a mint sprig.

Grey Wolf

Created by Julia Momosé

This cocktail brings together ingredients that aren't usually mixed: Japanese whisky, plum extract, and French herbal liqueur. But this unique combination works, and has become one of Julia Momosé's signature cocktails. It was first published in the James Beard Award–winning *The Way of the Cocktail*, which Momosé wrote with Emma Janzen.

INGREDIENTS

2 ounces (60 ml) Mars Iwai Japanese Whisky
1 teaspoon Bénédictine
1 teaspoon Umé-su (Beksul plum extract)
2 dashes Angostura bitters
¼ ounce (5 ml) rich demerara syrup (2 parts demerara sugar, 1 part water)

GLASS: Old-Fashioned
GARNISH: Grapefruit peel

DIRECTIONS

Combine all of the ingredients in a mixing glass and fill it with ice. Stir, then strain into an Old-Fashioned glass with an ice ball in it. Express the oils of a grapefruit peel over the top of the drink and discard the peel.

Irish Flip

Created by John Lermayer

John Lermayer was truly a special bartender. Take for proof his signature Irish Flip. Despite Guinness's international reputation and global distribution, there are shockingly few cocktails that call for the creamy stout. This is the only recipe I know of that uses it in a cocktail that you'll actually enjoy drinking.

Not only was Lermayer extremely creative behind the bar, coming up with a number of original drinks (and winning a slew of cocktail competitions in the process), but he also inspired many with his motto, "Pursue Happiness."

While he was originally from New York, he helped build Miami's modern cocktail scene. At first, he led the drinks programs at several South Beach hotels, before finally opening his now legendary Sweet Liberty bar, which is still a must-visit. Tragically, Lermayer passed away in 2018, at the age of just forty-five.

INGREDIENTS
  1 ounce (30 ml) Jameson Irish Whiskey
  1 ounce (30 ml) Heering cherry liqueur*
  1½ ounces (45 ml) Guinness Stout Beer
  1 dash chocolate bitters
  1 large egg

GLASS: Cocktail
GARNISH: Nutmeg

DIRECTIONS
Combine all of the ingredients in a shaker and fill it with ice. Shake, then strain into a chilled cocktail glass and garnish with a sprinkle of grated nutmeg.

You can substitute the Spanish licorice-flavored liqueur Licor 43 for Heering cherry liqueur, which is how Lermayer sometimes made the drink.

Iron Ranger

Created by Erick Castro

Pineapple juice, lemon juice, and Velvet Falernum are a famous trio that show up in a number of tropical drink recipes. But what makes Erick Castro's cocktail unique is that it calls for bourbon and not the perennial tiki favorite, rum. The Iron Ranger is a refreshing cocktail that is perfect on hot summer nights.

INGREDIENTS
  2 ounces (60 ml) bourbon
  ½ ounce (15 ml) Velvet Falernum
  2 dashes Angostura bitters
  ¾ ounce (20 ml) lemon juice
  1 ounce (30 ml) pineapple juice
  ½ ounce (15 ml) simple syrup
     (1 part sugar, 1 part water)

GLASS: Hurricane
GARNISH: Grated cinnamon and a mint sprig

DIRECTIONS
Combine all of the ingredients in a Hurricane glass and fill it with crushed

or pebble ice. Stir, then garnish with grated cinnamon and a mint sprig.

Le Sang et Sable

Created by Toby Cecchini

It's no secret that one of my favorite drinks is the classic Scotch cocktail, the Blood and Sand. I am definitely in the minority, since many craft bartenders don't think it is balanced and won't deign to drink one, or even make one. Fortunately, Toby Cecchini, acclaimed bartender and owner of Brooklyn's beloved Long Island Bar, is another fan of the cocktail. Not only does he make a delicious Blood and Sand (complete with a homemade brandied cherry), but he has taken the time to create his own spin on the classic recipe, which calls for a few key, flavorful changes. His drink, Le Sang et Sable, includes not just Scotch but also Cognac. Instead of using regular orange juice, he prefers the aptly named blood orange juice and adds a bit of acidic brightness with lemon juice. It's so good that it just might get some folks to reconsider the original Blood and Sand.

INGREDIENTS

¾ ounce (20 ml) unpeated Scotch, such as Compass Box Artist Blend

¾ ounce (20 ml) Cognac, such as Hine H or Park Carte Blanche

¾ ounce (20 ml) sweet vermouth, such as Carpano Classico or Volume Primo

¾ ounce (20 ml) freshly squeezed blood orange juice

½ ounce (15 ml) lemon juice

½ ounce (15 ml) Heering cherry liqueur

GLASS: Coupe

GARNISH: Lemon peel and a brandied cherry

DIRECTIONS

Combine all of the ingredients in a shaker and fill it with ice. Shake, then strain into a chilled coupe glass. Express a lemon peel over the glass and discard the peel. Garnish with a brandied cherry.

Little Italy

Created by Audrey Saunders

If you like your Manhattan to have a bit more bite and backbone, try famed bartender Audrey Saunders's Little Italy. To the spicy and potent 100-proof (50 percent alcohol by volume) Rittenhouse Rye she adds Cynar, a bitter Italian amaro flavored with artichoke. Saunders then balances the drink with a "dribble" of syrup from the Luxardo Original Maraschino Cherries jar, which gives the Little Italy a charming, bittersweet flavor and a delicious, porklike undertone. How much cherry syrup you add depends on the rye you're using. You need a muscular whiskey that has plenty of flavor, which will stand up to the supersweet syrup.

INGREDIENTS

- 2 ounces (60 ml) Rittenhouse Bottled-in-Bond Rye Whiskey
- ½ ounce (15 ml) Cynar
- ¾ ounce (20 ml) Martini & Rossi Sweet Vermouth

GLASS: Small cocktail glass
GARNISH: 2 Luxardo maraschino cherries

DIRECTIONS

Combine all of the ingredients in a mixing glass and fill it with ice. Stir, then strain into a small chilled cocktail glass. Garnish with 2 Luxardo maraschino cherries and a dribble of syrup from the Luxardo Original Maraschino Cherries jar.

The Mastodon

Created by Alex Smith

One of the best tiki bars in the world is located on a nondescript street in San Francisco. If you're not paying attention, you run the risk of walking right by Smuggler's Cove. But once you go inside, you'll know from the nautical bric-a-brac, floral shirts, fez hats, and flaming volcano-style drinks that you're in the right place. Bartender Alex Smith created this tropical tipple for the award-winning establishment. It's a tasty combination of tropical ingredients, licorice-flavored Spanish liqueur, and bourbon.

INGREDIENTS

- 1½ ounces (45 ml) bourbon
- 1½ ounces (45 ml) blended aged rum, such as Appleton Estate Reserve or Mount Gay XO
- ½ ounce (15 ml) Licor 43
- ½ ounce (15 ml) maraschino liqueur
- 2 dashes Peychaud's Bitters
- 3 ounces (90 ml) pineapple juice
- 1 ounce (30 ml) passion fruit puree
- ½ ounce (15 ml) lime juice

GLASS: Bottom half of a hollowed-out pineapple

DIRECTIONS

Combine all of the ingredients in a blender and fill it with crushed ice. Blend until smooth, then pour the contents into a hollowed-out pineapple.

Moto Guzzi

Created by John Gertsen

While New York, San Francisco, and London got most of the press for leading the craft cocktail movement, Boston, Massachusetts generally doesn't get the credit it deserves. During the early 2000s, the city developed a small community of dedicated and talented bartenders. One of the key players was John Gertsen, who ran several influential bars. When he worked at No. 9 Park in Beacon Hill, he created a classic: the Moto Guzzi. Given that it has just two ingredients, it seems deceptively simple. On the contrary, few folks would dare to try to balance cask strength Booker's Bourbon in any cocktail, let alone with just a single ingredient. It's a task akin to performing a high-wire act without a net. But Gertsen was more than up for the challenge and dreamed up this recipe for one of his regulars, who named it after the elegant Italian motorcycle brand.

INGREDIENTS

1½ ounces (45 ml) Booker's Bourbon
1½ ounces (45 ml) Punt e Mes vermouth

GLASS: Rocks

DIRECTIONS

Combine both ingredients in a mixing glass and fill it with ice. Stir, then strain into a chilled rocks glass.

Not So Rusty Nail

Created by Iain McPherson

How do you reinvent a classic cocktail that has just two ingredients? That was the challenge facing Edinburgh bartender Iain McPherson when he decided to put his own spin on the classic Rusty Nail, which is traditionally a mix of Scotch and the Scotch-based liqueur Drambuie. The one thing for certain was that the Scotch had to stay. But while the drink is usually made with a smooth and quaffable blended Scotch, McPherson went in the opposite direction with the peaty and briny Islay malt Bunnahabhain Toiteach A Dhà. The whisky gives his recipe a newfound power. And instead of Drambuie, he adds some Bruadar Single Malt Whisky Liqueur, made with Scottish honey and sloe berries. While McPherson's riff on the Rusty Nail is very different from the original recipe, you can still tell that they're related, proving he got it right.

INGREDIENTS

1½ ounces (45 ml) Bunnahabhain Toiteach A Dhà Scotch
¾ ounce (20 ml) Bruadar Single Malt Whisky Liqueur
2 dashes Angostura bitters

GLASS: Rocks

DIRECTIONS

Combine all of the ingredients in a mixing glass and fill it with ice. Stir, then strain into a rocks glass with a single cube of ice in it.

Paniolo

Created by Jeff Berry

Jeff "Beachbum" Berry is the dean of tiki cocktail bartenders, and his establishment, Latitude 29, is a must for anyone visiting New Orleans, Louisiana. So, leave it to Berry to turn a seemingly disparate group of ingredients into a wonderful cocktail that deserves consideration as the official drink of Thanksgiving. The name of Berry's recipe is the Hawaiian term for cowboy; I hope that after a long day of herding cattle, today's paniolos now fix themselves this drink.

INGREDIENTS

- 1½ ounces (45 ml) Four Roses Yellow Bourbon
- ½ ounce (15 ml) Trader Vic Macadamia Nut Liqueur
- Dash Fee Bros. Aztec Chocolate bitters
- ½ ounce (15 ml) lime juice
- ½ ounce (15 ml) L29 Cranberry Syrup*

GLASS: Double rocks
GARNISH: 2 fresh or frozen cranberries and a lime peel, skewered

DIRECTIONS

Combine all of the ingredients in a shaker and fill it with ice. Shake, then strain into a double rocks glass with two large ice cubes in it. Garnish with a cranberry and lime peel skewer.

*L29 Cranberry Syrup

INGREDIENTS

- 1 part organic cane sugar
- 1 part unsweetened cranberry juice

DIRECTIONS

Combine both ingredients in a small saucepan over medium-high heat and simmer until the sugar dissolves. Remove the syrup from the heat and let it cool. Store the syrup in a bottle in the refrigerator.

Paper Plane

Created by Sam Ross

You couldn't engineer a better recipe for the modern drinker than the Paper Plane. It includes some of the trendiest types of spirits today: bourbon, amaro, and Aperol. But when the cocktail was created in 2008 by all-star Australian bartender Sam Ross for Chicago's award-winning Violet Hour bar, it would have

been a hard sell for many customers. At the time, the bourbon boom was just taking off and the drink's overall flavor was very different from what most establishments were serving. Fast forward nearly two decades, and Italian bitters have gone mainstream and are now appearing in a range of historic and modern drinks around the country. As a result, the Paper Plane has become increasingly popular and is now considered a modern classic.

INGREDIENTS

¾ ounce (20 ml) bourbon
¾ ounce (20 ml) Amaro Nonino
¾ ounce (20 ml) Aperol
¾ ounce (20 ml) lemon juice

GLASS: Cocktail

DIRECTIONS

Combine all of the ingredients in a shaker and fill it with ice. Shake, then strain into a chilled cocktail glass.

Penicillin

Created by Sam Ross

The Penicillin is one of the most successful whiskey drinks to be created since the rebirth of the cocktail. The recipe was thought up by Sam Ross when he was working at the pioneering New York bar Milk & Honey. (This is the same Sam Ross who created the Paper Plane.) The secret of the drink is also its most unusual element—a drop of smoky Islay Scotch. It pairs beautifully with the ginger, lemon, and honey, and turns a decent cocktail into a modern classic. The Penicillin proves that big-and-bold Scotch deserves to be used in more cocktails.

INGREDIENTS

2 ounces (60 ml) Scotch
¼ ounce (5 ml) Islay Scotch
¾ ounce (20 ml) lemon juice
¾ tablespoon (10 ml) honey syrup (3 parts honey, 1 part water)
¾ tablespoon (10 ml) sweetened ginger juice (4 parts ginger juice, 3 parts sugar)

GLASS: Rocks
GARNISH: Candied ginger

DIRECTIONS

Combine all of the ingredients except the Islay Scotch in a shaker and fill it with ice. Shake, then strain into a rocks glass filled with ice. Float the Islay Scotch on top by pouring it over the back of a spoon. Garnish the rim of the glass with a piece of candied ginger.

Pickleback

Created by Reggie Cunningham

The Pickleback was created in 2006 by Reggie Cunningham, a Brooklyn bartender, and became a sensation in every hipster enclave from Williamsburg to Portland, Oregon. While it was originally made with Old Crow Bourbon, the drink was soon co-opted by Jameson Irish Whiskey. This version became super popular, and was even a "bartender's handshake"—a drink made by bartenders for other bartenders. Read the full history of this drink on page 342.

INGREDIENTS

2 ounces (60 ml) Jameson Irish Whiskey

2 ounces (60 ml) pickle brine

GLASS: 2 shot glasses

DIRECTIONS

Pour each ingredient into its own shot glass. Shoot or sip the whiskey and then shoot or sip the pickle brine.

Plum Sazerac

Created by Kenta Goto

Slivovitz, the Eastern European plum brandy, rarely shows up in cocktails because it doesn't pair easily with anything. Undeterred by the spirit's tough reputation, award-winning bartender Kenta Goto features it in his delectable and expertly balanced Plum Sazerac.

INGREDIENTS

1 ¾ ounces (50 ml) bourbon

¼ ounce (5 ml) Slivovitz

⅛ teaspoon Pastis

1 drop Peychaud's Bitters

¼ ounce (5 ml) demerara syrup (2 parts demerara sugar, 1 part water)

GLASS: Brandy snifter

DIRECTIONS

Combine all of the ingredients in a mixing glass and fill it with ice. Stir 60 times and strain into a brandy snifter glass.

Revolver

Created by Jon Santer

Besides the White Russian and the Espresso Martini, there aren't many popular cocktails that call for coffee liqueur these days. But Jon Santer's cocktail, the Revolver, makes a strong case that perhaps we should take another look at the caffeinated liqueur. The coffee flavor pairs beautifully with the sweet woody and vanilla notes of the bourbon. The orange bitters and the flamed orange peel add a bit of brightness and tie all the ingredients together. While Santer is based in the San Francisco Bay area, his drink has gone national and shows up on bar menus across the United States.

INGREDIENTS

2 ounces (60 ml) bourbon
½ ounce (15 ml) coffee liqueur
2 dashes orange bitters

GLASS: Coupe or Nick & Nora
GARNISH: Flamed oval piece of orange peel

DIRECTIONS

Combine all of the ingredients in a mixing glass and fill it with ice. Stir, then strain into a chilled coupe or Nick & Nora glass. Garnish with a flamed orange peel.

Rob Royce

Created by Iain McPherson

The classic Scotch cocktail the Rob Roy is all about subtlety and balance. The Scotch should embrace the vermouth without overpowering it and the sweet vermouth should enrobe the Scotch without suffocating it. This detente doesn't leave much room for creativity or innovation, which is what is so impressive about Edinburgh bartender Iain McPherson's Rob Royce. His variation adds a bit of depth and complexity to the drink with some tawny port, which pairs beautifully with Scotch.

INGREDIENTS

1½ ounces (45 ml) GlenDronach 15-Year-Old Revival Single Malt Scotch
½ ounce (15 ml) Valentian Rosso Vermouth
½ ounce (15 ml) Port of Leith Distillery Reserve Tawny Port

GLASS: Coupe
GARNISH: Orange zest

DIRECTIONS

Combine all of the ingredients in an insulated water bottle and place it in the freezer for 4 hours. Pour into a chilled coupe glass and garnish with an orange zest.

Smoke and Mirrors

Created by Alex Day

According to its creator, Alex Day from the Death & Co family of bars, the secret to this cocktail is the mint and the absinthe. These two ingredients are able to pull together the two seemingly incongruent types of Scotch and the acidic lime juice. (Day recommends making it with the Famous Grouse Blended Scotch and Bowmore Legend or Bowmore 12.)

Inspired by the classic Daiquiri, Day created the Smoke and Mirrors in 2010.

INGREDIENTS

¾ ounce (20 ml) simple syrup
   (1 part sugar, 1 part water)
5 mint leaves
1 ounce (30 ml) blended Scotch
1 ounce (30 ml) Islay Scotch
2 dashes Absinthe
¾ ounce (20 ml) lime juice

GLASS: Double Old-Fashioned
GARNISH: Mint sprig

DIRECTIONS

Place the simple syrup and mint leaves in a shaker and lightly muddle them. Add the rest of the ingredients and fill the shaker with ice. Shake, then strain into a double Old-Fashioned glass. Garnish with a mint sprig.

Whiskey Smash

Created by Dale DeGroff

Dale DeGroff never liked the Whiskey Smash that was included in Jerry Thomas's pioneering 1862 cocktail book *How to Mix Drinks or The Bon Vivant's Companion*. So, in 2005, when DeGroff was asked to come up with a drink menu for celebrity chef Bobby Flay's new midtown Manhattan bistro, Bar Americain, he decided to revise the Whiskey Smash to his liking. A bourbon cocktail would perfectly accompany one of Flay's signature dishes, a take on the historic and decadent Louisville, Kentucky, sandwich the Hot Brown. So DeGroff dialed back the sugar and added muddled lemons, which gave the cocktail brightness and made it less syrupy. DeGroff included the recipe in the second edition of his pioneering book *The Craft of the Cocktail*, which was published in 2020.

INGREDIENTS

Half a lemon, cut into four pieces
2 or 3 mint leaves
¾ ounce (20 ml) simple syrup
   (1 part sugar, 1 part water)
2 ounces (60 ml) Maker's Mark Bourbon

GLASS: Old-Fashioned
GARNISH: Sprig of mint and a lemon wheel

DIRECTIONS

Put the lemon, mint leaves, and simple syrup in a shaker and muddle them. Add the bourbon and fill the shaker with ice. Shake, then strain into an Old-Fashioned glass filled with crushed ice. Garnish with a mint sprig and lemon wheel.

Wildest Redhead

Created by Meaghan Dorman

When it comes to cocktail names, generally anything including *redhead* is not what anyone with red hair would find charming or ever order—I speak from personal experience. So I was delighted when my fellow redhead Meaghan Dorman took back the term in this delicious drink. It has an almost tropical flavor and a good amount of St. Elizabeth Allspice Dram, a favorite of tiki bartenders.

INGREDIENTS

1½ ounces (45 ml) Monkey Shoulder Blended Malt Scotch

¼ ounce (5 ml) St. Elizabeth Allspice Dram

¾ ounce (20 ml) lemon juice

½ ounce (15 ml) honey syrup (3 parts honey, 1 part water)

GLASS: Rocks

GARNISH: ¼ ounce (5 ml) Heering cherry liqueur

DIRECTIONS

Combine all of the ingredients in a shaker and fill it with ice. Shake, then strain into a rocks glass filled with ice. Drizzle the Heering cherry liqueur over the surface of the drink.

SOURCES & FURTHER READING

Arthur, Stanley Clisby. *Famous New Orleans Drinks and How to Mix 'Em*. New Orleans: Harmanson, 1937.

Ashcraft, Brian. *Japanese Whisky: The Ultimate Guide to the World's Most Desirable Spirit*. Rutland, Vermont: Tuttle, 2018.

Baker, Charles H., Jr. *The Gentleman's Companion*. New York: Derrydale, 1939.

Bernheim, Isaac W. *History of the Settlement of Jews in Paducah and the Lower Ohio Valley*. London: Forgotten Books, 2012.

Blum, Deborah. *The Poison Squad: One Chemist's Single-Minded Crusade for Food Safety at the Turn of the Twentieth Century*. New York: Penguin, 2018.

Bodenheimer, Neal and Emily Timberlake. *Cure: New Orleans Drinks and How to Mix 'Em*. New York: Abrams, 2022.

Boudreau, Jamie and James O. Fraioli. *The Canon Cocktail Book: Recipes from the Award-Winning Bar*. New York: Houghton Mifflin Harcourt, 2016.

Broom, Dave. *Gin, How to Drink it*. London: Mitchell Beazley, 2020.

Broom, Dave. *A Sense of Place: A journey around Scotland's whisky*. London: Mitchell Beazley, 2022.

Broom, Dave. *The Way of Whisky: A journey around Japanese whisky*. London: Mitchell Beazley, 2017.

Broom, Dave. *Whisky: The Manual*. London: Mitchell Beazley, 2014.

Broom, Dave. *The World Atlas of Whisky*. London: Mitchell Beazley, 2010.

Bryson, Lew. *Tasting Whiskey: An Insider's Guide to the Unique Pleasures of the World's Finest Spirits*. North Adams, MA: Storey, 2014.

Bryson, Lew. *Whiskey Master Class: The Ultimate Guide to Understanding Scotch, Bourbon, Rye, and More*. Boston: Harvard Common Press, 2020.

Bulleit, Tom. *Bulleit Proof*. With Alan Eisenstock. Hoboken, NJ: Wiley, 2020.

Bullock, Tom. *The Ideal Bartender*. St. Louis, MO: Buxton & Skinner, 1917.

Buxton, Ian. *Glenfarclas: An Independent Distillery*. Glasgow: Angels' Share, 2011.

Caiafa, Frank. *The Waldorf Astoria Bar Book*. New York: Penguin, 2016.

Campbell, Sally Van Winkle. *But Always Fine Bourbon: Pappy Van Winkle and the Story of Old Fitzgerald*. Louisville, KY: Limestone Lane, 1999.

Carson, Gerald. *The Social History of Bourbon*. Lexington, KY: University Press of Kentucky, 2010.

Checkland, Olive. *Japanese Whisky, Scotch Blend*. Edinburgh: Scottish Cultural Press, 1998.

Craig, Charles H. *The Scotch Whisky Industry Record*. Dumberton, Scotland: Index Publishing, 1994.

Cobb, Irwin. *Irvin S. Cobb's Own Recipe Book*. Louisville, KY: Frankfort Distilleries, 1934.

Cooper, Ambrose. *The Complete Distiller*. London, 1757.

Crowley, Henry G. *Kentucky Bourbon: The Early Years of Whiskey Making*. Lexington, KY: University Press of Kentucky, 2008.

Davis, Marni. *Jews and Booze: Becoming American in the Age of Prohibition*. New York: NYU Press, 2014.

Day, Alex, Nick Fauchald and Dave Kaplan. *Cocktail Codex*. New York: Ten Speed, 2018.

Dewar, Thomas R. *A Ramble Round the Globe*. London, 1894.

DeGroff, Dale. *The New Craft of the Cocktail*. New York: Clarkson Potter, 2020.

Dynner, Glenn. *Yankel's Tavern: Jews, Liquor, and Life in the Kingdom of Poland*. New York: Oxford University Press, 2014.

Ensslin, Hugo R. *Recipes for Mixed Drinks*. 2nd ed. New York: Fox Printing House, 1917.

Forbes, R. J. *Short History of the Art of Distillation: From the Beginnings Up to the Death of Cellier Blumenthal*. Leiden, Netherlands: Brill, 1948.

Gils, Marcel van and Hans Offringa. *200 Years of Laphroaig, 1815–2015*. Islay, Scotland: Conceptual Continuity, 2015.

Grimes, William. *Straight Up or On the Rocks: The Story of the American Cocktail*. New York: North Point, 2001.

Harwell, Richard Barksdale. *The Mint Julep*. Charlottesville, VA: University of Virginia Press, 2005.

Jennings, David. *American Spirit: Wild Turkey Bourbon from Ripy to Russell*. Herndon, VA: Mascot Books, 2020.

Kergommeaux, Davin de. *Canadian Whisky: The New Portable Expert*. 2nd ed. Vancouver: Appetite by Random House, 2017.

Kergommeaux, Davin de and Blair Phillips. *The Definitive Guide to Canadian Distilleries: The Portable Expert to Over 200 Distilleries and the Spirits they Make (From Absinthe to Whisky, and Everything in Between)*. Vancouver: Appetite by Random House, 2020.

Kokoris, Jim. *The Big Man of Jim Beam: Booker Noe and the Number-One Bourbon in the World*. Hoboken, NJ: Wiley, 2016.

MacDonald, Aeneas. *Whisky*. Edinburgh: Birlinn, 2016.

Maeda, Yonekichi. *Kokuteeru*. Chippenham, England: Mixellany, 2022.

Magee, Malachy. *1000 Years of Irish Whiskey*. Dublin: O'Brien Press, 1980.

Mahoney, Charley. *Hoffman House Bartender's Guide*. New York: Richard K. Fox, 1912.

Maloney, Toby and Emma Janzen. *The Bartender's Manifesto: How to Think, Drink & Create Cocktails Like a Pro*. New York: Clarkson Potter, 2022.

McElhone, Harry. *ABC of Mixing Cocktails*. London: Dean & Son, 1921.

McElhone, Harry. *Barflies and Cocktails*. Paris: Lecram, 1927.

McGuire, E. B. *Irish Whiskey: A History of Distilling in Ireland*. Dublin: Gill & Macmillan, 1973.

Miller, Gregory H. *Whisky Science: A Condensed Distillation*. Cham, Switzerland: Springer Nature, 2019.

Mitenbuler, Reid. *Bourbon Empire: The Past and Future of America's Whiskey*. New York: Penguin, 2015.

Mersman, Joseph J. *The Whiskey Merchant's Diary*. Athens, OH: Ohio University Press, 2007.

Mew, James and John Ashton. *Drinks of the World*. London: Leadenhall, 1892.

Momosé, Julia. *The Way of the Cocktail: Japanese Traditions, Techniques, and Recipes*. With Emma Janzen. New York: Clarkson Potter, 2021.

Morgan, Nicholas. *A Long Stride: The Story of the World's No. 1 Scotch Whisky*. London: Canongate, 2020.

Morgenthaler, Jeffrey. *Drinking Distilled: A User's Manual*. Berkeley: Ten Speed, 2018.

Moss, Michael S. and John R. Hume. *The Making of Scotch Whisky: A History of the Scotch Whisky Distilling Industry*. Edinburgh: James & James, 1981.

Nettleton, J. A. *The Manufacture of Spirit: As Conducted at the Various Distilleries of the United Kingdom*. London: Marcus Ward, 1893.

Noe, Fred. *Beam Straight Up: The Bold Story of the First Family of Bourbon*. Hoboken, NJ: Wiley, 2012.

Norton, Charles. *Modern Blending and Rectification*. Rev ed. Chicago: 1913.

Okrent, Daniel. *Last Call: The Rise and Fall of Prohibition*. New York: Scribner, 2010.

Rannie, William F. *Canadian Whisky: The Product and the Industry*. Lincoln, Ontario: W.F. Rannie, 1976.

Regan, Gary and Mardee Haidin. *The Book of Bourbon and Other Fine American Whiskeys*. New York: Houghton Mifflin Harcourt, 1995.

Robins, William. *A Plot Against the People: A History of the Audacious Attempt by Certain Kentucky "Straight Whiskey" Interests to Pervert the Pure Food Law in Order to Create a Monopoly for their Fusel Oil Whiskies and to Outlaw all Refined Whiskies*. Walkerville, Ontario: Hiram Walker & Sons, 1911.

Peachee, Carol. *The Birth of Bourbon: A Photographic Tour of Early Distilleries*. Lexington, KY: University Press of Kentucky, 2015.

Rothbaum, Noah. *The Art of American Whiskey: A Visual History of the Nation's Most Storied Spirit, Through 100 Iconic Labels*. Berkeley: Ten Speed, 2015.

Rothbaum, Noah. *The Business of Spirits: How Savvy Marketers, Innovative Distillers, and Entrepreneurs Changed How We Drink*. New York: Kaplan, 2007.

Rorabaugh, W. J. *The Alcohol Republic: An American Tradition*. New York: Oxford University Press, 1979.

Simonson, Robert. *Modern Classic Cocktails: 60+ Stories and Recipes from the New Golden Age in Drinks*. New York: Ten Speed, 2022.

Taketsuru, Masataka. *On the Production Methods of Pot Still Whisky*. Edinburgh: Humming Earth, 2021.

Thomas, Jerry. *How to Mix Drinks or the Bon Vivant's Companion*. New York: Dick & Fitzgerald, 1862.

Walker, Hiram Incorporated. *The Hiram Walker Outline of the Distilled Spirits Business*. Detroit, 1946.

Weir, Ronald. *The History of the Distillers Company, 1877–1939*. Oxford: Clarendon Press, 1996.

Wiley, Harvey W. *Beverages and Their Adulteration*. Philadelphia, PA: P. Blakiston's Son, 1919.

Willkie, Herman Frederick. *Beverage Spirits in America: A Brief History*. New York: Newcomen Society, 1949.

Willkie, Herman Frederick and Harrison C. Blankmeyer. *An Outline for the Industry*. Springfield, IL: Charles C Thomas, 1944.

Willkie, Herman Frederick and Paul John Kolachov. *Food for Thought*. Indianapolis, IN: Indiana Farm Bureau, 1942.

Willkie, Herman Frederick and Paul John Kolachov. *Fundamentals of Distillery Practice: A Handbook on the Manufacture of Ethyl Alcohol and Distillers' Feed Products from Cereals*. Louisville, KY: Joseph E. Seagram & Sons, 1943.

Willkie, Robert T. and Rolland S. Mather. *Distillers' Grain Manual Compiled*. Louisville, KY: Joseph E. Seagram & Sons, 1942.

Wilson, James Boone. *The Spirit of Old Kentucky*. Louisville, KY: Glenmore Distilleries Company, 1945.

Wondrich, David. *Imbibe! From Absinthe Cocktail to Whiskey Smash, a Salute in Stories and Drinks to "Professor" Jerry Thomas, Pioneer of the American Bar*. Rev ed. New York: TarcherPerigee, 2015.

Wondrich, David. *Punch: The Delights (and Dangers) of the Flowing Bowl*. New York: TarcherPerigee, 2010.

Wondrich, David with Noah Rothbaum. *The Oxford Companion to Spirits & Cocktails*. New York: Oxford University Press, 2021.

Young, Al. *Four Roses: The Return of a Whiskey Legend*. Louisville, KY: Butler Books, 2010.

ACKNOWLEDGMENTS

One Friday afternoon in January 2020, I received an email from John Meils of Workman inquiring if I might be interested in writing a book on whiskey. He'd been tipped off by his colleague, the PR and marketing maven Rebecca Carlisle, that I was "quite the whiskey obsessive." It took me all of eight minutes to respond. We chatted on the phone later that same afternoon about *The Whiskey Bible*.

Although I was incredibly intrigued, at first I wasn't sure if this was the project for me. For one thing, David Wondrich and I were still scrambling to finish up *The Oxford Companion to Spirits & Cocktails*. For another, as a huge fan of Karen MacNeil's *The Wine Bible*, I knew that this sister book on whiskey had to measure up to the incredibly high bar it set and recognized the amount of work it would take to properly tackle this vast subject. I didn't want to just rehash the same well-known and tired chestnuts, myths, and legends about whiskey—I wanted to break new ground.

I quickly came to my senses and realized that this opportunity was too good to pass up. Taking on this project, of course, wasn't just a decision that affected me, but my whole family. On countless days, my wife, Ingrid, took our two sons, Aksel and Theo, out to explore New York City while I stayed home to write and research, barely leaving my desk for hours at a time. I couldn't have written this book without their love, support, and, above all, patience. *The Whiskey Bible* is dedicated to the three of them. I hope I've made them proud.

I also couldn't have done this without the support of my parents, sister, aunt, and Midwestern family. Their excitement for the project was invaluable.

The unwavering support and sage counsel of my superstar agent, Rica Allannic, at the David Black Literary Agency, was also incredibly important. Thank you for always having my back.

Creating a book of these epic proportions is kind of like sailing a homemade boat on a transatlantic crossing, with enough dramatic twists and turns to make you seasick before land finally comes into focus. I thank you, John Meils, for going on this journey with me. And thank you, Maisie Tivnan, for guiding me through the final miles of this journey and running point for the book's production.

I also owe a great debt of gratitude to the Hachette team, including Lia Ronnen, Julia Perry, Beth Levy, Becky Terhune, Suet Chong, Doug

Wolff, Barbara Peragine, Annie O'Donnell, Bart Dawson, and Katherine Pepper. It is thanks to all of you that this book exists. Thanks also to photo researchers Michelle Wolfe and Kate Osba, at Look See Photo. And this would be a much duller book without Tom Woolley's charming illustrations.

While I hoped to break new ground, I soon realized that there was a river of documents, books, and articles that no one had read in years or decades. (Thank you to all the librarians who helped me!) I was soon drowning in information, and experiencing epiphanies that made me rethink many of my fundamental beliefs about whiskey history and culture. Fortunately, I had my crew of personal advisers to turn to, chiefly: David Wondrich, Todd Leopold, Nicole Austin, Allen Katz, Dave Mitton, and Ewan Morgan. They were usually willing to drop what they were doing to ponder one of my ideas or discuss a new finding.

Countless folks across the drinks industry were willing to answer questions, provide key information and photos, and offer moral support, including: Brian Ashcraft, Sarah Bessette, David Blackmore, Dave Broom, Campbell P. Brown, Lew Bryson, Paddy Caulfield, Dan Cohen, Greg Cohen, Emma Cullen, Laura Cullen, Rob Dietrich, Leah Doyle, Colum Egan, Shinji Fukuyo, Josh Hafer, Amanda Hathaway, Lisa Hawkins, Gareth Howells, Doug Kragel, Kate Laufer, Dr. Don Livermore, Bernie Lubbers, Dr. Bill Lumsden, Stephanie Macleod, Joe Magliocco, Dave Mandler, Reid Mitenbuler, Dr. Nick Morgan, Helen Mulholland, Brian Nation, Lauren Cherry Newcomb, Conor O'Driscoll, Jessica Rodriguez, Manuela Savona, Gia Vecchio, Charlotte Voisey, Jennifer Webb, Andrew Wiehebrink, and Maggie Quinn.

I'm also grateful to the bartenders who allowed me to share their amazing whiskey cocktail recipes in this book: Eric Alperin, Tiffanie Barriere, Jeff Berry, Neal Bodenheimer, Jamie Boudreau, Frank Caiafa, Erick Castro, Toby Cecchini, Reggie Cunningham, Alex Day, Dale DeGroff, Meaghan Dorman, St. John Frizell, John Gertsen, Kenta Goto, Lynn House, Don Lee, John Lermayer, Toby Maloney, Iain McPherson, Julia Momosé, Jeffrey Morgenthaler, Garret Richard, Sam Ross, Jon Santer, Audrey Saunders, T.J. Siegel, Joaquín Simó, Alex Smith, and Chad Solomon.

And, of course, thank you to all the distillers and blenders who are making whiskey around the world. This book celebrates your work.

Cheers!

INDEX

A

A. Ph. Stitzel distillery, 98, 152
Abasolo distillery, 456–457, 476–477
ABC of Mixing Cocktails (McElhone), 557
Aberargie, 246
Aberfeldy, 196, 282, 284–286
Aberlour, 264–265, 300
absinthe, 566
Absolut Vodka, 274, 545
A'bunadh, 264
ABV. See alcohol by volume
ACSA (American Craft Spirits Association), 132
Adulteration of Liquors (Cotter), 84
aging process. See maturation process
Akadama Port Wine, 443
Akashi, 452–453
Akuto, Ichiro, 416, 454
Albert (prince), 256
Alberta Distillers, 532
Alberta Prime distillery, 368
Alberta Rye Whisky Dark Batch, 400
alcohol by volume (ABV)
　barrel entry proof, 31
　distiller's beer and wash, 25
　"low wines," 29
　proof vs., 49
Alcoholic Republic, The (Rorabaugh), 74, 78
Allardice, James, 274
Alliance Global Group, 297
Allied Domecq, 265, 274, 292, 294, 540, 543
Allied-Lyons, 292
Alperin, Eric, 556, 568
Alsop, Joseph, 109, 112
American Brands, 295, 542
American Craft Spirits Association (ACSA), 132

American Heritage magazine, 383
American Honey, 157
American Single Malt Whiskey Commission, 67
American whiskey, 57–194
　Bacardi, 173–174
　Blackened Whiskey, 181–182
　blended whiskey, 69
　bottled-in-bond, 80, 86–87
　bourbon
　　high-rye bourbon, 80
　　inventing, 74, 77
　　overview, 59–60
　　small batch bourbons, 121–126
　　wheated bourbon, 81
　Brown-Forman, 145–149
　Campari, 154–158
　cask strength, 80
　Castle & Key, 182
　Constellation Brands, 176–178
　corn whiskey, 68–69
　craft distilling, 341
　Deutsch Family Wine & Spirits, 178–179
　Diageo, 149–154
　distiller's beer, 25
　drinking recommendations, 503–505, 508
　Edrington, 180–181
　family tree, 133–194
　　FEW, 138–139
　　Frey Ranch, 182–183
　　Heaven Hill, 133–138
　　High Wire Distilling, 183–184
　　Hotaling & Co., 179–180
　　Illva Saronno, 178
　　Jim Beam, 139–145
　　Keeper's Heart, 184–185
　　Kings County, 185–186
　　Kirin, 174–176
　　Leopold Bros., 186–187
　　Lock Stock & Barrel, 187

INDEX

Michter's, 187–189
New Riff, 189
New York Distilling Company, 189–190
Pernod Ricard, 158–162
Pinhook Bourbon, 190–191
Proximo, 162–164
Rémy Cointreau, 164
Sazerac, 165–172
St. George Spirits, 191–192
Uncle Nearest, 192
Westward Whiskey, 192–193
WhistlePig, 193–194
Willett, 194
William Grant & Sons, 172–173
history of, 70–132
    American revolution, 71
    Bottled-in-Bond Act of 1897, 86–87
    Brown-Forman, 88
    chamber stills, 78–79, 82–83
    Civil War, 77–78
    decline, 118–121
    distiller's beer, 79
    doublers, 79, 82
    early American spirits, 70–74
    farm distillery and craft movement, 129–132
    Green, Nathan "Nearest," 76
    Hamilton, Alexander, 75
    high-rye bourbon, 80
    Hiram Walker, 115
    inventing bourbon, 74
    Korean War, 116
    medical whiskey, 88, 96–97
    National Distillers, 115
    new barrel requirement, 107–109, 112–113
    Old Forester, 88
    post-World War II, 115–116
    Prohibition, 12, 96–97, 102
    rectifiers, 93
    role of immigrants, 90–92
    rum, 74
    rye, 126–129
    Schenley, 115–117
    Seagram's, 115
    slavery, 73, 76–77
    small batch bourbons, 121–126
    temperance movement, 11–12
    Van Winkle, Julian "Pappy," 98–101
    Washington, George, 72–73
    wheated bourbon, 81
    whiskey purity issue, 88–89, 93–94
    Whiskey Rebellion, 75
    World War I, 95–96
    World War II, 113–116
imposter whiskey, 84
light whiskey, 118–119
mash bill, 80
mashing process, 24
medical whiskey, 85
moonshine, 57
overview, 57–58
rectifiers, 85
rickhouse, 81
rye, 60–61, 64
single barrel whiskey, 81
single malt, 67–68
small batch whiskey, 81
sour mash, 21
straight, 81
sweet mash, 21
Tennessee whiskey, 64–67
three-chamber still, 62–63
unique methods and traditions, 59
whiskey purity issue, 85
whisky regions, 54–55
white dog, 81
American white oak (*Quercus alba*), 45

Amis, Kingsley, 267
Amrut Distilleries, 456–457, 472–473, 543
anaerobic digesters, 16
Anchor Distilling Company, 179, 538
Ancient Age, 432, 538, 541
Anderson, Hugh, 341
Andrews, Lavone Dickensheets, 353–354
Andrews, Mark Edwin, 353–354
Andrews, Mark, III, 354
Angel's Envy, 173–174, 442
Angostura, 130
Antique Collection, 166
Apprentice, The (TV series), 193
aqua vitae, 207–208, 315, 520
Arbikie, 246
Ardbeg, 196, 203, 234, 292–295, 511, 540, 542–543
Ardmore, 288–289
Ardnahoe, 203
Armorik distillery, 456–457, 470
arrack, 9
Arran distillery, 469
Arrow Cordials, 541
Art & Decadence, 303
Art of Blending and Compounding Liquors and Wines, The (Fleischman), 85
Arthur, Stanley Clisby, 567
Arvin, Will, 182
Asahi, 447–448
Ashburn, Bill, 397
Ashcraft, Brian, 424, 442
Asian whisky. *See also* Japanese whisky
  arrack, 9
  early alcohol beverages, 7
  East Asia, 456–457, 465–466
  India, 456–457, 472–473
Associated Press, 236

Athyr Single Malt, 475
Auchentoshan, 29, 202, 259, 272, 287–288, 439, 539
Aultmore, 282
Austin, Nichols, 155, 536
Austin, Nicole, 54–55, 152
Australian newspaper, 462
Australian whisky
  Lark, 456–457, 460–461
  Morris Single Malt Whisky, 462
  Starward, 456–457, 461–462, 518
  Sullivans Cove's, 456–457, 461

B

B. Daly distillery, 354
Baby Blue Corn Whisky, 154
Bacardi, 173–174, 239, 282–287, 363–364, 540
  Aberfeldy, 285–286
  Craigellachie, 286
  Dewar's, 283–285
  Last Great Malts collection, 282
  Royal Brackla, 286–287
  Teeling, 363–364
backset, 21
Baileys Original Irish Cream, 354–356
Baker, Charles H., 564
Baker's Bourbon, 126, 141
Balance, and Columbian Repository, 521
Balblair, 239
Balcones, 154
Ballantine's, 543
Balmoral Castle, 256
Baltimore Sun, 225
Balvenie, The, 20, 196, 202, 241, 254, 277–279, 525, 533, 547
  Caribbean Cask, 278

INDEX

Classic, 278
DoubleWood 12, 278, 539
Founder's Reserve, 278
origin of, 277
Balzer, Robert Lawrence, 239
Banzer, Emma, 151
BAR 1661, 317
Barflies and Cocktails (McElhone), 555, 563
Barkley, Alben W., 112
barley
flavor notes and attributes, 18
malt, 18–19
Barnard, Alfred, 214–217, 258, 261, 266, 290, 294, 298, 303, 319, 350, 356–357, 525
Barnum, Eli, 6
barrel entry proof, 31
barrels, 34–36
American white oak, 45
bilge, 36
bilge hoop, 36
bourbon barrels, 40–41
bung hole, 36
charring process, 45
corn whiskey, 108
craft distilleries versus big makers, 490–491
croze, 36
effect on flavor, 41, 44
finishing, 241
French oak, 46
Garry oak, 47
head, 36
head hoop, 36
Japanese mizunara oak, 46, 442
location and rate of maturation, 44–45
new barrel requirement for American whiskey, 107–109, 112–113
quarter hoop, 36

reusing, 45
sherry casks, 39
stave, 36
using multiple barrels, 47
Barrie, Rachel, 272
Barriere, Tiffanie, 573
Bartender's Manifesto, The (Maloney), 571
Barterhouse, 153
Basil Hayden, viii, 126, 141
Bass, Heather, 161
Beam, Baker, 141
Beam, Carl, 122, 141
Beam, Charles L., 91
Beam, Earl, 26
Beam, James Beauregard "Jim," 25, 103, 140
Beam, John Henry "Jack," 91, 171, 528
Beam, Joseph L., 91
Beam, Parker, 542
Beam, Straight Up (Noe), 25–26
Beam Global
Alberta distillers, 400–401
Canadian Club, 398–400
Beam Suntory, 359–361, 543, 547. *See also* Jim Beam; Suntory
Connemara, 359–360
Kilbeggan, 360–361
Tyrconnell, 360
Bearface Canadian whisky, 412
Beckham, David, 253
Beckmann family, 320
Bell, Geoff, 271, 547
Bell, Max, 400, 532
Ben Nevis, 439, 449, 538
Benchmark, 537
Benriach, 271–274, 547
Bensonhurst, 569–570
Benton's Old-Fashioned, 570–571
Bergeron, Walter, 567
Bernheim, 538, 541

Bernheim, Bernard, 110, 532
Bernheim, Isaac Wolfe, 92, 110–111, 136, 153, 532
Bernheim Bros., 110–111
Bernheim Forest, 111
Bernheim Original Wheat Whiskey, 136
Bernstein, Barry, 414
Berry, Jeff "Beachbum," 581
Berry Bros. & Rudd, 270–271, 301, 468
Bever, Megan L., 77
Bhakta, Raj, 193
Big Ginger, 514
Big Shanty Corn, 111
Biggie Smalls, 417
bilge hoops, barrel, 36
bilges, barrel, 36
biofuel, 16
Birthday Bourbon, 148
Black Band distillery, 105
Black Bowmore, 290, 539
Black Bush, 335, 347
Black Velvet, 368, 411
Blackened Whiskey, 69, 181–182, 548
Blackpitts Peated Single Malt, 344
Blackwell, Scott, 183–184
Blade and Bow, 99, 152–153
Bladnoch whisky, 202
Blankmeyer, Harrison C., 109
Blanton, Albert B., 167
Blanton's, 126, 432, 536, 538, 546
blenders (rectifiers), 85, 93
blends
   American whiskey, 50, 69
   Canadian whisky, 50, 370, 390–393
   Irish whiskey, 311, 321, 323–325, 331–332, 334, 340
   Japanese whisky, 120, 125
   overview, 49–50

Scotch whisky, 50, 204, 211–214, 216–217, 228–229, 235–236, 244
Blinker, 571
Blood and Sand, 554
Bloody Caesar, 515
Bloom, Moses, 110
Blue Blazer, 553
Blue Spot, 343, 351–352
Bobby Burns cocktail, 554
Bodenheimer, Neal, 566–567
Boehm, Johannes Jakob (Jacob Beam), 91
Boilermaker, 555
Bombay Gin, 282
Bonaparte, Charles Joseph, 93, 380
Bonfort's Wine and Spirit Circular, 93, 379
   Bernheim Bros., 111
   chamber stills, 79
   charcoal filtration, 65–66
Bonnie Prince Charlie (Charles Edward Stuart), 196, 279–280
Booker's, viii, 122–124, 126, 140, 537
Boothby, William "Cocktail," 84–85
"Bootleg Paradise" (Curtis), 383
Bordeaux, Peter, 165
Borwick, George, 269
Borwick, James, 269
Borwick, Robert, 269
Boss Hog whiskey, 194
Boston Globe, 218
Botanist Gin, The, 296, 546
Botsford, Constantine & Gardner, 427
Bottled-in-Bond Act of 1897, 86–87, 526
bottled-in-bond whiskey, 86–87
bottling
   glass bottling, 100, 377–378, 526
   proofing down and, 51–52
Boudreau, Jamie, 573

Boulevardier, The, 555
bourbon
   high-rye bourbon, 80
   inventing, 74, 77
   new barrel requirement, 107–109, 112–113
   overview, 59–60
   small batch bourbons, 121–126
     Baker's, 126
     Basil Hayden, viii, 126
     Blanton's Bourbon, 126
     Booker's Bourbon, 122–124
     Knob Creek, 126
     rise of, 121–126
   wheated bourbon, 81
bourbon barrels, 34, 40–41
Bourbon Hall of Fame, 546
Bourbon Institute, 533–535
Bourbon Milk Punch, 557
Bourbon Renewal, 571–572
Bourbon Rickey, 556
Bourbon Trail, 540
Bourbon Trail Craft Tour, 540
Bow Street, 306, 316, 521, 535
Bowmore, 20, 196, 203, 272, 287, 289–290, 439, 511, 520, 539
Boxergrail rye whiskey, 161
Branca Menta, 576
Brenne Estate Cask, 470
Brenne Single Malt, 470–471
Brenne Ten, 470
Brimstone whiskey, 154
Briscoe, Robert, 330
British Wine & Spirit Brand Association, 531
Brittany whisky, 470
Bronfman, Abe, 385
Bronfman, Allan, 385
Bronfman, Harry, 385, 387
Bronfman, Mindel, 385
Bronfman, Sam, 385
Bronfman, Yechiel, 385
Bronfman family, 130, 384–387, 526, 529, 541
Brooks, Benjamin, 6
Broom, Dave, 202, 299, 432, 451, 517
Brora, 233, 252, 256, 536, 547, 549
Brown, Campbell, 148
Brown, George Garvin, 88, 145, 548
Brown, J.T.S., Jr., 88, 145
Brown, Mark, 165, 167
Brown Derby cocktail, 556
Brown-Forman, 88, 96–97, 432, 508, 528, 532, 547
   Benriach, 272–273
   Birthday Bourbon, 148
   Early Times, 171–172
   Frost 8/80 Dry White Whiskey, 118
   GlenDronach, 274–275
   Glenglassaugh, 275–276
   Jack Daniel's, 146–147
   Old Forester, 148, 508
   Slane Irish Whiskey, 362–363
   Woodford Reserve, 148–149
Brownstoner, 572
Bruichladdich, 203, 295–296, 344, 365, 539, 542, 546
Bryson, Lew, 188, 352, 400–401
Buchanan, George C., 66
Buchanan's, 218, 284, 529
Buena Vista Cafe, 328–330, 513, 532
Buffalo Trace, 54–55, 100–101, 167, 361, 432, 538, 541, 543
Bukowski, Charles, vi
Bulleit, Augustus, 151
Bulleit, Hollis, 151
Bulleit, Tom, 150–151
Bulleit Bourbon, 16, 128, 150–151
Bullock, Tom, 505–506, 528, 561
bung holes, 36
Bunnahabhain, 203

Bureau of Internal Revenue. *See* Internal Revenue Service
Burns, Robert, 196, 301, 554
Bushmills, 306, 309, 313–314, 316, 319–320, 331, 333–336, 341, 344–347, 520, 536, 543, 546
Bushwick Country Club, 342
Business Week, 229
Butler, Victoria Eady, 76, 192
butts (sherry casks), 35, 39
Buxton, Ian, 281
Buzza, George, Jr., 556
Byrne, Alicia, 522
Byrne, Murtagh, 522

C

C&C Group (Cantrell & Cochrane), 357–358, 546
Cab Calloway cocktail, 573
Cabin Still, 531
Cadbury's, 355
Caelum Capital, 303
Caiafa, Frank, 568
Calder, John, 236
Call, Dan, 76, 146, 192
Cambus, 233
Cameronbridge, 196, 247, 252–253
Cameron's Kick, 512, 514, 557
Campari, 154–158, 298–300, 358, 545, 547
  American Honey, 157
  Canadian whisky, 397
  Longbranch bourbon, 156–157
  Russell's Reserve, 157
  Wild Turkey Bourbon, 155–156
  Wilderness Trail, 157–158
Campari, Gaspare, 397
Canadian Club, 374–375, 377–382, 516, 527, 543
  Beam Global, 398–400
  evolution of, 378–379
  knockoffs, 379
  legal challenge to, 379–382
  origin of, 377–378
Canadian Mist, 368, 409
Canadian Rye Whisky, 379
Canadian whisky, 368–414. *See also* Seagram's
  Alberta Prime distillery, 368
  Black Velvet distillery, 368
  Canadian Club, 398–400
  Canadian Mist distillery, 368
  Corby distillery, 15, 368
  Crown Royal, 368, 371, 394
  drinking recommendations, 515–516
  Eau Claire distillery, 368
  family tree, 397–414
    Beam Global, 398–401
    Campari, 397
    Diageo, 406–407
    Eau Claire distillery, 412–413
    Forty Creek, 397–398
    Found North distillery, 413–414
    Glenora distillery, 414
    Heaven Hill, 411
    Jose Cuervo, 404, 406
    Mark Anthony Group, 411–412
    Pernod Ricard, 401–404
    Sazerac, 408–411
    Still Waters distillery, 414
  Glen Breton distillery, 368
  Gooderham & Worts distillery, 368
  Hiram Walker distillery, 368–370
  history of, 374–396
    American Prohibition, 382–384
    blends, 390–393
    Bronfman family, 384–387
    Canadian Club, 374–375, 377–382

INDEX 599

end of American Prohibition, 389–390
Hatch, Harry, 387–389
industrialization, 374
origins, 374
World Wars, 390–391
modern makeover, 394–396
9.09 percent rule, 373, 412
Regal Apple Whisky, 371
regions, 368
Still Waters distillery, 368
types of, 371–372
Canadian Whisky (Kergommeaux), 374, 403
Canon (bar), 573
Canterbury Tales (Chaucer), 9
Cantrell & Cochrane (C&C Group), 357, 546
Caol Ila, 196, 203, 242–243, 252, 255–256
carbon neutral distilleries, 16
Cardhu, 197, 248, 258–259, 276
Caribou Crossing, 408
Carlisle, 525, 528
Caro, Robert, 170
Carson, Gerald, 134, 378
casks (wooden barrels), 30. *See also* barrels
Castle & Key, 54–55, 182, 548
Castle Brands, 160, 354, 548
Castro, Erick, 156, 577
Causeway, 347
Cavehill Kentucky Straight Bourbon Whiskey, 161
Cecchini, Toby, 511, 555, 578
Celtic Tiger economic boom, 338
chamber stills, 62–63, 78–79, 82–83
Chambord Liqueur, 127
charcoal filtration, 47, 64–67, 409
Charles Edward Stuart (Bonnie Prince Charlie), 196, 279–280
Charles III, 256, 290, 469

charring process, 45
Charter, 541
Chasko, Alex, 363
Checkland, Olive, 422
Chicago Tribune, 224, 379
Chichibu, 416, 435, 454
Childs, Marquis, 112
chill filtration, 48–49
Chinese whisky, 463–464, 518
Chuan, 456–457, 463–464
early alcohol beverages, 7
Eryuan, 456–457, 464
Chita, 416, 419, 426, 444–445, 535
Chivas, James, 236
Chivas, John, 263
Chivas Brothers, 430, 439, 449–450
Chivas Regal, 50, 204, 218, 234, 262–264, 272–273, 277, 300, 335, 430, 440, 486, 512, 532
Christian Brothers, 541
Christie's, 500
Chuan, The, 456–457, 463–464, 549
Churchill, Winston, vi, 116, 226–227
Churchill Downs distillery, 54–55, 140, 507–508
Cisco Brewers, 542
Civil War, 77–78, 524
Clynelish, 252, 256–257
Cocker, Joe, 231
Cocktail Techniques (Uyeda), 435
cocktails, 503–505, 508–518
American whiskey, 503–505, 508
Canadian whisky, 515–516
classic, 553–569
Blood and Sand, 554
Blue Blazer, 553
Bobby Burns, 554
Boilermaker, 555
Boulevardier, The, 555
Bourbon Milk Punch, 557
Bourbon Rickey, 556
Brown Derby, 556

600 INDEX

Cameron's Kick, 557
Highball, 558
Hot Toddy, 558
Irish Coffee, 559
Mamie Taylor, 559
Manhattan, 560
Mint Julep, 560–561
Modern, 561
New York Sour, 562
Old Pal, 563
Old-Fashioned, 562–563
Presbyterian, 563
Remember the Maine, 564
Reverse Manhattan, 564
Rob Roy, 565
Rusty Nail, 512, 565
Sazerac, 566
Uncle Angelo's Eggnog, 566–567
Vieux Carré, 567
Waldorf, 568
Ward Eight, 568
Whiskey Sour, 569
early definition of, 521
Irish whiskey, 512–515
Japanese whisky, 516–518
modern, 569–586
    Bensonhurst, 569–570
    Benton's Old-Fashioned, 570–571
    Blinker, 571
    Bourbon Renewal, 571–572
    Brownstoner, 572
    Cab Calloway, 573
    DuBoudreau Cocktail, 573
    Emerald Old-Fashioned, 574
    Fitzgerald Fizz, 575
    Flannel Shirt, 574
    Gold Rush, 575
    Good Night, Irene, 576
    Grey Wolf, 576
    Irish Flip, 577
    Iron Ranger, 577–578
    Le Sang et Sable, 578
    Little Italy, 579
    Mastodon, The, 579
    Moto Guzzi, 580
    Not So Rusty Nail, 580
    Paniolo, 581
    Paper Plane, 581–582
    Penicillin, 582
    Pickleback, 583
    Plum Sazerac, 583
    Revolver, 583–584
    Rob Royce, 584
    Smoke and Mirrors, 585
    Whiskey Smash, 585–586
    Wildest Redhead, 586
Scotch whisky, 508–512
world whiskey, 518
Coffey, Aeneas, 32, 82, 211–213, 306, 319, 321, 448–449, 522
Coffey Grain Whisky, 449
Coffey Malt Whisky, 449
Coffey stills, 311, 319, 321–325, 522. *See also* column stills
Cognac, 89
Cohn, Roy, 117
Cold Cut Bourbon, 139
Colere, 164
Collaboration Blend, 187
collecting whiskey, 500–502
   social media, 501
   storage, 501–502
Collingwood, 408–409
coloring, 50–51
column stills, 30–33, 522
   barrel entry proof, 31
   doublers, 33
   effect on flavor, 35, 37
   Hiram Walker's use of, 377
   hybrid column/pot still, 33
   Irish whiskey, 311, 319, 321–325

INDEX 601

Scotch whisky, 211–212, 216, 221–222, 253, 320
Compass Box, 302–303, 542
conglomerates
  Brown-Forman, 88
  Hiram Walker, 115
  National Distillers, 115
  Norton Simon, 99
  Schenley, 115–117
  Seagram's, 115
Conhurst, William F., 82
Connemara, 359–360, 546
Connery, Sean, 429
Constellation Brands, 176–178, 547
Continental Distilling, 135
Conyngham, Alex, 362
Cook & Bernheimer, 526
Cooley distillery, vii, 306, 313, 337, 344, 359, 361–362, 365, 537
Cooper, Katie, 187
Cooper, Rob, 187, 395–396, 400
Cooper, Robert, 127–128, 187, 395–396, 400
Cooper King distillery, 467–468
copper pot stills, 27–30
Coppola, Sofia, 446, 543
Cor, John, 9, 207, 520
Córas Tráchtála, 330
Corby distillery, 15, 24, 368, 380
Core Collection (Sagamore Spirit), 178
cork breakage, 501–502
Cork Distilleries Company, 332, 350, 352, 358, 361, 534
corn, flavor notes and attributes, 18
Corn Laws, 212, 523
corn whiskey, 68–69
  Baby Blue Corn Whisky, 154
  barrels, 108
  Mellow Corn, 138
Corsair Quinoa Whiskey, 15
Cotswolds distillery, 468

Cotter, Oliver, 84
Coughlin, Simon, 295
Cowan, Jessie Roberta. *See* Taketsuru, Rita
Cowdery, Chuck, 143
Craddock, Harry, 554, 556
craft distilling
  American whiskey, 129–132, 341
  big makers versus, 489–491
  Irish whiskey, 337–338, 341, 343–344
Craft of the Cocktail, The (DeGroff), 542, 567, 585
Cragganmore, 259
Craig, Elijah, 134
Craigellachie, 282, 286
Crampton, Charles Albert, 527
Crestmore, 111
Crock o' Gold Whiskey, 331
Crockett, Barry, 352–353
Crow, James, 143
Crow Light, 118
Crown Royal, 368, 371, 394, 516, 531, 534, 549
crozes, 36
Cruikshank, John, 270
Cueno, Martin, 508
Cuervo y Valdés, José Antonio de, 345
Cumming, Helen, 197, 259
Cumming, John, 259
Cunningham, Reggie, 342, 583
Currie, Paul, 456–457, 469
Curtis, Wayne, 383
Cutty Sark, 229–230, 270–271, 301

D

D. M. distillery, 119
Dahlby, Tracy, 439
Dai Nippon Kaju, 426, 447

Daily Beast, 401
Daily Record, 226
Daily Telegraph, 217
Dál Riata, 203
Dallas Dhu, 233
Dalmore, The, 297–298, 534, 545
Dalwhinnie, 249–250, 259, 526
Dand, David, 355
Daniel, Jack, 76, 146–147, 524, 527
Dareringer bourbon, 161
David Sherman Corporation, 541
Davis, Sammy, Jr., 429
Day, Alex, 585
DCL (Distillers Company Limited), 249, 252, 256, 258, 285–286, 440, 529
Dead Rabbit, The, 329, 513, 546, 559
DeFazio, David, 180
DeGroff, Dale, 242, 542, 553, 567, 585
DeKuyper Peachtree Schnapps, 356
Delaplane, Stanton, 326, 328–330, 532
Delola, 348
Denmark and Sweden
  Mackmyra, 456–457, 479–480
  Stauning, 456–457, 478–479
Derbomez, Seb, 279
Desmarais, Jules, 387
Deutsch Family Wine & Spirits, 178–179
Deveron, 282
Devil's Cut, 141–142
Dewar, John, 283–286, 522
Dewar, John Alexander, 283–285
Dewar, Thomas "Tommy," 219, 283–285
Dewar's, 50, 204, 216, 218–219, 228, 239, 277, 282, 286, 363, 442, 486, 512, 529, 540

Diageo, 526, 538, 540–541, 543, 546–549
  avoiding monopoly status, 282, 297
  Baileys, 354–356
  Balcones, 154
  Blade and Bow, 152–153
  Brora, 252
  Bulleit Bourbon, 16, 150–151
  Caol Ila, 255–256
  Cardhu, 258–259
  Clynelish, 256–257
  Cragganmore, 259
  Crown Royal, 406–408
  Dalwhinnie, 249–250
  Distill Ventures, 462
  George Dickel, 151–152
  Glenkinchie, 259
  Haig Club Single Grain Whisky, 252–253
  I.W. Harper, 111, 153
  J&B Rare Blended Scotch Whisky, 250–251
  Johnnie Walker, 247–249
  Lagavulin, 257–258
  Linkwood, 258
  merger with Grand Metropolitan and Guinness, 239
  Mortlach, 254–255
  Oban Single Malt Scotch Whisky, 251
  Orphan Barrel Whiskey Distilling Co., 153–154
  overview, 149–150
  Port Ellen, 260
  purchase of Bushmills, 346
  Roe & Co, 356–357
  role in rebirth of rye, 128
  Royal Lochnagar, 256
  Talisker, 253–254
Dick, Robert, 270
Dickel, George A., 92, 151, 533

Dickel distillery, 54–55
Dietrich, Rob, 181–182
Dingle Irish Whiskey, 365
Distill Ventures, 462, 479
Distilled Spirits Council of the United States (DISCUS), 243, 348, 535, 544
Distilled Spirits Institute, 114, 535
Distillers Company Limited (DCL), 249, 252, 256, 258, 285–286, 440, 529
Distillery Row, 148
distilling, 5. *See also* stills
  advantages of, 9
  barrel entry proof, 31
  distiller's beer, 26
  distilling on the grains, 24
  early history of, 7–8
  impact of world wars on, 12, 14
  recycling waste, 17
  transition from medicinal tinctures to recreational drinks, 8
Distilling Act of 1779, 319
Dom Pérignon, 499
Domaine des Hautes Glaces, 456–457, 471
Don Julio Tequila, 346, 546
Donohoe, Mike, 123
Dorman, Meaghan, 586
Double Eagle Very Rare bourbon, 167
doublers (thumpers), 33, 79, 82
Downing, Emmanuel, 91, 520
Dr. McGillicuddy's, 166, 409–410, 537, 542
draff, 207–208
Drambuie, 279–280, 565
Drinks Ireland, 343
Dublin Distillers Company Ltd., 357
Dublin Liberties, 344

Dublin Whiskey Distillery Company, 357
DuBoudreau Cocktail, 573
Duff, John, 272
Duffy, Patrick J., 284
Dukes of Hazzard (TV series), 57
Dunbar, 439
Dunphy, 335
Dutch immigrants, role in American whiskey industry, 90

E

Eagle Rare, 167, 537
Early Times, 91, 96–97, 171–172, 432, 528
Eau Claire distillery, 368, 412–413
eau-de-vie, 207–208
Eaves, Marianne, 182
Economist, 296
Edrington, 180–181, 265–271, 275, 281, 301
  Glenrothes, The, 270–271
  Highland Park, 265, 268–269
  Macallan, The, 265–268
Edward, William, 263
Egan, Colum, 320, 346
E.H. Taylor, Jr., 168
Eigashima Shuzo, 416, 452–453
Eight Immortals oolong tea, 139
Eighteenth Amendment, US Constitution, 12
Eisenhower, Dwight D., 533
Elijah Craig bourbon, 134–135, 530
Elizabeth (queen mother), 531
Elizabeth I, 315
Elizabeth II, 256, 264, 278, 547
Emerald Old-Fashioned, 574
Emperador, 297
Empire Rye program, 13

English whisky
    Cooper King, 467–468
    Cotswolds, 468
    English distillery, The, 456–457, 469
    Lakes distillery, The, 456–457, 469
Ensslin, Hugo, 554
environmental issues, 16–17
Erenzo, Ralph, 128–129, 542, 548
Eryuan, 456–457, 464
Esquire, 235, 325, 329, 337
Estate Oak Rye, 193–194
Evan Williams Bourbon, 135, 530
Evening Standard, 225
Everyday Drinking (Amis), 267
Excise Act of 1823, 209, 317, 522

F

FAA (Federal Alcohol Administration), 107–108, 531
Famous Grouse, The, 235, 280–281, 486
Famous New Orleans Drinks and How to Mix 'Em (Arthur), 567
FarmStock Rye, 193–194
Farnsley, Alex, 98, 531
Federal Alcohol Administration (FAA), 107–108, 531
feints stills, 29
fermentation process, 24–26
    distiller's beer, 25
    fermenters, 24
    role of yeast in, 25–26
    wash, 25
    washbacks, 24
FEW, 138–139
filtration process
    chill filtration, 48–49

Lincoln County Process, 47–48, 64–67
Financial Times, 464, 466
Fireball, 409–410, 537, 542
Firestone, Leonard, 161
Fistful of Bourbon, 172
Fitzgerald, F. Scott, 575
Fitzgerald, John E., 137
Fitzgerald Fizz, 575
Flannel Shirt, 574
Flarsheim, A. B., 111
Fleischman, Joseph, 85
Fleischmann's Preferred, 69
Fleming, James, 264
floor malting, 19–20
Fly Market Hotel, 522
Flying Dog brewery, 162
Food + Wine magazine, vii
Forand Bill, 533
Ford, Henry, 92
Forman, Louis, 188
Fortune Brands, 292, 543
Forty Creek, 397–398, 515, 535, 547
Found North distillery, 413–414
Four Roses, 91, 174–176, 432, 541
Four Roses (Young), 174
Foynes Flying Boat Station, 327, 513
Frankfort Distilling Company, 175
Fraser, William, 287
French oak (*Quercus robur*), 46
French Oak Single Cask whisky, 461
French whiskey, 470–471
    Armorik, 456–457, 470
    Brenne Single Malt, 470–471
    Domaine des Hautes Glaces, 456–457, 471
Frey, Ashley, 182
Frey, Colby, 182
Frey Ranch, 182–183
Frost, Doug, 501
Frost 8/80 Dry White Whiskey, 118

INDEX 605

FTC (US Fair Trade Commission), 441
Fuji, 416, 430, 435, 439, 449–450
Fukuyo, Shinji, 444
Fusion whisky, 473

G

Galyean, Tag, 161
Garry oak (*Quercus garryana*), 47
Garryana, 164
genever, 90
Gentleman Jack, 147
Gentleman's Companion, The (Baker), 564
Geoffroy, Richard, 499
George Dickel, 64, 92, 151–152
George T. Stagg distillery, 166–167, 170
George VI, 531
German immigrants, role in American whiskey industry, 91–92
Gertsen, John, 580
ghost distilleries, 232, 260, 488
Gilmore, Eddy, 236
gin, 90, 208, 211, 213
Gin Lane (Hogarth), 211, 213
Glaser, Amy, 302
Glaser, John, viii, 302, 542
glasses, 499
Glen Albyn, 277
Glen Breton, 368, 414
Glen Garioch, 439, 539
Glen Grant, The, 298–300
Glen Moray, 292–293, 543
Glen Moray-Glenlivet, 238
GlenAllachie, 272
Glencairn, 499
Glendalough, 364
GlenDronach, 271, 273–275, 547

Glenfarclas, 230, 259, 303–304
Glenfiddich, 196, 202, 230, 241, 254, 259, 276–277, 279, 343, 525, 533–534
Glenglassaugh, 271, 273–276, 547
Glenkinchie, 202, 259
Glenlivet, The, 196, 202, 209, 216, 239, 260–262, 272, 299–300, 438–440, 522, 524–525, 536
Glenmorangie, 29–30, 47, 196, 230, 234, 238, 241, 272, 292–295, 540, 543
Glenmore Distilleries Company, 82
Glenora, 414, 538
Glenrothes, The, 270–271, 301
Gloag, Matthew, 280–281
Gluckman, David, 355
Goa, 9
Gold Rush cocktail, 575
Goldring, Newman, 165
Goldring, Stephen, 165
Goldring, William, 165–166
golf, 218
Good Friday Agreement, 338
Good Night, Irene, 576
Gooderham, Elizabeth, 403
Gooderham, William, 403, 523
Gooderham & Worts Ltd., 368, 388, 403–404, 523, 529
Gordon, Charles Grant, 235
Gordon, James, 264
Gordon & MacPhail, 258
Goslings Rum, 354
Goto, Kenta, 435, 558, 583
GQ, 266, 331
Graber, Jess, 162
Graham, Walter, 291
Graham, William, 228
grain whisky, 253
  Irish whiskey, 311–312
  Japanese whisky, 419–420
  Scotch whisky, 201, 204

Grand Marnier Orange Liqueur, 356
Grand Metropolitan, 155, 239, 247, 337–338, 355, 536–537, 540
Grant, Charles, 274
Grant, James, 269, 299
Grant, John, 299, 303
Grant, William (cofounder of The Glenrothes), 270
Grant, William (founder of Glenfiddich and Balvenie), 254–255, 259, 274, 276–277, 525
Grant's, 235, 277–279
Great Depression, 107, 529
Great Jones Distilling Co., 163–164
Great Northern, 306, 337, 365
Green, Nathan "Nearest," 54–55, 67, 76, 146, 192, 548
green initiatives, 16–17
Green Spot, 343, 351–352
Green Stripe, 523
Greenberg, Emanuel, 266, 331–332
Greene, Richard Leighton, 315
Grey Goose Vodka, 363
Grey Wolf, 576
Grupo Estévez, 268
Guinness, 239, 247, 357, 540, 548
Gwynne, Erskine, 555

H

Haas, John E., 561
Haig, John, 253, 349
Haig, Margaret, 349
Haig & Haig, 253
Haig Club Single Grain Whisky, 252–253, 284
Hakata, 454
Hakushu, 416, 424, 433–434, 437, 444–446, 535

Hall, John, 397–398
Hamilton, Alan, 440
Hamilton, Alexander, 75, 521
Hamm, Jon, 544
Hanyo, 454
hard seltzer, 411
Harmsworth, John, 526
Harper's Weekly Gazette, 214, 216
Harvey, John, 295
Harvey, Robert, 295
Harvey, William, 295
Haskell, David, 185
Hatch, Harry, 387–389, 399, 403–404, 529
Hatozaki, 453–454
Hay, Robert, 303
Hayden, R. B., 141
Hazelburn, 203, 418, 422–423, 447
head hoops, 36
heads, barrel, 36
Heaven Hill, 91–92, 102–103, 541, 543
  Bernheim Original Wheat Whiskey, 136
  Black Velvet, 411
  Bourbon Heritage Center, 54–55
  column stills, 33
  Elijah Craig Bourbon, 134–135
  Evan Williams bourbon, 135
  founding of, 530
  Henry McKenna Single Barrel Bourbon, 138
  Larceny Kentucky Straight Bourbon, 137–138
  Mellow Corn, 69, 138
  Mellow Corn whiskey, 68–69
  1996 fire, 539
  Old Fitzgerald Bourbon, 137
  Parker's Heritage Collection, 137
  Pikesville Rye, 136
  Rittenhouse Rye, 135
Hedonism, 302–303

Heigold Bourbon, 161
Heilmann, Pam, 188
heirloom grains, 13, 18
Hemingway, Ernest, vi
Henderson, Lincoln, 173, 180
Henderson & Turnbull, 225
Henry McKenna Single Barrel Bourbon, 138
Herbsaint, 566
Heriot-Watt University, 293
Heritage, 528
Herlihy, Tim, 365
Hibiki, 434, 444, 446, 537, 545
High, Joel, 119
High West, 69, 547
High West Saloon, 177–178
High Wire Distilling, 183–184
Highball, 497, 510, 514, 516–518, 545
  cocktail recipe, 558
  Japanese whisky, 445
  Scotch whisky, 218–220, 226
Highland Distillers, 265, 267, 269–270, 275, 281
Highland Park, 196, 239, 265, 268–269
Hikari, 416, 454
Hillrock Estate, 548
Hills, Nicholas, 438
Hilton, Conrad, 544
Hioki, 451
hipsters, 14
Hiram Walker, 368–370, 375, 439, 546. *See also* Canadian Club
  acquisitions, 106, 115, 265, 294
  Canadian Club, 377–379, 399–401
  Deluxe Straight Rye, 378
  end of Prohibition, 529
  origin of, 377, 523
  Peoria distillery, 104
  Pernod, 543
  post-Prohibition, 390–391

Hitchcock, Alfred, 429
Hletko, Paul, 138
Hobbs, Joseph, 295
Hochstadter's Slow & Low Rock & Rye, 187
Hoffman, Ahlers & Co., 377
Hoffman House Bartender's Guide, 561
Hofmann, Matt, 164
Hogarth, William, 211, 213
hogshead barrels, 35
Hollywood Cocktails (Buzza), 556
Hombo family, 451
hooch (moonshine), 57
Hood River Distillers, 404, 406
Hoover, Herbert, 95
Horton rye, 13
Hospital, The, 220
Hot Scotches, 284
Hot Toddy, 510, 558
Hotaling & Co., 179–180
How to Blend Scotch Whisky (Barnard), 217
How to Make Old Kentucky Famed Drinks (Brown-Forman), 508
How to Mix Drinks or The Bon Vivant's Companion (Thomas), 507, 524, 553, 585
Hudson Whiskey, 129, 173
Hughes, Oliver, 365
Hunter, Ian, 210, 291
hybrid column/pot stills, 33

I

Ibrahim, Youssef, 239
Ideal Bartender, The (Bullock), 505, 528, 561
IDV (*See* International Distillers & Vintners)
Illva Saronno, 178

Immaculate Baking Company, 183
Immature Spirits (Restriction) Act of 1915, 222, 528
immigrants, role in American whiskey industry
    Dutch immigrants, 90
    German immigrants, 91–92
    Jewish immigrants, 92
Immortal Rye Whiskey, 139
Inatomi, Koichi, 446
Independent, 422
Independent Scotch Whisky Association, 228
independents, 364–366
Indian whisky, 472–473
    Amrut Distilleries, 456–457, 472–473, 543
    Paul John, 473
Innes, Peter, 422–423, 447
"Inside Marketing" (Moskowitz), 229
Internal Revenue Service, 41, 63, 107, 186, 527
International Distillers & Vintners, 355
Invergordon Distillers, 295–298
Irish Coffee, 326–331, 512–513, 532, 559
Irish Distillers Limited, 332–333, 335–337, 339–340, 343, 346, 348–350, 352–353, 358–359, 361, 534–537
Irish Distillers Museum, 334
Irish Flip, 577
Irish Potato Famine, 317
Irish Times, 324, 329, 331, 333, 337, 340, 351, 353, 355
Irish whiskey, 306–366
    drinking recommendations, 512–515
    early whisky distilling, 8
    family tree, 345–366
        Bacardi, 363–364
        Beam Suntory, 359–361
        Brown-Forman, 362–363
        Diageo, 354–357
        independents, 364–366
        Mark Anthony Brands, 364
        Pernod Ricard, 348–354
        Proximo, 345–348
        Sazerac, 361
        William Grant & Sons, 357–359
    floor malting, 19
    history of, 313–344
        American consumption, 308
        blends, 321, 331–332, 334, 340
        booms and growth, 308, 313, 335, 338
        Coffey stills, 319
        column stills versus pot stills, 321–323
        competition from blended Scotch, 323–325
        craft distilling, 337–338, 341, 343–344
        downturns, 313, 317, 321–326
        growth of whiskey-drinking in England, 217
        Irish Coffee, 326–331
        Irish Distillers Limited, 332–333
        Irish versus Scotch origins, 206–207, 314
        large stills, 319
        Midleton, 333–334
        pot still whiskey, 340, 343
        rise of modern industry, 316–318
        taxes, 318–319
        World War II, 313, 321–322
    myth of potatoes in, 325
    number of distillations, 29
    Pickleback, 342
    regions, 306

INDEX 609

religious division, 320
Scotch whisky versus, 308, 318–319, 332, 335–336, 339–340
types of, 309–312
  blended whiskey, 311
  grain whiskey, 311–312
  pot still whiskey, 310–311
  single malts, 309–310, 319
use of malted and unmalted barley, 20
what makes Irish whiskey Irish, 307–308, 318–319, 332, 344
Irish Whiskey: A History of Distilling, the Spirit Trade, and Excise Controls in Ireland (McGuire), 358, 361
IRS (*See* Internal Revenue Service)
Islay Single Malt Scotch Whisky, 304
Israeli whiskey, 474
I.W. Harper, 111, 153, 532
Iwai, Kiichiro, 416, 451–452
Iwai Whisky, 452
izakaya restaurants, 516–517

J

J&B Rare Blended Scotch Whisky, 218, 229–231, 239, 250–251
Jack Daniel's, 54–55, 146–147, 271, 527, 531–532, 548
  chamber stills, 79
  column stills, 33
  Gentleman Jack, 147
  Lincoln County Process, 47, 64–67
  Old No. 7 80-proof, 147
  Sinatra Select, 147
Jackson, Michael James, 422, 544
Jagdale, Neelakanta Rao, 473
Jago, Tom, 238, 355–356
James IV, 207, 520
James of Hereford, 323

James Stuart & Co., 270
Jameson, 543–544
  advertising and promotion, 325, 332, 340
  Black Barrel, 340, 350
  blends, 311, 349
  Bow Street distillery, 306, 312, 316, 521, 535
  as definition of Irish whiskey, 307–308, 344
  Irish Distillers Limited, 332, 534
  Local pub and restaurant, 514, 544
  makeover and relaunch, 334–335, 339, 534
  origin of, 349
  Pernod, 543
  Pickleback, 342
  religious division, 320
  1780, 335
  Single Pot Still Whiskey, 350
Jameson, Andrew, 323, 349
Jameson, John, 253, 316, 320, 349, 521
Jameson, William, 357
Jameson's blends, 37
Janzen, Emma, 576
Japan Spirits & Liqueurs Makers Association, 418–420, 438, 548
Japan Times, 428
Japanese Harmony, 446
Japanese mizunara oak (*Quercus mongolica*), 46, 442
Japanese whisky, 233, 416–454
  drinking recommendations, 516–518
  family tree, 443–454
    Akashi, 452–453
    Chichibu, 454
    Fuji, 449–450
    Hakata, 454

Hatozaki, 453–454
Kanosuke, 450–451
Kikori, 453
Mars Iwai, 451–452
Nikka, 446–449
Suntory, 443–446
future of, 441
history of, 421–441
  advertising, 427–429
  American market, 427–428
  blending system, 425
  collapse, 431–432, 440
  modern era, 433–440
  regulation scandal, 417, 437–438, 441
  successes and growth, 417
  Taketsuru, 421–424, 426
  Torii, 423–424
  World War II and postwar growth, 426–427
monozukuri and wabi-sabi, 436
regions, 416
types of, 418–420
  blended whisky, 420
  grain whisky, 419–420
  malt whisky, 418–419
what makes Japanese whisky Japanese, 418
Japanese Whisky (Ashcraft), 424, 442
Japanese Whisky, Scotch Blend (Checkland), 422
Jaume, Christopher, 468
Jaywalk Year rye whiskey, 13
Jefferson's Bourbon, 158–160, 354, 548
Jennings, Waylon, 57
Jewish immigrants, role in American whiskey industry, 92
Jim Beam, 92, 103, 126, 139–145, 287–288, 292, 297, 337, 359, 362, 365, 435, 497, 516, 537, 546–547

Jim Downey's Steak House, 330
Jimmy Red Straight Bourbon Whiskey, 184
Johansson, Scarlett, 429
John Jameson & Son, 323, 350–351, 358, 361, 534. *See also* Jameson
John Power & Son, 323, 350, 358, 361. *See also* Power's
John Walker & Sons, 259
Johnnie Walker, 284
  advertising and promotion, 216
  Black Label, 238, 248–249, 254–255, 512, 526
  blending of single malts, 50, 204, 218, 255, 259, 277, 486
  Blue Label (Oldest), 238, 249, 537
  bottle and label, 248
  Compass Box, 302, 542
  Distillers Company Limited, 284, 529
  Double Black, 249
  High Rye bottling, 249
  Highballs, 248–249
  Kilmarnock grocery store, 247–248
  Old Highland Whisky, 248, 523, 527
  origin of, 211, 247–248, 522
  rebranding, 248
  Red Label, 227, 238–239, 248, 526
  square bottle, 524
  striding man logo, 248–249, 527
  Walker's Whisky, 248
  White Label, 248, 526
Johnny Drum bourbon, 194
John's Lane, 306, 316, 334, 350, 535
Johnson, Dwayne "The Rock," 348
Johnson, Hugh, 239
Johnson, Lyndon B., 170
Johnston, Alexander, 290
Johnston, Donald, 290

Johnston, John, 257
Jones, Lawrence, 175
Jones, Paul, Jr., 174–175
Jones, Saunders, 175
Jose Cuervo, 162, 320, 404, 406, 546
Joseph E. Seagram & Sons, 71, 529. *See also* Seagram's
Josephs, Sean, 190–191
Journal of Southern History, 77
J.P. Wiser's, 402–403
Jungle, The (Sinclair), 93
Junipero, 180
Jura, 295, 298
Justerini & Brooks, 229, 250. *See also* J&B Rare Blended Scotch Whisky

K

Kaikyō, 416, 453
Kakubin, 424, 426, 444–445, 516, 531
Kandar, Michael, 178
Kanosuke, 416, 450–451
Katz, Allen, 128, 189–190
Kavalan, 456–457, 465–466
Kaye, Danny, 329
Keeper's Heart, 69, 184–185
Keiswetter, Wayne, 271, 547
Kentucky Bourbon Hall of Fame, 542
Kentucky Derby Fizz, 508
Kentucky Distillers' Association, 525, 540, 542
Kentucky Iced Tea, 497–498
Keogh, Olive, 337
Kergommeaux, Davin de, 373–374, 376–377, 396, 403
Khrushchev, Nikita, 234, 263
Kieft, Willem, 71, 520
Kikori, 453

Kilbeggan, 306, 360–361, 546
Kilchoman, 203, 304
Kings County, 185–186, 545
Kininvie, 279
Kintner, Robert, 109, 112
Kirin, 174–176, 432, 439, 449–450, 541
Kittling Ridge Estate Wines and Spirits, 397–398
Knappogue Castle, vii, 353–354, 548
Knob Creek, viii, 126, 141
Koeppler, Jack, 330
Komagatake, 416, 452
Korean War, 116
korn spirit, 91
Kotobukiya Limited, 444, 529–531
Krogstad, Christian, 192–193
Kulsveen, Drew, 182, 194
Kulsveen, Even, 194

L

La Martiniquaise-Bardinet, 271, 300–301
Ladyburn, 233
Lagavulin, 196, 203, 209, 239, 257–259, 277, 291
LaHart, Liam, 365
Lakes, The, 456–457, 469
Lamb, Emerson, 164
Laphroaig, 20, 196, 203, 210, 239, 245, 272, 288, 290–292, 543
Larceny Barrel Proof, 138
Larceny Kentucky Straight Bourbon, 137–138
Lark, Bill, 456–457, 460–461, 538
Lark, Lyn, 456–457, 460–461
Lark distillery, 456–457, 460–461, 538
Lawrenceburg Distillers Indiana (LDI), 130

Le Sang et Sable, 578
Lebanese whisky, 475
Ledrede, Richard de, 314
Lee, Brian, 132
Lee, Don, 570
Lee, Elmer T., 125–126, 167–168, 536, 542, 546
Lee, Tien-tsai, 465
Lee, Yu-ting, 465–466
Leestown Company Inc., 151
Legent bourbon, 143
Leighton, Billy, 351
Lem Motlow, 531
Lennon, John, 355
Leopold, Scott, 186
Leopold, Todd, 22, 186
Leopold Bros., 22, 54–55, 186–187, 549
Lermayer, John, 577
Lewis, Ken, 189
Licensed Beverage Industries, Inc., 535
Liggett Group, 155, 536
Lincoln, Abraham, 84
Lincoln County Process, 47, 64–67, 409
Lineage Single Malt Whisky, 154
Linkwood, 258
Little, John, 161–162
Little Italy cocktail, 579
Livermore, Don, 396, 401–402, 546
Local pub and restaurant, 514, 544
Lock Stock & Barrel, 187
Loeb, Bloom & Co, 110
Loeb, Reuben, 110
Logan, Graham, 298
Long Stride, A (Morgan), 208, 226, 238, 248, 509
Longbranch, 156–157
Longmorn, 300, 422, 447
Lopez, Jennifer, 348
Los Angeles Times, 239, 335, 427

Lost in Translation (movie), 429, 446, 543
Lost Irish, 311, 344, 365
Lot No. 40, 401–402, 515, 546
Low Flyer, 235
"low wines," 29
Lumsden, Bill, 196, 241, 278, 293–294, 539
Lundborg, Rikard, 479
LVMH. *See* Moët Hennessy Louis Vuitton
Lynn House, 575
Lyrics of the Red Book of Ossory, The (Greene), 315

M

Macallan, The, 29, 196, 202, 239, 245
   collectible bottlings, 268
   Fine & Rare Collection, 268, 542
   modern facility, 266
   new identity, 267–268
   opening of, 522
   origin of, 266
   overview, 265–266
   popularity in United States, 266–267
   Suntory and, 439
MacAskill, Hugh, 253
MacAskill, Kenneth, 253
Macdonald & Muir, 238, 293
Macdougall family, 294
Macfarlane & Townsend, 265
MacGregor, Rob Roy, 565
Machado, Gerardo, 564
Machir Bay, 304
Machrihanish, 203
Mackall, Lawton, 235, 325
Mackay, Charles, 297
Mackenzie, Andrew, 297–298

Mackenzie, Charles, 297–298
Mackenzie, Compton, 210
Mackenzie, William, 298
Mackie & Co., 286, 291
MacKinnon, John, 280
Mackmyra, 456–457, 479–480, 540
Macleod, Stephanie, 285
Mad Men (TV show), 544
madeira drum barrels, 34
Magee, Malachy, 319
Magliocco, Joe, 188–189, 540
Magnolia Marketing Company, 165, 532
Maker's Mark, 16, 47, 54–55, 106, 142, 485, 517, 533, 543, 545, 548
"making cuts" process, 37–38
Malcolm, Dennis, 300
Mallya, Vijay, 297
Maloney, Toby, 571
malt and malting
   defined, 18
   floor malting, 19–20
   peat and, 20, 22
   single malt, 18
Malt Whisky Trail, 199
maltsters, 19
Mamie Taylor cocktail, 559
Manchester, William, 226
Manhattan, 504–505, 512, 515, 540, 560
Margarita, 511
Mark Anthony Group, 364, 411–412
Market Watch, 410
Marquess of Stafford, 252
Mars Iwai, 435, 451–452
Marshall, Ann, 183–184
Marshall, William J., 120
Martell Cognac, 273, 356
mashing
   defined, 22
   mash bill, 23

mash tuns, 23
wort, 24
Masters of Whiskey Series, 182
Mastodon, The, 579
Matheson, Alexander, 297
Matheson, William, 292
maturation process, 38–47
   barrels
      American white oak, 45
      bourbon barrels, 40–41
      charring process, 45–46
      effect on flavor, 41, 44
      French oak, 46
      Garry oak, 47
      Japanese mizunara oak, 46
      location and rate of maturation, 44–45
      reusing, 45
      sherry casks, 39
      using multiple barrels, 47
   overview, 38, 40
Maytag, Fritz, 54–55, 179–180, 538
Mayville, Drew, 408
McCall, Elizabeth, 149
McCarthy, Denis, 366
McCarthy, Ger, 366
McCarthy, Steve, 67
McCarthy, Thomas, 155
McClure's, 342
McConaughey, Matthew, 156
McDermond, Bill, 178
McElhone, Harry, 555, 557, 563
McEwan, Jim, 296
McGarry, Jack, 546
McGovern, Patrick, 7
McGowan, Jack, 335
McGregor, Connor, 348
McGuire, E. B., 358, 361
McKee, Dan, 188
McKenna, Kenneth, 235
McKerrow, Neil, 237–238
McMahon, Frank, 400, 532

McPherson, Iain, 580, 584
Mead, Brad, 180
Mead, Kate, 180
medicinal whiskey, 85
   Canadian Club, 399
   Four Roses, 97, 175
   Mint Julep, 505, 560
   Old Forester whiskey, 88
   Prohibition and, 96–98
   Scotch, 220
Mega Highball, 517
Mellow Corn, 138
Merchant, The, 546
Mesopotamia, 7
Metallica, 181–182
Mexican whisky, 475–477
   Abasolo, 456–457, 476–477
   Oaxaca, 477
   Sierra Norte, 456–457, 477
MGP Ingredients Inc., 54–55, 106, 128, 130–131, 341, 530
Michter's, 187–189, 538, 540
Midleton, 29, 37, 306–307, 310, 313, 333–334, 336, 340, 346, 350, 352–353, 535–536
Midwinter Night's Dram, A, 177–178
Mike's Hard Lemonade, 411
Milam & Greene, 69
Milk & Honey, 456–457, 474, 544
Miller, Arthur, 327, 329
minibottles, 486–487
Mint Julep, 505–508, 511, 528, 560–561
Miquelon island, 382–384
Mitchell & Son, 306, 351–352
Mitsuya, Naomi, 454
Miyagikyo, 416, 447–449
mizunara oak, 46, 442
Mizuwari, 516
Modern cocktail, 561

Moët Hennessy Louis Vuitton (LVMH), 193, 234, 292–295, 543
Moir, James, 275
Molloy, Michael, 358
Momosé, Julia, 576
"Monkey Mixer," 279
monkey shoulder, 19–20, 279
Monkey Shoulder Blended Scotch Whisky, 279
Monopole, 281
monozukuri, 436
Monroe, Marilyn, 327, 329
Montreal Club, 379
Montreal Daily Star, 378
moonshine (hooch; white lightning), 57
Morgan, Nicholas, 208, 226, 238, 248, 509, 526
Morgenthaler, Jeffrey, 571, 574
Morgenthau, Henry, Jr., 387
Morris, Chris, 148–149
Morris Single Malt Whisky, 462
Morrison, Alexander, 275
Morrison, William, 275
Morrison Bowmore, 272, 439
Mortlach, 37, 254–255, 276
Moskowitz, Milton, 119, 229
Mosley, Peter, 365
Motlow, Lem, 527
Moto Guzzi, 580
Mount Vernon, 72–73
Mountcharles, Henry, 362
Muirhead's, 229
Muldoon, Sean, 546
Murphy, 335
Murray, Bill, 429, 543
Murray, Wes, 182
Murray McDavid, 295–296
Myers, Kevin, 351
Myers's Rum, 356

N

Naarangi whisky, 473
Nally, Steve, 180
Nantucket Vineyard, 542
Nashville American, 66
National Bourbon Heritage Month, 544
National Distillers, 105–106, 115–116, 535, 537
National Wholesale Liquor Dealers' Association, 89
Neilson, Abbie, 468
Nelstrop, Andrew, 469
Nelstrop, James, 469
New Amsterdam, 90
New Riff, 189
New York Daily News, 235, 238, 510
New York Distilling Company, 13, 87, 128, 189–190
New York Sour, 562
New York Sun, 218
New York Times
   bootlegging on Saint-Pierre and Miquelon islands, 384
   Canadian Club advertising, 398–399
   Chivas advertisement, 263
   comments from Tadeo Onishi, 429
   Dewar's White Label Scotch advertisement, 284
   Diageo's sale of Dewar's to Bacardi, 239
   Famous Grouse, The, 281
   Gotemba distillery, 439
   Mexican distilleries, 476
   Nikka advertisement, 428, 447
   obituary of Harry Hatch, 389
   Scotch and golf, 218
Newcomb-Buchanan Company, 66
Newett, George A., 505
Nikka, 425–426, 428–430, 434–435, 439, 446–449, 451, 530–531, 538
Nikka Kakubin (Square Bottle), 426
Nilsson, Harry, 355
9.09 rule, 373, 412
nixtamalization method, 477
Noe, Booker, viii, 54–55, 122–124, 126, 140, 497–498, 542–543
Noe, Fred, 25–26, 141
North Star Pub, 267
Norton Simon conglomerate, 99
Not So Rusty Nail, 580
Notch, The, 67, 542

O

Oaxaca, Mexico, 477
Oban, 251, 259
Oberholtzer, Henrich, 92
Oberholtzer, Henry, 144
Ocean bourbon, 159
O'Connell, John, 366
Octomore, 22, 296
O.F.C. distillery, 168, 525, 528
off notes, 493
Offerman, Nick, 257–258
O'Flaherty, Patrick J., 361
O'Gallachoir, Donal, 364
Okura, 432, 439
Old Bardstown, 194
Old Blowhard, 153
Old Crow, 118, 143, 342
Old-Fashioned, 503–504, 508, 511–512, 515, 544, 562–563
Old-Fashioned glasses, 499
Old Fitzgerald, 99, 137, 531, 541
Old Forester, 88, 148, 524, 548
Old Grand-Dad Bourbon, 144

Old No. 7, 147, 527
Old Overholt, 54–55, 92, 144–145, 522
Old Pal, 563
Old Potrero, 179–180, 538
Old Rip Van Winkle, 100, 168–169, 535, 543
Old Roan, 111
Old Suntory Whisky, 427, 429, 431
Old Taylor, 525, 528, 535, 537
Old Waldorf-Astoria Bar Book, The, 568
Old Whaler, 82
Omakase, 454
Omar, 456–457, 466
On the Production Methods of Pot Still Whisky (Taketsuru), 421
100 Pipers Blended Scotch, 266
1000 Years of Irish Whiskey (Magee), 319
Onishi, Tadeo, 429
Orphan Barrel Whiskey Distilling Co., 153–154
Ottawa Journal, 224
Outline for Industry, An (Willkie and Blankmeyer), 109
Outline of the Distilled Spirits Business (Walker), 388
Outpost Range line, 164
Overholt, Abraham, 144, 522
Owen Sound Sun Times, 403
Owens, Michael J., 526
Oxford Companion to Spirits & Cocktails, The, 501

P

Paddy's, 311, 361
Pan Am, 327
Paniolo, 581
Paper Plane, 581–582

Pappy Van Winkle, 98–101, 432, 539
Parker's Heritage Collection, 137
Parks and Recreation (TV show), 257
patent stills, 311, 331, 522. *See also* Coffey stills; column stills
Paterson, Richard "The Nose," 297, 534
Patino, Chris, 342
Pattison, Elder & Co., 303
Paul John distillery, 456–457, 473
Peacock Alley bar, 568
Pearse Lyons, 344
peat, 20, 22
Peat Monster, The, 303
Peerless distillery, 21
Pegu Club, 435
Pendleton Whisky, 404–406
Penicillin cocktail, 544, 582
Penny Bridge, 264
Peoria distillery, 104–105
Perkins, David, 177, 185
Perkins, Jane, 177
Pernod Ricard
  Aberlour, 264–265
  avoiding monopoly status, 274
  Blue Spot, 343, 351–352
  building relationship with bartending trade, 342–343
  carbon footprint pledge, 16
  Chivas Regal, 262–264
  Chuan, The, 549
  formation of, 535
  Glenlivet, The, 260–262
  Gooderham & Worts Ltd., 403–404
  Gotemba distillery, 450
  Green Spot, 343, 351–352
  Irish Distillers and, 337–338, 346, 537
  Jameson, 320, 349–350
  Jefferson's Bourbon, 158–160
  J.P. Wiser's, 402–403

Knappogue Castle, 353–354
Lawrenceburg distillery, 130
Lot No. 40 Rye Whisky, 401–402
Midleton Very Rare, 352–353
overview, 348–349
partnership with Fortune Brands, 543
Pike Creek, 404
Power's, 350
purchase and sale of The Glen Grant, 300
purchase of Castle Brands, 548
purchase of Seagram's spirit brands and distilleries, 541
purchase of Wild Turkey, 155, 536
Rabbit Hole, 160–161
Red Spot, 343, 351–352
Redbreast, 350–351
sale of GlenAllachie, 272
sale of Tullamore D.E.W., 358
Scapa, 265
Smooth Ambler, 161–162
TX Whiskey, 161
Vin & Spirit, 545
Yellow Spot, 343, 351–352
Perrier, 511, 526
Perry, Matthew C., 523
Peterson, Art, 151
phenolic parts per million (PPM), 22
Philadelphia Inquirer, 228
phylloxera, 10–11, 214, 216, 220, 248, 250, 508, 510, 515, 524
Pickerell, David, 126, 128, 181, 193, 395–396, 400, 548
Pickleback, 342, 544, 583
Pike Creek, 404
Pikesville Rye, 136, 530
Pinhook Bourbon, 190–191
pipes (port casks), 35
Plank, Kevin, 178
Plum Sazerac, 583
PM Blended Whiskey, 116

poitín, 207, 317–318
Pope, Christy, 187
port casks (pipes), 35
Port Ellen, 233, 260, 536, 547, 549
Port Wood Finish Scotch, 294
Porter, Sylvia, 120
Porterhouse Brewing Company, 365
Porto Cruz, 301
Portsoy, 276
pot stills, 8, 27–30
  effect on flavor, 37–38
  hybrid column/pot stills, 33
  Irish whiskey, 318–319, 321–325, 331, 340, 343
  Scotch whisky, 207–208, 211–212, 221–222, 230
Power, James Talbot, 323, 350
Power, John, 316
Power's, 306, 316, 330, 332, 334–335, 344, 350, 534–535
PPM (phenolic parts per million), 22
Pratt, Willie, 188
Presbyterian cocktail, 563
Prohibition, 12, 92, 95, 102, 220, 222–226, 250, 285, 382–384, 508, 528–530
proof
  ABV vs., 49
  proofing down, 51–52
Proper No. Twelve, 348
Proximo, 162–164, 345–348, 546
  Bushmills, 345–346
  Great Jones Distilling Co., 163–164
  Proper No. Twelve, 348
  Sexton, The, 347–348
  Stranahan's Colorado Whiskey, 162–163
  Tincup Whiskey, 163
Publicker, Harry, 135
puncheon barrels, 34

Pure Food and Drug Act of 1906, 93, 380, 526
purity of whiskey, 85, 88–89, 93–94

Q

quarter hoops, barrel, 36
Quercus alba (American white oak), 45
Quercus garryana (Garry oak), 47
Quercus mongolica (Japanese mizunara oak), 46, 442
Quercus robur (French oak), 46

R

R. H. Macy's, 82
Rabbit Hole, 160–161
Rainbow Room, 242
Ramble Round the Globe, A (Dewar), 284
Rebel Yell, 531, 541
Recipes for Mixed Drinks (Ensslin), 554
rectifiers (blenders), 85, 93
"Red Book of Ossory," 9, 207, 314–315, 520
Red Rooster restaurant, 572
Red Spot, 343, 351–352
Redbreast, 37, 310, 340, 343, 350–351, 355
Redemption Whiskey, 178–179
Regal Apple Whisky, 371
Regan, Gary, 267
Reid, Alexander, 266–267, 522
Remember the Maine cocktail, 564
Rémy Cointreau, 164, 267, 295–296, 365, 471, 546
Reserve Series (Sagamore Spirit), 178
Restoration Rye Whiskey, 182
Restriction (Immature Spirits) Act of 1915, 222, 528
Reuters, 440
Reverse Manhattan, 504, 564
Revival Rye, 183–184
Revolver cocktail, 583–584
Reynier, Mark, 295–296, 344, 365–366, 542, 546
Riachi, 456–457
Rice, Jack, 332
Rickey, Joseph Kerr, 556
Rieder, Otto, 397, 535
Rieder distillery, 397
Risen, Clay, 548
Ritchie, Guy, 253
Rittenhouse Rye, 135, 530
Rob Roy, 511, 565
Rob Royce cocktail, 584
Robert Brown, 439
Roberts, Glenn, 184
Robertson, David, 269
Robertson, Troy, 161
Robertson, William "Sparrow," 563
Robertson & Baxter, 265
Robertson Trust, The, 265
Robins, Nelson, 223
rocks glasses, 499
Roe, George, 357, 520
Roe, Peter, 356, 520
Roe & Co, 306, 344, 356–357, 520, 529, 548
Rohr McHenry Distilling Co., 94
Roosevelt, Franklin D., 97, 102
Roosevelt, Theodore, 93, 380–382, 505–507, 528
Rorabaugh, W. J., 74, 78
Rosebank, 233
Rosenstiel, Lewis, 116–117, 119–120, 152, 529, 533–534
Ross, John, 280
Ross, Sam, 544, 581–582

Royal Brackla, 282, 286–287
Royal Canadian, 358
Royal Commission on Whiskey and Other Potable Spirits, 208, 214, 221, 225, 322, 349, 527
Royal Lochnagar, 256
Royal Whisky, 428, 430
rum, 71, 74
RumChata, 356
Rupf, Jörg, 191
Russell, Bruce, 128–129
Russell, Eddie, 155, 157
Russell, Jimmy, 54–55, 128–129, 155–157, 532, 542
Russell's Reserve, 157
Rusty Nail, 280, 511–512, 565
Rutledge, Jim, 151
rye
   Canadian whisky, 371–372
   column stills, 83
   flavor notes and attributes, 18
   new barrel requirement, 107–109, 112–113
   overview, 60–61, 64
   rebirth of, 127–129
   three-chamber stills, 82

S

saccharification, 23
Sagamore Spirit, 178
Saint-Pierre island, 382–384
Saji, Keizo, 427, 430, 445–446
Saji, Nobutada, 444
Saldaña, Iván, 456–457, 476
Samuels, Bill, Jr., 542, 545
Samuels, Bill, Sr., 106, 142, 533, 545
Samuels, Margie, 106, 142, 533, 545
Samuels family, 103, 106
Samuelsson, Marcus, 572
San Francisco Chronicle, 326, 328, 532
Sandend, 276
Sands, Neil, 365
Santer, Jon, 583
Saunders, Audrey, 576, 579
Savoy Cocktail Book, The (Craddock), 554, 556
Sazerac, 271, 361, 532, 537–538, 541–542
   Blanton's Bourbon, 166–167
   Buffalo Trace Bourbon, 167
   Canadian Mist, 409
   Caribou Crossing, 408
   Collingwood, 408–409
   Eagle Rare Bourbon, 167
   Early Times, 171–172
   E.H. Taylor, Jr., 168
   Fireball Cinnamon, 409–410
   George T. Stagg bourbon, 170
   Old Rip Van Winkle, 168–169
   Sazerac Rye 18 Year, 100–101, 170
   Seagram's VO, 410–411
   single barrel Elmer T. Lee, 168
   W.L. Weller, 170–171
Sazerac cocktail, 505, 508–509, 566
Sazerac Coffee House, 505, 508
Scaent Group, 275–276
Scapa, 265, 298
Schenley, 92, 115, 529, 533
   support role during World War II, 114
   whiskey tax fight, 116–117
Schlitz beer, 165
Schmier, Dave, 178
Schur, Michael, 257
Scotch Julep, 511
Scotch whisky, 10, 196–304
   age of, 236–237
   climate, 197–199
   cutting peat logs, 20

distilleries
  downturn in the '80s and '90s, 198
  map of, 196
  regions, 202–203
drinking recommendations, 502–512
expensive versus better, 486–487
family tree, 247–304
  Bacardi, 282–287
  Brown-Forman, 271–276
  Campari, 298–300
  Diageo, 247–304
  Edrington, 265–271
  independents, 301–304
  La Martiniquaise-Bardinet, 300–301
  LVMH, 292–295
  Pernod Ricard, 260–265
  Rémy Cointreau, 295–296
  Suntory Global Spirits, 287–292
  Whyte & Mackay, 297–298
  William Grant & Sons, 276–281
finishing, 241
floor malting, 19
future of, 244–245
hallmarks of, 199–200, 204
history of, 205–243
  advertising, 216, 218, 228–229
  American consumption, 199
  American restrictions on domestic production, 227
  American rye and bourbon, 225–226
  blends, 50, 211–214, 216–217, 228–229, 244
  booms and growth, 216–218, 224–225, 228–229, 243
  challenges from Irish whiskey industry, 221
  column stills, 211
  decline in popularity, 230–233
  Diageo conglomerate, 239
  early distilling, 9
  early ingredients, 206–208
  early spirits, 206–207
  endorsement of consumption by medical community, 220
  ghost distilleries, 232
  golden age, 243–244
  golf and Highballs in America, 218–220
  growth of whisky-drinking in England, 217
  immature whisky, 228
  invented traditions, 216
  lighter-blend trend, 235–236
  Prohibition, 222–226
  promotion of old whisky, 233–234
  rebirth of the classic cocktail, 241–242
  regions, 209–211
  rise of single malts, 233–240, 244
  Scotch versus Irish origins, 206–207, 314
  steam-heated stills, 230
  taxes, 209, 211–212, 216, 223–224
  terminology, 208
  upscaling, 237–239
  "whisky ocean" surplus, 219–220, 224–225
  World War I, 222–223
  World War II, 14, 226–227
mashing process, 24
meteoric rise of, 198–199
non age statement whiskies, 245–246
number of distillations, 29
regions, 196, 202–203
  Campbeltown, 196, 203
  Highlands, 196, 203, 209–211
  Islay, 196, 203, 209
  Lowlands, 196, 202, 208–209
  Speyside, 196, 202, 209

types of, 200–201, 204
  blended scotch, 204
  grain whisky, 201, 204
  single malts, 200–201
washbacks, 24
what makes Scotch Scotch, 214–215, 221–222, 225
Scotch Whisky Association (SWA), 200, 203, 228–229, 296, 302–303, 414, 531
Scotch Whisky Industry Record, 11
Seager Evans and Co., 292
Seagram's
  acquisitions, 115, 262–264, 272–273, 300, 333–335, 438–439, 536
  Bulleit Bourbon, 151
  Chivas Regal, 262–264, 532
  Crown Royal, 531, 534
  dominance of, 106
  end of Prohibition, 385–387, 390, 530
  Four Roses, 432, 537
  Fuji distillery, 430, 449–450
  Jewish ownership, 92
  Lawrenceburg distillery, 130
  100 Pipers Blended Scotch, 266
  origin of, 526, 529
  post-Prohibition, 390
  sale of, 541
  Seagram's 7, 69, 515–516
  7 & 7, 515–516
  support role during World War II, 114
  VO Canadian whisky, 410–411
  whiskey tax fight, 117
Seikyo, 440
Settsu Shuzo, 421, 423, 444, 446–447, 451, 528
7 & 7, 515–516
Sex and the City (TV show), 540
Sexton, The, 347–348
Seymour-Davies, Hugh Reade, 355

Shakespeare, William, 286
Shannon Airport, 326–330, 513
Shapira, Max L., 102, 133
Shapira family, 530
Sheridan, Joe, 306, 327–329
Sherry Cask Matured, 469
sherry casks (butts), 35, 39
Shinji Fukuyo, 143
Shinjiro Torii, 529
Shirofuda (White Label), 424, 426, 433, 444, 529
shōchū, 431
Shwab, Victor Emmanuel, 151–152
Siegal, T.J., 575
Sierra Norte distillery, 456–457, 477
Simó, Joaquín, 574
Simon, Norton, 535
Sinatra Select, 147
Sinclair, Upton, 93
single malts
  American, 67–68
  Australian, 462
  defined, 18
  French, 469–470
  Irish, 309–310, 319, 341
  Scotch, 200–201, 233–240, 244
Slane Irish Whiskey, 362–363
slavery, American whiskey and, 73, 76
small batch bourbons
  Baker's, 126
  Basil Hayden, viii, 126
  Blanton's Bourbon, 126
  Booker's, viii
  Booker's Bourbon, 122–124
  Knob Creek, viii, 126
  rise of, 121–126
  Willett distillery, 194
Smart, Elizabeth, 117
Smith, Alex, 579
Smith, George, 196, 216, 261–262, 524–525
Smith, John, 259

Smith, John Gordon, 261, 524
Smoke and Mirrors, 585
"Smoke Gets in Your Nose" (Mackall), 235
Smokey Monkey, 279
Smooth Ambler, 161–162
Smuggler's Cove bar, 579
Snowflake Whiskey, 163
Snyder, John, 112
Social History of Bourbon, The (Carson), 134, 378
Solist Amontillado Sherry Single Cask Strength, 480
Solist Vinho Barrique whisky, 480
Solomon, Chad, 187, 569
sonic aging technique, 181
sour mash, 21
Southern Comfort, 271
Specialty Series (Redemption Whiskey), 179
Spice Tree, 303
spirit caramel, 51
Spirit of Old Kentucky, The (Wilson), 82
spirit stills, 29
Spirits Business, 250, 399, 407, 468
Spoelman, Colin, 185
Springbank, 203
Square Bottle (Nikka Kakubin), 426
St. Andrews, 197–199
St. George Spirits, 54–55, 67, 191–192, 540
St. Louis Post-Dispatch, 332, 507
St. Magdalene, 233
Stagg, George T., 166, 525, 536, 538, 546
Stagg Jr. bourbon, 170
Stalk & Barrel, 414
Standard Union, 223
Starward, 456–457, 461–462, 518, 544
Staub, John, 353

Stauning Danish Whisky, 456–457, 478–479 , 544
staves, barrel, 36
steam-heated stills, 230, 487–488
Stein, Barry, 414
Stein, Robert, 213, 319
Stevenson, James, 248
Stevenson, John, 250–251
Stewart, David, 196, 241, 278, 533, 539, 547
Stewart, Margaret, 264
St-Germain Elderflower Liqueur, 127, 187
Still Waters distillery, 368, 414
stillage, 21
stills. *See also* distilling
   Barnum and Brooks wooden chamber still, 6
   chamber stills, 78–79, 82–83
   column stills, 30–33, 377
   effect on flavor
      column stills, 35, 37
      overview, 33, 36
      pot stills, 37–38
   feints stills, 29
   hybrid column/pot still, 33
   Mesopotamia, 7
   pot stills, 8, 27–30, 37–38
   spirit stills, 29
   three-chamber stills, 62–63
   types of, 28
   wash stills, 29
Stitzel, Arthur Phillip, 531
Stitzel-Weller, 54–55, 98–99, 531, 535, 538
Stokes, Thomas L., 115
Stoneman, William H., 228
storing whiskey, 501–502
Stranahan, George, 162
Stranahan's Colorado Whiskey, 162–163
Strathisla, 263

Sullivans Cove, 456–457, 461, 547
Sunday News, 219
Suntory, 419, 424–431, 437–439, 529–531, 539, 543
   Chita distillery, 535
   fight over Glenlivet, 262
   getting US to recognize Japanese whisky, 533
   Hakushu, 446, 535
   Hibiki, 446, 537, 545
   Highball bars, 517
   Highball machines, 545, 547
   Kakubin, 444–445
   Macallan, The, 267
   mizunara casks, 442
   modern era, 433–435
   Old Suntory Whisky, 427, 429, 431
   overview, 443–444
   Pure Malt Whisky, 427
   Royal Whisky, 428, 430
   Signature, 430
   Toki, 445
   Yamazaki, 433, 445, 451, 536
Suntory Global Spirits, 272, 287–292, 399–400
   Ardmore, 288–289
   Auchentoshan, 288
   Bowmore, 289–290
   Laphroaig, 290–292
sustainability (environmental issues), 16–17
Sutherland, Margaret, 297
Svensk Ek Whisky, 480
SWA (Scotch Whisky Association), 200, 203, 228–229, 296, 302–303, 414, 531
Swan, Jim, 456–457, 474, 481–482
sweating, 142
Sweden. *See* Denmark and Sweden
Sweet Liberty bar, 577
sweet mash, 21

Swingers (movie), 240–241
Szor, Daniel, 468

T

tachinomi, 517
Taft, William Howard, 94, 323, 382, 527, 530
Takara Shuzo, 167, 432, 439, 538
Taketsuru, Masataka, 416, 421–423, 428, 443–444, 446–449, 451, 528–530
Taketsuru, Rita (Jessie Roberta Cowan), 416, 422–423, 447
Taketsuru Pure Malt 12 Year, 435
Tales of the Cocktail conference, 435
Talisker, 196, 199, 253–254, 259
"Tam o' Shanter" (Burns), 301
Tasmanian whisky, 460–461
tasting whiskey, 492–498
   adding ice or water, 496–498
   aroma, 494
   color, 492
   common flavors, 496
   finish, 495–496
   mouthfeel, 495
   off notes, 493
   sipping, 495
Tate, Chip, 154
Taylor, E. H., 54–55, 85, 93, 166, 168, 522, 525, 528, 535, 548
Taylor, Mayme, 559
Taylor, Nick, 413
Taylor, Zach, 413
Teacher's, 274, 288–289
Teeling, Jack, 339, 344, 363
Teeling, John, 306, 337, 359–360, 365, 537
Teeling, Stephen, 339, 344, 363
Teeling Bros., 306, 337–339, 344, 363–364

temperance movement, 11–12, 527
Tennessee whiskey, 64–67
　charcoal filtration, 64–67
　defined, 64
　George Dickel, 64
　Jack Daniel's, 64–67
Tepe Gawra, 7
Teremana Tequila, 348
That S*it Will Never Sell (Gluckman), 355
Thatcher, Margaret, 231
Thomas, Jerry, 507, 524, 553, 585
Thomas Street, 356
Three Chamber Rye, 549
Three Swallow, 350
three-chamber stills, 62–63
thumpers (doublers), 33, 79, 82
Time, 230–231, 326
Times of London, 210, 439–440
Tincup Whiskey, 163
Tito's Vodka, 511–512
Toddy, 509–510
Toki, 445, 516
Tolman, Lucius Moody, 527
Tomatin, 432, 439
Torii, Shinjiro, 416, 421–423, 427, 443–447, 451, 537
Toronto Star, 397
Torys Bars, 428
Trade Marks Registration Act of 1875, 525
triangular trade, 70–71
Trinitas, 297, 545
Triple Eight, 67, 542
Truman, Harry, 226
Trump, Donald, 193
Tsunuki, 416, 452
Tuaca, 271
Tullamore D.E.W., 306, 311, 344, 354, 357–359, 365, 546–547
Tuthilltown Spirits, 54–55, 132, 542, 548
T.W. Samuels brand, 142

21st Amendment, 102
Two-Fold Double Grain Whisky, 462
TX Whiskey, 161
Tyrconnell, 360, 546

U

U2, 338
UD (United Distillers), 149–150, 538
Uigeadail, 295, 511
uisge beatha, 4, 8–9, 208
UK (United Kingdom). *See* English whisky; Irish whiskey; Scotch whisky
umeshu, 434
Uncle Angelo's Eggnog, 566–567
Uncle Nearest, 76, 192, 548
United Distillers (UD), 149–150, 538
United Kingdom (UK). *See* English whisky; Irish whiskey; Scotch whisky
United Press International (UPI), 223, 226, 235
United States. *See* American whiskey
UPI (United Press International), 223, 226, 235
US Department of Agriculture, 88–89, 379, 381, 527–528, 530
US Fair Trade Commission (FTC), 441
US Federal Alcohol Administration, 225
US Food Administration, 222
Usher, Andrew, 523
Uyeda, Kazuo, 435

V

Van Winkle, Julian, 432
Van Winkle, Julian, III, 100, 539, 543

Van Winkle, Julian, Jr., 99–100, 169, 535
Van Winkle, Julian "Pappy," 54–55, 98–99, 168–169, 525, 531, 534–535, 538
Vancouver Sun, 330
Vasyma, 268
Vendome Copper & Brass Works, 29, 180
vermouth, 504–505
Victoria, 256
Vieux Carré, 567
Vin & Spirit, 274, 545
Vitale, David, 456–457, 462, 544
Vivendi, 262, 264, 273, 390, 541
vodka, 14, 207–208, 231, 233, 237, 277, 335, 342, 432
Volstead Act, 11–12

W

W&A Gilbey, 306, 331, 350, 354–356
wabi-sabi, 436
Waldorf Astoria Bar Book, The (Caiafa), 568
Waldorf cocktail, 568
Walker, Alexander (grandfather), 247
Walker, Alexander (grandson), 248, 523
Walker, Billy, 271–274, 276, 547
Walker, Brent, 297
Walker, George Herbert, 528
Walker, Hiram, 377, 388, 398–399, 523, 526
Walker, John, 247, 522–523
Walker family, 211
Walker Grocery Store, 196, 247–248
Walker's Club, 398–399
Wall Street Journal, 479
Walter, Robert, 100

Ward Eight, 568
Wartime Prohibition Act, 96
wash stills, 29
washbacks, 24
Washington, George, 54–55, 72–73, 521, 544
Washington Post, 477
water, role in distilling process, 22–23
Waterford, 296, 344, 365–366
Watt, Andrew Alexander, 360
Way of the Cocktail, The (Momosé and Janzen), 576
Way of Whisky, The (Broom), 432, 451, 517
Weaver, Fawn, 76, 192, 548
Weber, Bruce, 337
Welles, Orson, 429
Wells, Pete, vii
West, Dominic, 320
West Cork Distillers, 306, 365–366
Westland American Single Malt, 47
Westland distillery, 164
Westminster Budget, 283
Westward Whiskey, 192–193
W.G. Smith & Bros., 379
wheat, flavor notes and attributes, 18
whiskey, 483. *See also names of specific brands, distillers, and nationalities*
  collecting, 500–502
  craft distilleries versus big makers, 489–491
  debate about proper spelling, 4
  defining traits of, 3, 5
  drinking recommendations, 503–505, 508–518
  expensive versus better, 487–488
  finding your favorite, 484
  glasses, 499
  grains used for, 15
  history of, 6–14

how grain affects flavor, 15, 18
learning to appreciate, 485
off notes, 493
origin of, 3
phenolic parts per million, 22
tasting, 492–498
timeline of, 520–549
vodka vs., 5
what to spend on, 485–487
Whiskey Del Bac, 67
Whisky Distilleries of the United Kingdom, The (Barnard), 214–216, 258, 261, 266, 294, 319, 350, 525
Whiskey Ginger, 514
Whiskey Rebellion, 75, 521
Whiskey Smash, 585–586
Whiskey Sour, 569
WhiskyFest, viii
WhistlePig, 87, 126, 193–194, 548
White Claw, 364, 411
White Horse, 258, 286
White Label Bourbon, 140
white lightning (moonshine), 57
White Oak, 416, 453
white whiskey, 81. *See also* corn whiskey
Whyte, James, 297
Whyte & Mackay, 296–298, 534
Widow Jane, 139
Wild Turkey, 52, 54–55, 155–156, 532, 536, 545
Wilderness Trail, 21, 157–158
Wildest Redhead, 586
Wiley, Harvey W., 88–89, 93–94, 379–382, 527–528, 530
Wilkins, Christopher, 439
Willard, Frances Elizabeth, 138–139
Willett, Aloysius Lambert Thompson, 194
Willett, Martha Harriet, 194
Willett distillery, 194

William Grant & Sons, 276–281, 357–359, 533
 American market, 235, 343
 Balvenie, The, 277–278
 C&C Group, 546
 Drambuie, 279–280
 Famous Grouse, The, 280–281
 Fistful of Bourbon, 172
 Glenfiddich, 277
 Grant's, 278–279
 Highland Distillers, 265, 267
 Hudson Whiskey, 173
 Monkey Shoulder Blended Scotch Whisky, 279
 Tullamore D.E.W., 357–359
 Tuthilltown, 548
William IV, 287
William Teacher & Sons, 288
Williams, Daniel E., 358
Williams, Evan, 135
Williamson, Elizabeth "Bessie," 196, 210, 291–292
Willkie, H. F., 71, 78, 109
Wills, Anthony, 304
Wills, Kathy, 304
Wilmington Morning News, 112
Wilson, Thomas, 275
Windsor Daily Star, 331, 389
Wine and Spirit Trade Record, 255, 287, 296
Wine Trade Review, 299
Winters, Lance, 67, 191, 540
Winthrop, John, 91, 520
Wire, The (TV show), 320
Wiser, John Philip, 402
Witchburn, 203
W.L. Weller, 98, 170–171, 531, 541
Woldenberg, Malcolm, 165
Woldenberg, Mathilde, 165
Wondrich, David, 7, 79, 91, 327, 522, 553, 556–557
Wood, Pollard & Co., 218

Wooden Barrel, The, 120
wooden barrels (casks). *See* barrels
Woodford Reserve, 148–149
Woods, Ann Soh, 453
Wordsworth, William, 467
Working (Caro), 170
World Atlas of Whisky, The (Broom), 202
world whiskey
   Australian whisky
      Lark, 456–457, 460–461
      Morris Single Malt Whisky, 462
      Starward, 456–457, 461–462
      Sullivans Cove's, 456–457, 461
   Chinese whiskey
      Chuan, 456–457, 463–464
      Eryuan, 456–457, 464
   Denmark and Sweden
      Mackmyra, 456–457, 479–480
      Stauning, 456–457, 478–479
   drinking recommendations, 518
   East Asian whisky
      Kavalan, 456–457, 465–466
      Omar, 456–457, 466
   English whisky
      Cooper King, 467–468
      Cotswolds, 468
      English distillery, The, 456–457, 469
      Lakes distillery, The, 456–457, 469
   French whiskey
      Armorik, 456–457, 470
      Brenne Single Malt, 470–471
      Domaine des Hautes Glaces, 456–457, 471
   Indian whisky
      Amrut, 456–457, 472–473, 543
      Paul John, 473
   Israeli whiskey, 456–457, 474
   Lebanese whisky, 456–457, 475
   Mexican whisky
      Abasolo, 456–457, 476–477
      Sierra Norte, 456–457, 477
   whiskey regions, 456–457
World Whiskies Awards, 547
World's Drinks and How to Mix Them, The (Boothby), 84–85
Worts, James, 403
Wright, Gordon, 295
Wright, Jeffrey, 192
Wyoming whiskey, 179–180

Y

Yamazaki, 416, 419, 426, 430–431, 433–435, 442, 444–445, 447, 529, 536
Yang Tao, 464
yeast. *See also* fermentation process
   distiller's beer, 3, 25
   effect on flavor, 25–26
Yellow Spot, 310, 343, 351–352
Yoichi, 416–417, 426, 435, 447–448, 530
Young, Al, 174

Z

Zamanian, Kaveh, 160–161
Zoeller, Trey, 158–160

PHOTO CREDITS

STOCK:
Advertising Archive: Advertising Archive pp. 218, 228, 229, 249, 428, 429. **Alamy:** Ambling Images p. 447; Archive Pics p. 507; Artefact p. 211; Neil Baylis p. 522; David Bertho p. 417; Oksana Bratanova p. 355; David Burton p. 5; calebbodaniel p. 500; California Dreamin p. 328 (bottom); Chris Cooper-Smith p. 312; Ian Dagnall Computing p. 196 (middle left, bottom right); DGDImages p. 232; dpa picture alliance p. 326; ESPY Photography pp. 242-243; Greg Balfour Evans p. 333; Everett Collection Inc p. 382 (top); Horst Friedrichs p. 237; Tim Gainey p. 468 (bottom); Brent Hofacker pp. 510 (bottom), 556; Keith Homan p. 292; Peter Horree p. 459; Hum Images p. 6; Anwar Hussein p. 469; Iconographic Archive p. 206; Image Professionals GmbH p. 360 (bottom); John Frost Newspapers p. 325; Nicole Kandi p. 562; Leon Harris/Connect Images p. 494; LightField Studios Inc. p. 495 (bottom); LynnEnglandPhotography p. 281, Svyatoslav Lypynskyy p. 495 (top); Michael Marquand p. 560; Patti McConville pp. 398, 406, 409, 410, 503; Arthur Miller p. 11; Moviestore Collection Ltd p. 240; North Wind Picture Archives pp. 8, 70, 75; PA Images p. 46; Panther Media GmbH p. 449; Brent Peters p. 328 (top); picture that p. 39; Ben Pruchnie p. 107; Radharc Images p. 486 (bottom); Kay Roxby p. 467; Peter Sandground p. 288; David Sanger Photography p. 513 (top); Rebecca Schochenmaier p. 40; Science History Images p. 379; Nick Scott p. 360 (top); Steve Speller p. 322; Jeremy Sutton-Hibbert p. 287 (bottom); SvetlanaSF p. 559; The History Collection p. 89; The Reading Room p. 380; Roger Tillberg p. 502; Ognyan Trifonov p. 4 (top); Kristoffer Tripplaar p. 131; Mark Unsworth p. 289; Ivan Vdovin p. 10 (top); Weyo p. 574; Jeffrey Whyte p. 412 (bottom); WorldPix p. 470. Associated Press: Jim Beam Brands pp. 122, 123.
Getty Images: Studio Alcott p. 482; American Stock Archive p. 224; Archive Photos p. 94; Bettmann pp. 117, 282 (bottom), 391; bhofack2 p. 518; Bloomberg pp. 446. 460, 464 (bottom), 465; DEA / G. WRIGHT p. 20; Fototeca Storica Nazionale p. 217; Fox Photos p. 226; Getty Images p. 196 (top); Carla Gottgens p. 461; John Greim p. 73; Herb Kossover/Michael Ochs Archives p. 231; Steven Kriemadis p. 370 (top); Kyodo News p. 450; David Lefranc pp. 416, 422 (right), 423, 528; Library of Congress p. 223; Indranil Mukherjee p. 472; Tomohiro Ohsumi p. 448; Picture Post p. 283 (top); Qilai Shen p. 463; Universal History Archive pp. 324, 375. **Library of Congress:** p. 221.

Louisville Free Public Library: p. 78. **Shutterstock:** 5PH p. 53, 509, 566; Addictive Creative pp. 498, 576; Africa Studio p. 512; Applejak p. 442; AtlasStudio p. 521; Roman Chemeris p. 514; Danita Delimont p. 519; Maksym Fesenko pp. 497, 550, 565, 581; Fotofairy777 p. 508; Jeppe Gustafsson p. vii; Eric Harlow p. 585; Hero Images on Offset p. 14; Brent Hofacker pp. 505, 511, 513 (bottom), 555, 582; Jack Daniel's p. 147 (bottom); Kiko Jimenez p. 488; Igor Klyakhin p. Title Page; Krasula p. vi; Lukas Gojda p. 487; Margaret Bourke-White/The LIFE Picture Collection p. 12; Igor Normann p. 552; Alexander Prokopenko pp. 570, 578; July Prokopiv p. 56; Remizov p. 358; Bernd Schmidt p. 499; Ned Snowman p. 433; Heleno Viero p. 504; Aleksandr Vrublevskiy p. 1. **Wikimedia Commons:** The following images are used under a Creative Commons Attribution CC BY-SA 2.0 License (https://creativecommons.org/licenses/by-sa/2.0/deed.en) and belongs to the following Wikimedia Commons users: Phylloxerid Plant Louse p. 220; Stuart Yeates p. 256 (bottom). The following images are used under a Creative Commons Attribution CC BY-SA 3.0 License (https://creativecommons.org/licenses/by-sa/3.0/deed.en) and belongs to the following Wikimedia Commons users: 663highland p. 453 (top); Johnny Controletti p. 306 (top right); Cooley Distillery p. 359; Dwstultz p. 170. The following images are used under a Creative Commons Attribution CC BY-SA 4.0 License (https://creativecommons.org/licenses/by-sa/4.0/deed.en) and belongs to the following Wikimedia Commons users: DixieLiquor p. 166; Masterofmalt pp. 213, 306; Shckwv p. 111; Kenneth C. Zirkel p. 145. **Public Domain:** Atlas of Mutual Heritage p. 90; BrineStans p. 152; Canadian Science and Technology Museum, CN Images of Canada Gallery p. 407; Eason Photographic Collection p. 520 (left and right); Imperial War Museums p. 113; Internet Archive Book Images pp. 144, 172; Jack Daniel's p. 147 (top); Louisville Free Public Library p. 78; Metropolitan Museum of Art p. 72; National Archives and Records Administration p. 114; National Library of Ireland p. 318; OpenStreetMap p. 315; US FDA p. 379; Rudolphous p. 220; Whisky Distilleries of the United Kingdom p. 316.

COURTESY USE:
Abasolo Whisky p. 455, 476; Aberfeldy pp. 198, 285; Angels Envy p. 173; August Images p. 99; Balvenie pp. 196, 278; Bar Goto/

PHOTO CREDITS

Daniel Krieger p. 435; Benriach p. 19; Blackened Whiskey p. 181; Brenne Whisky p. 471; Brown-Forman pp. 119, 148, 272, 275, 331, 362 (top and bottom); Brown-Forman/BenRiach pp. 272, 273 (bottom), 273 (top); Brown-Forman/GlenDronach p. 271, 274, 275, 276 (top); Bruichladdich p. 295; Buffalo Trace pp. 98, 101, 125, 168; Bushmills Irish Whiskey pp. 309, 310, 313, 314, 334, 345, 346; Campari pp. 58, 486 (top); Campari/Wild Turkey pp. 156 (bottom), 156 (top), 157; Campari/Wilderness Trail p. 158; Caribou Crossing p. 408; Chichibu p. 454; Liz Clayman p. 329; Compass Box pp. 302, 303; Cooper King Distillery p. 468 (top); Cooper Spirits p. 395; Craigellachie pp. 282, 286; Crown Royal p. 385 (bottom); Cultural Heritage Images/Universal Images Group p. 105; Dewar's pp. 204, 283 (bottom), 284; Diageo p. 23, 24, 215, 252, 260, 464 (top); Diageo/Baileys p. 354; Diageo/Balcones p. 154; Diageo/Blade and Bow p. 153 (top); Diageo/Bulleit p. 150; Diageo/Cardhu pp. 197, 201, 248, 258; Diageo/Dalwhinnie p. 250; Diageo/IWHarper p. 153 (bottom); Diageo/Johnnie Walker p. 247; Diageo/Lagavulin p. 44; Diageo/Lagavulin pp. 200, 209, 257 (top); Diageo/Mortlach p. 254 (bottom), 255; Diageo/Oban p. 251; Diageo/Port Ellen p. 549; Diageo/Roe & Co. p. 548 (right); Diageo/

Talisker pp. 205, 253, 254 (top), 510 (top); Dingle Irish Whiskey p. 365; Drambuie p. 280; Eau Claire p. 413; Edrington/Macallan p. 266; Ralph Erenzo p. 128; Everett p. 393; Forty Creek p. 397; Found North pp. 413 (bottom), 491; Four Roses pp. 25, 97, 175; Foynes Flying Boat & Maritime Museum p. 306 (left); Frey Ranch p. 121, 183, 489; Gallery Stock p. 445 (bottom); Glendalough pp. 108, 364, 400, 412 (top), 490; Glenfarclas p. 304; Glenfiddich pp. 276 (bottom), 277; Glenlivet pp. 196 (top right), 261 (bottom), 262; Glen Grant pp. 299, 300; Hakushu: pp. 444, 516; Heaven Hill: pp. 68, 102, 136 (top and bottom), 138, 492 (top); Highland Park: pp. 268, 269; Hill Rock Distillery: p. 127 (bottom); Hiram Walker & Sons: pp. 372, 376, 377, 378, 392-393, 394, 396, 399, 401, 402, 403, 404, 515; Holly Booth, Model: Joshua Novaski/Courtesy High West p. 177; Hudson Whiskey pp. 129, 172, 492 (bottom); Ichiro p. 416 (top right); Irish Distillers Ltd pp. 302 (top), 307, 311, 336, 342, 343 (left), 349 (top and bottom), 351 (top); Iwai Tradition Japanese Whisky p. 452; Jack Daniel's p. 66, 76; Jameson p. 340; Jaywalk p. 13; Jean Pierre Andrieux Collection pp. 383, 386; Jim Beam p. 59; Kanosuke Distillery p. 451; Keepers' Heart p. 36; Keeper's Heart Whiskey p. 184; Kikori p. 453 (bottom);

PHOTO CREDITS

Kings County Whiskey p. 185; Knappogue Castle FB site p. 353; Laphroaig Collector p. 196 (bottom left); Leopold Bros pp. 62, 63, 186; Library and Archives Canada, Acc. No. R9266-1617 Peter Winkworth Collection of Canadiana p. 388; Library UCLA pp. 370 (bottom), 387; Lock Stock & Barrel p. 127 (top and bottom); LVMH pp. 10, 203, 293 (bottom), 293 (top), 294; Macallan pp. 245, 267, 439; Mackmyra pp. 479 (bottom), 480; Maker's Mark pp. 103, 142, 485; Michter's Distillery pp. 187, 188; Milk & Honey pp. 456, 474; Monkey Shoulder p. 279; Montclair Film p. 257 (bottom); New Riff p. 189; Newscom p. 105; Nikka Whisky p. 238; Nikka/Yoichi p. 421; Old Fitzgerald p. 137 (top); Old Overholt pp. 61, 91; Old Portrero pp. 93, 180; Pernod /Jefferson's p. 159; Pernod Ricard pp. 5, 109, 160, 161, 162 (bottom), 162 (top); Pernod/Aberlour p. 234, 264, 265; Pernod/Chivas pp. 263 (bottom), 263 (top); Pernod/Glenlivet p. 261 (top), 438; Pernod/Midleton pp. 341, 352; Pernod/Spot Whiskeys p. 341 (bottom); Pinhook Bourbon p. 190; Gabi Porter p. 517; Proximo/Proper No. Twelve pp. 163 (top and bottom), 320 (bottom), 327, 347 (top and bottom), 405, 481; Frey Ranch p. 18; Redemption FB page p. 179; Remy-Cointreau p. 471 (bottom); Benriach p. 19; Riachi p. 475; Rittenhouse Rye p. 135; Roe and Co p. 356; Rosemary Gilliat Eaton /
Library and Archives Canada pp. 385 (top), 389; Royal Brackla p. 22, 195, 287; Sazerac pp. 21, 83, 165, 169, 361, 411, 473; Sierra Norte p. 477; St George pp. 34, 48, 191; Starward Distillery p. 462; Stauning Danish Whisky p. 478; Suntory pp. 81, 87, 291, 416 (bottom), 422 (left), 424 (bottom), 424 (top), 441; Suntory/Basil Hayden p. 141; Suntory/Beam pp. 139, 143; Suntory/Booker's p. 140; Suntory/Hibiki p. 434; Suntory/Yamazaki pp. 425, 426, 430-431; Talisker p. 205; TEELING Whiskey Company pp. 338, 339, 363; Tullamore D.E.W. p. 27, 357; Uncle Nearest pp. 66 (bottom), 192, 548 (left); Waterford Whisky pp. 164, 343 (right), 366; Westward Whiskey pp. 15. 17, 29, 31, 51, 134, 137 (bottom), 193 (top); Whistle Pig pp. 126, 193; William Grant & Sons pp. 202, 484; Woodford Reserve p. 149 (top); Yamazaki pp. 43, 415, 419, 420, 436, 437, 443, 445 (top).